POIRIER

DIGITAL SYSTEMS:
HARDWARE ORGANIZATION AND DESIGN
SECOND EDITION

DIGITAL SYSTEMS:
HARDWARE ORGANIZATION
AND DESIGN
SECOND EDITION

FREDRICK J. HILL
Professor of Electrical Engineering
University of Arizona

GERALD R. PETERSON
Professor of Electrical Engineering
University of Arizona

JOHN WILEY & SONS
New York • Chichester • Brisbane • Toronto • Singapore

The need for a book on digital computer hardware design that is really an engineering textbook was evident at the time of the writing of the first edition. Traditionally, enginering textbooks are concerned with imparting a skill—with teaching the student how to do something. By contrast, most books on computer design are little more than descriptive surveys of existing computer hardware. In reading such books, the student is an observer rather than a participant.

In this book, we involve the student in the design process rather than just describe the end product. The principal vehicle for this involvement is a register-transfer and control-sequence design language. Various languages of this kind have been proposed, but none have met with general acceptance. We devised A Hardware Programming Language (AHPL), some of whose basic operators closely resemble those of APL (A Programming Language). A Hardware Programming Language is revised in this second edition to further clarify its relationship to hardware. Now, when the designer writes an AHPL expression, he is able to picture clearly the hardware that will eventually result. Using this language, we explore the design of a wide variety of digital hardware systems and present concrete design examples as liberally as possible throughout the book.

This book is written for the computer scientist and systems programmer, as well as the electrical engineer. Undoubtedly, many users of this book will never be responsible for actual hardware design, but the design point of view is a fascinating one even for the student whose primary objective is to become familiar with hardware organization and system architecture. We have used this text in classes divided almost equally between computer science students with no engineering background and electrical engineering students with prior courses in switching theory and electronics. The responses from both groups have been positive and most gratifying.

v

The only topics specifically prerequisite to this book are programming in a high-level language, the binary number system, Boolean algebra, and Karnaugh maps. We assume that the instructor will have no difficulty presenting a brief introduction to these topics if necessary. The material covered in Chapters 2, 4, and 6 of our book on switching theory would be ample for this purpose.* With the addition of this material, the only prerequisites for a course based on this book would be programming experience, a certain degree of intellectual maturity, and a serious interest in computers.

Electrical engineers who hope to design digital hardware should master switching theory and sequential circuits, as well as the material presented in this book. For these students, a prior course covering material similar in scope to the first 15 chapters of our switching theory book is highly desirable. The engineer on his or her first job is far more likely to be confronted with the logical design of a small system of sequential circuits than with the design of a complete computer.

The chart below illustrates the relationship between the various chapters of the book. Chapter 6 and certain sections of Chapter 7 serve as a focal point. In Chapter 6 a minicomputer, SIC, is described in the design language AHPL. The design language is developed and illustrated in Chapters 4 and 5. The minicomputer SIC is defined, and its assembly language is presented in Chapter 2. Sections 7.3 and 7.7 are prerequisite to most of the rest of the book. The remaining sections of Chapter 7 consider topics in hardware implementation that will be of interest to readers with a background in digital circuits. On the other hand, to

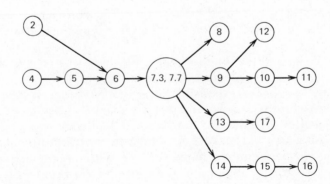

*F. J. Hill and G. R. Peterson, *Introduction to Switching Theory and Logical Design*, 2nd ed., Wiley, © 1974, New York.

readers with an electronics bacground some of the material in Chapter 3 may seem oversimplified. This chapter has been included primarily as an introduction for students whose previous background has been in programming and computer science.

Chapter 8 is a complete treatment of microprogramming. Chapters 9, 10, and 11 introduce intersystem communication and develop the input/output structure for SIC. Chapter 12 is a treatment of a typical microprocessor.

Section 7.7 on combinational logic unit descriptions is utilized in Chapters 13 to 17. Chapters 14, 15, and 16 contain discussions of computer arithmetic. Chapter 13 is a treatment of memory organizations for large machines and Chapter 17 treats other large machine topics.

The instructor is at liberty to select material from Chapters 8 to 17 constrained only by the prerequisite arrows indicated in the chart. The first 9 or perhaps, 10 chapters can be used to form a one-semester course. However, the book is now sufficient for a two-semester course with or without supplementary material provided by the instructor.

Chapters 11 and 12 are new in the second edition, and Chapters 4 to 8 are extensively rewritten and supplemented. The syntax of AHPL and its interpretation as hardware are now much more carefully developed in Chapters 4 and 5. The control delays of the first edition have been eliminated and have been replaced by a level-oriented control unit that can be realized by using available integrated circuit components. A section on the hardware compiling process has been added to Chapter 7. The material on memories has been reorganized and consolidated in Chapter 13, and a complete treatment of virtual memory hardware has been added to this chapter. A complete summary of AHPL is given in Appendix A. Appendix B now lists ASC II equivalents of the AHPL character sets.

Our objective in this book is to introduce system into the design process. However, it is not our intention in any way to reduce this process to a cookbook procedure. A premium is placed on the imagination of the designer. This is immediately evident in the problem sets of Chapter 6 and subsequent chapters. A variety of problems is essential to any meaningful course, and we have included a broad selection. Problem solution, however, has not been reduced to the formalism of switching theory. For many problems, a variety of correct solutions is possible.

Compiler and simulator programs have been written for the version of AHPL described herein. Information about the availability of these programs may be obtained by writing the authors.

Fredrick J. Hill
Gerald R. Peterson

CONTENTS

4 DESIGN CONVENTIONS

5 INTRODUCTION TO A HARDWARE PROGRAMMING LANGUAGE (AHPL)

6 MACHINE ORGANIZATION AND HARDWARE PROGRAMS

7 HARDWARE REALIZATIONS

8 MICROPROGRAMMING

9 INTERSYSTEM COMMUNICATIONS

10 INTERRUPT AND INPUT/OUTPUT

Contents

DIGITAL SYSTEMS:
HARDWARE ORGANIZATION
AND DESIGN
SECOND EDITION

1

INTRODUCTION

1.1 OBJECTIVES OF THE BOOK

The basic objective of this book is, quite simply, to teach the reader how to design complex digital systems. There is certainly no shortage of books on digital systems, but few deal directly with the problem of systems design. Books on digital systems fall primarily into three categories: (1) largely software, (2) primarily switching theory, and (3) computer architecture from a descriptive point of view. It is the authors' contention that the first two categories deal with subjects quite distinct from, although related to, digital systems design. Books in the third category, although useful as an introduction to digital systems, fail to involve the reader in the design process.

Our primary resolve in writing this book has been to avoid merely describing computer hardware. Wherever possible we have tried to emphasize the designer's point of view, starting with a problem to be solved and then considering possible means of solution. Our primary vehicle for involving the reader in the design experience is a *hardware design language*, utilized in writing the *control sequence*, a step-by-step description of the functioning of the digital system. The control sequences are easily translated into control unit hardware. Once this is accomplished, the *digital system*, except for electronic circuit details, is designed.

We have used the term *digital system* without providing a definition. In the broadest sense, *digital* simply means that information is represented by signals that take on a limited number of discrete values and is processed by devices that normally function only in a limited number of discrete states. Further, the lack of practical devices capable of functioning reliably in more than two discrete states has resulted in the vast majority of digital devices being binary, i.e., having signals and states

1

limited to two discrete values. Any structure of physical devices assembled to process or transmit digital information may be termed *a digital system*. This includes, for example, teletypes, dial telephone switching exchanges, telemetering systems, tape transports and other peripheral equipments, and, of course, computers. Often the word *system* is thought of as implying a large or complex system. For the present our definition will be the broader one just presented. In later chapters *large* or *complex* may find its way into our meaning of *system* as we seek to distinguish a complete computing facility from its various components, such as a memory unit.

The characteristics of digital systems vary, and the approach to their design sometimes varies as well. Consider the very general model of a digital system shown in Fig. 1.1. Although in practice the distinction may not always be apparent, we shall arbitrarily separate the information that enters and leaves a digital system into two categories: (1) information to be processed or transmitted and (2) control information. Information in the first category usually occurs in the form of a time-sequence of information vectors. A vector might be a *byte*, 8 binary bits; it might be a word of 16 to 64 bits; or it might be several words. In any case a large number of wires are required to handle a vector in a physical system. Usually, the bits of a vector are treated within the system in some uniform manner, rather than each bit being treated in a completely separate way.

The second category, control information, usually occurs in smaller quantities, involving physically one to a very small number of wires. Control information is self-defining. It is information that guides the digital system in performing its function. Sometimes, control information is received only. In other cases control pulses are sent out to control the function of some other equipment.

Certain digital systems handle only control information. The controller for an elevator is a good example. Systems of this type may be designed as *sequential circuits*. The procedures for sequential circuit de-

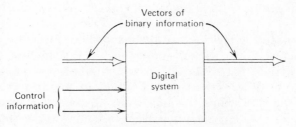

Figure 1.1. Types of digital information.

sign are well defined and are discussed in a number of introductory textbooks. See, for example, References 3 and 4. Classical sequential circuit techniques have not proved satisfactory for designing systems to process vectors of information. Consequently, computers have never been designed that way.

The control portion of a more general digital system is a sequential circuit and may be treated as such. For more complex systems, particularly computers, the portion that may be treated effectively as a classical sequential circuit is a relatively small part of the whole. Even certain kinds of control information can be assembled into vectors and transmitted and stored as such. Our approach has been to restrict control hardware to a few standard forms, which may be analyzed once and used repeatedly. We are then in a position to investigate and develop design procedures for almost any form of equipment for processing information vectors.

Digital computers certainly form the most important class of digital systems. Nearly every day we are reminded of the ways in which computers have basically altered our society, and the case for their importance can hardly be overstated. In this book we shall be primarily concerned with digital computers and their peripheral equipments for two reasons. First, computers are the most important type of digital system. Second, virtually every aspect of digital design is encountered in computer design, so that the person well-versed in computer design should be capable of designing any type of digital system.

For the computer scientist, whose primary interest is software, this book may stand alone as an engaging (we hope) introduction to the philosophy of hardware design. With more imaginative use of microprogramming, the overlap of hardware and software functions becomes increasingly apparent. A familiarity with hardware at the level of detail presented herein will be increasingly required of individuals going into the area of systems programming. Further, the steadily increasing importance of the microprocessor creates a real need for designers with competence in both the hardware and software aspects of digital systems design.

For the electrical engineer it is certainly not our intention to minimize the importance of a companion course in switching theory and sequential circuits. As contrasted with the computer scientist, the electrical engineer has the responsibility of making the hardware work. Particular circuit technologies generate intricate fundamental-mode problems in situations that have been idealized in this volume. Interface (connection between digital equipments) design will continue to occupy ever-increasing amounts of engineering effort. This area will always overlap system techniques (see Chapters 9 to 12), sequential circuits, and even circuit design. The computer engineer should have coursework background in all three of these areas.

1.2 EVOLUTION OF THE COMPUTER

The history of mechanical aids to computation goes back many centuries. The development of the abacus apparently predates recorded history. In the 17th century Pascal and Leibniz developed mechanical calculators, the ancestors through hundreds of years of development of today's desk calculators. The first device that was a computer in the modern sense was proposed about 1830 by Charles Babbage.

Babbage, an eccentric English mathematician, was one of the most fascinating characters in the history of science. He was concerned with improving the methods of computing mathematical tables. Until the advent of the digital computers, mathematical tables were computed by teams of mathematicians, grinding away endlessly at desk calculators, performing the same calculations over and over to produce the thousands of entries in tables of logarithms, trigonometric functions, etc. Babbage was working on some improved log tables, and so despaired at ever getting the job done that he resolved to build a machine to do it.

The result of his first efforts was the Difference Engine, the first description of which he published in 1822. The Difference Engine carried out a fixed sequence of calculations, specified by mechanical settings of levers, cams, gears, etc. Even data had to be entered mechanically, and results were printed out immediately on computation. The Difference Engine was funded by the British government and was partially completed when Babbage conceived the idea of using punched cards, invented by Jacquard in 1801, to provide the input and storage of results. He proposed that instructions be read from one set of cards and data from another set, with the results stored on still another set. The proposed machine, which he called the Analytical Engine, even had a primitive decision capability. Although instructions had to be executed in the order read from the cards, an instruction could specify alternative actions, based on a test of previous results.

Babbage first started work on the Analytical Engine about 1830; the remainder of his life (he died in 1871) was spent in a fruitless effort to get the machine built. His ideas were a hundred years ahead of technology. The mechanical technology of the day was inadequate to meet the requirements of his designs. Indeed, it is doubtful if the Analytical Engine could be realized by mechanical means even today. The reali-

4

zation of Charles Babbage's dreams had to await the development of electronics.

In 1937, Howard Aiken, of Harvard University, proposed the Automatic Sequence Controlled Calculator, based on a combination of Babbage's ideas and the technology of the electromechanical calculators then being produced by IBM. Construction of this machine, more generally known as Mark I, was started in 1939, sponsored jointly by Harvard and IBM. The completed machine was dedicated August 7, 1944, a date considered by many to mark the start of the computer era.

Mark I was primarily electromechanical, being constructed mostly of switches and relays, a factor that severely limited its speed. Scientists at the Aberdeen Proving Ground, concerned with the development of ballistic tables for new weapons systems, recognized the need for a faster computer than Mark I. As a result, a contract was awarded in 1943 to the University of Pennsylvania to develop a digital computer using vacuum tubes instead of relays. The result was ENIAC, the world's first electronic digital computer. The ENIAC development team was led by J. P. Eckert and J. W. Mauchly, and the mathematical consultant to the group was John von Neumann, one of the most creative mathematicians of this century. The development of the digital computer involved the efforts of many brilliant individuals, and no one person can be said to have invented the computer. Nevertheless, many people consider von Neumann to be the single most important figure in the history of the computer.

Although Mark I is generally considered to be the first digital computer, its structure was very little like that of present-day computers. It essentially consisted of many electromechanical calculators, working in parallel on a common problem, under the direction of a single control unit. This paralleling of many calculating units was made necessary by the slow speed of the electromechanical devices. The control unit read the instructions from a paper tape and, like the Analytical Engine, could execute them only in the sequence received.

ENIAC was essentially an electronic version of Mark I, with many parallel calculating elements and a sequential control unit. During the development of ENIAC two new concepts emerged. One was the realization that the great speed of electronic devices made it unecessary to have many parallel calculating elements. The second was the idea that storing the program in memory, in much the same manner that data are stored, would make it possible to branch to alternate sequences of instructions, rather than being tied to a fixed sequence. These two concepts, together with some new developments in electronics, led to the proposal for a new machine, the EDVAC computer.

The development of the EDVAC proposal was a team effort, and it is difficult to assign credit for specific ideas to specific persons. Nevertheless, it was von Neumann who tied all the ideas together for the first time, in the *First Draft for a Report on EDVAC*, issued in June 1945. In this document von Neumann set forth the basic logical structure of the *stored-program computer*. The following five criteria essentially define the computer, in terms of the capabilities it must have.

1. It must have an *input* medium, by means of which an essentially unlimited number of operands or instructions may be entered.
2. It must have a *store*, from which operands or instructions may be obtained and into which results may be entered, *in any desired order*.
3. It must have a *calculating* section, capable of carrying out arithmetic or logical operations on any operands taken from the store.
4. It must have an *output* medium, by means of which an essentially unlimited number of results may be delivered to the user.
5. It must have a *control unit*, capable of interpreting instructions obtained from memory, and capable of choosing between alternative courses of action on the basis of computed results.

The basic structure resulting from these criteria is known as the *von Neumann structure*, and virtually all computers built since that time have utilized this structure.

The ENIAC/EDVAC team broke up in 1946, Eckert and Mauchly leaving to found their own company, and von Neumann going to the Institute for Advanced Study at Princeton. The departure of many key people seriously slowed development of EDVAC, and it was not finally completed until 1950. Building on the basic structure of EDVAC, Eckert and Mauchly developed the first commercially produced computer, UNIVAC I, the first unit of which was delivered in 1951. At Princeton, von Neumann led the development of the IAS computer, which was also completed in 1951. During the course of this project, von Neumann contributed another basic concept in digital computing, that of modifying the address portion of instructions so that a single set of instructions can be applied to many sets of data elements.

In succeeding years, the power and speed of computers has increased by many orders of magnitude, and computers now exercise a pervasive influence on modern society. The recent development of the microprocessor will greatly increase this influence, probably to the point where virtually every person will have almost daily direct contact with computers. But the improvements in computers have been due chiefly to improved devices and technology. The basic organization of most computers still conforms closely to the criteria set forth by von Neumann.

1.3 BASIC ORGANIZATION OF DIGITAL COMPUTERS

Any computer meeting the criteria set forth in the previous section will be basically organized as shown in Fig. 1.2. The exact nature of the components making up the five basic sections of the computer may vary widely, and the sections may overlap or share components; but the five functions associated with the five sections may be clearly identified in any digital computer.

The memory is the central element of the computer, in the sense that it is the source or destination of all information flowing to or from the other four sections of the computer. The memory may be regarded as a collection of storage locations for information; with each location is associated an *address*, by means of which that location may be accessed by the other sections of the computer. The amount of information that can be stored in an individually addressable location, expressed in terms of the number of bits (binary digits), is known as the *word length* of the memory. Nomenclature here is sometimes confusing, and you will hear such terms as *byte-organized* and *variable word length* applied to memory. Whatever the type of organization, we use *memory word* to signify the smallest amount of information that can be individually accessed, or

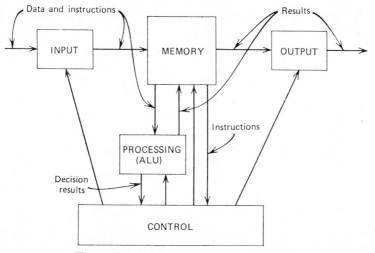

Figure 1.2. Basic computer organization.

addressed, in memory. Word lengths in various modern computers typically range from about 8 bits to 64 bits.

A great variety of devices is used for memory, ranging from fast, low-capacity devices with a high cost per bit, to slow, high-capacity devices with a low cost per bit. A single computer may employ a whole hierarchy of memory devices of varying speed/capacity ratios. The main memory, i.e., that portion of memory in most direct communication with the control and processing sections, is usually a high-speed random access memory with a capacity in the range of about 4000 to a million or more words. This may be backed up by any number of slower devices, such as disk or tape, which may make bulk transfers of large numbers of words to or from main memory.

The basic functions of the input and output sections are quite obvious; but they have two subsidiary functions, buffering and data conversion, which are not quite so obvious. The buffering function provides the interface between the very fast processing section and the comparatively slow "outside world." For example, a human operator may punch data onto cards at a rate of a few characters per second. A stack of these cards may be read onto tape at a rate of a thousand characters per second. The tape may then be read into main memory at a rate of 100,000 characters per second, and main memory can communicate with the processing unit at the rate of a million words per second.

The data conversion can be illustrated in the same example. When the operator punches written information onto cards, it is converted into the Hollerith code. While the Hollerith code is fine for punched cards, it is not particularly suitable for magnetic tape; so the characters are translated to another code as they are transferred to tape. While tapes are character-organized, main memory is word-organized, with a word generally made up of several characters. So the characters are grouped into words as the tape is read into memory. The reverse operations take place on output.

The processing section, which we shall refer to as the arithmetic-logical unit (ALU), implements the various arithmetic and logical operations on operands obtained from memory. ALU's vary considerably in the number of different operations implemented. The minimum possible set of operations for a general-purpose computer is a subject of some theoretical interest; as few as two may be sufficient, but most ALU's have a repertory in the range of 16 to 256 commands.

The control section receives instruction words from memory, decodes them, and issues the appropriate control signals to the other sections to cause the desired operations to take place. It also receives the results of various tests on data made by the ALU, on the basis of which it may choose between alternate courses of action. The combination of the ALU and the control unit is often referred to as the *central processing unit* (CPU).

1.4 INSTRUCTION FORMATS

We can get an idea of what information must be included in an instruction word by considering how we might give instructions to a person who is to do some computing for us. We could provide him with a ledger sheet of data and a sheet of instructions. Then a typical instruction might read, "Take a number from column 1, add it to a number in column 2, enter the sum in 3, and proceed to line 4 of the instruction sheet for the next step." In computer terms, this is a *four-address* instruction.

An instruction word, which is simply a string of 0's and 1's, is divided up into several sections, each of which is interpreted to have some specific significance by the control unit. The format of a four-address instruction is shown in Fig. 1.3a. The *op code* is the numeric code, typically 4 to 6 bits, indicating the operation—add, subtract, shift, etc.—to be performed. The remainder of the word provides the four addresses in memory required for the two operands, the result, and the next instruction.

The main problem with the four-address instruction is the amount of space required to accommodate four addresses. Since accessing instructions takes time, it is highly desirable that only one memory access be required to obtain an instruction. Thus the pressure is strong to limit the complexity of the instructions so they may fit into a single memory

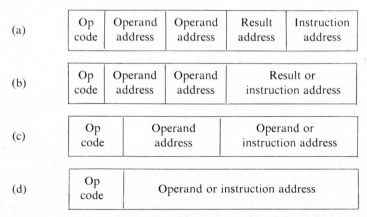

Figure 1.3. Typical instruction formats.

word. The size of an address is determined by the size of the memory: the more locations in memory, the more bits will be required to specify an address. For example, a 32,000-word memory, a typical size, requires 15-bit addresses; so a four-address instruction will require 60 bits just for addresses. Only the very largest machines have memory words this long.

The number of addresses in the instruction word can be reduced by letting some of the information be "understood." Computer programs usually proceed in a fixed sequence most of the time, branching to an alternate path only occasionally. We therefore specify that the instructions shall be stored in sequentially numbered locations; and the next instruction will be taken from the next sequential location, unless otherwise specified. This concept leads to the three-address instruction (Fig. 1.3b), which will typically have the meaning, "Take the operands from the first two addresses, store the result at the third address, and take the next instruction from the next sequential location." Deviation from the fixed sequence requires a *branch* instruction, which could have the meaning, "Compare the operands taken from the first two addresses: if they are equal, take the next instruction from the third address; if not, take the next instruction from the next sequential location."

The number of required addresses can be further reduced by allowing the destination of the result to be "understood." The two-address instruction (Fig. 1.3c) takes on two standard forms.

The *replacement* instruction typically has the meaning, "Take the operands from the two addresses, store the result at the second address (replacing the second operand), and take the next instruction from the next sequential location." This type of instruction is inconvenient if both operands need to be preserved for further operations. The problem can be avoided by specifying a standard register in the ALU, usually known as the *accumulator*, as the destination for results. Then a typical two-address instruction will have the meaning, "Take the operands from the two addresses, place the result in the accumulator, and take the next instruction from the next sequential location." With this form we must also have a *store* instruction, of the form, "Store the contents of the accumulator in one of the two specified addresses." In either case, the branch instruction might take the form, "Compare the contents of the first address with the contents of the accumulator: if they are equal, take the next instruction from the second address; if not, take the next instruction from the next sequential location."

Finally, there is the single-address format (Fig. 1.3d), which allows the source of the second operand to be "understood." Now the typical instruction will have the meaning, "Take the first operand from the addressed location, the second from the accumulator, place the result in the accumulator, and take the next instruction from the next sequential location." A typical branch instruction might take the form, "Test the contents of the accumulator: if they are zero, take the instruction from the addressed location; if not, continue in sequence." Most machines also have an unconditional branch that causes the next instruction to be taken from the addressed location regardless of the contents of the accumulator.

The choice of an instruction format is a difficult one, requiring the balancing of a number of conflicting factors. The single-address is obviously most efficient in terms of the amount of memory space required for each instruction. However, a program written in single-address instructions will certainly have more instructions than a corresponding one written in multiple-address instructions. Obviously, the more information we can put in each instruction, the fewer instructions we require to accomplish a given task. But even this is not a simple relationhip, since there are some types of instructions for which more than one address is not needed. The *store* instruction discussed earlier is an example. Another is the *shift* instruction, causing the contents of the accumulator to be shifted left or right a specified number of places. In this case the "address" portion of the instruction is not an address at all, but may be interpreted as a binary number, indicating the number of places to be shifted.

In the class of small machines generally known as minicomputers, the word length is usually 16 to 20 bits, making the single-address format really the only practical choice. As we increase the word length, we obviously increase our options. In some large computers with long memory words, two or more single-address instructions may be packed into a single word, thus reducing the number of memory accesses required for fetching instructions. Other large machines use two-address instructions. Still others do both, placing two single-address or one two-address instruction in each word. This makes the control unit more complex, but gives the programmer more flexibility.

Three-address instructions are seldom, if ever, used for addressing memory directly. Several machines use shorter addresses to select the operands and destination from eight or more operating registers. Thus a three-address instruction can specify two operand registers and one result register, using only 9 bits. This approach also requires a two-address format for transferring information between memory and the operating registers. We know of no machines using the four-address format.

In microprocessors the word length is commonly 8 bits, sometimes only 4 bits. These devices normally use a variant of the single-address format, with the op code in one word and the address in one or more additional words, stored sequentially immediately following the op code.

The number of combinations and variations on these formats is practically unlimited, and virtually any combination or variation you might think of has probably been tried by somebody. However, the single-address format is used in more different models of computers than any other; and, with a few exceptions, it is the format we shall use in this book.

1.5 SOFTWARE

Programs written in the form of instructions discussed in the previous section, strings of binary 1's and 0's, are known as *machine language* programs. All programs must be ultimately placed in this form, since these are the only kind of instructions the control unit can interpret. Writing programs in this form is incredibly difficult. First, binary strings are cumbersome, inconvenient, and downright unnatural to humans. Second, the programmer must assign binary addresses to all the data and instructions, and, even worse, keep track of all these addresses.

In the early days of computers, programmers had to work in machine language; and many despaired of computers ever being of much use because it was virtually impossible to get a really useful program running. As we know, the problem was solved by writing programs to get the computers to do most of the drudgery of programming. The class of "programs to process programs" is known collectively as software. Software is so important to successful operation of a computer that the success of a particular model is often determined more by the quality of the software than by the quality of the hardware, i.e., the machine itself. Many of the developments in computer organization have come about in response to the need for efficient processing of the software.

Software initially developed in a fairly natural and straightforward manner, but has recently become quite complex. As we noted, binary strings are inconvenient, if only because they are so long. The first simplification, suggested by von Neumann in 1945, is to convert instructions to octal form, treating each group of 3 bits as a binary number, and replacing each group with the equivalent octal digit. And it was a simple matter to equip the input section with the capability of converting each octal digit to the equivalent binary form.

Once we recognize that the computer can convert from one form to another, it is quite natural to replace the numeric op codes with mnemonic names, such as ADD, MULT, DIV, etc., and write a program to enable the computer to convert these names to the equivalent codes. Next, as we assign variables to memory locations, we make up a table giving the addresses corresponding to the variable names. In the address portion of the instructions we simply write the variable name, instead of the actual address. When we feed the program into the computer, we also feed in the address table, and let the computer replace variable names with the appropriate addresses.

Next we note that assigning addresses is routine bookkeeping job, just as well given to the computer. Now our programs need contain little more than instructions consisting only of operation names and variable names. At this point, we have an *assembly language*. The program that assigns the addresses and converts the instructions to machine language form is known as an *assembler*.

Assembly language is an immense improvement over machine language, but there are still many problems. The main problem is that an assembly language is computer-oriented. Each assembly language statement corresponds to one machine language statement, so that the programmer must be familiar with the instructions and internal organization of the particular computer. Knowledge of how to program one computer will be of little value in programming any other computer. We would prefer a language in which we could write programs that could be run on virtually any computer. This leads us to the concept of *problem-oriented* or *high-level* languages, such as FORTRAN, ALGOL, COBOL, PL/I, APL, etc.

Problem-oriented languages (POL) permit us to write programs in forms as close as possible to the natural, "human-oriented" languages that might be appropriate to the particular problems. Thus, a mathematical formula such as

$$s = (-b + \sqrt{b^2 - 4ac})/2a$$

may be evaluated by a single, closely analogous program statement in FORTRAN.

The evaluation of a formula such as the above will obviously require many machine language instructions. There are two distinct methods for converting POL programs into machine language programs. In one method, as the program is executed, each POL statement is converted into a corresponding set of machine language instructions, which are immediately executed, before proceeding to the next POL statement. A system functioning in this manner is known as an *interpreter*.

Interpreters are inefficient for programs with repetitive loops. For example, in FORTRAN we use DO loops to apply the same set of instructions over and over to a whole set of data. An interpreter has to translate the instructions in the DO loop on every pass through the loop, which is clearly inefficient since the translation is the same on every pass. This fault is corrected by *compilers*, which translate the complete POL program into a complete machine language program that is executed only after the complete program has been compiled.

Since interpreters and compilers translate into the machine language, they must be written separately for each computer. However, the compiler or interpreter for a given language may be written for any machine having adequate memory capacity to hold the software. Thus a programmer writing in a popular language, such as FORTRAN, can run his program on practically any computer.

Another important class of software is the control program. In the early days of computers, each program run had to be initiated and terminated by an operator. With modern computers capable of executing a complete program in a fraction of a second, such human intervention is obviously impractical. So we have *executive* routines and *monitors*, which control the actual running of the computer. For example, a card reader may be loaded with large stacks of cards, representing hundreds of programs. The executive or monitor will separate the programs, assign them to tapes, schedule compilation and execution, assign memory, schedule printing, etc., all automatically. Except for dealing with emergencies, about all the operators have to do is load the cards and tear off the printer sheets.

There, are many specialized types of software that we have not discussed. Although the hardware and software of a computer make up an integral and inseparable whole, software represents a complete area of study in itself. In this book we are concerned with software only to the extent that some understanding of software is essential to good hardware design. A knowledge of programming, at least in a problem-oriented language, is a prerequisite to this book; any person seriously interested in computer design must also study software design.

REFERENCES

1. Morrison, P., and E. Morrison, eds., *Charles Babbage and His Calculating Engines*, Dover Publications, New York, 1961.

2. Bowden, B. V., *Faster than Thought*, Putnam, London, 1953.

3. Hill, F. J., and G. R. Peterson, *Introduction to Switching Theory and Logical Design*, 2nd ed., Wiley, New York, 1974.

4. McClusky, E. J., *Introduction to the Theory of Switching Circuits*, McGraw-Hill, New York, 1965.

5. Aiken, H. H., "Proposed Automatic Calculating Machine," *IEEE Spectrum*, Vol. 1, August 1964, pp. 62–69.

6. Serrell, R., et al., "The Evolution of Computing Machines and Systems," *Proc. I.R.E.*, Vol. 50, May 1962, pp. 1040–1058.

7. Dill, F. Y., "Battle of the Giant Brains," *Popular Electronics*, Vol. 34, April 1971, pp. 39–43.

8. Goldstine, H. H., *The Computer from Pascal to von Neumann*, Princeton University Press, Princeton, N.J., 1972.

9. Tropp, H., "The Effervescent Years: A Retrospective," *IEEE Spectrum*, Vol. 11, Feb. 1974, pp. 70–79.

2

ORGANIZATION AND PROGRAMMING
OF A SMALL COMPUTER

2.1 INTRODUCTION

This chapter contains a discussion of the organization and assembly
language programming of a minicomputer. At the risk of seeming trite,
we shall label this computer SIC for *Small Instructional Computer*. A
name will prove convenient, since frequent references to the machine
will be necessary.

The previous background of readers in assembly language programming will vary greatly. For the reader whose only programming experience has been in FORTRAN, COBOL, or some other high-level language, this chapter is intended to serve two purposes. First, it will serve
as an introduction to assembly language programming. Second, it provides a description of a minicomputer sufficiently complete to serve as
a basis for hardware design. The reader who is already familiar with
assembly language programming should be able to move rapidly
through the chapter. All readers must learn the organization and instruction codes of SIC so they can follow the design of the SIC control unit
in Chapters 6 and 7.

Historically, the development and use of computing machines preceded the invention of high-level languages. The development of these
languages was heavily influenced by the already existing machine languages. FORTRAN, for example, is really a union of the notation of
ordinary algebra with the control features of machine language. In this
chapter we shall proceed in reverse to uncover the machine language
counterparts of the basic FORTRAN operations. We shall not attempt to
illustrate all of the procedures involved in machine language program-

16

ming. Armed with an understanding of the relation between FORTRAN and machine language, the reader should be able to expound the list of machine language programming techniques to be presented. Some of the examples may resemble elementary compiler techniques. Our purpose is only to take maximum advantage of the reader's experience in a high-level language; compilers as such will not be treated in this book.

The SIC computer is typical of several existing minicomputers. Left out of this machine are many of the sophistications found in computers intended for high-speed, maximum throughput, batch-processing applications. All of the essential features that serve to identify a digital system as a general-purpose computer are included. We shall stay with this machine through the end of Chapter 7. In this way we hope to provide the reader with the basic tools of computer design without inundating him with details at the outset.

2.2 REMARKS ON NUMBER SYSTEMS

We assume that most readers will have had some previous experience with nondecimal number systems. One topic of the binary number system, namely that of handling negative numbers in two's-complement form, will appear several times in this chapter. We shall therefore review it briefly in this section.

The most straightforward way to store in memory a binary number, which may be positive or negative, is in sign and magnitude form. If a memory location is capable of storing n binary bits, one of these bits must be used to store the sign; so only $n - 1$ bits are available to store the magnitude. The disadvantage of sign and magnitude form is that signs must be checked separately prior to every addition or subtraction operation.

This difficulty is avoided by storing all numbers in memory in two's-complement form. If a number is positive, the two's complement of that number is merely the number itself. If a number, x, is negative, the two's complement of x is given by Eq. 2.1:

$$\text{two's complement } (x) = 2^n - |x| \quad (x < 0) \qquad (2.1)$$

In this chapter n will be the number of bits in a storage location. In order to distinguish positive and negative numbers, we require that $|x| < 2^{n-1}$. If this restriction is satisfied, the leftmost bit of a positive number will always be 0.

Suppose that $n = 6$. Then the number -25 (decimal) may be expressed

17

in two's-complement form as follows. First, 25 expressed in 6 binary bits is 011001. Thus, using Eq. 2.1 we obtain

$$
\begin{array}{r}
1000000 \\
-011001 \\
\hline
100111
\end{array} = \text{two's complement } (-25).
$$

Notice that the leftmost bit is a 1. This will always be the case for a negative x, where $|x| < 2^{n-1}$. That is,

$$2^n - |x| > 2^n - 2^{n-1} = 2^{n-1}. \tag{2.2}$$

We note that 2^{n-1} expressed as n binary bits has a 1 in the leftmost bit and 0 in the other bits. From Eq. 2.2 we conclude that the leftmost bit of $2^n - |x|$ must be 1 also.

The advantage of the two's-complement approach is that two's-complement addition is the same as the addition of two positive arguments. Suppose, for example, that a negative number, x, in two's-complement form is added to a positive number, y, of smaller magnitude as given in Eq. 2.3. The result is, as it should be,

$$(2^n - |x|) + y = 2^n - (|x| - y) \tag{2.3}$$

a negative number in two's-complement form. Whether the arguments are positive or negative, the result of an addition will always be the correct two's-complement form if the magnitude of the result remains $<2^{n-1}$. The four possible cases are illustrated in Fig. 2.1. Notice that in two of the examples of Fig. 2.1 a one appears in the 7th bit position. Physically, two's-complement addition will be modulo-2^n. That is, the $(n + 1)$st bit will not fit in the accumulator and will not be considered part of the result. The reader can verify that the rightmost 6 bits are the correct result in all cases.

Before leaving this section, we remark that the binary and octal number system will be used almost interchangeably in this book. Octal numbers will be used to represent binary numbers for convenience. For example, an 18-bit binary number may be expressed much more compactly as a 6-digit octal number. The familiar method of determining the octal equivalent of a binary number by arranging bits into groups of

$(-25) + 15$	$25 + (-15)$	$(-15) + (-14)$	$15 + 14$
100111	011001	110001	001111
001111	110001	110010	001110
110110	1 001010	1 100011	011101

Figure 2.1. Examples of two's-complement addition.

three and replacing each by an octal digit is illustrated as follows.

$$001 \quad 010 \quad 011 \quad 100 \quad 101 \quad 110$$
$$1 \quad\;\; 2 \quad\;\; 3 \quad\;\; 4 \quad\;\; 5 \quad\;\; 6$$

The binary and octal numbers shown are equal. Justification of this method is left as a problem for the reader.

2.3 LAYOUT OF A SMALL INSTRUCTIONAL COMPUTER (SIC)

In Chapter 1 it was established that every computer includes a memory for storing instructions and data in binary form. Associated with each memory location is an address. The method by which an address is used electronically to obtain the contents of a memory location will be discussed in the next chapter. SIC has $2^{13} = 8192$ memory locations whose addresses are numbered from 0 to $2^{13} - 1$. These addresses will be referred to as binary numbers or octal numbers. In octal, the range of addresses is from 0 to 17777. Each item stored in memory, whether data or instruction, has the form of an *18-bit* binary number.

The large number of memory locations required indicates that the memory must be realized physically by a set of relatively inexpensive memory elements. The speed at which a machine can execute instructions is dependent on the time required to electronically select a location and acquire or replace its contents. A memory in which any location can be accessed in the same short time interval is called a random access memory (RAM). One example of a reasonably inexpensive random access memory is a magnetic core memory.

The control unit shown in Fig. 1.2 must be capable of storing some information in order to execute instructions. The binary representation of the instruction being executed is stored in an instruction register. The address of the next instruction in memory is stored in the program counter. An accumulator for storing the results of computations is included in the arithmetic section as suggested in Chapter 1. Two additional registers called index registers are included. Two registers that need not concern us until Chapter 6 are a memory address register and a memory data register. All of these registers consist of electronic storage elements that function at the highest possible speeds. A discussion of the purpose of these registers follows.

A. Program Counter

The machine language instructions making up a program must all reside in the random access memory of the machine in order for the program to be executed.* In any machine it is possible to load a short program into memory utilizing switches on the control console. Usually, programs are loaded into memory from a card reader or a magnetic tape by a program called a *loader*, which might be part of the computer's software operating system. The *program counter* is a register that stores the address of the next instruction to be executed by the computer. At some point during the execution of most instructions the number in the program counter is increased by 1. Thus instructions are executed in the order of their locations in memory. The only exceptions occur in the event of machine language branch instructions analogous to the IF and GO TO statements. The program counter is a 13-bit register, in order that an instruction may be obtained from any of the 2^{13} memory locations.

B. Accumulator

The *accumulator* is utilized as temporary storage for the results of a computation. In some cases it may store one of the arguments as well. For example, addition is accomplished by adding a word from the random access memory to the contents of the accumulator and leaving the result in the accumulator. A 19th bit called the *link* is placed at the left of the accumulator to facilitate various arithmetic operations.

C. Instruction Register

In order for an instruction to be executed, it must be *read* from memory and placed in the *instruction register*. In this position the binary bits of the instruction are decoded to generate control signals, which are active throughout the period of execution. The instruction to be placed in the instruction register is determined by the contents of the program counter. The instruction register must store 18 bits.

D. Index Registers

Two index registers are included in the machine. We shall label these *Index Register A* and *Index Register B*. The contents of these registers may be added to the address portion of an instruction to permit repetition of that instruction on an array of data words. Special instructions are provided for incrementing the index registers following each pass through some sequence of instructions. In effect this permits convenient

---

*The exception to this rule is memory overlays. However, it is not possible to jump directly from one overlay to an instruction in another overlay.

execution of DO loops in FORTRAN. The mechanism of indexing will become clear in the next two sections. Index registers are 13-bit registers.

2.4 SIC INSTRUCTIONS

All 18 bits of an instruction word are necessary to completely define an instruction. Any 18-bit word placed in the instruction register will cause some sort of instruction to be executed. The computer cannot distinguish between an instruction word and a data word. If a programmer error causes a data word to be executed, the subsequent results become meaningless.

The basic instruction codes for SIC are shown in Fig. 2.2a. The first seven instructions are the *addressed* instructions, for which the complete instruction format is shown in Fig. 2.2b. All of the addressed instructions except JMP are *memory reference instructions*. Memory reference instructions always address an operand in the random access memory. Thus bits 5 to 17 are required to indicate the address of the operand in a memory reference instruction. Clearly, SIC is a single-address machine. Where two arguments are used and a result is computed as in TAD, for example, one of the arguments is found in the

Bits 012	Octal	Mnemonic	Description
000	0	ISZ	Increment and skip if zero
001	1	LAC	Load accumulator
010	2	AND	Logical and
011	3	TAD	Two's-complement add
100	4	JMS	Jump to subroutine
101	5	DAC	Deposit accumulator
110	6	JMP	Jump (GO TO)
111	7		Operate or input/output instructions

(a)

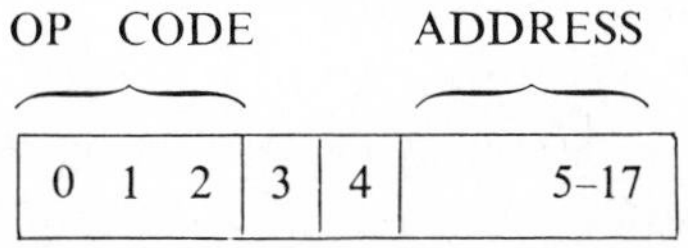

OP CODE   ADDRESS

| 0 | 1 | 2 | 3 | 4 | 5–17 |

(b)

Figure 2.2. Basic SIC instruction codes and format.

accumulator and the result is placed in the accumulator. For the JMP instruction the address specifies the next instruction.

The code 111 indicates that the instruction is an input/output (I/O) or operate instruction, for which no address is required. Bits 5 to 17 (also 3 and 4) may be used to further specify these instructions. Thus a very large number of input/output and operate instructions are possible. A list of important operate instructions will be presented later in this section. We shall defer the problem of input/output completely until Chapter 10. We are confident that the reader's experience with FORTRAN programming has left him generally familiar with the input/output process. Consideration of all of the sample programs in this chapter will be terminated with the results still in memory. In Chapter 10 we shall consider topics such as I/O busing, interrupts, and I/O software.

In order to facilitate our discussion we refer to binary instruction words by their octal equivalents. For example, the instruction

$$\begin{array}{c|c|c} \text{LAC} & & \text{ADDRESS} \\ 001, & 00 & 0,000,000,001,011 \end{array} \qquad (2.4)$$

which specifies "Load the accumulator with the contents of location 1011" and leave the contents of 1011 unchanged,* will be written

$$100013 \qquad (2.5)$$

For the time being, we are assuming that bits 3 and 4 are both zero so that the second octal digit from the left will always be zero or one. Still more convenient is the form

$$\text{LAC } 13 \qquad (2.6)$$

Throughout our discussion, LAC 13 shall have the same meaning as expressions 2.4 and 2.5. Clearly, it is necessary for LAC 13 to be translated to numerical form before it can be stored in memory. This is part of the function of a program called an assembler.

The remaining addressed instructions in Fig. 2.2a are explained in more detail as follows:

ISZ 13 means add 1 to (increment) the contents of memory location 13 (octal) and skip the next instruction if the result is zero.

AND 13 calls for "anding" each bit of the word in location 13 with the corresponding bits in the accumulator. The resulting word is left in the accumulator.

*This is the case with all instructions that place the contents of one register (including memory locations) in another register. The information remains in the first register as well. This is consistent with the nature of FORTRAN replacement statements.

TAD 13 causes the number in location 13 to be added to the number in the accumulator. A carry bit from the leftmost column of addition is placed in the link. The 18-bit addition will be correct if both arguments are in two's-complement form.

JMS 13 (jump to subroutine) causes the contents of the program counter to be incremented and placed in memory location 13. The next instruction to be executed is taken from memory location 14.

DAC 13 deposits the contents of the accumulator in memory location 13.

JMP 13 causes the next instruction to be taken from memory location 13.

Example 2.1

The execution of a TAD instruction is illustrated in Fig. 2.3. The memory locations of interest are shown in Fig. 2.3a. For convenience, only the actual

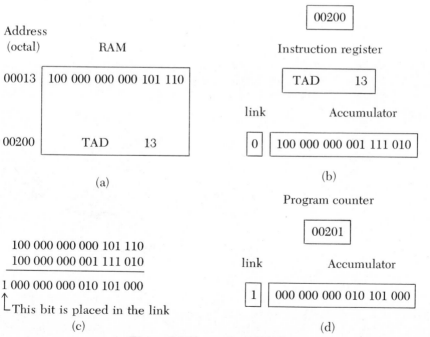

Program counter

00200

Address
(octal)   RAM

| 00013 | 100 000 000 000 101 110 |
| 00200 | TAD   13 |

(a)

Instruction register

TAD   13

link   Accumulator

| 0 | 100 000 000 001 111 010 |

(b)

```
  100 000 000 000 101 110
  100 000 000 001 111 010
─────────────────────────
1 000 000 000 010 101 000
↑
```
└This bit is placed in the link

(c)

Program counter

00201

link   Accumulator

| 1 | 000 000 000 010 101 000 |

(d)

Figure 2.3 Execution of TAD 13.

arguments of the addition are shown in binary. In reality, of course, the contents of location 200 would also be stored in binary form. The contents of the program counter and the accumulator prior to execution of the instruction are shown in Fig. 2.3b. The number in the program counter is given in octal form. The operation begins by reading the contents of memory location 200 (as specified by the program counter) from memory and placing them in the instruction register. The symbolic form of the binary contents of the instruction register is shown in Fig. 2.3b. Next, the address portion of the instruction (00013 octal) is used to obtain a binary argument from memory. The actual addition of this number to the contents of the accumulator is displayed in Fig. 2.3c. Notice that the result is 19 bits long. The leftmost bit is placed in the link. The presence of the link as a 19th bit of storage for the results of arithmetic and certain other operations will prove quite convenient. The result of the operation is shown in the link and accumulator in Fig. 2.3d. Also shown are the new contents of the program counter after it has been incremented to prepare for fetching the next instruction from memory.

It is possible to manipulate the contents of the accumulator and exercise certain control functions without referencing the random access memory. This is accomplished by the *operate* instructions, several of which are listed in Fig. 2.4. Because of the great number of these in-

HLT	Halt
NOP	No operation
CLA	Clear accumulator to zero
STA	Set accumulator to 777777
CMA	Complement bits of accumulator
CLL	Clear link to zero
STL	Set link to one
SKP	Skip next instruction if accumulator ≥ 0
SKZ	Skip next instruction if accumulator $= 0$
SZL	Skip next instruction if link $= 0$
RAR	Rotate accumulator right
RAL	Rotate accumulator left
DTA	Deposit contents of accumulator in index register A
DTB	Deposit contents of accumulator in index register B
DFA	Deposit contents of index register A in accumulator
DFB	Deposit contents of index register B in accumulator
INA	Increment index register A
INB	Increment index register B

Figure 2.4. Operate instructions. In RAR and RAL the link is included in the rotation operations. For RAR the link is rotated into bit zero of the accumulator, and bit 17 is placed in the link.

structions we shall identify them here in mnemonic form only. In Chapter 6 the bit codes for various operate instructions will become clear as we discuss their hardware implementation. We shall assume that the descriptions in Fig. 2.4 are self-explanatory. The use of the various instructions will be further clarified as we discuss programming.

2.5 PROGRAMMING

In order to avoid the presentation of an excessive number of programming examples, we shall illustrate how the basic FORTRAN operations could be accomplished in machine language. Thus the reader will be able to generate his own examples by drawing on his FORTRAN programming experience. In this section we only illustrate how the reader can use his ingenuity to replace FORTRAN routines with sequences of assembly language instructions. This falls significantly short of defining a compiler or a set of rules for accomplishing this task automatically.

Let us consider first a version of FORTRAN consisting of replacement statements ("IXX="), GO TO statements, arithmetic IF statements, DO statements, arithmetic expressions, and subroutine CALLS. The reader will recognize that any program can be written, although not necessarily conveniently, using only these statements.

The replacement statement can be accomplished using only the instruction DAC. Suppose the quantity to replace the variable IXX, which we shall assume has been assigned to memory location 100, has been calculated and placed in the accumulator. Then the instruction DAC 100 causes IXX to take on its new value.

The control statements IF and GO TO are implemented easily in machine language. The statement JMP 100 could mean identically GO TO 100 if the first statement of FORTRAN instruction 100 were stored in memory location 100.

Assume now that FORTRAN instructions 100, 110, and 120 begin in the respective SIC memory locations, and IXX is assigned to location 1000. Then we may implement the FORTRAN instruction

$$\text{IF(IXX)} \quad 100, 110, 120 \qquad (2.7)$$

as follows:

```
LAC 1000
SKP
JMP 100
SKZ
JMP 120
JMP 110
```

Notice that the argument of the IF statement is immediately placed in the accumulator. The instruction SKP causes the next instruction to be skipped if IXX $\geq$ 0. If JMP 100 is not skipped, then the next instruction is taken from location 100. If JMP is skipped, the next instruction is SKZ. Thus control jumps to location 110 if the accumulator is zero, and to 120 if the accumulator is greater than zero.

The only instruction that is obviously intended to accomplish arithmetic is TAD. However, any arithmetic expression can be accomplished using this instruction together with LAC and the various operate instructions. Consider, for example,

$$N = M1 + ABS(M2) - M3 \qquad (2.8)$$

The sequence of instructions in Fig. 2.5 can be used to compute the arithmetic expression on the right. Assume that M1 is assigned to 1001, M2 to 1002, and M3 to 1003, and that the number 001 is stored in 2000. Since we shall wish to follow the program through several jump instructions, it is necessary to indicate the location in memory at the left of each instruction.

The first instruction in Fig. 2.5 loads the argument, M2. If M2 is negative, the program jumps to location 200. The instruction CMA takes the one's complement of M2. Adding +1 as is specified by instruction 201 leaves the two's complement of M2 in the accumulator. Then the program jumps back to location 103. If M2 is positive, the instruction in location 102 is skipped. In either case the absolute value of M2 is in the accumulator just prior to the execution of instruction 103. Next, M1 is added to M2 and the result is temporarily stored in location 203. The instructions 105 to 107 leave the two's complement of M3 in the accumulator. Adding the contents of 203 completes the generation of the right side of Eq. 2.8. Including the replacement statement DAC 1004

100	LAC	1002		200	CMA	
101	SKP			201	TAD	2000
102	JMP	200		202	JMP	103
103	TAD	1001		203	xxxxxx	
104	DAC	203		.		
105	LAC	1003		.		
106	CMA			.		
107	TAD	2000		1001		
110	TAD	203		1002		
				1003		
				2000	000001	

Figure 2.5.

would complete the instruction in Eq. 2.8 by placing the new value of N in location 1004.

In our example of an arithmetic expression we have avoided floating point as well as the more complicated operations of multiplication, division, and exponentiation. All of these can be accomplished in terms of sequences of SIC instructions. At this point we leave these tasks to the reader. Of course, large machines contain hardware for the implementation of multiplication, division, and floating point. The reader may surmise that avoiding software routines for these operations results in a considerable improvement in a machine's overall capability. These topics are discussed in detail in Chapters 15 and 16.

Example 2.2

An interesting example of the use of the link is found in the short routine for double precision arithmetic shown in Fig. 2.6a. As 18 bits are equivalent in precision to approximately five decimal digits, it is not surprising that greater accuracy is required on occasion. Memory locations 1000 and 1001 contain a 36-bit binary number, which will serve as one of the arguments of addition. The least significant 18 bits are in location 1000. Locations 1002 and 1003 similarly store the other 36-bit argument. The 36-bit result will be placed in locations 1004 and 1005.

100	CLL			300	000,000,000,000,000,001
101	LAC	1000		.	
102	TAD	1002		.	
103	DAC	1004		.	
104	LAC	1001		1000	100,000,000,000,101,110
105	SZL			1001	000,000,000,000,000,100
106	TAD	300		1002	100,000,000,001,111,010
107	TAD	1003		1003	000,000,000,000,100,110
110	DAC	1005		1004	000,000,000,010,101,000
	.			1005	000,000,000,000,101,011

(a)

```
      100 000 000 000 101 110      000 000 000 000 000 100
      100 000 000 001 111 010      000 000 000 000 100 110
    1 000 000 000 010 101 000      000 000 000 000 101 010
    └→Temporarily stored in link ──────────────────────→ +1

                                    000 000 000 000 101 011
        (b)                                  (c)
```

Figure 2.6. Double precision addition.

The first instruction clears the link to prepare for a possible carry from the least significant 18 bits. These portions of the two arguments are added by instructions 101 and 102. The result is stored in location 1004. As illustrated in Fig. 2.6b for the particular example, a carry propagates into the link, where it remains after a new argument is placed in the accumulator. The addition of the most significant 18 bits of the arguments is accomplished by instructions 104 to 107, as illustrated in Fig. 2.6c. If the link contains a 1, one is added to this result. For the example shown, the link is 1, representing a carry from the least significant 18 bits to the most significant 18 bits. The addition of this carry is shown in Fig. 2.6c. If the link contains a 0, instruction 106 is skipped; and the most significant 18 bits of the result are placed in location 1005.

2.6 INDEXING AND INDIRECT ADDRESSING

In this section we shall see that DO loops can be implemented by a sequence of instructions that use indexing or indirect addressing or both. Both of these techniques may be used for other purposes. Indirect addressing, in particular, is useful in information retrieval and various types of simulations.

The reader will recall that bits 3 and 4 of the instruction have yet to be discussed. The meanings of these bits, which apply only in the case of memory reference instructions, may be found in Fig. 2.7. If bit 3 is 0 and bit 4 is 1, then the address specified in the instruction does not contain the actual argument of the operation. Instead, the instruction specifies the address of a memory location containing a word whose last 13 bits are the address of the argument. This technique is called indirect addressing. Consider, for example, a set of memory locations specified as in Fig. 2.8. Notice that the instruction in location 200 is LAC. Since bit 4 is a 1, indirect addressing is specified. Thus location 600 contains the address of the argument. This address is 700; finally, the number 000005 is loaded into the accumulator from that location.

In order to utilize our mnemonic notation without confusion, we in-

Bits	3	4	Meaning
	0	0	No indexing or indirect addressing
	0	1	Indirect addressing
	1	0	Add index register A to address
	1	1	Add index register B to address

Figure 2.7. Interpretation of bits 3 and 4.

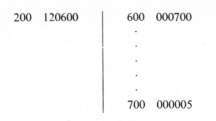

Figure 2.8.

dicate indirect addressing with an I. For example, the instruction in Fig. 2.8 could be represented by

LAC I 600

We shall refer to indexing in mnemonic fashion as well. The letters A and B will be used to indicate the addition of the respective index registers. For example, 140600 and LAC A 600 would both call for loading the accumulator with the word located at the address given by Eq. 2.9.

$$\text{Address} = 600 + \text{contents of } A \qquad (2.9)$$

Consider now the following DO loop:

```
          K = 0
          DO 90 J = 1, 6
          K = M(J) + K
          N(J) = K
      90  Continue
```

This set of instructions computes a sequence of partial sums of the elements in array M and leaves the result in array N. The instructions are found in locations 200 to 210. The array M is stored in 1000 to 1005 and the array N is stored in 1010 to 1015. The partial sums, which will be stored in these latter locations after execution of the routine, are shown there in Fig. 2.9b. Instructions 200 and 201 place in 776 the number –6 expressed in two's complement form. All numbers are given in octal form for brevity.

Instruction 202 established K = 0. Instruction 203 prepared for the DO loop by storing J = 0 in index register A. The first instruction of the DO loop loads K in the accumulator. The first execution of TAD A 1000 causes the contents of location 1000 to be added to the accumulator. The contents of the accumulator are then deposited in location 1010 as the first partial sum by the instruction DAC A 1010. Now the contents of index register A are increased by 1 by the operate instruction INA. The

200	LAC		(−6	776	777772 (−6)
201	DAC		776	1000	000007⎫
202	CLA			1001	000011⎪
203	DTA			1002	000001⎬ M
204	TAD	A	1000	1003	000021⎪
205	DAC	A	1010	1004	000005⎪
206	INA			1005	000006⎭
207	ISZ		776		
210	JMP		204		

(a)

1010	000007⎫
1011	000020⎪
1012	000021⎬ N
1013	000042⎪
1014	000047⎪
1015	000055⎭

(b)

Figure 2.9. Implementation of a DO loop.

function of ISZ 776 is to determine when six executions of the DO loop have been completed. This is done by incrementing the contents of 776 each time and then checking to see if the result is zero. If the result is still less than zero, the computer will jump back to the instruction in 204 to go through the loop again.

Since the contents of location 776 are initially −6, this quantity will be incremented six times. Each time through the loop the contents of index register A will also be increased by one. Thus the instruction TAD A 1000 will successively call out the contents of 1000, 1001, down to 1005; and DAC A 1010 will effect storage in 1010 through 1015. After the sixth time through the loop, ISZ will cause JMP 204 to be skipped; and the next instruction following the DO loop will be executed.

Not all machines have index registers. It is possible to perform the function of a DO loop utilizing indirect addressing with a location in core memory substituting for an index register. The sequence of instructions given in Fig. 2.10 will perform the same function as those in Fig. 2.9. The reader should verify this fact. The data registers may be assumed to be the same as those given in Fig. 2.10, with the exception that locations 774 and 775 are now used to store addresses. Initially, these registers contain 1000 and 1010, respectively. Notice that the instruction ISZ is used to merely add one to an address. Since the address is a large positive number, a skip will never occur.

```
200  CLA                    210  ISZ    776
201  DAC      777           211  JMP    202
202  LAC      777
203  TAD   I  774
204  DAC      777           774  001000
205  DAC   I  775           775  001010
206  ISZ      774           776  777772        (−6)
207  ISZ      775           777
```

Figure 2.10. Implementation of a DO loop with indirect addressing.

The disadvantage of the routine in Fig. 2.10 with respect to Fig. 2.9 is that the ISZ instruction is a memory reference instruction requiring longer to complete than the operate instruction INA. Thus more time is required for each pass through the loop. In addition, the initial addresses in 774 and 775 are destroyed, making it impossible to repeat the DO loop of Fig. 2.10. It is possible to accomplish the function of a DO loop without using indexing or indirect addressing, by performing arithmetic on the instructions themselves. The index register method is clearly preferable, however, and repetitive loops of the sort discussed account for the inclusion of index registers in computers. Nested DO loops may be handled by the use of more than one index register. This situation often calls for the addition of a number other than one to the contents of an index register. This must be accomplished by first transferring the index to the accumulator, adding the number, and then transferring the result back to the index register.

Indirect addressing can be used to accomplish some of the more complicated control functions such as the computed GO TO. For example, the instruction

$$\text{GO TO } (100, 200, 300, 400) \text{ M}$$

can be accomplished by the SIC routine given in Fig. 2.11. For simplicity we assume that the beginnings of FORTRAN instructions 100, 200, 300, and 400 are stored in SIC locations 100, 200, 300, and 400,

```
501  LAC      506
502  TAD      507           1001  JMP    100
503  DAC      505           1002  JMP    200
504  JMP   I  505           1003  JMP    300
505                         1004  JMP    400
506  M
507  001000
```

Figure 2.11. SIC equivalent of ASSIGNED GO TO.

31

respectively. The integer, M, which ranges between 1 and 4, is stored at location 506. The reader will note that the number 1000 + M is placed in location 505. The instruction JMP I 505 causes the execution of instructions to continue from 100, 200, 300, or 400, depending on M.

2.7 USING THE JMS INSTRUCTION

In many programs there are certain calculations that have to be carried out at different points in the program, on different sets of data. Rather than duplicate the code for these calculations each time they are to be carried out, it is often convenient to use a *subroutine*, a group of instructions for the calculation that can be referred to, or *called*, whenever needed. In using subroutines, there are two main problems. One is the transfer of control, from the main program to the subroutine when it is called, and from the subroutine back to the main program when the subroutine is done. The second is the transfer of arguments, operands from the main program to the subroutine, and results from the subroutine to the main program. The procedures for dealing with these problems are often referred to as the *subroutine linkage* and the *calling sequence*. The JMS instruction is provided to simplify the writing of subroutine linkages and calling sequences.

As a first example of a subroutine, Fig. 2.12 shows a subroutine (starting at location 1000) for computing the inclusive-OR by the use of De Morgan's theorem, as given by Eq. 2.10,

$$A \vee B = \overline{\overline{A} \wedge \overline{B}} \qquad (2.10)$$

The segment of the main program starting at location 200 calls the subroutine to compute the OR of operands stored at 300 and 301, and stores the result at 302.

Main Program			Subroutine		
200	LAC	300	1000	0000	
201	DAC	204	1001	CMA	
202	LAC	301	1002	DAC	1011
203	JMS	1000	1003	LAC I	1000
204	0000		1004	ISZ	1000
205	DAC	302	1005	CMA	
	·		1006	AND	1011
	·		1007	CMA	
	·		1010	JMP I	1000
			1011	0000	

Figure 2.12. Using the JMS Instruction.

The first two instructions in the main program obtain one operand and load it into the location immediately following the JMS instruction. The next instruction obtains the other operand and leaves it in the accumulator. Instruction 203 then calls the subroutine by executing JMS 1000. The JMS instruction increments the program counter to 204 and stores this address at location 1000. Then 1001 is placed in the program counter and the next instruction is taken from that location. The JMS instruction thus provides the first half of the linkage, the transfer of control to the subroutine.

The calling sequence in this example uses two methods of transferring data. One is through the accumulator. The JMS instruction has no effect on the accumulator, so the operand loaded into the accumulator at step 202 is still there. Steps 1001 and 1002 complement this operand and store it temporarily. Step 1003 performs an indirect LAC through 1000. Recall that 1000 contains 204 as a result of the JMS operation, so the second operand is brought from 204 into the accumulator. Before processing this operand, location 1000 is incremented to 205, in preparation for the return to the main program. The next steps (1005 to 1007) complement the second operand, AND it with the complement of the first operand, and complement the result, leaving the OR of the operands in the accumulator. Instruction 1010 now completes the linkage by jumping indirect through 1000, which now contains 205. Control then returns to 205, which stores the result, left in the accumulator by step 1007, in location 302.

As noted, the above example illustrates two techniques used in calling sequences. One operand or result can always be passed through the accumulator. Additional operands can be placed in locations following the JMS instruction and obtained by the subroutine by LAC I instructions, as in the above example. Results can be similarly transferred by using the DAC I instruction to place results in locations immediately following the JMS instruction. When arrays of operands or results are needed, the preferable technique is to place the starting addresses of the arrays in locations immediately following the JMS instruction. The subroutine can then obtain these addresses by LAC I operations, and then use them as pointers to the arrays. Note that each time an indirect LAC or DAC is executed, the address stored in the first location of the subroutine by JMS must be incremented, so that that address will always point to the next location in the main program that must be accessed by the subroutine.

2.8 ASSEMBLY LANGUAGE

So far, relatively few memory locations have been required and the assignment of numbers to these locations has not been difficult. In writing programs in assembly language, the task of allocating memory locations for data storage and program storage in advance is not pleasant. Should a routine require more storage or use more constants than envisioned at first, it may become necessary to reassign an entire region of storage.

For most machines the assembler provides a way around this problem. As well as translating mnemonic instructions to a binary code, this program will assign actual storage locations. The programmer need only specify a string of characters representing a variable, and the assembler will assign a memory location. It may be desired to jump to an instruction whose numerical memory location is not known precisely. It is possible to label any statement by a string of characters, AAA, for example, and then write the statement JMP AAA, which will cause a jump to the instruction in AAA. The programmer is usually allowed to label a statement with a specific (numbered) memory location, or symbolically with a character string, or omit the label. If there are no contradictions between memory locations specified by number, the assembler will fit it all together in memory.

To make the assembly process as efficient as possible, most assemblers require distinct characters to separate a fixed location from its contents and a variable location from its contents. We shall use the convention that a number followed by a slash, "/", represents a fixed memory location. A string of characters beginning with a letter will indicate a location to be assigned by the assembler and will be separated from the contents of the location by a comma. Thus

$$200/ \text{ LAC AAA} \tag{2.11}$$

causes LAC AAA to be stored in location 200 while

$$\text{AAA, 0} \tag{2.12}$$

lets the assembler assign a location to AAA in which a zero is stored. Once the location corresponding to AAA has been assigned, the assembler must replace AAA with the number of the assigned memory location in all instructions such as LAC AAA.

In writing a program, it is not necessary to precede each program line with either a fixed or variable location. Lines following locations specified as in either Eq. 2.11 or 2.12 will be assigned, in order, to succeeding memory locations. For example, the four instructions in Fig. 2.11 could be listed by the programmer in the two distinct forms given in

Fig. 2.13. In the case of Fig. 2.13b the assembler will assign LOC1 to a memory location and will place the LAC instruction in that location. TAD 1000 will be placed in the next location, and so on. Notice that it has been possible to avoid labeling the two data locations at the end of the routine. Since these will be stored in the 4th and 5th locations after LOC1, the assembler allows them to be referred to as LOC1 + 4 and LOC1 + 5. This technique is convenient when handling arrays of data.

501/	LAC	506	LOC1,	LAC LOC1 + 5
	TAD	1000		TAD 1000
	DAC	505		DAC LOC1 + 4
	JMP I	505		JMP I LOC1 + 4
				0
				M
	(a)			(b)

Figure 2.13. Program list in assembly language.

One more convenient feature is found in most assemblers. If the programmer finds it necessary to use a particular constant, he need not consider the storage of that constant. Expression 2.13 is an example of the special notation for this situation, which we shall assume to be understandable by the assembler:

$$\text{LAC} \ (-6 \qquad\qquad (2.13)$$

The parenthesis indicates that the number which follows is a constant. The assembler assigns a location and stores the two's complement of 6 in that location. Suppose, for example, that this location is 763. Then LAC 763 is substituted for LAC (−6 when the program is loaded in the computer.

We conclude this section with a longer programming example, which would be very tedious to write without assembly language techniques.

Example 2.3
Write a program that will accomplish the multiplication of two 18-bit numbers in SIC. Assume that these numbers are stored in two's complement form.

Solution
The multiplication routine as presented in Fig. 2.14 assumes that the multiplier and multiplicand are stored in MLTR and MLTD, respectively. Thirty-six bits must be allowed for storage of the product. The most significant 18 bits will be found in PROD1 and the least significant bits in PROD2. For purposes of explanation the program has been separated by brackets into four sections. The first section merely provides for initializing the index and setting the product initially to zero.

The second section takes the absolute value of both MLTR and MLTD and stores the sign of the final product in SIGN. The actual multiplication is accomplished in the third section of the program. The method used is similar to the usual pencil and paper method. The multiplier is first rotated right, placing the least significant bit in the link. If the contents of the link are 1, the multiplicand is added to PROD1. Whether or not an addition is performed, PROD2 and PROD1 are then shifted right. The rightmost bit of PROD1 is temporarily stored in the link before being rotated into the leftmost bit of PROD2. Seventeen more repetitions of this process leave the final product stored as described above in PROD1 and PROD2.

		LAC	(−18		JMP	LOC4
		DAC	INDEX	LOC3,	LAC	PROD1
1		CLA			TAD	MLTD
		DAC	PROD1		DAC	PROD1
		DAC	PROD2	LOC4,	CLL	
		DAC	SIGN		LAC	PROD1
		LAC	MLTR		RAR	
		SKP			DAC	PROD1
		JMP	COMP1	3	LAC	PROD2
		JMP	LOC1		RAR	
2	COMP1,	CMA			DAC	PROD2
		TAD	(1		ISZ	INDEX
		DAC	MLTR		JMP	LOC2
		LAC	SIGN		LAC	SIGN
		CMA			SKP	
		DAC	SIGN		JMP	LOC5
	LOC1,	LAC	MLTD		HLT	
		SKP		LOC5,	LAC	PROD1
		JMP	COMP2	4	CMA	
		JMP	LOC2		DAC	PROD1
	COMP2,	CMA			LAC	PROD2
		TAD	(1		CMA	
		DAC	MLTD		CLL	
		LAC	SIGN		TAD	(1
		CMA			DAC	PROD2
		DAC	SIGN		LAC	PROD1
3	LOC2,	LAC	MLTR		SZL	
		RAR			TAD	(1
		DAC	MLTR		DAC	PROD1
		SZL			HLT	
		JMP	LOC3			

Figure 2.14. Multiplication.

The fourth section is included solely to establish the final sign of the product. If SIGN contains 777777(-1), the 36-bit product is replaced by its two's-complement. This operation utilizes the link to store a possible overflow from the two's-complementing of PROD2.

With only slight modification, the program in Fig. 2.14 could take the form of a subroutine. When called, the subroutine would develop a product as described above. It would then be the function of the main program to use as many of the 36 bits in the fixed point product as required.

PROBLEMS

2.1 Prove that adding the two's-complement forms of two negative numbers will give the proper two's-complement result if the sum of the magnitudes is less than 2^{n-1}. Note that the addition is physically addition modulo 2^n.

2.2 Suppose that indexing were eliminated from SIC so that 14 memory reference instructions could be permitted. List some additional memory reference instructions that you think would be of value.

2.3 Suppose that a computer is to be designed with the same memory reference instructions as SIC but with eight index registers. How could indirect addressing be employed so that 8192 words of random access memory could still be used? Suggest a bit layout for the instruction in such a machine.

2.4 Suppose that the number of I/O instructions and operate instructions in SIC are the same. In this case what would be the maximum number of distinct operate instructions that could be specified?

2.5 Devise a sequence of SIC assembly language instructions that will effect a branch to one location if the contents of an index register are zero, and to another location if the contents are nonzero.

2.6 Devise a sequence of SIC instructions that will accomplish the equivalent of the DO loop in Fig. 2.9 without using either indexing or indirect addressing.

2.7 Write in SIC assembly language a program for adding the rows of a 10×10 matrix. Use index registers insofar as possible to imitate a nested DO loop approach.

2.8 Suggest a routine that depends on indirect addressing to perform a search of a list.

2.9 Write a short sequence of instructions, utilizing any SIC instructions except ISZ, that will accomplish the same function as an ISZ instruction.

2.10 Write a sequence of SIC instructions that will reorder the bits of a word in memory as follows:

9 10 11	0 1 2	15 16 17	6 7 8	3 4 5	12 13 14

(*Hint:* Use the instruction AND to accomplish masking and use rotate instructions.)

2.11 Suppose two floating-point numbers are stored with 18-bit characteristics located immediately following 18-bit mantissas in memory. Assume that the binary point is between bit-0 and bit-1 for both mantissas. The characteristics need not be equal. Write a sequence of SIC instructions that will accomplish addition of the two floating-point numbers.

2.12 Write a sequence of instructions that will accomplish multiplication of two floating-point numbers, such as discussed in Problem 2.11.

2.13 Write a SIC assembly language version of a FORTRAN subroutine call. Include the mechanism for the transfer of arguments. Write routines that could tolerate separate compilations of the main routine and the subroutine.

2.14 Write a sequence of instructions that will call a subroutine without using the JMS instruction. Assume that no transfer of arguments is required.

2.15 Write in SIC assembly language a sequence of instructions that will illustrate the accomplishment of a simple FORTRAN function subroutine.

2.16 Write in SIC assembly language a sequence of instructions that will accomplish division of two 18-bit, fixed-point numbers.

2.17 Write in SIC assembly language routines that will perform bit-by-bit the following Boolean operations on two 18-bit words.
(a) OR
(b) exclusive-OR
Set the operations up as subroutines that will use the accumulator and one word of memory as arguments.

2.18 Justify the method of converting a binary number to octal form given in Section 2.2.

3

l_____

SYSTEM COMPONENTS

3.1 INTRODUCTION

In this chapter we shall present a brief and rather general discussion of some of the basic types of logic and memory devices used in digital computers. The actual design of these devices is not the concern of the system designer, who generally regards them as "black boxes" with certain known characteristics. On the other hand, intelligent selection and application of these devices does require some understanding of their operation and an appreciation of their limitations. In addition, without some physical interpretation of registers, memory, etc., much of the material in following chapters may seem too abstract to many readers. Readers who are already familiar with digital hardware may skip the majority of the topics in this chapter without loss of continuity.

Logic circuits are implemented in a tremendous variety of technologies. There is diode-transistor logic (DTL), transistor-transistor logic (TTL), MOS logic, emitter-coupled logic (ECL), etc. These various types differ in matters of speed, cost, power consumption, physical dimensions, immunity to environmental influences, etc.; but they all accomplish the same basic purpose, and from the point of view of this book, the differences are of little importance. All of them accept input signals in which the voltage levels represent the values of certain logical (binary) variables and produce output signals in which the voltage levels correspond to logical functions of the input variables. Until recently, single logic circuits usually implemented very simple functions, such as AND, OR, and NOT. With the advent of integrated circuits, more complex functions are available in single packages.

The purpose of logic circuits, then, is to process signals and produce outputs that are functions of the inputs. The outputs are available only during the duration of the input signals. The purpose of memory devices

39

is to store information for later use, generally returning it without alteration, in the same form as it was originally stored. The definition of memory is elusive. We shall simply settle for the intuitive idea that a memory device is any device that we place in a specific, identifiable physical state for the specific purpose of preserving information, without alteration, until a later time.

Memory devices may be classified in a number of different ways. First, most may be classified as being either magnetic or electronic. Magnetic devices utilize ferromagnetic materials, which can be placed in a specific magnetic state by the passage of electric currents through them or near them, and which then maintain these states indefinitely, until interrogated. The chief types of magnetic memory are tape, disk, and core. Electronic memory devices are primarily transistor and diode circuits in which the outputs can be set to certain voltage levels by the application of certain input signals and will be maintained even when the input signals are removed. A common electronic memory device is the bistable latch, which can be used to construct *register memories* (RM).

Memories may also be classified by the type of access to the stored information. In *random access memories* (RAM), all stored information is equally accessible, in the sense that any given piece of information may be retrieved in exactly the same length of time as any other piece of information. Core memory and semiconductor memories are usually classified as RAM. Tape, by contrast, is a *sequential memory* (SM), in which information can be retrieved only in the same order it was stored. When you want a particular piece of information off tape, you simply start running the tape until the desired information comes into position to be read. The access time is thus dependent on where the desired information is located relative to the starting point.

Between these two categories are disk and shift register memories, which are *semirandom access memories* (SRAM). In these devices, any given area, or sector, of the memory can be accessed at random in a relatively long access time. Once accessed, all of the information in the sector can be read or written at a faster rate.

A final special category, which resembles logic as well as memory, is the *read-only memory* (ROM). The stored information is actually built into the structure of the device. The stored information can then be read out electronically but can be changed only by alteration of the structure of the device.

The above classification and listing is quite broad and general and is not intended to be complete. There are many other specialized memory devices, some fitting into the above categories, some not really fitting into any category.

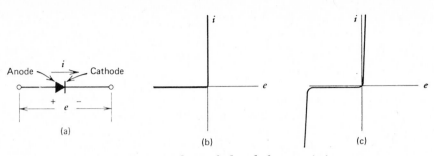

Figure 3.1. Diode symbol and characteristics.

3.2 DIODE LOGIC

The simplest type of electronic logic is diode logic. A diode is a device that can conduct current in only one direction. The schematic symbol for a diode is shown in Fig. 3.1a. Ideally, a diode offers zero resistance to the flow of current from anode to cathode (forward direction) and infinite resistance to current flow from cathode to anode (reverse direction). The ideal current-voltage characteristic would thus be that shown in Fig. 3.1b. A typical characteristic for an actual semiconductor diode is shown in Fig. 3.1c. When the diode is conducting in the forward direction, there is a small, nearly constant, positive voltage across the diode. When the voltage across the diode goes negative, a very small reverse current flows. When the voltage goes sufficiently negative, a phenomenon known as the *Zener* breakdown* occurs, and the reverse current increases sharply. In normal switching circuit applications, diodes are never operated in the Zener range. For purposes of analyzing diode circuits it is simplest just to remember that the anode cannot be more positive than the cathode. Consider the diode symbol as an arrowhead and remember that if the anode attempts to go positive, current will flow in the arrow direction until there is essentially zero voltage across the diode.

Logical values are usually represented in digital circuits in the form of voltage levels. There is more than one possible way to define the relation between logical values and voltage levels. In order to minimize the possibility of confusion, assume that a positive voltage, usually 1 to 10 volts, represents logical 1 while a voltage very near zero volts represents logical 0. This convention, which is an example of *positive logic*,

---

*There are actually two types of breakdown, *Zener* and *avalanche*, which are due to quite different physical phenomena. From an external point of view, however, there is no important difference.

will be used throughout this chapter. The opposite situation in which the more negative voltage represents logical 1 and the more positive voltage represents logical 0 (negative logic) may also be encountered in practice.

The circuits for the two basic forms of diode gates are shown in Fig. 3.2. The supply voltage, V_H, is positive and slightly greater than V_+, which represents logical 1. The voltage inputs to the circuit are e_1 and e_2 representing logical variables A and B, respectively. The output voltage, e_o, represents logical variable Z. First consider the circuit of Fig. 3.2a. With the diodes connected in this direction, e_o cannot be more positive than the smaller of e_1 and e_2. First assume that both e_1 and e_2 are equal to V_+. Since V_H is more positive than V_+, enough current will flow, in the direction shown, through the resistor R and the diodes to set up a voltage drop across R equal to $V_H - V_+$; so $e_o = V_+$. Now assume that either e_1 or e_2, or both, goes to 0 (approximately zero). Then the current flow through R will increase until the drop is equal to V_H, and $e_o = 0$. This behavior is summarized in Fig. 3.2b.

In the circuit of Fig. 3.2d, the direction of the diodes is reversed and the voltage connected to R is changed to 0. Thus some current will always flow through R in the direction indicated. With the diode connected in this manner, neither signal voltage, e_1 or e_2, can be more positive than e_o; so e_o must be equal to the larger of e_1 or e_2. This behavior is summarized in Fig. 3.2e.

The corresponding values for Z as a function of A and B are shown in Fig. 3.2c and f. We recognize the AND* operation in Fig. 3.2c. Thus we identify the circuit of Fig. 3.2a as an AND gate. Throughout the text we shall use the symbol of Fig. 3.2.g for the AND gate. Similarly, we see that the circuit of Fig. 3.2d realizes the OR operation. This will be symbolized as in Fig. 3.2h.

We have shown only two inputs on the gates of Fig. 3.2. This is not a necessary limitation. For example, in the gate of Fig. 3.2a, if we connect more diodes, in parallel to the two shown and in the same direction, the circuit will still have an output $e_o = V_+$ only if *all* inputs are at the V_+ level. For positive logic this would correspond to an ANDing of all the inputs.

Diode gates can be connected together to implement more complex logic functions, as shown in Fig. 3.3. For positive logic we have two AND gates driving an OR gate, and the function realized is

$$Z = (A \wedge B) \vee (C \wedge D).$$

---

*The reader not familiar with these logical operations and with Boolean algebra and Karnaugh maps should digress at this point to study a suitable reference, such as Hill [1]

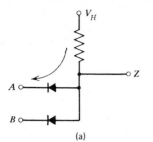

e_1	e_2	e_o
0	0	0
0	V_+	0
V_+	0	0
V_+	V_+	V_+

(b)

A	B	Z
0	0	0
0	1	0
1	0	0
1	1	1

(c)

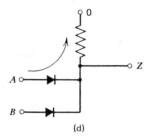

e_1	e_2	e_o
0	0	0
0	V_+	V_+
V_+	0	V_+
V_+	V_+	V_+

(e)

A	B	Z
0	0	0
0	1	1
1	0	1
1	1	1

(f)

$Z = A \wedge B$

(g)

$Z = A \vee B$

(h)

Figure 3.2. Diode Gates.

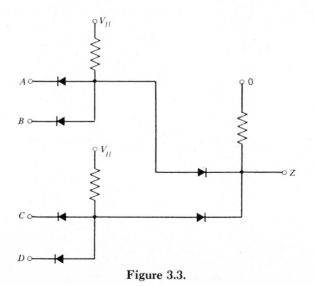

Figure 3.3.

If the diodes were ideal, there would be no limit on the number of inputs on a single gate (fan-in), or on the number of other gates a single gate could drive (fan-out), or on the number of gates that could be connected in series, one after another (levels of gating). However, the voltage across conducting diodes and the finite reverse current of nonconducting diodes result in continual degradation of signal level as the circuit complexity increases. For example, even in a single gate the output voltage will always be slightly different from the input voltages because of the drops across the conducting diodes. Because of the loading problems, diode logic is rarely used. It has been introduced here as a preliminary to the discussion of a more practical type of logic, diode-transistor logic.

3.3 DIODE-TRANSISTOR LOGIC

Shown in Fig. 3.4 is one type of transistor, the NPN bipolar transistor. This device and the diode are the basic components of diode-transistor logic (DTL). Of the various logic families DTL is most easily understood; therefore, we use DTL to illustrate for the unfamiliar reader the functioning of one type of logic circuit.

Transistors are used as switches in logic circuits. In the NPN transistor, if the base is driven slightly negative with respect to the emitter, the transistor will be *cut off*, thus acting as an open circuit to the current flow from the collector to the emitter. If the base is driven slightly positive with respect to the emitter, the transistor will be *saturated*, thus acting essentially as a short circuit to current flow from collector to emitter. In the inverter circuit of Fig. 3.5a a very small base voltage e_b, will be sufficient to cause enough current to flow through R_c to drop the

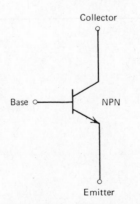

Figure 3.4. Bioplar NPN transistor.

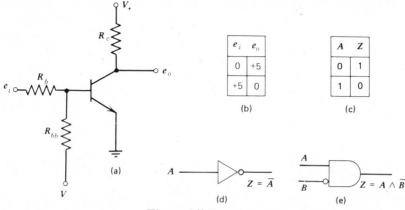

Figure 3.5. Inverters.

output voltage e_o almost to 0 volts. Typically, when the transistor is in saturation $e_o = 0.1$ volts. When e_b is 0 or slightly negative, no current will flow in R_c; and e_o will be almost 5 volts.

In the circuit of Fig. 3.5a R_b and R_{bb} are chosen so that, when $e_i = 5$ volts, e_b is positive and $e_o = 0$. If $e_i = 0$, e_b is negative and $e_o = 5$ volts. This behavior is summarized in Fig. 3.5b. If 5 volts represents logical 1, the circuit is described by the truth table of Fig. 3.5c. There are two ways of showing inversion on logic diagrams. We may use a separate symbol, as shown in Fig. 3.5d, or a small circle at the input or output of another gate, as shown in Fig. 3.5e.

In order to correct the loading deficiencies of the diode gates, we may simply let the output of each gate drive an inverter, as shown in Fig. 3.6. Consider the circuit of Fig. 3.6a, which consists of a diode AND gate driving a NPN inverter. If one or more inputs are at 0, e_g will also be at 0, and the voltage at the base will be negative with respect to the emitter. The transistor will be cut off, so $e_o = +5$. If both inputs are at $+5$, the voltage at e_g, which will depend on the circuit parameters in the base circuit, will be such as to drive the base positive with respect to the emitter. The transistor will conduct, and $e_o = 0$. This behavior is summarized in the table of Fig. 3.6b. For positive logic, this results in the truth table of Fig. 3.6c, which is seen to be the table for NOT-AND, or NAND. In a similar fashion the diode OR gate connected to an inverter will provide NOR for positive logic. The logic symbols for NAND and NOR are shown in Figs. 3.6d and 3.6e.

The addition of the transistor inverters considerably alleviates the loading problems associated with diode logic, but it does not entirely eliminate them. A gate whose output is 0 must draw current from each

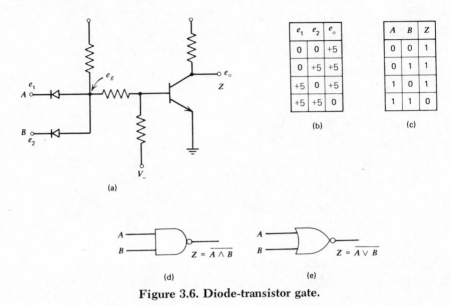

e_1	e_2	e_o
0	0	+5
0	+5	+5
+5	0	+5
+5	+5	0

(b)

A	B	Z
0	0	1
0	1	1
1	0	1
1	1	0

(c)

$Z = \overline{A \wedge B}$

(d)

$Z = \overline{A \vee B}$

(e)

Figure 3.6. Diode-transistor gate.

gate to which its output is connected. The amount of current that can flow into the collector of a gate is limited. If this amount is exceeded, the device will operate in the linear region and the output voltage will rise noticeably above 0. A typical inverter will be able to draw current from at least eight gates, so that the fan-out restriction is considerably relaxed for DTL logic.

The fan-in can also be considerably increased over that possible with diode logic. The finite back resistance of the diodes will still cause deterioration in signal level at the gate output, but now the gate voltage, e_g, need only have enough swing to provide reliable control of the transistor. As long as we observe the fan-in and fan-out restrictions, there will be no deterioration of signal level through successive levels of diode-transistor gating.

Diode-transistor logic is an easily understood type of logic but is no longer commonly used. Among the more popular logic types are emitter-coupled (ECL), transistor-transistor logic (TTL), and MOS and CMOS which use field effect transistors. The internal functioning of these types is somewhat more complex than DTL, but they implement the same logical functions; the difference between them, in such matters as speed and cost, need not concern us here.

The logical inversion noted in DTL occurs in most types of electronic logic, so that NAND and NOR are often cheaper and more convenient to realize than AND and OR. In this book we shall find it convenient to

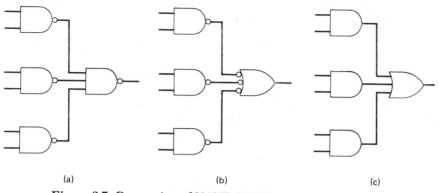

(a)   (b)   (c)

Figure 3.7. Conversion of NAND-NAND to AND-OR circuit.

rely on the AND and OR functions. This does not present a problem, since networks of AND, OR, and NOT gates can always be converted to NAND or NOR networks.

Consider the simple logical circuit of Fig. 3.7a, which consists of three NAND gates driving another NAND gate. From De Morgan's law,

$$\overline{X \wedge Y \wedge Z} = \overline{X} \vee \overline{Y} \vee \overline{Z}$$

we see that the final NAND gate can be replaced by an OR gate with inversion on the inputs (Fig. 3.7b). Next,

$$\overline{\overline{X}} = X$$

so that the two successive inversions on the lines between the input and output gates cancel, giving the circuit of Fig. 3.7c. Thus we see that a two-level NAND circuit is equivalent to a two-level AND-OR circuit. In a similar fashion, we can show that a two-level NOR circuit is equivalent to a two-level OR-AND circuit.

3.4 SPEED AND DELAY IN LOGIC CIRCUITS

Faster operation generally means greater computing power, so that there is a continual search for faster and faster logic circuits. The development of faster circuits is the province of the electronic circuit designer, but the systems designer must have some understanding of the delays in logic circuits, since they profoundly affect the operation of the entire system.

Figure 3.8 shows a grounded-emitter inverter and the response to a positive pulse at the base, taking the transistor from cutoff to saturation and back. There are a number of complex physical factors entering into the determination of this response, of which we can consider only a few.

47

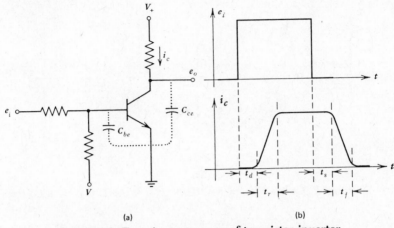

Figure 3.8. Transient response of transistor inverter.

First, from the time of the start of the base pulse, there is a delay time, t_d, before the collector current starts to rise. This delay is primarily caused by the effective base-to-emitter capacitance of the transistor (shown dotted in Fig. 3.8a). This capacitance must be charged to a positive level before the transistor starts to turn on. After the transistor starts to conduct, there is a finite rise time, t_r, primarily controlled by the collector capacitance. On the trailing edge of the base pulse, there is again a delay, t_s, before the collector current starts to drop. This delay is due to the base-to-emitter capacitance, as well as the storage of charge in the base region during saturation. The delay due to the storage effect t_s is longer than t_d. Finally, there is a finite fall time, t_f, again due to the collector capacitance.

The digital system designer will usually not be concerned with the distinction between rise time and delay. The two effects will usually be lumped together and be represented by an *ideal delay*, as illustrated in Fig. 3.9. In this book we shall assume that the change in a gate output will always follow a change in a gate input by a period of time, t_d.

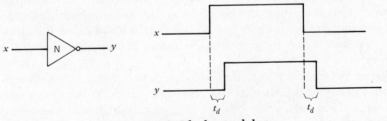

Figure 3.9. Ideal gate delay.

3.5 FLIP-FLOPS AND REGISTER MEMORY (RM)

As we have seen, memory, the ability to store information, is essential in a digital system. The most common type of electronic memory device is the *flip-flop*. Figure 3.10 shows the circuit for a flip-flop constructed from two NOR gates, and the timing diagram for a typical operating sequence. We have also repeated the truth table for NOR for convenience in explaining the operation.

At the start, both inputs are at 0, the Q output is at 0, and the P output at 1. Since the outputs are fed back to the inputs of the gates, we must check to see that the assumed conditions are consistent. Gate 1 has inputs of $R = 0$ and $P = 1$, giving an output $Q = 0$, which checks. Similarly, at gate 2 we have $S = 0$ and $Q = 0$, giving $P = 1$. At time t_1, input S goes to 1. The inputs of gate 2 are thus changing from 00 to 01. After a delay (as discussed in the last section) P changes from 1 to 0 at time t_2. This changes the inputs of gate 1 from 01 to 00, so Q changes from 0 to 1 at t_3. This changes the inputs of gate 2 from 01 to 11, but has no effect on the outputs. Similarly, the change of S from 1 to 0 at t_4 has no effect. When R goes to 1, Q goes to 0, driving P to 1, thus "locking-in" Q, so that the return of R to 0 has no further effect.

Note that it is the change of an input (S or R) from 0 to 1 that initiates the change of state of the flip-flop. The return of the signal to 0 has no effect; therefore, it could occur at any time after the output change has stabilized. In Fig. 3.10, if S returned to 0 before time t_3, the input to OR-

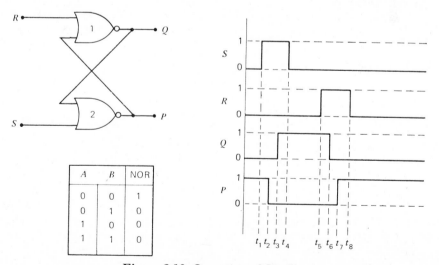

Figure 3.10. Operation of flip-flop.

2 would again be 00, tending to cause P to return to 1. In this situation the operation of the circuit would be unpredictable.

In short, the timing of signals controlling flip-flops is quite critical, so that it is the usual practice to use specially timed pulses, called *clock pulses*, to control the setting of flip-flops in computer systems. A *pulse* is simply a signal that normally remains at one level (usually zero) and goes to the other level only for a very short duration. By contrast, a *level* signal is one that may remain at either the 1 or 0 level for indefinite periods of time and changes values only at intervals long compared to the pulse duration. Just what is meant by "very short" depends on the speed of the circuits, but is normally about the same as the delay time of the flip-flops.*

By adding two gates to the *S-R* flip-flop of Fig. 3.10, the significance of the inputs is changed resulting in the circuit of Fig. 3.11, which is commonly referred to as a *latch*. In Fig. 3.10 we see that $P = \overline{Q}$ whenever the circuit is in the steady state. In Fig. 3.11 we have relabeled the outputs as Q and $\overline{Q}$.

In the latch circuit the input labeled D may be regarded as the data input. A logical 1 on line *enable* will allow the data and its complement to flow into the flip-flop. In this case $R = \overline{D}$ and $S = D$, so that the output Q will after a delay assume the value of D. In *enable* = 0, the data is shut out of the latch; and the output Q remains constant in spite of changes on the data input line, D.

Without extremely precise control of the duration of a logical 1 pulse on line *enable*, the input to a latch cannot be a logical function of its own output. Thus the latch is unsatisfactory as the primary memory element for digital system design. It is, however, used in random access memories, where the output is not used during the time interval in which new data is being written.

As we shall see in Chapter 4, register memory must be implemented using flip-flops all of whose outputs change at the same instants of time. These flip-flops are called clocked. A change in the output of a clocked flip-flop can occur only at the time of a transition on the clock line. If the change can take place at the time of a 0 to 1 clock transition, then the flip-flop is said to be *leading-edge-triggered*. If the output change can take place upon a 1 to 0 clock transition, then the flip-flop is *trailing-edge-triggered*.

The type of flip-flop that we shall rely on almost universally in this book is the clocked D flip-flop. This flip-flop has a single data input and

---

*For a more thorough discussion of timing problems in flip-flops, refer to Chapter 9 of Reference 1.

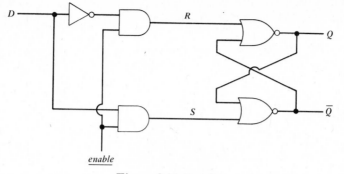

Figure 3.11. Latch.

a clock input that is conventionally labeled C. At the time of the appropriate clock transition the flip-flop output takes on the value of the *D* input present at that time instant. A timing diagram for a trailing-edge-triggered, *D* flip-flop is illustrated in Fig. 3.12a. Circuit diagrams for clocked flip-flops will not be given here but, in general, will consist of a pair of cross-coupled output gates as in Fig. 3.10 and several additional gates.

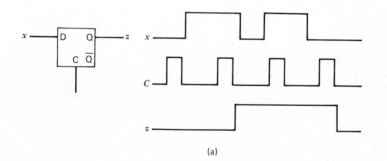

(a)

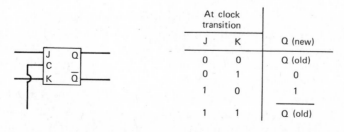

At clock transition		Q (new)
J	K	
0	0	Q (old)
0	1	0
1	0	1
1	1	Q (old)

(b)

Figure 3.12. Functioning of standard flip-flops.

A second type of flip-flop, which we shall see occasionally, is the *J-K* flip-flop. The behavior of the *J-K* device at the time of an appropriate clock transition is illustrated in Fig. 3.11b. This type of flip-flop is useful when it is necessary to cause a constant 0 or 1 to be stored rather than a data value.

Flip-flops may be used individually to store single bits, in which case they are often referred to as *indicators*, or they may be used to construct *registers*. A register is simply a set of *n* flip-flops, used to store *n*-bit words, where *n* may range from 2 to 100 or more. For example, in SIC, the accumulator is an 18-bit register, the program counter is a 13-bit register, etc. Registers may be constructed with any type of flip-flop; we shall use *D* flip-flops in this book. The nomenclature here is not completely standard. Some manufacturers use the word *register* to signify any storage location permanently assigned to the processing unit for some specific purpose and not addressable in the same sense as ordinary memory locations. Thus, they may speak of a computer as having several hundred registers, when, in fact, these "registers" are simply reserved locations in random access memory. There is nothing wrong with this practice, and it may reflect a tendency for the functions of memory and processing to merge in some designs. However, we shall use the term *register memory* (RM) exclusively to denote independent vectors of flip-flops.

3.6 RANDOM ACCESS MEMORY (RAM)

Flip-flop registers are the fastest memory devices available. Until about 1970 the cost of semiconductor memories was appreciably greater than the slower magnetic core memories to be discussed first in this section. More recently, with the continued improvement of large-scale integrated circuits (LSI), the cost of certain semiconductor memory configurations has been reduced dramatically. Still the cost of such memories varies directly with their speed. Although semiconductor memories now surpass core memories in terms of speed/cost ratio, core memories still find application. One advantage of cores is that information is not lost when the power goes off. That is, they are *nonvolatile*. Further, the vast number of core memories in already installed systems guarantees our interest in them for some time to come. When we talk of the *main* memory of a computer, we generally refer to a relatively large store in which we can place entire programs or operating systems. Also, the main memory should feature *random access*, i.e., the access time to any given location in memory should be the same as to any other location. If access is not random, then the programmer must carefully specify storage lo-

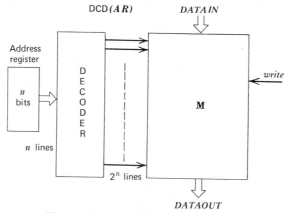

Figure 3.13. An electronic memory.

cations for data and instructions so as to minimize access times, a requirement that makes programming much more difficult. The magnetic core memory is an example of a random access memory.

A model of what will be termed *clocked electronic RAM* is depicted in Fig. 3.13. Associated with this memory is an address register. Except for a short time delay following the change of contents of the address register and a short period following a *write in memory* operation, the word in memory specified by the binary number in the address register appears continuously on lines *DATAOUT*. If a control pulse appears on the line *write*, the word currently represented on lines *DATAIN* will be stored in the memory location specified by the number in the address register. For small memories, this storage operation can be completed with the new word appearing on lines *DATAOUT*, within one clock period following the pulse on line *write*. Characteristic of the clocked RAM is that old contents of a RAM location may be used during the same clock period in which information is being written into that location. The read and write operations are assumed to take place at the same clock transition.

The *decoder* illustrated in Fig. 3.13, is an essential component of every random access memory. The decoder has n input lines and 2^n output lines. One and only one output line will have the value logical 1 for each combination of input values. A simple implementation of a 3 to 2^3 or 3-bit decoder is illustrated in Fig. 3.14a. Notice that the output of the top AND gate, for example, will be 1 if and only if $a_3 = a_2 = a_1 = 0$.

In theory, the networks of 3.14a could be extended directly to any number, n, inputs using 2^n gates with n inputs each. In practice, a fan-in limitation will eventually be reached in any technology. Thus some

54

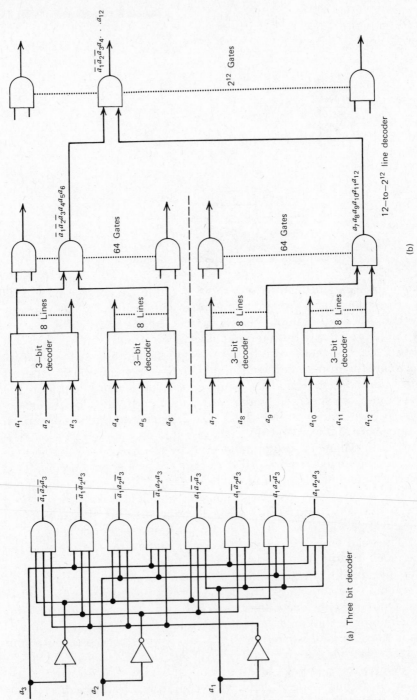

(a) Three bit decoder

(b)

Figure 3.14. Decoders.

type of multilevel network must be employed in large decoders. An example of a 12 to 2^{12} line decoder based on four 3-bit decoders is shown in Fig. 3.14b.

To keep the diagram readable, only a few connections are actually shown. The 3-bit decoders may be considered to be copies of the circuit of Fig. 3.14a in integrated circuit form. There are 64 pairs of output lines, one from each of the upper two 3-bit decoders. These pairs form the inputs to the upper 64 second-level AND gates. The outputs of these gates are the 64 possible minterms of the variables a_1, a_2, a_3, a_4, a_5, and a_6. The lower 64 second-level gate outputs are the minterms of a_7, a_8, a_9, a_{10}, a_{11}, and a_{12}. The 2^{12} twelve-bit minterms are formed by using all possible pairs of outputs of the second level gates (one from the upper 64 and one from the lower 64) to form inputs to the final 2^{12} AND gates. The total cost of the network is almost entirely reflected in the 2^{12} gates in the final level of the network. Hence the network is arranged so that these gates are two-input gates. Also we may conclude that the cost of the network is approximately proportional to the number of output lines rather than the number of input lines. As an example, a 12 to 2^{12} line decoder would be much more expensive than a 6 to 2^6 line decoder.

A segment of a clocked memory implemented using D flip-flops is illustrated in Fig. 3.15. Only words $i-1$, i, and $i+1$ out of 2^n words and only the first 3 bits of each word are shown. Each bit is stored in a D flip-flop. Notice that only the bits of one word will be gated through the AND gates at the output of the flip-flops of that word. This will be the word corresponding to the number in the address register. The word line from the decoder for this word will carry a logical 1. All other word lines will be 0. The addressed word will propagate through the chains of OR gates to **DATAOUT**. In practice the ORing function may be organized using multi-input gates or a wired NOR configuration to significantly reduce the number of logic levels and hence the time delay following a change in the contents of the address register.

A pulse on line **write** will pass through only one of the 2^n gates to which it is connected. This will be the gate that is connected to the word line carrying a logical 1 and corresponding to the number in the address register. Thus this pulse will reach only the clock inputs of the flip-flops in the addressed word. This pulse will cause the vector **DATAIN** to be clocked into the flip-flops of that data word. We see that the memory of Fig. 3.15 functions in the manner prescribed for the model of Fig. 3.13 for both read and write operations.

The model just discussed accurately describes a fast electronic memory that can be accessed in one clock period within relatively fast central processors. The ability to read and write simultaneously in a RAM is of

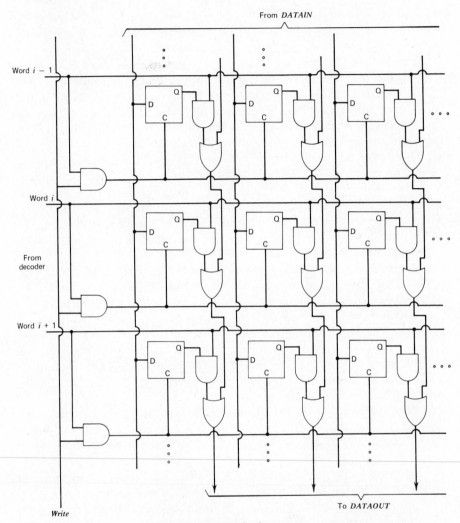

Figure 3.15. Clocked memory.

value only in a limited range of applications. Usually, read and write are separate operations just as are LAC and DAC at the assembly language level. On the other hand, the economics of the random access memory is very much dependent on the complexity of the individual memory element. The memory of Fig. 3.15 consisting of relatively complex clocked flip-flops would be expensive to manufacture.

By relaxing the clocked memory specification, we could replace the clock flip-flops in Fig. 3.15 with the latches as shown in Fig. 3.11 and

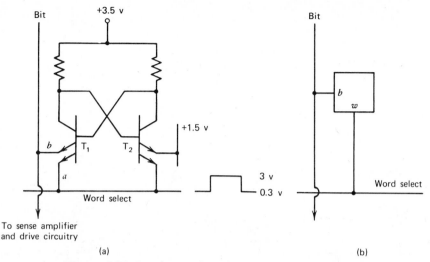

Figure 3.16. Bipolar random access memory element.

reduce the memory cost by at least a factor of 2. The line **write** would then be relabled **write enable**, and the signal on this line would not necessarily be a clock pulse but could be of longer duration. Now the memory output could not be used during, or for a short time after, **write enable** = 1 but would otherwise be continuously available.

The latch of Fig. 3.11 is still not the most economical memory element to manufacture. Most bipolar memories are in fact arrays of bistable elements similar to the one shown in Fig. 3.16. The functioning of this example circuit may be explained as follows. In the cell's normal state when not selected for a read or write operation, the **word select** line is at a potential of 0.3 volts and the emitter labeled b is held at about 0.5 volts. In this situation either transistor T_1 or transistor T_2 will be cutoff and the other turned on. If T_1 is turned on, a 1 is stored in the memory element. If T_2 is on, a 0 is stored. When the value stored in this memory element is to be read, the **word select** line is raised to 3 volts. This prevents current from flowing from the emitter labeled a. If T_1 were turned on, the current in this transistor would necessarily flow from emitter b onto the "bit" line where it would be detected by a *sense amplifier*. If T_1 had been turned off, no current would have flowed from either a or b and none would have been detected by the sense amplifier. Thus the output of the sense amplifier will equal the value stored in the memory element as long as the word select is held at 3 volts.

No voltage is externally imposed on line **bit** during a read operation, so that the cell returns to its former operating condition when **word**

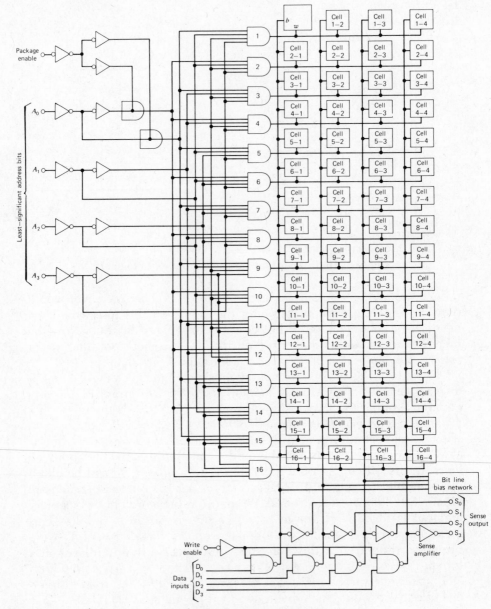

Figure 3.17. A 16 × 4 RAM.

select returns to 0.3 volts. To write in the cell, a voltage is imposed on line *bit* and then *word select* is raised to 3 volts. If b is held at 0 volts, T_1 will be turned on and T_2 turned off. If b is held above 1.5 volts, T_1 is turned off and T_2 on. The circuit remains in its new state after *word select* is returned to 0.3 volt.

A simplified representation of the RAM memory element is given in Fig. 3.16b. Making b serve as both an input and an output for the cell requires some special circuitry in each integrated circuit memory package. This includes sense amplifiers and circuitry that can impose three separate voltages on the bit lines. This may nonetheless be the most efficient approach to the design of a bipolar LSI memory.

A 64-bit RAM package composed of sixteen 4-bit words complete with decoder is depicted in Fig. 3.17. For a longer word length it is only necessary to connect several such packages in parallel. The *package enable* line makes it possible to use additional packages to increase the number of words in a complete memory. This line will be 1 only when it is desired to address a word in the particular package. If *write enable* is 0 (and *package enable* = 1), the addressed 4-bit word will appear on the output lines S_0, S_1, S_2, and S_3. A *write enable* = 1 will cause the input data word on D_0, D_1, D_2, and D_3 to be written into the addressed location. The output of the sense amplifiers is not meaningful while *write enable* = 1.

Bipolar RAM packages are available containing as many as 1024 or more bits. To best take advantage of available output pins, this type of memory might be organized as 1024 one-bit words. Another approach to efficient pin utilization is to let the data input and data output share a common set of pins. This is made possible by using an internal busing network. In this case an additional control line, which might be called *read* (*read* = 1 for READ and *read* = 0 for WRITE), would be required to switch the data bus between input and output. This is a common approach in MOS memories that typically contain more bits but are slower than bipolar RAMs.

Some, typically the lowest cost, random access memories function slower than and, therefore, asynchronously with the systems they serve. A typical asynchronous memory model is shown in Fig. 3.18. For a read operation the central processor will place the address of the desired word on the *ADDRESS* input lines to *MAR* and request a read by issuing signal on the line *read*. When the *read* level is observed, the memory loads the address in *MAR* and sets output line *busy* to 1. At the completion of the read operation the desired data is placed in *MDR* and *busy* is cleared to 0. The CPU is thus notified that the desired data may be accepted from lines *DATAOUT*.

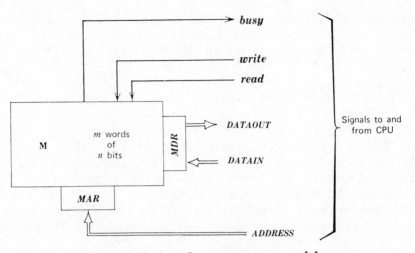

Figure 3.18. Asynchronous memory model.

For the WRITE operation the CPU will provide an address and will place the data to be stored on lines **DATAIN**. It will then place a signal on line **write**. The **busy** line will immediately go to 1 and will remain at this value until the write operation has been completed.

An example of an asynchronous memory is the 3-*D* or coincident current magnetic core memory depicted in Fig. 3.19. A 0 or 1 is stored in each individual core depending on the direction of flux in the core. A minimum amount of current, the *full-read current,* must flow in wires oriented in the same direction through the core to cause the flux to change direction. Changing the direction of the flux is the method of reading from, as well as writing in, a core. To read a core, the *full-read current* is applied to wires in the core so as to cause the flux to assume the direction corresponding to a stored logical 0. If the core initially stored a 1, the change in flux direction will induce a voltage on a wire leading to a sense amplifier. If the flux was initially in the 0 direction, no such voltage is observed. To write a 1 in the core, the same amount of current now in the *"full-write current"* must pass within the core in the opposite direction.

The memory consists of *n* bit-planes, each of which is a square array of *m* cores. The drive lines are divided into two groups, the *X*-lines, and the *Y*-lines, which run through all *n* bit-planes. To select a word, we select one *X*-line and one *Y*-line. The cores at the intersections of the selected lines, one core in each of the *n* bit-planes, represent the *n* bits of the selected word. In addition, there is a sense/inhibit winding on each plane, which passes through all the cores on that plane.

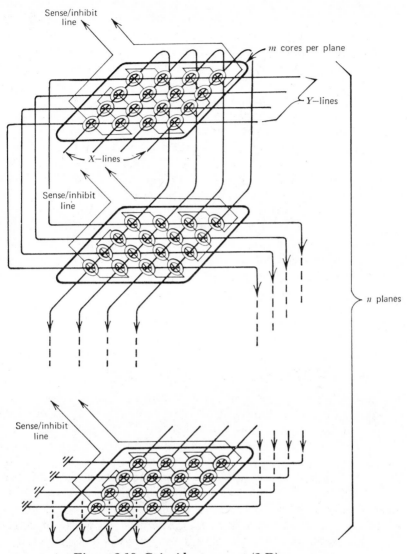

Sense/inhibit line

m cores per plane

Y-lines

X-lines

Sense/inhibit line

n planes

Sense/inhibit line

Figure 3.19. Coincident-current (3-D) memory.

For reading, each sense/inhibit line is connected to a sense amplifier, which in turn drives a corresponding bit-position of the **MDR**. To select a word, we pass half-read currents along one X-line and one Y-line so that the cores of the selected word, at the intersection of the selected lines, receive a full-read current. Where a 1 has been stored, the core will switch and induce a voltage on the sense line for that plane, thus setting the corresponding position of the **MDR**. To write, we pass half-write currents through the selected drive lines. The selected cores would thus see a net full-write current and switch. Where a 0 is to be written, we pass an *inhibit* current (equal to half-read) through the sense/inhibit line for that plane. This results in a net half-write current for the selected core in that plane so that it does not switch. All other cores in a plane subject to an inhibit current see a net drive of zero or half-read, neither of which changes the setting of any core.

A write operation must always be preceded by a read to initialize the bits of the addressed word to 0's. A read must be followed by a write to restore the cores to these original states. Thus in all cases the *busy* line will remain 1 until both read and write operations have been completed.

One advantage of the coincident current core memory is that the X and Y address lines are decoded separately, eliminating the cost-dominating last stage of the decoder. In effect the cores themselves act as AND gates, responding only when *half-read* or *half-write* currents exist on two separate lines. This *coincident current* feature has been applied with some success in semiconductor memories.

Various MOS memory configurations are also described by the model of Fig. 3.18, but space limitations preclude their treatment in this section.

3.7 SEMIRANDOM ACCESS MEMORY (SRAM)

In many computer systems there is a requirement for very large capacity memory at lower cost than random access memories. *Disk* memories, which we shall classify as *semirandom access,** are widely used to meet this requirement. The basic structure of a small disk memory is shown in Fig. 3.20. A metal disk coated with a ferromagnetic material rotates under one or more read/write heads. The speed of rotation is typically 1800 to 3600 rpm. The manner in which information is stored or recovered is indicated in Fig. 3.21, in which we show a cross section of a read/write head and the disk passing under it. To write information, we pass a current through the coil of the read/write head, which in turn sets up a magnetic flux in the armature (Fig. 3.21a). When the flux crosses the gap in the armature, it passes through the magnetic coating of the disk, thus magnetizing a small area on the disk. The size of the magnetized area depends on the speed of the disk and the duration of the write current. Bit density on disks runs from several hundred to several thousand bits per inch. For reading, the coil is used as a sense

*MOS shift registers and delay lines also exhibit many of the external characteristics of semirandom access memories.

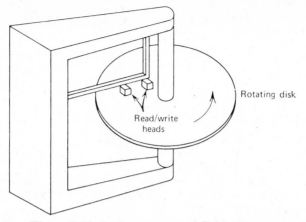

Figure 3.20. Basic structure of disk memory.

winding. As the magnetized area passes under the head, the motion of the flux field relative to the head causes a flux change ($d\phi/dt$) in the gap, which induces a voltage in the sense winding (Fig. 3.21b). This voltage is detected by a sense amplifier and used to set a register. This reading process is nondestructive, since there is no current flowing to alter the stored flux pattern. There are a number of different ways of coding the information on the disk. Different directions of magnetiz ion may be used for 0's and 1's, or 1's may be indicated by a change of flux direction and 0's by no change of flux, etc. The reader is referred to the literature for details on recording processes.

There are several ways of arranging the heads. There may be a large number of heads mounted in fixed positions distributed radially across the surfaces (both sides are used) of the disk. This is known as a one-head-per-track system, where a *track* is simply the circular pattern re-

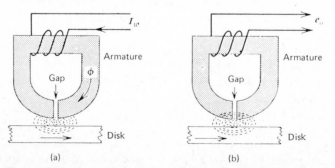

Figure 3.21. Write and read operations on a magnetic disk.

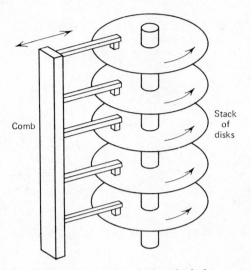

Comb

Stack
of
disks

Figure 3.22. Basic structure of multidisk memory.

corded by a single head. This system is most widely used in single-disk systems. Multidisk systems have a number of disks arranged in a stack. The heads are mounted on the arms of a *comb*, which moves in or out radially to position the heads over selected tracks (Fig. 3.22). Both sides of the disks are used, but we have shown heads on only one side for clarity.

All data transfer in disk memories is sequential in the sense that data move in or out sequentially as the disks move by the heads, but individual words may be transferred either in serial or parallel. In a one-head-per-track system, we may select a single head, in which case words are transferred serially, one bit at a time. Or, we may select n heads, one for each bit position, in which case words are transferred in parallel, each bit in a separate track. In a multidisk system, a given track is selected by mechanically positioning the heads. Once the track has been selected, a single head may be selected, providing serial transfer, or parallel transfer can be obtained by taking one bit from each head, i.e., storing each bit on a different disk.

The access to a disk memory is termed *semirandom*, indicating that the access time to a selected word is partially, but not wholly, dependent on its location. A head, or group of heads, can be selected electronically in one clock time; but once the track is selected, it is necessary to wait for the desired location to rotate into position under the head. The average waiting time is known as the *latency* time. With one set of heads, the latency time is the time for half a revolution, 16⅔ msec for an 1800-

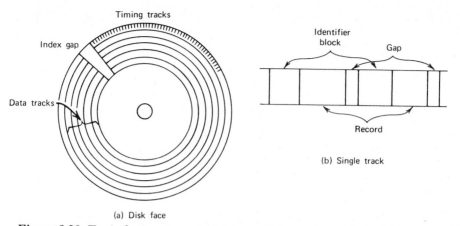

(a) Disk face

(b) Single track

Figure 3.23. Typical arrangement of data on disk memory. (*a*) Disk face. (*b*) Single track.

rpm disk. Some disks will have several sets of heads spaced around the disk to reduce latency time. If the heads have to be moved to select a track, this adds to the access time; this added time is a function of the relative locations of the desired track and the current track.

There are probably as many different ways of arranging data on a disk as there are different models of disk memories, but a typical arrangement is that shown in Fig. 3.23. The index gap is used to reset the timing circuits once each revolution. The timing track, usually engraved during manufacturing, provides the clock pulses used for synchronizing all read and write operations.

Data is usually stored on disk in units of eight bits or *bytes*. Usually, each track is single-bit serial so that each byte is stored as 8 consecutive bits on a track. A track address register is provided into which a disk controller or interface can place the address of a track to be accessed. The track address register can have sufficient bits so that a track can be selected on any one disk of a multiple-disk system.

Within a track, information is usually organized in records. A record may consist of any number of bytes, limited only by the storage capacity of a track. The record length will vary so as to be most meaningful in terms of the type of information to be stored. Usually, several records will be stored on a single track. The addressing of records within a track is commonly not a hardware function. So that records can be identified by software, each record is preceded by an identifier block as illustrated in Fig. 3.23b. The format of the identifier block will vary with the system. The sequence of bytes in each identifier block is checked and then ignored by software until some type of descriptor identifying the desired record is encountered.

Note that the circumference of a track obviously depends on its radial location. If we record at maximum bit density on the innermost track, the outer tracks will be recorded at lower densities, thus "wasting" space. This problem can be alleviated by dividing the disk radially into zones, each zone having its own timing and word mark tracks, with the number of words per track decreasing as we move toward the center of the disk.

A special type of disk memory that has become increasingly popular is the "floppy disk." This disk is characterized by less-stringent mechanical tolerances and slower operating speeds, sometimes only 360 RPM. The floppy disk itself is relatively inexpensive and can be removed from the disk drive to serve as a permanent record, just as a tape cassette can be removed from a cassette drive.

Because data is usually stored in bytes in disk memories, capacity and speed of disk memories are usually stated in terms of Kilobytes (Kbytes) or Megabytes (Mbytes). For single-disk, head-per-track systems, capacity ranges from 1 to 40 Mbytes, with access times of 5 to 10 msec. For multiple-disk moving head systems, capacities range from 40 to 1000 Mbytes, with access times of 30 to 200 msec. Data rates for rigid (non-floppy) disk systems range from 1 to 10 MHz. For floppy disks, capacity per disk ranges from 400 to 800 Kbytes, with access times of 250 to 500 msec, and data rates of 200 to 500 KHz.

Because of the long access time, data are nearly always transferred in and out of SRAM in large blocks of hundreds or thousands of bytes, which will be stored in sequential locations. Thus, it may take anywhere from 5 to 200 msec. to access a particular block of data; once accessed, and providing no further head movement is required, data can be transferred at rates up to 10 Mbytes/sec. The typical model of a disk SRAM, shown in Figure 3.24, is based on the assumption that data will be transferred in large blocks.

When a logical 1 is observed on line *seek*, the lines labeled **INPUT** are treated as the address of the track that must be accessed. Once the SRAM has located a read head on the desired track, it will indicate with a signal on *ready*. The controlling system will respond with a signal on line *read*. Each data byte appearing on the 8 lines **DATAOUT** will be signaled by a pulse on line *time*. Successive bytes will be examined until the desired record description is encountered. If information is to be read from the SRAM, the reading continues with the data bytes routed to the CPU. No timing signals will appear while a gap is under the read/write head. During this time a logical-1 level can be placed on

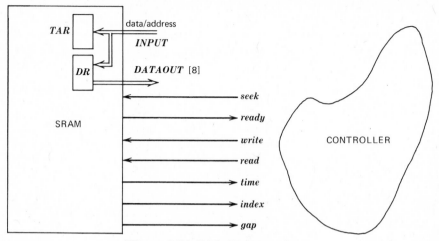

Figure 3.24. Disk SRAM model.

line **write** causing a new record to be written beginning at the current spot in the tract.

Note that data transfer proceeds at a fixed rate determined by the speed of the disk and independent of the clock rate of the CPU. It is thus vital that the control of the CPU be such that there is no possibility of failing to respond to a signal on line **time**.

One method of handling this problem is to provide a controller, or synchronizer, between the SRAM and the CPU, which will have a small *buffer* memory of its own that can temporarily store a small block of data, thus giving the CPU more time to respond. Also, disk transfer instructions may include the number of bytes to be transferred, and the controller may be used to keep track of the number of bytes transferred.

A new form of SRAM just coming into use at the time of this writing is the *magnetic bubble memory.* Magnetic bubbles are minute magnetic domains that can be created or destroyed in certain magnetic materials by the application of perpendicular magnetic fields. Once set up, these bubbles are stable in the absence of a field, thus forming the basis for a nonvolatile memory. To detect the bubbles, they must be made to move. For this purpose a loop pattern of segments of permalloy is deposited on the surface of the memory chip. Then, setting up a rotating magnetic field in a plane parallel to the surface of the chip will cause the bubbles to circulate around the permalloy loop, thus forming a magnetic shift register. The movement of the bubbles past a specific point can be detected by several methods. Note that there is a rather direct analogy to a disk, in that we again have circular movement of data, the

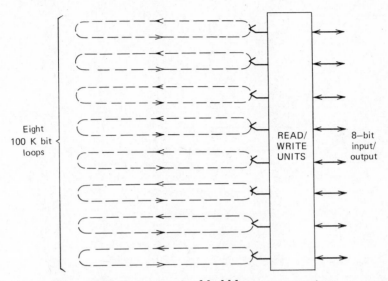

Figure 3.25. Byte-organized bubble memory system.

difference being that the movement is magnetic rather than mechanical.

Figure 3.25 shows the basic organization of one of the first commercial bubble memories to appear, a 100-Kbyte unit. The memory is organized as eight loops of 100 Kbits each, 1 loop for each of the 8 bits forming a byte. The eight loops rotate in synchronism, with the 8 bits making up each byte passing the read/write station simultaneously. It takes 1 sec to complete a full revolution of a loop, so that the data rate is 100 Kbytes/sec, with an average access time of one-half second. Bubble memories offer great advantages over disk memories in size and, potentially, cost. Bit densities of 10^5 bits/cm^2 are common today and densities in excess of 10^8 bits/cm^2 are forecast for 1985. Single-chip systems with capacities equal to current floppy disks should be available within a few years. Present data rates and access times do not match those of better disk systems, but improvements in speed and access time are sure to come as the technology advances. Many people believe that bubble memories will entirely supplant disks by 1985.

3.8 SEQUENTIAL MEMORY (SM)

Sequential memories, of which magnetic tape is the most common type, fill the need for very large capacity memory of very low cost. Digital magnetic recording tape is plastic tape coated with a magnetic surface, identical except in size and quality to the tape used for home recording.

68

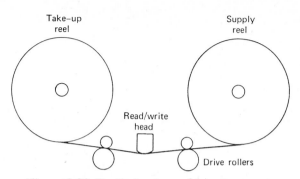

Figure 3.26. Basic structure of tape transport.

The tape is wound on reels and passes from one reel to another past a read/write head (Fig. 3.26). Digital tape transports are similar in principle to home tape recorders but provide for much faster and more precise control of tape movement. The method of reading and writing is identical to that used in disk memories.

The general arrangement of data on a tape is shown in Fig. 3.27. Data is recorded in groups of 7 to 13 bits, known as *characters,* arranged laterally across the tape. One of the bits is normally a *parity* bit, selected to be 1 or 0 so that the total number of 1's in a character will be odd. This is used as a means of detecting errors, which are primarily caused by imperfections in the tape surface. When the data are read, if the total number of 1's in a character is not odd, an error is known to have occurred.

When tape is written, consecutive characters will continue to be written at uniform intervals as long as data continue to be made available. All the characters written in a single WRITE operation will constitute a *record.* When the WRITE operation ends, an *end-of-record mark* will be generated to establish longitudinal parity over each bit position in the record, and the tape will come to a stop. When another WRITE operation is initiated, the tape will come up to speed and this process

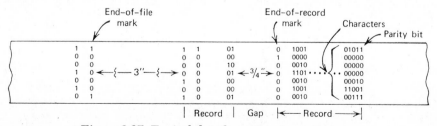

Figure 3.27. Typical data format on magnetic tape.

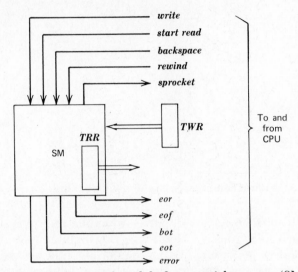

Figure 3.28. Terminal model of sequential memory (SM).

will be repeated. Because it takes time to stop and start the tape, there will be a blank interval (usually 1.9 cm) between records, known as the *interrecord gap*. In addition, most systems provide for a special one-character record known as the *end-of-file mark*, where a *file* is simply a set of records that have some logical connection. Thus all the payroll records of a firm might be one file, all the sales records another file, etc. The end-of-file mark is usually placed 3 inches after the end of the last record in the file; and since it is considered a one-character record, it has its own end-of-record mark associated with it.

The general model for a sequential memory is shown in Fig. 3.28. The CPU or tape controller will initiate a write operation by a signal on line *write*. When the tape transport has reached operating speed it will respond with a signal on line *sprocket** and accept the first character from the tape write register *TWR*. New characters will be placed in *TWR* in response to each sprocket signal until *write* is returned to 0. During a write operation the sprocket signal is generated by a clock within the SM. The SM keeps track of longitudinal parity and writes the EOR character on tape at the termination of the write operation.

The sequential memory will respond to a start read pulse by accel-

---

*The term *sprocket signal* is apparently derived from the sprocket holes in paper tape, which actually control the mechanical movement of the tape; it has become fairly standard in referring to magnetic tape. The sprocket signals serve the same function as the signals derived from the timing track of a disk, that of marking the position of each character.

erating the tape in a forward direction. The tape will have reached operating speed before the 1.9 cm gap is exhausted and the first character of the next record is encountered. Each character will be deposited in the tape read register, **TRR**, and its availability is indicated by a signal on line **sprocket**. During the read operation the timing of the sprocket signal is determined by the characters as they read from tape. In the simplest method of recording this signal is merely the OR combination of the bits in each character. The sprocket signal would thus be 1 for each character, since all characters are odd parity. When the SM senses the end-of-record gap, the tape is stopped and this fact is signaled on line **eor**.

There are a number of error conditions, such as parity errors, attempts to write past the end of the tape, etc., which can only be detected by the tape unit. Therefore we indicate an **error** output on our general model, with the understanding that in any particular model there may be a number of error lines, depending on the number of error conditions defined by the designer.

Note that there is no means of addressing locations on tape. READ and WRITE operations start wherever the tape happens to be. We can move forward or backward on the tape a desired number of records. If we want to skip a record, for example, we simply issue a **start read** command but ignore the data being read. The **backspace** command will move the tape back to the immediately preceding inter-record gap, i.e., one record back. We can provide for locating specific records by writing identification characters as the beginning of the record. We can then search the tape by looking for the correct identification. The **rewind** command rewinds the entire tape onto the supply reel. The completion of this command will be indicated by a signal on line **bot** (beginning of tape). Both ends of the tape should be indicated by marks on the tape which can be sensed by the SM.

There are three basic types of magnetic tape units used in computer systems today. Reel-to-reel units provide the highest performance at the highest cost, and are generally found only in large systems. Recording density in reel-to-reel units ranges from 200 to 1600 bytes/in., with tape speeds from 10 to 200 in./sec, providing data rates of 2 to 320 Kbytes/sec. The number of bytes on a tape will depend on the number of records or files, since the gaps take up space. A standard 10½ in. reel of tape holds 2400 ft, providing a capacity of about 0.5 to 2.5 Mbytes per tape. The format, model, and operating sequences described above apply primarily to reel-to-reel systems.

In smaller systems, where the cost of reel-to-reel units can rarely be justified, *cassettes* and *cartridges* have achieved considerable popularity. There are two sizes of cassettes, the full-size (Phillips) cassette and the minicassette. The full-size cassette typically provides a capacity of 200 to 800 Kbytes per cassette, with a data transfer rate of 24 Kbytes/sec. Minicassettes provide a typical capacity of 64 Kbytes at a transfer rate of 2.4 Kbytes/sec. There are also two sizes of cartridges. Full-size cartridges typically provide 2 to 3 Mbytes capacity, while minicartridges provide 0.5 to 1 Mbytes capacity, both at data rates of 48 Kbytes/sec. Data formats in cassette and cartridge system are different from those used in reel-to-reel systems, and there are usually fewer signals and control functions. Nevertheless, the basic model of Figure 3.28 will still apply with only minor modifications.

3.9 READ-ONLY MEMORY (ROM)

The read-only memory is a device in which the stored information either is permanently fixed during fabrication or can be altered only by changes in the device structure. The basic form of the typical read-only memory is shown in Fig. 3.29. The coupling devices are usually transistors but in some cases may be passive circuit elements.

The address in the **MAR** is decoded to select one word line, as was illustrated for the electronic memory of Fig. 3.13. A voltage is applied to the selected word line, which in turn is coupled through to a bit line wherever a coupling element is connected. Wherever a coupling device is connected, a 1 is considered to be stored; wherever there is no connection, a 0 is considered to be stored. The coupling device may be connected during fabrication, in which case the information storage is permanent. Alternately, coupling devices may be placed at each intersection with means provided for the user to destroy connections where the operator wishes 0's to be stored. Sometimes this is done by the user of the ROM passing large currents (sufficient to destroy the devices) through unwanted coupling devices.

In the static ROM the coupling devices can be regarded simply as connections to a single ORing operation to generate the data output bits. This viewpoint is illustrated in Fig. 3.30a. This figure closely resembles the clocked RAM of Fig. 3.15 with the write line **DATAIN**, and the memory elements removed. Most ROM's are transistor-coupled as illustrated in Fig. 3.30b. In this figure the word lines are vertical rather than horizontal, as in the previous illustrations. At each point where a 1 is to be stored a transistor is connected, the emitter to the bit line, the base to the word line. All collectors are connected to a common supply voltage. All word lines are normally held at a sufficiently negative level to cut off all the transistors so that the bit lines are at 0 volt. When a word

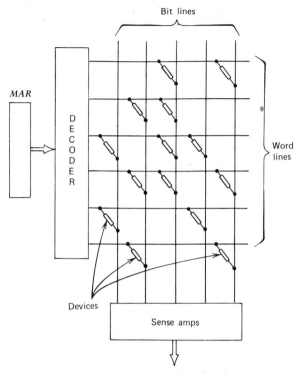

Figure 3.29. Basic structure of read-only memory.

line is selected, it is raised to a sufficiently positive level to switch the transistors on, thus raising the bit lines where a transistor is connected to a positive level. This type of ROM is commonly available in integrated circuit form. Integrated circuit ROM's are available in both bipolar and MOS types, with capacities up to several thousand words, including address decoding logic, in a single IC package. Depending on type, MOS or bipolar, access times range from about 1 μsec to less than 10 nsec. The direct compatibility, both in speed and logic levels with ordinary gates is an obvious advantage. The transistor-coupled ROM may be the only type of ROM ever encountered by many designers.

3.10 SUMMARY AND PERSPECTIVE

As we stated at the beginning of the chapter, this is not intended to be an exhaustive survey. There is at least one whole category of memory that we have not treated: mass memory to handle the problems of very large stores such as census or tax records. At present, magnetic tape is

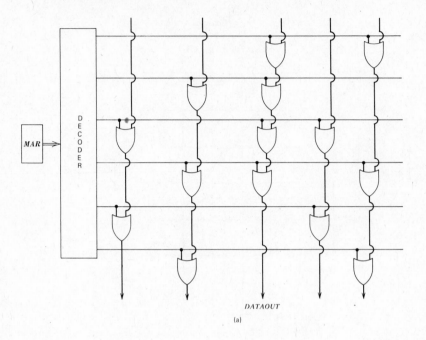

(a)

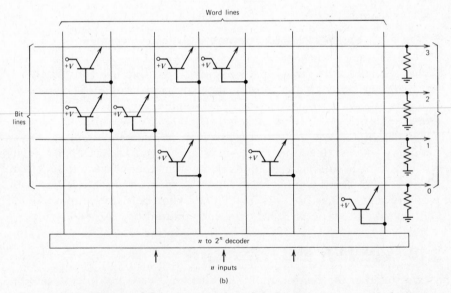

(b)

Figure 3.30. ROM models. (*a*) **General model.** (*b*) **Transistor-coupled ROM.**

74

the dominant medium for such applications. Its capacity is unlimited, but it has the disadvantage of requiring manual handling of the tapes. A mass memory in which the computer could have access to any part of the store without human intervention would have obvious advantages. Most research in this area has centered on optical and photographic techniques. A few systems have been developed, but this is basically an area with many difficult problems and few solutions.

Even with better access, the problems of searching very large files are formidable, and there has been much interest in the *associative,* or *content-addressable,* memory. As an example, in a hit-run investigation it might be desired to search the license plate files for all owners of cars of a certain make, year, and color. But these files would be indexed under license number or owner's name so that a complete search of the entire file would be required. In an associative memory we would simply input the desired identifying characteristics, and all records with matching characteristics would be immediately identified, without exhaustive search. Many techniques for implementing this type of memory have been suggested, but none has even approached the low cost required for very large files. The associative memory that seems so inviting as a means of handling large files may also be used as a high-speed buffer memory. This application will be discussed in Chapter 13.

Even within the categories we have discussed, we have treated only those types that seem to have the greatest present and continuing importance. However, continued technical developments will undoubtedly produce new devices and change the relative importance of existing devices. Rather than attempt to prophesy the future (with our very cloudy crystal ball), we shall try to give the reader some perspective on the cost-speed relationships among the various categories of memory. These relationships are, hopefully, somewhat independent of exact form of implementation and may, therefore, have some continuing validity.

In Fig. 3.31 we show a logarithmic plot of memory speed vs. cost per bit. The four main types of memory—register, random access, semirandom access, and sequential—are represented by dark areas on the graph, since there are wide variations in speed and cost in each category. Even with these variations, however, it is notable that there are distinct intervals between the four categories, a fact that presumably accounts for the continuing importance of all four types over the past 15 to 25 years. Over this period the graph as a whole has shifted down and to the left, i.e., toward the cheaper and faster; but the relative position of the four types has not changed significantly.

A variety of electronic RAM's together with core memories occupy the lower section of the RAM area in Fig. 3.31. These lower-cost devices

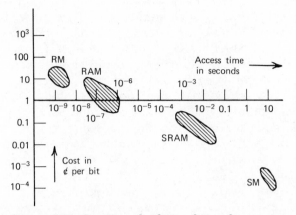

Figure 3.31. Cost/Speed relationships of memory.

form the principal random access memory of most large computer systems. In time, core will probably be limited to very large memories and to applications in which its nonvolatility is important. (The relative importance of volatility in memories is a subject of spirited debate among computer designers.)

The MOS and CCD (charged coupled device) shift register organizations are possible replacements for disk memories. These organizations may eventually fall between the SRAM and nonstatic RAM of Fig. 3.31 or extend the SRAM area to the left. They offer faster speed and greater logical flexibility, but their volatility may be a problem. Advocates of semiconductor RAM have suggested that the loss of volatile main memory in case of power failure may be avoided by providing sufficient standby battery power to unload the volatile memory onto the disk. This option is obviously ruled out if the disk is replaced by volatile memory types. Whatever the future of MOS shift registers, it is unlikely that they will significantly change the cost/speed position of SRAM.

There appears to be nothing in prospect to replace tape; magnetic tape may very likely prove to be the most durable of all memory types.

We noted earlier that it is a matter of choice as to whether magnetic tape should be regarded as a storage medium or an input/output medium. Similarly, ROM could equally well be regarded as stored logic, and electronic RAM is just a special case of register memory. It is important that the designer recognize these multiple points of view and remain flexible in his attitudes about the possible applications of specific devices. Rigid classification of devices leads to rigid thinking and stereotyped design.

REFERENCES

1. Hill, F. J., and G. R. Peterson, *Introduction to Switching Theory and Logical Design,* 2nd ed. Wiley, New York, 1974.

2. *Disc File Applications,* American Data Processing Inc., Detroit, Michigan, 1964.

3. French, M., "Rotating Discs and Drums Set Peripheral Memories spinning," *Electronics,* Vol. 42, No. 11, May 26, 1969, pp. 96–101.

4. Burroughs Corp., *Digital Computer Principles,* 2nd ed., McGraw-Hill, New York, 1969.

5. Husson, S. S., *Microprogramming,* Prentice-Hall, Englewood Cliffs, N.J., 1970

6. Kolk, A. J., "Low-Cost Rotating Memories: Status and Future," *Computer,* Vol. 9, No. 3, Mar. 1976, pp. 30–35.

7. McDermott, J., "Semi Conductor Memories," *Electronic Design,* Vol. 24, No. 12, June 1976, pp. 78–82.

8. Allan, R., "Semi Conductor Memories," *IEEE Spectrum,* Vol. 12, No. 8, Aug. 1975, pp. 40–45.

9. Joseph, E. C., "Memory Hierarchy: Computer System Considerations," *Computer Design,* Vol. 8, No. 11, Nov. 1969, pp. 165–169.

10. Mrazek, D., "Shrink Delay Line Costs with MOS," *Electronic Design,* Vol. 17, No. 5, Mar. 1, 1969, pp. 50–57.

11. Sebestyan, L. E., *Digital Magnetic Tape Recording for Computer Applications,* Chapman and Hall, London, 1973.

12. Flores, I., *Peripheral Devices,* Prentice-Hall, Englewood Cliffs, N.J., 1973.

13. Hoff, M. E., "MOS Memory and Its Application,"*Computer Design,* Vol. 9 , No. 6, June 1970, pp. 83–87.

14. Bryant, R. W., et al., "A High-Performance LSI Memory System," *Computer Design,* Vol. 9, No. 7, July 1970, pp. 71–77.

15. Bonn, T. H., "Mass Storage: A Broad Review," *Proc. IEEE,* Vol. 54, No. 12, Dec. 1966, pp. 1861–1869.

16. Pohm, A. V., "Electronic Replacements for Head-per-Track Drums and Disks," *Computer,* Vol. 9, No. 3, Mar. 1976, pp. 16–20.

17. Luecke, G., J. P. Mize and W. N. Carr, *Semiconductor Memory Design and Application,* McGraw-Hill, New York, 1973.

4

DESIGN CONVENTIONS

4.1 INTRODUCTION

Subsequent to the publication of the first edition of this book there has been a noticeable increase in interest in computer hardware description languages [1,2,3]. These languages have been recognized as vehicles for communications of ideas in the early stages of design. They have served as the bases of design automation processes. They have proved useful in product description, for training purposes, and in maintenance documents.

The procedure that we shall propose for digital system design will be based on one such hardware description language called AHPL. Most of this language will be presented in the next chapter. The purpose of this chapter is to interpret certain of the more basic conventions in terms of hardware. Enough of the language will be presented to permit the design of a simple vector-processing digital system. The need for a more sophisticated notation and a carefully constructed set of conventions for translating this notation into hardware will become evident in the process.

The utility of AHPL or any hardware language is based on the fact that most digital systems can be partitioned into a control section and a section containing data registers and logic as shown in Fig. 4.1. The control circuit will cause register transfers to take place in the data section by sending signals on a set of control lines. In some systems the sequencing of control will be influenced by branching information fed back from the data section. Usually, memory elements in the data section are arranged as registers. A single control level will typically cause the results of a logical computation to be transferred into all of the flip-flops of one or more registers. Since the bits of registers are often treated

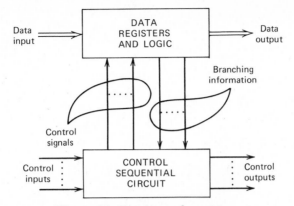

Figure 4.1. Data/control partition.

uniformly, these logical computations can be conveniently expressed in the vector notation of APL.*

4.2 REGISTER TRANSFERS

Much of the activity of a vector-handling digital system consists of transferring vectors of information from one register to another. A computation, for example, consists of placing some Boolean function of the contents of argument registers into a destination register. It is quite possible to view a digital computer simply as a collection of registers among which data may be transferred, with logical manipulations taking place during the transfers. As we shall see, a major part of the description of a computer will consist of a schedule defining each transfer and specifying the ordering and timing in which these transfers will take place. In this section we shall describe the hardware mechanism through which a register transfer can be accomplished. The notation for expressing the simplest of these transfers as design language steps will also be presented.

Registers will be noted by strings of boldface italic capitals, such as *MA, PC, AC,* etc. Transfer of the contents of one register into another is indicated by an arrow, e.g.,

$$AC \leftarrow MD$$

signifies that the contents of *MD* are transferred to *AC*. The contents of the source register, i.e., *MD* in the above example, are not affected by

---

*APL is *A Programming Language* invented by K. E. Iverson. This language will be discussed in Chapter 5.

the transfer; but any previous information in *AC* is, of course, destroyed. The notation

$$AC \leftarrow 0, 0, 0, 0$$

will indicate that all the flip-flops in *AC* are cleared, if *AC* is a 4-bit register, while

$$AC \leftarrow 1, 1, 1, 1$$

will indicate that all the flip-flops in *AC* are set.

Throughout the book we shall utilize the two types of flip-flops discussed in Chapter 3, the clocked *D* flip-flop and the clocked *J-K* flip-flop. The large majority of register transfers in digital systems are clocked, that is, synchronized by a system master clock. Many *J-K* flip-flops are equipped with master set and/or master clear inputs. These inputs are unclocked, and register transfers implemented through the use of these inputs are necessarily unclocked transfers.

We assume that the control section as well as the data section of Fig. 4.1 is synchronized by the system clock. Therefore, all logic level changes on output lines from the control unit will be assumed to take place at the time of the leading or the trailing edge of a clock pulse. We shall arbitrarily choose to synchronize all state changes in both the control and data units with the trailing edge of a clock pulse. Thus master slave or trailing-edge-triggered flip-flops will be used throughout, and the system will be referred to as *trailing-edge-triggered system*. With only slight complication one could choose leading-edge-triggered flip-flops to form a leading-edge system.

A single control level output from the control sequential circuit is illustrated in Fig. 4.2a. The assumed relationship between this control signal, which we shall label CSL, and the system clock is illustrated in

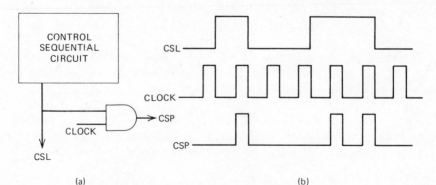

(a)   (b)

Figure 4.2. Control levels and control pulses.

Fig. 4.2b. A close correspondence exists between a control level and each clock pulse that occurs while this control level is 1. These clock pulses will be used to effect the register transfers specified by the corresponding control levels. Very often, the AND combination of a control signal and the clock will be implemented explicitly. ANDing the line CSL with the clock results in a line labeled CSP on which pulses approximately synchronized with the clock appear as shown in Fig. 4.2b.

The implementation of a clocked transfer from the 4-bit register **AR** to the 4-bit register **BR** caused by control level CSL is illustrated in Fig. 4.3a, where each register is composed of J-K flip-flops. The realization of a similar transfer into a register composed of *D* flip-flops is illustrated in Fig. 4.3b. It can be seen that both transfers are effected by the trailing edge of pulses on line CSP. *During clock periods when a pulse does not appear on this line the contents of the register **BR** remain unchanged.* This is emphasized in Fig. 4.4 which is applicable to the circuits in both Fig. 4.3a and b. This simple mechanism for assuring that the contents

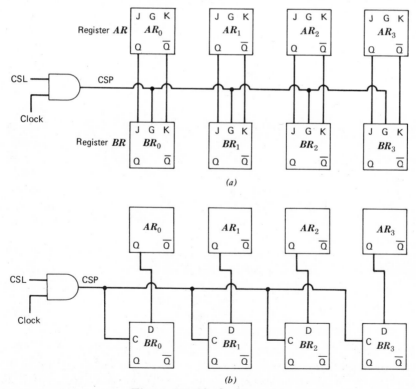

Figure 4.3. Clocked transfer.

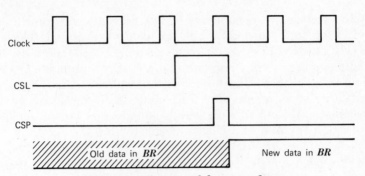

Figure 4.4. Timing of data transfers.

of register change only when a control level is present is extremely important and corresponds to the situation in software language when a variable remains unchanged until it appears on the left of an executed step. Consistent with the notation introduced in the first paragraph of this section, we represent the transfer of *AR* into *BR* by

$$BR \leftarrow AR$$

Each time the control sequential circuit is in a state corresponding to an AHPL step containing this expression, the logic level CSL will be 1 causing the transfer to take place.

Very often there will be more than one vector to be transferred into the same register in a given digital system. As we shall see in Section 4.7, these transfers may take place in separate steps in a control sequence or they may be expressed in the same step as a *conditional transfer.* That is, the vector to be transferred in a given step will be contingent to the value of one or more control inputs or feedback variables to the control circuit. In either case there will be a separate control line from the control sequential circuit for each vector to be directly transferred into each register. Suppose, for example, that any one of three vectors can be transferred into a 4-bit register *DR*. If CSL1 = 1, *AR* will be transferred into *DR*; if CSL2 = 1, *BR* will be transferred into *DR*; and if CSL3 = 1, then *CR* will be transferred into *DR*. The implementation of these three transfers is illustrated in Fig. 4.5a for D flip-flops. A similar implementation is given in Fig. 4.5b for J-K flip-flops. In both cases the output of the banks of AND gates will be 0 unless the corresponding control signal is 1. It will normally be assumed that no more than one control signal will be 1. Thus if one control level, e.g. CSL1, is 1, the vector *AR* will be routed to the output of the bank of OR gates. The same control level will enable a clock pulse to reach the "C"

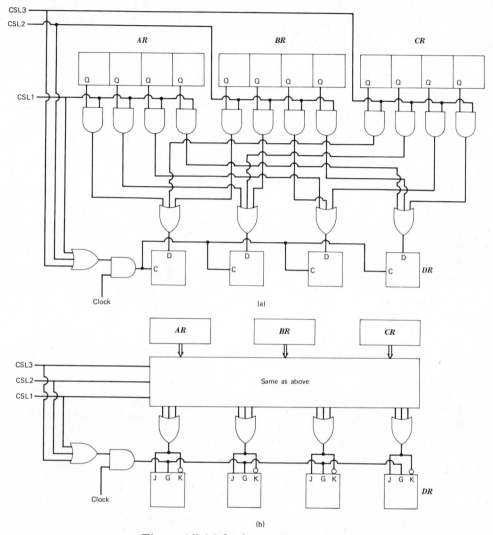

Figure 4.5. Multiple transfers into *DR*.

inputs of the **DR** flip-flops, thereby clocking **AR** into **DR** with timing as illustrated in Fig. 4.4. The principal difference between the two configurations of Fig. 4.5 is the set of four inverters required to generate the K inputs to the **DR** flip-flops. This suggests that D flip-flops are preferable when two or more data vectors are to be transferred into a register.

It is often necessary to clear all of the flip-flops of a register to 0 or to set them to 1. We have already presented notation for these two operations. It is unlikely that only these two operations would appear in a control sequence for a given register. Let us, therefore, consider the situation in which a 4-bit register of D flip-flops **AR** is to be set to 1 if CSL1 = 1, where **AR** is to be cleared if CSL2 = 1, and where the contents of **BR** are to be transferred into **AR** if CSL3 = 1. A Karnaugh map for the next value of flip-flop **AR**, applicable whenever a control pulse reaches the clock input of this flip-flop, is given in Fig. 4.6. We assume that no more than one of the three control signals will be 1 simultaneously giving us four of the "don't-care" entries on this map. Since a clock pulse will be gated to the flip-flop clock input if and only if one of the three control signals is 1, the upper left square of the map is also a "don't-care" condition.

From the Karnaugh map we determine expression 4.1 for the D input of flip-flop AR_i. A logic block diagram of the

$$D_{AR_i} = \text{CSL1} \vee (BR_i \wedge \text{CSL3}) \tag{4.1}$$

input network of register **AR** is given in Fig. 4.7. A similar network using J-K flip-flops will require additional gates. The determination of such a network will be left as a problem for the reader. The savings of hardware in Fig. 4.7 when compared to the standard three control level configuration of Fig. 4.5a is evident. Such savings are possible and a Karnaugh map approach is justified whenever one or more of the input vectors is all 0's or all 1's.

Not all data transfers involve every flip-flop of a register. Subscripts are used in AHPL to select individual flip-flops of a register. Consistent with Figures 4.3 and 4.7 the left most flip-flop of a register is denoted by subscript 0 with subscripts increasing to the right. Similarly, registers and flip-flops may be *catenated* using separating commas to form longer vectors. Thus expression 4.2 is a valid AHPL expression specifying the placing of

$$DR_2, DR_3, CR_0 \leftarrow AR_3, AR_4, AR_5 \tag{4.2}$$

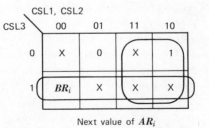

Next value of AR_i

Figure 4.6. Karnaugh map for ith D flip-flop of AR.

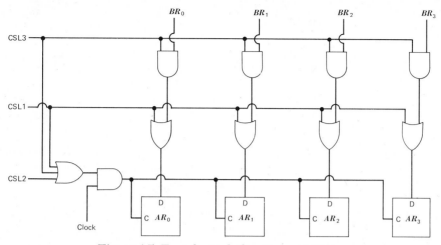

Figure 4.7. Transfer including Set and Clear.

the contents of AR_3 in DR_2, the contents of AR_4 in DR_3, and the contents of AR_5 in CR_0. A long segment of a register may be specified by indicating the first and last flip-flops of the segment, separated by a colon. As an example the string AR_2, AR_3, AR_4, AR_5 could be denoted $AR_{2:5}$. Expression 4.3, therefore specifies the same data transfer as does expression 4.2.

$$DR_{2:3},\ CR_0 \leftarrow AR_{3:5} \qquad (4.3)$$

Critical to the design of any digital system is the ability to perform logical computations on the contents of registers and flip-flops as they are transferred into other memory elements. Expression 4.4, for example, calls for transferring the complement of the contents of a register BR into AR of the same dimension. Expression 4.5 calls for ORing the contents of AR and BR and placing the result in CR while expression 4.6 would place an AND combination of these same two registers into CR. A circuit realization of the

$$AR \leftarrow \overline{BR}$$

$$\qquad (4.4)$$

$$CR \leftarrow AR \vee BR \qquad (4.5)$$

$$CR \leftarrow AR \wedge BR \qquad (4.6)$$

latter is given in Fig. 4.8, where AR, BR, and CR are 3-bit registers. For simplicity the AHPL transfer notation is used to identify the correspond-

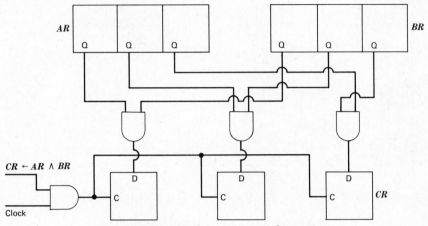

Figure 4.8. Logical operation and transfer.

ing control line. A complete listing of the logical operations available in AHPL and the corresponding notation will be given in Chapter 5.

4.3 BUSING

In the examples of Section 4.2 we considered primarily the gating between a single pair of registers. Many times we must provide for the gating of any one of several registers into several other registers. For example, suppose that we have two registers, *AR* and *BR*, both of which we must be able to gate to either of two other registers, *CR* or *DR*. The direct extension of the method of Fig. 4.5 to this requirement is shown in Fig. 4.9a. For each transfer desired there must be a set of AND gates to combine the register outputs and the control levels, and there must be a set of OR gates at the input of each receiving register.

As the number of registers increases, the above method gets very expensive. For example, with four registers to be gated to any one of four other registers, 16 sets of AND gates will be required; and the OR gates must all have four inputs. An alternate method that is generally less expensive is the use of an interconnection bus, as shown in Fig. 4.9b. In some cases, depending on the electrical characteristics of the AND gates, the OR gates may be replaced by direct connection on bus wires.

The notation for a bus will be the same as for a register, i.e., italic capitals, except that the name of a bus will always end in the word "*BUS*." For example, the bus in Fig. 4.9b will be referred to as the *IBUS*. This natural similarity will not prove inconvenient as a bus ex-

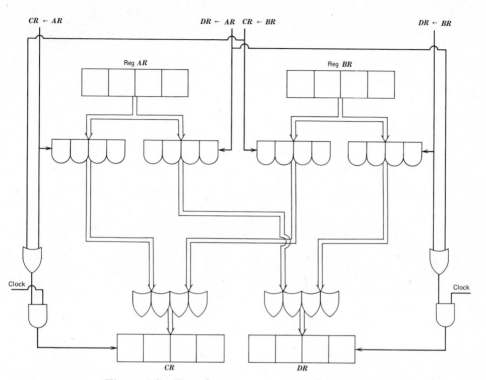

$CR \leftarrow AR$ $DR \leftarrow AR$ $CR \leftarrow BR$ $DR \leftarrow BR$

Reg AR Reg BR

Clock   Clock

CR DR

Figure 4.9a. Transfer among a group of registers.

hibits many of the characteristics of a register. The transfer of data through a bus is a two-step process. Both steps can be accomplished in one clock period. The first step uses the control level to route the data to the output of the bus. This operation differs from a transfer in that data is *not* stored by a bus. A data vector will remain at the output of a bus only *as long as the control level remains 1*. This distinction between a register and a bus must not be forgotten. The symbol "=" will be used to denote the routing of a data vector to the output of a bus. Thus the two possible connection statements routing data onto the bus in Fig. 4.9b are denoted

$$IBUS = AR \text{ and } IBUS = BR$$

The second step of triggering the bus output into the destination register is usually accomplished by the same clock pulse that terminates the control level holding the data on the bus. This operation does not differ from that of transferring the contents of a register into a destination register. The two possible clocked transfers of the output of *IBUS* in Fig. 4.9b and the corresponding control lines will be designated

87

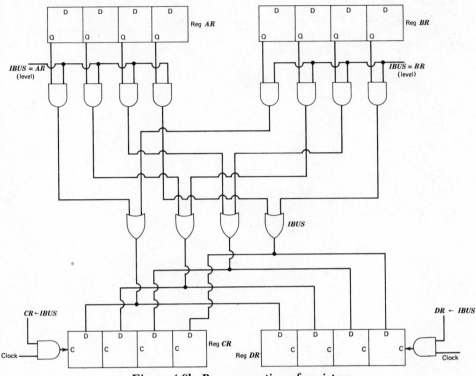

Figure 4.9b. Bus connection of registers.

$CR \leftarrow IBUS$ and $DR \leftarrow IBUS$

From the above we conclude, for example, that the transfer of data from AR to DR through the $IBUS$ can be expressed by the simple AHPL step (5) given in expression 4.7. The timing

$$\textbf{5.} \quad \textbf{\textit{IBUS} = \textit{AR}} \qquad\qquad\qquad\qquad (4.7)$$
$$\textbf{\textit{DR} $\leftarrow$ \textit{IBUS}}$$

of this operation is illustrated in Fig. 4.10, where CSL5 is the control level corresponding to step 5.

The actual physical realization of a bus may be more complex than a simple set of gates, as implied by Fig. 4.9b. The exact form will depend on the type of input and output gates used, the number of registers connected, and a variety of other factors. The results of gating more than one register onto the bus at a time will depend on the exact form of the bus. In some cases the results may be a logical ORing of the data; in others the result may be unpredictable. In this book we shall assume

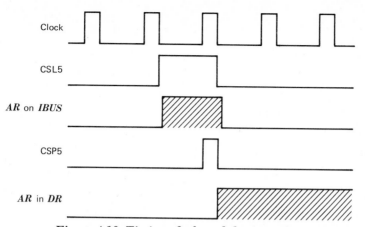

Figure 4.10. Timing of a bused data transfer.

that only one register may be gated onto the bus at a time. It is permissable to pulse the data on a bus into any number of registers simultaneously.

Both methods of register interconnection, separate gating and busing, are used. To suggest the possible hardware saving achieved through the use of a bus, suppose that it is desired that a path be made available for the transfer of information *from any one of n registers to any one of m destination registers.* If busing is not used, $n \cdot m$ banks of AND gates will be required together with m banks of OR gates. If we assume b bits in each register and a unit cost for each AND gate and each OR gate, the cost of the data paths, if busing is not used, is given by Eq. 4.8.

$$\text{cost without busing} = m \cdot b \ (n + 1)$$

(4.8)

If busing is employed, only n banks of AND gates and one bank of OR gates will be required, so that the cost of the data paths with busing is given by Eq. 4.9.

$$\text{cost with busing} = b(n + 1)$$

(4.9)

Thus, when interconnections between three or more registers are required, the use of busing will permit a savings in hardware. Where not all possible paths between registers are needed, the situation is more complicated, but the analysis is similar.

Before proceeding, it will be necessary to have a simplified diagrammatic form for representing these interconnections; diagrams showing all the individual lines, as in Fig. 4.9b, are obviously impractical. The simplified equivalents to these figures are shown in Fig. 4.11. Single

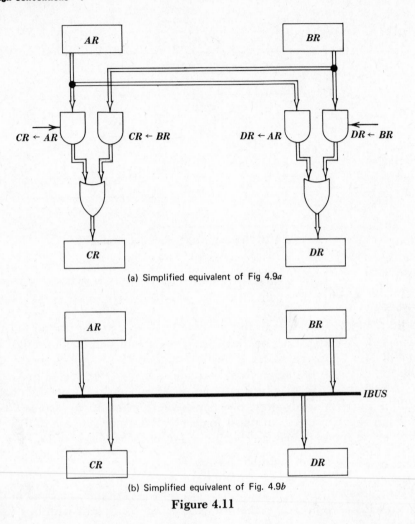

(a) Simplified equivalent of Fig 4.9*a*

(b) Simplified equivalent of Fig. 4.9*b*

Figure 4.11

lines indicate individual data or control wires; double lines indicate sets of wires; and solid lines indicate buses. When the inputs to gates are sets of wires, the gate symbol is understood to indicate the appropriate set of gates. In the case of direct connections, the control gates may be shown, as in Fig. 4.11a, or they may be omitted for clarity, since their use is generally clearly implied by the very existence of the interconnections. For bus systems, Fig. 4.11b, the control gates will not be shown because the use of a bus always requires the input and output gating as shown in Fig. 4.9b.

4.4 INTERSYSTEM BUSING

The reader may previously have heard the term *bus* used to refer to the cables used to physically interconnect separate digital systems. Such a bus will be called a *communication bus*. Communications buses are used to make possible a savings in the number of wires interconnecting the separate equipments. Distances between devices can be as much as several hundred feet, and the buses will almost always transmit 8 or more bits. Often the cost of wire and associated installation problems will dwarf the cost of integrated circuit components used to gate vectors onto the buses. The concept of a bus as a bank of OR gates realized in any technology is inadequate if the purpose of the communications bus is assumed to be one of minimizing the cost of interconnecting cables.

To illustrate two approaches to intersystem bus wiring, let us consider four digital systems A, B, C, and D, each of which must have the capability to connect one vector to the input of a bus called the *IOBUS*. Each of the four systems must have access to the output of the *IOBUS* as well. We shall assume that the four systems are physically separated, with each system located several feet from its nearest neighbor. It will be sufficient to illustrate just 1 bit of the bus for each of the four systems along with the corresponding individual wires of the interconnecting cable. Additional bits imply only identical repetitions of the 1-bit configurations.

Using the hardware suggested by Fig. 4.9b to satisfy the above design problem results in a configuration 1 bit of which is given in Fig. 4.12a. The data lines from each of the four units must be ORed together to form the corresponding bus output bit. This is accomplished by three OR gates in systems A, B, and C as shown so that only two wires are required to connect each pair of systems within a linear arrangement. One of these routes the inputs to the OR gate whose output constitutes the bus. The other routes the bus output back to each system.

Figure 4.12b symbolizes a system with only one interconnecting wire. Such a system could function properly if each of the elements represented by circles could behave in the manner to be described for the element in system B. If the control line labeled *Bcontrol* is 1, the element must cause the interconnecting wire to assume the voltage representing the value of *Bdata*. If Bcontrol = 0, the device must permit the voltage on the interconnecting wire to be determined by a similar element in one of the other systems.

One commonly used physical realization that closely approximates the function described for Fig. 4.12b is the wired NOR* configuration of

---

*It is quite common to ignore all inversions and refer to this configuration as wired OR.

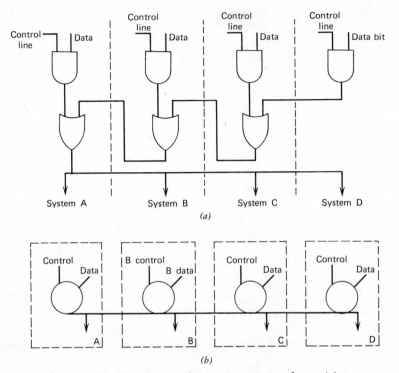

Figure 4.12. Two approaches to intersystem bus wiring.

DTL logic. Figure 4.13 illustrates 1 bit of a wired NOR bus with two input and two output parts. This circuit effectively realizes expression 4.10.

$$f = \overline{(\text{CSL1} \wedge \textit{data1}) \vee (\text{CSL2} \wedge \textit{data2})} \tag{4.10}$$

Although the actual interconnecting bus wire is f, the value $\overline{f}$ represents the bus output and is available in both systems. Clearly, $f = \overline{\textit{data1}}$ if CSL1 = 1, and f = $\overline{\textit{data2}}$ if CSL2 = 1. If CSL1 = CSL2 = 0, then $f =$ 0 as would be the case in Fig. 4.12a if all four control signals were 0. If CSL1 = CSL2 = 1, the value on the bus would not be meaningful in the context of intersystem communications. Clearly, some coordination scheme must be used to ascertain that no more than one system tries to use the bus at a given time. This matter will be considered in Chapters 10, 11, and 12.

Another commonly used single-wire busing device is the tristate element, a considerably simplified version of which is given in Fig. 4.14. We shall refer to the two elements enclosed by rectangles and connected to +5 volts and 0 volts as controlled switches. There are a variety of

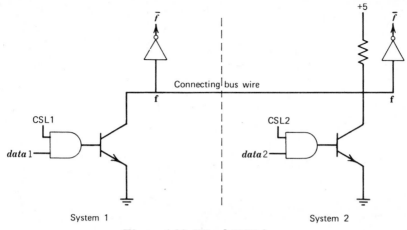

Figure 4.13. Wired NOR bus.

physical realizations of the tristate concept depending on the logic family and the voltage and impedance levels desired on the buses. The realization most closely corresponding to Fig. 4.14 is the TTL 74125 in which the controlled switches are merely transistors with a carefully designed input network to insure proper biasing. For our purposes it is sufficient to say that a controlled switch is *open* if the output of the corresponding AND gate is 0 and is *closed* if the output of the corresponding AND gate is 1.

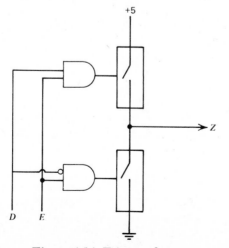

Figure 4.14. Tristate element.

The element has two inputs labeled D and E for data and enable, respectively, and one output Z. If $E = +5$ volts or logical 1 data is routed through the element to the output Z which may be thought of as 1 bit of a bus. If $E = +5$ volts and $D = 0$, the lower switch is closed while the upper switch remains open so that point Z is directly connected to 0 volts. If $E = +5$ volts and $D = +5$ volts, the upper switch is closed while the lower switch remains open so that Z is connected to $+5$ volts. The *third state* occurs whenever $E = 0$. In this case Z is left floating (not fixed at any value) by this element. However, Z may be fixed by some other tristate element connected to the same output line. Once again no two enable inputs to the tri state bus can be 1 simultaneously.

4.5 SEQUENCING OF CONTROL

We have carefully described the wiring and timing of control signals associated with the accomplishment of individual register transfers and the routing of data vectors through buses in advance of transfers. We have yet to discuss the mechanism by which a sequence of such transfers can be accomplished. It is this ability to execute and re-execute sequences of register transfers and the facility, comparable to software programming, to alter this sequencing as a function of results that makes possible the processing of algorithms via hardware. There must exist a hardware mechanism to provide for sequencing as well as notation for representing both fixed and conditional branches in sequences in our hardware description language. Sequencing notation is the subject of this section. Its realization in the form of the control sequential circuit of Fig. 4.1 will be the topic of Section 4.6. Before formally defining the branching notation of AHPL, let us illustrate the need with an example.

Example 4.1
Figure 4.15 is the system block diagram of a digital system B that provides for a selective data flow between system A and system C. A sequence of 12-bit data vectors will appear on the 12 wires forming the vector X to ultimately be accepted by system C. The function of system B is to delete those vectors for which

$$X_{0:3} \wedge X_{4:7} \wedge X_{8:11} = (0, 0, 0, 0) \tag{4.11}$$

The data flow is asynchronous; that is, system A places a new vector on line X after it receives a logical 1 of one-clock-period duration on line *inready*. Similarly, system C will accept a data vector from the set of 12 lines Z immediately after observing a logical 1 for one clock period on line *outready*. These control signals will appear well in advance of the need for new data on lines X

94

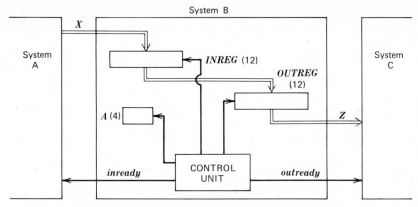

Figure 4.15. System block diagram of data selector.

and well before the data will be changed on lines **Z**. This will be the case, since several clock periods will be required for system B to perform its function.

The purpose of Fig. 4.15 is only to depict the general layout of the system and to serve as a list of all data registers to be used. It is not a complete wiring diagram of either the data paths or the control logic. The number of data flip-flops (28) might be considered excessive if the goal were the most economical realization of the data selector. The purpose here, however, is a straightforward sequence of transfers so that the functional sharing of registers has been disallowed.

The following is a sequence of numbered steps to be executed by the control unit of system B to implement the data selection function described above assuming the system to operate continuously. The first step accepts a data vector and places it in a working register *INREG*. At the same time a signal is generated to inform system A that a new data vector can now be placed on lines **X**. The realization of the signal *inready* requires only the routing of the line from the control unit representing step 1 directly to an output point and labeling the wire *inready* as illustrated in Fig. 4.16.

1. $INREG \leftarrow X$
   $inready = 1$
2. $A \leftarrow INREG_{0:3} \wedge INREG_{4:7}$
3. $A \leftarrow INREG_{8:11} \wedge A$
4. $s \leftarrow A_0 \vee A_1 \vee A_2 \vee A_3$
5. GO TO (step 6 if $s = 1$ or step 1 if $s = 0$)
6. $OUTREG \leftarrow INREG$
   $outready = 1$
7. GO TO 1
END SEQUENCE
$Z = OUTREG$

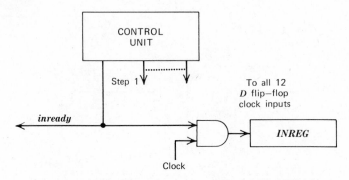

Figure 4.16. Generation of a one-period output.

Step 2 AND's together the first two 4-bit segments of *INREG* while the third segment is ANDed to this result at step 3. If the resulting four bits are all zero, flip-flop *s* will be zero following step 4. Otherwise *s* will be 1. Clearly, the operations of steps 2, 3, and 4 could have been condensed to one step, but it is instructive to illustrate a multistep sequence.

Following step 4 the vector in *INREG* may be deleted from the data flow depending on the contents of flip-flop *s*. The decision is made by the English language branch statement included as step 5. This step causes control to be switched back to step 1, if *s* = 0, so that the next vector may be placd in *INREG*. In this event the original contents of *INREG* are lost, and that vector is deleted from the sequence. If *s* = 1, control goes from step 5 to step 6; the data vector is placed in *OUTREG*; and system C is alerted to accept this vector by a 1 on line *outready*. Following step 6, control returns to step 1 for a new vector. This is accomplished by the unconditional branch symbolized by a FORTRAN-like GO TO in step 7. The last line is not a numbered step. The notation **Z** = *OUTREG* indicates that the vector of output lines is connected to this register at all times.

The sequence of steps generated in the previous example is an example of what shall be called a hardware *control sequence.* Notation is provided in all software languages to handle both fixed and conditional branches in the sequencing of transfer operations. Steps 5 and 7 of the control sequence for Example 4.1 suggest the need for expressing both concepts in our hardware description language AHPL. Including the corresponding notation in a hardware language yields a tool fundamentally as powerful as a software language.

The fixed transfer of GO TO operation will be denoted in AHPL by

$$\rightarrow (D)$$

where D is the statement number of the next statement to be executed. Following the approach used in APL, we also allow

$$\rightarrow (F)$$

where F is a function to be determined by a logical or algebraic computation. The form of function F to be used almost exclusively throughout the book is given by expression 4.12.

$$\rightarrow (f_1(x_1..x_k), f_2(x_1...x_k), \ldots f_n(x_1,..x_k))/(D_1, D_2..D_n) \tag{4.12}$$

The D_i's are statement numbers of the alternative statements that could be executed following completion of the branch statement. Each f_i is a Boolean function of the logic levels $x_1, x_2, \ldots x_k$, which are either control inputs or variables fed back from data unit. If the Boolean function $f_i = 1$, then D_i, the statement number in the corresponding position to the right of the "/", will be the number of the next statement to be executed. We assume for now that Eq. 4.13 will be satisfied for all i and j $(i \neq j)$

$$f_i(x_1, x_2, \ldots x_k) \wedge f_j(x_1, x_2, \ldots x_k) = 0 \tag{4.13}$$

so that only one D_i will be selected. If $f_i = 0$ for all i, it is assumed that control will continue to the next step in sequence. Expression 4.14 is an example in which control continues to step 18 if the flip flop $IR_0 = 1$ or returns to step 10 if $IR_0 = 0$.

17. $\rightarrow (\overline{IR}_0, IR_0)/(10, 18)$ (4.14)

The above rule allows us to rewrite this expression more compactly as given by 4.15.

17. $\rightarrow (\overline{IR}_0)/(10)$ (4.15)

The fixed branch in step 7 of Example 4.1 may now be expressed in AHPL as

$$\rightarrow (1) \tag{4.16}$$

The conditional of step 5 requires the notation suggested by expression 4.12 and may be written

5. $\rightarrow (s, \overline{s})/(6, 1)$ (4.17)

or as

5. $\rightarrow \overline{s}/(1)$ (4.18)

Each AHPL statement will consist of a transfer part and a branch *part*.* The transfer part will consist of any number (possibly zero) of transfers, output statements, or bus routes. The branch part will follow the format of expression 4.12 but will not explicitly appear if the following statement in the sequence is always to be executed next. Subject to this convention the control sequence of Example 4.1 may be rewritten completely in AHPL as shown in Fig. 4.17. Notice that the branch operation in the last step was combined with the preceding transfer operation to form a single step. It was not possible to combine steps 4 and 5, since the logical value on which the branch is based will not be found in s until after the step 4 transfer is completed. It will become clear in Section 4.6 that the clock pulse which executes a transfer at a given step also effects the branch operation at the same step. In some situations it is impossible to avoid a seemingly wasted step consisting of a branch and no transfer. In this example we can save one clock period by eliminating flip-flop s from the design and replacing steps 4 and 5 by

4. null
$$\rightarrow ((A_0 \vee A_1 \vee A_2 \vee A_3), \overline{(A_0 \vee A_1 \vee A_2 \vee A_3)})/(5,1)$$

Our goal is to generate from an English language description of a digital system of any complexity an AHPL *control sequence* or hardware program that completely and unambiguously describes that system. A hardware realization consisting of a control section and a data section can then be derived from the AHPL sequence. The data unit will be constructed as already described. The realization of the control unit will

1. $INREG \leftarrow X$
   $inready = 1$
2. $A \leftarrow INREG_{0:3} \wedge INREG_{4:7}$
3. $A \leftarrow INREG_{8:11} \wedge A$
4. $s \leftarrow A_0 \vee A_1 \vee A_2 \vee A_3$
5. null
   $\rightarrow (s, \bar{s})/(6, 1)$
6. $OUTREG \leftarrow INREG$
   $outready = 1$
   $\rightarrow (1)$

Figure 4.17. AHPL Control Sequence for Data Selector.

*This format is a significant departure from the first edition, where branch operations were always separate statements. The new format is, however, consistent with Chapter 15 of the 2nd edition for the authors' other book *Introduction to Switching Theory and Logical Design*.

be discussed in the next section. For now let us consider another simple example for which the AHPL sequence has already been determined.

Example 4.2

The following AHPL sequence describes a simple system that receives a vector X and makes it available as an output after a delay, subject to the control of input signals a and b. If $a=b=0$, the vector is not transferred. If $a=0$ and $b=1$, the vector is transferred without modification. If $a=1$, the vector is first rotated, one place right if $b=0$, two places right if $b=1$.

1. $R \leftarrow X$
   $\rightarrow (\bar{a} \wedge \bar{b}, a, \bar{a} \wedge b)/(1,2,4)$
2. $R \leftarrow R_2, R_{0:1}$
   $\rightarrow (\bar{b})/(4)$
3. $R \leftarrow R_2, R_{0:1}$
4. $ready = 1$
   $Z = R$
   $\rightarrow (1)$

Let us follow the functioning of the digital system described by the above control sequence assuming the control unit to be originally in the state corresponding to step 1. The first line of step 1 indicates that the step 1 control signal causes the 3-bit vector X to be placed in a register R, which we also assume to be 3-bits in length. The second line, or branch portion, of step 1 specifies the step to be executed following the completion of step 1. If $a = b = 0$, control remains at step 1, causing a new input vector to be placed in R, while the previously received vector is discarded. If $a = 1$, step 2 is executed next. If $a = 0$ and $b = 1$, control jumps to step 4.

Step 2 causes the contents of R to be rotated one position to the right, that is, $R_1 \leftarrow R_0, R_2 \leftarrow R_1$ and $R_0 \leftarrow R_2$. If input b is 1, control proceeds to step 3, where R is again rotated right. If b is zero, control jumps from step 2 directly to step 4. Following the execution of step 3 control always proceeds to step 4. Therefore, the branch portion of step 3 may be and is omitted. In step 4 the connection statement $Z = R$ effectively makes the contents of R available on the three lines corresponding to the output vector Z. This notation specifies that the output is available only during the one clock period while the control unit remains in the state corresponding to step 4. The same step 4 control signal causes a 1 to appear on another output line, *ready*, to indicate to any interacting digital system that a valid output vector currently appears on the lines Z.

The reader will notice that the control sequence as given in the above example is only a partial description of the system without certain information provided in the preceding paragraphs. The input and output lines, for example, were identified only in this verbal description. Also the number of bits in R was revealed only in this same manner. This situation will not be satisfactory in the long run. *It is our intention that the AHPL description stand alone as a compete specification of a digital system.* This will be possible through the use of declaration statements, which will, among other functions, specify register length and identify input output/lines. We shall defer this subject until the complete language is presented in Chapter 5.

4.6 ELECTRONIC REALIZATION OF THE CONTROL UNIT

Many realizations of the control unit are possible requiring varying numbers of flip-flops and varying amounts of combinational logic. In general there is a tradeoff between memory elements and combinational logic. At one extreme would be the classical, minimal state, sequential circuit realization. In most cases this would require extensive combinational logic with no unifying pattern. The microprogrammed control unit to be discussed in Chapter 8 is a nearly minimal state, sequential circuit. In one version of a microprogrammable control unit up to 2^n microprogram steps are available, where n is the total number of flip-flops in the control unit.

In this chapter and throughout the book we shall use a one flip-flop per control state model as the hard-wired realization of a control unit. At the other end of the spectrum from the microprogrammable version, this model employs far from a minimal number of flip-flops with correspondingly simple combinational logic. In this model only the flip-flop corresponding to the current control step will be in the 1 (set) state. All other flip-flops will contain 0 (reset state).

The one flip-flop per control state model is easily the most direct interpretation of an AHPL control sequence. Translating an AHPL sequence to this type of control unit will require no knowledge of formal sequential circuit synthesis. In spite of the lavish use of flip-flops we have found it difficult to improve on the overall economy of this approach. It pays additional dividends by easing maintenance problems later in the life of a digital system.

Let us first illustrate the translation of the following arbitrary step of an arbitrary control sequence to the corresponding portion of a control unit.

9. $B \leftarrow A$

    $\rightarrow (f_1, f_2, f_3)/(10, 20, 40)$ (4.19)

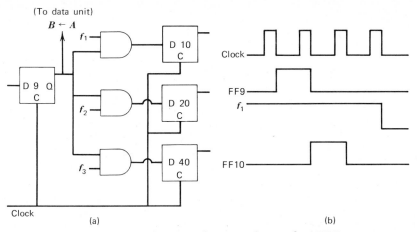

Figure 4.18. Control unit realization of a single AHPL step.

As illustrated in Fig. 4.18a, step 9 is represented by a single flip-flop. The realization of the transfer portion of the step requires only that the output of the step 9 D flip-flop be routed to the data unit to be utilized as described earlier in the chapter. The branch portion translates to an array of AND gates whose outputs lead to the flip-flops corresponding to the three possible steps to be executed following step 9. Since one and only one of the three functions f_1, f_2, or f_3 will be 1, the output of one and only one of the three AND gates will be 1 while control is in step 9. If control is not in step 9, the output of all three AND gates will be 0. In Fig. 4.18b the case in which $f_1 = 1$ and (although not shown) $f_2 = f_3 = 0$ is illustrated. Notice that the step 9 flip-flop is 1 for one clock period. The same clock pulse that executes the step 9 transfer also causes the step 10 control flip-flop to go to 1, where it remains during the following clock period. In this way the one period logical 1 can work its way around the control network with one and only one control flip-flop having the value 1 during any one clock period.

Example 4.2 continued

Let us further illustrate the process of translating an AHPL sequence into a control unit using the control sequence determined in Example 4.2, which for convenience is repeated here.

1. $R \leftarrow X$
   $\rightarrow (\overline{a} \wedge \overline{b}, a, \overline{a} \wedge b)/(1, 2, 4)$
2. $R \leftarrow R_2, R_{0:1}$
   $\rightarrow (\overline{b})/(4)$

3. $R \leftarrow R_2, R_{0:1}$
4. *ready* = 1
   $Z = R$
   $\rightarrow (1)$

The realization of both the control unit and the data unit is given in Fig. 4.19. Consider first the control section in the lower portion of the figure. Since both steps 1 and 2 include conditional branches, branching networks appear at the output of the two corresponding flip-flops. Notice that it is possible to go to step 4 from any of the first three steps. Consequently, an OR gate appears at the D input to step 4. If any of the three inputs to this OR gate is a 1 during a given clock period, the step 4 flip-flop will be 1 during the next clock period. The inputs to the OR gate originate in the branching networks from steps 1, 2, and 3. Similarly, an OR gate appears at the D input of the step 1 flip-flop with inputs

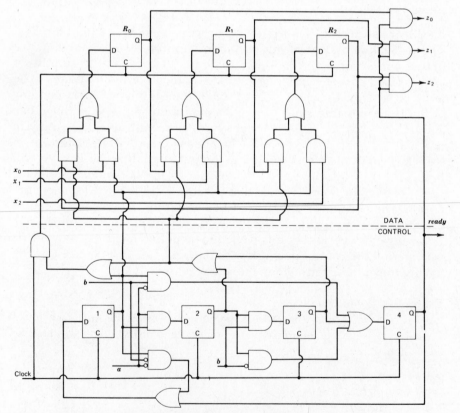

Figure 4.19. Realization of Example 4.2.

from the step 1 branching network as well as from step 4. If $a = b = 0$, when the step 1 flip-flop contains a 1, this 1 is routed back around to the D input of this same flip-flop. Therefore, this flip-flop value would remain 1. If one of the control flip-flops is initially 1 and the other three are zero, the single 1-level will propagate continuously through the network. We assume that the direct set or clear inputs can be used to establish the initial conditions.

Two control lines are routed into the data unit, one to transfer X into R, the other to rotate the contents of R to the right. The latter is the transfer specified by both steps 2 and 3. Notice that the control lines for these two steps are ORed together with only the result of this operation routed to the data unit to effect the transfer. The control line from step 4 is connected directly to the output line **ready**. It also routes the contents of R through a set of AND gates to form the output vector Z. Therefore, the output is $Z = R$ as specified when the step 4 flip-flop is 1. By implication $Z = 0, 0, 0$ at all other times.

4.7 THE CONDITIONAL TRANSFER

The conditional branch offers a method of choosing between two or more transfers, which might be accomplished at a particular point in time depending on which of a set of input or feedback control values are 1. Suppose, for example, that it is desired to transfer $A \leftarrow B$ if $a = 0$ or to transfer $D \leftarrow C$ if $a = 1$. This would be accomplished using conditional branch notation as follows.

1.
   $\rightarrow (\bar{a}, a)/(2, 3)$
2. $A \leftarrow B$
   $\rightarrow (4)$
3. $D \leftarrow C$
4.

This sequence will imply the control unit hardware illustrated in Fig. 4.20a. One of the two step 2 and step 3 flip-flops in this figure may seem immediately redundant. At a given point in time one of the two flip-flops will be 1. The output from either will cause the step 4 flip-flop to advance control to the next operation. Each flip-flop can be excited only following step 1 depending on the value of a. It would seem possible to save one control flip-flop in this case by assigning only one flip-flop, which will store a 1 during the clock period following step 1 and prior to step 4. As depicted in Fig. 4.20b, no information is stored at this step to indicate which of the two transfers $D \leftarrow C$ or $A \leftarrow B$ is to be executed.

103

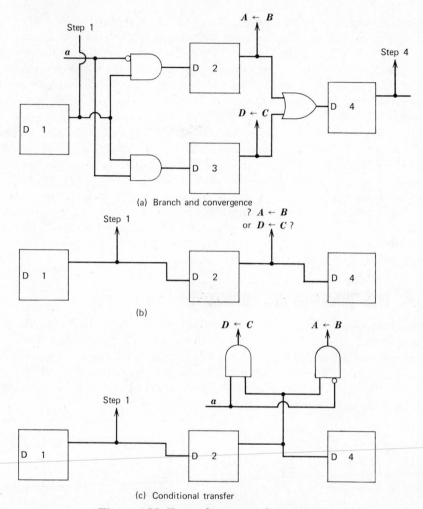

(a) Branch and convergence

(b)

(c) Conditional transfer

Figure 4.20. Equivalent control structures.

The information required to make this distinction was available as the value of a at the time of step 1.

In most cases the contents of flip-flop a will have remained unchanged between steps 1 and 2. If this is so, the logic level on line a can be used at step 2 to effect a choice between these two transfers. The hardware mechanism by which this is accomplished is given in Fig. 4.20c. Just as in 4.20a, a separate line is generated corresponding to each of the two transfers. A one-period logical 1 will appear on the line labeled $D \leftarrow C$

whenever this transfer is to be executed, and a similar level will appear on the line labeled $A \leftarrow B$ when that is the transfer to be executed.

The mechanism for which control is shown implemented in Fig. 4.20c will be called a *conditional transfer* and will be represented in AHPL by the notation

2. $A * \bar{a} \leftarrow B; \; D * a \leftarrow C$

The asterisk may be translated as "if." Therefore, $A * \bar{a} \leftarrow B$ may be interpreted as "The contents of B are placed in A if and only if $a = 0$." If $a = 1$, the contents of A will be unchanged. Transfers separated by a semicolon is the notation for simultaneous transfers. In this case one transfer will take place if $a = 1$ the other if $a = 0$. Since the two transfers are independent, it is not necessary that the two condition functions be mutually exclusive. For example, the following notation implies that both transfers take place if $y = 1$.

$$A * (y \vee f) \leftarrow B; \; D * (y \vee g) \leftarrow C$$

Sometimes only the destination of a transfer will vary with the values of a set of condition variables. In this case the notation of expression 4.20 may be used.†

$$(A \,!\, B \,!\, C) * (f, g, h) \leftarrow D \tag{4.20}$$

The asterisk representing "if" relates each of the registers separated by ! to the corresponding element of the vector at the right of the asterisk. If $f = 1$, then $A \leftarrow D$. If $g = 1$, then $B \leftarrow D$; and if $h = 1$, then $C \leftarrow D$. Again no transfer takes place if $f = g = h = 0$. If more than one of the values of f, g, and h are 1, then the contents of D are simultaneously transferred to more than one register.

An asterisk or condition function on the left side of a transfer expression always indicates that a control pulse will arrive at the clock inputs to the flip-flops of a register only if the corresponding condition function is 1. This is illustrated in Fig. 4.21.

Quite often the vector to be selected on the right side of a transfer or connection statement will be subject to the values of a set of condition variables. The notations of expressions 4.21 and 4.22 will both be assigned meaning.

$$D \leftarrow (A \,!\, B \,!\, C) * (f, g, h) \tag{4.21}$$

$$DBUS = (A \,!\, B \,!\, C) * (f, g, h) \tag{4.22}$$

---

†The use of this notation for a conditional transfer is actually a special application of the notation for catenating rows of a matrix, which will be introduced in Chapter 5.

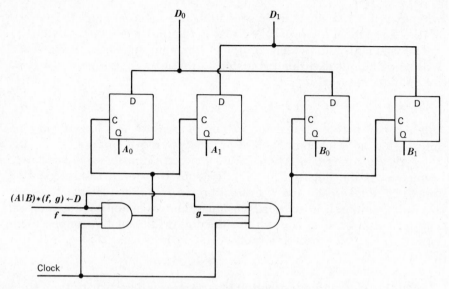

Figure 4.21. $(A!B) * (f, g) \leftarrow D$

The register A will be transferred into D or connected to the $DBUS$ if $f = 1$. Similarly, $D \leftarrow C$ or $DBUS = C$ if $h = 1$. When utilizing the forms in expressions 4.21 and 4.22, it must be ascertained that no two of the condition variables are 1 simultaneously. If $f = g = h = 0$ in this case, a vector of 0's is transferred into D or connected to $DBUS$. The implementation of a shortened version of expression 4.22 is given in Fig. 4.22. The logic network that determines the vector to be transferred into D in expression 4.21 is quite similar. The line labeled with the connection statement is connected directly to the output of a control flip-flop. In summary the asterisk on either side of a connection or transfer statement is used to specify conditions. *Conditions on the left control the clock inputs* to the registers. *Conditions on the right specify busing networks* for the data vectors.

Expression 4.23 fits naturally into the language to be presented in Chapter 5 and is logically equivalent to expression 4.21.

$$D \leftarrow (A \wedge f) \vee (B \wedge g) \vee (C \wedge h) \qquad (4.23)$$

There is a difference in hardware, however, since f, g, and h are considered data variables in expression 4.23. These variables are part of the combinational logic network and are not gated with the control signal generated for the control sequence step (Fig. 4.23). This distinction will be important when the process of compiling a control sequence into a sequential network is considered formally in Chapter 7.

106

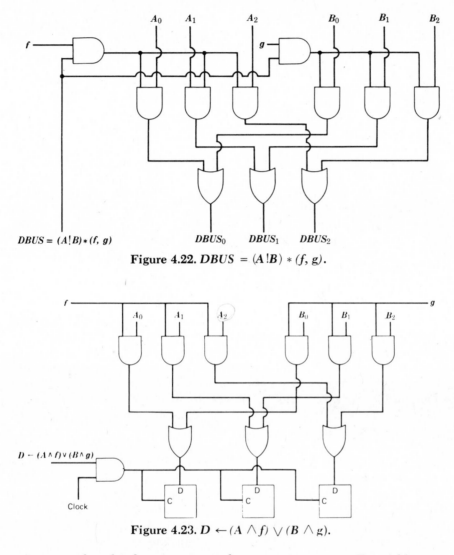

Figure 4.22. $DBUS = (A!B) * (f, g)$.

Figure 4.23. $D \leftarrow (A \wedge f) \vee (B \wedge g)$.

Suppose that the four-step control sequence given in Fig. 4.20 were specified in more detail to read

1. $a \leftarrow (X_0 \wedge X_1 \wedge X_2) \vee B_0$
2.
   $\rightarrow (\bar{a}, a)/(3, 4)$
3. $A \leftarrow B$
   $\rightarrow (5)$
4. $D \leftarrow C$

107

Notice that it is not possible to combine transfer step 1 and branch step 2, because the branch at step 2 must make use of the value of *a* determined by step 1. Thus three clock periods are required for the execution of steps 1, 2, 3, and 4 regardless of the value of *a*. The accomplishment of the same functions can be expressed as follows using conditional transfers.

1. $a \leftarrow (X_0 \wedge X_1 \wedge X_2) \vee B_0$
2. $A * \overline{a} \leftarrow B; D * a \leftarrow C$

Clearly, only two clock periods are required for executing this sequence. The saving is possible, because *a* is used at the time of the actual transfer rather than one period earlier. Situations in which flip-flop value is established immediately prior to its use as the determining argument in a conditional operation are not uncommon. Conditional transfer notation will prove valuable in tightening the timing in most such cases.

4.8 FLOW CHARTING

It is not always easy to think through a design concept while representing it only in the form of a one-dimensional language or list of branches and transfers. A two-dimensional format or a flow chart language sometimes provides a much better vehicle for guiding the thought process through the development of an algorithm. The designer should not hesitate to use the flow chart as an idea is crystallized, rendered clear, and firmly established in the designer's mind. Before a design is complete, it must be expressed in total detail in a form that can be communicated unambiguously to those involved in the later stages of the process of design construction and utilization of the system. A flow chart is less suitable as a communications tool than is a one-dimensional language description. Our procedure and a recommended procedure will be to use a flow chart, wherever convenient as a starting point in the development of a complete AHPL description.

If a flow chart is not given for some control sequence in a subsequent chapter, the reader may find it useful to translate all or part of an AHPL description back to some type of flow chart as part of the study and analysis of the system. This same strategy would be useful in any context in which it is necessary to analyze a design language description.

The following example is the first in which we begin with a word description of a design problem and follow through to an AHPL control sequence. A flow chart will be of considerable assistance in this process. This example will involve a simple form of communications between two separate digital systems. There are a number of special problems associated with intersystem communications that we will not allow to surface here. These will be the subject of Chapter 10.

Example 4.3

The register configuration of Fig. 4.24a illustrates the principal data paths of a special-purpose memory unit that must accept a stream of data and addresses continuously but asynchronously placed in the 8-bit input register **INR**. The communications system providing data to **INR** will not be part of the design. We need only know the sequence and timing of data placed in **INR** and the relationship of three control lines, *ready*, *accept*, and *word*, to this system. The memory consists of 2^{16} 32-bit words, an associated 32-bit data register **DR** and a 16-bit address register **AR**. Each time a logical 1 is placed on line *write*, the word in **DR** is written into memory at the address currently located in **AR**. We shall not be concerned with the internal implementation of the memory module. We shall similarly ignore the read-from memory capability, which we presume to exist using the same address and data registers.

The overall data transmission rate is sufficiently slow so that the memory interface for which an AHPL description is to be written will have ample time to deal will any 8-bit byte in **INR** before a subsequent byte is placed there. Each time a byte is placed in **INR**, a logical 1 will appear on line *ready* until the interface signals acceptance with a one-period level on line *accept*. The data

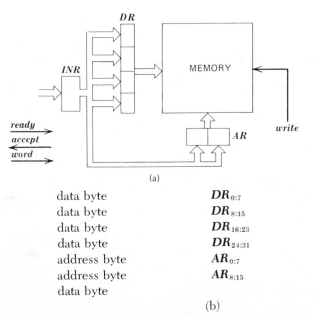

(a)

data byte	$DR_{0:7}$
data byte	$DR_{8:15}$
data byte	$DR_{16:23}$
data byte	$DR_{24:31}$
address byte	$AR_{0:7}$
address byte	$AR_{8:15}$
data byte	

(b)

Figure 4.24. Communications memory.

109

and corresponding addresses will appear in the order given in Fig. 4.24b. The 4 data bytes that are to be catenated to form a 32-bit word appear first beginning with the most significant 8 bits. The four data bytes are followed by the 16-bit address in 2 consecutive bytes. Each address is followed by the first byte of the next data word, and so on. The *ready* signal corresponding to each first data byte will coincide with a logical 1 on the line *word*. The latter control line provides a synchronizing capability.

Solution

Prior to transferring a data byte from *INR*, it is necessary to check for a 1 on line *ready*. This check and the subsequent transfer of a data byte are represented in the flow chart of Fig. 4.25a. Also included is a mechanism for checking for the fourth data byte to alert the system that the next 2 bytes will form the address. We continue the sequence by checking for the *ready* = 1 signaling the presence of the first address byte in *INR*. This is followed by a similar sequence corresponding to the second address byte. With the complete address in *AR* we let *write* = 1 for one clock period prior to returning control to the beginning in anticipation of another data word (Fig. 4.25b).

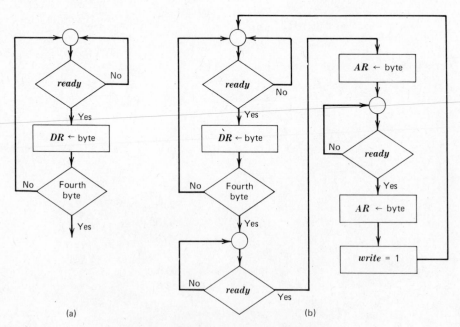

(a)　　　　　　　　　　(b)

Figure 4.25. Flow chart development.

So far no synchronizing mechanism has been included in the flow chart to ascertain that the 6 bytes are transferred to their correct places in **AR** and **DR**. A line, **word**, has been included in Fig. 4.24 for this purpose. Let us revise the sequence so that the interface will expect the first data byte whenever a 1 is observed on line **word**. This will permit the communications system to interrupt and resynchronize the sequence at any point to begin a new data word. A check of line **word** following each observation of **ready** is added to Fig. 4.25b to form Fig. 4.26. If a 1 is detected on the line **word**, control is routed to a point to prepare for handling the first byte as shown.

Although the sequence of events for the interface is accurately reflected in Fig. 4.26, there remain some details that can only be specified in the AHPL description. First, it is convenient to check both **ready** and **word** in a single-branch statement.

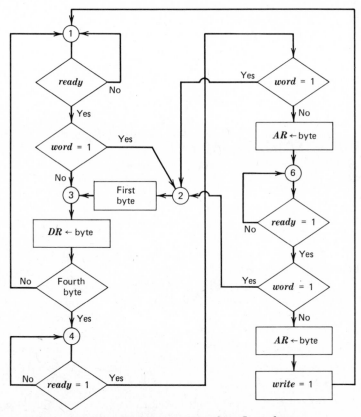

Figure 4.26. Memory interface flow chart.

1.
$$\rightarrow (\overline{ready}, ready \wedge word, ready \wedge \overline{word})/(1,2,3)$$
2. $CNT \leftarrow 0, 0$

In step 2 a 2-bit register CNT is introduced. This counting register will be utilized to store the number of the byte to next be transferred into DR. If step 2 is executed prior to step 3, the latter step will cause INR to be transferred into the left most 8-bits of DR. Step 3 also increases the number in CNT by 1, informs the communications system that the byte in INR has been accepted, and effects a branch depending on the old value of CNT. If CNT contains (1,1), control proceeds to step 4 to look for the first address byte. Otherwise control returns to step 1 in anticipation of another data byte. As before step 4 checks both $ready$ and $word$. If $ready = 1$ and $word = 0$, the first address byte is transferred into AR at step 5. This procedure is repeated in steps 6 and 7 for the second address byte. As indicated in the flow chart, the sequence is completed by the one period $write = 1$ in step 8.

3. $(DR_{0:7} \mathbin{!} DR_{8:15} \mathbin{!} DR_{16:23} \mathbin{!} DR_{24:31}) * ((\overline{CNT}_0 \wedge \overline{CNT}_1),$
$(\overline{CNT}_0 \wedge CNT_1),(CNT_0 \wedge \overline{CNT}_1),(CNT_0 \wedge CNT_1)) \leftarrow INR;$
$CNT \leftarrow (CNT_0 \oplus CNT_1), \overline{CNT}_1; \ accept = 1$
$\rightarrow \overline{(CNT_0 \wedge CNT_1)} /(1)$

4. $\rightarrow (\overline{ready}, ready \wedge word, ready \wedge \overline{word})/(4,2,5)$
5. $AR_{0:7} \leftarrow INR; accept = 1$
6. $\rightarrow(\overline{ready}, ready \wedge word, ready \wedge \overline{word})/(6,2,7)$
7. $AR_{8:15} \leftarrow INR; accept = 1$
8. $write = 1$
$\rightarrow (1)$

The above is not the only control sequence that will satisfy the design problem presented. For example, the similar tasks of selecting bytes for the data register and for the address register were handled in two distinct ways. A counter was provided to count through the 4 bytes to be loaded in DR. Two consecutive two-step sequences were employed to load the 2 address bytes in AR. The latter approach adds hardware to the control unit while avoiding a register analogous to CNT in the data unit. The larger the number of similar activities, the greater the likelihood that using a counter will be the best approach. Choosing the overall best approach from the array of alternatives is perhaps the most difficult step in the design process.

The time intervals between data bytes in the above example will not necessarily be uniform. It therefore is not possible to time the information transfers with any sort of periodic signal. We term data exchanges under these circumstances as *asynchronous*. We have followed a standard technique using two control lines to communicate the availability and acceptance of data between two systems. Various forms of the control step

1. $\overline{}$ (4.24)
   $\rightarrow (\overline{ready}) / (1)$

will appear throughout the book as a means retaining control at one point in a control sequence while waiting for a control input from another system as part of an asynchronous data transmission. The straightforward realization of expression 4.24 is given in Fig. 4.27a. An equivalent and slightly more economical version is given in Fig. 4.27b. It will be left as a problem for the reader to show the equivalence of these two networks.

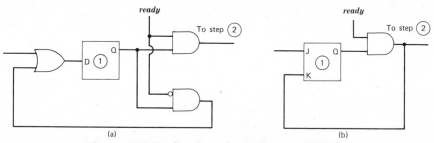

Figure 4.27. Realization of asynchronous WAIT.

4.9 ECONOMICS OF DIGITAL SYSTEM DESIGN

Most tasks that are accomplished by vector-handling digital systems are sufficiently complex that a variety of approaches are possible. The costs (both production and design) are likely to vary with the approach chosen. So will the amount of time required by the digital system to perform a given task.

In many cases the digital system must interact with some very slow system, either physical or biological. Two examples might be desk calculators or a controller for a chemical process. For such cases the speed of the digital system is not important. The most economical approach consistent with adequate reliability should be chosen.

Occasionally, a digital system must interact with a very fast system. In such cases only the fastest solution may be satisfactory.

The above are the two extreme examples of what may be called *real-time* digital systems. In general the speed at which a real-time digital system must operate is dictated by some other system with which it must interact. The appropriate design approach is the most economical one that will operate at the required speed.

The situation is quite different for *non-real-time* systems, of which the general purpose computer is the most common example. Such systems can operate at various *levels of performance*. In batch processing, for example, performance might be measured in terms of the dollar value of jobs executable per hour. Dollar values can be estimated when there is a past history of other digital systems performing the same type of job.

In designing a digital system, many of the choices that affect cost and speed are choices of whether to perform sets of similar operations simultaneously or sequentially. The choices range from handling bits in a word serially or in parallel to the possibility of processing more than one job at a time by the computer. Simultaneous or *parallel* operations almost always imply larger numbers of components and, therefore, greater overall cost. In addition, choices must be made between component technologies on the basis of speed and cost.

There are a finite number of essentially different combinations of choices that might be made in the design of a particular digital system. It is possible to analyze all of these alternatives in sufficient detail to estimate their cost and speed. The effort one would actually devote to this would depend on the number of copies of the system to be constructed, as well as the cost of this effort in relation to the overall design cost. If such an analysis were made, the result might appear in the form of Fig. 4.28.

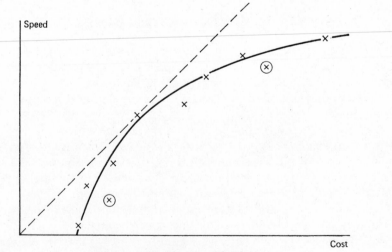

Figure 4.28. Cost/speed relation.

Each cross on the figure represents a design based on some set of choices. The solid line on the figure is not a minimal mean square error fit of the data points but is rather a smooth curve approximately joining points with the lowest cost/speed ratios. The two points that are circled on the figure represent design choices, which need not be considered seriously. There are higher-speed–lower-cost alternatives available.

Notice that the dashed tangent line passes through the point on the curve that has the optimum cost/speed ratio. If cost/speed ratio were the only criterion, then the design point nearest this tangent point might be chosen. When system performance must be matched to some other system, it may be necessary to move in one direction or the other from the optimum. As mentioned, this is common in the case of real-time systems. If the designs of several subsystems of a larger system are projected to depart significantly from the economic optimum, a reconfiguration of overall system *architecture* may be in order.

Vector-handling systems which are not computers are more likely to be described by Fig. 4.28. In a complete computer, storage capacity as well as data handling speed is a factor in overall system performance. For some jobs there is a trade-off between speed and memory capacity. The analysis of overall computer performance in terms of cost/speed characteristics and storage capacities of subsystems is an interesting but difficult problem. In many cases it is not possible to complete as accurate an analysis as might be desired. We postpone further discussion of this topic until Chapter 7.

PROBLEMS

4.1 Construct a logic block diagram similar to Fig. 4.3b illustrating the transfer

$$AR \leftarrow AR_1, AR_2, AR_0$$

4.2 Construct a timing diagram for Problem 4.1 using leading-edge-triggered data flip-flops. Assume that the initial value of AR is (1, 0, 0).

4.3 Construct the logic block diagram of hardware associated with the register AR providing for the accomplishment of either of the transfers

$$AR \leftarrow \overline{AR}$$
$$AR \leftarrow BR$$

given the proper control signal. Both AR and BR are 4-bit registers.

4.4 Assume a set of register transfers as depicted in Fig. 4.6. Determine

Karnaugh maps and Boolean expressions for J_{ARi} and K_{ARi} in a J-K flip-flop implementation of this set of transfers.

4.5 Determine a minimal expression for D_{ARi} similar to Eq. 4.1, where

AR_i must be the destination of the following four transfers:

$$AR \leftarrow 0,0,0$$
$$AR \leftarrow 1,1,1$$
$$AR \leftarrow \overline{AR}$$
$$AR \leftarrow BR$$

4.6 Repeat Problem 4.5 using J-K flip-flops.

4.7 Suppose that the transfer $AR \leftarrow AR_2, AR_{0:1}$ is to be accomplished if the control signal CSL1 is 1 and $AR \leftarrow AR_{1:2}, AR_0$ is to be accomplished if CSL2 = 1. Construct a logic block diagram of the input network for the register AR that will provide for both of these transfers.

4.8 Let AR, BR CR, and DR all be 8-bit registers that form part of a digital system. Included at various points in the control sequence for the system are the following transfers:

$BR \leftarrow AR$	$AR \leftarrow BR$
$CR \leftarrow AR$	$CR \leftarrow BR_{1:7}, BR_0$
$DR \leftarrow AR_{1:7}, AR_0$	$AR \leftarrow DR$
$BR \leftarrow \overline{AR}$	$BR \leftarrow DR$

Construct a busing diagram of the form of Fig. 4.11 showing paths for all listed transfers. Determine the total number of AND gates required to provide paths for these transfers by both methods of interconnection.

4.9 Write the AHPL control sequence from which the control unit of Fig. P4.9 was derived.

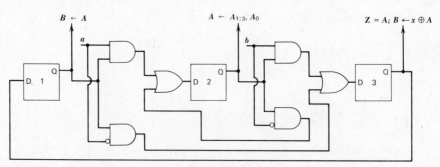

Figure P4.9.

4.10 Construct a control unit realization corresponding to the following AHPL sequence.

1. $Z = X \lor A$
   $\rightarrow (a, \bar{a} \land b, \bar{a} \land \bar{b})/(2,3,4)$
2. $A \leftarrow X$
   $\rightarrow (1)$
3. $A \leftarrow X_{13}, X_0$
   $\rightarrow(4)$
4. $A \leftarrow A_{13}, A_0$
   $\rightarrow(1)$

4.11 Construct a detailed logic block diagram of the hardware realization of both the control and data units specified by the following AHPL description, where a and b are flip-flops, x is an input, and z a single output line.

1. $a \leftarrow x \lor b$
2. $b \leftarrow x$
   $\rightarrow (a, \bar{a})/(1, 3)$
3. $z = 1; b \leftarrow x \oplus b$
   $\rightarrow (1)$

4.12 Assume the control unit of Fig. 4.19 initially stores 1, 0, 0, 0 in the four control flip-flops from left to right. Construct a timing diagram for the contents of these four flip-flops spanning eight consecutive clock periods in which the control inputs are successively $a, b = 00, 01, 11, 10, 10, 11, 01, 00$.

4.13 Redraw the control unit block diagram of Fig. 4.19 with the leftmost D flip-flop replacd by a J-K flip-flop.

4.14 Apply the input sequence given in Problem 4.12 to the control unit of Fig. P4.9 with the three flip-flops from left to right initially in the states 1, 0, and 0. Obtain timing diagrams for a and b, and the output of each control flip-flop.

4.15 Construct logic block diagrams of the data unit realizations of expressions 4.20 and 4.21.

4.16 Obtain an AHPL control sequence for the sequential network of Fig. P4.16 assuming the network to be partitioned into control and data sections as shown.

4.17 The digital system described by the following AHPL control sequence has one output line z, an input vector X, and three single inputs a, b, and c. Operation of the system starts when a goes to

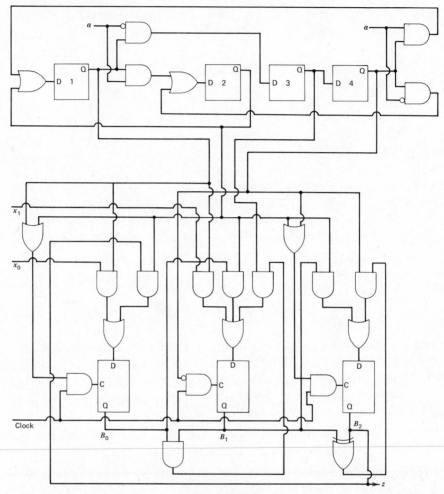

Figure P4.16.

1 for one clock period. The system then carries out the transfers indicated and then raises z for one clock period as a signal that operations are complete. The external system will then establish new values of b, c, and x, and then send a 1-period level on a to start a new cycle. Reduce the sequence to an equivalent three-step sequence by employing conditional transfers. Is it possible to describe the system in fewer than three steps? Why or why not?

1. $\rightarrow (\bar{a})/(1)$
2. $\rightarrow (\bar{b})/(4)$
3. $B \leftarrow X \vee B$
    $\rightarrow (\bar{c})/(5)$
4. $D \leftarrow A \wedge B$
5. $A \leftarrow X \oplus B$
6. $z = 1$
    $\rightarrow (1)$

4.18 A digital system controlling a bank of four lamps is to be driven by a very slow clock with a period equal to 0.2 sec. The lamps will be allowed to assume only one of the seven numbered patterns given in Fig. P4.18 where a circle indicates that a lamp is on, and an unlighted lamp is represented by a blank. If the only input to the system $x = 0$, then the light patterns are to cycle as follows with a change each clock period.

$$1 \rightarrow 2 \rightarrow 3 \rightarrow 4 \rightarrow 4 \rightarrow 5 \rightarrow 6 \rightarrow 7 \rightarrow 1 \rightarrow 2, \text{ etc.}$$

If $x = 1$, the sequence is

$$1 \rightarrow 7 \rightarrow 6 \rightarrow 5 \rightarrow 4 \rightarrow 4 \rightarrow 3 \rightarrow 2 \rightarrow 1 \rightarrow 7, \text{ etc.}$$

Write an AHPL sequence to describe a controller for these lamps. Let the 4-bit vector L [4] represent the outputs to the lamps. **Hint:** Consider an eight-step control sequence with no data flip-flops.

Pattern	1	2	3	4	5	6	7
Lamp 1	0	0	0	0			
Lamp 2		0	0	0	0		
Lamp 3			0	0	0	0	
Lamp 4				0	0	0	0

Figure P4.18.

4.19 A digital system has an 8-bit vector, X, of input lines together with another input line **ready**. The system will have two output lines z and **ask**. Following each one period level placed on line **ask**, a new vector will become available on lines X. The availability of such a vector will be signaled by a one-period level on line **ready**. Each time an input vector is exactly the same as either of the two previous input vectors, the output z should be 1 for four clock periods prior to another signal on line **ask**. The line z should be 0 at all other times. Write an AHPL sequence describing this digital system. Define the data registers as required.

4.20   (For students with background in state table minimization.) Determine a four-state (two flip-flop) realization of the control unit shown in Fig. P4.16.

REFERENCES

1.   Proceedings 1975 *Symposium on Computer Hardware Description Languages*, IEEE catalog no. 75CH 1010-8c, New York, Sept. 1973.

2.   Chu, Y., "Why Do We Need Hardware Description Languages?" *Computer*, Dec. 1974, pp. 18–22.

3.   Lipovski, G. J., "Hardware Description Languages," *Computer*, June 1977.

4.   Hill, F. J., and G. R. Peterson, *Introduction to Switching Theory and Logic Design*, 2nd ed., Wiley, New York, 1974.

5

INTRODUCTION TO A HARDWARE PROGRAMMING LANGUAGE (AHPL)

5.1 INTRODUCTION

A digital computer is a very complex device, and a complete description of a computer is going to be correspondingly complicated. We have already seen in Chapter 2 that it can take a lot of words to describe even a few of the operations of a very simple computer. Certainly, something better than the English language is going to be needed if we are to achieve efficient and concise descriptions of the design and functioning of digital computers.

There are many levels at which computers can be described: block diagrams, wiring tables, etc. We are concerned here with a description of what the computer does in terms of the sequencing of operations and the flow of information from one point to another in the computer. Developing this description is the fundamental job of the designer. Once this description has been completed, the development of logic diagrams, schematics, wiring tables, etc., becomes largely a mechanical procedure, subject to considerable automation, as we shall discuss in later chapters.

In Chapter 4 we saw that hardware register transfers could be expressed in programming language form. We also observed that program branches could be realized as hardware. In the process we established a few of the conventions of AHPL, the design language that will be used throughout the book. In this chapter we shall assemble AHPL as a complete language and consider the hardware realization of those AHPL constructions not already treated in Chapter 4.

In the early stages of the development of AHPL several languages were evaluated as to their suitability for hardware design. A suitable hardware language must permit sufficient detail to describe even bit-by-bit operations and must at the same time have sufficient power to permit concise descriptions of complex operations. The language that seemed best able to meet these requirements had been developed by K. E. Iverson, and was known simply as *A Programming Language* or APL [1]. Although APL is now primarily used for interactive programming, hardware description was one of the applications originally envisioned by Iverson. APL has subsequently been implemented with various modifications on several computer systems, the most widely used version being APL/370, which is available on several IBM computer systems.

Although APL lacks a number of features that are needed to represent hardware level operations, many of the standard APL conventions used with binary arguments could represent the common logic networks very well. We thus decided to adopt as many APL conventions as possible and add other hardware related features as needed to form a new hardware programming language, AHPL.

In Sections 5.2 and 5.3, prior to presenting the complete syntax of AHPL, we shall provide the meaning for some of the notational conventions of both APL and AHPL. The majority of the conventions presented will be common to both languages. A few are designated as included in AHPL only. *Many APL operations do not suggest unique hardware realizations, and these are not permitted in AHPL.* A few such conventions will prove helpful in subsequent discussions and have, therefore, been included in Section 5.3. These "APL only" entries are clearly marked as they are presented in tabular form. APL is notationally a very rich language. Thus many of its features do not relate to the objectives of this book and will not be mentioned. This situation is summarized in Fig. 5.1.

In view of the obvious opportunity for confusion between the two languages and the fact that the design language AHPL is the principal topic of this chapter, the reader may wonder why APL is mentioned at all. The richness of APL makes it valuable as an expository aid. Another and more specific reason is illustrated in Fig. 5.2. When the analyst first

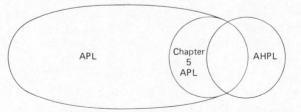

Figure 5.1. Sets of notation.

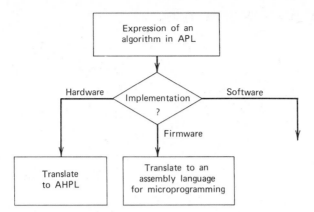

Figure 5.2. Implementation of an algorithm.

formulates an algorithm unambiguously in program form, it is usually immaterial whether the implementation of that algorithm is to be in the form of hardware, software, or in the form of a microprogramming language. The power and flexibility of APL make it one of the most convenient mediums for this initial expression of an algorithm. Once an APL formulation has been obtained, it can be translated into AHPL if the implementation is to be through hardware. Since the AHPL version will be constrained by its one-to-one correspondence to an ultimate hardware realization, this latter form may consist of many more steps than the original APL version. If the algorithm is to be implemented on a microprogrammable machine, the APL version will ordinarily be translated to some form of microassembly language prior to its reduction to microcode. Microprogramming will be the subject of Chapter 8 of this book. In that chapter we shall present a microassembly language called MICRAL which will be applicable to a particular microprogrammable computer. MICRAL will also be based on APL but will differ materially from AHPL. Several of the "APL only" conventions of this chapter will be useful in Chapter 8.

The reader must approach the next three sections making the assumption that of the two languages AHPL is far more critical to the overall objective of the book. One can go forward with a superficial knowledge of APL, but AHPL must be mastered. Also it should be remembered that the emphasis in these three sections is on semantics. The reader will not be expected to have formed a complete picture of exactly what is permitted in AHPL until the end of Section 5.7. In this section a complete syntax of this language is presented with as much rigor as possible given the expected background of most readers.

5.2 OPERAND CONVENTIONS

In any programming system there are a number of different types of operands, and some system must be used to distinguish between them. In FORTRAN, for example, the different types of variables must be declared. In print, however, it is more convenient to use different typographic conventions for different kinds of operands. The conventions to be used in APL and AHPL are shown in the table in Fig. 5.3.

For handwritten or typed material where italics are unavailable or inconvenient, our convention has been to underline lower case strings for scalars, underline upper-case strings for vectors, and double underline upper-case strings for matrices.

The distinction between variables and literals is very important. In conventional programming systems a variable is a *name* by which we refer to operands; a literal is an actual value for an operand. Thus, in FORTRAN we write

$$X = Y + 1$$

meaning "The new *value* of X is to be equal to the *value* of Y plus one," i.e., Y is a variable and 1 is a literal. *In AHPL a variable may be the name of a register*, the *contents* of which are referred to in a program statement; a *literal* is the actual data to be placed in a register. For example,

$$MA \leftarrow PC$$

means to transfer the *contents* of *PC* to *MA*, while

Type of Operand	Printed Representation
Literal	
Numeric	Standard numerals
Alphanumeric	Standard letters or numerals set off by apostrophes
Variables	
Scalar	Bold lower-case italic letters
Vector	Bold upper-case italic letters
Matrix	Bold upper-case Roman

Figure 5.3. Typographic conventions for APL and AHPL.

$$MA \leftarrow 0,1,0,1,0,0,0,0,1,1,1,1,0$$

means to store the string of bits shown in **MA**. In APL, as illustrated, letters or strings of letters indicate variables while numerals indicate literals. For this reason, as in FORTRAN, operators must not be omitted. Thus **MA** is the name of a single variable and should in no case be interpreted as $M \times A$.

A *vector* is simply a collection of operands arranged in a one-dimensional array. The number of elements (operands) in a vector is known as the *dimension* of the vector and will be denoted by ρ. Registers of more than one bit are considered to be vectors, since they consist of a number of bit positions, the contents of which are generally independent of one another. Thus, if the **PC** register has 18 bits, then $\rho PC = 18$; and the individual bit positions are denoted (PC_0, PC_1, $PC_2 \cdots PC_{17}$), with PC_i denoting the bit in the ith position. Note that the first position of the vector is denoted PC_0, a procedure that is known as a 0-origin indexing. In some programming systems, such as FORTRAN, 1-origin indexing is used. In this book 0-origin indexing will always be assumed unless otherwise specifically stated.

A matrix is a two-dimensional array of operands as illustrated in Fig. 5.4. The vector (M_0^i, $M_1^i \cdots M_{\rho_1-1}^i$) is known as the ith row vector of **M**, denoted by $\mathbf{M}^i$. Its dimension $\rho_1 M$ is known as the row dimension of the matrix. The vector (M_j^0, $M_j^1, \cdots M_j^{\rho_2-1}$) is known as the jth column vector of **M**, denoted by $\mathbf{M}_j$. Its dimension $\rho_2 M$ is known as the column dimension of **M**. The operand M_j^i is known as the (i, j)th element of **M**.

The matrix most commonly encountered in AHPL is the memory matrix, **M**, which is considered to have ρ_2 words, each of ρ_1 bits length. Thus, for a memory of 4096 eighteen-bit words, $\rho_2 M = 4096$ and $\rho_1 M = 18$. Note that in this convention each word is a row of the matrix so that $\mathbf{M}^i$ denotes the ith word in memory. In a similar manner, a stack of registers could be considered a matrix.

As discussed in Chapter 4, the subscript and superscript notation has been extended in AHPL to permit selection of subvectors and submatrices. That is, $\mathbf{M}^{i:k}$ is a matrix consisting of row i through k of **M** while

$$\begin{bmatrix} M_0^0 & M_1^0 & M_2^0 & \cdots & M_{\rho_1-1}^0 \\ M_0^1 & M_1^1 & \cdots\cdots\cdots & M_{\rho_1-1}^1 \\ \cdot & & & & \cdot \\ \cdot & & & & \cdot \\ \cdot & & & & \cdot \\ M_0^{\rho_2-1} & \cdots\cdots\cdots & & M_{\rho_1-1}^{\rho_2-1} \end{bmatrix}$$

Figure 5.4. Matrix.

$A_{i:k}$ is a vector consisting of elements i through k of A. This convention is not part of APL.

5.3 APL AND AHPL OPERATORS

The primitive operators are those which are primarily defined in terms of scalars (i.e., operands that are single numbers) although they all may be extended to vectors and matrices. The primitive operators are listed in the table of Fig. 5.5. Notice that some operators (unary) operate on only one argument while others (binary) relate two arguments. In a complete version of APL [1] [5], most symbols have both unary and binary meanings. In some cases these meanings are unrelated. Fortunately, we have managed to avoid this possible source of confusion. All of the operations extend to vectors on an element-by-element basis.

Operation	Name	Meaning	Comments
$x + y$	Addition	Algebraic sum of x and y	In APL only
$x - y$	Subtraction	Algebraic difference	In APL only
$x \times y$	Multiplication	Algebraic product	In APL only
$x \div y$	Division	x divided by y	In APL only
$\lvert x$	Absolute value	Absolute value of $\lvert x$	In APL only
$\overline{x}$	NOT		
$x \wedge y$	AND		
$x \vee y$	OR		
$x \oplus y$	Exclusive OR		
$(x \mathscr{R} y)$	Relational operator		In APL only

Figure 5.5. Primitive Operators.

A set of examples illustrating the use of the operators in Fig. 5.5 follows. The reader will note that the literals in these examples are represented in decimal form and may take on all real values. In AHPL every literal element in a register transfer statement must be either 1 or 0. Only these two values can be stored in a flip-flop, which is the hardware counterpart of a scalar variable. In the following examples, let $x = 1$, $y = -5$, $W = (3, 5, -1, 4)$, and $U = (1, 0, -1, -1)$.

Statement	Meaning
$z \leftarrow x + y$	$z = -4$
$z \leftarrow \bar{x}$	$z = 0$
$Z \leftarrow W + U$	$Z = (4, 5, -2, 3)$
$Z \leftarrow W \times U$	$Z = (3, 0, 1, -4)$
$Z \leftarrow U \div W$	$Z = (0.33, 0, 1, -0.25)$

The operators extend to matrices in an analogous fashion. When both operands are vectors or matrices, the dimensions must conform, as shown in the above examples. However, it is permissible to mix scalars and vectors or matrices. For example,

$$Z \leftarrow x + W$$

indicates that x is to be added to each element of W.

The logical operators AND, OR, and NOT differ from the other primitive operators in that they are defined only in terms of logical variables, i.e., variables that take on only the values 0 or 1. In operating versions of APL an attempt to apply a logical operator to a variable having a value other than 0 or 1 will result in a *domain error*. On the other hand, there is no distinction made between logical and arithmetic variables with regard to the arithmetic operators. When an arithmetic operator is applied to a variable that takes on the value 0 or 1, it is treated as a numeric 0 or 1, whatever the programmer's intent as to the meaning of the variable may have been. In the following examples, $U = (1,0,0,1,0,1)$ and $V = (0,1,1,1,0,1)$.

Statement	Result
$Z \leftarrow \bar{U}$	$Z = (0,1,1,0,1,0)$
$Z \leftarrow U \wedge V$	$Z = (0,0,0,1,0,1)$
$Z \leftarrow U \vee V$	$Z = (1,1,1,1,0,1)$
$Z \leftarrow U + V$	$Z = (1,1,1,2,0,2)$

The relational operator $(x \mathcal{R} y)$ evaluates to 1 if the relation $\mathcal{R}$ is satisfied and to 0 if the relation is not satisfied. The relation $\mathcal{R}$ may be any of the relations that typically compare numbers such $=, >, \geq, <,$ or $\leq$. For example

$$(4 > 3) = 1$$

since 4 is indeed greater than 3. Similarly,

$$(4 < 3) = 0$$

127

Much of the special power of APL derives from the mixed operators, which operate on various combinations of scalars, vectors, and matrices. There are a great many of these in APL, some of considerable complexity. A few of the more important ones are listed in Fig. 5.6.

The CATENATE operator simply joins vectors together to form larger vectors. Thus, if $X = (1, 2, 3)$ and $Y = (4, 5, 6)$ then

$$Z \leftarrow X, Y$$

specifies that $Z = (1, 2, 3, 4, 5, 6)$. The notation $M!N$ indicating row catenation has been added to AHPL. This operation is valid only if M and N have the same number of columns. The result is a matrix whose first $\rho_2 M$ rows are the rows of M and whose last $\rho_2 N$ rows are the rows of N. One or more of the arguments of row catenation may be a vector as illustrated by the example

$$M^{1:2}! \, M^0 = \begin{bmatrix} 0 & 1 & 1 \\ 1 & 1 & 1 \\ 0 & 0 & 1 \end{bmatrix}$$

where

$$M = \begin{bmatrix} 0 & 0 & 1 \\ 0 & 1 & 1 \\ 1 & 1 & 1 \end{bmatrix}$$

The take and drop operations of Fig. 5.6 are consistent with APL and will prove helpful in the discussion of Chapter 8. Letting $A = (1, 2, 3, 4, 5)$, we illustrate these operations as follows

$$2 \uparrow A = (1, 2)$$
$$2 \downarrow A = (3, 4, 5)$$

These operations will not be included in AHPL, since the same results can be accomplished by subscripting. For example,

$$A_{0:1} = (1, 2) \text{ and } A_{2:4} = (3, 4, 5)$$

The binary encode and decode operations of Fig. 5.6 are special cases of the standard APL encode and decode operations. The result of the binary decode operation $\perp X$ is a decimal scalar equal to the binary number formed from the respective bits of X. Clearly, $\perp X$ is valid only if each element of X is a 1 or a 0. The binary encode operation, $n \top p$, is almost the reverse. That is, $n \top p$ expresses the binary equivalent of the decimal number p as an n-element vector. The least significant bit of

Notation	Name	Meaning	Comment
X, Y	CATENATE	$X_0, X_1 \cdots X_{\rho x-1}, Y_0,$ $Y_1, \cdots Y_{\rho y-1}$	
$M \,!\, N$	ROW CATENATE	A matrix with $\rho_2 M + \rho_2 N$ rows with the rows of M above the rows of N	In AHPL only
$k \uparrow X$	TAKE	The first k elements of X	In APL only
$k \downarrow X$	DROP	All but the first k elements of X	In APL only
$\perp X$	BINARY DECODE	The decimal equivalent of the vector X of 1's and 0's interpreted as a binary number	In APL only
$n \top p$	BINARY ENCODE	An n element binary vector formed from the base-2 representation of p	
$\odot /X$	REDUCTION	$X_0 \odot X_1 \odot X_2 \cdots \odot X_{\rho X-1}$	
$Z = \odot /M$	ROW REDUCTION	$Z_i = \odot /M^i$	
$Z = \odot //M$	COLUMN REDUCTION	$Z_i = \odot /M_i$	
$Z = U/X$	COMPRESS	Z obtained from X by suppressing each X_i for which $U_i = 0$	In APL and in AHPL combinational logic unit descriptions only
$A = U/M$	ROW COMPRESS	$A^i = U/M^i$	
$A = U//M$	COLUMN COMPRESS	$A_j = U/M_j$	

Figure 5.6. Mixed Operators in APL and AHPL.

the binary number is the rightmost element of $n \top p$. This notation will provide a convenient method of expressing constants in APL. For example,

$$8 \top 100 = (0, 1, 1, 0, 0, 1, 0, 0)$$

and

$$8 \top 0 \quad = (0, 0, 0, 0, 0, 0, 0, 0)$$

The decode notation $\perp X$ will be used in APL only, since the result is a decimal number that cannot be stored in a hardware register:

$$\perp (0, 1, 1, 0, 0, 1, 0, 0) = 100$$

An operation that is applied to all elements of a vector or matrix to produce a simpler structure is called a *reduction*. The reduction of a vector is denoted by

$$z \leftarrow \odot / X$$

where $\odot$ may be any binary operator, and signifies that

$$z = (\cdots ((X_0 \odot X_1) \odot X_2) \cdots) \odot X_{\rho-1}).$$

For example,

$$z \leftarrow +/X$$

is equivalent to

$$z = \sum_{i=0}^{\rho-1} X_i$$

Reduction is a very powerful operation and can be used in many ingenious ways. For example, if V is a logical vector,

$$z \leftarrow +/V$$

will give a count of the 1's in V,

$$z \leftarrow \vee/V$$

will be 0 if and only if every element of V is 0, and

$$z \leftarrow \wedge/V$$

will be 1 if and only if every element of V is 1.

Reduction is extended to matrices in two ways. *Row reduction* is denoted

$$X \leftarrow \odot / M$$

and signifies that each row is reduced individually, producing a vector dimension $\rho_2 M$. Column reduction is denoted

$$X \leftarrow \odot // M$$

and signifies that each column is reduced individually, resulting in a vector of dimension $\rho_1 M$. For example, if

$$M = \begin{bmatrix} 1 & 1 & 0 & 1 \\ 1 & 0 & 0 & 1 \\ 0 & 1 & 0 & 0 \end{bmatrix}$$

then $+/M = (3,2,1)$, $+//M = (2,2,0,2)$, and $+/(+//M) = 6$.

Effective use of vectors and matrices in APL depends not only on operators for handling them but also on the ability to select specific elements from them. Single elements can be selected through the use of indices, as in PC_i, M^i, M_j, or M^i_j, but often we need to select a group of elements. For this purpose we define the *compression* operator, denoted by

$$Z \leftarrow U/X$$

where U is a logical vector. The vector Z is obtained by suppressing from the vector X each element X_i for which $U_i = 0$. For example, if $U = (1, 0, 0, 1, 0, 1)$ and $X = (1, 2, 3, 4, 5, 6)$, then

$$Z \leftarrow U/X$$

results in $Z = (1, 4, 6)$.

As will be shown in Section 5.4, the power of the compression operator U/X is most evident when U is allowed to be a variable data vector. There is, however, no simple hardware realization of U/X when U is a data register. Most applications of compression with constant U can be adequately described using superscripting and subscripting. For this reason compression will be omitted from the allowed AHPL syntax to be presented in Section 5.7.

5.4 APL PROGRAMMING*

In APL many very complex operations can be expressed as a single line. Often we discover a single-line representation after we have first expressed an operation as a multistep APL program. As is the case with any language, a branching notation is needed to permit the writing of efficient programs. This makes it possible to determine the next program step as a function of computed data.

The standard branch in APL will take the form

$$\rightarrow (\text{APL expression})$$

*This section has been included to provide a glimpse of the power of APL programming for the interested reader. It may be omitted without loss of continuity.

The APL expression above may be any expression that properly computes the number of the next program step to be executed. If the result is a vector, the next step will be the first element of the vector. If the vector is empty, i.e., a vector of no elements, then the program continues to the next step in sequence. We have been using one example of the branch notation given above. The expression

$$\rightarrow (P/A)$$

uses compression to determine a next step from a vector A of next steps. So far we have insisted that P be a vector of Boolean expressions one of which must have the value 1. This restriction need not apply in APL.

To emphasize the advantage of reducing an APL program to a single step and to provide a first example of such a program, consider the following sequence of steps that computes U/X.

1. $j \leftarrow 0$
2. $i \leftarrow 0$
3. $\rightarrow (\bar{U}_i, U_i)/(6, 4)$
4. $Z_j \leftarrow X_i$
5. $j \leftarrow j + 1$
6. $i \leftarrow i + 1$
7. $\rightarrow (i < \rho X)/(3)$
8.

Notice that branch operations are separate numbered steps in APL. The branch at step 7 is based on a relational operator. If this relation is satisfied, step 7 reads $\rightarrow 1/3$ or $\rightarrow (3)$ so the program loops back to step 3. If the relation is not satisfied, each element of U having been examined, then step 7 reads $\rightarrow 0/3$ or $\rightarrow$ (an empty vector); and the program goes on to step 8.

List searching and matrix operations are two types of programs that can be expressed very concisely in terms of APL. Both are involved in the following example.

Example 5.1
Write an APL program that will search a list of words in memory for words, the leftmost 3 bits of which are all ones. These words should be assembled into a separate list.

Solution
Let the list of words be represented by the matrix, N, whose elements are all ones and zeros. We assume an 18-bit memory so that $\rho_1 N = 18$. We let $\rho_2 N$, the

number of words, be some unspecified large number. The following short program will accomplish the search:

1. $U \leftarrow \rho_2 N \top 0$
2. $i \leftarrow 0$
3. $\rightarrow ((\wedge/(3 \uparrow N^i)) = 0)/(5)$
4. $U_i \leftarrow 1$
5. $i \leftarrow i + 1$
6. $\rightarrow (i < \rho_2 N)/(3)$
7. $Z \leftarrow U//N$

A vector U is created with an element corresponding to each row of N. A one is stored in each element of U which corresponds to a word in N whose first 3 bits are ones. All other elements of U remain zero. The inspection of words in N is carried out at step 3. At step 7, U is used to select the desired list Z.

The power and flexibility of APL becomes even more apparent as the reader recognizes that the following shorter program will accomplish this same job:

$$Z \leftarrow (N_0 \wedge N_1 \wedge N_2)//N$$

5.5 AHPL CONVENTIONS FOR COMBINATIONAL LOGIC

Having presented the primitive operations for AHPL and some of those of APL, we now leave APL to concentrate on completely defining the structure of AHPL. In the next section we shall begin a semiformal development of the AHPL syntax. It is first convenient to introduce one more concept which will be found in that syntax, an abbreviated notation for complex combinational logic expressions.

Consider the moderately complex combinational logic vector given by expression 5.1.

$$C \leftarrow (A_0 \wedge B_0) \oplus ((A_1 \wedge B_1) \wedge (A_2 \wedge B_2) \wedge (A_3 \wedge B_3)),$$
$$(A_1 \wedge B_1) \oplus ((A_2 \wedge B_2) \wedge (A_3 \wedge B_3)),$$
$$(A_2 \wedge B_2) \oplus (A_3 \wedge B_3), (A_3 \wedge B_3) \quad (5.1)$$

If this expression appeared only once within an AHPL control sequence, it could be written as given. If the same expression appeared more than once, added clarity and a saving in effort would result if the expression were replaced by an abbreviation, with the logic function defining the abbreviation presented only once. For example, expression 5.2 could be substituted for expression 5.1.

$$C \leftarrow \text{LOGIC}\ (A;\ B) \quad (5.2)$$

The form LOGIC $(A;\ B)$ is similar to subroutine notation in a programming language. Here we shall refer to LOGIC $(A; B)$ as a *function* or a *combinational logic unit*. This notation will be restricted to refer *only* to combinational logic networks.

The description of the network defined by LOGIC $(A; B)$ will be set apart by the heading and END notation.

UNIT: LOGIC $(A; B)$
connections

.
.
.

END

The above is the format of a *combinational logic unit description*. The combinational logic description of LOGIC $(A; B)$ may consist of a single *connection statement* or a series of connection statements.

If notation for a single, combinational logic unit appears more than once with the same arguments, only one network needs to be constructed with multiple connections to its output. Thus the combinational logic unit description is a vehicle for minimizing cost through the reuse of logic networks. If the notation for a given function appears more than once but with different arguments, then the network must be constructed separately for each distinct set of inputs.* Only one combinational logic unit description is required in any case. If the function is to be used with more than one set of arguments, dummy variables may appear in the heading of the combinational logic unit description.

Some special features will be allowed within a combinational logic unit description to simplify the expression of particularly complex networks. The writing of combinational logic unit descriptions and their compilation into hardware will be considered further in Chapter 7.

In this section we shall be content with a single example of the use of combinational logic unit notation.

Example 5.3
The sequences of Fig. 5.7 represent typical inputs and the corresponding output for an eight's complementing sequential circuit. This circuit can be realized using only two data flip-flops.

*We shall see in Chapter 6 that a complex combinational logic network can be shared by declaring buses as its arguments.

START 0 0 0 0 1 0 0 0 0 0 0 0 0 0

x 1 0 1 1 1/0 0 1/1 1 0/0 0

z 0 0 0 0 0 0 0/1 1 1/0 1 0

Figure 5.7. Input/Ouput of 8's Complementer

Following a 1 on line START, subsequent 3-bit sequences on input line x are to be interpreted as octal digits. The eight's complement of these digits is to appear on the output line z with a delay of two clock periods. For example, the first 3 bits as separated by diagonal lines represent octal 1. The corresponding output bits after a two-period delay represent octal 7. The outputs prior to the first start pulse following "power on" will be ignored.

An AHPL control sequence for a sequential network based on a two flip-flop shift register, Y, and satisfying this specification is given below. Notice that steps 2 and 3 call for shifting x into Y_1, and Y_1, into Y_0, and letting Y_0 be the output. At step 4 a translation of the 3-bit character Y, x into its eight's complement takes place. The most-significant bit is outputted immediately, and the two least-significant bits represented by $COMP_{1:2}$ are placed in Y. The word COMP is notation for an eight's complementing combinational logic network that will be discussed in detail in the following paragraphs. Following step 4, control returns to step 2 and the process is repeated. Step 1 is provided to restart the process after each start signal. Consecutive start signals hold the circuit at this step causing 0 outputs.

1. $Y \leftarrow 0, x; z = 0$
   $\rightarrow (start, \overline{start}) / (1,3)$
2. $Y \leftarrow Y_1, x \; ; \; z = Y_0$
   $\rightarrow (start) / (1)$
3. $Y \leftarrow Y_1, x \; ; \; z = Y_0$
   $\rightarrow start / (1)$
4. $z = COMP_0 (Y, x);$
   $Y \leftarrow COMP_{1:2} (Y, x)$
   $\rightarrow (start, \overline{start}) / (1,2)$

With the exception of the combinational logic network, COMP, the reader should have no difficulty generating realizations of both the control and data units from the above AHPL description. As illustrated in Fig. 5.8, this network has inputs x and Y with outputs gated by the step 4 control signal into Y and to the output z. The gate inputs for register Y are connected directly to the clock, since the contents of Y are changed at each control step.

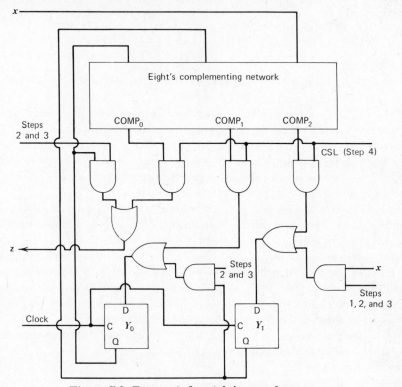

Figure 5.8. Data unit for eight's complementer.

The designer who first formulates a system design in AHPL and then translates it to hardware manually can easily incorporate a combinational logic circuit which has been derived in any manner into the network. The network COMP, for example, need not necessarily ever be expressed in AHPL. In order to show the relation between combinational logic unit descriptions and their representation within the control sequence, we shall generate a series of connection statements for the eight's complementing network.

Recall that in Example 5.3 the most significant bit arrives first so that during the clock period in which COMP is employed the most-significant bit is in Y_0, the next in Y_1 and the least-significant bit is x. The output $COMP_0$ is the most-significant bit; $COMP_1$ is next; and $COMP_2$ is least significant. The map in Fig. 5.9 is a tabulation of these three output values as a function of the inputs x and Y. As verified by the table, the least-significant bit of a number is the same as the least-significant bit of its eight's complement. That is, if a number is odd, its

136

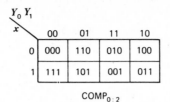

$$COMP_{0:2}$$

Figure 5.9. Complementing functions.

eight's complement is odd; if a number is even, its eight's complement is even. Therefore,

$$COMP_2 = x \tag{5.3}$$

Individual Karnaugh maps for the remaining two functions are given in Figs. 5.10 and 5.11. The reader can verify from these maps that $COMP_0$ and $COMP_1$ are given by the multilevel logic expressions 5.4 and 5.5.

$$COMP_0 = ((x \vee Y_1) \wedge \overline{Y}_0) \vee (Y_0 \wedge \overline{Y}_1 \wedge \overline{x}) \tag{5.4}$$

$$COMP_1 = (x \vee Y_1) \wedge \overline{(x \wedge Y_1)} \tag{5.5}$$

Since there is one term common to these expressions, they lead to a realization with one less gate than a sum of products from. We can now express the network in the form of a combinational logic unit description or list of connection statements.

UNIT: COMP $(Y; x)$
          $wa = x \vee Y_1$
          $wb = wa \wedge \overline{Y}_0$
          $wc = Y_0 \wedge \overline{Y}_1 \wedge \overline{x}$
        $COMP_0 = wb \vee wc$
          $wd = \overline{x \wedge Y_1}$
        $COMP_1 = wd \wedge wa$
        $COMP_2 = x$
END

$Y_0 Y_1$ x	00	01	11	10
0	0	1	0	1
1	1	1	0	0

Figure 5.10. $COMP_0$.

$Y_0 \, Y_1$

x	00	01	11	10
0	0	1	1	0
1	1	0	0	1

Figure 5.11. $COMP_1$.

Notice that the outputs of earlier connection statements serve as inputs to subsequent statements. Finally, the outputs forming COMP (Y, x) are generated. The term END will separate the series of steps defining COMP from any succeeding network descriptions.

There are a small set of combinational logic units that are used repeatedly in a variety of digital systems. These will be introduced as needed. Perhaps the most common of these combinational logic unit descriptions is the increment function

$$INC \, (REG)$$

which is an n bit vector representation of a binary number determined by increasing by 1-modulo-2^n the number given by the APL expression $\perp REG$. In hardware terms

$$REG \leftarrow INC(REG)$$

merely means treating REG as a counter and incrementing that counter. The AHPL connection description representing INC and the corresponding hardware realization will be a homework problem in Chapter 7.

5.6 SYSTEM MODULES

A typical large digital system will consist of a number of interconnected subsystems or modules. Although a design problem will often be limited to a single module, it will usually be important to see clearly the relationships of that module to other modules within the system. There will be wires interconnecting modules that must have labels as outputs in one module as well as inputs in another. Certain memory elements may be capable of receiving data that might be clocked in by the control unit of more than one module. It is also important to be able to collect the transfer and connection statements associated with one subsystem so that they are immediately recognized as part of that module and no other.

We have already presented some of the AHPL conventions at the level of the individual statement. Before presenting the complete syntax, we

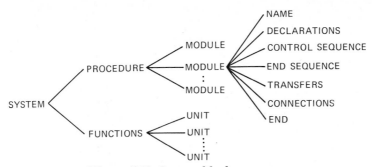

Figure 5.12. System block structure.

shall consider the relationship of the individual statement to the overall system description, which may include many modules as well as combinational logic units. Not all systems are isolated with easily defined boundaries. Some may even be connected through communications links into seemingly never ending networks. In such cases a system boundary must be imposed by the designer. Often bounds can be established at points of interface with equipment which is primarily nondigital. In the end, however, the designer is free to establish any system boundary that may prove convenient.

In Fig. 5.12 we see an informal illustration of a syntax for subdividing a bounded system with the system itself as the root. The first level of branching in the tree indicates that the procedural AHPL descriptions of the modules containing memory and control precede the FUNCTIONS consisting of combinational logic only. The outputs of a combinational logic unit may be used within any procedural module or nonrecursively within any other functional unit. The format for describing a simple unit was described in the previous section. A more detailed treatment of the syntax for these connection descriptions will be deferred until Chapter 7.

As indicated in Fig. 5.12, the AHPL description of a module will consist of a name, a list of declarations, a control sequence, a list of individual connection statements, and a termination. The declarations include

MEMORY (flip-flops, registers, and arrays)
INPUTS
OUTPUTS
BUSES
LABELS
ONE-SHOTS
COMBUS

All flip-flops, registers, and memory arrays that will appear in the control sequence of a given module must be dimensioned in a MEMORY declaration. Vectors of input and output lines as well as individual lines must be declared. The source of each input line together with any different label in its module of origin may be given. Each BUS must be declared and dimensioned. A *communications bus* as discussed in Chapter 4 may now be formally defined as a bus on which the contents may be determined by more than one module. A communications bus must be declared separately as a COMBUS, thus recording the fact that this bus must be connected to a set of input/output lines from the module. It is not necessary to also include a communications bus among the INPUT and OUTPUT declarations.

The **LABELS** declaration may be used to rename portions of larger registers. It may also be used to call for a particular hardware realization of a register such as an MSI part. As will be discussed in Section 5.9 a monostable multivibrator or "one shot" may appear in AHPL descriptions in much the same way as a flip-flop. A declaration must be provided to distinguish a one shot from a flip-flop and to specify the duration of its output.

To illustrate the use of declaration statements, the initial steps of a formal AHPL description of the data selector of Example 4.1 will be given as follows.

MODULE: DATA SELECTOR
  MEMORY: *INREG* [12]; *OUTREG* [12];
  A [4]; *s*
  INPUTS: X [12]
  OUTPUTS: Z [12]; *inready*; *outready*

The above example illustrates the declaration of registers and individual memory elements. An *array will be dimensioned as* $M[m, n]$ where m is the number of rows and n is the number of columns. If **M** is a memory array, we shall assume it to have m words of n bits each.

Following the declarations is the control sequence which will consist of a series of action statements, the syntax of which will be defined in the next section. The control sequence will be terminated by END SEQUENCE. This indicator may be followed by individual transfers and connection statements that are intended to be applicable at all times regardless of the step in the control sequence active during the current clock period. A combinational logic network generating an output as a function of the registers in a module might be included following the END SEQUENCE statement. In this case the same output function would apply continuously regardless of state of the control unit.

In some systems it is necessary to keep track of time in parallel with any other activities that might be in progress. This can be accomplished by incrementing a counter every clock period. Such a counting function can be specified by inserting a statement like

COUNT ← INC (**COUNT**)

following the END SEQUENCE statement. All connection statements and transfers may be subject to conditional expressions consistent with the syntax to be presented in the following section. In the following partial example a counter is incremented whenever the data flip-flop a = 1. The output statement is valid every clock period.

END SEQUENCE
COUNT ∗ a ← INC(**COUNT**)
$Z = X \wedge$ **REG**
END

Finally, as illustrated by this example the overall module description must be terminated by END.

5.7 AHPL STATEMENTS

Only those APL operations that satisfy the constraints imposed by available hardware are included in AHPL. We wish to make this point in the strongest possible way. Every AHPL step written down by the designer will represent some action on some already-specified hardware elements. The designer will always have a mental picture of the hardware involved prior to writing an AHPL step. In the remainder of this chapter we shall develop hardware related features for AHPL that are not in APL.

The syntax and semantics of individual statements in an AHPL control sequence will be presented in this section. The syntax will be presented in outline form, gradually working inward from the overall program sequence to the individual operations. First, however, let us look briefly at the notation on either side of the arrow in a simple transfer statement.

$$DV \leftarrow OCLV \qquad (5.6)$$

The vector **DV** represents what we shall call the destination vector. It may be a single register or a vector of one or more memory elements assembled by any of the list of already discussed *selection operators* tabulated in Fig. 5.13. The subscripts and superscripts appearing in these selection operators must be constants.

A_j	The jth element of A
$A_{m:n}$	Elements m through n of A
,	Catenation
$A!B$	Row catenation
M^j	The jth row of M
$M^{m:n}$	Row m through row n of M

Figure 5.13. AHPL Selection Operators.

The vector **OCLV** on the right-hand side of expression 5.6 represents what will be called an *origin combinational logic vector*. Each element of an **OCLV** is a combinational logic expression whose arguments may be elements from any of the following:

1. Memory elements
2. Inputs
3. FUNCTIONS
4. buses
5. Constants

Only 0, 1 and the n bit encoding of a decimal number d ($n \top d$) will be used as constants. Particular arguments for combinational logic expressions may be selected from the above using any of the selection operators in Fig. 5.13. These arguments may then be related by any of the logic operators listed in Fig. 5.14.

$\wedge$	And
$\vee$	Or
Overbar	Not
$\wedge/$	And over elements of a vector
$\vee/$	Or over elements of a vector
$\oplus$	Exclusive Or
SYN	Synchronization

Figure 5.14. AHPL Logic Operators.

In order to minimize the need for parentheses in the formation of OCL expressions, the AHPL selection and logic operators will be used according to the following *precedence structure*.

1. Not and syn
2. All selection operators except catenate
3. $\wedge$

4. $\vee$ or $\oplus$

5. Catenate

An operation in the lower-numbered category will have the highest precedence and will be executed first. When the issue is otherwise unresolved, parentheses will be employed. In this book parentheses may be used in some places when not absolutely required in order to ensure clarity.

We are now ready to examine the syntax of a control sequence step. Any number of such steps may be listed to form the control sequence of Fig. 5.12. Each control sequence step will consist of an action statement followed by a branch as suggested by Fig. 5.15. This figure also indicates the four possible compositions of the action statement. In effect the action statement may consist of any number of clocked transfers and/or connection statements. The first alternative, "null," allows for steps consisting only of a branch statement.

The branch portion of a step in a control sequence may take on any of the four possible forms given in Fig. 5.15. The meanings of the first three have already been discussed. The statement DEAD END indicates that no other control state will follow the current state. This might be used to effect a HALT instruction, for example, or to terminate various paths within a set of simultaneous or parallel control sequences. The concept of parallelism will be considered in Chapter 9.

In Fig. 5.15, F represents a vector of Boolean expressions that serve as conditionals. The elements of an F vector may be generated in the same way as those of an **OCLV**, and S is a vector of statement numbers.

The three possible forms of a clocked transfer are given in Fig. 5.16,*

---

*The forms $\to (f_1 \times b_1 + f_2 \times b_2)$ for conditional branch of the first version of AHPL is still in use but will prove inconvenient in a few applications of the newer notation.

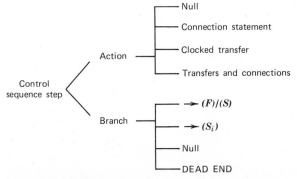

Figure 5.15. Syntax of a control sequence step.

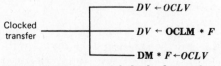

$$DV \leftarrow OCLV$$

Clocked transfer

$$DV \leftarrow \mathbf{OCLM} * F$$

$$\mathbf{DM} * F \leftarrow OCLV$$

Figure 5.16. Forms of clocked transfers.

and the four forms of a connection statement are given in Fig. 5.17.*
The simplest clocked transfer merely transfers an origin combinational
logic vector into a destination register of the same length. The remaining
two forms are conditional transfers. The array **OCLM** is merely a matrix
whose rows are vectors of combinational logic expressions. If the **OCLM**
is $(A\,!B\,!C)$, if $F = (f, g, h)$, and the DV is D, then the second transfer form
represents the transfer previously given as expression 4.21.

$$D \leftarrow (A\;!\;B\;!\;C) * (f, g, h)$$

Similarly, if the *destination matrix*, **DM**, were to represent $(A\;!\;B\;!\;C)$
and the **OCLV** were D, the third transfer form would coincide with
expression 4.20.

$$(A\;!\;B\;!\;C) * (f, g, h) \leftarrow D$$

In all cases the expression will have meaning only if the vector of expressions selected on the right has the same number of elements as the
destination vector selected on the left.

In Fig. 5.17 we distinguish the connection to a predeclared bus from
a connection statement that routes an **OCLV** to a vector of module outputs when it appears in a control sequence. There is no logical difference between a connection to an output vector **Z** and connection to a
bus. Where the number of anticipated inputs is very large, one would
usually use a predeclared bus. Where output networks route only a few
data vectors, the notation $Z = OCLV$ may be used.

Expression 5.7 is a conditional connection to a bus of 2-bit length, the

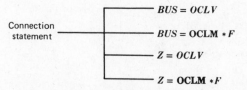

$$BUS = OCLV$$

Connection statement

$$BUS = \mathbf{OCLM} * F$$

$$Z = OCLV$$

$$Z = \mathbf{OCLM} * F$$

Figure 5.17. Connection statements.

*The form $B \leftarrow A * f_1 \lor C * f_2$ for conditional transfer of the first version of AHPL is
still in use but will prove inconvenient in a few applications of the newer notation.

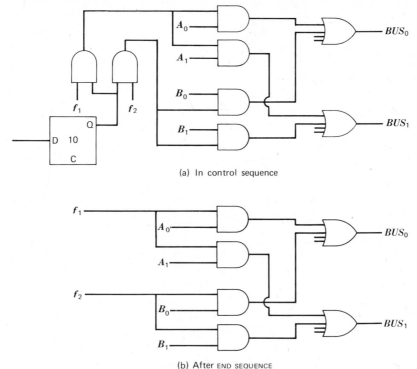

(a) In control sequence

(b) After END SEQUENCE

Figure 5.18. Conditional connections to a BUS.

hardware realization of which is depicted in Fig. 5.18a. The same expression following END SEQUENCE would not require ANDing the condition variables f_1 and f_2 to the output of a control flip-flop resulting in the network given in Fig. 5.18b. The reader should note the similarity to the transfer network of Fig. 4.5.

$$10. \quad BUS = (A \; ! \; B) * (f_1, f_2) \qquad (5.7)$$

Ordinarily, only connection statements of the form $Y = OCLV$ will appear in combinational logic unit descriptions.

5.8 HANDLING OF MEMORY ARRAYS IN AHPL

The selection operators listed in the previous section serve the function of selecting arguments from flip-flops, registers, and arrays so that they may be permanently wired into the data unit, either providing input data to a transfer or serving as the destination of a transfer. These se-

145

lection operators imply permanent connections only, not logical operations or computations. This is the reason that subscripts and superscripts
must be constants. Wired connections are inherently constant. Often it
is necessary to select a word from a memory array as a function of the
contents of a register as in the case of a random access memory (RAM).
The conditional transfer notation of Fig. 5.16 has been provided in part
for this purpose. Suppose that the array M in Fig. 5.19 consists of 2^n
words stored in 2^n static semiconductor registers. Let F be a vector of 2^n
elements, one and only one of which will be logical 1. In this case
expression 5.8 specifies transferring the contents of the memory data
register MD into one of the words of memory.

$$M * F \leftarrow MD \qquad (5.8)$$

By constraining the value of the elements of F such that one and only
one of these values is logical 1, only one of the 2^n memory registers is
clocked each time the step in expression 5.8 is executed. Usually, the
location of the word in memory to be replaced will be specified by the
binary number stored in an address register, labeled AR in Fig. 5.19. To
complete the notation for a write-in memory operation, we must replace
F in expression 5.8 by the output of a combinational logic network,
which we shall call DCD. This network must be constructed in such a
way that $DCD_i = 1$ and $DCD_j = 0$, where $j \neq i$ if the binary number
stored in AR is i. The network DCD, as depicted in Fig. 5.19b, is usually
referred to as an n-2^n line decoder. Decoding networks are treated in
most books on switching theory and were considered briefly in Chapter
3. In Chapter 7 a combinational logic unit description of the network
DCD will be developed. The write in memory operation can, therefore,
be expressed in AHPL as

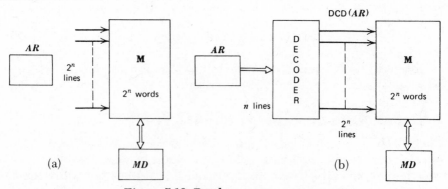

Figure 5.19. Random access memory.

$$M * DCD\,(AR) \leftarrow MD$$

The logic network for reading from a static memory as was depicted in Chapter 3 is much the same as a busing network. For a hypothetical four-word memory the read from memory operation is given by expression 5.9.

$$MD \leftarrow (M^0 \wedge DCD_0\,(AR)) \vee (M^1 \wedge DCD_1\,(AR)) \vee (M^2 \wedge DCD_2\,(AR))$$
$$\vee (M^3 \wedge DCD_3\,(AR)) \tag{5.9}$$

A shorter form is clearly necessary to represent this operation for a memory of practical size. Again we fall back on the combinational logic function notation introduced in Section 5.5. Since the two level AND-OR network implementing expression 5.9 is in effect a busing network, we use the notation BUSFN to express a generalization of expression 5.9.

$$MD \leftarrow BUSFN\,(M;\ DCD\,(AR)) \tag{5.10}$$

As with DCD, an AHPL combinational logic unit description for BUSFN will be given in Chapter 7.

Previously, AHPL has used

$$MD \leftarrow M^{\perp AR}$$

and

$$M^{\perp AR} \leftarrow MD$$

to represent memory read and write operations, respectively. While these are legitimate APL expressions, they have no status in AHPL, since they imply nothing about the form of hardware. They may occasionally be used, as in Chapter 8, where it is desired to indicate a read or write operation without implication as to the type of memory hardware.

Making up the remainder of this section are two design examples. These are included to illustrate two approaches to the manipulation of small data arrays. They will also be the first complete module descriptions presented and the first opportunity to take advantage of the complete AHPL syntax as presented in the previous section.

Example 5.4

A simple machine tool controller is to be designed using a read-only memory to store sequences of tool positions. Eighteen-bit numbers are used to specify the tool position in three dimensions in a way that need not concern us here.

147

There are four possible sequences, any of which may be requested by an operator at any time. Each sequence is 256 words long. The system hardware must include an 18-bit register, **PR**, for storing the current tool position. The tool electronics continually monitor this register through three digital-to-analog converters. Communications with the operator is provided using a start-stop flip-flop, **ss**, and a 2-bit register, **SQR**, which specifies the desired sequence. The bit combinations 00, 01, 10, and 11 in **SQR** indicate that the sequence presently being utilized (if any) is A, B, C, or D, respectively. Setting the flip-flop **ss** to 1 will cause the controller to begin reading out the sequence specified by **SQR**. If the operator causes the flip-flop **ss** to be reset to 0, the controller responds by terminating the sequence in progress and storing a vector of 18 zeros in **PR**. Upon completing a sequence, the controller must reset **ss** and store zeros in **PR**. A synchronizing mechanism has been provided so that the contents of **ss** and **SQR** will never change during a controller clock pulse.

Solution

The only required storage registers in addition to those described above are a 10-bit address register for the read-only memory and the read-only memory itself. These devices may be represented by the vector **AR** and the matrix **ROM**, respectively. The complete register configuration is given in Fig. 5.20. The read-only memory (**ROM**) contains 1024 eighteen-bit words in all. Sequence A is stored in locations 0 to 255 (decimal). In decimal, the first addresses of sequences B, C, and D are 256, 512, and 768, respectively.

The frequency of the clock source has been established compatible with the required data rate of the tool and is, therefore, slower than the **ROM**. Thus a word can be read from the **ROM** in one clock period. The one following is a module description of the machine tool controller.

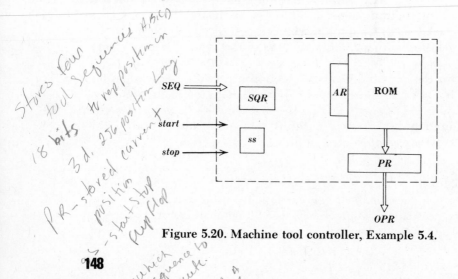

Figure 5.20. Machine tool controller, Example 5.4.

MODULE: MACHINE TOOL CONTROLLER
MEMORY: **ROM**[1024, 18]; **PR**[18]; **AR**[10]; **SQR**[2]; *ss*
INPUTS: **SEQ**[2]; *start*; *stop*
OUTPUTS: **OPR**[18]

1. $SQR \leftarrow SEQ$
   $\rightarrow (\overline{ss}, ss) / (1, 2)$
2. $AR \leftarrow SQR_0, SQR_1, 8\top 0$
3. $PR \leftarrow$ BUSFN (**ROM**; DCD(**AR**))
4. $AR \leftarrow$ INC(**AR**)
   $\rightarrow ((\wedge/AR_{2:9} \wedge ss), \overline{ss}, (\overline{\wedge/AR_{2:9}} \wedge ss)) / (5, 6, 3)$
5. $ss \leftarrow 0$
6. $PR \leftarrow 18 \top 0$
   $\rightarrow (1)$

END SEQUENCE
   $ss * (start \vee stop) \leftarrow (1!0) * (start, stop)$
   $OPR = PR$
END

Step 1 provides a waiting loop to start operation. Notice the conditional transfer following END SEQUENCE, indicating that the *start* and *stop* lines are continuously monitored. Anytime the operator pulses the *start* line, the next clock pulse will set *ss*, and the following clock pulse will branch from step 1 to step 2 to start the sequence. Step 1 also gates the input **SEQ** into **SQR**, so that whenever the sequence starts, **SQR** will contain the number of the sequence most recently specified by the operator.

Depending on the two bits in **SQR**, the right side of step 2 will reduce to one of the four 10-bit vectors: 10 $\top$ 0, $\top$256, $\top$512, or $\top$768, which indicates whether the desired sequence is A, B, C, or D. For example,

$$\top 768 = 1, 1, 0, 0, 0, 0, 0, 0, 0, 0$$

Step 3 is an example of what will become a familiar read-from-memory notation. The contents of the address in **ROM** specified by **AR** are placed in **PR**.

Step 4 is our first encounter with the function INC. This step causes one to be added to the binary number in **AR** so that the next word in sequence may be obtained from **ROM**. In APL the step might have been expressed as

$$AR \leftarrow (10)\top((\perp AR) + 1)$$

This form is not included in the AHPL syntax because it gives no hint of the form of the combinational logic required to implement the operation. Step 4 also causes a branch to step 5 if a 256-word sequence has just been completed. Notice that although the contents of **AR** are being incremented by this same step, the branch is a function of the old value of **AR**. That is, when the last number is

149

read from the **ROM** the last 8 bits of *AR* will all be 1's. Steps 5 and 6 clear *ss* and initialize the position information in *PR* before returning control to step 1 to await another user request. If step 4 encounters *ss* = 0 at any point, the process in progress is aborted by clearing *PR* at step 6 and control returns to step 1.

The previous example illustrates one method of manipulating data in an array, that of treating the array as a memory and accessing individual words using an address register and an accompanying decoding network. A second commonly used approach is to treat the array as a bank of shift registers and rotate the desired word to the output. A single upward rotation of the rows of a 16-row array is given by

$$M \leftarrow (M^{1:15} \mathbin{!} M^0) \tag{5.12}$$

A downward rotation would be similarly expressed.

A design based on rotation of rows is closely related to a semirandom access memory and is, therefore, slower than a design based on the addressing of words in an array. Example 5.5 illustrates the use of row rotation of an array of limited size in an application in which speed is not a primary consideration.

Example 5.5

A digital module is to be designed to check for duplicate characters in a stream of 8-bit data characters. The circuit has an input line **data** that will be 1 whenever a new data character is available on a vector of input lines **CHAR**. Transitions on these input lines are synchronized with the clock of the duplicate character checker. An output line **accept** must be provided on which a one-clock-period level will occur following acceptance of a data vector from the line **CHAR**. The only other output line is to be connected to a flip-flop *y* *that is to contain a 1 if and only if the most recently received character is a duplicate of any one of the 16 immediately previous characters.* The value of *y* should return to 0 when **accept** goes to 1 indicating reception of the next character. It may be assumed that the time interval between data characters will be ample to permit checking for duplicates serially.

Write a complete description of the character checker module including declarations and control sequence.

Solution

The duplicate character checker will be based on an array **SRM** of eight 16-bit shift registers. Also required are an 8-bit input data register **INR** and a 4-bit counter **CNT**. Each character received in **INR** is compared with each of the 16 characters stored in **SRM** as they are rotated to the top row. The number of rotations is monitored by **CNT** causing the process to terminate after all 16 characters are checked. Following the last cycle of the checking operation, the character in **INR** is entered in SRM^{15} and the oldest word, which had previously been stored in SRM^0, is lost. As soon as a duplicate character is received, y is set to 1.

The following is an AHPL description of the duplicate character checker.

MODULE: DUPLICATE CHARACTER CHECKER
   MEMORY: **SRM** [16,8]; **INR**[8]; **CNT**[4]; y
   INPUTS: **CHAR**[8]; $data$
   OUTPUTS: $accept$; y

1. $\rightarrow \overline{(data}, data)/(1,2)$
2. $accept = 1; y \leftarrow 0;$
    $INR \leftarrow CHAR; CNT \leftarrow 4 \top 0$
3. $y * \overline{\vee/(INR \oplus SRM^0)} \leftarrow 1;$
    $CNT \leftarrow INC\ (CNT);$
    $SRM \leftarrow (SRM^{1:15}\ !\ SRM^0)$
    $\rightarrow (\wedge/CNT, \overline{\wedge/CNT})/(4, 3)$
4. $SRM \leftarrow (SRM^{1:15}\ !\ INR)$
    $\rightarrow (1)$
END SEQUENCE
END

5.9 ASYNCHRONOUS SUBSYSTEMS*

A digital system to be designed in terms of AHPL is presumed to be a synchronous system. That is, all memory elements within the system are assumed to change values only on a common edge (in our case the trailing edge) of the same clock pulse. Within many systems there are subsystems for which this assumption is not true. A few logic levels may change values at random without regard to the system clock. Distance between modules of a single system may make it impossible to synchronize them with the same clock. This problem is most likely to occur at high clock frequencies, where the clock period may be of the same order of magnitude as the propagation delay in typical wire connections.

An asynchronous subsystem is depicted in Fig. 5.21a. The design can be expressed in AHPL by separating the asynchronous subsystem and identifying it as a separate module as illustrated in Fig. 5.21b. As illustrated, a synchronizer is placed on each control line from module A to

*This section has been included to provide meaning for the last of the logical operators given in Fig. 5.14. It will not be necessary to utilize the synchronization operator until Chapter 9. Some readers may wish to skip this section for now and return when they reach that point.

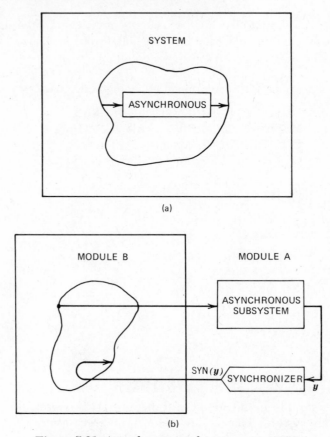

Figure 5.21. Asynchronous subsystems in AHPL.

module B, where module A is assumed to be asynchronous with respect to the module B clock. It is necessary that signals on line y be synchronized to the module B clock before they can be used in that system. Synchronization of the control line y can be accomplished very easily using the circuit shown in Fig. 5.22 if we assume at least two clock periods between level changes on y. The output $SYN(y)$ will change only on the appropriate edge of the module B clock just as would be the case if it were an internal variable in module B. The function $SYN(y)$ was included in AHPL syntax, and for each variable on which it is used a simple hardware compiler will include a circuit of the form of Fig. 5.22 in the network. When y changes at approximately the time of a module B clock transition, the corresponding change in $SYN(y)$ may be delayed for one complete clock period. In most cases this synchronization delay will easily be tolerated.

152

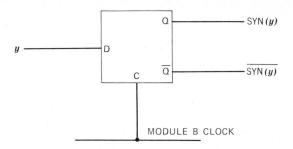

Figure 5.22. Control level synchronizer.

Certain components that are commonly used in digital system design are inherently asynchronous, such as one-shots and deliberately inserted gate delays. Of these only the one-shot has been included in the standard AHPL syntax. A one-shot can be treated by the language in much the same manner as a flip-flop. The designer must remember that the output of a one-shot will return to its stable value after a period of time, but this is no greater burden than remembering the state of other system components. The output pulse width of the one-shot in an integral number of clock periods would normally be declared in advance to permit inclusion of the proper component values in the circuit of Fig. 5.23a to realize

$$ysyn \leftarrow 1$$

The first clock pulse occurring while the control level is 1 will trigger the one-shot and set **ysyn** to 1. Following the trailing edge of the one-shot pulse, **ysyn** will return to zero synchronized with the clock.

A typical timing diagram for the synchronized one-shot is given in Fig. 5.23b. A pulse appears at point T in Fig. 5.23a coinciding with the clock pulse which terminates the level on the line **ysyn** ← 1. This pulse triggers the one-shot and $\overline{y}$, the complement of the one-shot output, goes to 0. The flip-flop whose output is **ysyn** will be set to 1 by this same clock pulse. The line $\overline{y}$ will remain 0 a period of time determined by the time constant of the RC network shown. The first clock pulse after $\overline{y}$ returns to 1 will clear the synchronizing flip-flop, thus returning **ysyn** to 0. A hardware compiler will generate the network of Fig. 5.23a in response to the declaration statement

ONE-SHOT: **ysyn** (6)

which specifies a time interval of six clock periods. Clearly, this assumes that the resistor and capacitor can be chosen with sufficient precision to assure a one-shot output duration between five and six clock periods. If this precision is impossible, the one-shot may still be used when a tol-

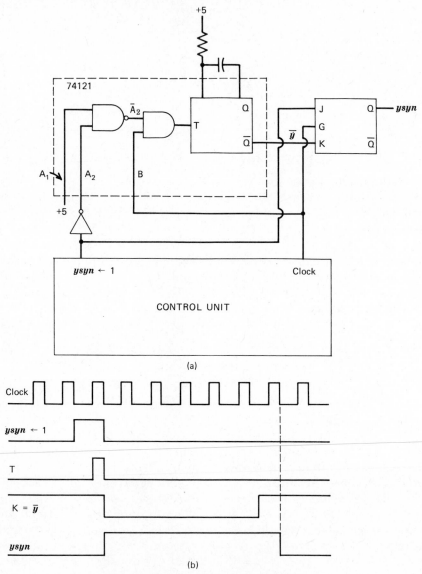

(a)

(b)

Figure 5.23. Synchronized one shot.

erance of a few clock periods in its output is acceptable. In any case *ysyn* will always change state in synchronism with the clock.

It is possible to add notation to AHPL to permit specification of extra gate delay on control lines that interconnect modules not synchronized by the same clock. Sometimes delay can be employed to shorten a con-

154

trol loop by an entire clock period. This is of value in systems that must operate at the maximum possible speed. We leave it to the ingenuity of the reader to add features of this kind to the language.

5.10 A TIMING REFINEMENT

Often a flow chart of a system will be developed in such a way that operations which can be accomplished at the same time or when timing is not critical are represented by separate steps. A second pass through the AHPL sequence may reveal potential changes that could both speed up its execution and save control flip-flops. Interrelated branches can make this process more difficult than one of merely combining steps. Often the hoped-for timing improvements can be accomplished using conditional transfers as discussed in Sec. 4.7. Another approach we shall explore in this section is that of eliminating the delay associated with an individual step in the control sequence. We shall specify this in AHPL by appending the comment NO DELAY to the action portion of the step.

The one-clock-period delay associated with an AHPL step may be eliminated if neither the branch portion or the action portion is dependent on the result of a transfer in an immediately preceding step and if such action will not destroy the proper timing relationship on input and output lines connected to other modules. In the following three-step sequence a time delay is unnecessary at step 2, since the

1.
$$\to (\bar{a})/(1)$$
2. $A \leftarrow B$ NO DELAY
3. $C \leftarrow X \vee A$

transfer uses only information available prior to the previous step. The delay associated with step 3 cannot be eliminated since this step depends on the result of step 2. A realization of the control unit for this three-step partial sequence is illustrated in Fig. 5.24a. From the figure it can be seen that step 2 is accomplished during the last clock period for which control remains in step 1. The following two-step sequence with a conditional transfer associated with step 1 will provide timing

1. $A * \underline{a} \leftarrow B$
$$\to (\bar{a})/(1)$$
2. $C \leftarrow X \vee A$

identical to that specified by Fig. 5.24a. A realization of this sequence is given in Fig. 5.24b. For this simple case the two AHPL sequences

155

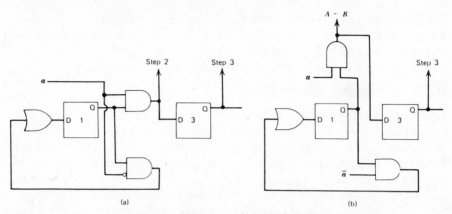

Figure 5.24. Partial control unit.

result in identical control units. This will not always be so as the number of control gates compiled by a conditional transfer step will depend on the designer's facility with multiple-output combinational logic min̄imization.

The advantage of the NO DELAY notation over that of the conditional transfer lies in the ease of application. Often it will not be worthwhile to undertake the analysis necessary to reformulate a sequence in terms of conditional transfers even though the result might be more compact. This would be particularly true in the case of complicated systems.

Example 5.6

A peripheral equipment will often be required to output signals on a number of control lines as a function of stored data. It is often convenient to interrogate this data and generate the control signals sequentially even in cases where there is no precise timing relation between the output signals. Such is the case for the following control sequence. It was subsequently discovered that none of steps 2, 3, 4, and 5 required separate clock periods for execution so that these steps are marked NO DELAY.

1.

$\rightarrow (\overline{a}) \, / \, (1)$

2. $out1 = 1$ NO DELAY

$\rightarrow (B_0, B_1, \overline{B_0 \vee B_1}) \, / \, (3,4,5)$

3. $out2 = 1$ NO DELAY

4. $out3 = 1$ NO DELAY

5. $A \leftarrow X$ NO DELAY

6. $BUS = A$

$B \leftarrow BUS_{4:7}, BUS_{0:3}; \rightarrow (1)$

156

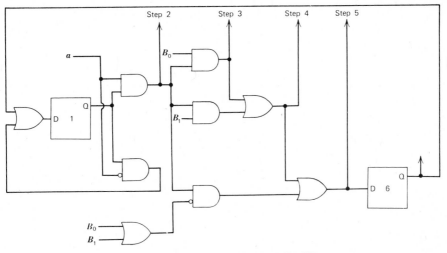

Figure 5.25. Realization of NO DELAY steps.

A realization of the control unit corresponding to the above sequence is given in Fig. 5.25. Notice that delay flip-flops are required for steps 1 and 6. The former is necessary to hold control at one point while waiting for control input a to go to 1. The latter establishes a bus route whose argument is dependent on the result of step 5.

A two-step sequence equivalent to the one given above can be written using conditional transfers. We leave it as a problem for the reader to develop and obtain a realization of such a sequence.

5.11 CONCLUSIONS

We have now presented most of AHPL along with the corresponding hardware realization. We have provided a number of small design examples to assist the reader in developing a facility for the use of the design language. We are now ready to consider more complex and more important design examples. The remainder of the book will be devoted to digital computer systems and their related peripheral equipment.

PROBLEMS

In Problems 5.1 to 5.7 the result of carrying out the specified operations is to be determined. The following values for the operands are to be used:

$$w = 2, u = 1, x = 5, y = -2 \qquad N = \begin{bmatrix} 0 & 1 & 3 \\ 2 & -1 & 0 \\ 4 & 3 & 2 \\ 1 & -3 & 4 \end{bmatrix}$$

$$U = (1, 0, 0, 1) \qquad V = (1, 0, 1, 1)$$
$$W = (1, 3, 7, 8) \qquad X = (0, 1, -1, 3)$$
$$Y = (2, 4, 8, 16)$$

5.1 (a) $z \leftarrow -y$ (b) $z \leftarrow \times/W$
    (c) $Z \leftarrow |X$ (d) $Z \leftarrow U \div W$

5.2 (a) $X \leftarrow x + X$ (b) $Z \leftarrow u \vee U$
    (c) $Z \leftarrow U/V$ (d) $Z \leftarrow \top (1 + \bot U)$

5.3 (a) $Z \leftarrow \bar{U}$ (b) $Z \leftarrow U \wedge V$
    (c) $Z \leftarrow U \vee V$ (d) $Z \leftarrow \bar{u} \vee V$

5.4 (a) $A \leftarrow -N$ (b) $A \leftarrow w \times N$
    (c) $A \leftarrow |N$ (d) $z \leftarrow ((1 + \bot U) > y)$

5.5 (a) $Z \leftarrow +/N$ (b) $Z \leftarrow \times//N$
    (c) $z \leftarrow \wedge/U$ (d) $Z \leftarrow +//|N$

5.6 (a) $Z \leftarrow U/Y$ (b) $Z \leftarrow V/X$
    (c) $A \leftarrow U//N$ (d) $A \leftarrow (V/U)/N$

5.7 (a) $z \leftarrow +/(X > 0)$ (b) $M \leftarrow (U!V)$
    (c) $3 \uparrow U$ (d) $2 \downarrow V$

5.8 Given two lists of numbers, X and Y. Write a concise program in APL to obtain those elements of Y having the same position numbers as those elements of X whose value is greater than 12.

5.9 It is desired to obtain that element of a matrix A which is the minimum of the row-by-row maxima of the elements. Write an APL program to compute this element.

5.10 The number of combination of n items taken k at a time may be computed from
$$C(n, k) = C(n - 1, k) + C(n - 1, k - 1)$$
where $C(n, 0) = C(n, n) = 1$.
(a) Prove this assertion.
(b) Write in APL a program that will compute $C(n, k)$ for all pairs n, k such that $k \leq n$.

5.11 A matrix, M, has 20 rows and 6 columns. Write in APL a program that will determine a scalar value, x, which is the number of a row in M such that the sum of the elements in that row is greater than or equal to the sum of the elements of every other row.

5.12 A combinational logic priority network has a vector of six input wires X [6] and vector of six output wires PRI [6]. An output PRI_j is to be 1 if and only if X_j is 1 and each $X_i = 0$ for all $i < j$. Write an AHPL combinational logic unit description for this 6-bit priority network.

5.13 Suppose that a network realizing the function INC is to be constructed allowing for only six inputs and outputs.
(a) Write an AHPL combinational logic unit description for this 6-bit INC network.
(b) Construct a hardware combinational logic network realizing the function description obtained in part (a).
(c) Can you suggest a capability that might be added to the concept of a combinational logic unit description to make the writing of such description easier for complex but repetitive networks?

5.14 Construct a hardware realization of the combinational logic unit description of the combinational logic network COMP derived in Section 5.5.

5.15 Add declarations to form a complete module description in AHPL for the eight's complementer of Example 5.3.

5.16 Which of the following are legitimate AHPL action statements or parts of action statements? Register A [2] has two flip-flops, B [3] and C [3] have three, X [2] is a vector of two input lines, a and b are individual inputs, and BUS is a 3-bit bus.
(a) $b \leftarrow a$
(b) $B \leftarrow ((A, a) \mathbin{!} (A, b)) * (C_0, \bar{C}_0)$
(c) $(A_0, B_{0:1}) * a \leftarrow C$
(d) $BUS \leftarrow C$
(e) $B \leftarrow BUS + C$
(f) $BUS = 0, 1, 0$
$\quad C \leftarrow BUS$
(g) $C \leftarrow 4 \mathbin{\top} 0$
(h) $B \leftarrow (B \oplus (A, a)) \oplus C$
(i) $a * B \leftarrow C$
(j) $B * a \leftarrow (X, b)$
(k) $\wedge/B, A \leftarrow C$
(l) $(0, 1, 0)/B, A \leftarrow C$
(m) $A, C_0 \leftarrow INC(B)$
(n) $SYN(b) \leftarrow a$
(o) $C \leftarrow (\bar{C} \mathbin{!} B) * (SYN(a), C_0);$
$\quad (B \mathbin{!} C) * (A_0, A_1) \leftarrow X, a$

5.17 Let **N** be a memory array consisting of 2^{10} eighteen-bit words. Write an AHPL sequence that will accomplish economically a search on this array similar to that described in Example 5.1. Let **A** [10] be the 10-bit register specifying the address of a read or write operation on **N** and declare other registers as needed. If $n + 1$ is the number of words in **N** in which the first 3 bits are 1's, then these words should be stored in $N^{0:n}$ at the conclusion of the process. Word $n + 1$ should consist of all zeros and the contents of the remaining $2^{10} - n - 2$ words may be considered immaterial.

5.18 Modify the AHPL module description of the machine tool controller of Example 5.4 to incorporate the following improvements:
(a) The system will stop and wait for the start of a new sequence if $\top(2^{18} - 1)$ is encountered in **PR**.
(b) Expand the memory to 2048 words so that eight 256-word sequences can be included.

5.19 A digital communications buffer contains 32 eighteen-bit words. The buffer has its own control unit. Part of the function of the buffer is to check for longitudinal parity (i.e., parity over the 32 bits in each bit position of the word). If a parity error in one of the 18-bit positions is found, a flip-flop *pf* is to be set to 1. Write a partial control sequence in AHPL that accomplishes this parity check in an economical sequential manner. Declare memory elements as required. Consider using an array composed of eighteen 32-bit shift registers.

5.20 Let **M** be a memory consisting of 1024 eighteen-bit words with a 10-bit memory address register **AR**. Write an AHPL control sequence that will compute $\vee/\wedge/M$ in an economical sequential manner.

5.21 A random sequence generator is driven by an external clock source. This generator provides a level, z, which is constant between clock pulses, and may or may not change, on a random basis, when triggered by a clock pulse or leading edge of a one-period level. A special-purpose computer is to be designed employing a 1-MHz clock. This computer is to provide an output clock to drive the random process at a frequency of 1 kHz. The computer must also compute the number of level changes in the random process each second. The computer must also compute and display the average number of level changes per second over the first 2^8 seconds following the depression of its start button. Write in AHPL a complete module description of the above special-purpose computer. Declare counters and other registers as required. Accomplish division by shifting.

5.22 Two small memory arrays **M** and **N** each consisting of 256 eighteen-bit words form part of a special-purpose digital system. The arrays have memory address registers *ARM* and *ARN*, respectively. At the beginning of a partial control sequence **M** contains 256 random numbers, which are to be transferred to **N** and arranged in the order of magnitude. The largest is to be placed in N^0. Write a partial AHPL control sequence that will accomplish this operation. Declare additional registers as required. Assume that a two-output function LARGER(A, B), where A and B are 18-bit vectors, is available. The outputs of LARGER as a function of its inputs are tabulated as follows.

LARGER

$\perp A > \perp B$	0 1
$\perp A < \perp B$	1 0
$\perp A = \perp B$	0 0

5.23 Consider a simple digital module whose primary data element is a one-shot *ten*. The module has one input x that is synchronized with the module clock. The only output z is to remain zero except for the occurrence of a 1-clock-period level exactly 10 clock periods following each change in the logic level on line x. Changes in the value of line x will be separated by at least 15 clock periods. Write in AHPL a complete module description for this device. Declare additional data elements as required.

5.24 Can the comment NO DELAY be added to any of the steps in the control unit of Example 5.3? Why or why not? Is there excess delay anywhere in the control sequence for Example 5.4?

5.25 Write a two-step control sequence equivalent to the sequence of Example 5.6 by using conditional transfers to eliminate the steps designated NO DELAY. Obtain a complete logic block diagram of the corresponding control unit. Compare the number of gates with the nine gates of Fig. 5.25. Which is the most economical realization? Can the more costly circuit be minimized through Boolean manipulation to compare more favorably?

REFERENCES

1. Iverson, K. E., *A Programming Language,* Wiley, New York, 1962.

2. Hellerman, Herbert, *Digital System Principles,* 2nd ed., McGraw-Hill, New York, 1973.

3. Friedman T. D., and S. C. Yang, "Methods Used in Automatic Logic

Design Generator (ALERT)," *IEEE Trans. Computers,* Sept. 1969, p. 593.

4. Schoor, H., "Computer Aided Digital System Design and Analysis Using a Register Transfer Language," *IEEE Trans. Electronic Computers,* Dec. 1964, pp. 730–737.

5. Gilman, L., and A. J. Rose, *APL an Interactive Approach,* 2nd ed., Wiley, New York, 1975.

6. Hill, F. J., "Introducing AHPL," *Computer,* Dec. 1974, pp. 28–30.

7. Hill, F. J., and G. R. Peterson, *Introduction to Switching Theory and Logical Design,* 2nd ed., Wiley, New York, 1974.

8. Duley, J. R., and D. L. Dietmeyer, "A Digital System Design Language (DDL)," *IEEE Transactions on Computers,*" Vol. C-17, Sept. 1968, pp. 850–861.

9. Piloty, Robert, "Segmentation Constructs of RTS III, A Computer Hardware Description Language Based on CDL," *Proceedings of the 1975 International Symposium on Design Languages and Their Applications,* New York, Sept. 3–5.

6
MACHINE ORGANIZATION AND HARDWARE PROGRAMS

6.1 INTRODUCTION

In Chapter 5 we introduced a new language, AHPL, with the justification that computer hardware could be described in terms of this language. In Chapter 2 we discussed in detail a small digital computer, SIC. In this chapter we propose to design a computer that will function in the manner attributed to SIC in Chapter 2. The design will be expressed as a program in AHPL. Translation of this program into a hardware description or a logic block diagram must wait until Chapter 7.

We shall continue to use SIC as the vehicle to illustrate what is actually a completely general procedure. Because SIC is sufficiently simple, a reasonably complete design can be presented without burdening the reader with detail. There are, however, many important features of large-scale computers that are not found in SIC; AHPL routines describing many of these features will be presented in later chapters. Having seen the details of a complete computer tied together in Chapters 6 and 7, the reader should be able to visualize the incorporation of these individual features into the overall design of a larger-scale computer.

It is our conviction that AHPL is not only an excellent vehicle for teaching computer organization but is also a practical design language. We have already shown some correspondences between AHPL conventions and digital hardware. We shall continue this in Chapter 7, to show how a complete AHPL description of a computer can be directly translated into corresponding hardware. This process can be done automatically, and programs have been written to compile AHPL programs, i.e., to translate them into hardware form. But our basic goal is to provide the reader with the tools required to perform the translation himself if required. Once he has progressed to this point, the reader will have a basic understanding of computer organization and design.

6.2 BASIC ORGANIZATION OF SIC

The instruction set and the main operating registers of SIC were specified in Chapter 2. We also need two registers in association with the memory: the memory data register, *MD*, and the memory address register, *MA*. On a memory read cycle, the address of the desired word is first loaded into *MA*, and the word stored at that location is then read into *MD*, from whence it is available to be processed in whatever manner may be desired. For a memory write operation, the address is loaded into *MA*; the word to be stored is loaded into *MD* and then stored at the addressed location.

Given the instruction set, the next step is to specify the register interconnections and ALU capabilities necessary to realize the instruction set. Some readers may wonder how we know, "in advance," that a certain organization is required. The answer is that one usually does not. The experienced designer may be able to make a very accurate estimate of the requirements, but this is not necessary. As we shall see, it is quite practical to start with a very minimal specification, gradually expanding and refining the design as our understanding of the required sequence of operations increases.

The *arithmetic-logic unit* (ALU) contains the various logic circuits—usually combinational—that perform the necessary operations on the contents of the various registers. Since the instruction set includes TAD and AND, the ALU must include an adder and an 18-bit logical AND circuit. It will probably include other capabilities, but this is all that will be assumed to start.

For TAD and AND, the operands will be taken from the accumulator (*AC*) and the memory data register (*MD*) so that these two registers must be connected to the two ALU inputs. The adder will also be used for index addressing, to add the contents of the selected index register to the address portion of the instruction register. Thus we must be able to connect either *IA* or *IB* to one input of the adder, and *IR* to the other. Since we need to connect several different registers to the ALU inputs, it is likely that busing will be advantageous. Therefore, two 18-bit buses, *ABUS* and *BBUS*, are specified, the outputs of which will provide the inputs to the adder and AND circuits of the ALU.

In assigning registers to the two buses, the only constraint is that registers which are to be arguments of the same operation cannot be on the same bus. We shall initially put **MD** and **IR** on the **ABUS**, and **AC**, **IA**, and **IB** on the **BBUS**, recognizing that we may later find that some other arrangement is preferable. It is difficult to anticipate the input networks to each register at this point. For now, we shall leave these unspecified and proceed with the control sequence, on the assumption that any needed connections can be provided. These input networks will be implicitly defined in the process of generating the control sequence. Also, it is not clear that **PC** needs to be connected to the ALU, so we shall leave its connections unspecified for now. On the basis of these considerations, a preliminary block diagram of SIC will appear as shown in Fig. 6.1.

The memory will be designated **M**, consisting for purposes of this discussion of 2^{13} row vectors of 18 bits each. Thus M^i will refer to row i as the ith numbered word in memory; **MD, AC,** and **IR** are 18-bit registers, while **MA, PC, IA,** and **IB,** which are used for addresses only, are 13-bit registers. The *link* flip-flop, *lf*, is a 1-bit register. One function of the link is to receive the output carry in addition, and a flip-flop serving this purpose is sometimes referred to as the *carry flag*. However, the link also serves other purposes in SIC, and we prefer the less-restrictive name, *link*. The connections required for the link are not clear at this point and will be left unspecified.

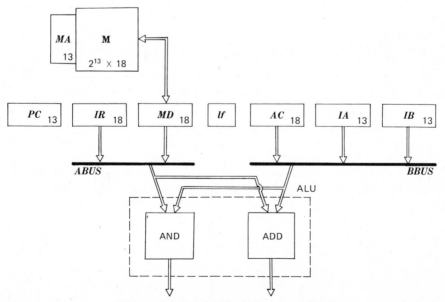

Figure 6.1. Initial block diagram of SIC.

6.3 REGISTER TRANSFERS

The execution of an instruction by a computer such as SIC consists of a series of transfers of data from register to register, with the data being processed by the ALU as required during the transfer operations. Several such register transfers will be required to accomplish a single machine language instruction such as LAC.

As discussed in Chapter 4, when registers are interconnected by buses the execution of a single-register transfer requires the generation of several control signals, to connect the various buses and registers. For the SIC organization specified above, signals must be generated to determine which registers are placed on the buses, and to determine which ALU output is gated into which register. For example, a basic operation is the AND transfer, in which the contents of *MD* and *AC* are ANDed and the result is placed in *AC*. The control signals and interconnections involved in this transfer are depicted in Fig. 6.2.

According to the syntax presented in Chapter 5, the AHPL step describing this AND transfer would be written as follows:

$$8. \quad ABUS = MD;\ BBUS = AC;\ AC \leftarrow ABUS \land BBUS$$

Given the SIC bus organization, much of the notation in the above register transfer description would be repeated in every transfer statement. The inputs to the ALU are always *ABUS* and *BBUS*, and the input bus routings are known, since each register can drive only one bus. Therefore, in discussions of SIC we shall use an abbreviated form of register transfer statement, for example,

$$AC \leftarrow MD \land AC$$

with the register on the *ABUS* listed first for two-operand transfers.

This form of abbreviated notation is suitable in any case in which the bus organization is such that there is no ambiguity in determining the bus connections required. In such situations one might rely on the hardware compiler to generate the necessary bus connections. The only special precaution is that the designer must not specify an operation that is impossible because of the bus connections. For example,

$$AC \leftarrow AC \land IA$$

is impossible, since *AC* and *IA* are both on the *BBUS*. In cases in which there is any possible ambiguity, as, for example, if a register is connected to more than one bus, the designer must fully specify the bus routing.

Memory read and write operations are quite different from normal register transfers, as they do not involve the buses or the ALU, and often require a much longer time than conventional transfers. However, they

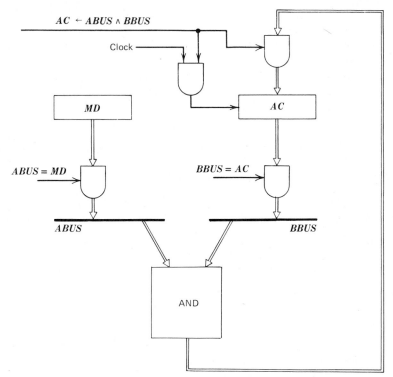

Figure 6.2. Control of AND transfer.

will be regarded as single transfers, represented by the transfer state- *taking out of mem*
ments,

and

$$MD \leftarrow BUSFN \ (M; \ DCD(MA))$$ *taking out of mem*

$$M * DCD(MA) \leftarrow MD$$ *putting into mem*

for read and write, respectively. As discussed in Chapter 5, the notation
$M * DCD(MA)$ represents the selection of word M^i where i is the address
given by the contents of MA, interpreted as a binary number.

6.4 CLASSIFYING INSTRUCTIONS

We are now ready to proceed with the first step in the design of a control
unit for SIC, the writing of a control sequence. This will be an AHPL
program consisting of routines to execute the SIC instructions. The complete sequence of operations required to carry out a single instruction
will be referred to as an *instruction cycle*. Each instruction cycle will
consist of two parts, *a fetch cycle* and an *execute cycle*. In the fetch

167

cycle, a new instruction is fetched from memory. The operations required by that instruction are then carried out in the execute cycle.

During the fetch cycle the contents of the program counter, *PC*, are first shifted to the memory address register, *MA*. The memory executes a read operation, leaving the addressed word in *MD*. The instruction is then transferred from *MD* to *IR*. These steps of the fetch cycle are common to all instructions. The succeeding steps depend on what the instruction is.

There are two basic approaches to the design of a computer sequence for a computer. In one, following the above steps in the fetch cycle, the sequence branches to a completely separate set of steps for each instruction. The other approach, which we shall follow, is to classify the instructions according to various features and to share common operations wherever possible. The instructions of any single-address computer may be divided into five basic categories:

1. Input–output
2. Operate
3. Read operand
4. Store
5. Branch without read

Instruction categories 3, 4, and 5 are the *addressed instructions*, consisting of an op-code and a memory address. Categories 1 and 2 are the *nonaddressed instructions*, in which the whole instruction may serve as an op-code. For these instructions the fetch cycle is complete when instruction has been moved to *IR*. For addressed instructions the fetch cycle continues if modification of the address is called for, as with indexing or indirect addressing. The fetch cycle for addressed-instruction is complete when the *effective address*, the address actually to be used in the instruction, has been obtained.

Instruction groups 3 and 4 comprise the *memory reference instructions*. For these instructions, the execute cycle will include one or more references to memory, to obtain an operand or store a result. For group 5 branch instructions no memory reference is made during the execute cycle; rather, the address is simply transferred to *PC* to be used in the next fetch cycle. The branch may be unconditional (JMP) or depend on the contents of certain registers.

Any system of classification of instructions is to some degree arbitrary, and there are likely to be some instructions that do not fit exactly into any category. Some conditional branch instruction may require a test of a word read from memory. Other instructions may involve both a read and write. For SIC, the only such "hybrid" instruction is ISZ, which we

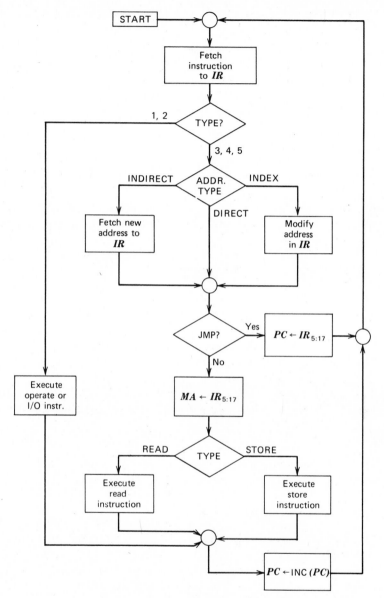

Figure 6.3. Overall control flow chart.

shall assign to group 3, since a read is carried out first, followed by a store and a test for a possible skip.

Figure 6.3 shows the overall flow chart of the control sequence for SIC. The fetch cycle is complete. The execute cycle is not detailed except for JMP, which involves only one step. For groups 1 and 2 instructions, control branches to the execute cycle following fetch of the instruction. For addressed instructions (groups 3, 4, and 5) indexing or indirect addressing is next carried out if required. For JMP, the effective address is immediately transferred to *PC*, completing this instruction cycle. For groups 3 and 4, the effective address is transferred to *MA* in preparation for the memory reference, after which the read or store instruction is executed. Following the execution of instructions other than branch, control converges to cause the contents of the program counter to be increased by one. Control then returns to block 1 to begin the fetch cycle for the next instruction.

6.5 AHPL CONTROL PROGRAMS

We are now ready to expand the flow chart of Fig. 6.3 into a control program, a sequence of steps in AHPL. In the next chapter this sequence will be translated into a hardware control unit to generate the necessary signals to implement the sequence of steps. We begin the AHPL control sequence for SIC with the declaration statements. These declarations include only that hardware anticipated at this point as being required for the addressed instructions and the operate instructions. Hardware required only for Input/Output will be considered in Chapter 10.

MODULE: SIC
MEMORY: *AC* [18]; *MD* [18]; *PC* [13]; *IR* [18]; *IA* [13];
IB [13]; *MA* [13]; *lf* ;
M [8192,18]
INPUTS: *start*
BUSES: *ABUS* [18]; *BBUS* [18]

The *start* input is a pushbutton signal, which, after synchronization, will start the control sequence.

The reader will recall from Chapter 2 that the bits of a SIC instruction word are grouped as follows. Bits 0 to 2 specify the operation code while bits

0 to 2	3	4	5 to 17
OP CODE			ADDRESS

5 to 17 specify the address for memory reference instructions. Bits 3 and 4 are used to specify indexing and indirect addressing. Bit combination

Bits	0	1	2	Octal	Mnemonic	Group
	0	0	0	0	ISZ	3
	0	0	1	1	LAC	3
	0	1	0	2	AND	3
	0	1	1	3	TAD	3
	1	0	0	4	JMS	4
	1	0	1	5	DAC	4
	1	1	0	6	JMP	5
	1	1	1	7	Operate or I/O	1, 2

Figure 6.4. Instruction set.

01 specifies indirect addressing, while 10 and 11 specify indexing, and 00 calls for neither indexing nor indirect addressing, i.e., direct addressing.

The instruction list is repeated in Fig. 6.4. The function of the first seven instructions is as discussed in Chapter 2. If the OP code is 111, then bits 5 to 17 no longer refer to an address but may be used to specify particular input/output or operate instructions. The reader will note that the bit codings were carefully assigned to group the instructions. Notice that bit zero is 0 for all group 3 instructions. Bit zero is 1 and bit one is 0 for group 4 instructions. As will become apparent soon, these instruction bits specify many of the branch functions within the SIC control sequence. The convenient bit assignments of Fig. 6.4 will simplify these operations.

The first step of the control sequence is a waiting loop for the *start* signal. The next three steps fetch a new instruction to the *IR* register.

1. $\rightarrow (\overline{SYN(start)})/(1)$
2. $MA \leftarrow PC$
3. $MD \leftarrow BUSFN(M; DCD(MA))$
4. $IR \leftarrow MD$
5. $\rightarrow (IR_0 \wedge IR_1 \wedge IR_2)/(25)$
6. NO DELAY
   $\rightarrow ((\overline{IR_3} \wedge \overline{IR_4}), (\overline{IR_3} \wedge IR_4), IR_3)/(13, 7, 10)$

Note the branch at step 5, which tests the op code to determine if the instruction is group 1 or 2 (nonaddressed), or group 3, 4, or 5 (addressed). This cannot be included as the branch portion of step 4, since it is dependent on the transfer carried out by step 4. For addressed instructions, the fetch cycle continues at step 6 with a test for the type of addressing. The reader will note that the separate branches of steps 5 and 6 could be combined into a more complex single branch. However,

171

in terms of clarity and ease of interpretation of the control sequence, it is better to restrict the complexity of the branches. In this case, step 5 branches on the type of instruction, while step 6 branches on the type of address. To mix the two would obscure the logic of the control sequence. Since the delay required for the loading of *IR* was provided at step 5, step 6 is a NO DELAY step.

The next three steps implement indirect addressing, fetching the effective address to *IR* from the location specified by the original instruction address.

   7. $MA \leftarrow IR_{5:17}$
   8. $MD \leftarrow \text{BUSFN}(M; \text{DCD}(MA))$
   9. $IR_{5:17} \leftarrow MD_{5:17}$
      $\rightarrow (13)$

Steps 10, 11, and 12 implement index addressing, adding the contents of *IA* or *IB*, as determined by IR_4, to the original address to produce the effective address.

  10. NO DELAY
      $\rightarrow (IR_4)/(12)$
  11. $IR_{5:17} \leftarrow \text{ADD}(IR_{5:17}; IA)$
      $\rightarrow (13)$
  12. $IR_{5:17} \leftarrow \text{ADD}(IR_{5:17}; IB)$

Before continuing with the control sequence, it will be instructive to consider a possible alternate sequence for address modification.

Example 6.1

Design an indirect addressing cycle that will require one less register transfer (therefore requiring less time to accomplish) than the cycle illustrated in Fig. 6.3.

Solution

A solution is shown in Fig. 6.5. The saving in time is achieved by moving the transfer of the address to *MA* from step 15 to step 6, immediately following the decision that an address is required. Then, in the index and indirect address cycles, the effective address is transferred directly to *MA*, rather than to *IR*. The modified control sequence follows.

   6. $MA \leftarrow IR_{5:17}$
      $\rightarrow ((\overline{IR_3} \wedge \overline{IR_4}), (\overline{IR_3} \wedge IR_4), IR_3)/(12, 7, 9)$
   7. $MD \leftarrow \text{BUSFN}(M; \text{DCD}(MA))$
   8. $MA \leftarrow MD_{5:17}$
      $\rightarrow (12)$

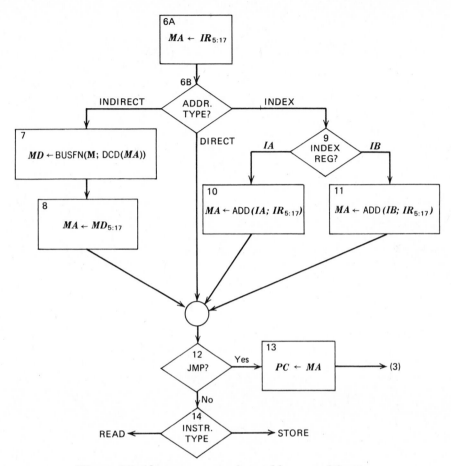

Figure 6.5. Alternate approach to address modification.

9. NO DELAY
    $\rightarrow(\overline{IR_4}, IR_4)/(10, 11)$
10. $MA \leftarrow ADD(IR_{5:17}; IA)$
    $\rightarrow(12)$
11. $MA \leftarrow ADD(IR_{5:17}; IB)$
12. NO DELAY
    $\rightarrow((IR_0 \wedge IR_1), (\overline{IR_0 \wedge IR_1}))/(13, 14)$
13. $PC \leftarrow MA$
    $\rightarrow(3)$
14. NO DELAY
    $\rightarrow(\overline{IR_0}, IR_0)/(15, 20)$
    . . . Continue execute cycle . . .

Note that on JMP the address is loaded into PC from MA, which allows step 2 to be skipped on the next fetch cycle.

There are some paths (i.e., $MA \leftarrow MD$ and $PC \leftarrow MA$) that would not otherwise be used, but this requires no extra hardware with the bus organization that has been assumed. There will be a time penalty in that the load of MA (step 6) is wasted for JMP instructions, except in the case of indirect addressing. Thus a choice between the two sequences might depend on the expected relative frequencies of JMP instructions and relative addressing. One should also check the possible effect of this change in the execute cycle for group 3 and 4 instructions. (See Problem 6.4.)

We shall assume the original sequence (Fig. 6.3) as we continue the specification of SIC. The fetch cycle is now complete, and we continue with the execute cycle for the addressed instructions (groups 3, 4, and 5). Step 13 separates the JMP instruction from the memory reference instructions and Step 14 executes the JMP by transferring the jump address to PC and returning to fetch another instruction.

13.   NO DELAY
      $\rightarrow (\overline{IR_0 \wedge IR_1})/(15)$
14. $PC \leftarrow IR_{5:17}$
      $\rightarrow (2)$

If the instruction requires a memory reference, step 15 moves the effective address to MA and branches to execute a read or store instruction.

15. $MA \leftarrow IR_{5:17}$
      $\rightarrow (IR_0)/(21)$

Before continuing with the control sequence, let us consider more carefully the branches at steps 5, 13, and 15, branches based on the type of instruction. The AHPL branch functions are based on the op code, and the manner in which the bit combinations are determined may be more easily understood with the aid of the Karnaugh map of Fig. 6.6. Across the top and along the side of the map are listed the various possible values of the 3 bits of the op code so that each square corresponds to a distinct combination of bit values. For example, the lower-left square corresponds to $IR_0 \, IR_1 \, IR_2 = 001$, etc. The SIC instructions corresponding to each op code have been entered in the appropriate square.

At step 5 the branch is based on whether or not the instruction is a nonaddressed (Operate or I/O) instruction. These are identified by the single-bit combination $IR_0 \, IR_1 \, IR_2 = 111$, and the branch tests for this combination. At step 13 the branch is to distinguish between JMP and

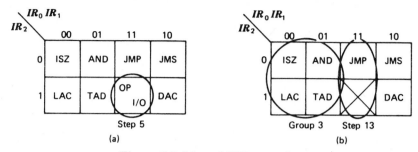

Figure 6.6. Map of SIC op codes.

any of the other addressed instructions. The code for JMP is 110, but we note that if the code had been 111, we would never have reached this point in the sequence due to branch at step 5. Thus the combination $IR_0 IR_1 IR_2 = 111$ is now a "don't care" as shown in Fig. 6.6b; we need test only for $IR_0 IR_1 = 11$. Step 15 must distinguish between read and store instructions. The read instructions (ISZ, LAC, AND, and TAD) are clearly identified by $IR_0 = 0$. If $IR_0 = 1$, at step 15, the command is JMS or DAC, since codes 110 and 111 are "don't cares," i.e., cannot occur at this point in the sequence.

We now proceed with the execute phase for the read and store instructions, for which the flow chart is shown in Fig. 6.7. For group 3 instructions, step 16 retrieves the data word from memory and separates control for the ISZ instruction from that for the other three instructions:

16. $MD \leftarrow BUSFN(M; DCD(MA))$
$\rightarrow (\overline{IR_1} \wedge \overline{IR_2})/(18)$

17. $AC \leftarrow (MD \mathrel{!} (MD \wedge AC) \mathrel{!} (ADD_{1:18}(MD; AC)))$
$* ((\overline{IR_1} \wedge IR_2), (IR_1 \wedge \overline{IR_2}), (IR_1 \wedge IR_2));$
$\textit{lf} * (IR_1 \wedge IR_2) \leftarrow ADD_0 (MD; AC); \rightarrow(24)$

Results from the AND, TAD, and LAC operations must be gated to AC, so that these instructions are implemented in a single conditional transfer. ADD($MD; AC$) represents a combinational logic function that accomplishes addition of two 18-bit arguments. The corresponding combinational logic unit description will be considered in Chapter 7. The addition of two 18-bit arguments can result in a 19-bit sum so that ADD($MD; AC$) must be regarded as a 19-bit vector. The leftmost bit, which can be regarded as a carry from the most significant bit, will be stored in $\textit{lf}$ as part of the addition operation. This is accomplished as a separate conditional transfer in step 17. Following the transfer, control branches to the *convergence point*, or common point for all instructions

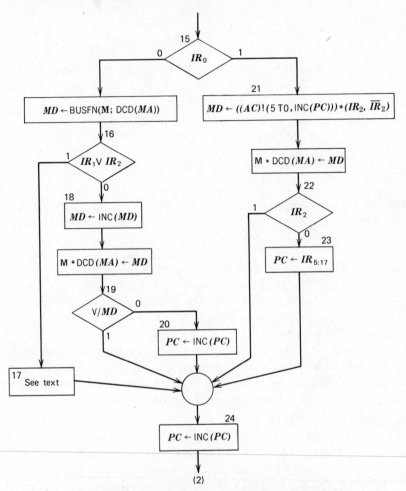

Figure 6.7. Execution of group 3 and 4 instructions.

except JMP, at which PC is incremented in preparation for fetching the next instruction.

The TAD instruction may require more than one clock time for execution. Since AND and LAC can be accomplished in one clock interval, one could choose to separately control the three instructions. The following would be an alternative AHPL sequence applicable if addition requires two clock periods.

17. $\quad \rightarrow ((\overline{IR_1} \wedge IR_2), (IR_1 \wedge \overline{IR_2}), (IR_1 \wedge IR_2))/(18, 19, 20)$

18. $\quad AC \leftarrow MD$
$\quad\quad \rightarrow$(convergence point)

19. $AC \leftarrow MD \wedge AC$
$\rightarrow$(convergence point)
20. null
21. $lf,AC \leftarrow ADD(MD;AC)$

We note this approach also simplifies the handling of the link. The hardware difference implied by these two approaches will be investigated later.

Continuing with the former version, we may implement the ISZ instruction by the following sequence:

18. $MD \leftarrow INC(MD)$
19. $M * DCD(MA) \leftarrow MD$
$\rightarrow (\vee/MD)/(24)$
20. $PC \leftarrow INC(PC)$
$\rightarrow(24)$

Steps 18 and 20 call for incrementing the contents of MD and PC, respectively. At this point we have not yet specified how this operation will be realized. We might add increment logic to the ALU, or we might just use the adder to add 1 to the contents of the specified register. For the present, we shall indicate the operation by the functional notation INC and defer a decision on realization until the control sequence is complete. Also note step 19, the first instance in which control branches as a function of a data word rather than an instruction. This will present no particular difficulty with respect to hardware implementation as we shall see in Chapter 7.

The instructions DAC and JMS have a common memory write cycle, so let us continue them as a single control sequence. Step 21 loads the memory data register with AC in the case of DAC and the contents of the program counter in the case of JMS. The reader will recall that the contents of $PC + 1$ must be stored in memory by JMS so that the computer can return to the proper point in the program following the completion of the subroutine.

21. $MD \leftarrow (AC \ ! \ (5 \top 0, INC(PC))) * (IR_2, \overline{IR_2})$
22. $M * DCD(MA) \leftarrow MD$
$\rightarrow(IR_2)/(24)$
23. $PC \leftarrow IR_{5:17}$
24. $PC \leftarrow INC(PC)$
$\rightarrow(2)$

The DAC instruction is completed after the memory write cycle of step 22; and control branches to line 24, the point of convergence for instructions other than JMP. Step 23 concludes JMS by transferring the

13 address bits from *IR* to the program counter. The program counter will be incremented at step 24, and the next instruction will be taken from the memory location immediately following the one addressed by JMS.

6.6 OPERATE INSTRUCTIONS

If bits 0, 1, and 2 of the op code are all 1's, then another bit must be inspected to distinguish between I/O and operate instructions. Let us assume that bit 3 will be 1 for I/O instructions and 0 for operate instructions. Then the fourteen bits 4 through 17 may be used to specify the specific instruction. In this section only operate instructions will be considered.

The value of the operate instructions should be clear. By using the instruction bits normally set aside for addressing, we can specify a very large number of operations on the data registers of the machine. In fact, using 14 bits we may specify 2^{14} or over 16,000 instructions. If we were to assign these instructions arbitrarily in a list of 16,000, it would be necessary for the programmer to refer to a dictionary in writing each instruction. Instead let us visualize each possible operate instruction as a sequence of lesser *microcoded* instructions. In microcoding, rather than assign arbitrary combinations of the available bits to each instruction, we assign specific meaning to individual bits or small groups of bits. Although there are some features in common, this should not be confused with *microprogramming*, which will be treated in Chapter 8.

Operate instructions do not require a time-consuming separate memory reference during execution. Similarly, individual microcoded segments can be accomplished in a single clock interval. Therefore, they can reasonably be handled in sequential fashion. For SIC, each operate instruction will consist of three register transfers or branch operations executed in sequence. The execution cycle will still require less time than the fetch cycle.

Of the 14 available bits, one is applicable to all three event times. Five bits describe the first event time, and 4 bits describe each of the last two event times. The coding is tabulated in Table 6.1. The reader will quickly conclude that not all of the information available in 14 binary bits is utilized. Considerably fewer than 16,000 meaningful instructions can be assembled from Table 6.1. However, the coding scheme used is convenient both from the user's and from the designer's point of view; and a large number of instructions are possible.

Considerably more instructions are possible than the 18 listed in Fig. 2.4. Various schemes can be used for incorporating more of them into

TABLE 6.1 Coding of Operate Instructions

Bit(s)		
4	0	If rotate is specified, the rotate is left
	1	Rotate right

		First Event Time
5	0	No Rotate
	1	Rotate AC
6, 7	00	NO OP
	01	Set Link
	10	Clear Link
	11	Halt
8, 9	00	NO OP
	01	Set AC
	10	Clear AC
	11	Complement AC

		Second Event Time
10	0	NO Rotate
	1	Rotate AC
11, 12, 13	000	NO OP
	001	SZL (also skips Third Event Time)
	010	DFA
	011	DFB
	100	DTA
	101	INA
	110	DTB
	111	INB

		Third Event Time
14	0	NO Rotate
	1	Rotate AC
15	0	NO OP
	1	Skip if number in $AC < 0$
16	0	NO OP
	1	Skip if number in $AC = 0$
17	0	NO OP
	1	Skip if number in $AC > 0$

the assembly language. We shall not discuss that topic here. Any assembler will allow the programmer to specify an instruction in octal machine code as a last resort.

A general statement would be that any combinations of bits that do not result in a logical conflict may be specified for the three event times. The valid combinations will become apparent as the design of the control sequences for operate instructions is worked out.

Before we proceed to an example instruction, a few general comments regarding Table 6.1 are in order. Note that a rotation of 3 bits in either direction is possible if rotate is specified each event time. Bit 4 is applicable only if rotation is specified in one of the three event times. In that case it gives the direction of rotation. More than one operation can be accomplished in a single event time. For example, the link and accumulator could be cleared simultaneously during the first event time. Similarly, various combinations of SKIP instructions can be worked out using bits 15, 16, and 17. If bits 5 to 17 are all zero, then no operation will be performed. The option may be useful to a programmer in sequences designed to test for completion of asynchronous IOT Operations.

As an example, the instruction

$$7 \quad 0 \quad 5 \quad 6 \quad 0 \quad 6$$

would cause the link to be cleared and AC complemented followed by a rotation of AC left. If the resulting AC contents were less than or equal to zero, the next instruction would be skipped.

As we proceed with the development of the control sequencer, we shall tend to disallow bit combinations that would require more than one register transfer in sequence per event time. Our primary reason will be to avoid obscuring our discussion with detail. This might well be the approach in practice, as the problem of explaining the various sequences of operations to the user could easily outstrip the worth of the added versatility. A designer would be free, however, to allow considerably more complicated sequences of microcodes.

In Section 6.5 we saw that control branched to point 25 in the case of an operate or IOT instruction. At that point it is necessary to establish whether the instruction is operate or IOT. The operate sequence begins at step 26.

25. NO DELAY
   $\rightarrow(IR_3)/(\text{I/O sequence})$

In accordance with the above paragraph, control is restricted to one of the 30 possible paths between point A and point D in Fig. 6.8. Branching

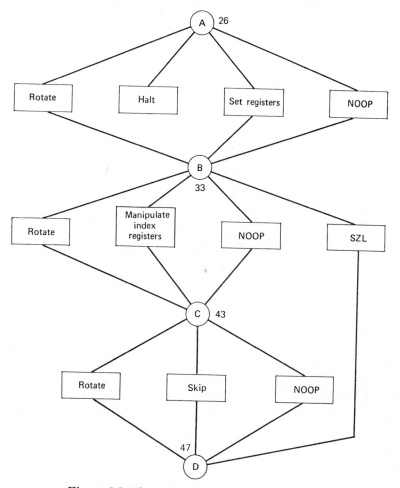

Figure 6.8. Flow chart for operate instructions.

to select a path between points A and B must begin at step 26. The rotate instruction is conveniently separated first. Step 27 separates the HALT instruction, which is executed at step 28. The physical implementation of

26. NO DELAY
$\rightarrow(IR_5)/(30)$
27. NO DELAY
$\rightarrow (\overline{IR_6 \wedge IR_7})/(29)$
28. DEAD END

181

29. $AC * (IR_8 \lor IR_9) \leftarrow (\overline{18 \top 0} ! 18\top0 ! \overline{AC}) * ((\overline{IR_8} \land IR_9),$
$(IR_8 \land \overline{IR_9}), (IR_8 \land IR_9));$

$lf * IR_6 \leftarrow 0; lf * IR_7 \leftarrow 1$
$\rightarrow(33)$

30. $\rightarrow(IR_1)/(32)$ NO DELAY

31. $lf, AC \leftarrow AC, lf$
$\rightarrow(33)$

32. $lf, AC \leftarrow AC_{17}, lf, AC_{0:16}$

HALT will be considered in Chapter 7. The five possible operations on *lf* and *AC* are all expressed by step 29. If nothing is changed in either *lf* or *AC*, the operation is effectively NO OP.

For the rotate instruction it is necessary to inspect bit IR_1 to determine the direction of rotation. The left or right rotations are accomplished at steps 31 and 32, respectively. The rotate operations will require special logic not yet specified. Again, we shall defer a final decision on implementation until completion of the control sequence. Following the rotate steps, control converges to step 33, which corresponds to point *B* of Fig. 6.8. In event time two, control is first separated for rotate, as before. The eight instructions specified by IR_{11}, IR_{12}, and IR_{13} may be separated into four pairs. Notice that the destination register of DFA and DFB is *AC*, while the destination register of DTA and INA is *IA*, and the destination register of DTB and INB is *IB*. Thus each of these pairs may be executed as a single program step. Branching to the four steps is accomplished by step 34.

33. NO DELAY
$\rightarrow(IR_{10})/(40)$

34. NO DELAY
$\rightarrow((\overline{IR_{11}} \land \overline{IR_{12}}),(\overline{IR_{11}} \land IR_{12}),(IR_{11} \land \overline{IR_{12}}),$
$(IR_{11} \land IR_{12}))/(35, 37, 38, 39)$

35. NO DELAY
$\rightarrow (IR_{13} \land \overline{lf})/(43)$

36. $PC \leftarrow INC(PC)$
$\rightarrow(24)$

If $IR_{13} = 1$ indicating SZL and $lf = 0$, then the program counter is incremented causing the next instruction to be skipped. If the skip is successful, the third event time is skipped also to eliminate the possibility of skipping two instructions. Otherwise control proceeds directly from step 35 to event time 3. Execution of instructions DFA and DFB is accomplished at Step 37. Similarly, DTA and INA are handled at step 38.

37. $AC_{5:17} \leftarrow (IA ! IB) * (\overline{IR_{13}}, IR_{13})$
  $\rightarrow (43)$
38. $IA \leftarrow (AC_{5:17} ! INC (IA)) * (\overline{IR_{13}}, IR_{13})$
  $\rightarrow (43)$
39. $IB \leftarrow (AC_{5:17} ! INC(IB)) * (\overline{IR_{13}}, IR_{13})$
  $\rightarrow (43)$

The three-step rotate instruction will be identical to steps 30 to 32 as detailed for event time one. These steps would merely be repeated on lines 40 to 42.

40.
  . (Rotate)
  .
43. $\rightarrow (IR_{14})/(45)$ NO DELAY

Control is separated at step 43 for a third possible rotation. At step 44 the contents of the **AC** are examined to determine if a skip should be executed.

44. $\rightarrow (f, \bar{f})/(36, 24)$

Equation 6.1 is the logical expression generated in step 44. It is presented separately to avoid writing it twice. If the criterion specified in Table 6.1 is satisfied for one of bits $IR_{15}, IR_{16},$ and IR_{17}, which is specified as 1, then

$$f = (AC_0 \wedge IR_{15}) \vee ((\overline{\vee/AC}) \wedge IR_{16}) \vee (\overline{AC_0} \wedge (\vee/AC) \wedge IR_{17}) \qquad (6.1)$$

and **PC** is incremented at step 36. Otherwise control passes to step 24, the point of convergence for all (except JMP) instructions.

Once again the rotate execution is the same as in event time one. Steps 45 to 47 are allowed for this operation. This completes the AHPL listing for the operate instructions.

45.
  . (Rotate)
47.
  $\rightarrow (24)$

6.7 COMPLETION OF DATA TRANSFER CONNECTIONS

With the completion of the control sequence, we can now determine exactly what interconnections and logic are required to implement the addressed and operate instructions. Further refinements may be required by the input/output instructions, but the basic structure of the

computer can be fully specified at this point. Referring to the partial
block diagram of Fig. 6.1, the reader will recall that we made no specification whatever of the input connections to the registers. We now go
through the control sequence and list the inputs to all the registers, as
tabulated in Table 6.2. The destinations include all registers in the computer. The sources include register contents (direct transfers), constants
($18 \top 0$ and $\overline{18 \top 0}$), and functions of various registers (AND, INC, etc.).
The link connections are not explicitly listed, but will be considered in
the discussion to follow.

TABLE 6.2 Register Interconnections in SIC

Destinations	Sources
MA	PC $\quad IR_{5:17}$
IR	MD $\quad ADD(IA; IR_{5:17})$ $\qquad ADD(IB; IR_{5:17})$
PC	$IR_{5:17}$ $\quad INC(PC)$
AC	MD $\quad ADD(MD; AC)$ $\quad AND(MD; AC)$ $\quad 18 \top 0$ $\quad \overline{18 \top 0}$
	$lf, AC_{0:16}$ $\quad AC_{1:17}, \, lf$ $\quad IA$ $\quad IB$ $\quad \overline{AC}$
MD	$INC(MD)$ $\quad INC(PC)$ $\quad AC$
IA	$AC_{5:17}$ $\quad INC(IA)$
IB	$AC_{5:17}$ $\quad INC(IB)$

From Table 6.2 we note that every register has at least two inputs so
that direct gating (in the manner of Fig. 4.9a) would require a bank of
OR gates at the input to every register. Clearly, the use of a common
bus to drive all registers will be preferable. This bus, the *OBUS*, will
have its output connected to the input of every register. A transfer will
involve gating the desired source vector onto the *OBUS* and then clocking the *OBUS* contents into the specified destination register.

Next we must consider whether our original assignment of registers
to the *ABUS* and *BBUS* is appropriate. We note that four registers—*PC*,
MD, *IA*, and *IB*—require incrementing. If we put these four registers
on the same bus, they can share the increment logic. In Fig. 6.1, *MD* is
not on the same bus as *IA* and *IB*. Therefore, we shall move *MD* to the
BBUS and add *PC* to the *BBUS*. Since ADD and AND require *AC* and
MD to be on different buses, we also move *AC* to the *ABUS*.

All registers that serve as sources are now on either the *ABUS* or

BBUS. Direct transfers will be implemented by gating the source register onto *ABUS* or *BBUS*, gating *ABUS* or *BBUS* to the *OBUS* to the destination register. For increment transfers, the specified register will be gated onto the *BBUS* and the *BBUS* incremented to the *OBUS*. The incrementing could be done with special increment logic or by adding 1 in the adder. The latter approach will require gating 1 onto the *ABUS*. This requires only one gate, to gate logic 1 to $ABUS_{17}$; the remaining 17 bits are set to logic 0 simply by not gating anything. In view of the simplicity of this method we shall use the adder for incrementing.

Only one register, *AC*, requires complementing. This could be done by gating the complement outputs of *AC* to the *ABUS* and gating *ABUS* directly to *OBUS*, or by gating *AC* directly to *ABUS* and complementing *ABUS* to *OBUS*. The latter method requires more logic (18 inverters), but it will be used as it simplifies the generation of the all 1's constant. For both constants, the *ABUS* will be set to all 0's by gating nothing to it. For the constant 18 $\top$ 0 (all 0's), *ABUS* will be gated directly to the *OBUS*; for the constant $\overline{18 \top 0}$ (all 1's), *ABUS* will be complemented to the *OBUS*.

Since there are 18-bit registers on both *ABUS* and *BBUS*, both buses will be 18-bits in length. The 13-bit registers *PC*, *IA*, and *IB* will be connected to the low-order 13 bits of *BBUS*, i.e., $BBUS_{5:17}$. To accommodate the ADD and rotate operations, which involve the link, the *OBUS* will be 19 bits in length. All connections to the *OBUS* will be right-justified, i.e., $OBUS_{1:18}$ will drive 18-bit registers and $OBUS_{6:18}$ will drive 13-bit registers; $OBUS_0$ will drive the link. The output of the link will not be on any bus but will drive the adder and shifting network within the ALU directly. Shifting will be accomplished between the *ABUS* and *OBUS*, by gating each bit one place to the right or left.

All of the above discussion may be summarized in the block diagram of Fig. 6.9 and the bus connection table, Table 6.3. The *OBUS* input table also specifies the functions to be performed by the ALU. The ALU will consist of the gates and logic required to provide the specified *OBUS* inputs. Most of the connections listed should be self-explanatory in light of the preceding discussion. The last two *OBUS* inputs represent the rotate operations. Note that for all input connections in which the source is shorter than the bus, the remaining bits are specified as zeros, which simply means that these bits are not connected.

The direct connection of *ABUS* or *BBUS* to *OBUS* is specified in Table 6.3. These connections could be eliminated and direct transfers accomplished through the adder. For example, connecting all zeros (18 $\top$ 0) to the *ABUS* and the output of the adder to the *OBUS* would transfer

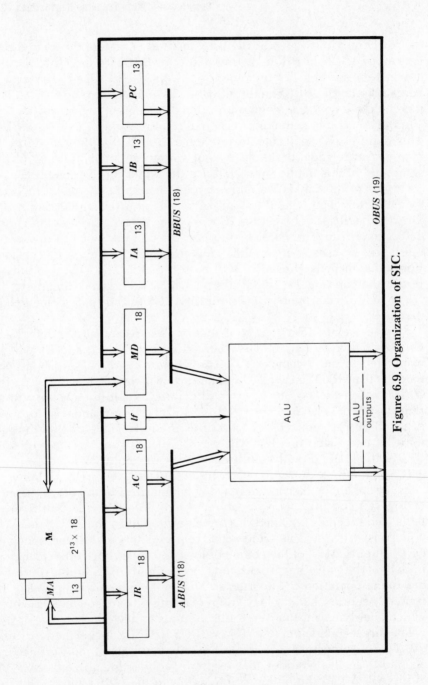

Figure 6.9. Organization of SIC.

BBUS to *OBUS*. A similar procedure for transferring *ABUS* to *OBUS* would require that 18 ⊤ 0 be added to the list of *BBUS* inputs. Depending on the design of the adder, we find that this method might be slower than direct connection; but it is an option that the designer of the ALU should consider.

TABLE 6.3   Bus Connections for SIC

ABUS Inputs	*BBUS* Inputs
ABUS = *AC* *ABUS* = *IR* *ABUS* = 18 ⊤ 0 *ABUS* = 18 ⊤ 1	*BBUS* = *MD* *BBUS* = 5 ⊤ 0, *IA* *BBUS* = 5 ⊤ 0, *IB* *BBUS* = 5 ⊤ 0, *PC*
OBUS Inputs	*OBUS* Outputs
OBUS = 0, *ABUS* *OBUS* = 0, *BBUS* *OBUS* = 0, $\overline{ABUS}$ *OBUS* = ADD(*ABUS*; *BBUS*) *OBUS* = 0, *ABUS* ∧ *BBUS* *OBUS* = *ABUS*, *lf* *OBUS* = *ABUS*$_{17}$, *lf*, *ABUS*$_{0:16}$	$AC \leftarrow OBUS_{1:18}$ $MD \leftarrow OBUS_{1:18}$ $IR \leftarrow OBUS_{1:18}$ $IR_{5:17} \leftarrow OBUS_{6:18}$ $IA \leftarrow OBUS_{6:18}$ $IB \leftarrow OBUS_{6:18}$ $PC \leftarrow OBUS_{6:18}$ $MA \leftarrow OBUS_{6:18}$ *lf*, $AC \leftarrow OBUS$

The addition of the *OBUS* will require the generation of additional bus control signals, and the full AHPL description will be correspondingly more complex. For example, the full description of the transfer

$$AC \leftarrow AC \wedge MD$$

would be

$$ABUS = AC;\ BBUS = MD;\ OBUS = 0, (ABUS \wedge BBUS)$$
$$AC \leftarrow OBUS_{1:18}$$

For more complex transfers, particularly conditional transfers, it becomes clear why a complete design must fully specify the bus connections. Consider as an example the conditional transfer at step 21.

21. $MD \leftarrow (AC\ !\ (5 \top 0, INC\ (PC))) * (IR_2, \overline{IR_2})$

The complete statement, specifying all bus connections, would be the following.

187

21. $ABUS = (AC \: ! \: 18 \top 1) * (IR_2, \overline{IR_2}); BBUS = 5 \top 0, \underline{PC};$
     $OBUS = ((0, ABUS) \: ! \: \text{ADD} \: (ABUS; BBUS)) * (IR_2, \overline{IR_2})$
     $MD \leftarrow OBUS_{1:18}$

For $IR_2 = 1$, AC is gated onto the $ABUS$ and in turn onto the $OBUS$, and then clocked into MD. For $IR_2 = 0$, $18 \top 1$ (binary 1) is gated onto the $ABUS$, and added to PC from the $BBUS$ to increment PC) the result is then clocked into MD. In either case, PC is gated onto $BBUS$ but affects the $OBUS$ only if $IR_2 = 0$.

It is conceivable that a hardware compiler could be sufficiently complex to generate the bus connections for all but the most complex conditional transfers. However, manually converting the abbreviated transfer statements into the complete form is a good way for the designer to verify that his list of interconnections is adequate to realize the control sequence. We shall leave it as an exercise for the reader to verify that all the transfers in the SIC control sequence can be realized with the bus connections of Table 6.3 (see Problem 6.9).

6.8 OPTIONS IN COMPUTER STRUCTURES

In the preceding sections we have studied the design of the SIC computer in considerable detail. We have done so because we believe that it is pedagogically advantageous to follow through the design of at least one specific machine in a consistent and comprehensive manner. The concentration on this particular machine is not intended to imply that this is in any sense the only reasonable design or even a preferable design. Although SIC has many features in common with various minicomputers, the number of possible variations and options in organization is virtually unlimited. Now that the reader has the essential features of one specific design well in hand, it is appropriate to look briefly at some possible options.

Any attempt to classify options would be most difficult without some bounds on the nature of the system under discussion. As noted in Chapter 1, the basic characteristics and structure of digital computers were first set forth in a systematic manner by the mathematician John von Neumann, in 1945. Since that time, computers conforming generally to the organization he set forth have been classified as *von Neumann machines*, and it is a measure of the significance of his contributions that the vast majority of computers built over the years have been von Neumann machines. In this section we shall restrict our discussion to features consistent with the general notion of a von Neumann organization. Elsewhere in the book we shall consider other possibilities.

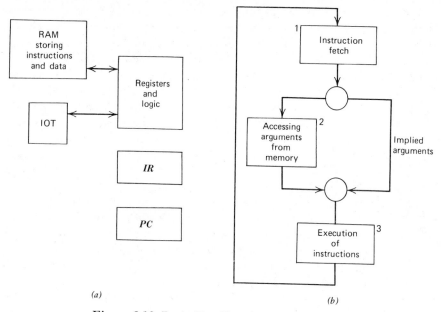

Figure 6.10. Basic Von Neumann organization.

Von Neumann's analysis dealt with very general concepts, and it is difficult to arrive at a precise definition of what is or is not a von Neumann machine. The characteristic most commonly cited as distinguishing the von Neumann organization is the storage of data and instructions in the same form, in the same random access memory. This characteristic in turn implies other structural features, including separation of registers and logic from memory, a program counter and an instruction register, and input/output facilities. Figure 6.10a illustrates the essential features of a von Neumann structure. This structure also implies the division of the instruction cycle into three basic parts, as shown in Fig. 6.10b. Clearly, SIC includes all these features.

Available options with the von Neumann organization can be classified in terms of options in structuring the three blocks of Fig. 6.10b. The number of options available in the instruction execution block is essentially unlimited. Some possible categories of instructions were discussed earlier. One particularly important group of instructions, the arithmetic instructions, will be discussed in detail in Chapters 15, 16, and 17. Options in the accessing of arguments will be the subject of the next section.

Within the instruction fetch cycle there are basically two types of options available. The first concerns the manner in which the address of the next instruction is obtained. One method is to include the address of the next instruction in each instruction. Then the instruction fetch requires moving the next instruction address from the instruction register to the memory address register and reading the new instruction into the instruction register. This option was employed in a few early computers, but the standard technique used today is that used in SIC. The program is assumed to be stored in sequential locations in memory, and a program counter is used to keep track of the next instruction address. Branch instructions can change the next instruction address, but they do so by modifying the program counter so that the fetch cycle uniformly refers to the program counter for the instruction address.

The second option in the fetch cycle is in the number of words per instruction. As in the case of SIC, computers with word lengths in the range of 16 to 32 bits usually use one-word instructions. Machines with longer words may pack two or more instructions in a word, while machines with shorter word lengths, especially microprocessors, may require several words per instruction. The basic structure of the fetch cycle for a machine with more than one instruction per word is shown in Fig. 6.11a. If an instruction has m-bits, the usual technique is to execute the instruction in the most-significant m-bits of the instruction register. After the fetch of an instruction word, each individual instruction must in turn be shifted into the correct position. Also note that n is not necessarily a constant for a given machine; i.e., some instructions may occupy a full word, others only part of a word. In such cases the op code will contain information to set the appropriate value of n.

The basic fetch cycle for the case in which more than one word may be required per instruction is shown in Fig. 6.11b. This time n indicates the number of words per instruction and, again, it is not necessarily constant for a given machine. If this is the case, the number of words in the instruction will usually be specified in the first instruction word. As shown in Fig. 6.11b, if additional words are required they are fetched from successive memory locations until n words have been assembled into the instruction register.

Example 6.2
Write in AHPL the steps of the control sequence that specify the instruction fetch for a computer which employs a twelve-bit 2^{18}-word RAM. Instructions that require an operand from memory must consist of 24 bits, i.e., two computer words. Instructions such as operate instructions, which do not require an argument from memory, are 12-bit instructions. Bit $IR_0 = 0$ for one-word instructions, and $IR_0 = 1$ for two-word instructions.

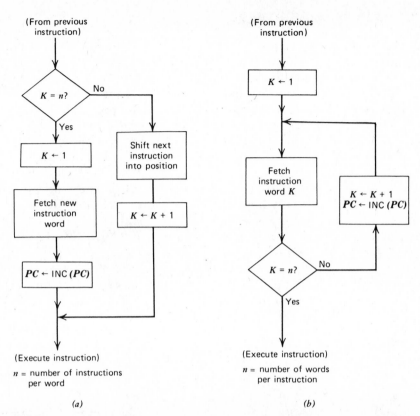

Figure 6.11. Fetch cycles for partial-word and multiple-word instructions.

Solution

Since the following is only a partial control sequence, declarations are omitted. As implied, *PC* and *MA* are 18-bit registers while *IR* is 24 bits and *MD* is 12 bits. The first instruction word is always placed in $IR_{0:11}$.

1. $MA \leftarrow PC$
2. $MD \leftarrow \text{BUSFN (M; DCD } (MA))$
3. $IR_{0:11} \leftarrow MD$
4. $\rightarrow (\overline{IR_0})/$ (execution of 1-word instructions)
5. $PC \leftarrow \text{INC}(PC); MA \leftarrow \text{INC } (PC)$
6. $MD \leftarrow \text{BUSFN (M; DCD } (MA))$
7. $IR_{12:23} \leftarrow MD$
8. Accessing of argument

The above control sequence is clearly an example of Fig. 6.11b, where *n* is restricted to the values 1 and 2.

191

6.9 ADDRESSING OPTIONS

Let us now turn our attention to the options available in the accessing of arguments in block 2 of Fig. 6.10b. The term *argument* is used in a very broad sense here, to include operands to be processed, results to be stored, and addresses for branch operations. Thus every instruction requires access to at least one argument. In the interest of simplicity we have shown the access to arguments only once in Fig. 6.10b although the storing results will usually occur after the execute phase.

Arguments may be broadly grouped into two classifications, addressed and implied. Implied arguments are the contents of registers whose use is specified by the op code itself. Such instructions as the operate instructions in SIC use only implied operands; for example, CMA clearly implies the accumulator contents as the argument. Also, addressed instructions commonly imply some arguments. For instance, TAD and AND imply the accumulator as the source of one operand and the destination of the result. This mode of access is indicated by a straight-through line in block 2 of Fig. 6.10b because no steps are required to move the arguments into position for execution. The processing of the registers implied by the op code automatically accesses these arguments.

Addressed arguments are those which require access to memory. There is complication here in that registers are memory devices, and in many modern computer systems the memory may include a whole hierarchy of devices rather than just one main memory as in SIC. Here we use the term *memory* in the basic von Neumann sense: to denote a separate section of the computer system consisting of 2^n information storage locations, identified by n-bit addresses. An addressed argument requires the generation of an n-bit address, which is in some way specified by the instruction. This address generation and memory access is indicated as block 2 in Fig. 6.10b. The options available in this block are the subject of the remainder of this section.

The design decisions that must be made in setting up an addressing scheme have been separated into the four degrees of freedom listed in Fig. 6.12. The tree in this figure is provided as a means of graphically depicting the great variety of combinations of approaches to address determination that are available. Each terminal node of the tree corresponds to one combination. The ordering of the four degrees of freedom was selected solely for the convenience of illustration.

The first option is how many arguments are to be accessed in memory. As discussed in Chapter 1, the single-address format, in which one argument is addressed and the others are implied, is the most common. However, some machines do use two- or three-address formats. Multi-

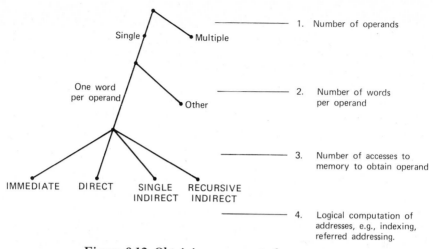

Figure 6.12. Obtaining arguments from memory.

ple-address instructions are often stored in several words, as discussed in the last section. The options of single or multiple arguments are depicted as separate branches from the root node of the tree depicted in Fig. 6.12. Although a continuation is shown only for the single-address branch, a complete tree would have branches corresponding to the next degree of freedom from each nonterminal node. Thus terminal nodes would exist corresponding to all combinations of choices for the four addressing parameters.

The next choice (the second level of branching) is the number of words per argument. The amount of information obtained from each location in the memory is assumed to be one word. Most machines use one word per operand, but in some machines operands may be spread over several consecutive locations. In such machines the instruction usually specifies the location of the first word in the operand; accessing then continues through successive locations until the entire operand has been processed.

The next choice (third degree of freedom) is how many accesses to the memory must be made to obtain each operand (or each word of an operand). The leftmost branch on the decision tree represents *immediate addressing*, in which the argument is a part of the instruction so that no additional accesses to memory are required. This form of addressing may seem out of place on the decision tree, since no address is generated nor is a memory access made. A reasonable argument could be made that this is a form of implied addressing, except that the use of an im-

193

mediate argument is not usually implied by the op code, but is rather specified by an address mode bit, in the same way that indirect or index addressing was specified in SIC. This is simply a special case that does not fit neatly in either of the two categories, addresed and nonaddressed instructions.

Direct addressing and single-level indirect addressing, which are used in SIC, require one and two additional memory accesses, respectively. *Recursive indirect addressing*, which is not provided in SIC, will allow any number of successive memory accesses before the operand is finally obtained. This is accomplished by replacing the indirect addressing specification bit as well as the address in *IR* after each successive memory access. The operand is not read from memory until a 0 in this bit position is encountered (see Problem 6.1).

The fourth and final degree of freedom is less convenient to depict in the tree structure because of the large number of possibilities. Indexing is allowed in SIC which calls for an address to be formed by adding the contents of an index register to a vector from *IR*. In general, addresses can be generated *as combinational logic functions of any registers or combinations of registers*. Another example of this fourth degree of freedom is the use of the op code to specify a register within the CPU that contains the address. We shall call this *referred addressing* or *pointer addressing*.

The third and fourth degrees of freedom are logically independent in that the third provides for the determination of addresses by successive operations in time while the fourth involves a single, one-time determination of the address in terms of combinational logic. The examples in this section and Section 6.10 will illustrate various combinations of these two types of options.

Multiple-address instructions are often used in larger machines. Machines in the minicomputer or microcomputer class are usually single-address machines but often resort to more complex address generation in order to increase the amount of memory that can be addressed without increasing the word length. The techniques most often used for increasing address capacity are indirect or referred addressing, which offer the means of obtaining longer addresses. For example, when an indirect address cycle is executed in SIC, a full 18-bit word is fetched but only 13 bits are used. If SIC were to be modified to use the full 18 bits, its address capacity would be increased to $2^{18} = 262k$ words. To accomplish this, we must increase the size of *MA* and *PC* to full word length and use an addressing cycle similar to that discussed in Example 6.1, in which addresses are routed directly to *MA* or *PC* rather than to *IR*.

This modification does not fully solve the problem because an address is still needed in the instruction, even with indirect addressing. The usual procedure is as follows. During the fetch cycle a full length address (18 bits in SIC) is transferred from *PC* to *MA* and an instruction fetched. During execution of an addressed instruction, a partial address (13 bits in SIC) is transferred to the corresponding position of *MA* and catenated to the most significant position (5 bits in SIC) left in *MA* by the instruction fetch.

When such a scheme is used, it is usual to consider the memory as being divided into *pages*. The most significant portion of an address, which is left unchanged by direct addressing, is known as the *page number*; the least significant portion, normally taken from the instruction, is known as the *page address*. The complete, full word address is known as the *absolute address*. In the case of a 2^{18}-word SIC, the upper 5 bits are the page number and the lower 13 bits the page address so that the 262k memory is divided into 32 pages of 8192 words each. For example, if the first 5 bits are 00000, we are on a page-0, with addresses ranging from 000000 to 017777 (octal), i.e., the first 8k words of memory. For the first 5 bits 00001, we are on a page-1, with addresses ranging from 020000 to 037777, etc.

The page number designated by the leading bits of *PC* is known as the *current page*. As long as direct addressing is used, the program will be executed on the current page. Indirect addressing need not be used unless it is necessary to move off the current page. For machines with large pages, such as the 8k pages in SIC, many programs could be executed without leaving the current page. When necessary, however, indirect addressing on memory reference instructions can refer to data locations on any page. Indirect jumps will reset the program counter providing a new current page number as required.

The above paragraphs describe the basic principles by which indirect addressing can be used to increase the addressing capacity of computers. In machines using this technique, additional refinements are often incorporated to provide for simpler programming. Let us now consider as an example a machine similar to the PDP-8, which has a word length of only 12 bits, making the problem of address capacity particularly severe.

Example 6.3
Figure 6.13 shows the basic organization of a 12-bit, 4k computer.

Devise an instruction format for addressed instructions and a page addressing scheme. Also devise a convenient means to use memory locations to serve the function of index registers.

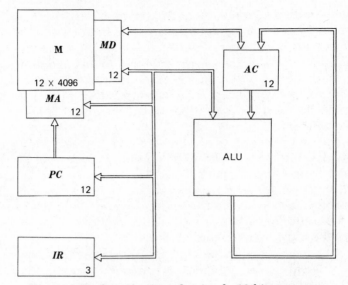

Figure 6.13. Organization of a simple 12-bit computer.

Solution

Three bits is about the minimum possible for op codes if the machine is to do anything at all, and 1 bit will be required to designate indirect addressing. Thus we have a maximum of 8 bits available for page addresses, which would allow for 16 pages of 256 words each. However, as a matter of programming convenience, we shall instead divide the memory into 32 pages of 128 words each, with bit 4 used to choose between the current page or page-0, as shown in Fig. 6.14. Thus, if $Z/C = 0$, the page address is taken on page 0; if $Z/C = 1$, the page address is taken on the current page.

This zero-current page choice does not increase address capacity. With an 8-bit page address, the direct addressing range would be 256 words. With this method, the range is still 256 words, 128 on page-0 and 128 in the current page. But there is a programming advantage. Many locations on page-0 will be used as *pointers*, containing the addresses of standard subroutines or tables of constants. For example, we might have standard subroutines for multiplication and

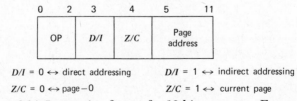

Figure 6.14. Instruction format for 12-bit computer, Example 6.3.

division. These could be stored at convenient places in memory, and their starting addresses could be stored on page-0. Then programs located anywhere in memory could refer to these routines by an indirect reference through page-0.

The page-0 feature also makes it convenient to provide an indexing feature using standard memory locations. The first eight locations on page-0 (absolute addresses 0000_8 to 0007_8) will be used as *autoindex* registers. When an indirect reference is made to these locations, the contents will be incremented by one and rewritten in the same location, and the incremented number will be used as the effective address. For example, if the contents of location 0004_8 were 2163 and the command were

LAC I Z 4 (Z indicates page-0)

then 2163 would be read from location 4 and incremented to 2164, 2164 would be rewritten in location 4, and the contents of location 2164 would be loaded into the accumulator. It can be seen that this feature would provide a very convenient means of stepping through an array of data.

The basic flow chart for the fetch cycle of this machine is shown in Fig. 6.15. We shall leave the task of writing an actual control sequence as an exercise for the reader. (See Problem 6.13.)

Another technique for address modification, found primarily in larger machines, is *base addressing*. In this scheme, at least one *base address register* is provided.

Whenever an argument is accessed in memory, a page address from **IR** is added to or catenated with a base address register to form the absolute address. The above operation will usually be transparent to the user although an instruction for loading each base address register must be provided.

In addition to increasing addressing capacity, base addressing also facilitates *relocatability*, a characteristic important in large machines operated in either a batch or a multiprogramming mode by executive or monitor software. The executive or monitor is responsible for allocating memory in the most efficient manner, so as to accommodate as many programs as possible. A compiler does not anticipate the best arrangement in memory for a program and associated data files. Usually, it assumes each program to begin at address 0. The executive or monitor then loads a starting address in a base address register assigned to the program at load time to locate the program where it fits best in terms of the current state of memory. Because all program addresses are relative to the base address, this technique is sometimes referred to as *relative addressing.**

---

*Addressing may be relative to any register. In Chapter 12 we shall see that it is customary in microprocessors to refer to relative addressing as relative to the program counter.

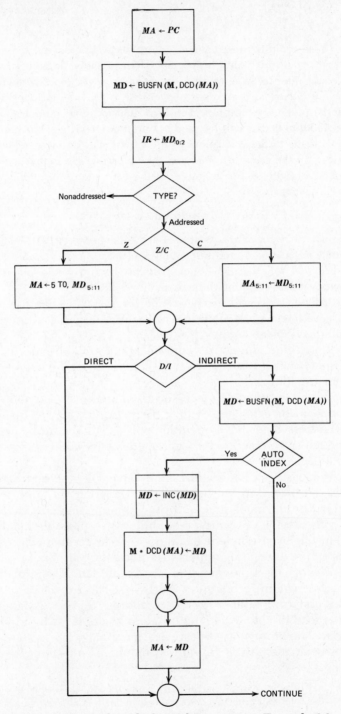

Figure 6.15. Fetch cycle for 12-bit computer, Example 6.3.

Example 6.4

Relative addressing can be included in SIC by adding a 13-bit base address register, *BASE*, and an operate instruction DBA, which will transfer $AC_{5:17}$ to *BASE*. By executing the following instructions, a SIC system monitor could then initiate a program that has been loaded with its first instruction in a location for which the address has been stored in location START.

$$
\begin{array}{ll}
\text{LAC} & \text{START} \\
\text{DBA} & \\
\text{JMP} & 0
\end{array}
$$

This assumes that *BASE* has been set to zero prior to the LAC command. In the execution of all addressed instructions, the contents of *BASE* will be added to the address specified in the instruction. The above JMP command will thus load the address in START into *PC* causing the computer to jump to the starting location of the program. Specify any changes in the SIC control sequence required to implement this form of relative addressing and suggest possible improvements in the approach.

Solution

The basic modification required is that all addresses obtained from $IR_{5:17}$ must be added to the contents of *BASE* before being used. For indirect addressing, step 7 must be changed to:

   7. $MA \leftarrow \text{ADD}(BASE; IR_{5:17})$

To implement the jump, step 14 is changed to

   14. $PC \leftarrow \text{ADD}(BASE; IR_{5:17})$

and step 15 is similarly modified for memory reference instructions.

   15. $MA \leftarrow \text{ADD}(BASE; IR_{5:17})$

Finally, step 23 in the JMS sequence must be changed to

   23. $PC \leftarrow \text{ADD}(BASE; IR_{5:17})$

The operate sequence would also have to be changed to implement the DBA instruction, but we shall not consider that here. The alert reader may note that this approach may cause problems in return from subroutines. We shall leave consideration of this problem as an exercise for the reader. (See Problem 6.15.)

Depending on the speed of the adder available, this approach may result in some loss of speed. At the price of somewhat less flexibility, relative addressing can be accomplished without addition by catenating a page address from the instruction with a page number in the base address register. For SIC we could divide the memory into eight 1K pages, with 10-bit page addresses in the instructions. Then *BASE* would be a 3-bit register containing a page number. Step 7 would then be changed to

7. $MA \leftarrow BASE, IR_{8:17}$

and steps 14, 15 and 24 would be similarly modified. Although this approach does place some constraints on program relocation, it has the advantage of releasing 3 bits for more complex op codes.

6.10 ARGUMENT ACCESS IN A MULTIREGISTER ORGANIZATION

As we have noted, memory speed is one of the main limiting factors in the speed of computers. Even with developing memory technology, it is likely that there will always be a gap between the speed of large capacity memory and the speed of registers and logic. One consequence of this fact is that instructions involving only register transfers are much faster than those requiring a memory access. We have already taken advantage of this in SIC, with each operate instruction allowing up to three register transfers with execution times that would still probably be less than for a single memory reference instruction.

If programs could be arranged to do many operate (register-to-register) instructions for every memory reference, overall execution time would be greatly reduced. The more registers that are available, the more that can be done between memory references. With only two full-length registers, as in SIC, not much can be done before having to obtain a new operand or store a result.

As the number of high-speed registers increases, it becomes convenient to organize them as a small but fast static memory. Arguments can then be specified by short addresses, eliminating the need for separate op-codes for similar operations on different registers such as INA and INB. Since the number of registers is small, they can be addressed with a small number of bits, making two-address or three-address instruction formats practical.

Let us now consider a typical, multiple-register organization for which the basic block diagram is shown in Fig. 6.16a, where *MA, IR,* and *PC* serve the usual purpose; *AR* and *BR* will store the final (effective) addresses of the respective arguments and, eventually, the arguments themselves. There are eight general-purpose registers, *R0* to *R7*, arranged as array **R**. There is no memory data register. Instead the output of the static memory is connected directly to the *ABUS*. Although no other connections to the buses are shown, it is assumed that all transfers take place through the busing structure.

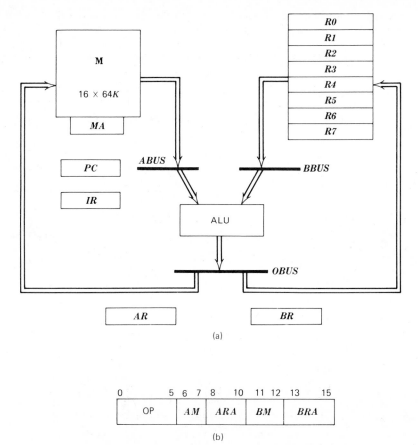

Figure 6.16. Organization of a multiple-register computer.

The basic instructions of the machine are of the two-address replacement type, in which the operands are delivered to **AR** and **BR** from the general-purpose registers or memory, and the result is returned from **BR** to the source of the second operand. The instruction format is shown in Fig. 6.16b, where **AM** and **ARA** specify the source of the first operand, **BM** and **BRA** the source of the second operand and the destination of the result, and **ARA** and **BRA** each specify the number of one of the general-purpose registers. Finally, **AM** and **BM** are the *address mode* bits specifying how the contents of the corresponding register are to be used, as given in Fig. 6.17.

This is a rather complex addressing scheme but one that provides great flexibility and power in a short instruction word. We have 6 bits

AM or BM	Mode	Function
00	Register	Register contains operand.
01	Referred	Register contains address of operand.
11	Auto increment	Register contains address of operand; register is incremented after reference.
10	Index	Contents of register are added to contents of memory location immediately following instruction to form operand address. If both addresses are in the index mode, the next two locations are used.

(*a.*) Definition

AM or BM	Interpretation of Argument Access Parameters
00	Multiple argument; implied mode
01	Multiple argument; referred addressing
11	Multiple argument; referred addressing; logical incrementing of address
10	Multiword instruction; multiple argument; address is logical function of two vectors

(*b.*) Interpretation of argument access parameters

Figure 6.17. Addressing Modes.

available for the op code, allowing up to 63 addressed instructions (assuming that one code must be set aside to designate nonaddressed instructions.) We have the power of the two-address instruction, permitting us to obtain two operands from memory and store a result in memory in a single instruction. Although it is not evident at this point, this two-address (memory-to-memory) capability will allow us to set up variable-word-length instructions, a feature normally found only in very large machines. (This topic will be discussed in Chapter 17.)

In spite of the apparent complexity, each of the four addressing modes can be assigned to a terminal node in the argument access parameter tree of Fig. 6.12. As shown in Fig. 6.17b, all four modes are multiple argument. Mode 00 does not call for a reference to memory to obtain an argument and is therefore the implied mode discussed in connection with Fig. 6.10b. Mode 01 is the special case of logical computation of an address in which a designated register simply contains the address. We called this referred addressing. Mode 11 is similar except that the register is incremented after reference to memory. Incrementing is a combinational logic function with just one register argument. Mode 10 calls for either a two, or three word instruction as illustrated in Fig. 6.11b, with addresses determined by the addition of two vectors.

As is usually the case, there is a price to pay for the advantages of the addressing scheme just described. A reference to memory requires that an address first be loaded into a register by some other command. For programs with a large number of individual data elements, this is a serious disadvantage. For many programs, however, data are primarily in arrays. For arrays we need load only the starting address into a register and then step through the array by autoincrement addressing. By combining index addressing with autoincrement addressing, one can step through a whole set of arrays in parallel, using one register to provide the offset from the starting address of the arrays stored in the locations following the instructions.

The basic flow chart for this machine is shown in Fig. 6.18. The first five steps fetch the instruction and check for instruction type in the same manner as SIC. Step 6 checks AM for the address mode on the first operand. For register mode (AM = 00), step 7 moves the first operand from the row of $\mathbf{R}^i$ specified by ARA, through the bus structure to AR.

6. NO DELAY
    $\rightarrow((\overline{IR_6} \wedge \overline{IR_7}),(IR_6 \wedge \overline{IR_7}), IR_7)/(7, 8, 11)$
7. $BBUS = \mathrm{BUSFN}(\mathbf{R}; \mathrm{DCD}(IR_{8:10})); OBUS = BBUS;$
    $AR \leftarrow OBUS$
    $\rightarrow (14)$

The bus connections will be specifically cited only in AHPL steps involving $\mathbf{M}$ or $\mathbf{R}$. For other transfers the use of the bus structure will be implicit, as in the early sections of this chapter. Following step 7, control jumps to step 14, the first step in the fetch sequence for the second operand.

For index mode, step 8 increments PC to obtain the address of the location following the instruction. Step 9 places this vector in MA, and step 10 adds the addressed numbers in $\mathbf{M}$ and $\mathbf{R}$ placing the result in MA. For the deferred or autoincrement modes, step 11 places the address in MA and, for autoincrement, step 12 increments this address in $\mathbf{R}$.

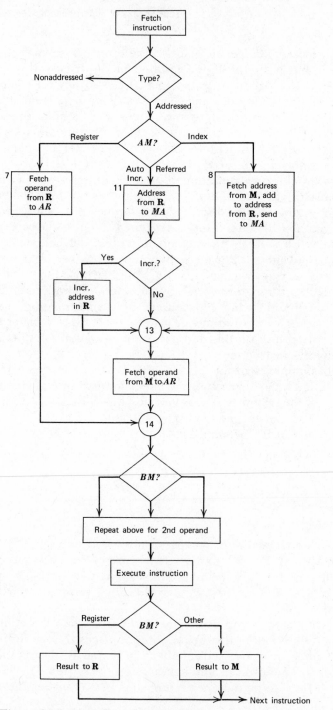

Figure 6.18. Basic flow chart, multiple-register computer.

8. $PC \leftarrow INC(PC)$
9. $MA \leftarrow PC$
10. $ABUS = BUSFN(M; DCD(MA))$
    $BBUS = BUSFN(R; DCD(IR_{8:10}))$
    $OBUS = ADD(ABUS; BBUS)$
    $MA \leftarrow OBUS$
    $\rightarrow (13)$
11. $MA \leftarrow BUSFN(R; DCD(IR_{8:10}))$
    $\rightarrow (\overline{IR_6})/(13)$
12. $R * DCD(IR_{8:10}) \leftarrow INC(BUSFN(R; DCD(IR_{8:10})))$

Finally, step 13 obtains the actual operand from memory and places it in AR.

13. $AR \leftarrow BUSFN(M; DCD(MA))$

This process is then repeated for the second operand, after which the instruction is executed, leaving the result in BR. Next BM is checked again to determine the destination. For register mode the contents of BR are transferred to the register respecified by BRA. For the other modes, the address of the destination is still in MA so that the result is simply stored.

As a final comment, it is interesting to note that the multiple-register principle does not seem to be limited to any particular class or size of computer. One of the earliest examples of multiple-register architecture is found in the CDC-6000 series, which are very large machines with a 60-bit word length. By contrast, probably the most popular computers of this type today are in the PDP-11 minicomputer series. The PDP-11 architecture is similar to the organization just described.

6.11 MULTIPLE-CYCLE INSTRUCTIONS

Now that the instruction fetch and argument access have been treated in some detail, let us now turn our attention briefly to the third or execution phase. The memory reference instructions considered so far were executed by a single transfer of information from one register to another register. The operate instructions required no more than three consecutive changes of state in a register. In later chapters, as we consider instructions useful in computers with particular problem distributions, we shall find that some instructions require many consecutive register transfers.

In general, the approach to designing the control sequencing hardware will be the same, regardless of instruction complexity. Let us illustrate, using fixed-point multiplication as an example. There are various possible approaches to the multiplication of numbers that may be negative. Since storage may be in the form of one's complements, two's complements, or sign and magnitude, various schemes are used to effect multiplication in all of these formats. To preserve continuity, let us defer a discussion of the various alernatives until Chapter 15.

The simplest, although not necessarily the fastest or least-expensive, approach to multiplication is keeping track of signs and multiplying the magnitudes. Here let us assume that numbers are stored as two's-complement integers. Thus, prior to multiplication, the sign of the product will be determined, and all two's-complement negative numbers will be replaced by magnitudes.

Since the fixed-point multiplication of two 18-bit numbers may result in a 36-bit product, another register, the **MQ** register, must be added to store the 18 least-significant bits of the product. It will be necessary to count the number of bits of the multiplier that have been treated at any given stage in the process; so a 5-bit counter, designated **MC**, will be added. The link will be used for storage of the sign. The described hardware configuration may be found in Fig. 6.19.

Only the basic data paths involved in multiplication are shown in fashion Fig. 6.19. In practice busing would almost certainly be used. As we have seen, however, we need not concern ourselves with the bus arrangement in writing the control sequence. We shall assume that the bus configuration is such that all transfers required in the following sequence can be implemented.

The multiplication instruction is not included in SIC. Similarly, several of the registers in Fig. 6.19 are not available in SIC. Therefore, let us visualize multiplication as part of another computer, encompassing all of the features of SIC but with an extended arithmetic capability, including multiplication.

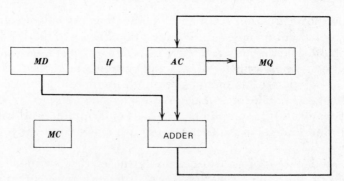

Figure 6.19. Multiplication hardware.

Let us pick up the operation at a point in the control sequence following the fetch cycle and the identification of the instruction. The multiplier is in the AC from the previous instruction. The multiplicand has just been read from storage and placed in MD. Control has diverged to the point of the actual beginning of the instruction. The operation begins with the clearing of the link to prepare for sign determination. The first four steps convert the multiplier to sign and magnitude form, leaving the magnitude in MQ and the sign in lf. The next four steps place the magnitude of the multiplicand in MD and leave the sign of the final product in lf. Two's complements, where necessary, are obtained by complementing individual bits and adding one to the least-significant bit. Notice that lf, which was initially reset to 0, is complemented once if the multiplier is negative and once if the multiplicand is negative. Thus it ends up 0 if and only if the signs are the same.

1. $lf \leftarrow 0$
   $\rightarrow (\overline{AC_0})/(4)$
2. $lf, AC \leftarrow \overline{lf}, \overline{AC}$
3. $AC \leftarrow \text{ADD}_{1:18}(AC;(18 \top 1))$
4. $MQ \leftarrow AC$
5. $AC \leftarrow MD$
   $\rightarrow (\overline{AC_0}, AC_0)/(8, 6)$
6. $lf, AC \leftarrow \overline{lf}, \overline{AC}$
7. $AC \leftarrow \text{ADD}_{1:18}(AC; (18 \top 1))$
8. $MD \leftarrow AC$

Before proceeding, let us consider the basic multiplication process in some detail. Since the basic arithmetic process of a computer is addition, multiplication is generally carried out by successive addition. In this technique the decimal multiplication of 203×576 would be carried out as shown in Fig. 6.20a. For the binary case, the process is even simpler, since the only multiplier bits are zero or one. Thus, for each multiplier bit, the multiplicand is either added once or not added at all. A typical binary multiplication is shown in Fig. 6.20b.

From this, it is seen that the basic binary multiplicative process involves inspecting each multiplier bit in turn, adding and shifting for a 1, and shifting without adding for a 0. As shown in Fig. 6.20, the partial products are successively shifted left before addition, finally resulting in a product having twice as many bits as the initial operands. This process would be impractical in a computer, since it would require a double-length adder, for example, a 36-bit adder for a machine with 18-bit operands.

To avoid this difficulty, addition, if required, is performed as each bit

$$
\begin{array}{r}
576 \\
\times\ 203 \\
\hline
576 \\
576 \\
576 \\
000 \\
576 \\
576 \\
\hline
\text{(a)}\quad 116{,}828
\end{array}
\qquad
\begin{array}{r}
0110 \\
0101 \\
\hline
0110 \\
0000 \\
0110 \\
0000 \\
\hline
\text{(b)}\quad 0011110
\end{array}
$$

Figure 6.20. Multiplication by successive addition.

of the multiplier is inspected; and the resultant sum is then shifted right, providing a relative left shift of the next partial product. To provide for the double-length product, the *AC* and *MQ* registers are catenated for right shifting. The multiplier is initially loaded into *MQ*, the multiplicand into *MD*, with *AC* initially cleared. As the product is shifted into *MQ*, the multiplier is shifted out so that the multiplier bit to be inspected is always in the low-order position of *MQ*. This process of multiplication is illustrated in Fig. 6.21 for the same multiplications as Fig. 6.20b. The dotted line in *MQ* indicates the boundary between the developing partial product and the remainder of the multiplier.

The first step in the implementation of this process stores a string of zeros in *AC* and sets the multiplication counter, *MC*, to zero. This is followed by a loop that adds a product vector to *AC* and shifts the result right. This loop will be executed 18 times. When $\perp(MC) = 18$, the process will terminate. Thus, at the conclusion of 18 cycles, the product will be found with the least-significant bits in *MQ* and the remaining bits in *AC*. The *AC* will not overflow at any step, since the magnitude of the multiplicand is less than or equal to $2^{17}-1$.

9. $MC, AC \leftarrow 23 \top 0$

10. $\rightarrow (MC_0 \wedge MC_3)/(15)$

11. $\rightarrow (MQ_{17})/(13)$

12. $AC, MQ \leftarrow 0, AC, MQ_{0:16}$
     $\rightarrow (14)$

13. $AC, MQ \leftarrow \text{ADD}(AC; MD), MQ_{0:16}$

14. $MC \leftarrow \text{INC}(MC)$
     $\rightarrow (10)$

Notice that a separation of control is specified depending on whether a given bit of the multiplier is 1 or 0. The reason for this is a physical one: the shift operation will require less time than the add followed by

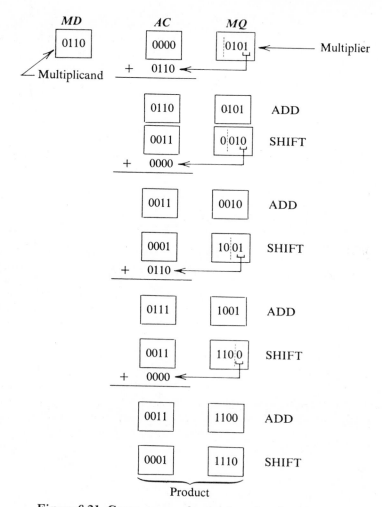

Figure 6.21. Computer mechanization of multiplication.

a shift (perhaps 5:1). Thus, if half the multiplier bits are zero, this approach will reduce the overall multiplication time by a factor of almost 2. Step 13 may appear to be dimensionally inconsistent. However, it should be recalled that the ADD function produces a 19-bit sum, the leading bit indicating overflow. Since the multiplicand is in positive form, the leading bit (the sign bit) is 0 so that there can be no overflow. Hence the leading bit of the sum will always be 0, as desired for shifting into AC_0.

After consideration of all 18 bits, the contents of both MQ and AC are complemented if the link is 1. The process of complementing a double-length result is rather cumbersome. This alone might suggest looking for another approach to multiplication. For completeness, the following sequence, although awkward, does complete the process.

15. $\rightarrow (\overline{lf})/(22)$
16. $MD \leftarrow AC$
17. $lf, AC \leftarrow 0, \overline{MQ}$
18. $lf, AC \leftarrow \text{ADD} (AC; 18 \top 1)$
19. $MQ \leftarrow AC$
20. $AC \leftarrow MD$
21. $lf, AC \leftarrow \text{ADD} ((17 \top 0, lf); AC)$
22. Exit to next instruction

6.12 SUMMARY

In this chapter we have presented a language with which the engineer can approach the design of a computer or a computer subsystem. It is not an algorithmic design procedure. The designer is not relieved of the responsibility of optimizing this AHPL description of the control unit for a particular application.

It is hoped, however, that this chapter and Chapter 7 will provide him with a place to start. We have developed the complete control sequence (except for IOT) for a typical single-address machine. We have also introduced some more complex systems of addressing and a basic multiple-register organization. We have hardly scratched the surface in terms of possible computer organizations, and many other possibilities will be discussed in succeeding chapters.

PROBLEMS

6.1 Multiple indirect addressing is possible. Such a scheme would allow an address obtained by indirect addressing to be the address of another address, which might be the data address or the address of another address, etc. The SIC control sequence can easily be modified to allow this option by replacing IR_1 as well as the address portion of IR. Modify steps 6 to 9 of the SIC control sequence (Appendix C) to provide multiple indirect addressing.

6.2 Suppose that a computer with a register configuration similar to that shown in Fig. 6.1 has an instruction JMP A if $\perp AC \geqslant 0$, where A is the address portion of the instruction. Write the control sequence for this instruction in AHPL, beginning at a point where control has diverged to separate this instruction from all other instructions.

6.3   Some computers, particularly microprogrammed computers, branch at one point to separate sequences for all instructions, rather than share steps as is done in SIC. Rewrite the SIC control sequence so that a branch at step 15 branches to separate sequences for LAC, DAC, AND, TAD, ISZ, and JMS. Compare the number of AHPL steps required by the two approaches.

6.4   Assume that the alternate address modification sequence given in Example 6.1 has been adopted for SIC. Determine what changes, if any, will be required in that portion of the control sequence implementing the memory reference instructions.

6.5   Write an AHPL control sequence for a machine similar to SIC but with the instruction set given. Consider all instructions except for IOT and OPR. The instruction format will be the same as for SIC, and the fetch cycle (steps 1 to 12, Appendix C) will be the same as for SIC except for the branch at step 5.

Op Code	Mnemonic	Operation
000	OR	$AC \leftarrow AC \vee MD$
001	TAD	
010	JPA	Jump if $\perp AC \geqslant 0$
011	JMP	
100	JMS	
101	DCA	Deposit and clear AC
110	IOT	
111	OPR	

6.6   Another variant on indirect addressing is indexed indirect addressing. If indirect addressing brings back IR_3 and IR_4 along with the address, then the indirect address can be indexed. Modify the control sequence of SIC to provide indexed multiple-level indirect addressing.

6.7   A certain computer has only 8-bit instruction and data words. If the first 3 bits of an instruction are all 1's, the instruction is an operate instruction to be executed in two event times. Bits 3, 4, and 5 control the first event time and bits 6 and 7 the second. If bit 3 is a 0, the first event time is a NO OP. If bit 3 is a 1, bits 4 and 5 specify rotate or shift (enter a 0 in the vacated bit position) operations as follows:

Bit	4	5	
	0	0	Rotate AC left
	0	1	Rotate AC right
	1	0	Shift AC left
	1	1	Shift AC right

The action of the second event time is specified as follows:

Bit	6	7	
	0	0	No operation
	0	1	Set AC
	1	0	Clear AC
	1	1	Complement AC

Write an AHPL sequence to implement these operate instructions.

6.8 A certain computer makes no distinction between operate and memory reference instructions. All but the IOT instructions are accomplished through a form of microcoding on the basic op code. The first 7 bits are set up to specify the flow chart of the instruction cycle as shown in Fig. P6.8. If IR_i controls a branch operation, the question is answered yes if and only if $IR_i = 1$. Bits IR_1 and IR_2 specify the computation in block 3 as follows. Similarly, bits IR_3 and IR_4 specify the operations on AC in block 4. Although not necessarily a useful machine, this computer illustrates that various combinations of instructions may be microcoded as a single-memory reference instruction. Write an AHPL control sequence for all but the IOT instructions of this machine.

IR_1	IR_2		IR_3	IR_4	
0	0	NO OP	0	0	NO OP
0	1	LAC	0	1	$AC \leftarrow AC_{1:17}, AC_0$
1	0	AND	1	0	$AC \leftarrow AC_{17}, AC_{0:16}$
1	1	TAD	1	1	$AC \leftarrow \overline{AC}$

6.9 To verify that the bus connections specified in Table 6.3 are sufficient to realize the SIC sequence, convert all register transfers in the SIC sequence (steps 1 to 47, Appendix C) to a form completely specifying the bus connections. If you find that the connections specified in Table 6.3 are not sufficient, specify additional connections as required.

6.10 In the discussion of the bus connections in Section 6.7, it is assumed that the various operations of the ALU (AND, ADD, ROTATE, etc.) are carried out by separate logic units, each with its

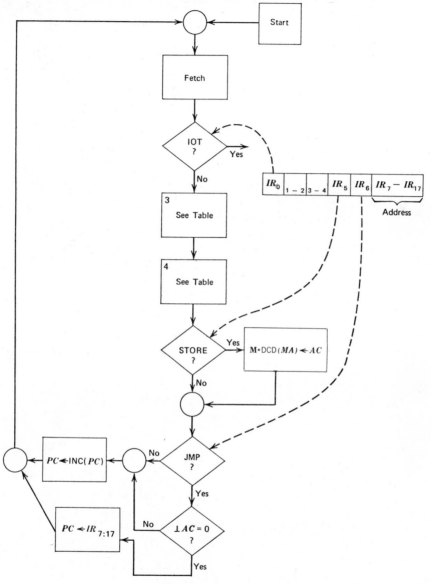

Figure P6.8.

own output. The operation performed is determined by which of these outputs is gated to the *OBUS*. An alternative approach would be to use an integrated circuit logic unit, such as the SN74181. This is a 4-bit, general-purpose, arithmetic-logic circuit, which can perform over 40 different arithmetic and logical operations, including most of those required in SIC. By cascading 74181's, a complete ALU for any word length can be constructed very economically. The 74181 has two 4-bit data inputs, $A(4)$ and $B(4)$; one data output, $F(4)$; an output carry, *cout*; and six control inputs that determine which function of A and B will appear at F.

Let us assume that an 18-bit ALU has been assembled from 74181's. This unit will have two 18-bit inputs, $A(18)$ and $B(18)$, and a 19-bit output, ALU(19). For all functions other than addition, $ALU_{1:18}$ will be the functional output; for addition $ALU_{1:18}$ will be the sum and ALU_0 the carry out. To simplify the problem, we shall use only those functions needed for the SIC control sequence and will add external logic so that only four control bits, $C(4)$, will be required. The control codes and corresponding functions are

C_0	C_1	C_2	C_3	Function
0	0	0	0	$\bar{A}$
0	0	0	1	INC(A)
0	0	1	1	0
0	1	0	1	$\bar{B}$
1	0	0	1	ADD(A;B)
1	0	1	0	B
1	0	1	1	$A \wedge B$
1	1	0	0	1
1	1	1	1	A

For notational convenience we shall assume that the ALU has been declared as a separate module so that the control lines, $C(4)$, can be declared as outputs of the CPU module. Thus the following notation would specify the TAD operation:

17. $ABUS = AC$; $BBUS = MD$; $C = 1,0,0,1$;
    $OBUS = \text{ALU}(ABUS; BBUS; C)$
    $lf, AC \leftarrow OBUS$

First modify the bus connection list, Table 6.3, as required to accommodate the use of this ALU. Then repeat Problem 6.9, assuming this ALU, i.e., convert all transfer statements to forms similar to the above.

6.11 In some computers the index registers are automatically incremented each time they are referenced; as a result, instructions like INA and INB are not required. This procedure may be called *autoindexing.*

(a) What are the advantages and disadvantages of this approach?

(b) How might one set up the instruction set so as to enjoy the advantages without the disadvantages?

(c) Rewrite the SIC fetch sequence to provide for autoindexing.

6.12 As discussed in Section 6.9, indirect addressing is often used to increase the addressing capacity of a computer. Modify the register configuration and control sequence for SIC so that indirect addressing can be used to access a memory of 2^{18} words.

6.13 Write the AHPL control sequence for the fetch cycle of the computer of Example 6.3.

6.14 Example 6.4 specifies an instruction DBA, which would be needed to implement base-addressing in SIC. To accommodate this new operate instruction, we shall eliminate the third rotate so that $IR_{14} = 1$ will call for DBA. Modify the SIC control sequence as required to implement this new instruction.

6.15 The base addressing scheme developed in Example 6.4 may cause difficulties in returns from subroutines. Discuss carefully the nature of these difficulties and how they can be avoided, either by programming or further modifications to the hardware.

6.16 As pointed out in Section 6.10, register-to-register instructions would not be of much value in SIC, with only two full-length registers, *AC* and *MD*. However, if we make *IA* and *IB* also full length (18-bit) registers, we can then add a class of microcoded register instructions which will considerably increase the flexibility of the machine. For this purpose we shall divide the operate instruction ($IR_{0:3} = 1, 1, 1, 0$) into two types: $IR_4 = 1$ will signify register-to-register instructions, and $IR_4 = 0$ will signify other types of operate instructions such as skip, rotate, etc. This problem is concerned only with the register-to-register instructions ($IR_{0:4} = 1, 1, 1, 0, 1$).

The remaining 13 bits will be used to indicate the operation according to the following scheme: $IR_{5:8}$ will specify the destination of the transfer; $IR_{9:11}$ will specify the operation to be performed; $IR_{12:17}$ will specify the source of the transfer. The codes are as follows.

215

Destinations		Sources		IR_9	IR_{10}	IR_{11}	Operations
IR_5	AC	IR_{12}	AC	0	0	0	No Op
IR_6	MD	IR_{13}	MD	0	0	1	$DST \leftarrow SRC$
IR_7	IA	IR_{14}	IA	0	1	0	$DST \leftarrow \overline{SRC}$
IR_8	IB	IR_{15}	IB	0	1	1	$DST \leftarrow INC(SRC)$
		IR_{16}	18T0	1	0	0	$DST \leftarrow AC \wedge SRC$
		IR_{17}	18T1	1	0	1	$DST \leftarrow AC \vee SRC$
				1	1	0	$DST \leftarrow AC \oplus SRC$
				1	1	1	$DST \leftarrow ADD(AC;SRC)$

For sources and destinations, a 1 in the bit indicated will select that register; any number of destination bits may be 1 but only one source bit may be 1. You may assume that the ALU has been modified to provide the inclusive-and-exclusive-OR functions.

Indicate necessary modifications to the bus connections in Table 6.3 and write an AHPL control sequence to implement these register transfer instructions, in the fully expanded form showing bus connections for each statement.

6.17 A computer is to be designed in which the basic word length is 8 bits. With this limitation it is impossible to fit both an op code and an address into a single word. Therefore, an instruction may consist of either one or two words. If it is an instruction that does not require an address, then the instruction will consist only of an op code, contained in one word. If it is an instruction requiring an address, the instruction will be contained in two words, the op code in the first word, the address, Y, in the next sequential location in memory. The significance of the first two bits of the op code, b_0 and b_1, will be as follows:

0 0	Operate instruction, no address required
0 1	IOT instruction, no address required
1 0	Memory reference instruction, direct addressing
1 1	Memory reference instruction, indirect addressing

For operate instructions, the remaining 6 bits are microcoded: bits 2, 3, and 4 controlling event time 1, and bits 5, 6, and 7 controlling event time 2, as follows:

Bits 2	3	4		
0	0	0	No op	NOP
0	0	1	Clear link	CLL

0	1	0	Set link	STL
0	1	1	Complement link	CML
1	0	0	Increment *AC*	INA
1	0	1	Clear *AC*	CLA
1	1	0	Set *AC*	STA
1	1	1	Complement *AC*	CMA

Bits 5 6 7

0	0	0	No op	NOP
0	0	1	Skip if $AC \geqslant 0$	SPA
0	1	0	Skip if $AC < 0$	SMA
0	1	1	Skip	SKP
1	0	0	Rotate *AC* left	RAL
1	0	1	Rotate *AC* right	RAR
1	1	0	} Not used	
1	1	1		

The memory reference instructions are also microcoded, but there is only one event time. If bit 2 is 0, the operation is a jump; if bit 2 is 1, the instruction calls for an operation on *AC*. The codes are as follows.

MRI Codes

Bit	Value	Jumps (Bit-2=0)	AC Ops (Bit-2 = 1)	
3	0	No op	Load *MD*	LMD
	1	Jump if $AC = 0$ JZA	Store *AC*	DAC
4	0	No op	No op	
	1	Jump if $AC > 0$ JPA	Clear *AC*	CLA
5	0	No op	No op	
	1	Jump if $AC < 0$ JMA	$MD \wedge AC$	AND
6	0	No op	No op	
	1	Return jump, store contents of *PC* at $Y, Y + 1$, take next instruction from $y + 2$ RJP	Two's complement Add	TAD

Bit 7 is not assigned and is available for expanding the op codes. Part of the design task is to specify what should happen, in what order, if the programmer specifies two or more *AC* operations in a single instruction. The memory size is 8k words. Means must be provided through indirect addressing to reference any word in memory. Assume the register configuration of Fig. 6.1, except for size and omitting the index registers; but you may add or delete registers or data paths as you wish, provided only that you be able to justify any changes.

(a) Draw a hardware flow chart for the machine.

(b) Write a detailed AHPL routine for the control sequences. Let IOT branch to an unspecified sequence.

6.18 This problem is concerned with writing the AHPL description of a two-address machine. That is, two arguments may be obtained from the random access memory or one argument can be read from memory and a result deposited in memory by one instruction. For simplicity, we assume that the random access memory contains only 2^{10} twenty-four bit words. Unless bits $IR_0 = IR_1 = IR_2 = 1$, the instruction word will take the following form.

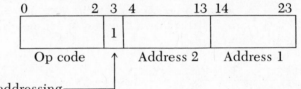

Indirect addressing

It will be observed that indirect addressing is allowed while indexing is omitted for convenience. Arbitrarily, we shall assume that when indirect addressing is specified it refers to ADDRESS 1 only.

Of the seven possible memory reference instructions, two are of particular interest. These are

010   AND   AND the contents of the memory location specified by ADDRESS 1 with *AC* and deposit the result at the location specified by ADDRESS 2; *AC* is left unchanged.

011   JMP   JMP to ADDRESS 2 if and only if the contents of the location specified by ADDRESS 1 are ≥ 0.

The machine has a 24-bit instruction register, *IR* a single 10-bit memory address register, *MA* (only one memory access can be performed at a time), a 24-bit memory data register, *MD*, a 24-bit accumulator, *AC*, an extra 24-bit working register, *WK*, and a 10-

bit program counter, *PC*. Write an AHPL sequence representing a hard-wired control unit for the above machine. Include the fetch cycle and allow for indirect addressing. Carry through the execute cycle for only the two instructions AND and JMP listed above. Indicate the point where control diverges for the operate and I/O instructions represented by op code 111, and indicate the point where control for the instructions AND and JMP diverges from that of the other memory reference instructions.

REFERENCES

1. Chu, Y., *Computer Organization and Microprogramming*, Prentice-Hall, Englewood Cliffs, N.J., 1972.

2. Kline, R. M., *Digital Computer Design*, Prentice-Hall, Englewood cliffs, N.J., 1977.

3. Blaauw, G. A., *Digital System Implementation*, Prentice-Hall, Englewood Cliffs, N.J., 1976.

4. Mowle, F. J., *A Systematic Approach to Digital Logic Design*, Addison-Wesley, Reading, Mass., 1976.

5. Mano, M. M., *Computer System Architecture*, Prentice-Hall, Englewood Cliffs, N.J., 1976.

6. Hellerman, H., *Digital Computer System Principles*, 2nd ed., McGraw-Hill, New York, 1973.

7. Bartee, T., *Digital Computer Fundamentals*, 4th ed. McGraw-Hill, New York, 1977.

8. Tannenbaum, A. S., *Structured Computer Organization*, Prentice-Hall, Englewood Cliffs, N.J., 1976.

9. Dietmeyer, D. L., *Logical Design of Digital Systems*, Allyn and Bacon, Boston, 1971.

10. Hill, F. J. and G. R. Peterson, *Introduction to Switching Theory and Logical Design*, 2nd ed., Wiley, New York, 1974.

7 HARDWARE REALIZATIONS

7.1 INTRODUCTION

In the last chapter we showed how the functioning of a digital system can be described in terms of an AHPL control sequence. The next step in the design process is to translate this description into hardware. Some of this has already been done. In Chapter 6 we developed the basic data structure of the system, i.e., the internal organization of registers, buses, and processing logic, in parallel with the writing of the control sequence. Another major part of the design process is the development of the control unit. In Section 4.6 a particular form of hardwired control unit was introduced. For readers whose primary objective is to gain an understanding of computer functioning from the user's point of view, the material on hardware in preceding chapters will be adequate for most purposes. Such readers may prefer to skim over the material in this chapter rather quickly. Sections 7.3 and 7.6 introduce some extensions of AHPL that will be needed in later chapters and should be covered in some detail. The remaining sections are directed primarily to the reader who expects to design digital systems and has the objective of filling in some of the fine points of hardware realizations that are not evident from previous chapters.

Section 7.2 deals with the problems of starting and stopping complex digital systems. Although not essential to the developments in succeeding chapters, this material is important if real systems are to be built. Section 7.3 deals with the problems of controlling devices that cannot respond in a single clock period. This material is very important to the designer, as is the material in Section 7.4, which explores the hardware implications of conditional transfers in considerable detail.

Section 7.5 deals with hardware compilers. The use of computers to mechanize parts of the design process is virtually a necessity in the design of computers or other systems of comparable complexity. It is easy to write a statement such as

$$20. \, If, AC \leftarrow \text{ADD} \, (AC; MD)$$

and it is clear what is to occur. But the actual implementation will require the wiring of hundreds of connections, every one of which must be individually specified. The manner in which computers take over such detail work is discussed in this section. This material is not essential to later chapters but is very helpful in providing a clearer picture of the manner in which the necessary hardware can be determined from the control sequence.

Section 7.6 provides a detailed analysis of propagation delays in the data paths and the control unit. This material is critical, since it is these delays that set the basic limit on the speed of any digital system. Another important consideration is the design of the processing logic, particularly in the Arithmetic-Logic Unit. The basic tool here is the combinational logic subroutine, the basic concepts of which were introduced in Section 5.5. In Section 7.7 we shall expand these concepts and apply them to the design of complete units of considerable complexity. Except for clarifying matters of notation, this material is not essential for later chapters. Finally, Section 7.8 presents a complete design example. Although not essential, this example is useful in demonstrating the integration of concepts developed in the other sections.

As a final note, most of the material in this chapter is based on the use of a hardwired control unit. This type of control unit offers maximum speed and is usually preferable for special-purpose, low-volume applications. Another type of control unit is the microprogrammed control unit. These are usually slower than hard-wired units but will often be more economical for high-volume applications. Microprogramming will be treated in Chapter 8.

7.2 STARTING, STOPPING, AND RESETTING

One of the more subtle problems associated with the design of a control unit is how to get it started. With the control unit design we have so far assumed, once a single-clock-period level has been established at the input to any single D flip-flop, the desired sequence of levels will propagate through the sequence of control flip-flops. But the reader may well have wondered just how that sequence of levels is initiated.

The reader will recall that the first step in the control sequence for SIC was a waiting loop for a synchronized *start* signal,

$$1. \rightarrow \overline{\text{SYN}(start)}/(1)$$

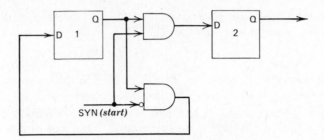

Figure 7.1. Implementation of SIC step No. 1.

Figure 7.1 shows the direct hardware realization of this step. Note that the presence of a *start* signal is not by itself sufficient to start the sequence. Unless flip-flop No. 1 is set, the output of both AND gates will be 0, regardless of the value of *start*. One possibility might be to add an OR gate at the D input to flip-flop No. 1 to allow application of some special signal to set that flip-flop. However, we must also assure that all other control flip-flops are reset in order to prevent several control signals from propagating through the system at the same time. In other words, the whole system must be reset before it can be started.

Most systems include provision for manually resetting the entire system in preparation for starting. Appropriate signals could be OR'ed into the D inputs of the control flip-flops, but it is more usual to use the direct SET and RESET inputs. Figure 7.2 shows the realization of the first few steps of the SIC control sequence, with the reset line added, and also shows the timing of a typical reset-start sequence, in which we have assumed that the computer happened to be at step 3 of the sequence at the time of the reset.

When the *reset* line goes low (on most flip-flops the direct inputs are activated by the signal going low) flip-flop No. 1 is set and all other flip-flops in the control unit are reset. When the *reset* line goes high, step 1 is enabled and the *start* signal is tested. As long as *start* is low, control will remain at step 1. When *start* goes high, control moves to step 2 to start the normal sequence. This reset action will be indicated by the statement

CONTROL RESET (1)

appearing after the END SEQUENCE statement, with the number in parentheses indicating the control step to which the system returns when reset.

The above system of start and reset will be suitable if control step 1 can be entered only by means of control reset. This may be the case in

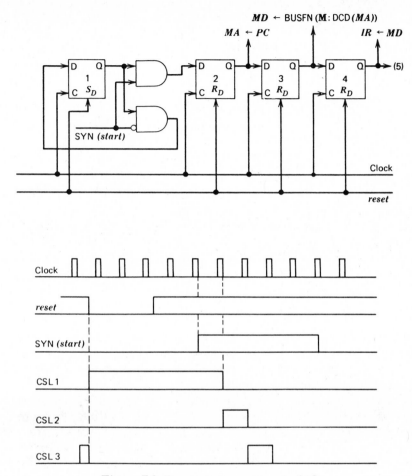

Figure 7.2. Reset-start sequence in SIC.

some systems but not necessarily in computers in which the implementation of various HALT commands must be considered. In Chapter 6, the HALT instruction was indicated at step 28, but consideration of the realization was deferred. The simplest way to implement HALT command would be with a DEAD END at step 28, indicating that propagation of the control level is simply terminated. The hardware implementation of steps 26 to 28 is shown in Fig. 7.3. Note that there is no gate at step 27 corresponding to the term $(IR_6 \wedge IR_7)$, so that if that condition occurs, indicating a HALT, the sequence simply terminates, leaving all control flip-flops in the reset state. Thus DEAD END is a dummy statement in the sense that it indicates no hardware, included

223

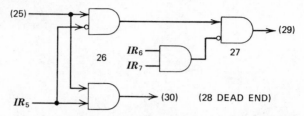

Figure 7.3. Implementation of HALT by DEAD END.

for clarity and to satisfy the syntactical requirement that all branch statements must go somewhere.

Since DEAD END as described above will leave all control flip-flops
reset, the computer cannot be started again without a control reset, to
enable step 1. If a reset operation affected nothing but the control unit,
this would be satisfactory; but a computer reset is often used to shut
everything down and start over when something goes wrong. In addition
to resetting the control unit, it may also reset the I/O devices, the interrupt system, the status indicators, even the data registers. HALT is often
used to stop a program to give the operator a chance to intervene, without otherwise affecting the status of the program, so that a computer
reset would be undesirable. We shall, therefore implement HALT by
returning control to step 1, to wait for a *start* signal without otherwise
affecting the status of the computer. This is done at step 27, as shown
in Fig. 7.4, and step 28 is eliminated.

With the above implementation of HALT, the timing of the *start* signal
must be considered more carefully. A modern computer executes an
instruction in a few microseconds or less and can execute a complete
program in a small fraction of a second. If a *start* signal is derived directly from a manual pushbutton, it may last thousands of microseconds.
Thus, when the start button is pushed, the computer might complete
the program, execute a HALT, and return to step 1 before the button has
been released, in which event it would start again. Such false restarts
can be prevented by the use of a *single-level generator*. Although the

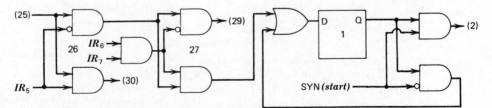

Figure 7.4. Implementation of HALT by return to step 1.

single-level generator consists of only one flip-flop, it must be represented in AHPL as a separate module.

MODULE: SL (*a*)
        INPUT: *a*
        OUTPUTS: SL
        MEMORY: *slf*
END SEQUENCE
        $slf \leftarrow \overline{a}$
        $SL = \overline{slf} \wedge a$
END

The module has no control flip-flops and only one data flip-flop. The single-level module with a synchronized start level as its input is illustrated in Fig. 7.5a; the corresponding timing diagram is shown in Fig. 7.5b. The output of the single level module is 1 from the time its input goes to 1 until the arrival of the next clock pulse. Since SYN (*start*) is synchronized, the output SL(SYN(*start*)) is a 1-period level. Step 1 may now be written

$$1. \rightarrow (\overline{SL(SYN(start))})/(1)$$

The reader will note that the SL module has been called in the same manner as a combinational logic function, although it is a sequential circuit. This is possible because the SL module, although sequential, has no independent control section. It operates directly under the control of the computer, and is thus treated in the same manner as a combinational logic function, as though it were a part of the main computer, rather than as a separate module.

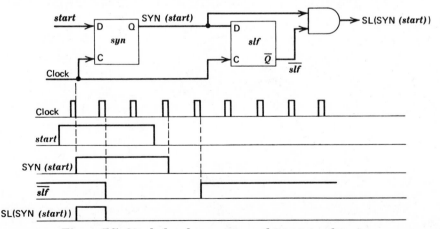

Figure 7.5. Single-level generator and input synchronizer.

7.3 MULTIPERIOD OPERATIONS

In writing the SIC control sequence in Chapter 6, we assumed that all transfer operations could be completed in one clock period. However, there are many cases in which transfers or logic operations may require more than one clock period. Memory access is one such situation. Because of cost, main random access memory is often realized in technology that is slower than register memory. Since the majority of transfers involve registers, the clock rate is set accordingly, and any slower transfers will require multiple clock periods.

As discussed in Chapter 3, many different technologies may be considered for implementing random access memories. These many types of memories differ greatly in signal and timing requirements. In terms of the control sequence steps required to control them, the majority of memory systems can be grouped into three categories, which we shall refer to as *clocked, slow synchronous,* and *asynchronous.* The clocked memory is the simplest to handle, being logically equivalent to an array of clocked registers. Normally realized in TTL or ECL technology, such a memory is fully compatible in speed with the control unit. The general model for a clocked memory is shown in Fig. 3.13. There are address lines, separate input and output lines for data, and a single control line, *write enable*, which is equivalent to the clock line for a register.

To apply such a memory in SIC, the address lines would be driven by the output of MA, the data in lines would be driven by the output of MD, and the data out lines will drive the input of MD. For a read operation, if an address is applied to the address lines by loading MA in one clock period, then the data is available to be transferred to MD at the end of the next clock period. Thus a pair of statements such as

   2. $MA \leftarrow PC$
   3. $MD \leftarrow \text{BUSFN}(\mathbf{M}; \text{DCD}(MA))$

is sufficient to specify a read operation. For a write operation, if the address and data to be written are supplied in one clock period, applying the next clock pulse to the *write enable* line will complete the operation. Thus two statements of the form

  21. $MD \leftarrow AC; MA \leftarrow IR_{5:17}$
  22. $\mathbf{M} * \text{DCD}(MA) \leftarrow MD$

are sufficient to specify a write operation.

Such clocked memories are generally limited to rather small size by cost factors. For larger memories, the slow synchronous or asynchronous

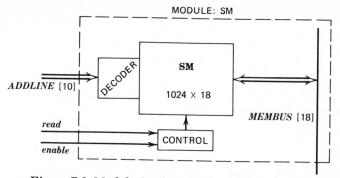

Figure 7.6. Model of a slow synchronous memory.

memories are usually preferable in terms of cost. The slow synchronous memory type, of which the static MOS memory is the most common example, is not clocked by short pulses in the manner of registers but instead requires level control signals extending for one or more clock periods. We consider such memories to be synchronous in the sense that the timing of control signals is entirely controlled by the central control unit. Such units also commonly share a single bus for both input and output of data. Figure 7.6 shows the basic model for a typical memory of this type, consisting of 1024 words of 18 bits each. Addresses are provided over 10-bit *ADDLINE*; data are transferred over the 18-bit *MEMBUS*. There are two control lines, *read* and *enable*. The line *read* must be at the 1-level for a read operation, at the 0-level for a write. For a read operation, the address must be stable on *ADDLINE* for a minimum of one clock period before *enable* goes to 1 and must remain stable as long as *enable* is up. The output data will be available two clock periods after *enable* goes up and will remain available as long as *enable* is up. The line *read* must be stable for the same period as the address. For a write operation, the data to be written must be stable for the same period as the address, for one period before *enable* goes up and for two periods after.

Because of the bus and separate control lines, the memory must be declared as a separate module and the communication lines must be added to the declarations for SIC.

OUTPUTS: *ADDLINE*[10]; *read* ; *enable*
COMBUS: *MEMBUS*[18]

These lines would similarly be declared as INPUTS and COMBUS in the description of the memory module. We shall assume that *ADDLINE* will be driven by the low-order 10 bits of *MA*, as specified by the statement

$$ADDLINE = MA_{3:12}$$

after END SEQUENCE.

With this model and connections as indicated, a typical read sequence would appear as follows.

2. *MA* ← *PC*
3. *read* = 1
4. *enable* = 1; *read* = 1
5 *enable* = 1; *read* = 1; *MD* ← *MEMBUS*

The clock pulse at the end of step 2 establishes the address in *MA* and thus on *ADDLINE*. At the beginning of step 3, *read* is set to 1. At the start of step 4, after a delay of 1 period, *enable* is set to 1, and *read* continues at 1. This condition is held through step 5, until the data word is transferred into *MD* from *MEMBUS* by the clock pulse at the end of step 5, two clock periods after *enable* was set to 1.

A typical write sequence would appear as follows.

8. *MA* ← *PC*; *MD* ← *AC*
9. *MEMBUS* = *MD*; *read* = 0
10. *MEMBUS* = *MD*; *enable* = 1; *read* = 0
11. *MEMBUS* = *MD*; *enable* = 1; *read* = 0

The most common forms of asynchronous memory in use at this time are core memory and dynamic MOS memory. These types of memories will usually have their own timing and control circuitry, and are best treated as separate asynchronous modules. Such a module will probably have its own intrinsic address and data registers, which cannot be treated as CPU registers. Let us now consider how a typical asynchronous memory organization could be incorporated in the SIC control sequence.

The organization of the memory module is shown in Fig. 7.7. The memory module includes the memory itself (8192 × 18); address and data registers (*MAR* and *MDR*); address and data input lines (*MEMADDR*[13] and *DATAIN*[18]; data output lines *DATAOUT*[18]; control input lines (*read* and *write*) and a control output line, *busy*. The control lines are at the 0-level when the memory is not in use. To initiate a memory operation, the CPU will set *read* or *write* to logic 1 and gate appropriate information onto the address and data lines. The memory will respond by gating *MEMADDR* into *MAR* and, for a write operation, *DATAIN* into *MDR*, and will then raise *busy* to the 1-level. At this point

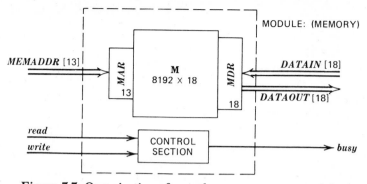

Figure 7.7. Organization of asynchronous memory module.

the CPU may lower *read* or *write* and clear the address and data lines. When the memory cycle is complete and, for a read operation, the requested word is on the **DATAOUT** lines, *busy* will return to the 0-level. It is important to note that the CPU "sees" the memory only in terms of the communications lines. The existence of the **MAR** and **MDR** registers will not be indicated in the CPU sequence in any way. We have mentioned them solely for the sake of clarity in the discussion of memory operation.

The first modification required in the SIC control sequence is to add the memory communications lines to the INPUT and OUTPUT and BUS declarations.

> INPUTS: *busy; DATAOUT*[18]
> OUTPUTS: *read; write; MEMADDR*[13]; *DATAIN*[18]
> BUS: *MEMADBUS*[13]

The register **MA** is no longer required in the CPU. In the CPU sequence, **MA** appears only as a destination for transfers from **PC** or **IR**. It never serves as a source, nor are its contents ever manipulated. Steps could be saved by eliminating transfers to **MA** and declaring a **MEMADBUS**. The outputs of either **PC** or **IR** may be connected to **MEMADBUS**, and the **MEMADDR** lines to memory are permanently connected to **MEMADBUS** by the statement

> **MEMADDR = MEMADBUS**

following END SEQUENCE. If **MA** remains in the CPU, we would write

> **MEMADDR = MA**

following END SEQUENCE.

Although we could dispense with the *MA* register, it is desirable to retain the *MD* register. In the implementation of the ISZ command the contents of *MD* must be manipulated, independent of any memory operations. This cannot be done in *MDR*, since that register cannot be controlled by the CPU. We shall also find a separate *MD* register useful in I/O operations. On the other hand, there is no longer any need to route all memory operations through *MD*. Instead, *DATAOUT* can be an input to the *OBUS*, and *DATAIN* an output of the *OBUS*.

The use of an asynchronous memory will also necessitate changes in the body of the control sequence. Assuming no *MA*, let us consider the modifications necessary to the SIC control sequence steps that fetch a new instruction. The original steps (from Chapter 6) and the new steps are shown side-by-side for ease of comparison.

2. *MA* ← *PC*   2. *MEMADBUS* = *PC*; *read* = 1
                                          → SYN(*busy*)/(2)

3. *MD* ← BUSFN(M; DCD(*MA*))   3. null
                                          → SYN(*busy*)/(3)

4. *IR* ← *MD*   4. NO DELAY
                                      OBUS = 0, *DATAOUT*;
                                        IR ← *OBUS*$_{1:18}$

         (Old sequence)   (New sequence)

Since we no longer have an *MA* register, the new step 2 connects the output of *PC* to *MEMADBUS*. Step 2 also sets *read* to 1 and waits for *busy* to go up, acknowledging the read request. Step 3 then waits for *busy* to go down, signaling completion of the memory cycle; step 4 then transfers the word from *DATAOUT* to *IR*, via the *OBUS*. Note that there is no need to pass the instruction word through *MD*, so we take advantage of the connection of *DATAOUT* to the *OBUS* to move the instruction directly to *IR*.

The control unit and timing diagram for these new steps are shown in Fig. 7.8. The logical 1 on *read* is provided by connecting CSL2 to the *read* line through an OR gate. The other inputs to the OR gate will be control levels from other read steps in the sequence. Control holds at step 2 until *busy* goes up and then holds at step 3 until *busy* goes down. Note that CSL4 overlaps CSL3, a situation characteristic of NO DELAY steps. The interaction in this sequence, raising *read* and then waiting for *busy* to go up as an acknowledgment, and then waiting for *busy* to go down, as an indication that the operation is complete, is an example of a *handshaking interchange*. This is a standard technique of communications between systems, and it will be more fully discussed in Chapters 9 and 10.

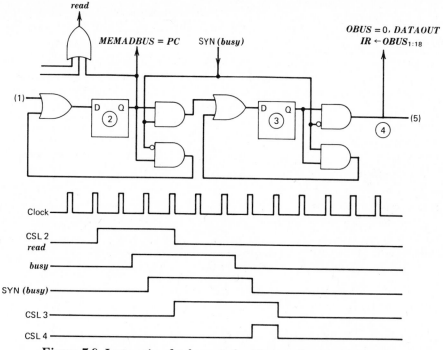

Figure 7.8. Instruction fetch control with asynchronous memory.

The reader may recall from Chapter 3 that in a read operation in a core memory, the data word read is available about halfway through the memory cycle, since the word has to be rewritten after being read. Because of this, a core memory will often have another output line, *data-ready*, indicating when the requested word is available on the *DA-TAOUT* lines. Obviously, the operation of the computer can be speeded up if the CPU picks up the word as soon as this signal appears, rather than wait for the end of the complete memory cycle. However, doing so will create certain complications. Since the sequence proceeds without waiting for the end of the memory cycle, it is possible that the sequence may reach another step requiring a memory operation before the previous cycle is complete. Similar considerations apply to write operations, in which it would be possible for the CPU to proceed to other nonmemory operations as soon as *busy* goes up, acknowledging receipt of the data to be stored. Modification of the SIC control sequence for other memory operations and consideration of the problems of overlapping CPU operations and memory operations will be left as exercises for the reader. Throughout the remainder of the book, the clocked memory will be assumed except where otherwise specifically indicated.

Multiperiod delays will also be required if there are logic operations that need more than one clock period to complete. One place where this situation may occur is in the adder. For reasons of delay in combinational logic, as will be discussed later in this chapter, the time from the gating of the operands to the adder inputs to the appearance of the correct sum at the output may be much longer than the time required for a simple register transfer. In the case of SIC, this would require that the outputs of *AC* and *MD* be held on the *ABUS* and *BBUS* for several clock periods.

In Chapter 6 an alternative control sequence was presented, which branched to separate steps for each of the AND, TAD, and LAC operations. This approach can more easily handle unequal timing of operations than can the conditional transfer approach. The corresponding steps 17 to 20 with busing connections given explicitly are

17. NO DELAY
   $\rightarrow ((\overline{IR_1} \wedge IR_2), (IR_1 \wedge \overline{IR_2}), (IR_1 \wedge IR_2))/(18, 19, 20)$
18. $BBUS = MD; OBUS = 0, BBUS; AC \leftarrow OBUS_{1:18}$
   $\rightarrow (24)$
19. $ABUS = AC; BBUS = MD; OBUS = 0, (ABUS \wedge BBUS);$
   $AC \leftarrow OBUS_{1:18}$
   $\rightarrow (24)$
20. $ABUS = AC; BBUS = MD$
   $OBUS = \text{ADD}(ABUS; BBUS); If, AC \leftarrow OBUS$
   $\rightarrow (24)$

Let us also assume an adder that requires three clock periods to develop a sum. Since we have separated control for the ADD step, only step 20 need be modified. To allow for the extra delay, we replace the above step 20 with the following three steps.

20-1. $ABUS = AC; BBUS = MD$
20-2. $ABUS = AC; BBUS = MD$
20-3. $ABUS = AC; BBUS = MD;$
   $OBUS = \text{ADD}(ABUS; BBUS); If, AC \leftarrow OBUS$
   $\rightarrow (24)$

The corresponding control circuit is shown in Fig. 7.9. Note that the outputs of the three step-20 flip-flops are OR'ed to hold *AC* and *MD* on the *ABUS* and *BBUS* for the three clock periods required to allow for adder propagation.

The above approach is satisfactory for short delays but would be very expensive for long delays. For long delays it will generally be preferable to count the required number of clock periods or use a one-shot to generate an arbitrary delay.

As an example of the former approach, let us consider the same sequence as above, but let us now assume that eight clock periods are required for adder propagation. We shall provide a 3-bit counter, *ADDCNT*, to count the eight periods of delay. *ADDCNT* will be reset to zero at step 16, at the same time *MD* is loaded with the memory output. The original step 20 will be replaced by the following.

20. *ABUS* = *AC*; *BBUS* = *MD*; *ADDCNT* ← INC (*ADDCNT*);
     OBUS = ADD(*ABUS*; *BBUS*);
     (*lf*, *AC*) * ($\wedge$/*ADDCNT*) ← *OBUS*
     →($\overline{\wedge/ADDCNT}$), ($\wedge$/*ADDCNT*)/(20, 24)

Step 20 provides a waiting loop that holds at this step, incrementing *ADDCNT* each clock time, until the count reaches 111. Since the branch is on the value of *ADDCNT* prior to incrementing, a count of 111 indicates that the sequence has held at this step for eight clock periods. At this time the transfer is completed and control branches to step 24.

As an example of the use of a one-shot, let us consider another adder requiring 10 clock periods for propagation delay. We shall declare a synchronized one-shot, *addsyn*.

ONE-SHOT: *addsyn*(10)

This one-shot will be triggered at step 17, by adding the transfer statement

17. *addsyn**($IR_1 \wedge IR_2$) ← 1 NO DELAY

Step 20 will now be

20. *ABUS* = *AC*; *BBUS* = *MD*;
     OBUS = $\underline{ADD}$(*ABUS*; *BBUS*)
     (*lf*, *AC*) * $\underline{addsyn}$ ← *OBUS*
     → ($\overline{addsyn}$, *addsyn*)/(20, 24)

Thus the operation will be the same as in the counter realization except that step 20 will wait for the end of the 10-period delay generated by *addsyn*.

We have seen three methods of providing multiperiod delays. The choice among these methods will be based primarily on cost. For delays of four periods or less, the first approach, adding extra delay flip-flops will generally be preferable. For longer delays, the one-shot approach will probably be cheaper than the counter approach. However, it should be noted that one-shots are prone to erroneous triggering due to noise, and some designers feel they should be avoided at all costs.

7.4 CONDITIONAL TRANSFERS AND CONNECTIONS

In Chapter 4 it was shown that the use of the conditional transfer can shorten certain control sequences and often save control hardware. Since that point we have introduced the SIC busing structure. When busing is used, the bus connection statements as well as transfers may be conditional. The availability of conditional connections as well as transfers extends some of the techniques we have considered thus far. As a first example, let us consider again the implementation of AND, TAD, and LAC in the SIC control sequence. To simplify the problem, let us initially assume that we have a fast adder, which requires only one clock period for propagation of the sum. With this simplification the alternate three-way branch implementation of these three operations would be as shown in Fig. 7.9 except that there would be only one control flip-flop for step 20 and no OR gate.

A comparison of the three steps shows that they differ only in the connections to the *OBUS* and in the fact that the ADD instruction requires a transfer into the link. Step 18 does not gate *AC* onto the *ABUS*, but it would make no difference if it did, since only *BBUS* is gated to *OBUS*. It thus appears that it is likely to be advantageous to combine these steps into a conditional transfer and eliminate two of the control flip-flops. The conditional transfer form of these three transfers, in terms of bus connections, would be as follows.

17. $ABUS = AC; BBUS = MD;$
    $OBUS = ((0, BBUS) \; ! \; (0, ABUS \wedge BBUS) \; ! \; (ADD \; (ABUS; BBUS)))*$
    $((\overline{IR}_1 \wedge IR_2), (IR_1 \wedge \overline{IR}_2), (IR_1 \wedge IR_2));$
    $AC \leftarrow OBUS_{1:18}; \; lf * (IR_1 \wedge IR_2) \leftarrow OBUS_0$
    $\rightarrow (24)$

The control unit realization of this conditional transfer is shown in Fig. 7.10. The reader will note, by comparison with Fig. 7.9, that the basic change we have made is to delay the decision as to what transfer is to be made; the same decision logic is required, but the decision is made one clock period later. This emphasizes an important point that is often confusing. The transfer in any given step is completed by the clock pulse at the *end* of the control period associated with that step. The delay of one clock period is to allow time for the results of the

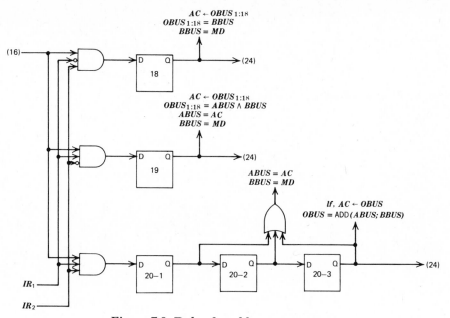

Figure 7.9. Delay for adder propagation.

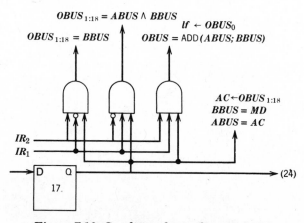

Figure 7.10. Conditional transfer at step 17.

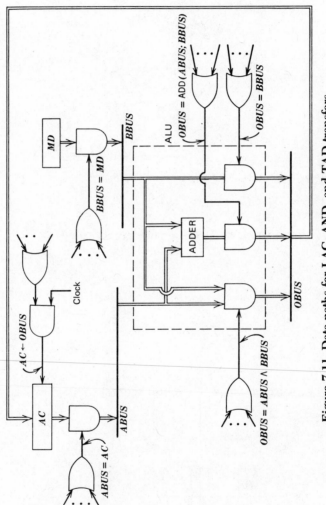

Figure 7.11. Data paths for LAC, AND, and TAD transfers.

previous transfer to propagate. In this case all three transfers must await the propagation of the new contents of *MD*, which was loaded at step 16. Since all three steps are waiting for the same thing, it is clearly wasteful to provide three separate delays. The conditional transfer is essentially equivalent to a delay for *MD* propagation followed by a branch to three separate NO DELAY transfers.

It is clear then that the use of a conditional transfer can simplify the control unit by eliminating delay flip-flops. Let us now consider the effect of this approach on the data section. Figure 7.11 shows the data paths involved in these three transfers (neglecting the link for the present). The inputs to the OR gates will be the control signal levels from all steps requiring that particular connection or transfer. If we adopt the approach of three separate transfers, the OR gate driving the AND gate that gates *MD* onto *BBUS* will receive inputs from steps 18, 19, 20, as will the OR gate controlling the loading of *AC*. But if the conditional transfer approach is used, only the signal from step 17 is needed for all three transfers. We also note that steps 18, 19, and 20 all branch to step 24, requiring three inputs to an OR gate at step 24, compared to one input from step 17, if the conditional transfer is used.

In this particular instance the use of a conditional transfer appears to be clearly preferable to a branch to separate transfers. Recall, however, that we simplified the problem by assuming an adder fast enough to complete addition in one clock period. If this is not the case, the conditional transfer approach will require that step 17 be a multiple-delay step. This delay can be realized by any of the techniques discussed in the last section, but it will result in slowing the LAC and AND transfers down to the speed of the ADD transfer, which will in turn slow the execution of programs.

As an example of conditional bus connections, let us consider step 29, which implements the various operate instructions that manipulate *AC* and the link. The connection of the output of $OBUS_0$ to *lf* can be used for setting and clearing *lf*. Manipulation of *AC* will take place through the *ABUS* and connections of *ABUS* or $\overline{ABUS}$ to $OBUS_{1:18}$ leaving $OBUS_0$ $= 0$. By connecting a control line directly to an input of the $OBUS_0$ OR gate, we can enforce $OBUS_0 = 1$. A survey of Table 6.3 reveals that this OR gate has only four inputs so that fan-in will not be a problem. Since control has branched to a separate step for HALT ($IR_6 \wedge IR_7 = 1$), the link can be clocked whenever $IR_6 \vee IR_7 = 1$. By establishing $OBUS_0 = 1$ if and only if $IR_7 = 1$, the link will be set and cleared as appropriate.

The expressions for generating the new value of *AC* are determined from the maps in Fig. 7.12. We note first from Table 6.1 and Fig. 7.12a that no operation is to take place if $IR_8 = IR_9 = 0$. Thus *AC* is not clocked

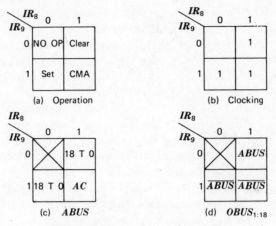

Figure 7.12. Analysis of step 29.

for this case which then becomes a "don't care" in determining control expressions for the bus connections. In Fig. 7.12c we note that 18 ⊤ 0 is connected to the *ABUS* when *AC* is to be set or cleared. In turn, $\overline{ABUS}$ or *ABUS* is connected to *OBUS* for set or clear *AC*, respectively. To complement *AC*, the input to *ABUS* is *AC*, and *ABUS* is then complemented enroute to the *OBUS*. From Fig. 7.12c we see that the condition for connecting *AC* to the *ABUS* is $IR_8 \wedge IR_9$. If no control signal is issued, the output of *ABUS* will be 18 ⊤ 0. From Fig. 7.12d we see that *ABUS* is connected to *OBUS* if $IR_9 = 0$, and $\overline{ABUS}$ to *OBUS* if $IR_9 = 1$. Therefore, step 29 appears as follows.

29. $ABUS = AC * (IR_8 \wedge IR_9)$
      $OBUS_{1:18} = (\overline{ABUS} \,!\, ABUS) * (\overline{IR_9}, IR_9)$
      $AC * (IR_8 \vee IR_9) \leftarrow OBUS_{1:18}$
      $OBUS_0 = IR_7$
      $lf * (IR_6 \vee IR_7) \leftarrow OBUS_0$

We have seen that the conditional transfer can provide hardware savings in situations where transfers that occur at the same point in the sequence have some bus connections in common. As another example let us consider the rotate operations, which were initially implemented by branches to separate transfers. With the bus connections specified, the rotate operations in the first event time are given by the following step:

30. $\rightarrow (\overline{IR}_4, IR_4)/(31, 32)$
31. $ABUS = AC; OBUS = ABUS, lf; lf, AC \leftarrow OBUS$
      $\rightarrow (33)$

32. $ABUS = AC$; $OBUS = ABUS_{17}$, lf, $ABUS_{0:16}$;
lf, $AC \leftarrow OBUS$

In considering the conditional transfer at step 17, we saw that the conditional form eliminated two control flip-flops by consolidating the delays in three steps into one delay. In this case it appears that no delay flip-flops are needed. Recall again that the purpose of delay in a control step is to allow time for the propagation of the results of a previous transfer. The **IR** register was loaded at step 4, and the delay at step 5 allowed for propagation of the results. Since rotate is an operate instruction, **AC** must have been loaded by another instruction. Thus all three steps can be NO DELAY steps, the control circuit for which is shown in Fig. 7.13a.

Considering this control circuit, we see that the only thing IR_4 controls is what is gated onto the **OBUS**. Control proceeds to step 33; **AC** goes onto the **ABUS**; and **OBUS** is loaded into lf, **AC**, regardless of the value of IR_4. The same results can be accomplished more simply by the following conditional transfer.

30. $ABUS = AC$; NO DELAY
$OBUS = ((ABUS, lf) \ ! \ (ABUS_{17}, lf, ABUS_{0:16})) * (\overline{IR}_4, IR_4)$;
lf, $AC \leftarrow OBUS$
$\rightarrow (33)$

In this case no control flip-flops are eliminated, but one OR gate is saved in the control unit, and two OR-gate inputs will be saved in the data unit.

Let us next consider whether the same conditional transfer should be used for the rotates in event times 2 and 3. If we consider the flow chart for the operate instructions (Fig. 6.8), we note that the steps in event time 2 (except for NOOP) alter or are affected by the contents of lf and **AC**. We further note that **AC** and lf are altered in event time 1, except in the event of HALT or NOOP, so that we must allow delay time before proceeding with further transfers or the SZL branch. There are several steps in event time 2 that must wait for the same thing, for the changes in **AC** and lf in event time 1 to propagate. As was the case with steps 18, 19, and 20 above, it would be wasteful to associate a separate delay with each step. We shall therefore add a delay to step 33; the first step in event time 2 and all the other steps in this event time will be NO DELAY steps. Similarly, we shall make step 43 a DELAY step and all the other steps in event time 3 will be NO DELAY steps. With the elimination of the delays, the rotates in event times 2 and 3 can, as shown in Fig. 7.13b, be realized by the same conditional transfer as in event time 1.

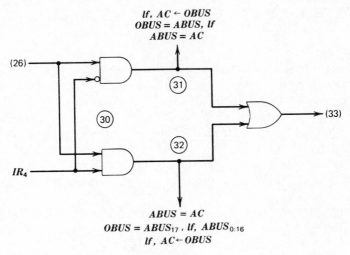

If, AC ← OBUS
OBUS = ABUS, If
ABUS = AC

ABUS = AC
OBUS = ABUS$_{17}$, If, ABUS$_{0:16}$
If, AC← OBUS

(a)

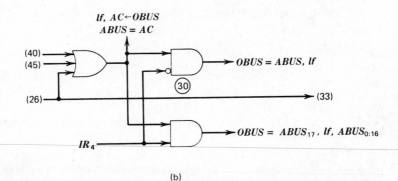

If, AC←OBUS
ABUS = AC

OBUS = ABUS, If

OBUS = ABUS$_{17}$, If, ABUS$_{0:16}$

(b)

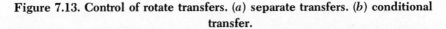

Figure 7.13. Control of rotate transfers. (*a*) separate transfers. (*b*) conditional transfer.

The reader may wonder why we did not use these conditional transfers and shared delays when we first developed the operate sequence
in Chapter 6. The reason is that a designer will never see all the possible
consolidations the first time through a control sequence. Design, as we
have noted before, is an iterative process. The first time through a control sequence, the designer should keep it simple. If he is not sure
whether a conditional transfer is practical, he should branch to separate
steps. If he is not sure if a delay is needed, he should leave it in. When

the sequence is complete, he will then develop the circuit for the corresponding control unit, either manually or with the aid of a hardware compiler program. The designer will then check through this circuit, just as we did above, to look for places where it can be simplified. When he makes changes, he will correct the control sequence accordingly. If he is using a hardware compiler, he will probably recompile the circuit and then check to see that it came out the way he intended. Depending on the skill of the designer, he may go around this loop several times before he is satisfied that the design is as simple as he can get it. The design of a digital system is a very complex task; you should not expect to get it right the first time.

7.5 HARDWARE COMPILERS

In the last section and elsewhere we have mentioned *hardware compilers*, without any indication of just what they are or do, beyond a general implication that they somehow mechanize the design process. Because the design and manufacture of a computer is such a complex process, a great deal of effort has been directed toward developing ways to use computers themselves in the design process, primarily because the speed and accuracy of computers is essential to handle the thousands, even millions, of small details involved in the process of designing and building a computer. Every computer manufacturer has an array of programs to assist in the design process. Every manufacturer does it somewhat differently and nomenclature in this field is not at all standardized. We use the term *hardware compiler* to signify a program that accepts as an input an AHPL control sequence and certain sequence-independent information and produces a complete network description of the system. A network description may take a variety of forms but will probably include block diagrams and wiring lists. Block diagrams, as we have seen, show the relationships between various elements in pictorial form, in varying degrees of detail. Wiring lists are lists of the connections between every input and every output of every element— gates, registers, flip-flops, etc.—in the system.

The basic input to the compiler is the AHPL sequence. The declaration section of the AHPL description directly specifies the registers and buses, the inputs and outputs. However, the logic elements required to implement the control unit and the interconnections required in the data unit are only indirectly specified, by the sequence itself. In preceding chapters we have discussed a type of control unit in which there is a very direct relationship between each step in a control sequence and the corresponding hardware in the control unit. We have also discussed the gating in the data unit and the manner in which the control signals control the data flow. Clearly, the hardware compiler must include a set of rules for translating the control sequence into a corresponding hardware configuration. This set of rules will be based on the designer's choice of the form of hardware realization to be used so that the design of the compiler itself is a basic component of the computer design.

The task of generating a wiring list for a sequential module divides naturally into the following two phases.

   I. Generation of Data Network
  II. Wiring of Control Network and
      Connecting to the Data Network

Generation of the data network is the most interesting, and we shall consider this phase first. A flow chart detailing the subtasks of the data network generation process is given in Fig. 7.14. The following control sequence was chosen as a brief example that suitably illustrates each of the data network compiler subtasks. The module is concerned with the input and output and shifting of data within an 18-bit register. The reader should not be concerned with the function of the module, since it has been devised only as a vehicle for illustrating the compiler.

$$\text{MODULE:}\quad \text{MULTISHIFT}$$

MEMORY: $A[18]; CNT[3]$
INPUTS: $a; b; X[6]$
OUTPUTS: $z; look; A_{0:5}$

1. $A \leftarrow 0, A_{0:16}$
   $\rightarrow (a)/(3)$
2. $A \leftarrow 0, A_{0:16}$
   $\rightarrow (1)$
3. $CNT \leftarrow a, b, 0;$
   $A_{0:11} \leftarrow X, A_{0:5}$
   $\rightarrow (b)/(1)$
4. $A \leftarrow 1, A_{0:16}$
   $CNT \leftarrow \text{INC}(CNT)$
   $\rightarrow (\wedge/CNT)/(4)$
5. $A_{0:5} \leftarrow ((A_{6:11} \wedge A_{12:17}) \,!\, (A_{6:11})) * (\bar{b}, b);$
   $A_{6:17} * b \leftarrow X, A_{0:5}; look = 1$
   $\rightarrow (1)$

END SEQUENCE
   $z = A_{17}$

END

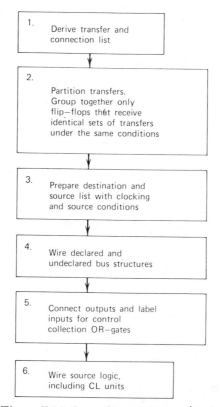

Figure 7.14. Compiling of data network.

The data network compiler is not concerned with branch statements or the order of execution of transfers and connection. Step 1 of Fig. 7.14 causes a table of all transfers to be formed without regard to order but with a list of source conditions and clock conditions. The transfer table for the above control sequence is given in Fig. 7.15. Notice that transfers which may occur at the same step with the same destination are listed separately. For example, $A_{0:5}$ is always clocked at step 5. However, two separate transfers are listed with this destination, one with source condition $5 \wedge \overline{b}$ the other $5 \wedge b$. The later notation indicates that $A_{6:11}$ is connected to the data inputs of $A_{0:5}$ if and only if control is in step 5 and $b = 1$. Notice that the same transfer appears in both steps 1 and 2. This transfer is listed only once with source and clock conditions $1 \vee 2$.

The second step of the compiling process is to partition the destination vectors so that only flip-flops with potentially identical input networks

Destination	Source	Source Conditions	Clock Conditions
1.	$A \leftarrow 0, A_{0:16}$	$1 \vee 2$	$1 \vee 2$
2.	$CNT \leftarrow a, b, 0$	3	3
3.	$A_{0:11} \leftarrow X, A_{0:5}$	3	3
4.	$A \leftarrow 1, A_{0:16}$	4	4
5.	$CNT \leftarrow INC(CNT)$	4	4
6.	$A_{0:5} \leftarrow A_{6:11} \wedge A_{12:17}$	$5 \wedge \bar{b}$	5
7.	$A_{6:17} \leftarrow X, A_{0:5}$	5	$5 \wedge b$
8.	$look = 1$	5	N/A
9.	$A_{0:5} \leftarrow A_{6:11}$	$5 \wedge b$	5
10.	$z = A_{17}$	ALL	N/A

Figure 7.15. Transfer Table.

are grouped together. This involves inspection of the destinations in the transfer table to identify blocks of flip-flops that are common destinations of various transfers. For example, the flip-flops of $A_{12:17}$ are all destinations of transfers in entries 1, 4, and 7 of Fig. 7.15 and of no other transfers. Thus $A_{12:17}$ remains a group. The right sides of transfers must be examined also to identify parts of transfers which are actually identical. The last 17 bits of transfers 1 and 4 in Fig. 7.15 are identical, but the first bits are not. Therefore, the destination flip-flop A_0 will have a different input network than flip-flops $A_{1:17}$ and must be treated separately. Continuing this process gives the following list of destinations:

$$A_0 \quad A_{1:5} \quad CNT \quad A_{6:11} \quad A_{12:17} \quad look \quad z$$

Once partitioning has been accomplished, step 3 of Fig. 7.14 calls for the tabulation of each group of destination flip-flops with a list of all conditions for which this group of flip-flops is clocked. For each group a list of all source vectors and corresponding source conditions is also tabulated. For the above example, this table is given in Fig. 7.16.

There are two destination entries in Fig. 7.16 for which clocking conditions do not apply: the output connections z and $look$. The same would be true for declared buses whose outputs fan out to various destination flip-flops. All declared outputs, memory elements, and buses should appear as destination entries in the table.

For each group of destination flip-flops the source list forms the inputs to an undeclared busing network. Step 4 of the compiling process generates the busing networks from the destination and source list of Fig. 7.16. As an illustration, the input network for the single-destination flip-flop A_0 is given in Fig. 7.17. Only three AND gates are required to

Destination Group	Source	Source Condition	Clock Condition
A_0	0	$1 \vee 2$	$1 \vee 2 \vee 3 \vee 4 \vee 5$
	X_0	3	
	1	4	
	$A_6 \wedge A_{12}$	$5 \wedge \bar{b}$	
	A_6	$5 \wedge b$	
$A_{1:5}$	$A_{0:4}$	$2 \vee 4 \vee 1$	$1 \vee 2 \vee 3 \vee 4 \vee 5$
	$X_{1:5}$	3	
	$A_{7:11} \wedge A_{13:17}$	$5 \wedge \bar{b}$	
	$A_{7:11}$	$5 \wedge b$	
CNT	$a, b, 0$	3	$3 \vee 4$
	$INC(CNT)$	4	
$A_{12:17}$	$A_{11:16}$	$1 \vee 2 \vee 4$	$1 \vee 2 \vee 4 \vee (5 \wedge b)$
	$A_{0:5}$	5	
$A_{6:11}$	$A_{5:10}$	$1 \vee 2 \vee 4$	$1 \vee 2 \vee 3 \vee 4 \vee (5 \wedge b)$
	$A_{0:5}$	3	
	X	5	
look	1	5	N/A
z	A_{17}	ALL	N/A

Figure 7.16. Destination and Source List.

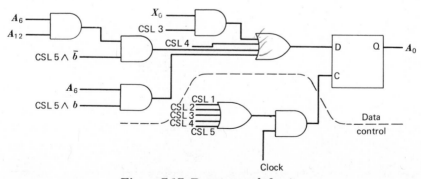

Figure 7.17. Data network for A_0.

accommodate data inputs X_0, A_6, and $A_6 \wedge A_{12}$. The step 4 control signal CSL4, is connected directly to the OR gate to cause a 1 to be loaded into A_0. The flip-flop will be clocked for steps 1 and 2 while all inputs to the data OR gate are 0, causing 0 to be loaded into the flip-flop. Enclosed by dashed lines in Fig. 7.17 is the only source logic gate generated by step 6 of the hardware compiler. The OR gate whose inputs are the five clocking conditions is generated by step 5. Since the only other source with more than one condition is 0, no other control collection OR gate is required.

The complete Destination and Source List for SIC would be too lengthy to be presented here. A few entries are listed in Fig. 7.18 to illustrate the compiling of a network organized around a set of declared buses. Notice that only source conditions are applicable to inputs to the **BBUS**. Only clocking conditions are listed for the register, **PC**, since it receives data only from $OBUS_{6:18}$. Therefore, its data inputs may be permanently connected to this source. The resulting data input networks for **BBUS** and **PC** are shown in Fig. 7.19.

The second step of the compiling process is the generation of the control unit, including branching interconnections between the control flip-flops and control levels to be connected to the data unit. One could proceed in a manner analogous to the compilation of data section logic, by focusing on the inputs to the control flip-flops, but this would make it difficult to maintain the identity of the individual steps. First, NO DELAY steps have no control flip-flops. Second, the gates controlling the inputs to given steps are in the branch sections of other steps. It is important to maintain the direct correspondence between the sequence and the control logic in the interests of efficient design verification and trouble-shooting.

Destination	Source	Source Conditions	Clock Conditions
$BBUS_{0:4}$	$MD_{0:4}$	$4 \vee 9 \vee 17 \vee 18$	
$BBUS_{5:17}$	PC	$2 \vee 20 \vee 21 \vee 24 \vee 36$	
	$MD_{5:17}$	$4 \vee 9 \vee 17 \vee 18$	
	IA	$11 \vee (37 \wedge \overline{IR}_{13}) \vee 38$	
	IB	$12 \vee (37 \wedge IR_{13}) \vee 39$	
PC	$OBUS_{6:18}$		$14 \vee 20 \vee 23 \vee 24 \vee 36$

Figure 7.18. Partial Destination/Source List for SIC.

246

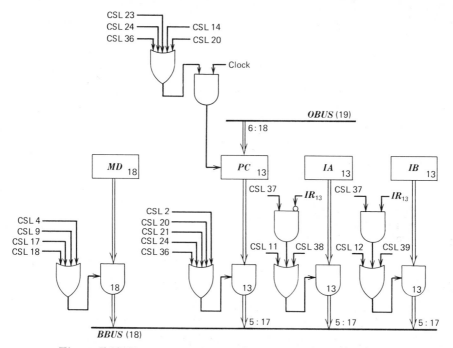

Figure 7.19. Data connections and control for *BBUS* and *PC*.

The compilation procedure to be described will specify the logic and interconnections for each step independently. For each step the following information must be specified:

1. The inputs and outputs of the control flip-flop if any
2. The equations of the branch logic if any
3. The steps that branch into this step
4. The steps to which this step branches
5. The identity of the control state level (CSL) for this step
6. Logical expressions for control outputs.

The control output expressions differ from the control state expressions of item 5 only in the case of conditional transfers. The last item is not needed in the generation of the control unit itself but provides the identification of the outputs of the control unit to the data unit, which is needed to complete the interconnections between the two units.

The required information could be presented in a variety of ways. The tabular listing developed in the following is compact and simple to interpret. For each step there will be four entries. The first column will give the equation of the D-input to the control flip-flop. If there is no control flip-flop (NO DELAY), a zero will be entered in this column. The second column will identify the control signal level. The third column will give the equations for the branch outputs. The fourth column lists the control output expressions. The D-input and Q-output of a control flip-flop at step n will be denoted Dn and Qn, respectively. The notation for branch outputs will be $n\,Bm$, denoting a branch *at* step n, *to* step m.

As a specific example let us develop the control table for the following sequence.

1. $A \leftarrow \text{INC}(A)$
2. $\rightarrow (A_0 \wedge A_1 \wedge A_2)/(1)$
3. NO DELAY
   $\rightarrow (A_3 \vee A_4)/(6)$
4. NO DELAY
   $B \leftarrow \bar{A}$
5. $B \leftarrow (\text{INC}(B) \, ! \, 8 \, \top \, 0) * (x, \bar{x})$
   $\rightarrow (B_0)/(5)$
6. $B \leftarrow \bar{B}$
   $\rightarrow (1)$

Again the reader should not be concerned with the process implemented by the control sequence. It should be regarded as an example sequence, developed to illustrate the compilation of all basic types of AHPL steps, transfer and branch, transfer or branch alone, with or without delay. The completed control table is shown in Fig. 7.20.

We start by noting that step 1 is not a NO DELAY step, so a control flip-flop is needed. Scanning the sequence, we find that steps 2 and 6 branch to step 1 so that the input equation for this step is

$$D1 = 2B1 \vee 6B1$$

For steps with a control flip-flop, the control signal level is always the output of the flip-flop, in this case,

$$CSL1 = Q1$$

This step does not branch but proceeds unconditionally to step 2 so that the output equation is

$$1B2 = CSL1$$

A scan of the sequence shows that only step 1 leads to step 2 so that

$$D2 = 1B2$$

and

$$CSL2 = Q2$$

Step	D	CSL	Branch Outputs	Control Outputs
1	$D1 = 2B1 \vee 6B1$	$CSL1 = Q1$	$1B2 = CSL1$	$CSL1$
2	$D2 = 1B2$	$CSL2 = Q2$	$2B1 = (A_0 \wedge A_1 \wedge A_2)$ $\wedge CSL2$ $2B3 = \overline{(A_0 \wedge A_1 \wedge A_2)}$ $\wedge CSL2$	
3	0	$CSL3 = 2B3$	$3B4 = \overline{(A_3 \vee A_4)} \wedge$ $CSL3$ $3B6 = (A_3 \vee A_4) \wedge$ $CSL3$	
4	0	$CSL4 = 3B4$	$4B5 = CSL4$	$CSL4$
5	$D5 = 4B5 \vee 5B5$	$CSL5 = Q5$	$5B5 = B_0 \wedge CSL5$ $5B6 = \overline{B_0} \wedge CSL5$	$CSL5 \wedge x$ $CSL5 \wedge \overline{x}$
6	$D6 = 3B6 \vee 5B6$	$CSL6 = Q6$	$6B1 = CSL6$	$CSL6$

Figure 7.20. Example Control Table.

Step 2 has a branch, to step 1 on the condition given or, by implication, to step 3 on the negation of that condition so that we have two branch outputs.

$$2B1 = (A_0 \wedge A_1 \wedge A_2) \wedge CSL2$$
$$2B3 = \overline{(A_0 \wedge A_1 \wedge A_2)} \wedge CSL2$$

Step 3 is a NO DELAY step so that a zero is entered in the D column. For NO DELAY steps, the control signal level is always the input from the preceding step or steps, in this case,

$$CSL3 = 2B3$$

Step 3 is another two-way branch so that the output equations are formed in the same general manner as for step 2. Step 4 is similar to step 3 except that the output goes unconditionally to step 5. Steps 5 and 6 are similar to steps 1 and 2, and the entries are developed in the same general manner.

Steps 2 and 3 do not specify a transfer or data connection; therefore, no control output is listed for these steps. In steps 1, 4, and 6 the control output is the same as the control state. Only in the case of step 5, which

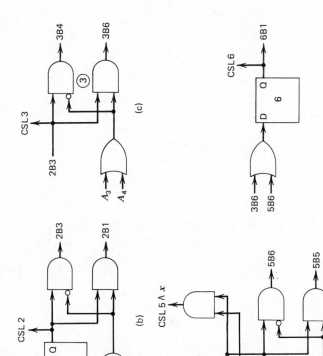

Figure 7.21. Development of control logic from control table.

includes a conditional transfer, are the control output expressions more complex.

Let us now see how the hardware for each step can be developed from the entries in the control table. Step 1 requires a flip-flop with an OR-gate at its input to combine the inputs from steps 2 and 6. The flip-flop output is labeled as CSL1 and 1B2, the unconditional branch output to step 2 (Fig. 7.21a). Step 2 also requires a flip-flop, but no OR-gate, as the only input is 1B2. The branch logic requires an AND-gate to develop the term $(A_0 \wedge A_1 \wedge A_2)$, which is gated with CSL2 to develop the branch outputs 2B1 and 2B3 (Fig. 7.21b)

Step 3 is a NO DELAY step, so the input 2B3 is labeled as CSL3 and gated with the condition term $(A_3 \vee A_4)$ to develop the branch outputs (Fig. 7.21c). Step 4 is a NO DELAY transfer without branch, which requires nothing more than the relabeling of a wire (Fig. 7.21d). Steps 5 and 6 are realized in much the same manner as steps 1 and 2 except that step 5 requires two additional AND gates to represent the conditional output control levels (Figs. 7.21e and 7.21f). All that remains to complete the design is to connect the various nBm branch outputs to the inputs of the appropriate destination steps.

The compilation process described in this section should not be taken as an exact description of any specific compiler. We have overlooked many details and simplified many steps in the interest of clarity. Our intent has been to illustrate the basic character of the compilation process and to show that a control sequence can be converted to a hardware design by a completely algorithmic procedure, not dependent in any way on human insight or intuition. This algorithmic character is necessary in a computer program, but it is a serious limitation on the flexibility of the designer. It is not possible to provide rules to deal in an optimum fashion with every possible design problem that may arise. The application of a limited number of standard procedures by the compiler will result in designs that will be accurate but often less than optimum. To allow for optimization, the designer can be provided with opportunities to intercede and modify the designs produced by the computer.

By procedures such as that described above, the compiler will develop an initial design. The designer will then review the design, making modifications if they are necessary. At this point, assuming a good compiler, we shall have a design that will accurately implement the sequence written by the designer, but this is no guarantee that the system will meet all the initial specifications. Therefore, the next step may be a simulation to verify correct operation. There are many kinds of simulations; one possibility would be to perform a logic simulation at the individual instruction level. Inputs corresponding to each instruction would be fed to a computer model of the system logic, and the logic flow for the entire sequence would be simulated to verify that the system did what it was supposed to do. If the simulation reveals errors, the designer will correct the design and repeat the process until no further errors are found.

The next steps in the process will depend on the electronic and mechanical realizations chosen by the designer. As an example let us assume the use of discrete IC logic elements mounted on printed circuit boards, which will in turn be plugged into sockets on a backplane, with the backplane wiring to be done by an automatic wiring machine. The designer will provide the compiler with a list of available IC's, and the compiler will assign specific IC types to all the various logic elements. This may seem simple in principle, but it is in reality a very complex job. In drawing block diagrams, we have just assumed the availability of whatever gates we needed. In practice the number of different gates may be very limited, possibly to only one type (NAND or NOR) with only two or three different input combinations. In that event the compiler must transform the logic into equivalent forms realizable in terms of the available elements. Also, elements such as gates and flip-flops usually come several to a package so that the compiler must decide how to make the best use of elements in each package. The compiler will probably also run loading checks to be sure that the number of logic inputs connected to each logic output does not exceed the drive capacity.

When the logic assignment is complete, the designer will be provided another opportunity to intervene and make corrections. Another simulation may then be run, to verify the logic transformations and to check on the effect of circuit delays. The next step is to assign the IC's to cards and to arrange the cards on the backplane. The designer must indicate the number of pins on the cards and the maximum number of IC's per card. This phase of the design is likely to be very interactive, with the designer intervening frequently to group IC's on certain cards or to specify standard cards, and to group cards on the backplane. The final output of this phase will be wiring lists, specifying the connections to every pin of every IC and every card socket. This would terminate the compiler phase of the design process. Computer software will often play a role in the manufacturing phase, generating tapes to control the wiring machines, generating the artwork and drilling plans for the PC boards, etc.

From the preceding description we can see clearly that the hardware compiler must have available a large amount of information beyond that provided by the control sequence itself. The sequence identifies the major components of the system and specifies what the system is to do. But this description could correspond to a variety of physical realizations. As we saw when we wrote the sequence for SIC in Chapter 6, the designer can write a control sequence with only a rather vague picture of the hardware configuration.

As we noted earlier, the compiler structure includes the rules of correspondence between various types of control sequence steps and a specific hardware realization. Thus, when the designer designs the compiler he is specifying the hardware details. In writing the compiler, he will have in mind the type of sequences to be realized, just as he will have some sort of hardware in mind when he writes the sequence. The compiler can be used to realize a variety of sequences, and a given sequence can be realized in a variety of ways. Thus the two phases of the design are carried out separately, but they are not independent of each other.

One question that the designer of a compiler must resolve is what information should be built into the structure of the compiler, and what information should be provided as input data. For example, when we wrote the original control sequence for SIC, we did not specify the bus connections and indicated that this would be satisfactory as long as there were no ambiguity about what bus connections were intended. But let us consider what information the compiler would need to determine the bus connections. If the only information provided is the original source and final destination of each transfer and the fact that there are three buses, it seems very unlikely that any set of rules could be devised to determine the exact bus configuration. For the compiler to do this, it would be necessary to provide the equivalent of the bus connections in Table 6.3 as an additional input. The alternative is for the designer to specify the bus connections in every transfer statement and let the compiler generate the bus connection table. The designer must decide which approach he prefers.

Consider the matter of specifying the actual logic elements to be used. Should this be built into the compiler or should one of the inputs be a list of IC's to be used in a given system? If an input list is to be used, should the designer be able to specify any IC's from any family of logic, or should he be restricted to a single family of logic, or even to a subset of elements within a single family? Allowing the widest possible range of elements increases the versatility of the compiler but makes it more complicated, since it has to have rules for dealing with a variety of situations. Restricting the compiler to a limited number of elements will make it simpler but will limit its applicability.

All these factors pose difficult problems for the designers of compilers and other software used in computer design and manufacture. The design of such software is a very big job and represents a sizable investment. To get the maximum return on the investment, it should be as flexible and versatile as possible. But the more flexible and versatile it is, the more it costs in the first place. Further, no matter how versatile it may be, many new developments cannot be anticipated. Inevitably, technological innovations will come along that offer significant improvements in cost or performance but cannot be incorporated into existing software. Then the designers must decide if the projected improvements warrant the cost of developing new software. In spite of all these problems it is safe to predict that computer aids to computer design are here to stay, simply because the job cannot be done without them.

7.6   PROPAGATION DELAYS AND CLOCK RATE

We have noted in previous sections that one purpose of the delay provided by control flip-flops is to allow the results of previous transfers to propagate. Let us now look at this problem more closely, to determine what kind of delays may be encountered and what other factors may be involved. As an example, consider the following two steps, which might be encountered in a multiplication sequence. At step 6 an argument is transferred to AC. If this number is positive, it is transferred to MQ at step 7. If not, the logical complement, or 1's complement, is transferred to MQ. We assume a bus organization similar to SIC.

6. $BBUS = MD$; $OBUS = 0, BBUS$;
   $AC \leftarrow OBUS_{1:18}$
7. $ABUS = AC$; $OBUS = ((0, ABUS) \mathbin{!} (0, \overline{ABUS})) * (\overline{AC_0}, AC_0)$;
   $MQ \leftarrow OBUS_{1:18}$

Figure 7.22 shows the control and data circuitry involved in these transfers, and a partial timing diagram. In this figure t_n will denote the time of the trailing edge of the clock pulse controlling the transfers in step n, and P_n will denote the corresponding pulse applied to the clock input of the destination register.

As discussed in chapter 3, all logic elements introduce delay. For master-slave flip-flops, which are assumed here, the delay is from the trailing edge of the clock pulse until the resultant change appears at the output. For gates the delay is from the time of any input change until any resultant change at the output. Although there will be some differences in delays for different logic elements, within any given family (such as TTL), the delays for all elements will be similar. For simplicity

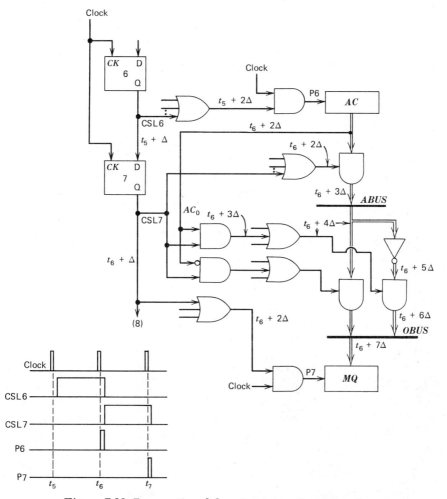

Figure 7.22. Propagation delays in conventional transfer.

in the following discussion we shall assume a uniform delay, Δ, for all elements.

The clock pulse at t_5 turns on control flip-flop 6 so that CSL6 goes up at $t_5 + \Delta$, passes through an OR-gate that combines signals from all steps loading the AC register, and arrives at the AND gate that controls the clocking of AC at $t_5 + 2\Delta$. If it is assumed that the logic inputs to AC are stable, the next clock could arrive at any time after this. The clock pulse at t_6 turns off CSL6 and turns on CSL7 at $t_6 + \Delta$. This same clock pulse also passes through the AND gate and clocks AC at $t_6 + \Delta$ so that the new value of AC is available at $t_6 + 2\Delta$. Then CSL7 passes through an OR-gate and reaches the bank of AND-gates between AC and $ABUS$, also at $t_6 + 2\Delta$ so that the new value of AC is available at the input to the $ABUS$ at $t_6 + 3\Delta$.

Next, we must note that buses are logic elements, generally banks of AND/OR-gates, and also introduce delays. Therefore, the output of the $ABUS$ does not reach its new value until $t_6 + 4\Delta$. There are two paths to the $OBUS$, for direct and inverted transfer. For inverted transfer the output of the inverter bank is available at $t_6 + 5\Delta$, at which time it can be gated through to the $OBUS$, provided that the control signal is available. Also, CSL7 is applied to the AND gates controlling the conditional transfer at $t_6 + \Delta$, but the AC_0 signal is not available until $t_6 + 2\Delta$ so that the outputs of the AND gates are available at $t_6 + 3\Delta$ and pass through the OR-gates to the AND-gate banks, controlling the $OBUS$ inputs at $t_6 + 4\Delta$. For the inverted transfer the data arrives after the control level and is available at the input to the $OBUS$ at $t_6 + 6\Delta$. Finally, the $OBUS$ introduces its own delay so that the new data is not available at the logic inputs to MQ until $t_6 + 7\Delta$. The level controlling the clock has been available since $t_6 + 2\Delta$, but the clock interval must be at least 7Δ for proper operation.

In the above example the minimum interval between clock pulses was seven times the delay of a single logic element. Of this time, only two delay times were needed for the actual loading of the register; the remaining times were associated with the delays in the control and data paths involved in the succeeding transfer. This raises a question as to how the propagation delays affect a "NO DELAY" transfer. As an example of this, let us consider the original rotate sequence for SIC, which was discussed in Section 7.4. The steps that must be considered in analyzing the timing of the step 30 transfer are the following.

4. $BBUS = MD$; $OBUS = 0, BBUS$; $IR \leftarrow OBUS_{1:18}$
5. Null
   $\rightarrow (IR_0 \land IR_1 \land IR_2)/(25)$
25. NO DELAY
   $\rightarrow (\overline{IR_3}, IR_3)/(26, \text{I/O Seq.})$
26. NO DELAY
   $\rightarrow (IR_5)/(30)$
30. $ABUS = AC$;
   $OBUS = ((ABUS, lf) \mathbin{!} (ABUS_{17}, lf, ABUS_{0:16})) * (\overline{IR_4}, IR_4)$
   $lf, AC \leftarrow OBUS$; NO DELAY
   $\rightarrow (33)$
33. $\rightarrow (IR_{10})/(40)$

Step 4 loads the instructions into *IR*; step 5 is the branch for addressed or nonaddressed instructions; step 25 is the branch for operate or I/O instructions; step 26 is the branch for rotate or non-rotate instructions in event time 1; step 30 is the rotate transfer; and step 33 is the initial branch in event time 2. Figure 7.23 shows the control circuitry and data paths for these steps. The clock pulse at t_4 loads *IR* and also turns on CSL5. However, the ANDing of the first three bits of *IR* is not available until $t_4 + 3\Delta$ so that the output of the step 5 branch logic is not available until $t_4 + 4\Delta$. This signal must then propagate through the logic for steps 25 and 26 so that CSL30, which controls the rotate transfer, is not available until $t_4 + 6\Delta$. To this delay must be added the propagation delay through the data paths so that the *OBUS* output is not available for loading into *lf*, *AC* until $t_4 + 11\Delta$, four delay times later than in the simpler transfer of Fig. 7.22.

A first reaction to this might be that this is just one special case in the control sequence and would not slow down the machine that much in a typical mix of instructions. But if we are to have a uniform clock rate, allowing the same time for all steps, we have to allow for the worst case. Thus, even if this were the only situation requiring 11Δ, and all other steps could be completed in the 7Δ determined in the previous example, we would be required to slow the system clock to allow for this case.

It may be that such a slowing of the clock, in this case by about 40 percent cannot be tolerated. If so, what are the alternatives? One approach is to consider this as a special case requiring the insertion of extra delay, just as we did with the add operation in Section 7.4. In this case, the simplest solution would probably be to make step 30 a delay step, i.e., insert a control flip-flop at step 30. This would not speed up this particular sequence of operations but would spread it over two clock periods, one associated with step 5, the other with step 30.

Alternately, we may note that step 30 is carried out in the same clock period as step 5. Even though CSL30 is delayed relative to CSL5, the step 30 transfer is completed by the same clock pulse, at t_5, that would have completed any transfers at step 5 had there been any. Thus we see that NO DELAY transfers and branches are essentially extensions of the branch logic of the preceding delay step. There is no theoretical reason why we could not consider all the logic associated with steps 25, 26, and 30 as a part of the step 5 logic, described by a complex conditional transfer and multiway branch at step 5. (See Problem 7.10.) Recognizing that this is the case, we then see that the number of levels of logic could be reduced by combining terms, with a resultant decrease in the propagation delays. In Chapter 6 we noted that we made several decisions sequentially that could have been combined in a single multiway

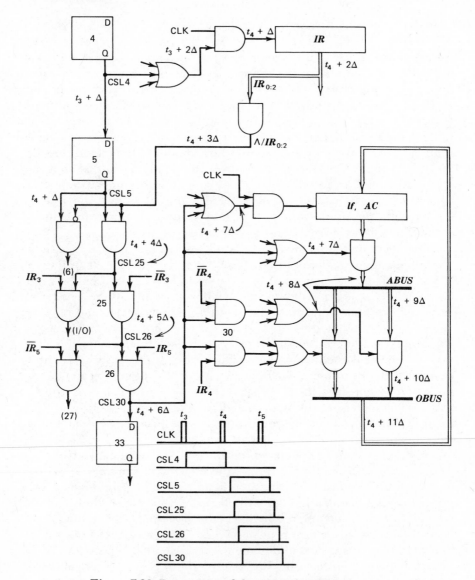

Figure 7.23. Propagation delays in **NO DELAY** steps.

branch, in the interests of clarifying the structure of the sequence. We see now that such sequential decisions exact a time penalty even though NO DELAY steps may be used. The designer must decide in each case whether the extra time is justified.

7.7 COMBINATIONAL LOGIC UNIT DESCRIPTIONS

Referring to Fig. 5.12, the reader will recall that the complete AHPL description of a system is broken up into two parts, *procedures* and *functions*. The procedure section describes the operation of *modules*, systems or subsystems having data and control sections. The function section consists of descriptions of the wiring of purely combinational *units*, which may be referred to in the procedural descriptions of the modules. In the procedural description of SIC we referred to two such units, the ADD unit and the INC unit. In Chapter 6 we simply noted that these references indicated the use of combinational logic units for performing the operations of addition and incrementing. Let us now consider just how such units can be described in AHPL.

In Chapter 5 we saw how a sequence of connection statements could be used to describe a simple combinational unit such as a full adder. We must now formalize the syntax of such descriptions and develop additional features that will permit us to describe much more complex units. The basic structure of the unit descriptions is shown in Fig. 7.24, and is seen to be similar to the structure of module descriptions. Each unit description consists of a name, declarations of inputs and outputs, a sequence of steps, and an END statement. Each step will consist of a connection statement or a *compile time operation*. Compile time operations provide the means of extending the basic concept to large iterative networks.

In this discussion we shall accept any legal APL transfer as a *compile time transfer*. Variables in compile time expressions will be called *index variables* and will always be expressed as integers in base 10. An index variable that appears on the left side of a compile time transfer need not have been declared. It is first defined by an initializing transfer statement. Once an index variable has appeared on the left side of a compile time transfer, it may be used in expressions on the right side of similar transfers. These same index variables are the branch functions in *compile time branch* statements. Any legal APL branch will be regarded here as a legal compile time branch. To avoid confusion, the symbols ⇐ and ⇒ are used to represent compile time transfers and branches, respectively. We thus emphasize the fact that these operations are indeed

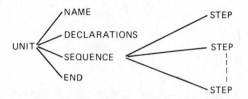

Figure 7.24. Structure of unit descriptions.

executed at compile time in contrast to the operations represented by ← and →.

One heretofore unmentioned primitive operator which will be admitted in compile time operations is the exponential operator, ↑. The algebraic expression i^n is thus represented in compile time expressions as *

$$i \uparrow n \qquad\qquad (7.1)$$

A completely defined syntax for AHPL combinational logic unit descriptions will be found in discussions of the AHPL hardware compiler. The range of compile time operations acceptable to a hardware compiler will be a limited subset of the APL operations accepted in this discussion. We allow the broader range of APL operators here to avoid a lengthy treatment of syntax.

The syntax for a connection statement in a combinational logic unit description is the same as in a control sequence with two exceptions. The compression operators R/A, R/M and $R//M$ will be allowed in combinational logic unit descriptions. These should be added to the list of selection operators given in Fig. 5.13. Subscripts may be variables, in particular, the index variables assigned by compile time transfers.

As a first example of a combinational logic unit description, let us develop a description of a circuit to perform the binary ADD function used at several points in the SIC sequence. There are many adder designs, but probably the simplest and most commonly used is the "ripple-carry" adder, which utilizes n identical stages to add two n-bit numbers. The n identical stages are called *full adders*.

---

*Although the exponential operator is available in APL, ↑ is not the symbol. This symbol was borrowed from a preliminary version of CONLAN (Consensus Design Language).

Example 7.1
Develop an AHPL combinational logic unit description of a full adder.

Solution
The term full adder refers to a circuit that accomplishes the addition of two corresponding bits, one from each argument vector connected to the input of the complete adder. This process entails accepting a carry bit from the full adder stage which adds bits just lower in significance and generating a sum bit and a carry bit to the next-most-significant full adder. If we denote the inputs as x, y, and cin, the minimal second-order equations for the sum and carry are as follows:

$$sum = (x \wedge \overline{y} \wedge \overline{cin}) \vee (\overline{x} \wedge y \wedge \overline{cin}) \vee (\overline{x} \wedge \overline{y} \wedge cin) \vee (x \wedge y \wedge cin)$$
$$cout = (x \wedge y) \vee (x \wedge cin) \vee (y \wedge cin)$$

These forms can be implemented directly as AND-OR circuits, but a simpler adder circuit can be obtained by factoring the above equations into the following forms:

$$sum = x \oplus y \oplus cin$$
$$cout = ((x \oplus y) \wedge cin) \vee (x \wedge y)$$

The implementation of these forms can be described by the AHPL unit description given below.

UNIT: FULLADD $(x; y; cin)$
        INPUTS: $x; y; cin$
        OUTPUTS: FULLADD [2]
        1. $a = x \oplus y$
        2. $b = x \wedge y$
        3. $sum = a \oplus cin$
        4. $c = a \wedge cin$
        5. $cout = b \vee c$
        6. $FULLADD_0 = cout$
        7. $FULLADD_1 = sum$
END

Note that the first five statements specify connections of gates, while the last two simply label the outputs.

The above example involves no compile time operations, only connection statements. The complete 18-bit ripple-carry adder could be similarly described, essentially repeating the above description 18 times, the only change being that cin at each stage would be the FULLADD$_0$ from the previous stage. However, this would be very inefficient and it would clearly be preferable to provide some means of iteration to eliminate the repetition. This is the function of the compile time operations.

Only the connection statements will generate actual hardware. Variable subscripts will appear on both sides of these connection statements permitting them to be reused in the generation of multiple copies of identical subnetworks with distinct inputs and outputs. The compile time operations will be actually *executed* during the compile process. The APL transfer statements will assign values to the variable subscripts. The branch statements control the order in which the steps in the sequence are executed. Let us now consider the ripple carry adder example, which will illustrate the use of the compile time operations.

Example 7.2

Write a description of a combinational logic unit to perform the two's complement ADD function required in SIC.

Solution

A satisfactory routine may be listed as follows:

UNIT: ADD $(X; Y)$
INPUTS: X [18]; Y [18]
OUTPUTS: ADD [19]
1. $\boldsymbol{C}_{18} = 0$
2. $i \Leftarrow 17$
3. $\boldsymbol{C}_i = \text{FULLADD}_0\,(\boldsymbol{X}_i;\ \boldsymbol{Y}_i;\ \boldsymbol{C}_{i+1})$
4. $\boldsymbol{S}_i = \text{FULLADD}_1\,(\boldsymbol{X}_i;\ \boldsymbol{Y}_i;\ \boldsymbol{C}_{i+1})$
5. $i \Leftarrow i - 1$
6. $\Rightarrow (i \geq 0)/(3)$
7. $\text{ADD} = \boldsymbol{C}_0,\ \boldsymbol{S}_{0:17}$

END

The declarations indicate that this unit requires two 18-bit inputs and produces a 19-bit output, since the addition of two 18-bit numbers can produce a 19-bit sum. Step 1, a connection statement, causes a line connected to logic 0 (assumed to be ground for this example) to be labeled $\boldsymbol{C}_{18}$, as shown in Fig. 7.25a. The compile time operation at step 2 assigns an initial value of 17 to the subscript i. With this value for i, the connection statements at steps 3 and 4 cause $\boldsymbol{X}_{17}$, $\boldsymbol{Y}_{17}$, and $\boldsymbol{C}_{18}$ to be connected as the inputs to a FULLADD circuit described by the sequence of Example 7.1, with the outputs labeled $\boldsymbol{C}_{17}$ and $\boldsymbol{S}_{17}$. The connections to this point are shown in Fig. 7.25b.

The compile time operation at step 5 now decrements i to 16; step 6,

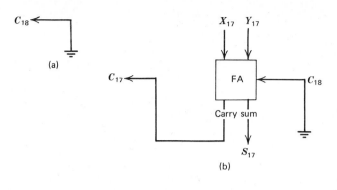

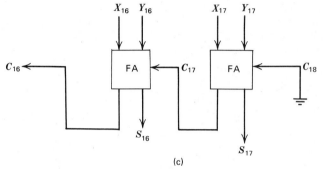

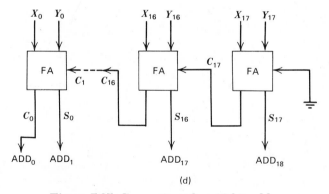

Figure 7.25. Generation of an 18-bit adder.

also a compile time operation, checks the value of i. Since i is greater than 0, the sequence returns to steps 3 and 4, to connect another FULLADD circuit to produce C_{16} and S_{16} (Fig. 7.25c). This process continues until $i = -1$ at which time step 7 assigns the output as the catenation of the output carry, C_0, and the 18 sum bits (Fig. 7.25d).

Note again that the compile time operations are so named because they are effective only when the circuit is actually being compiled. They do not generate logic directly, and the variables named in them are not variables in the circuit generated. They are strictly instructions to the compiler program on how to execute the compilation. It is for this reason that they may utilize the full range of APL, rather than restricted to AHPL. Recall that AHPL is restricted to a subset of APL forms because it is intended to describe hardware, and many APL forms have no direct hardware connotations. But compile time operations are instructions to the computer and can be any operation a computer can perform. Thus we can use arithmetic processing of subscripts, as in step 5. We can compare a subscript to a number as in step 6, since we are not concerned with generating the logic to make the comparison. In a unit description the only hardware statements are connection statements; transfer statements and branch statements will always be compile time operations.

The reader may wonder why we list arguments of the function in the name declaration, since these arguments are also listed in the input declaration. This is done to facilitate linkage with the module descriptions that use the unit. For example, the statement

$$lf, AC \leftarrow \text{ADD } (AC; MD)$$

in a module description tells the compiler that the outputs of AC and MD are to be connected to the inputs designated X and Y in the description of the unit ADD. Notice also that the outputs of the unit have the same name as the unit, for the same reason, to facilitate linkage between the module and unit descriptions. Finally, the reader should note that a unit description may refer to another unit, a fact that is essential to efficient iterative generation of complex circuits.

There are three other combinational logic functions, INC, DCD, and BUSFN, that were used in the last chapter and will continue to be used throughout the book. The first of these we leave as a homework problem for the reader; the latter are considered in the following two examples.

Example 7.3
Write a combinational logic unit description representing DCD(A), where A is a vector of n bits.

Solution

It is necessary to use the exponential operation $\uparrow$ in dimensioning the outputs of DCD(A) as well as within a compile time branch, since the number of outputs is 2^n. The following simple decoder description requires only four steps but uses 2^n n-input AND gates. A more economical description will be left as a problem for the reader.

UNIT: DCD (A)
        INPUTS: $A[n]$
        OUTPUTS: DCD$[2 \uparrow n]$
        1. $i \Leftarrow 0$
        2. $DCD_i = \wedge/ \, ((n \top i)/A, \overline{(n \top i)}/\bar{A})$
        3. $i \Leftarrow i + 1$
        4. $\Rightarrow (i < 2 \uparrow n)/2$
END

The first step initializes the index i. The second step generates a decoder output for each value of i by ANDing the appropriate elements from the vectors A and $\bar{A}$. For example, if $n = 4$ and $i = 5$, step 2 may be evaluated as follows.

$$
\begin{aligned}
DCD_5 &= \wedge/ \, ((4 \top 5)/A, \overline{(4 \top 5)}/\bar{A}) \\
&= \wedge/ \, ((0, 1, 0, 1)/A, (1, 0, 1, 0)/\bar{A}) \\
&= \wedge/\bar{A}_0, A_1, \bar{A}_2, A_3 = \bar{A}_0 \wedge A_1 \wedge \bar{A}_2 \wedge A_3
\end{aligned}
\tag{7.2}
$$

Equation 7.1 gives the correct expression for DCD_5. Steps 3 and 4 cause an AND gate similar to that represented by Eq. 7.2 to be generated for each value of i between 0 and $2^n - 1$.

When a memory is simply an array of flip-flops, the memory read operation may be expressed as

$$MD \leftarrow \text{BUSFN} \, (\mathbf{M}; \text{DCD}(MA)) \tag{7.3}$$

One possible combinational logic unit description for BUSFN with an arbitrary argument in place of the decoder output is given in Example 7.4.

Example 7.4

Write a combinational logic unit description for BUSFN applicable to an r-word memory with p bits per word.

Solution

    UNIT: BUSFN (**M**; R)
            INPUTS: **M**[r , p]; R[r]
            OUTPUTS: BUSFN[p]
            1. $\mathbf{N}^0 = \mathbf{M}^0 \wedge R_0$
            2. $i \Leftarrow 1$
            3. $\mathbf{N}^i = (\mathbf{M}^i \wedge R_i) \vee \mathbf{N}^{i-1}$
            4. $i \Leftarrow i + 1$
            5. $\Rightarrow (i < \mathbf{r})/(3)$
            6. BUSFN $= \mathbf{N}^{r-1}$
    END

The above description uses only 2-input OR gates. To reduce delay and reduce network costs, various other arrangements using multi-input OR gates are possible. The approach adopted will probably depend on the particular technology from which the memory is constructed.

7.8   A COMPLETE DESIGN EXAMPLE

So far in chapters 6 and 7 we have been concerned almost exclusively with the computer SIC. Because of the scope of this system it may not have seemed like a single design problem to the reader. The discussion of SIC should, however, have equipped the reader with the tools required to make the design decisions in less-complicated systems.

It remains to illustrate how these tools can be applied step-by-step to arrive at the design of a complete digital system. We shall do this in terms of a small priority storage unit that might be used to store a queue of instructions awaiting execution in a large overall system.

Although this priority store would form a part of some larger system, we shall design it as a complete self-contained system. We assume that the clocks of this unit may be synchronized with the main system clock so that transfers to and from the priority store are synchronized with internal transfers.

Example 7.5
A control sequence is to be designed for a priority store. This system is to provide temporary storage for 32 18-bit words on a priority basis. The leftmost 3 bits of each word indicate the priority of that word, priority 7 being highest. An output register *DR* is provided to store a data word waiting to be accepted by the requesting device. Input data words are accepted on a vector of lines *DATAIN*.

Two control inputs are provided. A level on line *inreq* indicates that a word to be added to the store is ready on lines *DATAIN*. A level on line *outreq* indicates that a word is desired from the store. Two control flip-flops, a and b, must also be included. The following status conditions are indicated by the corresponding values of a and b.

a	b	
0	0	idle, waiting for external request
0	1	
1	0	busy
1	1	output data available in DR

A memory space becomes available when the word it contains is placed in DR. Words below this space in memory must then be shifted up to fill the space. In this way new words are always entered at the bottom of the stack. When a request is made for data output, the highest priority word available is to be placed in DR. If more than one word of this priority is present, the first word received is selected.

Two additional control flip-flops are required. If all 32 words in the store are full, a third flip-flop, *full*, will be set to 1 to discourage requests to input data to the store. If there are no data words in the store, a flip-flop *empty* is set to 1 to prevent read requests. We assume that these flip-flops are examined by the external system before a read or write request is made.

Design this system assuming that a relatively slow system response time is tolerable. Add registers and flip-flops as required.

Solution

As usual, the first step is to determine a list of all storage devices that will be required in the design. Next we should list the important combinational logic subroutines required. Once these steps have been accomplished, we can proceed to write the control sequence.

For this example most of the rest of the hardware will depend on the approach chosen for the implementation of the 32 word × 18-bit store itself. The number of words in the store (32) falls in the gray area where RAM and register memory overlap so that a variety of possible approaches might be considered.

First, we assume that only a single copy of our system is to be produced so that it would not be economical to design a special LSI (large-scale integrated circuit) unit. Of the various approaches using "off the shelf" parts that might be considered, we shall mention only three. The approach offering the greatest flexibility would use 32 × 18 individual IC flip-flops (2 to 4 per package). In this way we could connect to the inputs and outputs of individual registers at will. A second approach would be to use a standard, small RAM, which might be available in the form of two or three IC's on a printed circuit card. A third approach might involve a bank of eighteen 32-bit, integrated-circuit shift registers. If standard parts are available , either of the latter two approaches will be more economical than the individual flip-flop approach.

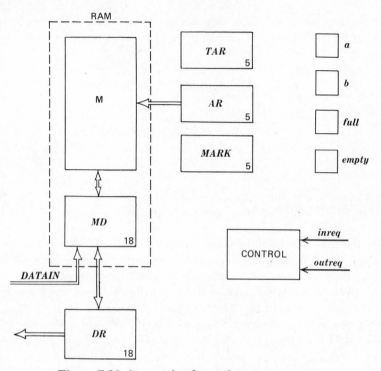

Figure 7.26. Storage hardware for priority store.

We now assume that discussions with vendors have led us to select a 32-word RAM as the primary component of our system. With this choice we must accept the usual constraints imposed by a RAM, that data may be entered and received only through the memory data register **MD**. As shown in Fig. 7.26, **MD** is part of the RAM. Addresses must reach the RAM on five level lines as shown. There- fore, an external 5-bit address register, **AR**, must be provided.

Two additional 5-bit registers are required. The register **MARK** contains the address of the first available space at the bottom of the data list. The basic strategy in servicing a READ request will be to store the highest priority word found so far in **DR**. As the memory is searched from address 0 to $\perp$ **MARK**, **DR** will be updated as higher priority words are found. The 5-bit trial address reg- ister **TAR** must contain the address of the word in **DR** at the end of the search. Data words below this address must be shifted up to fill this space.

A combinational logic subroutine LARGER will be used to compare the prior- ity of words in the store. Its arguments will be the first three bits of **MD** and **DR**. LARGER($MD_{0:2}$; $DR_{0:2}$) = 1 if and only if $MD_{0:2} > DR_{0:2}$. An AHPL de- scription of the priority store begins with the following declarations. The first step is a waiting loop for an input or output request. Steps 2 to 4 service an input request while service of a request for output data begins at step 5.

MODULE: PRIORITY STORE
  INPUTS: DATAIN[18]; *inreq*; *outreq*
  MEMORY: *MD*[18]; *DR*[18]; *TAR*[5]; *AR*[5];
              MARK[5]; *M*[32,18]; *a*; *b*; *full*; *empty*
  OUTPUTS: *DR*[18]; *a*; *b*; *full*; *empty*
  1. $(a, b) * (inreq \lor outreq) \leftarrow 1, 0$
       $\rightarrow ((\overline{inreq \land outreq}), inreq, outreq)/(1, 2, 5)$
  2. **MD** ← **DATAIN**; *empty* ← 0; **AR** ← **MARK**
  3. **M** *(DCD(AR) ← **MD**; **MARK** ← INC(**MARK**)
  4. $(full)*(\lor/MARK) \leftarrow 1; a \leftarrow 0$
       → (1)

Input is accomplished using **MARK** as the address of a WRITE operation, after which **MARK** is incremented. If **MARK** is found to equal 5 ⊤ 0, the store is full; and the flip-flop *full* is set to 1.

Steps 5 to 12 accomplish the search for the earliest-received maximum-priority word. This sequence begins with 0's in both **TAR** and **AR** so that they both point at the first word in memory, as depicted in Fig. 7.27a. Following step 12, the desired word is in **DR** and the address of this word is stored in **TAR**, as depicted in Fig. 7.27b. **AR** contains the same address as **MARK**. At step 12, *a* and *b* are set to 1 to indicate data available in **DR**.

  5. **AR** ← 5 ⊤ 0; **TAR** ← 5 ⊤ 0; *full* ← 0
  6. **MD** ← BUSFN (**M**; DCD (**AR**))
  7. **DR** ← **MD**
  8. **AR** ← INC(**AR**)

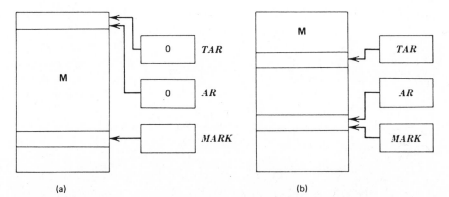

(a)   (b)

Figure 7.27. Search of store.

9. $\to \overline{(\bigvee/(AR \oplus MARK))}/(13)$

10. $MD \leftarrow \text{BUSFN}(\text{M}; \text{DCD}(AR))$

11. $\to \overline{(\text{LARGER}(MD_{0:2}; DR_{0:2}))}/(8)$

12. $DR \leftarrow MD; TAR \leftarrow AR;$
    $\to (8)$

Steps 13 to 20 shift each word in the store below the space marked TAR in Fig. 7.27b up one space. It is possible that the read operation has emptied the store. If so, *empty* is set to 1 at step 20.

13. $AR \leftarrow TAR; b \leftarrow 1$

14. $AR \leftarrow \text{INC}(AR)$

15. $\to \overline{(\bigvee/(AR \oplus MARK))}/(19)$

16. $MD \leftarrow \text{BUSFN}(\text{M}; \text{DCD}(AR));$
    $AR \leftarrow \text{DEC}(AR)$

17. $\text{M* DCD}(AR) \leftarrow MD$

18. $AR \leftarrow \text{INC}(AR)$
    $\to (14)$

19. $AR \leftarrow \text{DEC}(AR)$

20. $MARK \leftarrow AR; empty*\overline{(\bigvee/AR)} \leftarrow 1;$
    $a, b \leftarrow 0, 0$
    $\to (1)$

END

PROBLEMS

7.1 Modify steps 1 to 47 of the SIC control sequence (Appendix C) as required to accommodate the slow electronic memory of Fig. 7.6 and accompanying discussion. Consider the possibility of carrying out other steps in parallel while waiting for the memory to complete operations.

7.2 Repeat Problem 7.1 for the core memory of Fig. 7.7 and the accompanying discussion. Since the core memory is treated as a separate module, the *read* and *write* will have to be specified directly in the sequence.

7.3 Repeat Problem 7.2, but now assume that the core memory has a *dataready* signal, and that it is desired to transfer words into MD as soon as this signal appears rather than wait for *busy* to go down. Assume that *dataready* will go up as soon as the word is available, and down at the same time as *busy*. Assume that the delay between the time *dataready* goes up and the time *busy* goes down will never exceed six clock periods.

7.4 Show the hardware realization for steps 37 to 39 of the SIC control sequence. Since these steps all concern the same registers, the index registers and the accumulator, it may be that the use of conditional transfers will simplify these steps. Simplify these steps as much as possible by the use of conditional transfers. Show the modified AHPL steps and the corresponding hardware realizations.

7.5 Repeat Problem 7.4 for steps 10 to 12, which execute indexed addressing.

7.6 Show the hardware realization for the complete fetch sequence, steps 2-2 to 12 in Appendix C. Use conditional transfers wherever possible to simplify the hardware and speed up operations.

7.7 Repeat Problem 7.6 for steps 13 to 24, implementing the addressed instructions.

7.8 Repeat Problem 7.6 for steps 25 to 47, implementing the operate instructions.

7.9 Construct a Destination/Source list for SIC, similar to Fig. 7.18, considering only steps 13 to 24 and assuming a synchronous memory requiring no extra delays. From this develop a block diagram showing data connections and control in the same manner as Fig. 7.19.

7.10 In Section 7.6 the delays involved in the execution of a rotate instruction in the first event time are discussed. Because of a sequence of decisions at steps 5, 25, 26, and 30, the delay associated with the execution of this instruction, from the time the instruction is available in *IR*, is 11Δ, where Δ is the assumed uniform delay through any single level of logic. Some of this delay could be eliminated by combining these multiple decisions into a single complex decision and conditional transfer step. By so combining steps, speed up the execution of this rotate sequence as much as possible. Show the resultant AHPL steps and corresponding hardware. Comment on the increase in hardware complexity and the amount of time saved.

7.11 Write a combinational logic unit description for the function INC(A), where A is an n-bit register.

7.12 Write a combinational logic unit description for the decrement function, DEC(A), where A is an n-bit register. The function DEC decreases the binary value stored in A by one.

7.13 Write a combinational logic unit description of a 12-line decoder as shown in Fig. 3.14b. Use the description of Example 7.3 for the 3-bit decoders.

7.14 Show by a block diagram similar to Fig. 7.25 how the logic unit description of Example 7.4 generates BUSFN(**M**; **R**). For simplicity, consider **M** to be made up of eight 3-bit words. Then determine how the circuit might be simplified if OR-gates with any number of inputs up to and including eight are available. Modify the logic unit description as required to implement these simplifications.

7.15 Write a combinational logic unit description for the function LARGER described in Example 7.5.

7.16 The adder developed by the logic unit description ADD in Example 7.2 is an example of a *parallel* adder, so-called because all bits of both operands are presented at the inputs simultaneously, *in parallel*. In *serial* addition, a single full adder is used and the corresponding bits of the two operands are added *serially*, i.e., in sequence. First, the two least-significant bits are added, producing the least-significant bit of the sum and the carry-out, if any, is temporarily stored. The next two bits are then added, along with the carry from the first addition, again producing a single bit of the sum and a carry that is temporarily stored. This process is repeated until all bits have been added. The operand registers must be shift registers so that the individual bits can be shifted in and out. This approach is commonly used in such applications as pocket calculators, in which speed is less important than economy. Assuming that *AC* and *MD* are shift registers, show a serial adder configuration suitable for use in SIC. Then write the AHPL sequence to implement serial addition of 18-bit numbers.

REFERENCES

1. Hill, F. J., and G. R. Peterson, *Introduction to Switching Theory and Logical Design,* 2nd ed., Wiley, New York, 1974.

2. Dietmeyer, D. L., *Logical Design of Digital Systems,* Allyn and Bacon, Boston, 1971.

3. Mowle, F. J., *A Systematic Approach to Digital Logic Design,* Addison-Wesley, Reading, Mass., 1976.

4. Breuer, M. A., ed., *Design Automation of Digital Systems,* Prentice-Hall, Englewood Cliffs, N.J., 1972.

5. Swanson, R., Z. Navabi, and F. J. Hill, "An AHPL Compiler/ Simulator System," *Proc. 6th Texas Conference on Computing Systems,* Austin, Tex., 1977.

8

MICROPROGRAMMING

8.1 INTRODUCTION

The concept of a microprogram was first presented by M. V. Wilkes of Cambridge University Mathematical Laboratory in 1951 [1,2,3,4]. This may seem particularly remarkable if one recalls that the vacuum tube and the relay were the only switching devices available at that time. This was only eight years after the introduction of the first electrical computing machine, which incidently utilized the relay as the principal component. The concept was utilized infrequently until the introduction of the IBM system 360 in 1964. All but the fastest and most sophisticated model in the 360 series relied on microprogramming in the control unit design. A primary reason for this approach was to permit reasonably efficient emulation of earlier IBM computers on the system 360. The assurance that existing customer programs could be used directly on the new computer was no doubt a valuable marketing technique for IBM.

In Chapter 6 we learned to express the control function for a digital system as a sequence of AHPL steps very much like a program. Why not store this program in some type of memory and read the AHPL steps out in program sequence? Each time such an AHPL step is read, it could cause a branch (within the AHPL program) or a register transfer within the computer. This is microprogramming. In effect the control unit of a microprogrammable computer consists principally of a memory rather than a large network of flip-flops and logic. Most often this memory will be a read-only memory (ROM). The instructions stored in the ROM are called *microinstructions*. Each microinstruction corresponds to an AHPL step. Usually, a ROM will be cheaper than a read-write memory with the same access time.

In addition to possible economy, other advantages of a microprogram include the possibility of modifying the instruction code and the apparent architecture of the machine. Also, a ROM may make possible cheaper storage and faster execution of frequently used subroutines such as multiplication, division, and, in the case of scientific applications, trigonometric functions. In the early stages of the design process the designer must carefully weight the above factors against certain drawbacks, to be pointed out in succeeding sections, in the context of the intended application for the proposed computer. The designer will then decide to what extent, if any, microprogramming will be utilized in the design of the control unit.

8.2 CONTROLLING THE MICROPROGRAM

It is easy to say "Store the AHPL program in read-only memory," but how is this done? There are two basic problems we must consider. First, some correspondence must be established between the vectors of 1's and 0's that can be stored in memory and the AHPL program steps. Second, we must control the reading of program steps from memory and their execution. Clearly, it is impossible to avoid including a certain amount of hard-wired control circuitry.

In Fig. 8.1a we see a simplified diagram of the essential items of SIC hardware. The items of hardware that would be found in a microprogrammable version of SIC are shown in Fig. 8.1b. The most important observation to make from Fig. 8.1 is that the two versions of SIC are identical except for the control units. Even the terminal characteristics of the control unit are the same. That is, precisely the same sequence of transfer pulses appears on the same control lines in both versions. Only the means by which these control signals are generated is different.

The performance similarity of microprogrammed machines and non-microprogrammed machines should not be pushed too far. The control sequences for the two machines of Fig. 8.1 must necessarily be identical because both machines were defined to be SIC. This is not to say that the type of control unit, microprogrammed or hard-wired, will not influence the layout of the other parts of a digital system. As we shall see in subsequent sections, the choice of a microprogrammable control unit of realistic cost will impose certain constraints on the form of a control sequence that can be implemented. These constraints are not imposed by a hard-wired control sequencer.

The control sequencer of Fig. 8.1a is replaced by a ROM, two registers *MAR* and *MIR*, a *microsequencer*, and a network of decoding logic. Much of this chapter is devoted to demonstrating how these components might function as a control unit. The microsequencer is a small, hard-wired, control sequencer. This is necessary to facilitate the transfer of

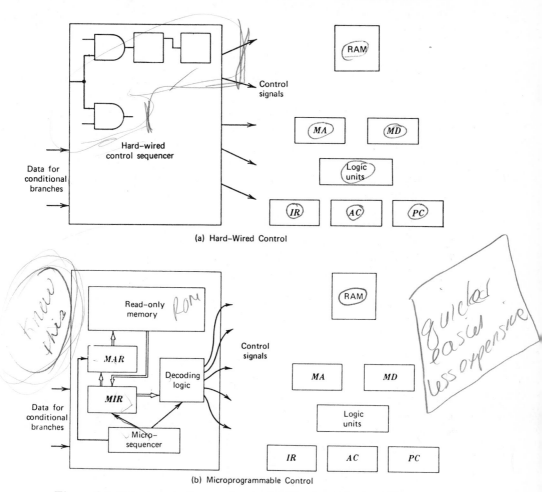

Figure 8.1. Two types of control unit. (*a*) **Hard-wired control** (*b*) **Microprogrammable control.**

vectors between the ROM, **MIR**, and **MAR** within the control unit. Only instructions are stored in the read-only memory.* Therefore, a word may be read from the ROM directly into the *microinstruction register, MIR*. No special memory data register for the read-only memory is required. The **MIR** stores the microinstruction currently being executed. This microinstruction will either cause a transfer pulse to be issued from the control unit or will cause a branch within the control sequence. The

---

* For some machines this constraint is modified to permit the reading of constants from the ROM.

275

microaddress register, MAR, functions as both a program counter and an address register for the read-only memory. Again this is possible because every address is the address of an instruction. The reader may observe that a microprogrammable control unit is almost a computer within a computer.

Under certain circumstances the microinstruction register *MIR* will not be required. If the control memory or ROM is a static memory, that is, the output word is continuously available as a function of *MAR*, the output lines from this memory can themselves be used to effect the proper transfer and branch operation without first transferring the information into *MIR*. With a static ROM the microprogrammable control unit can be represented as shown in Fig. 8.2. This configuration assumes that each microinstruction specifies a branch, if necessary, as well as a transfer and is deliberately arranged in the form of a classical Moore model sequential circuit. The register *MAR* stores the current state of the machine. The sequential circuit has only one state per word in the ROM or potentially one state per step in the control sequence. If, as is usually the case, no other microprogram would result in the same sequence of output control levels, the circuit of Fig. 8.2 is the minimal state control sequential circuit. That is, a 2^n state control sequence is realized by a control circuit consisting of n flip-flops rather than up to 2^n flip-flops as could be the case in a hard-wired control sequencer. As

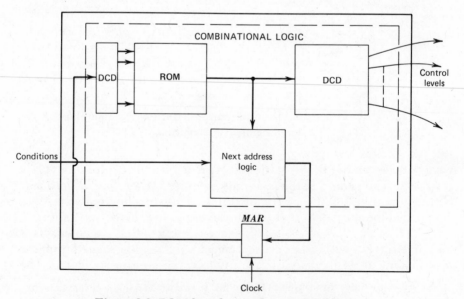

Figure 8.2. ROM-based control sequential circuit.

mentioned previously, the minimal state realization of a control circuit is not necessarily the best, or even the overall most economical realization.

There are inputs to the control unit that serve to control conditional branches within the *microprogram*. Very often these lines, which are shown in Fig. 8.1b, come from the instruction register, *IR*.

It is the decoding logic of Fig. 8.1b, in conjunction with the microsequencer, that makes it possible to interpret the vector in *MIR* as an AHPL step. Our approach here will be to gradually uncover the structure of these units and the reasons why they are so structured. We shall not start by showing all the details of the coding of a microinstruction but rather shall specify these details only as they arise naturally in the discussion. When an *MIR* is employed, the execution of a microinstruction is a two-step process:

1. Place a word from the ROM in *MIR*
2. Issue a control level and/or update *MAR*.

If no asynchronous transfers are specified two clock periods are required per microinstruction. By contrast, in a machine with a hard-wired control sequencer or in the circuit of Fig. 8.2, each step in the control sequence will be executed in one clock period.

The reader might conclude that the use of an *MIR* would decrease the speed of a microprogrammable computer by a factor of two. This would not necessarily be the case, since the clock rate to be established for the configuration of Fig. 8.2 will depend on the propagation delay through the ROM and the decoding logic in series with any combinational logic in the data unit. The inclusion of *MIR* will break this logic into two parts, each with a maximum delay shorter than the original maximum delay. Thus the clock frequency could be increased, although probably not doubled, if *MIR* is used. We shall see that it is possible to extend the complexity of the microsequencer beyond the simple, two-step procedure described here. In this case the faster clock rate would be advantageous. We have chosen to use *MIR* throughout the rest of the chapter primarily to simplify notation. Most of the subsequent discussion is equally applicable to the model of Fig. 8.2 with each instance of *MIR* translated as the output of the ROM.

The delay associated with the ROM will probably always make the microprogrammable approach slower than the fastest hard-wired control sequencer. We shall find that the number of microinstructions necessary to accomplish a task will usually exceed the number of steps in a control sequence for a hard-wired implementation of the same task. Various sophisticatons can be added to lessen the time penalty inherent in microprogramming. We shall see in Section 8.4 that the penalty is less severe in bus-oriented machines. It is safe to say that a machine with a hard-wired sequencer can always be made to operate faster than an apparently identical machine that relies on microprogramming.

There are three basic types of microinstructions that must be separated by the microsequencer: branch operations, synchronous transfers, and asynchronous transfers. We assume that if $MIR_0 = 1$, the microinstruction is a branch. If $MIR_0 = 0$, the microinstruction calls for a register transfer. For transfer microinstructions $MIR_1 = 0$ indicates synchronous transfers, and $MIR_1 = 1$ indicates asychronous transfers.

Because of the above alternatives, the *microcontrol sequence*, i.e., the sequence that is executed by the microsequencer to control the execution of a microinstruction, will require more than two steps. The basic form of the microsequence follows. The corresponding microsequencer, illustrated in Fig. 8.3, controls the functioning of the control unit.

1. $MIR \leftarrow BUSFN \ (ROM; \ DCD \ (MAR))$
2. $\rightarrow (MIR_0)/(4)$
3. $MAR \leftarrow ((INC \ (MAR)) \ ! \ (MIR_{8:19})) * (\bar{g}, g) \ \text{NO DELAY}$
   $\rightarrow (1)$
4. $MAR \leftarrow INC \ (MAR) \ \text{NO DELAY}$
   $\rightarrow (MIR_1)/(6)$
5. $DM \leftarrow OCLM * MIR_{4:19} \ \text{NO DELAY}$
   $\rightarrow (1)$
6. $read, write = MIR_{2:3}$
   $\rightarrow (busy)/(6)$
7. $MD * (busy \wedge MIR_2) \leftarrow DATAOUT$
   $\rightarrow (busy, \overline{busy})/(7, 1)$

The first step reads a microinstruction from the ROM and places it in *MIR*. A delay of one clock period must be allowed before a decision can be made on the basis of the bits of this microinstruction so that a separate step 2 is included to distinguish between a branch and a transfer. In order that a microinstruction be accomplished in two clock periods, no additional delays can be included in the loops that effect branches and synchronous transfers. Thus steps 3, 4, and 5 include the comment NO DELAY and translate into a network of gates as shown in Fig. 8.3. If the function g is 1, the last 12 bits of *MIR* are placed in *MAR* at step 3 causing a branch to another point in the microprogram. If $g = 0$, *MAR* is incremented, causing the next microinstruction in sequence to be executed. As we shall see, g, is a function of both the first 8 bits of *MIR* and condition functions from outside of the control unit that determine

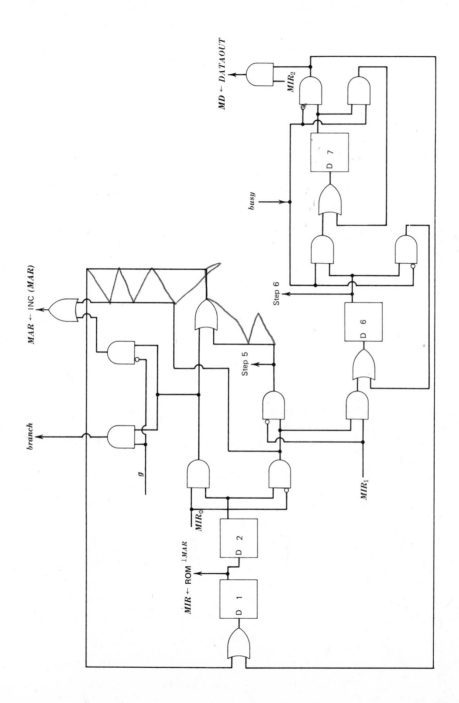

whether or not a branch is satisfied. This approach permits only two-way branches. A bidirectional branching capability will be sufficient to permit the implementation of a microprogrammable minicomputer in the next section. More complicated branching schemes are, however, used in larger microprogrammed computers such as System 370, so that the topic of branching will be explored again in more detail in Section 8.7.

For transfer instructions, step 4 increments *MAR* so that the next microinstruction will be fetched following the transfer. The microsequencer then proceeds to step 5 for synchronous transfers, or step 6 for asynchronous transfers. Step 5 causes any of 16 synchronous transfers to be executed, depending on which of the last 16 bits of *MIR* are 1. The conditional expression at step 5 is an extrapolation of the AHPL Syntax, which we shall find convenient to employ at only this one point in the text. It should be interpreted as if $((A \mathbin{!} B) \leftarrow (C \mathbin{!} D)) * (f_1, f_2)$ were defined as equivalent to $A * f_1 \leftarrow C; B * f_2 \leftarrow D$. Step 6 assumes that the only asynchronous instructions are READ and WRITE in the RAM. Consistent with the asynchronous memory model of Chapter 7, step 6 holds either *read* or *write* at 1 until a *busy* signal is observed from the memory module. Step 7 waits for *busy* to return to 0 before accepting data in the case of a READ operation. Step 6 could be expanded to send out signals to initiate other asynchronous operations. The line *busy* could be replaced in the branch expressions of steps 6 and 7 by the OR combination of similar lines from other modules.

It is not necessary to include the facility for providing timing for asynchronous operations within the microsequencer. If the microprogrammable control unit of Fig. 8.2 with its trivial one-state microcontrol sequence is used, a short microprogram loop can be written to wait for the completion of a multi-clock-period operation. As the complexity of the microsequencer increases, the number of steps in each microprogram decreases. Clearly, microsequencers can range in complexity from one state to a complete control unit without a ROM. Some of the various possibilities will be the topic of Section 8.6.

Example 8.1
Suppose that the addresses at which microinstructions are stored in the ROM are the binary equivalents of the corresponding AHPL steps. Thus the AHPL step

$$(67)$$

might be represented by the microinstruction

$$1XXXXXXX000001000011$$

The 7 bits represented by X will be specified so as to indicate that the branch is unconditional. When the above vector is read into **MIR**, the decoding network will sense from the 7 bits that the branch is unconditional and cause the 12-bit address to be placed in **MAR**. The 12 bits are the binary equivalent of 67 so that the next microinstruction read from the ROM will come from location 67.

We have not yet examined the implementation of the conditional transfer given in step 5. As shown in Fig. 8.1, there must be a control line leaving the control unit for each of the 16 possible transfers. The following example illustrates the simplicity of the decoding network necessary to implement

$$DM \leftarrow OCLM * MIR_{4:19}$$

Example 8.2

In small microprogrammable machines the number of transfers that can take place in the control sequence may be fewer than the number of bits in **MIR**. In this case each bit of **MIR** can correspond to a separate transfer. Then the portion of the decoding network that routes the transfer signals is trivial. Suppose that the last few bits of **MIR** specify transfers as given in Fig. 8.4a. The portion of

If $MIR_{19} = 1$ $\qquad A \leftarrow B$

If $MIR_{18} = 1$ $\qquad A \leftarrow C$

If $MIR_{17} = 1$ $\qquad D \leftarrow E$

(a.)

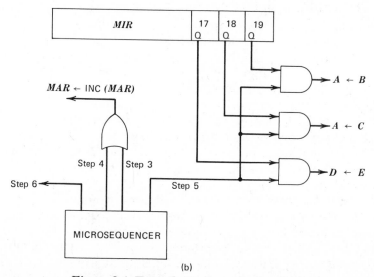

(b)

Figure 8.4. Typical synchronous transfers.

281

the microprogrammable control unit that effects these transfers is shown in Fig. 8.4b, in which the microsequencer of Fig. 8.3 is represented as a single block.

8.3 A MICROPROGRAMMED SIC

In this section we shall lay out a minicomputer to illustrate in more detail the most straightforward, although not necessarily the most efficient, approach to microprogramming. We shall restrict ourselves to two-way branches and list all transfers in the manner suggested by Example 8.2. Since the reader is already familiar with SIC, this is the natural choice for our first example of a microprogrammed machine. To make our first example as simple as possible, we omit the SIC busing structure. All of the transfers in SIC will be assumed to be accomplished through independent data paths.

For the microprogrammed SIC we choose, as a control memory, a ROM with 2^{12} 20-bit words. We assume a relatively fast ROM so that a microinstruction can be read from the ROM and placed in *MIR* in one clock period. In order to satisfy this assumption in practice, it may be necessary to choose a clock frequency somewhat lower than would otherwise be required. For this reason a microprogrammable machine will often have a built-in speed disadvantage when compared to a similar machine with a hard-wired control unit.

It will soon be apparent to the reader that the insistance on assigning one bit of a microinstruction to each possible transfer will preclude the implementation of a complete SIC. It is instructive, however, to proceed with the approach to the extent of implementing only the memory reference instructions. Our goal in this section will be to assure that this can be accomplished. Any additional capability will be regarded as a bonus. The approach would be quite different in the case of a machine designed to be microprogrammed by the user. There it becomes necessary to provide much more flexibility with regard to available branches and transfers that can be specified in microprograms the nature of which might not be anticipated in advance. We shall move gradually in this direction as we progress through the chapter.

A first step will be to list all branches and transfers that are utilized anywhere within the control sequence for the fetch cycle and addressed instructions. A list of all such branches is given in Fig. 8.5a. Recall that only two-way branches are allowed by the microsequencer of Fig. 8.3. Therefore, the three-way branch of step 6 of the SIC control sequence will have to be broken up into two two-way branches, one on IR_3 and one on IR_4. Similarly, there is no provision for conditional transfers in the microsequencer of Fig. 8.3. This is a feature that is not usually available in a microprogrammable computer. Thus the conditional transfers

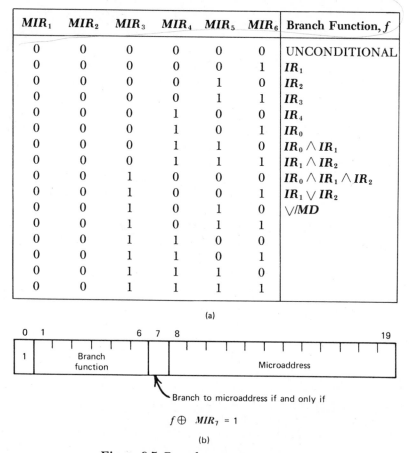

MIR_1	MIR_2	MIR_3	MIR_4	MIR_5	MIR_6	Branch Function, f
0	0	0	0	0	0	UNCONDITIONAL
0	0	0	0	0	1	IR_1
0	0	0	0	1	0	IR_2
0	0	0	0	1	1	IR_3
0	0	0	1	0	0	IR_4
0	0	0	1	0	1	IR_0
0	0	0	1	1	0	$IR_0 \wedge IR_1$
0	0	0	1	1	1	$IR_1 \wedge IR_2$
0	0	1	0	0	0	$IR_0 \wedge IR_1 \wedge IR_2$
0	0	1	0	0	1	$IR_1 \vee IR_2$
0	0	1	0	1	0	$\vee/MD$
0	0	1	0	1	1	
0	0	1	1	0	0	
0	0	1	1	0	1	
0	0	1	1	1	0	
0	0	1	1	1	1	

(a)

Branch to microaddress if and only if

$$f \oplus MIR_7 = 1$$

(b)

Figure 8.5. Branch operations in SIC.

of steps 17 and 21 must be represented by branches followed by transfers in the SIC microprogram. This will increase the number of words of ROM required to implement the SIC control sequence. It will also increase the time required to execute certain memory reference instructions in the microprogrammed SIC with respect to a realization of SIC with hard-wired control. In general the unavailability of conditional transfers is further reason for disqualifying microprogramming as an approach in applications in which speed is the highest-priority design goal.

The first five branch functions listed in Fig. 8.5a are sufficient in themselves to distinguish all memory reference instructions as well as indexing and indirect addressing. All of the branches in this figure are either unconditional or are determined by some Boolean function of the instruction bits or, in one case, a function of the bits in MD. The reader can satisfy himself that all branch operations in the control sequence of Section 6.5 are specified by one of the Boolean functions listed in the rightmost column of Fig. 8.5a. Counting the unconditional branch, there are 11 branch functions in all. Thus these functions could be represented by 4 microinstruction bits. Instead, 6 bits of MIR are used to code the branch microinstructions so that the same format can be used as additional branch functions are added in subsequent sections. Bits $MIR_{1:6}$ are used for this purpose. As previously indicated, bit MIR_0 serves to distinguish between branch and transfer microinstructions.

Once the branches of the SIC control sequence are reduced to bidirectional branches, one of the two possible next steps will follow immediately after the branch instruction in sequence. Thus we need only specify the branch function, f; the location of the alternate next step that does not follow in sequence; and a bit to assign functional values (1 or 0) to the two alternatives. If and only if the function, f, and the bit MIR_7 have opposite values, control branches to the address specified. That is, $MIR_7 = 0$ indicates that a jump will take place if the branch function is satisfied. $MIR_7 = 1$ indicates a jump when the branch function is not satisfied. If $f = MIR_7$, control passes to the next microinstruction in sequence. In effect we can use each function listed in Fig. 8.5 or its complement to specify a branch. As only 11 branch functions are found in an elementary SIC, 53 branch codes are unused in Fig. 8.5a. The complete branch instruction word is given in Fig. 8.5b. Since 12 bits are allowed to specify the microaddress, as many as 2^{12} instructions in the ROM can be reached by a branch.

Once the list of branch functions as given in Fig. 8.5 has been assembled, a network realizing the function g of steps 3 (repeated below) of the microsequences can be constructed.

3. $MAR \leftarrow (\text{INC } (MAR) \ ! \ (MIR_{8:19})) * (\overline{g}, g)$ NO DELAY

This step determines whether a new address will be placed in the microaddress register or whether this register will be incremented. A branch to a new address occurs when $g = 1$; thus g will be 1 for an unconditional branch. Also g will be 1 if the 6 bits $MIR_{1:6}$ take on the values corresponding to any one of the listed branch functions; that corresponding function is 1 if $MIR_7 = 0$ or 0 if $MIR_7 = 1$. Thus we may express the network g by the sum of products expression of Eq. 8.1.

$$g = \bigvee/(DCD_{0:10}(MIR_{1:6})) \wedge ((1, IR_1, IR_2, IR_3,$$
$$IR_4, IR_0, IR_0 \wedge IR_1, IR_1 \wedge IR_2, IR_0 \wedge IR_1 \wedge IR_2,$$
$$IR_1 \vee IR_2, \bigvee/MD) \oplus MIR_7) \tag{8.1}$$

Transfer Operation	Specifying Bit in MIR
$MD \leftarrow M^{\perp MA}$	2
$M^{\perp MA} \leftarrow MD$	3
$IR \leftarrow MD$	4
$MA \leftarrow IR_{5:17}$	5
$AC \leftarrow MD$	6
$AC \leftarrow AC \wedge MD$	7
$lf, AC \leftarrow \text{ADD}(MD, AC)$	8
$MD \leftarrow \text{INC}(MD)$	9
$PC \leftarrow \text{INC}(PC)$	10
$MD \leftarrow AC$	11
$MD \leftarrow 00000, \text{INC}(PC)$	12
$PC \leftarrow IR_{5:17}$	13
$MA \leftarrow PC$	14
$IR_{5:17} \leftarrow \text{ADD}_{6:18}(IR; IA)$	15
$IR_{5:17} \leftarrow \text{ADD}_{6:18}(IR; IB)$	16
$IR_{5:17} \leftarrow MD_{5:17}$	17
UNUSED	18
UNUSED	19

Figure 8.6. Transfer Microinstructions.

In the table of Fig. 8.6 are listed the 16 transfers that occur within the memory reference control sequence without regard to routes through the busing structure. We assume that the decoded control levels as illustrated in Fig. 8.4 are used to establish bus routes as well as effect the transfers or that each transfer is implemented using a separate data path. The order of the listing is arbitrary except that the read and write operations are listed first in agreement with step 6 of the microsequence. Bits 2 and 3 of MIR are assigned to these transfers. As previously suggested, bit $MIR_0 = 0$ for all transfers, bit $MIR_1 = 0$ for synchronous transfers, and $MIR_1 = 1$ for asynchronous transfers.

So far each of the activities discussed is a function performed by the designer of the microprogrammable computer. In order that these functions not be confused with microprogramming, which is about to be discussed, we have summarized the three phases of implementation and utilization for a microprogrammable machine in Fig. 8.7. So far we have considered only the hardware phase. This phase will have been completed once the unit leaves the manufacturer's installation. The task of supplying the microprogram may be accomplished by the manufacturer, may fall to the user, or may be done by the manufacturer according to

285

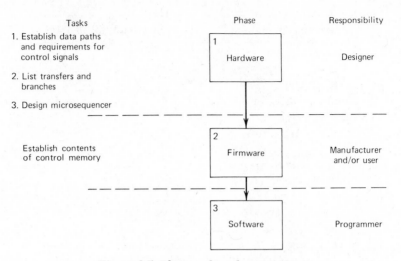

Figure 8.7. Phases of implementation.

the user's specification. A major selling point of a microprogrammable minicomputer is the potential to modify the control unit by supplying a revised microprogram. It is important to recognize that *supplying a microprogram is the limit of the user's ability to restructure the machine*. There is no provision for user modification of the microsequencer. For example, the list of branch functions is fixed. An exercise or example may call for augmenting the list of branch functions prior to writing a specific microprogram. In practice all such branches must be anticipated during the design process and included in the branch list. As a pedagogical tool we have chosen to introduce branch functions as needed rather than supply an exhaustive list in advance.

We are now ready to examine a short section of a microprogram. Using the tables of Figs. 8.5 and 8.6, we can translate the AHPL instructions of Section 6.5 into microcode form for storage in read-only memory. A program to accomplish this task would be somewhat less complicated than the hardware compiler proposed in Chapter 7. It would merely be required to generate a coded version of each AHPL instruction. Since address assignment would not be required, this program would, in that respect, be simpler than an assembler. An example of the assembly of a short sequence is given in Fig. 8.8. The vertical lines separate the 8 branch description bits from the 12 address bits in the case of branch microinstructions. The two bits that describe the type of transfer are similarly separated from the 15 bits that specify individual transfers.

The five steps of microcode in Fig. 8.8 actually implement the SIC

AHPL Instruction	Microcode
18 $MD \leftarrow$ INC (MD)	0 0 0 0 0 0 0 0 0 1 0 0 0 0 0 0 0 0 0
19 M^* DCD $(MA) \leftarrow MD$	0 1 0 1 0 0 0 0 0 0 0 0 0 0 0 0 0 0 0
19a $\rightarrow (\vee /MD)/(24)$	1 0 0 1 0 1 0 0 0 0 0 0 0 0 0 1 1 0 0 0
20 $PC \leftarrow$ INC (PC)	0 0 0 0 0 0 0 0 0 0 1 0 0 0 0 0 0 0 0
20a $\rightarrow (24)$	1 0 0 0 0 0 0 0 0 0 0 0 0 0 1 1 0 0 0

Figure 8.8. Example of microcode assembly.

increment and skip instruction. The sequence has been modified to the extent that each transfer and each branch are listed as separate steps. The write in memory operation is written as one step, since the "wait for a completion signal" is already incorporated in the microsequencer.

The first and fourth lines of microcode are synchronous transfers, as indicated by the two leftmost zeros in the microinstruction. Bit 9 of the first microinstruction is 1, since this bit corresponds to $MD \leftarrow$ INC (MD) in Fig. 8.6. The second transfer microinstruction is asynchronous, and the leftmost two bits are 01. The third and fifth microinstructions are branches to location 24 in the ROM so that the leftmost bit is 1 and the 12-bit address is the binary representation of 24. The third step is conditioned by $\vee /MD$. According to Fig. 8.5 this condition is imposed by making bits $MIR_{1:6} = 001010$ as shown. The last branch is unconditional; therefore, $MIR_{1:6} = 000000$.

8.4 MICROPROGRAMMING A BUS-ORIENTED MACHINE

The advantages of microprogramming may not seem apparent to the reader from the example of the previous section. There we added a massive ROM to replace most of a fairly simple, hard-wired control unit. In the process we have increased the execution time for each instruction considerably.

The discussion of the previous section was intended primarily as an introduction to some of the problems of controlling microprograms. The control unit discussed did not take advantage of the large ROM available. Once the hard-wired portion of the microprogram control unit has been included, it need not be increased regardless of the number of microinstructions stored in the read-only memory. It would seem, then, that the efficient use of microprogramming would imply sequences of microinstructions to execute complex operations such as multiplication, division, or other arithmetic or logical operations, or even long input-output or block data transfer sequences.

Although the op code could be changed, it would probably be difficult to devise microinstructions for the machine of Section 8.3 to substantially expand its performance beyond that of SIC. Only one branch condition that was a function of data registers was included, and only those register transfers specifically used in SIC were allowed. In order to permit a larger class of possible register transfers, data busing is almost universally used within machines employing microprogramming.

In this section we shall use the SIC busing structure together with certain additional branch conditions in a more general microprogrammable machine, which could include SIC as well as a much broader capability. Similarly, operate instructions could be microprogrammed. We shall still assume a 3-bit op code, which could be, but would not necessarily be, the SIC op code, depending on the microprogram. In this way we can use the 11 familiar branch conditions of Fig. 8.5a, adding as many additional branch functions as necessary. The unused bit combinations in operate instructions will be used to specify complex operations such as multiplication. These operations cannot involve memory references but must merely manipulate the contents of the high-speed registers. There is much to be said, of course, for a longer word length, which would allow 4 or more bits to specify the op code.

In Fig. 8.9 is an expanded list of branch functions, which we shall assume to be implemented by the microsequencer and available to the microprogrammer of a bus-oriented extended SIC. The last branch functions include the remaining bits of IR all of which are required to implement the SIC operate instructions. Functions 11, 12, and 14 are also needed within the operate instructions but will have other applications as well. Also MQ_{17} must be tested in multiplication while $\vee /(MC \oplus MAX)$ will make possible looping within a microprogram.

The register configurations and bus connections for the expanded SIC are given in Fig. 8.10. The index registers are now 18 bits so that they can be used for temporary storage as well as indexing. Three buses are used. The A and B buses serve as argument buses. The 19-bit $OBUS$, or output bus, also serves as the path for all direct transfers between registers. An *exclusive-OR* logic unit, designated XOR, has been provided. Most machines include this bit-by-bit operation. We shall find it convenient in various problems and examples. The only inputs to the $OBUS$ specifically shown are the combinational logic units that require both the A and B buses as arguments. Also not shown are the register connections into $ABUS$ and $BBUS$ and the output connections from $OBUS$. The connections between registers and buses will be specified in several tables to follow. The very large number of such connections would so clutter the diagram of Fig. 8.10 as to make it useless.

The configuration of Fig. 8.10 includes all registers found in SIC. Also

MIR_1	MIR_2	MIR_3	MIR_4	MIR_5	MIR_6	Branch Function, f
0	0	0	0	0	0	UNCONDITIONAL
0	0	0	0	0	1	IR_1
0	0	0	0	1	0	IR_2
0	0	0	0	1	1	IR_3
0	0	0	1	0	0	IR_4
0	0	0	1	0	1	IR_0
0	0	0	1	1	0	$IR_0 \wedge IR_1$
0	0	0	1	1	1	$IR_1 \wedge IR_2$
0	0	1	0	0	0	$IR_0 \wedge IR_1 \wedge IR_2$
0	0	1	0	0	1	$IR_1 \vee IR_2$
0	0	1	0	1	0	$\vee /MD$
0	0	1	0	1	1	$\vee /AC$
0	0	1	1	0	0	AC_0
0	0	1	1	0	1	MQ_{17}
0	0	1	1	1	0	lf
0	0	1	1	1	1	$\vee /(MC \oplus MAX)$
0	1	0	0	0	0	IR_5
0	1	0	0	0	1	IR_6
0	1	0	0	1	0	IR_7
0	1	0	0	1	1	IR_8
0	1	0	1	0	0	IR_9
0	1	0	1	0	1	IR_{10}
0	1	0	1	1	0	IR_{11} Needed in
0	1	0	1	1	1	IR_{12} operate
0	1	1	0	0	0	IR_{13} instructions
0	1	1	0	0	1	IR_{14}
0	1	1	0	1	0	IR_{15}
0	1	1	0	1	1	IR_{16}
0	1	1	1	0	0	IR_{17}
0	1	1	1	0	1	$IR_6 \wedge IR_7$

Figure 8.9. Expanded list branch conditions.

included are an 18-bit register MQ, which will be used in multiplication and other similar functions; and 6-bit registers MC and MAX, which are included primarily to count loops in a microprogram. We shall see shortly that all data paths available through the SIC busing structure of Chapter 6 will also be possible in the structure of Fig. 8.10. Many new data paths useful in a variety of microprograms will be possible as well.

It is of interest to examine in detail the hardware both in the control

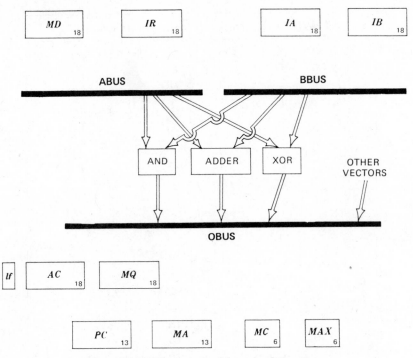

Figure 8.10. Register and bus configuration.

unit and the data unit for connecting data to a bus as specified by a set of bits in the microinstruction register. Presentation of a detailed network realization of Fig. 8.10 would be prohibitive. We can, however make all the same general observations on a less complex busing structure as is done in the following example.

Example 8.3

Figure 8.11 lists the vectors that must be connected to the 6-bit $QBUS$, one of the buses of a small microprogrammable computer. The vector to be connected to $QBUS$ by a particular microinstruction is specified by 3 bits of the microinstruction register, $MIR_{2:4}$. For example, if $MIR_{2:4}$ is 0, 0, 1, then zeros are to be connected to the first 3 bits of the $QBUS$, and $RA_{3:5}$ to the last 3 bits. Construct a detailed logic block diagram of the $QBUS$ including the decoder in the control unit that generates control levels to effect connections to the bus.

Solution

A single step in the AHPL description of the microsequencer will call for placing the appropriate vector from Fig. 8.11 on the $QBUS$. The array of bus inputs on

290

Vector to Be Placed on QBUS	$MIR_{2:4}$
RA	0, 0, 0
$3 \top 0, RA_{3:5}$	0, 0, 1
$RA_{0:2}, RB_{3:5}$	0, 1, 0
RB	0, 1, 1
$6 \top 0$	1, 0, 0
$6 \top 1$	1, 0, 1
$6 \top 8$	1, 1, 0
$6 \top 10$	1, 1, 1

Figure 8.11. Inputs to QBUS.

the right-hand side of the AHPL step given as expression 8.2 is abbreviated **QM** in Fig. 8.12.

$$QBUS = (RA \mathbin{!} 3 \top 0, RA_{3:5} \mathbin{!} RA_{0:2}, RB_{3:5} \mathbin{!} RB \mathbin{!} 6 \top 0 \mathbin{!} 6 \top 1 \mathbin{!} 6 \top 8 \mathbin{!} 6 \top 10)$$
$$* \text{DCD} (MIR)_{2:4}$$
$$= \text{QM} * \text{DCD} (MIR)_{2:4} \tag{8.2}$$

Only one step of the microsequence is shown in Fig. 8.12 along with that portion of the control unit that decodes $MIR_{2:4}$ and the realization of the **QBUS** in the data unit.

Notice that none of the OR gates making up **QBUS** has more than four inputs (three of the OR gates have only two inputs) even though eight vectors are listed in Fig. 8.11. By appropriate ORing of the control levels, the various combinations of bits from **RA** and **RB** result in only two connections to each **QBUS** OR gate. For example, only $RA_{0:2}$ and $RB_{0:2}$ need be routed to the first 3 bits of **QBUS**, since $3 \top 0$ is the $QBUS_{0:2}$ output if all input lines are 0. The routing of the constants listed as the last four entries in Fig. 8.11 is accomplished by connecting the respective control levels directly to the **QBUS** OR gates, much the same as in the implementation of a ROM. Notice that no connection to DCD_4 is required to cause $6 \top 0$ to be placed on the **QBUS**.

The vectors to be connected to the **ABUS** and **BBUS** of Fig. 8.10 are listed in Fig. 8.13. Three bits of the 20-bit microinstruction, $MIR_{3:5}$, are used to specify the **ABUS** input. Four bits $MIR_{6:9}$ are used to specify the **BBUS** input. In order to provide for rotation of *lf, AC* through the busing structure the ABUS *will consist of 19 bits* while the **BBUS** will have only 18 bits. As indicated in the table, many of the leftmost bits of the various vectors will always be 0's. As suggested by Example 8.3, these zeros will not result in actual input connections to the OR gates making

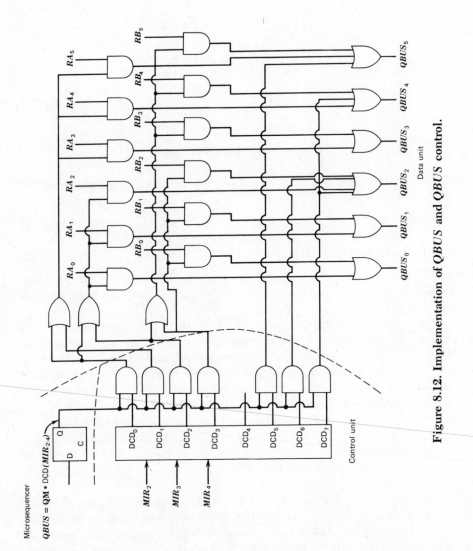

Figure 8.12. Implementation of *QBUS* and *QBUS* control.

MIR_3	MIR_4	MIR_5	ABUS Inputs
0	0	0	$19\top0$
0	0	1	AC_{17}, MQ
0	1	0	lf, AC
0	1	1	0, AC
1	0	0	$6\top0$, $IR_{5:17}$
1	0	1	$13\top0$, MC
1	1	0	$19\top1$
1	1	1	

MIR_6	MIR_7	MIR_8	MIR_9	BBUS Inputs
0	0	0	0	$18\top0$
0	0	0	1	MD
0	0	1	0	IA
0	0	1	1	IB
0	1	0	0	$5\top0$, PC
0	1	0	1	$18\top1$
0	1	1	0	$18\top2$
0	1	1	1	$18\top4$
1	0	0	0	$18\top16$
1	0	0	1	$18\top32$
1	0	1	0	$18\top18$
1	0	1	1	$18\top10$
1	1	0	0	$18\top100$
1	1	0	1	$18\top1000$
1	1	1	0	

(a)   (b)

Figure 8.13. Connections to the A and B buses.

up the buses. The input vectors listed in Fig. 8.13 include all SIC A and B bus connections as discussed in Chapter 6 as well as others useful in writing more complex microprograms. The constant 1 is available on both buses so that any of the listed registers can be incremented. Several commonly used constants are available on the *BBUS*. So far in the book we have not discussed SIC input-output. One may wish to assume that the unused bit combinations will specify the connection input-output registers to the *ABUS* and *BBUS*.

The *OBUS* is intended to supply a path for all register transfers. Therefore, one would expect a very large number of possible input and output connections to this bus. Four bits of *MIR* (10 to 13) are used to identify the input to the *OBUS*. The last 6 bits of *MIR* (14 to 19) specify the output connections from the *OBUS*. The bit combinations corresponding to particular connections to the *OBUS* are given in Fig. 8.14.

The layout of Fig. 8.14 provides a clue to our overall point of view. Notice that the output connections for the *OBUS* are listed in the form of register transfers. In fact, these are the only bused register transfers that can take place in the execution of a microinstruction. The execution of each microinstruction is accomplished in two steps. The first step utilizes bits 3 to 13 of *MIR* to gate a data vector to the output of the

(a)

$MIR_{10:13}$				Input Connection
0	0	0	0	$ABUS$
0	0	0	1	$0, BBUS$
0	0	1	0	$ABUS_{18}, ABUS_{0:17}$
0	0	1	1	$ABUS_{1:18}, ABUS_0$
0	1	0	0	$\overline{ABUS}$
0	1	0	1	$0, \overline{BBUS}$
0	1	1	0	$0, \text{AND} (ABUS_{1:18}, BBUS)$
0	1	1	1	$0, \text{XOR} (ABUS_{1:18}, BBUS)$
1	0	0	0	$\text{ADD} (ABUS_{1:18}, BBUS)$
1	0	0	1	$ABUS_{4:18}, MQ_{0:3}$

(b)

$MIR_{14:19}$						Output Transfer
0	0	0	0	0	0	$MD \leftarrow OBUS_{1:18}$
0	0	0	0	0	1	$IR \leftarrow OBUS_{1:18}$
0	0	0	0	1	0	$IA \leftarrow OBUS_{1:18}$
0	0	0	0	1	1	$IB \leftarrow OBUS_{1:18}$
0	0	0	1	0	0	$PC \leftarrow OBUS_{6:18}$
0	0	0	1	0	1	$MQ \leftarrow OBUS_{1:18}$
0	0	0	1	1	0	$If, AC \leftarrow OBUS$
0	0	0	1	1	1	$AC \leftarrow OBUS_{1:18}$
0	0	1	0	0	0	$If \leftarrow OBUS_0$
0	0	1	0	0	1	$MC \leftarrow OBUS_{13:18}$
0	0	1	0	1	0	$MAX \leftarrow OBUS_{13:18}$
0	0	1	0	1	1	$MA \leftarrow OBUS_{6:18}$

Figure 8.14. Connections to $OBUS$.

$OBUS$. This vector may be either a register or the combinational logic function of two registers depending on the particular bits in MIR.

This flow of data through the buses is determined by output lines from three decoders whose inputs are $MIR_{3:5}$, $MIR_{6:9}$, and $MIR_{10:13}$, respectively. For example, a data word will be gated onto the $BBUS$ by the one line from the 16-output decoder (inputs $MIR_{6:9}$) whose logical value is 1. The second step transfers bits from the $OBUS$ into one of the registers, as shown in Fig. 8.14b. The first step takes place when a transfer microinstruction is read from the ROM into MIR. Thus, as in the previous two sections, only two clock periods are required to execute a microinstruction. The clock period required to set connections to the buses is the same clock period in which a microinstruction is read from the ROM.

Again not all bit combinations are used in Fig. 8.14. Only those input connections and output transfers listed will be encountered in subsequent discussion. Many others could be added. In particular, many more connections to the output of the $OBUS$ can be specified. Since transfers from the $OBUS$ will require only ORing of control levels routing pluses to flip-flop clock inputs, a broader array of transfers can be provided quite economically. The only register with input logic is MD, which must also receive data from memory.

Not all data transfers can be accomplished through the busing network. Similarly, certain input-output instructions will require microinstructions that will generate control levels on lines constituting system outputs. We have provided for this situation by reserving two bits $MIR_{1:2}$ of the microinstruction to specify operations in addition to bused transfers. The meaning of these bits is summarized in Fig. 8.15. We shall not be concerned at this point with any specific operations in the second and third categories except the asynchronous references to the 8k RAM, $MD \leftarrow M^{\perp MA}$ when $MIR_3 = 1$ and $M^{\perp MA} \leftarrow MD$ when $MIR_4 = 1$.

$MIR_0 MIR_1 MIR_2$			Operation
0	0	0	Bused transfer
0	0	1	Other synchronous operations
0	1	0	Asynchronous Operations
0	1	1	$OBUS = ROM^{\perp 0,0, MIR_{3:13}};$
			$DM * DCD (MIR_{14:19}) \leftarrow OBUS$
1	X	X	Branch

Figure 8.15. Categories of operations in extended SIC.

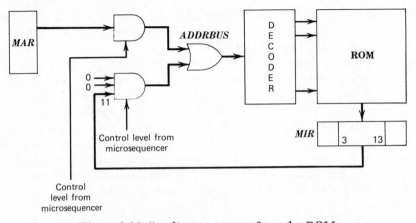

Figure 8.16. Reading a constant from the ROM.

The microsequencer that will effect the operations of Fig. 8.15 will be discussed in Section 8.6. For now let us consider briefly the fourth operation in the table, which causes a constant to be read from anywhere within the first 2k of ROM. This operation will require an extra clock period as well as a separate address path, as illustrated in Fig. 8.16. The two-input address bus, **ADDRBUS**, is entirely combinational, with two 13-bit banks of AND gates and a bank of OR gates as shown. The transfer of the constant from the **OBUS** into the desired register in **DM** is specified by $MIR_{14:19}$ exactly as listed in Fig. 8.14b. Thus the only additional hardware made necessary by this operation will be one gate for ORing two control lines at the output of the microsequencer.

With the machinery thus set up, consideration of examples of microprograms that can be accomplished by the expanded SIC would seem to be the next order of business. Clearly, however, we do not want to examine strings of 1's and 0's as we discuss these microprograms. In the next section we shall consider a version of APL as a possible assembly language for microprogramming. We shall not find it difficult to translate these assembly language programs to microcode where necessary. In instances in which a large variety of microprograms are to be written for a machine in production, the authors strongly recommend the use of a microassembler program. Such a program will be dependent on the machine to be microprogrammed but will not be difficult to write. As only line-by-line translation is required, many of the usual difficulties in writing an assembler are avoided. Certainly, such a program will be much less complicated than the hardware compiler mentioned previously.

8.5 AN ASSEMBLY LANGUAGE FOR MICROPROGRAMS

In this section we shall define an *assembly language for microprograms* for the machine just discussed called MICRAL (microassembly language). Each step of MICRAL will correspond to one microinstruction. The MICRAL representation of a transfer step must specify a connection to each bus and a transfer from the *OBUS* to a destination register. A bus connection will be omitted if and only if it is not one of the arguments of a logic network leading to the *OBUS*. A bus connection statement in MICRAL will have an abbreviation A, B, or OB for *ABUS*, *BBUS*, or *OBUS* on the left-hand side of the "=" with one of the vectors in Fig. 8.13 or Fig. 8.14a on the right. The abbreviated bus notation will also be used in the expressions to the right of the "=" sign. Since no ambiguity will result, leading zeros may be omitted in MICRAL. Similarly, the number of bits in a constant is constrained so that this number will not appear in MICRAL. Since the arguments of AND, XOR, and ADD are always the same, these will be omitted also. Where the rightmost bits of the *OBUS* are used in a transfer, the number of bits is fixed by the destination and will not otherwise be specified in MICRAL. The only two asynchronous operations, read and write in the **RAM** will simply be written in MICRAL as READ or WRITE.

None of the information omitted from MICRAL in the above discussion will be required by a *microassembler* program that will generate microcode from a MICRAL statement. The information provided in each statement will be sufficient to permit identification of the corresponding entry from Fig. 8.13 or Fig. 8.14.

As a first example, let us express the multiplication sequence of Section 6.11 in MICRAL. Each branch step and the MICRAL equivalent of each transfer microinstruction will be a numbered step. The reader will notice that to the extent permitted by this constraint, the routine of Section 6.11 is reconstructed in a step-by-step fashion. We begin with the sign determination routine.

1. $A = \top 0;\ OB = A$
   $lf \leftarrow OB_0$
2. $\rightarrow (\overline{AC_0})/(5)$
3. $A = lf,\ AC;\ OB = \bar{A}$
   $lf,\ AC \leftarrow OB$

The two-way branch format of step 2 will be used for all branches in MICRAL. Since all branches are two-way branches and one alternative is the next step in sequence, this special case of the AHPL branch notation will be sufficient.

Step 4 illustrates the use of the word ADD without arguments to specify the adder network. The arguments are always the A and B buses.

4. $A = lf, AC; B = \top 1; OB = \text{ADD}$
   $lf, AC \leftarrow OB$
5. $A = 0, AC; OB = A$
   $MQ \leftarrow OB$
6. $B = MD; OB = B$
   $AC \leftarrow OB$

The reader should compare the transfer portion of step 4, which uses all 19 bits of the $OBUS$, with step 6, which transfers only the last 18 bits into AC. The latter will be interpreted by a microassembler as the MICRAL abbreviation for $AC \leftarrow OBUS_{1:18}$.

7. $\rightarrow (\overline{AC_0})/(10)$
8. $A = lf, AC; OB = \bar{A}$
   $lf, AC \leftarrow OB$
9. $A = lf, AC; B = \top 1; OB = \text{ADD}$
   $lf, AC \leftarrow OB$
10. $A = 0, AC; OB = A$
    $MD \leftarrow OB$

Step 9 of Section 6.11 must be replaced by two separate two-step microinstructions. As we see, the $OBUS$ approach virtually excludes parallel operations. In general, we shall find that microprograms will include more steps and require more time for execution than hard-wired sequences. Microprograms, however, will require significantly less time than purely software approaches to the same operations. We replace step 9 by MICRAL steps 11 and 12.

11. $A = \top 0; OB = A$
    $AC \leftarrow OB$
12. $A = \top 0; OB = A$
    $MC \leftarrow OB$

A single branch condition has been provided that compares $\perp MC$ with $\perp MAX$. The rightmost 6 bits of any of the constants listed in Fig. 8.13 may be placed in MAX in advance. In this case we place the number 18 in MAX to count through the 18-bit multiplication.

13. $B = \top 18;\ OB = B$
     $MAX \leftarrow OB$
14. $\rightarrow (\bigvee / \overline{(MC \oplus MAX)}\ /(21)$
15. $\rightarrow (\overline{MQ}_{17})/(17)$

We have rearranged the original sequence so that the addition required when $MQ_{17} = 1$ appears ahead of the rotate right that is performed when $MQ_{17} = 0$. In this way we are able to write the 2-step rotate operation only once without adding an extra branch operation. Two steps are required for the rotate, since it involves two 18-bit registers AC and MQ. The MICRAL notation RR(A) means rotation of the $ABUS$ right and is an abbreviation for $ABUS_{18}, ABUS_{0:17}$, which appears in Fig. 8.14a.

16. $A = 0, AC;\ B = MD;\ OB = \text{ADD}$
     $lf, AC \leftarrow OB$
17. $A = AC_{17}, MQ;\ OB = \text{RR }(A)$
     $MQ \leftarrow OB$
18. $A = lf, AC;\ OB = \text{RR }(A)$
     $AC \leftarrow OB$
19. $A = MC;\ B = \top 1;\ OB = \text{ADD}$
     $MC \leftarrow OB$
20. $\rightarrow (14)$

The reader will recall that step 20 concludes the multiplication of the absolute value of the arguments. The following sequence takes the two's complement of AC, MQ if the sign of the product is to be negative.

21. $\rightarrow (\overline{lf})/(30)$
22. $A = 0, AC;\ OB = \bar{A}$
     $MD \leftarrow OB$
23. $A = AC_{17}, MQ;\ OB = \bar{A}$
     $AC \leftarrow OB$
24. $A = \top 0;\ OB = A$
     $lf \leftarrow OB_0$
25. $A = 0, AC;\ B = 1;\ OB = \text{ADD}$
     $lf, AC \leftarrow OB$
26. $A = 0, AC;\ OB = A$
     $MQ \leftarrow OB$
27. $B = \overline{MD};\ OB = B$
     $AC \leftarrow OB$

Step 21 of the original sequence uses the link as part of one of the arguments of addition. The tables of Fig. 8.14 do not provide for this situation so that this instruction must be replaced by a branch and the addition of a fixed argument to AC.

28. $\rightarrow \overline{(lf)}/(30)$
29. $A = 0, AC; \ B = \top 1; \ OB = \text{ADD}$
    $lf, AC \leftarrow OB$
30. END OF SEQUENCE

Example 8.4

Like SIC, most modern computers store data and perform arithmetic operations in straight binary form. Always present, then, is the problem of converting to and from binary-coded decimal notation for communication with the outside world. It is often necessary to recognize 6- to 8-bit alphanumeric characters as decimal digits and to convert strings of such digits to binary form. For purposes of illustration we shall simplify the problem as follows. Assume that the rightmost 16 bits of MQ represent four binary-coded decimal digits. Write a sequence of microinstructions that will convert this four-digit number to binary form.

Solution.

Our approach to the problem is suggested by the last three $ABUS$ arguments listed in Fig. 8.13. The four-digit number $D_3D_2D_1D_0$, which must be converted to binary, may be represented as

$$D_3 \times 1000_{\text{base ten}} + D_2 \times 100_{\text{base ten}} + D_1 \times 10_{\text{base ten}} + D_0 \qquad (8.3)$$

If each of the D_i and the powers of 10 are replaced by their binary equivalents and the above computation performed, the result will be the binary equivalent of $D_3 \ D_2 \ D_1 \ D_0$. Suppose, for example, that $D_1 = 9$. In this case the binary equivalent of $D_1 \times 10$ is given by Eq. 8.3.

$$
\begin{aligned}
\top (D_1 \times 10_{\text{base ten}}) &= 1001 \times (1010) \\
&= 1010000 \times 1 + 101000 \times 0 + 10100 \times 0 + 1010 \times 1 \\
&= 1010000 + 1010 = 1011010 \qquad (8.4)
\end{aligned}
$$

Thus the conversion process is very similar to multiplication. Each bit of the BCD digit multiples the power of 10 expressed binary. This process is carried out for all four digits with the results added together. As in multiplication, we consider each bit of MQ beginning at the right. The vector AC, MQ is rotated right each step. The following sequence handles the rightmost 8 bits, or two decimal digits. The reader is left to complete the microprogram for the remaining 8 bits. Step 10, which realigns the partial sum after the first digit multiplication, requires the special connection to the $OBUS$ found at the bottom of the list in Fig. 8.14a.

1. $A = \top 0$; $OB = A$
   $AC \leftarrow OB$
2. $A = \top 4$; $OB = A$
   $MAX \leftarrow OB$
3. $A = \top 0$; $OB = A$
   $MC \leftarrow OB$
4. $\rightarrow (\overline{MQ}_{17})/(6)$
5. $A = 0, AC$; $B = \top 1$; $OB = \mathrm{ADD}$
   $AC \leftarrow OB$
6. $A = AC_{17}, MQ$; $OB = \mathrm{RR}(A)$
   $MQ \leftarrow OB$
7. $A = 0, AC$; $OB = \mathrm{RR}(A)$
   $AC \leftarrow OB$
8. $A = MC$; $B = \top 1$; $OB = \mathrm{ADD}$
   $\mathbf{MC \leftarrow OB}$
9. $\rightarrow (\vee/(MAX \oplus MC))/(4)$
10. $A = 0, AC$; $OB = A_{4:18}, MQ_{0:3}$
    $\mathit{If}, AC \leftarrow OB$
11. $A = \top 0$; $OB = A$
    $MC \leftarrow OB$
12. $\rightarrow (\overline{MQ}_{17})/(14)$
13. $A = 0, AC$; $B = \top 10$; $OB = \mathrm{ADD}$
    $AC \leftarrow OB$
14. $A = AC_{17}, MQ$; $OB = \mathrm{RR}(A)$
    $MQ \leftarrow AC$
15. $A = 0, AC$; $OB = \mathrm{RR}(A)$
    $AC \leftarrow OB$
16. $A = MC$; $B = \top 1$; $OB = \mathrm{ADD}$
    $MC \leftarrow OB$
17. $\rightarrow (\vee/(MC \oplus MAX))/(11)$
18. Etc.

The reader may feel that the design of the machine described in the previous section has been tuned to the two examples that we have examined so far. To a certain extent this assertion would be correct although sufficient options are available to permit the writing of a large array of useful microprograms. Certainly, the last three arguments listed as available to the *BBUS* have limited utility. Other microprograms may require other constant vectors. A desirable modification of our machine would be a special transfer instruction that could read 18-bit constants from the ROM into high-speed constants temporarily as well as add to the overall capability of the machine. Another improvement would be the provision for more flexibility in branch microinstructions. These are the topics of the next sections.

8.6 FURTHER FLEXIBILITY

In Fig. 8.15 it was indicated that the microprogrammable extended SIC would have the capability of executing transfers outside of the bus structure as well as the capability of obtaining constants from the ROM. We assume that the ROM is static so that its output can be routed directly to the **OBUS** and from there transferred into any of the registers as provided in Fig. 8.14b. Because the ROM is static, no extra clock period is required to obtain the constant from the ROM. A very large number of constants may be stored in the ROM. These constants can be used for masking or in arithmetic operations.

The reader will recall that **MAR** serves as the microprogram counter as well as the microaddress register. Thus bits 3 to 13 of **MIR** are not placed in **MAR**. For simplicity we shall merely assume that the input to the address decoder can be switched by combinational logic as in Fig. 8.16. We shall use **OBUS** $\leftarrow$ **ROM**$^{\perp K}$ in MICRAL to refer to obtaining a constant from location $\perp K$ of the ROM.

It is often desirable to compare a data word with a list of constants stored in the ROM. This function can be greatly facilitated by adding an indexing capability for addresses in the ROM. To do this would require inclusion of an address register for the ROM separate from the program counting **MAR**. One approach would be to separate the ROM into a microprogram section and a separate section for storage of constants. The two sections would have completely separate address registers and decoders.

The ROM indexing and some other features for increasing the power of a microprogrammable machine will be considered shortly but will not be included in the extended SIC. The AHPL description of the microsequencer for the extended SIC is given as follows:

1. $ADDRBUS = MAR$
   $MIR \leftarrow \text{BUSFN}(\textbf{ROM}; \text{DCD}(ADDRBUS))$
2. $\rightarrow (\overline{MIR_0})/(4)$
3. $MAR \leftarrow (\text{INC}(MAR) \ ! \ MIR_{8:19}) * (\overline{g}, g) \ \text{NO DELAY}$
   $\rightarrow (1)$
4. $MAR \leftarrow \text{INC}(MAR) \ \text{NO DELAY}$
   $\rightarrow (\text{DCD}(MIR_{1:2}))/(5, 6, 7, 9)$
5. $ABUS = \textbf{OCLMA} * \text{DCD}(MIR_{3:5})$
   $BBUS = \textbf{OCLMB} * \text{DCD}(MIR_{6:9})$
   $OBUS = \textbf{OCLMO} * \text{DCD}(MIR_{10:13})$
   $\textbf{DM} * \text{DCD}(MIR_{14:19}) \leftarrow OBUS \ \text{NO DELAY}$
   $\rightarrow (1)$

In step 5 the rows of the origin combinational logic matrix **OCLMA** are the vectors tabulated in Fig. 8.13a. The rows of **OCLMB** and **OCLMO** are the vectors in Fig. 8.13b and Fig. 8.14a. The destination matrix, **DM**, consists of the registers on the left side of the transfers tabulated in Fig. 8.14b. Assume that rows of **DM** corresponding to registers with fewer than 19 are filled by dummy placeholders that do not receive data.

6. Control levels and transfers not specified NO DELAY
   $\rightarrow (1)$
7. *read, write* $= MIR_{3:4}$
   $\rightarrow (\overline{busy})/(7)$
8. $MD * (\overline{busy} \wedge MIR_3) \leftarrow DATAOUT$
   $\rightarrow (busy, \overline{busy})/(8,1)$
9. $ADDRBUS = 0, 0, MIR_{3:13}$
   $OBUS = BUSFN (ROM; DCD(ADDRBUS))$
   $DM * DCD(MIR_{14:19}) \leftarrow OBUS$ NO DELAY
   $\rightarrow (1)$

The realization of the above sequence as a microsequencer that differs only slightly from the basic sequencer of Fig. 8.3 is given in Fig. 8.17.

So far we have established a basic reference model in relationship to which other microprogrammable machines might be discussed. The use of this model as a standard for comparison is justified primarily by the simplicity of the microsequencer and the fact that no more than two clock periods are required for execution of a microinstruction. No attempt shall be made to consider any specific real-world microprogrammable machines. There are, however, features that have not been included in the extended SIC which might be valuable in a microprogrammable machine. We shall consider some of these features briefly in this section. Three possible categories of features are tabulated in Fig. 8.18. In general the incorporation of any of these features will increase the complexity of the microsequencer.

The features listed in categories I and II are clearly intended to enhance the overall capability of the machine in question. The basic clock rate at which the microsequencer can operate is a function of technology. If a static ROM is used so that most instructions can be executed in one clock period, there is clearly no further improvement to be made in the rate of execution of microinstructions. Thus the capability of a microprogrammable machine can be further enhanced only by providing an organization that can accomplish more in each individual microinstruction and will, therefore, require fewer microinstructions to accomplish

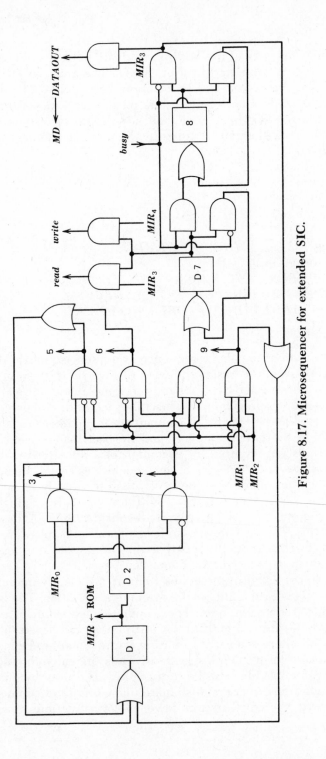

Figure 8.17. Microsequencer for extended SIC.

I.

    a. Simultaneous branches and transfers
    b. Parallel data paths
    c. Transfer and control functions in common microinstruction
    d. Multiple functions in data path
    e. Increased branching capability

II.

    a. Indexing within microprograms
    b. Microprogram subroutines

III.

    a. Economical approach to small special purpose jobs
    b. Convenience of user microprogramming

Figure 8.18. Desirable features for microprogramming.

a given higher-level function. In some sense this is the purpose of each of the features in categories I and II.

As has been mentioned, the incorporation of item Ia in the organization of a microprogrammable machine will increase (perhaps double) the number of bits in each microinstruction. Usually, this will result in an increase in the total number of bits of ROM. However, since the total number of microinstructions would be reduced, the speed at which the task would be accomplished would increase correspondingly. Items b, c, d, and e will generally have the same effect of increasing performance by shortening the microprograms for specific tasks at the price of increasing the number of bits in a microinstruction. The term *horizontal microprogramming* has been used to describe machines designed in accordance with this philosophy. An example of Ib might be two parallel busing structures so that any two data transfers could take place simultaneously. More commonly, there might be separate input/output data paths that could be used in parallel with a transfer through the busing network. In the extended SIC we have provided for distributing control levels to peripheral equipments via microinstructions for which $MIR_{0:2}$ = 0, 0, 1. With a longer instruction word this could be accomplished simultaneously with data transfers as suggested by Item Ic. Item Id will be illustrated by the following example while Item Ie is the subject of the next section.

Example 8.5

Suppose the extended SIC is to be redesigned somewhat so that every vector input to the *BBUS* may be shifted right either 0, 1, 2, or 9 bits before using it

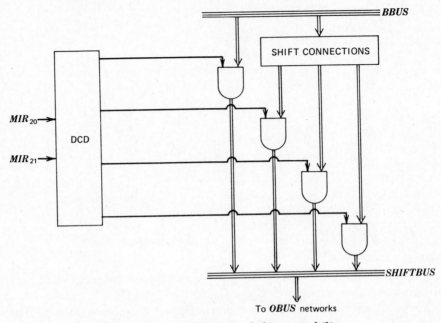

Figure 8.19. Simultaneous shifting capability.

as an argument of any of the networks leading to the $OBUS$. This shifting must be accomplished without increasing the number of clock periods required to execute a microinstruction. Rewrite the appropriate portion of the AHPL description of the extended SIC microsequencer to provide for this operation.

Solution
The cited shifting capability is made possible by adding a four-input 18-bit bus called the $SHIFTBUS$ that receives the shifted data from the $BBUS$ as shown in Fig. 8.19. The $SHIFTBUS$ will thus replace the $BBUS$ as an argument in all networks leading to the $OBUS$. It is also necessary to add 2 bits to each microinstruction. Thus the control memory is now dimensioned $ROM\ [22, 2^{13}]$. The two additional bits of the microinstruction register $MIR_{20:21}$ are decoded as shown in Fig. 8.19 to gate the desired data vector onto $SHIFTBUS$.

The matrix $OCLMSH$ listing the inputs to $SHIFTBUS$ is given by Eq. (8.5).

$$OCLMSH = (BBUS\ !\ BBUS_{17},\ BBUS_{0:16}\ !\ BBUS_{16:17},\ BBUS_{0:15}\ !\ BBUS_{9:17},$$
$$BBUS_{0:8}) \qquad (8.5)$$

Only step 5 of the extended SIC microsequencer, which describes synchronous transfers, needs to be modified. The new form of this step is given as follows.

5. $ABUS = \textbf{OCLMA} * \text{DCD}(MIR_{3:5})$
   $BBUS = \textbf{OCLMB} * \text{DCD}(MIR_{6:19})$
   $SHIFTBUS = \textbf{OCLMSH} * \text{DCD}(MIR_{20:21})$
   $OBUS = \textbf{OCLMO} * \text{DCD}(MIR_{10:13})$
   $DM * \text{DCD}(MIR_{14:19}) \leftarrow OBUS$
   $\rightarrow (1)$

The only delay added by incorporating the shifting operations is the two levels of gating making up **SHIFTBUS**. This may be short compared to the delay of the most complicated logic network leading to the **OBUS** and may not, therefore, necessitate lengthening the clock period.

In the above example a new resource, in this case a shifting network that could be controlled by separate bits of a microinstruction, was added. In general the greater the number of such independently-controlled resources, the more "horizontal" is the microprogramming approach [10].

One application of microprogramming is the design of special-purpose processors that will be permanently dedicated to one specific function, such as a communications terminal or a process control computer. Often the variety of operations specified for these machines is small, although these few operations may be quite complex, so that software can be kept to a minimum. Often the speed of execution specified for these instructions will be moderate as well.

Consider now a microprogrammable machine that might be designed to satisfy the range of applications discussed in the above paragraph. Usually, such a machine would be individually microprogrammed by the manufacturer or the user to accomplish a set of operations suitable to the individual application. In such a machine the features listed in category III of Fig. 8.18, namely, economy and ease of microprogramming, become most important. When low cost is a design criterion, it is desirable to reduce overhead associated with the control memory. This can be accomplished to some extent by reducing the word length and designing a microinstruction format in which all bits of **MIR** are meaningful in every microinstruction. Typically, a machine with a minimum word length will require a larger number of microinstructions to accomplish a given task than will a horizontal microprogrammable machine with longer word length. Thus the memory configuration of the former suggests the term *vertical microprogramming* as illustrated in Fig. 8.20a.

To partially compensate for the inability to accomplish multiple tasks in parallel, designers of vertical machines have succumbed to the

(a) (b)

Figure 8.20. Origin of terms in microprogramming. (*a*) **Vertical.** (*b*) **Horizontal.**

temptation to allow individual microinstructions to specify the multiple operations to be executed sequentially. Since microinstructon bits are not available to independently specify these sequential operations, the vertical microinstructions become inflexible, much like assembly language instructions. This inflexibility tends to make microprogramming easier (i.e., feature IIIb).

Sequential operations within microinstructions imply a more complicated multiclock-period microsequencer. One might argue that vertical microprogramming is not microprogramming at all. Less drastically, we might visualize a spectrum of microsequencers from the reference model of Fig. 8.17 to a complete control unit. We leave it to the reader to draw the line between microprogramming and programming in a primitive assembly language.

The category II features, indexing and subroutines within microprograms, are sufficiently useful to warrant inclusion in many vertical as well as horizontal microprogrammable machines. That these features can be realized while only slightly complicating the microsequencer will be illustrated by the following two examples.

Example 8.6
Modify the extended SIC control hardware and microsequencer to permit indexing the address of constants read from the control memory.

Solution
Indexing in the control memory can be accomplished only by providing for the addition of a stored number to the address $0, 0, MIR_{3:13}$. We choose to approach the addition using the adder already available in the bus structure rather than provide a separate adder. Under these circumstances indexing will require an extra clock period when executed by the microsequencer.

There must be a register for storing the index and a register for storing the resultant address following addition. We label these two 13-bit registers *IMIC* and *DMAR*, respectively. The register *DMAR* will thus replace $0, 0, MIR_{3:13}$ in the **ROM** addressing network as illustrated in Fig. 8.21a. The vector $0, 0, 0, 0,$

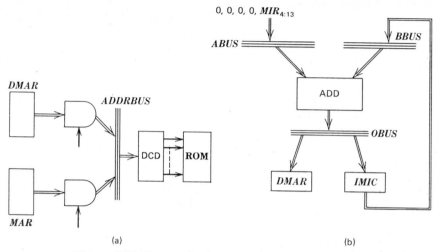

Figure 8.21. Data paths for control memory indexing.

$MIR_{4:13}$ must be connected as an $ABUS$ input; $IMIC$ must be a $BBUS$ input; and both $IMIC$ and $DMAR$ must be connected to the output of the $OBUS$. These connections are shown in Fig. 8.21b. Since loading $IMIC$ must be accomplished by a separate microinstruction, we must add the operation $IMIC \leftarrow OBUS_{6:18}$ to the list in Fig. 8.14 and assign it a code in $MIR_{14:19}$. It is important to emphasize that the connection of 0, 0, 0, 0, $MIR_{4:13}$ and $IMIC$ to the A and B buses need not be coded or listed in Fig. 8.13. These registers will not be available as arguments in transfer microinstructions but will be used only by the microsequencer. Similarly, the connection of the $OBUS$ output to $DMAR$ need not be listed.

In order to provide for specifying the indexing in microcode, we must use bit MIR_3 shown in Fig. 8.22. Thus the number of ROM words in which constants can be stored is reduced to 2^{10}.

MIR_0	MIR_1	MIR_2	MIR_3	Operation
0	0	0		
0	0	1		Transfers
0	1	0		
0	1	1	0	Read constant without indexing
0	1	1	1	Read constant with indexing
1	X	X	X	Branch

Figure 8.22. Microcoding of indexing.

The microsequencer is modified to execute indexing by changing step 9 to a conditional transfer and adding step 10 as follows.

9. $ABUS = 9 \top 0, MIR_{4:13};$
    $BBUS = 5 \top 0, IMIC$
    $OBUS = (ADD(ABUS; BBUS) \,!\, ABUS) * (MIR_3, \overline{MIR_3})$
    $DMAR \leftarrow OBUS_{6:18}$ NO DELAY
10. $ADDRBUS = DMAR$
    $OBUS = BUSFN(\textbf{ROM}; DCD(ADDRBUS))$
    $DM * DCD(MIR_{14:19}) \leftarrow OBUS$
    $\rightarrow (1)$

A portion of the microsequencer with the above modifications included is given in Fig. 8.23.

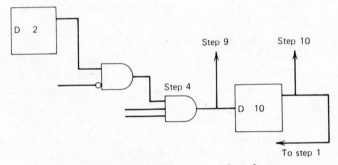

Figure 8.23. Microsequencer with indexing.

Indexing the control memory does reduce the number of words in which constants can be stored as well as complicating the microsequencer. In some cases this has led the designer to avoid the whole issue of storing constants in the control memory and depend instead on the main memory for the storage of constants.

Some provision for subroutines within the microprogram must be made in any machine where complex manipulations of blocks of data are to be accomplished by microprogram. In Chapters 12 and 13 we shall introduce a "stack" as a means of storage of return addresses for subroutines in ROM. A simpler, one-register approach is illustrated in the following example.

Example 8.7

Add to the control unit hardware and modify the microsequencer so as to include subroutine capability within the microprogram in the extended SIC.

MIR_0 MIR_1 MIR_2

0	X	X	Transfer
1	0	X	Branch
1	1	0	Branch to subroutine
1	1	1	Return from subroutine

Figure 8.24.   Microcode for subroutine branch.

Solution

Since the control memory is a **ROM**, some other provision must be made for storage of the address in **ROM** to which the microprogram must return following completion of the subroutine. The 13-bit register $SUBR$ will be used for this purpose. Because only one such address can be stored, only one level of subroutine is possible. That is, *a subroutine cannot be called from within a subroutine.*

There must be a microinstruction calling for return from a subroutine as well as a microinstruction for entering a subroutine. The corresponding microcodes are given in Fig. 8.24. Bit MIR_1 is now used to distinguish a branch from a subroutine call. The number of available branch functions must, therefore, be cut in half. Bits $MIR_{3:7}$ have no meaning in a "branch to subroutine" microinstruction, since only $MIR_{8:19}$ is required to specify the address of the subroutine. Only the first 3 bits of the "return from subroutine" microinstruction are meaningful.

The microsequencer can be modified to conform to Fig. 8.24 by merely writing a more complex step 3. Now one of three addresses, INC(MAR), $MIR_{8:19}$, or $SUBR$ is placed in MAR depending on bits $MIR_{1:2}$ and the branch conditions. If the microinstruction is a branch to subroutine, the incremented value of MAR is placed in $SUBR$.

2. $\rightarrow (\overline{MIR_0})/(4)$
3. $MAR \leftarrow (\text{INC}(MAR) \mathbin{!} MIR_{8:19} \mathbin{!} SUBR) *$
    $\qquad ((\overline{MIR_1} \wedge \overline{g}), (\overline{MIR_1} \wedge g) \vee (MIR_1 \wedge \overline{MIR_2}), (MIR_1 \wedge MIR_2))$
    $SUBR * (MIR_1 \wedge \overline{MIR_2}) \leftarrow \text{INC}(MAR)$
    $\rightarrow (1)$ \qquad\qquad NO DELAY

8.7 BRANCHING IMPROVEMENTS

In Section 8.4 we had no difficulty in providing for the coding of any register transfer that appeared to be useful. It was necessary in Section 8.5 to simplify the control sequence to conform to the lack of conditional transfers and the constrained branching format of the microprogrammable extended SIC. In general it is branching and conditional transfers that are most severely restricted by a microprogramming approach. The SIC control sequence of Chapter 6 liberally used instruction bits and data bits to branch at various points within the sequence. The wired approach makes it possible to connect directly to any bit or combination of bits of any registers in the machine to control a branch operation. For large machines with several high-speed data registers, the amount of information embodied in a particular branch condition is overwhelming. Consider, for example, a machine with 16 registers of 32 bits each. Let f_i be the Boolean function that gates a pulse through a particular path of a particular branch operation. The number of possible ways to specify this function is given in Eq. 8.6.

$$N(f_i) = 2^{2^{16(32)}} = 2^{2^{512}} \tag{8.6}$$

Thus, in the most general case, 2^{512} bits would be required to specify the function. Another $\rho(MAR)$ bits would be required to provide the address of the next microinstruction in the event the branch condition is satisfied. Compared to assembly language, a much larger number of branch functions is required in microprogramming.

In a microprogramming approach, the branch function and the branch address must be specified by the bits in a microinstruction. Clearly, not all functions enumerated in Eq. 8.6 would be of interest. However, if the designer of a large machine enjoyed the freedom of the hard-wired control approach, he would likely specify more branches than could be coded in a microinstruction if a large block of bits were set aside for the branch address.

We have not even discussed multiple branches as yet. Often it is desirable to provide a conditional branch to more than two points in the microprogram. When one considers the possibility of providing bits to specify more than one address in a microinstruction, the need for some other approach becomes obvious. There are many ways to add to the flexibility of branch commands. Two such schemes will be presented in this section. Both achieve this greater branching capability at the price of considerably more complex logic between the **ROM** and *MAR* and wasted space in the **ROM**. Before providing the reader with details of example of these two schemes, let us examine the general structure of address logic within the microprogrammable control unit.

In Fig. 8.25 we illustrate the logic structure associated with the two-way branching approach used so far. The OR gates that route the two alternative addresses to the input of *MAR* are represented as a bus. In Figs. 8.26a and 8.26b we see the logic structure for the two more-complex branching schemes mentioned. In both cases we have increased

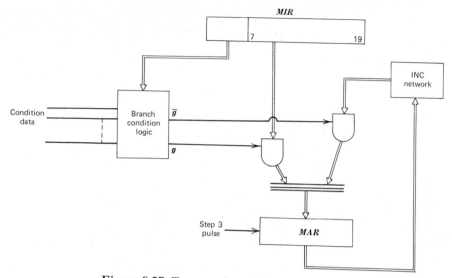

Figure 8.25. Two-way branch logic structure.

the number of alternative addresses that can be routed to the input of *MAR*. In both cases the addresses are completely generated by combinational logic so that the address is formed and placed in *MAR* in one clock period. The distinction between these two networks is primarily the handling of data that specify branch conditions.

In Fig. 8.26a the branch conditions are still selected by bits of *MIR* just as in the two-way branch scheme. The bits used to select branch conditions may vary, and multiway branches are possible, since more than two addresses are formed from bits in *MIR* and *MAR*.

In Fig. 8.26b there is no selection or condition function. Instead the vector $MIR_{1:3}$ is simply decoded to select one of, in this case, eight alternative addresses. The vector *MAR* is incremented only in the event of a transfer. Inputs from the machines data registers are used in the formation of alternative addresses.

Further discussion of the two approaches will consist of supplying the details of one example of each scheme.

Scheme I. Branch microinstructions in a particular system, employing an 18-bit, 2^{15}-word ROM, may take one of four forms depending on MIR_1 and MIR_2. These formats are illustrated in Fig. 8.27.

The first format specifies an unconditional branch to any address in the ROM. The second format is a two-option branch, with one option

313

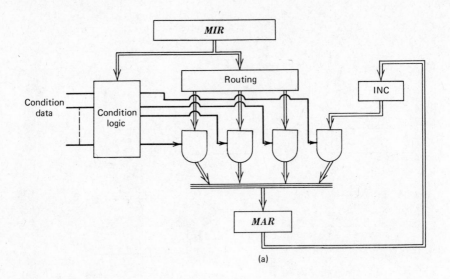

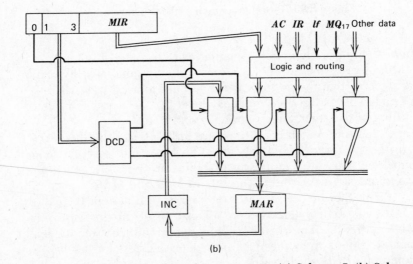

Figure 8.26. Alternative branching structure. (*a*) Scheme I. (*b*) Scheme II.

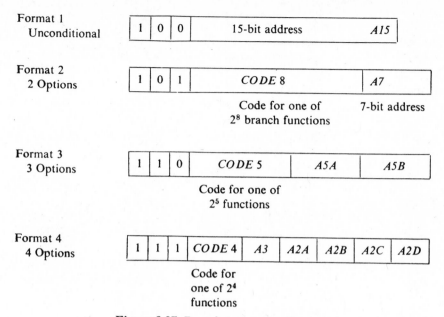

Figure 8.27. Branch instruction formats.

being the next instruction in sequence. Eight bits are provided to specify a branch function from a fairly long list of 2^8 such functions. If the branch condition is satisfied, the new 15-bit address is formed as given by expression 8.7,

$$MAR \leftarrow MAR_{0:7}, MIR_{11:17} \qquad (8.7)$$

Notice that the most significant 8 bits of *MAR* are not changed. The first two formats together provide an improvement over the approach of the previous sections. The longer list of branch functions is achieved at the price of only an occasional extra microinstruction.

Example 8.7

Suppose that the current address of a microprogram employing the branching scheme of this section is 32575 octal. From here it is desired to branch to 40000 if a branch condition, $f = 1$, is satisfied, and to continue in sequence otherwise. The two-step operation may be expressed in MICRAL as follows:

Octal address

$$32575 \qquad \rightarrow (\overline{f} = 1) / 32577.$$
$$32576 \qquad \rightarrow (40000)$$

The format-3 branch instruction provides for 32 possible three-way branches. Depending on functional values, the next microinstruction is taken from the next address in sequence or from an address formed from $A5A$ or $A5B$. Either of these 5-bit vectors can be used as the least significant 5 bits of an address as was done for format 2.

Format 4 provides for a four-way branch, as specified by one of 16 branch functions. The most significant 3 bits of the new address will always be $A3$; the next 2 bits will be $A2A$ or $A2B$ or $A2C$ or $A2D$; and the last 10 bits will always be zeros.

Most any three- or four-way branch can be accomplished using a format-3 or 4 branch microinstruction together with one or more unconditional branches. The principle disadvantage of the scheme discussed above is the long lists of branch functions. These lists would be difficult to remember. In addition, the associated decoding logic would be very costly.

Scheme II. The limitations mentioned above can be overcome by not storing the complete address of either alternative next instruction as bits of the branch microinstruction in the ROM. Instead, this address can be assembled from bits in various registers. Thus the branch is a function of these data bits, and multiple branches are possible.

We shall describe one possible approach to assembling a branch address. With this introduction the reader should be able to develop any number of similar schemes. Our approach is not optimized for any particular computer or for any prospective set of microprograms. In fact, it may not be particularly good in any application. It is convenient to explain, however, and it illustrates most types of options available to the designer. In this example, a ROM address will consist of 12 bits. We shall assemble this address by selecting three 4-bit blocks from a set of five such blocks and ordering them in a manner prescribed by the bits of the microinstruction. These blocks of 4 bits are taken from a variety of sources. The five available blocks of bits are listed in Fig. 8.28.

BLOC1	MIR_4, MIR_5, MIR_6, MIR_7
BLOC2	Assembled from zeros and the value of one of eight functions of various data bits
BLOC3	A special 4-bit register
BLOC4	0 or 1 *If*, $\overline{If}$,0, or 1 MQ_{17},$\overline{MQ}_{17}$,0, or 1 AC_0,$\overline{AC}_0$,0, or 1
BLOC5	IR_0, IR_1, IR_2 IR_3

Figure 8.28. Available blocks of microaddress bits.

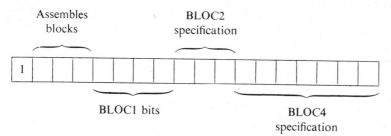

Figure 8.29. Branch microinstruction.

The 18-bit branch microinstruction is used to specify and assemble these blocks into a 12-bit address. The bits of MIR are utilized as shown in Fig. 8.29.

There are 3 bits that specify the assembly of blocks into an address. One bit combination specifies an unconditional transfer, so only seven permutations of three of the five blocks are allowed. These are given in Fig. 8.30 along with the bit combination that specifies each. For example, if bits MIR_1, MIR_2, and MIR_3 are all zero, then the address of the next microinstruction becomes

$$\text{BLOC3(4 bits), } MIR_4, MIR_5, MIR_6, MIR_7, \text{BLOC4(4 bits)}$$

Depending on how the bits of block 4 are assigned, this instruction would cause a branch to one of 16 adjacent addresses. If MIR_1, MIR_2, and MIR_3 are all 1, $MIR_{6:17}$ is taken as the address of an unconditional transfer.

The last 7 bits of MIR are used in a way that permits a great deal of flexibility in the composition of BLOC4. The bits of BLOC4 are assigned as shown in Fig. 8.31. Only 3 bits are available to control the composition of BLOC2. We, therefore, use the bits to choose one of eight functions of the data vectors. These functional values are inserted in BLOC2

MIR_1	MIR_2	MIR_3	First 4 Address Bits	2nd 4 Bits	3rd 4 Bits
0	0	0	Block 3,	Block 1,	Block 4
0	0	1	3,	1,	2
0	1	0	1,	3,	2
0	1	1	3,	4,	1
1	0	0	3,	4,	5
1	0	1	1,	5,	4
1	1	0	1,	3,	4
1	1	1	Unconditional Transfer		

Figure 8.30. Assembly of a microaddress.

317

MIR_{11}	0	1		
$BLOC4_0$	0	1		
MIR_{12}, MIR_{13}	00	01	10	11
$BLOC4_1$	0	1	lf	$\overline{lf}$
MIR_{14}, MIR_{15}	00	01	10	11
$BLOC4_2$	0	1	MQ_{17}	$\overline{MQ}_{17}$
MIR_{16}, MIR_{17}	00	01	10	11
$BLOC4_3$	0	1	AC_0	$\overline{AC}_0$

Figure 8.31. Assignment of bits in BLOC4.

as shown in Fig. 8.32. A particular f_i might be any useful function of the bits in the data register. For example, $\vee/AC$ would very likely be included.

The reader will immediately see ways to improve the scheme described herein. Our purpose has been to suggest a general approach and certain specific techniques that a designer may find useful in a particular design situation. One possibility, which we have not considered, would be the inclusion of blocks of bits from the present contents of *MAR* in an extended version of Fig. 8.30. No doubt the final choice of a branching scheme for a proposed computer would be the result of interaction between individuals or groups working on different aspects of the system design. One would expect modifications as the overall design of the computer progressed.

Consider, as an example, the branch microinstruction of Fig. 8.33a. Bits 1, 2, and 3 are 101; so the next address is given by blocks 1, 5, and

MIR_8,	MIR_9.	MIR_{10}	$BLOC2_0$,	$BLOC2_1$,	$BLOC2_2$,	$BLOC2_3$
0	0	0	0	0	0	f_1
0	0	1	0	0	0	f_2
0	1	0	0	0	0	f_3
0	1	1	0	0	0	f_4
1	0	0	0	0	f_5	0
1	0	1	0	0	f_6	0
1	1	0	0	0	f_7	0
1	1	1	0	0	f_8	0

Figure 8.32. Composition of BLOC2.

Assembles four blocks   BLOC2 Specification

1 1 0 1 1 0 0 1 0 0 0 0 0 0 0 0

BLOC1   BLOC4

(a)

$1,0,0,1, IR_0, IR_1, IR_2, IR_3, 0,0,0,0$

(b)

Figure 8.33. Sixteen-way branch.

4. BLOC1 is specified by the branch microinstruction as 1001. Since the last 7 bits of *MIR* are zero, BLOC4 is composed of all zeros. The 4 bits forming the center of the next address are taken as the first 4 bits of the instruction register, *IR*. Presumably, these bits are the op code of the instruction under execution. Thus the 16-way branch provides a method of simultaneously separating control into separate sequences for 16 instruction types. The addresses of the next microinstructions are the first words of 16 consecutive 16-bit blocks. The addresses of the first words in each block range from 4400 to 4760 octal.

It is assumed that the 16 separate instruction sequences will require no more than 16 operations before reconvergence or further branching. Certain of the alternate instructions sequences will likely require fewer than 16 operations. Thus unused ROM locations may remain in the various blocks. One of the unpleasant implications of any branch scheme of the type discussed in this section is that the use of these randomly distributed ROM locations elsewhere in the microprogram is very awkward.

Consider as a second example the microinstruction stored at 7430 in the ROM, as shown in Fig. 8.34. Bits 1, 2, and 3 of *MIR* are 011 so that the address of the next microinstruction is composed of blocks 3, 4, and

7430:   1 0 1 1 1 0 0 1 0 0 0 0 1 0 0 0 0 1

0 *lf* 0 1

BLOC3 = 1111   1 1 1 1   0 *lf* 0 1   1 0 0 1

Note 7430_{octal} = 1111 0001 1000

Figure 8.34. Single condition branch.

1, respectively. The BLOC3 register contains 1111 as shown in the figure. Similarly, the block 1 bits from *MIR* are placed in *MAR* as shown. The last 7 bits of *MIR* specify block 4 as *lf*, as indicated in the box in Fig. 8.34. These bits are also placed in *MAR* as indicated. Notice that if the link is zero, the 12 bits inserted in *MAR* differ from the original bits only in bit MAR_{11}. Thus if $lf = 0$, the next instruction in sequence is executed. If $lf = 1$, control branches to location 7531 of the ROM.

Thus it is possible to accomplish the simple, single-condition branch used exclusively in previous sections. Clearly, such branches cannot be specified with complete flexibility. The reader will agree that the expression of the branch microinstructions for this approach in MICRAL, or any other assembly language, will be awkward; the writing of the necessary assembler will also be much more difficult.

8.8 OBSERVATIONS

Microprogramming is a widely used method of controlling the execution of machine language instructions. It can be applied at a variety of levels with hard-wired control sequencers of greater or lesser complexity for controlling microprogram execution. The simplest application of microprogramming would limit the use of branching within the microprogram to separating all instructions at the beginning of the execution sequences. Assembly language branches could be accomplished by merely making a transfer to the program counter, *PC*, dependent on a data bit. We saw in Section 8.4 that a more elaborate microprogramming approach could be justified only by storing routines, which would otherwise be part of system software, in a large **ROM**.

When a **ROM** is used in the control unit, the overall machine speed is limited by the access time of the **ROM**. Thus wherever the cost per computation is a governing factor, the access time of the **ROM** must be of the same order of magnitude as the time required for a data transfer between high-speed registers. The clock rate would probably be specified according to this access time of the **ROM**. If the resulting clock period is significantly longer than the delay of the register transfers, the system will not be operating at maximum efficiency.

The cost-speed trade-off of the read-only memory is critical. Although speed of the **ROM** must be consistent with the speed of the other electronics, it must be sufficiently cheap to justify its use in place of a completely hard-wired control unit.

In order to improve machine speed, it is often found desirable to fetch a succeeding microinstruction from the **ROM** while one microinstruction is being executed. This overlap is similar to the more general notion of instruction look-ahead, which will be discussed in Chapter 17. As is the case for look-ahead, a branch microinstruction may cause a succeeding microinstruction already read from the **ROM** to go unused.

Microprograms will usually include a large number of branch operations. This can be verified by noticing the frequency of branches on the AHPL sequence of Chapter 6. In the hard-wired control unit, a branch instruction does not require a clock period. If every other operation were a branch, a 50 percent saving in execution time could be achieved if special references to the **ROM** memory for branch operations could be eliminated from the microprogramming approach. Thus branch and transfer operations are often combined in a single microinstruction, even though a register performing the function of *MIR* is included. The original Wilkes model followed this approach.

Whether or not branch and transfer operations should be combined depends on the frequency of branch operations and the cost of lengthening the **ROM** word to accommodate both operations. In the case of a transformer **ROM** with no *MIR*, this cost is negligible. The same number of transformers must be provided whether the two types of operations are done together or separately. A way to express the cost added to the **ROM** might be in the cost of storing zeros. A combined transfer and increment *MAR* microinstruction will contain mostly zeros in the branch section (in fact, mostly zeros altogether). In a semiconductor **ROM** an active device must be provided for each bit. This device is open-circuited in the last stage of the manufacturing process if the bit is 0.

Problems

8.1　Realize the control sequence of Example 4.2 as a microprogrammable control unit of the form suggested in Fig. 8.2. Your solution should consist of a complete bit pattern for the **ROM** as well as a gate-by-gate logic block diagram of the "Next Address Logic." A decoder for the output control levels will not be required.

　　Hint:　Let each microinstruction consist of 12 bits, 2 bits for each of four possible next addresses and 1 bit for each of the output control levels.

8.2　An alternative realization of a microprogrammable control sequential circuit is illustrated in Fig. P8.2. Realize the control sequential circuit of Example 4.2 according to this format. Your solution should define the layout of a microinstruction and include a complete bit pattern of the **ROM**.

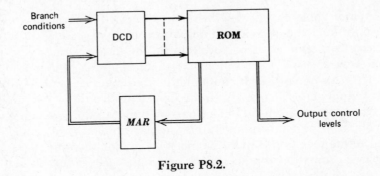

Figure P8.2.

8.3 It has been deemed desirable to change the instruction list of the microprogrammed SIC of Section 8.3 to agree with the list given for Problem 6.5. Write a control sequence for the execute phase of the memory reference instructions listed in Problem 6.5, which can be assembled in a one-to-one fashion into the microcode of Section 8.3. Use AHPL. Assemble the microcode of the short sequence of steps necessary to implement the OR instruction. Let the unused bit 18 of *MIR* (see Fig. 8.3) specify the transfer $AC \leftarrow \overline{AC}$. Let 1011 specify a branch with branch function, AC_0.

   Hint: It may be convenient to generate two simultaneous control pulses that will interchange *MD* and *AC*.

8.4 Discuss why a microprogrammable control unit cannot by itself be called a computer.

8.5 Rewrite the control sequence for the microsequencer in Section 8.2 such that it consists of only three steps with the appropriate conditional transfers.

8.6 Using the format of Section 8.3 microcode steps 7 through 12 of the SIC control sequence given in Section 6.5.

8.7 Obtain the most economical realization of the *ABUS* input logic as specified by Fig. 8.13. Include the control unit decoder as illustrated in Fig. 8.12.

8.8 (a) Is there a realization of the data unit that will permit simultaneous transfers to be specified by microinstructions for the machine discussed in Section 8.3? If so, describe the data unit.
   (b) Answer the same question for the extended SIC of Section 8.4.

8.9 An alternative approach to storing constants in the **ROM** is to use some of the bits of a microinstruction to specify this constant.

When such a microinstruction is identified, **MIR** will be connected to the **OBUS**. The last 6 bits of the microinstruction can then be used to specify the transfer of these bits into a data register.

(a) What would be the maximum number of bits available to specify such a constant in the extended SIC? Layout the format of this type of microinstruction. What value will be assumed by the leftmost bits if this constant is placed in a register?

(b) Revise the AHPL description of the microsequencer in Fig. 8.17 so that the constants are obtained as described above.

8.10 The microprogrammable bus-oriented machine described by Figs. 8.9, 8.13, and 8.14 is to be microprogrammed to form a special purpose computer for information retrieval applications. One special instruction is to be included that will search a list of words in the random access memory, beginning with the address specified by register **IA**. If one of these words is the same as the contents of index register **IB**, the instruction will terminate by leaving the corresponding address in **IA**. If no matching word is found, the instruction will leave $18 \top 0$ in **IA**. The number of words in the list is assumed to have been previously deposited in the register **MAX**. Assume that $MIR_3 = MIR_4 = MIR_5 = 1$ will cause $0, IB$ to be connected to the **ABUS**. Write in MICRAL a microprogram for the execution of the single instruction discussed. Assume that this instruction is coded like an operate instruction in SIC assembly language.

8.11 Translate AHPL steps 25 through 39 of Section 6.6, which execute part of the SIC operate instructions, to MICRAL. Microcode the MICRAL representation of AHPL steps 27 through 29 for the extended SIC of section 8.4.

8.12 Refer to the microprogrammable bus-oriented machine of Section 8.4. Write in MICRAL a control microprogram that will divide (discarding the remainder) a 17-bit positive integer in **AC** by $2^{\perp MAX}$. A number between 0 and 15 has been placed in **MAX** by a previous sequence. The answer will be left in **AC**. Microcode two instructions only: the first transfer microinstruction appearing in your sequence and the first branch microinstruction appearing in your sequence.

8.13 A proposed computer is to have 2^{13} sixteen-bit words of random access memory. Certain memory reference instructions are to be two-address instructions. For example, an instruction might call for adding the contents of two locations in the random access memory and leaving the result in a high-speed register. The machine will have eight high-speed registers, one of which must serve as a program counter and two of which must serve as an instruction register. The remaining five may serve as data registers (the output of the random access memory could be connected to a bus), accumulators, index registers, or whatever. A link is associated with only one register. The last 26 bits of the instruction registers contain the 13-bit addresses of the two arguments. The leftmost 6 bits may be used to specify the op code, indexing, and indirect addressing. The 26 address bits of the instruction register double as the memory address registers. Thus a fetch cycle would call for placing the contents of PC in the first 13 address bits and $\top(\bot\ PC + 1)$ in the other 13-bit address register.

Set up a system of buses to handle data in the machine under microprogram control. Devise a system of microprogram control branches and transfer operations to allow as much flexibility as possible. Use a 24-bit **ROM**. Make your specifications sufficiently complete to allow unambiguous coding of microinstructions.

8.14 Devise a suitable instruction list for the machine discussed in Problem 8.13. Include an instruction that will add two arguments from the random access memory and place the result in a high-speed register. Also include an instruction that will take the two's complement of a 16-bit word from a random access memory location and place the result in another location of the random access memory. Write microprograms for these instructions in an appropriate APL-like microassembly language.

8.15 Write in MICRAL the microprogram for the instruction fetch operation in the microprogrammed bus-oriented SIC. Provide for both indexing and indirect addressing. A transfer may be added to Fig. 8.14b.

8.16 Consider the microprogrammable extended SIC of Section 8.4 with the ability to retrieve constants from the **ROM**, as listed in Fig. 8.15, included. Suppose the rightmost 8 bits of the AC are a coded character that is the same as one of 20 eight-bit characters stored at consecutive locations in the **ROM**. Write in MICRAL a sequence of microinstructions that will compare AC with the list of characters until the identical character is found. A number between 1 and 20, which identifies this character, is to be left in IA. Note that no indexing capability is available for addresses in the **ROM**. Add your own MICRAL notation for reading the constant from **ROM**.

8.17 Repeat Problem 8.16 incorporating the indexing capability discussed in Example 8.6.

8.18 Assume the same hardware configuration described in Problem 8.17. Write in MICRAL a sequence of microinstructions that will accomplish the conversion of a 13-bit binary number stored initially in $AC_{5:17}$ into four binary-coded decimal digits.

8.19 Complete the last half of the microprogram for converting four BCD digits to a binary number as given in Section 8.5.

8.20 If the bus connections in the extended SIC were functions of *MIR* only and not the state of the microsequencer, an extra input to an AND gate or even an extra gate would be saved at every output in the *ABUS* and *BBUS* decoding networks. This modification can be made given some revision of the format of Fig. 8.15 and the layout of a transfer microinstruction. Every capability provided for in Fig. 8.15 must still be included. Make these format revisions and rewrite the AHPL description corresponding to the microsequencer of Fig. 8.17 to provide for the above hardware saving. Why is a similar saving not possible in the *OBUS* decoding network?

8.21 Suppose that the extended SIC microinstruction has been lengthened to 30 bits to provide greater horizontal microprogramming capability. Rewrite the AHPL description of the microsequencer in Fig. 8.17 so that the additional 10 bits can be used to specify one-period levels on any or all 10 control output lines to peripheral equipments.

8.22 "Indexing **ROM** addresses" can be added to the extended SIC without requiring the 13-bit register *DMAR*. Instead three flip-flops can be catenated to $MIR_{3:13}$ to provide for storage of the indexed 13-bit address. Rewrite steps 9 and 10 of example 8.6 to incorporate this saving.

8.23 Rewrite steps 9 and 10 of Example 8.6 as a single step taking full advantage of conditional transfer notation.

8.24 Revise Fig. 8.24 and the branch coding of Fig. 8.9 so that branching to and from subroutines in the **ROM** can be accomplished without making MIR_1 unavailable for coding branch functions. That is, it still must be possible to list approximately 2^6 branch functions.

8.25 Supply a detailed schematic diagram of the block labeled Routing in Fig. 8.26a to realize the precise branching format specified in Fig.

8.27. Show the 20 *MIR* flip-flops and the inputs to each AND gate leading to the address bus. Avoid any unnecessary gates.

8.26 Use one of the formats of Fig. 8.27 to specify the bit pattern of a microinstruction that will effect a four-way branch to one of the following four octal addresses.

$$36000 \qquad 30000 \qquad 34000 \qquad 32000$$

Assume the branch function code to be 1110.

8.27 Write the bit pattern of a scheme II microinstruction that will branch to 4322 if $MQ_{17} = 0$ and 4320 if $MQ_{17} = 1$.

8.28 Assume that a control unit is to be constructed using a **ROM** that will cost 1 cent per bit regardless of the length of a word. Suppose one step in the control sequence out of four is a branch. Twenty bits will be required to microcode a transfer operation, and 20 bits will be required to microcode a branch. Compute the costs of the **ROM** for separate branch and transfer operations, and for branches and transfers combined in the same microinstruction. Assume a total of 4000 branch and transfer steps in the control sequence. Assume that the cost of storing zeros is also 1 cent per bit. Neglect the decoder. What will be the percentage decrease execution time achieved by combining branches and transfers. If the cost of the **ROM** is 10 percent of the cost of the overall machine, compare the cost performance ratios for the two approaches.

REFERENCES

1. Husson, S. S., *Microprogramming Principles and Practice*, Prentice-Hall, Englewood Cliffs, N.J., 1970.

2. Wilkes, M. V., "The Best Way to Design an Automatic Calculating Machine," Report of Manchester University Computer Inaugural Conference," July 1951, pp. 16–18.

3. Wilkes, M. V., and J. B. Stringer, "Microprogramming and the Design of the Control Circuits in Electronic Digital Computers," *Proc. Camb. Phil. Soc.*, Vol. 49, Part 2, 1953, pp. 230–238.

4. Wilkes, M. V., W. Redwick, and D. Wheeler, "The Design of a Control Unit of an Electronic Digital Computer," *Proc. IRE*, Vol. 105, 1958, p. 21.

5. Gerace, G. B., "Microprogram Control for Computing Systems," *IRE Trans. Elec. Computer*, Vol. EC-12, 1963.

6. Tucker, S. G., "Emulation of Large Systems," *Commun. ACM*, Vol. 8, No. 12, Dec. 1965.

7. Katzan, Harry, Jr., *Microprogramming Primer,* McGraw-Hill, New York, 1977.

8. Bush, G. H., "Microprogramming," *IBM Technical Report*, No. 00-158L, SDD Division, Poughkeepsie, New York, March 7, 1967.

9. *A Guide to the IBM System 370, Model 165*, GC20-1730-0, June 1970.

10. Casaglia, G. F., and I. C. Olivetti, "Nonprogramming vs. Microprogramming," *Computer*, Jan. 1976, pp. 54–58.

11. Agrawala, A. K. and T. G. Rausher, "Microprogramming Perspective and Status," *IEEE Transactions on Computers*, Vol. C-23, pp. 817–837, Aug. 1974.

12. Clare, C. R. *Designing Logic Systems Using State Machines*, McGraw-Hill, New York, 1973.

13. *Microprogramming Handbook*, Microdata Corp., Santa Ana, Calif., 1971.

9

9.1 INTRODUCTION

All large data processing facilities constitute a network of interacting, vector-handling digital systems. Each of these systems includes at least an elementary control unit. These systems with their control units might be regarded as a set of separate intelligences organized to cooperate in accomplishing a computational task. One might observe a tenuous analogy with an industrial organization or committee of people, united to work on a particular problem.

Fortunately, the coordination of digital systems is less difficult, and their individual capacities are used more efficiently than is the case with most committees of people. The intelligence of certain digital systems (such as tape transports) is so rudimentary that they can function only in close communication with another system. In a computation facility there is nearly always a very strong committee chairman, usually but not always the central processor, which closely coordinates the activity of the individual digital systems.

Prior to our first major encounter with system interaction in the discussion of input/output in Chapter 10, it will be desirable to develop a means of describing intersystem communications. The problem of interconnecting two systems and providing for their communication is called *interfacing*. Problems arise in interfacing at the circuit design level, the sequential circuits level, and at the systems level. Although very real to the person who must design an interface, circuit problems, such as level conversion and impedance matching, can be conveniently divorced from a systems treatment. The sequential circuit problem involved in interfacing is *synchronization*. The discussion of this problem in Section 9.4 will be applicable throughout the book.

The remainder of the chapter will be devoted to an analysis of communications at the systems level. Some representation of the communications activity must be integrated in AHPL. Data lines and control lines that interconnect systems will be declared in both systems. This is, of course, consistent with the usual practice of constructing digital systems separately and connecting them as a final step.* The timing of communications between systems is part of the control function. We must, therefore, provide notation for sending and receiving signals in AHPL.

Closely related to multiple control is the notation of parallel processing. Parallel operations can be specified at several levels. Parallel operations can be handled with the notation already available. In its most sophisticated form, parallel processing clearly involves multiple control. It is an intermediate form, *parallel sequences* of operations, that will be considered in the next section. As parallel sequences become longer and more complex, the distinction between this format and multiple control becomes less clear.

9.2 PARALLEL OPERATIONS

No one can avoid the observation that performing a set of computing operations simultaneously or in parallel will require a shorter time than performing the same operations in sequence. In every context the degree of parallelism is limited by operations whose arguments are dependent on the results of other operations. In some cases this dependence is unavoidable. In others it is a function of a particular analysis or approach to a problem. It is often difficult to ascertain which is the case.

There are many ways in which parallelism can be built into a computer. The simplest, perhaps, is the processing of bits of data words simultaneously in arithmetic or logical operations, rather than serially. This form of parallelism is almost universal. Only in special-purpose computers, which are locked into situations in which continuous availability is required but computaion speed is unimportant, can the small savings in cost permitted by serial-by-bit operations be justified.

Other commonly employed parallelisms include simultaneous I/O and execution of different programs in a batch processing environment. Occasionally, two or more complete central processors share the same peripherals and memory, and operate in parallel. When look-ahead is employed, it is possible to have more than one machine in-

---

*Individually controlled systems are not always mounted in physically separate units. Certain system pairs must be mounted in very close (centimeters) proximity to maximize communications speed.

struction in various stages of execution at one time. The overall time saving achieved by this technique is heavily dependent on having an object program with a minimum of interdependence between consecutive operations. Another technique, which is even more problem dependent, involves the use of a single control unit to control the functioning of an array of processors that perform almost identical computations.

The benefit to be derived by executing machine instructions in parallel is contingent on factors beyond the control of the logical designer. Such, however, is not the case for the sequence of register transfers making up the execution of an individual instruction. In this case, parallelism of register transfers should be maximized. This observation is underscored when high-speed solid-state main memories or scratch-pad memories are employed. One cannot, then, point to slow memory cycles as determining execution times, making sequential register transfer times relatively unimportant.

In earlier chapters clarity was emphasized. Transfers were specified as parallel only when this did not interrupt the discussion. As a general rule the designer should arrange the AHPL sequence so as to minimize the number of delay flip-flops in each path through the control sequencer. Sequences of operations intended to be executed in parallel may be merged into a single sequence. Suppose, for example, that it is desired that the following two sequences be carried out in parallel:

1. $A \leftarrow INC(A)$ 1. $D \leftarrow \bar{A}$
2. $B \leftarrow \bar{A}$ 2. $E \leftarrow INC(D)$
3. $C \leftarrow B_{2:7}$

These sequences may be merged in the established notation as follows:

1. $A \leftarrow INC(A); D \leftarrow \bar{A}$
2. $B \leftarrow \bar{A}; E \leftarrow INC(D)$
3. $C \leftarrow B_{2:7}$

This tactic cannot be applied when asynchronous operations are involved, since the timing synchronism of the individual steps is destroyed. In this case it is necessary to permit more than one control pulse to propagate simultaneously through parallel paths in the control unit. Suppose that we have the situation in which the contents of an index register are to be added asynchronously to AC, while a reference to memory is being executed. The separate sequences each include a synchronous transfer as well. To handle this situation it is necessary to separate control into two separate paths. The existing AHPL branching notation can be used to specify branching control to two separate locations simultaneously if we allow more than one branch function to be 1.

8. $\rightarrow (\bar{a}, a, a)/(9, 10, 20)$ (9.1)

Expression 9.1, for example, would cause control to branch to steps 10 and 20 simultaneously if $a = 1$. An unconditional divergence to steps 10 and 20 could be written

$\rightarrow (1, 1)/(10, 20)$ (9.2)

For convenience we shall define the expression 9.3 to have the same meaning as 9.2.

$\rightarrow (10, 20)$ (9.3)

Let us return now to the asynchronous memory reference and asynchronous addition, which must be executed in parallel. We assume the former to be preceded by a synchronous transfer and the latter to be followed by a synchronous transfer.

1. $IA \leftarrow X$
     $\rightarrow (A2, B2)$
A2. $startadd = 1$
A3. $\rightarrow (\overline{sumready})/(A3)$
A4. $AC \leftarrow ADD(AC, IA)$ NO DELAY
A5. $AC \leftarrow AC_{17}, AC_{0:16}$
     DEAD END
B2. $MA \leftarrow PC$ NO DELAY
B3. $read = 1$
B4. $MD * dataready, \leftarrow DATAIN$
     $\rightarrow (\overline{dataready})/(B4)$
5. (Sequences continue)

In the above sequence it was assumed that the asynchronous addition would require less time for completion than the memory reference. When it is known that one or the other of the parallel sequences will always terminate first, there need be no hardware provision for convergence of the paths as illustrated in Fig. 9.1.

In many cases the relative completion times of two or more parallel sequences may be unknown. In this case a special convergence circuit must be provided. The symbol and application of such a circuit are illustrated very simply in Fig. 9.2. The output of the step 5 convergence circuit will be a one-period level coincident with the second of the one-period levels that arrive on each of the two input lines. It is assumed

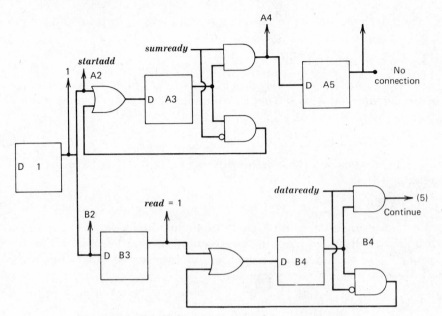

Figure 9.1. Parallel sequences without convergence.

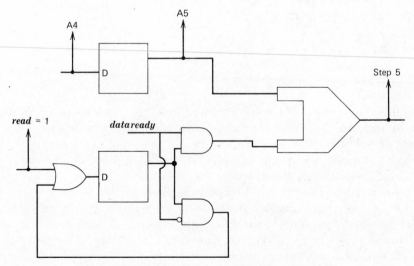

Figure 9.2. Convergence of parallel sequences.

332

that the inputs will always be connected to the outputs of control flip-flops whose values will remain 1 for only one clock period.

We introduce the term CONVERGE to specify the convergence hardware suggested in Fig. 9.2. This notation is illustrated as follows, now assuming the relative time delays of the addition and memory references of Fig. 9.1 to be unknown.

B4. $\rightarrow (\overline{dataready})/(\text{B4})$
5.   CONVERGE (A5, B4)
6.   etc.

A logic block diagram for one simple realization of the convergence circuit is given in Fig. 9.3 together with the corresponding state diagram. The control input lines, x_1 and x_2, are one-period levels from control flip-flops in the same module and are, therefore, synchronized to the same clock. As shown, the master clear input of the flip-flop in Fig. 9.3 must be connected to the system reset line in order to assure that it will be in the $Q = 0$ state prior to the occurrence of a 1-level on either input.

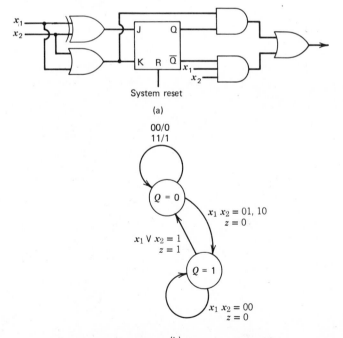

Figure 9.3. Convergence circuit.

We shall utilize the notation for divergence and convergence of control, as introduced above, as part of AHPL in the succeeding sections of this chapter. We shall not give further attention to the particular hardware approach to convergence.

Our attention throughout the remainder of the book will be restricted to developing control sequences. It will be convenient to not be concerned with the relative time required by parallel paths. Thus we use the same notation for all cases and leave the decision as to whether or not a hardware convergence circuit is needed to the "translation to hardware" step.

Example 9.1

A digital process controller is to be designed. The principal difference between this controller and the machine tool controller of Example 5.4 is that this controller must operate at the maximum-possible, data transfer rate. The register configuration for the controller is shown in Fig. 9.4. With each control level appearing on input line *request*, a word is read from the random access memory **M**. Each word is multiplied by a constant that is stored in register **KK** and is then placed in **CR**. The use of data vectors in **CR** by the external process is controlled by the exchange of signals of lines *ready* and *request*. The digital controller supplies a one-period *ready* level as soon as a new data vector is placed in **CR**. To indicate that the data has been accepted and that it is ready for another vector, the external process places a level on line *request*. The registers **KK** and **MA** can be loaded through control panel switches. The memory may be regarded as a separate module that holds a data word on the vector of output lines **DATA** until a subsequent *read* signal arrives.

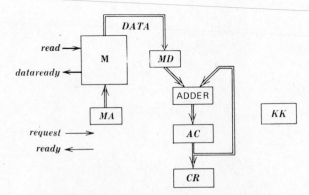

Figure 9.4. Registers for process controller.

Solution.

We shall examine two possible designs for the control unit of the process controller. The control sequences are given in Fig. 9.5. The sequence of Fig. 9.5a is straightforward. First, a word is read from memory; then it is multiplied by the constant in *KK*, and then it is placed in the register *CR*. The notation of step 19 indicates that a *ready* level is supplied to the external system and control waits at step 20 for a *request* level indicating that the external process is ready for a new word. Following a *request* level, control returns to step 1 to cause the next word to be read from memory.

The disadvantage of the sequence of Fig. 9.5a is that three time-consuming operations, read from memory, multiplication, and the asynchronous transfer, are done sequentially. In the sequence of Fig. 9.5b, these three operations are done in parallel for three different data words. This approach takes advantage of the register *DATA* in the memory module. In this way no register is involved in more than one of the three primary time-consuming operations. Each word from memory must pass through each of the three steps sequentially. However, while one data word is being read from *CR*, a second word is being readied for output through multiplication by *KK*, and a third data word is being read from memory. With each pass through the control sequence, each of three words advance one step in the process. After convergence, step 18 moves the data ahead and increments *MA*. Since the *request* level remains 1 until the next one-period *ready* level, convergence can be accomplished in two steps avoiding the necessity of a more complicated three-input convergence circuit. We have been

1. *read* = 1	$1 \rightarrow$ (A2, B2, C2)
2. $\rightarrow (\overline{dataready})/(2)$	A2. *ready* = 1
3. *MD* ← *DATA*	DEAD END
MA ← INC(*MA*)	B2. *read* = 1
4. First step of multiplication	B3. $\rightarrow (dataready, \overline{dataready})/(16, B3)$
.	C2. First step of multiplication
.	.
.	.
17. Last step of multiplication	C15. Last step of multiplication
18. *CR* ← *AC*	16. CONVERGE (B3, C15)
19. *ready* = 1	17 $\rightarrow (\overline{request})/(17)$
20. $\rightarrow (request, \overline{request})/(1, 20)$	18. *CR* ← *AC*; *MD* ← *DATA*;
	MA ← INC(*MA*)
	$\rightarrow$ (1)
(a)	(b)

Figure 9.5. Control sequences for process controller.

careful to ascertain that no register is involved in more than one of the three asynchronous operations. It is for this reason that the three parallel sequences must converge before data is moved synchronously from memory to the registers used in multiplication and between the AC that stores the product and CR.

When two parallel control sequences specify transfers involving the same set of registers, care must be taken to assure that the following two rules are always satisfied.

Rule 9.1. A single register can be the destination of no more than one transfer in the same clock period.

As pointed out in Chapter 4, the result of trying to transfer two vectors into a register simultaneously is unpredictable and cannot be tolerated. Rule 9.2 applies to registers that may be the destination of an asynchronous transfer. In Example 9.1 we were careful to cause the three sequences to converge before data were transferred at step 18 between registers involved in separate asynchronous sequences.

Rule 9.2. The contents of a register must not be read at a time when they might be in the process of change by an asynchronous sequence.

9.3 INTERACTING MODULES

As the user looks from the outside of a large digital system, he sees many input and output ports that seem to be simultaneously receiving and sending information. From the users' manuals he learns of many internal activities that are said to take place simultaneously. What is controlling all of these activities? How is it that these activities seem to cooperate rather than compete? Are these parallel operations controlled by a single intelligence or several?

That parallel control sequences and separate control might not be totally different can be argued in terms of the figurative model shown in Fig. 9.6. A portion of a control sequencer featuring three parallel sequences is represented by Fig. 9.6a. Only the paths of propagation of the control level within the control unit are shown. The transfers that take place are left to the imagination of the reader.

Figure 9.6b differs from Fig. 9.6a only in that the individual parallel branches have become more complicated. A control level can circulate in a path containing a loop for long periods of time. When such is the case for two or more loops, one might argue that the level convergence

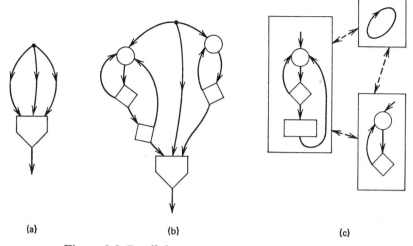

(a)   (b)   (c)

Figure 9.6. Parallel sequences and multiple control.

circuit serves to provide occasional communications between the separate control sequences embodied in these loops.

In Fig. 9.6c the individual control loops have been formally separated to form distinct control units. Two-way communications between these separate control units is indicated by the dashed arrows. Presumably, this communications capability is more flexible than could be provided by depending on the control level convergence circuit. To go further in comparing the details of interloop communications between Figs. 9.6a and 9.6b would be esoteric at best. The primary purpose of the rest of this chapter will be to develop the model suggested by Fig. 9.6c.

When control is separated into two or more different modules, most hardware compilers will require that the registers be partitioned and declared in the separate modules as well. Often it will be necessary for a control level from one module to cause a transfer to take place into a destination register in another module. A typical situation is illustrated in Fig. 9.7, where a data vector from system I serves as an input to system II. This vector, *DATAI*, is to be transferred into the register, *CRII*, within system II. Since two separate control sequences are involved, care must be taken to assure that *Rules 9.1 and 9.2 of the previous section are satisfied.* The control unit of system I will normally send a control signal to system II indicating when the former is ready for a vector to be read from *DATAI*. It may be expected that system I will ascertain that Rule 9.2 will be satisfied before sending such a control level.

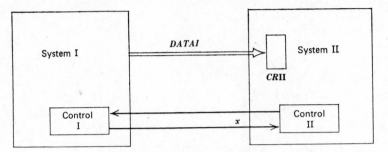

Figure 9.7. System interaction.

A control level, x, from system I intended to cause the transfer $CRII \leftarrow DATAI$ within system II can be handled by system II in two ways. The simplest approach is for the system II control sequence to wait for the signal on line, x, after which the system II controller would effect the transfer as illustrated in Fig. 9.8a. System II can easily ascertain that no other transfers into $CRII$ are attempted at the same time so that Rule 9.1 is satisfied. The disadvantage of this approach is that system II must have some information as to when a level might appear on line x or otherwise be willing to wait indefinitely at step 10 in its control sequence.

The second approach to the intermodule transfer uses x as the condition variable for a transfer that system II will allow to take place at any time. The responsibility of making certain that Rule 9.1 is satisfied thus falls to system I. To successfully discharge this responsibility, the system I control unit must have some knowledge of the state of affairs within system II. The only alternative would have no other transfers into $CRII$ possible at any time.

INPUTS SYSTEM II: $DATAI$[8], x INPUTS SYSTEM II: $DATAI$[8], x

$\cdot$ $\cdot$

$\cdot$ $\cdot$

$\cdot$ $\cdot$

$\cdot$ $\cdot$

10. $\cdot$

     $\rightarrow (\bar{x})/(10)$ END SEQUENCE

11. $CRII \leftarrow DATAI$ $CRII * x \leftarrow DATAI$

     NO DELAY

       (a) Approach I   (b) Approach II

Figure 9.8. Intermodule transfer.

Occasionally, it may be necessary for the control unit of one module, for example system I, to cause a data transfer to take place between two registers of another module (system II). Both approaches of Fig. 9.8 would still be applicable. However, using the approach of Fig. 9.8b would require system I to possess enough information about system II to insure the satisfaction of both Rules 9.1 and 9.2. Very often this knowledge will be included within information that system I would otherwise require in order to effect sensible and timely transfers within another system.

The example used in the previous section to illustrate parallel sequences may also be reworked in terms of interacting modules. This is done in Example 9.2, which illustrates the communication between modules using approach I of Fig. 9.8.

Example 9.2
Redesign the process controller in such a way that each of the three parallel sequences of Fig. 9.5b is accomplished by a separate module.

Solution
The process controller is laid out as three separate modules in Fig. 9.9. The memory had previously been treated as a separate module. The multiplication is now accomplished in a separate module leaving the third module to keep track of the memory address and to interact with the controlled process. Since

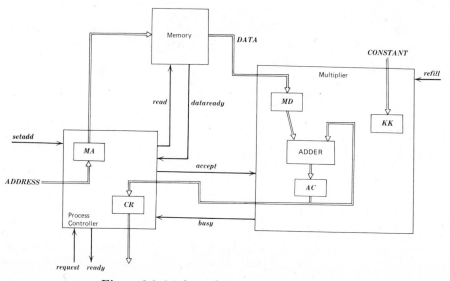

Figure 9.9. Multimodule process controller.

the memory will be integrated into the system as an off-the-shelf item, a detailed AHPL description of only the multiplier and process controller are given as follows.

    MODULE: MULTIPLIER
     INPUTS MEMORY: *DATA* [12]
     INPUTS SWITCHES: *CONSTANT* [6]; *refill*
     INPUTS PROCESS CONTROLLER: *accept*
     MEMORY: *AC* [18]; *KK* [6]; *busy*
     OUTPUTS: *AC; busy*
       1. $\rightarrow \overline{(accept)}/(1)$
       2. *busy* $\leftarrow$ 1; *MD* $\leftarrow$ *DATA*   NO DELAY
       3. First step of multiplication

              .
              .
              .

      16. Last step of multiplication
      17. *busy* $\leftarrow$ 0
          $\rightarrow (1)$
    END SEQUENCE
     KK * *refill* $\leftarrow$ *CONSTANT*
    END
    MODULE: PROCESS CONTROLLER
     INPUTS MULTIPLIER: *AC* [18]; *busy*
     INPUTS MEMORY: *dataready*
     INPUTS PROCESS: *ADDRESS* [12]; *request; setadd*
     MEMORY: *MA* [12]; *CR* [18]
     OUTPUTS: *CR; ready; read; MA; accept*
       1. *ready* = 1; *read* = 1
       2. $\rightarrow \overline{(dataready)}/(2)$
       3. $\rightarrow (busy)/(3)$
       4. $\rightarrow \overline{(request)}/(4)$
       5. *CR* $\leftarrow$ *AC*; *MA* $\leftarrow$ INC(*MA*); *accept* = 1
          $\rightarrow (1)$
    END SEQUENCE
     MA * *setadd* $\leftarrow$ *ADDRESS*
    END

    The above AHPL sequences are complete even to the point of providing for the external control signals, *setadd* and *refill*, by which the user can insert a new address in **MA** or a new constant in **KK**. It is assumed that such action will take place only when activity is held up by the withholding of a *request* signal. In this way Rule 9.1 is satisfied even though the AHPL specification of these loading operations is written following "END SEQUENCE." Once a new address signal has been placed in **MA** the corresponding number will appear in **CR** only after three *request* signals.

In this example the need to wait for completion of three separate functions (1. read from memory, 2. multiplication, and 3. use of data) has not been eliminated by separating the control unit into modules. In fact this is the primary function of the process controller module. No hardware convergence circuit is required, since now the **busy** level from the multiplier remains 0 and the **request** level remain 1 until responded to by the process controller. One possible timing sequence is illustrated in Fig. 9.10. Following receipt of the one-period *dataready* level, at least two more clock periods are required to check for *busy* = 0 indicating completion of multiplication and for *request* = 1. In Fig. 9.10 these lines have already assumed these respective values prior to the *dataready* signal and will retain the values until the check is made. Once all three signals have been received a one-period *accept* level is issued to the multiplier, which causes it to accept a new vector from lines **DATA**, begin multiplication, and set *busy* to 1. Signals on lines *read* and *ready* are also issued by the process controller and the chain of events is repeated.

It should be noted that the control signal *busy* from the multiplier proved very

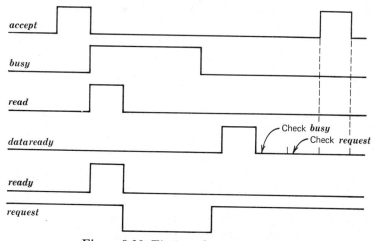

Figure 9.10. Timing of control signals.

convenient for the process controller, since it would remain zero indefinitely or until receipt of a subsequent one-period *accept*. This is contrasted with the line *dataready*, which must be watched constantly for the occurrence of a one-period level. This form of the signal *busy* is made possible by defining *busy* as a data flip-flop external to the control unit.

So far no mention has been made of Rule 9.2. The process controller assures that this rule is satisfied by executing the transfers

$$CR \leftarrow AC \text{ and } MA \leftarrow INC(MA)$$

and causing the transfer

$$MD \leftarrow DATA$$

to be executed by the multiplier during the two clock periods in which it knows that none of the three asynchronous operations are in progress.

9.4 SYNCHRONIZATION

Until now it has been assumed that all systems considered were timed by the same clock and that the physical distance between the subsystems was small. If either of these assertions is *not* true, a new set of problems arises. Suppose that a level from a separately clocked control unit I in Fig. 9.7 arrives at control unit I to indicate that a vector *DATAI* be placed in *CRII*. This system may introduce an unsynchronized level into the control unit of system II. Such unsynchronized levels can create havoc within a control unit.

As illustrated in Fig. 9.11, it is possible that expected transfers may not take place; it is possible that 1-levels may be caused to appear simultaneously at more than one point in the control unit. In Fig. 9.11 *x* is an unsynchronized control input that goes to 1 immediately ahead of the trailing edge of a clock pulse. A 1 signal appears at point *a* one gate delay after the transition on line *x*. The level at point *a* is used to gate a clock pulse that will cause the transfer, *CRII* ← *DATAI* to take place. The resultant control pulse may be a narrow spike as shown, which may or may not be sufficient to effect the desired transfer. Even in a case in which the step 11 transfer did not occur, the signal at point *a* may have appeared at the input of control flip-flop 12 in time for the trailing edge of the clock to set this flip-flop to 1. This situation is depicted in Fig. 9.11b by the shaded area on the step 12 waveform, which indicates that the value is uncertain. It is also possible that gate delays will be such that point *b* will still be 1 at the time of the trailing edge of clock pulse 1 even though *a* reached the value 1 prior to this edge. This could result in 1's appearing simultaneously in control flip-flops 10 and 12. These

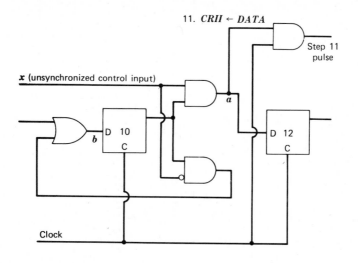

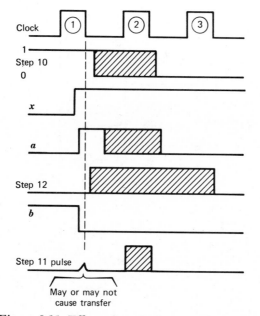

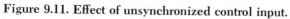

Figure 9.11. Effect of unsynchronized control input.

344

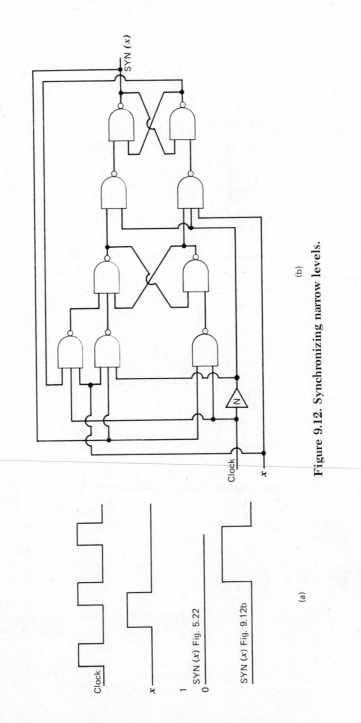

(b)

(a)

Figure 9.12. Synchronizing narrow levels.

two ones could then propagate independently within the control unit causing a sequence of erroneous transfers. On the other hand, a different combination of gate delays could cause 0's to appear at the input of both flip-flops 10 and 12 coincident with the trailing edge of the clock pulse. In this case the control level would be lost. Again, these various possibilities are represented by the shaded areas for steps 10 and 12.

If an input control level is one for a duration of two or more periods, it can be synchronized using a synchronizing flip-flop as shown in Fig. 5.22. This circuit will successfully synchronize a one-period level originating in a system with a lower clock frequency but will not prove satisfactory if the one-period level originated in a system with a slightly higher clock frequency. When both systems are driven by the same clock, a particular combination of gate delays could shorten a one-period level and cause it to fail to overlap the trailing edge of a clock pulse in the receiving system. That no output level would emerge from a simple flip-flop synchronizer in this case is illustrated in Fig. 9.12a. A synchronizing circuit that will generate an output whenever an input level overlaps any part of a clock pulse would function successfully under the circumstances just described. Such a circuit is illustrated in Fig. 9.12b. Notice that the synchronized level is delayed one clock period. Levels that can be synchronized by a synchronizing flip-flop will also be delayed one clock period.

Ordinarily, data input lines will not require synchronization. The transfer operation that places an input vector in a register of the receiving system in effect accomplishes synchronization. If one or more input data bits are changing at the time of such a transfer, the result can, however, be unpredictable. If the appearance of a binary vector approximately coincides with a clock pulse, some of the level changes may be clocked into the register while others may wait for the next clock pulse. If the register is sampled in the interim, an error may result.

Consider the machine tool controller of Chapter 5. The normal sequence of numbers transmitted to the controller might vary only slowly in magnitude. It might be tempting to supply the numbers to the tool in sequence without control communications. Suppose that two consecutive data numbers expressed in octal are 007765 followed by 010043. If the second number were only partially clocked into the tool register, some such number as 017767 might reside there for one clock period. This number is appreciably greater than the two correct numbers, which are close together in magnitude. An undesired transient in the movement of the controller might be the result. This problem could be most easily avoided by sending a control level to the machine tool indicating the availability of a stable data vector in *PR*.

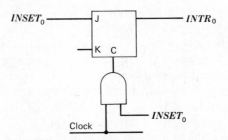

Figure 9.13. Setting an interrupt.

A control level signaling the availability of stable data on a vector of input lines will usually be connected to a branch or conditional transfer network within the control unit. Thus the control level must be synchronized. Once the synchronized level has propagated through the branching network, a transfer of the input data can be accomplished without further synchronization.

In Chapter 10 we shall encounter the AHPL form

END SEQUENCE
$$INTR_0 * INSET_0 \leftarrow 1$$

where $INTR$ has been declared as consisting of J-K flip-flops and $INSET_0$ has been declared as an input. Apparently, $INSET_0$ is a control input. Since $INTR_0$ is a J-K flip-flop, a typical hardware compiler might generate the network of Fig. 9.13 from the above AHPL expression. This approach treats $INSET_0$ as a data input and eliminates any need for independent synchronization if $INSET_0$ is at least one clock period in duration. The synchronization is accomplished by the data flip-flop.

9.5 INTERCONNECTION OF SYSTEMS

It is very often necessary to provide for the transfer of data among several independent modules. As suggested in Section 4.4, the most efficient method of implementing such a transfer network is through the use of a data bus. If one or more of the modules is a computer or a CPU, the most common arrangement for data transmission is the I/O bus, which from a logical point of view simply consists of a set of n lines providing bidirectional transfer of n-bit words between **MD** in the CPU and the data registers of the I/O devices as shown in Fig. 9.14. If there are no direct transfers between I/O devices, the principal saving achieved by the use of an I/O bus is in cabling. As shown in Fig. 9.14, the bus is routed serially from device to device rather than routing two cables

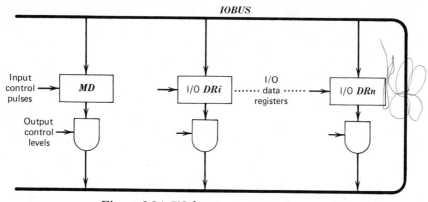

Figure 9.14. I/O bus interconnections.

between each device and the central processor. In addition the switching located at the input to the central processor is simpler (although the switching at each I/O device is more complicated).

Since the registers connected to the bus are located in separate devices, each module must generate the control levels required to place data on the IOBUS and to trigger data from the IOBUS into local registers. To accomplish the transfer of a data vector from device A to device B requires device A to first generate a 1 on the control line routing a data register to the *IOBUS*. This level must then remain 1 until system B clocks the vector from the *IOBUS* into its data register.

Clearly, some procedure must be provided through which a sending module will know when the *IOBUS* is not in use by another module and through which a receiving register will know when data is available on the bus. This coordinating procedure usually becomes the responsibility of one designated module. If one of the modules is a CPU, this unit will usually retain control of the *IOBUS*. Thus, in addition to the I/O bus, there must be paths provided for transmission of control information between the CPU and the I/O devices, which we shall refer to as the *control/status* lines. There are two distinct modes of interconnection possible. First, there may be a separate set of control/status lines to each I/O device, as shown in Fig. 9.15a. In this case the CPU addresses a specific I/O device by placing signals on the appropriate set of lines and determines which I/O device is signaling by noting which lines are active.

Second, there may be a single set of control/status lines connecting to all I/O devices as shown in Fig. 9.15b. With this arrangement, the control/status lines must include a set of address lines, with each device

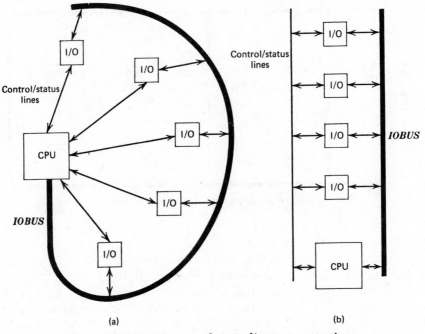

Figure 9.15. Basic types of control/status connections.

assigned an address, or *selector code*. To address a device, the CPU places its selector code on the address lines. Each device is equipped with a decoding circuit, by means of which it recognizes its own code and upon receipt of which it will gate in information from the other control/status lines. When a device signals the CPU, it must transmit its own code as a means of identification.

When the amount of status information that must be provided by a peripheral device is large and when the commands from the CPU are complex, implying a large number of control status lines, the approach of Fig. 9.15b will be the most economical. There are two distinct disadvantages associated with using the approach of Fig. 9.15b exclusively.

1. Communications can never be initiated by a module other than the supervising module (usually CPU).
2. Some provision must be made for parallel control within each module, since a module must be prepared to connect status information to the control status bus even though engaged in some other activity.

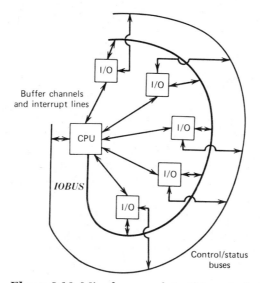

Figure 9.16. Mixed approach to I/O control.

That the second consideration can significantly complicate an otherwise simple control unit of a peripheral will be illustrated in an example to follow. Both *interrupt* and *buffered data transfer* (concepts to be discussed in Chapter 10) require communications to be initiated by a peripheral equipment. For this reason many systems employ a combination of the two approaches as illustrated in Fig. 9.16.

Example 9.3

A simple printing device has eight input lines designated as the vector *CHAR* and two control inputs labeled *print* and *feed*. Its only output is a single line labeled *wait*. Each time a one-period level is placed on line *print*, the character represented on lines *CHAR* in ASCII code will be printed. Each time a one-period level is placed on line *feed*, a combination carriage return and line feed is executed. Following either one-period level, the line *wait* will go to 1 until the operation is complete.

This printer is to be interfaced to a CPU that employs the I/O scheme depicted in Fig. 9.15a. Three control lines and the 18-bit *IOBUS* connect the printer interface to the CPU. The control line *ready* from the printer interface must be recognized as 1 by the CPU before a data vector is placed on the *IOBUS*. This will prevent another request when a printer operation is in progress. When a data word has been placed on the *IOBUS*, the CPU will so indicate with a 1-

level on a line *datavalid*. When the interface has accepted this data word, it must respond with a one-period level on the line *accept*. Each data word will contain two ASCII characters packed as vectors $IOBUS_{10:17}$ and $IOBUS_{1:8}$. Design an interface to satisfy these requirements.

Solution

The interface will utilize an 18-bit data register, *DR*, so it can release the *IOBUS*, together with an 8-bit register, *CR*, the outputs of which are permanently connected to the printer input lines, *CHAR*. A J-K flip-flop, *first*, will be used to indicate which of the two characters in a word is being printed. A J-K flip-flop is used, since this flip-flop is only set or reset in the sequence.

```
MODULE: PRINTER INTERFACE
      MEMORY: DR[18]; CR[8]; first(JK)
      OUTPUTS: CHAR[8]; ready; accept; print; feed
      INPUTS: datavalid; wait
      COMBUS: IOBUS[18]
  1.  ready = 1
      → (datavalid)/(1)
  2.  DR ← IOBUS; accept = 1; first ← 1
  3.  CR ← (DR₁₀:₁₇ ! DR₁:₈) * (first, first)
  4.  feed = RETURN(CR); print = RETURN(CR)
  5.  Null
  6.  → (wait)/(6)
  7.  first ← 0
      → (first, first)/(3, 1)
END SEQUENCE
      CHAR = CR
END
```

In step 3: $CR \leftarrow (DR_{10:17} \,!\, DR_{1:8}) * (first, \overline{first})$

In step 4: $feed = \text{RETURN}(CR)$; $print = \overline{\text{RETURN}(CR)}$

In step 7: $\rightarrow (first, \overline{first})/(3, 1)$

RETURN is a combinational logic function that is 1 if *CR* contains a carriage return character. Step 6 causes control to wait for the completion of the printing of the character. Step 5 is included to allow the printer an extra clock period to react by setting *wait*. After the completion of a printing operation, step 7 either returns control to step 3 to print the second character, or to step 1 to wait for another data word.

Two basic types of signaling are used in intersystem communications, *nonresponsive* and *responsive*. In *nonresponsive* signaling, the sending device simply places a signal on the communications lines for some fixed period of time and then proceeds, assuming that the receiving device has taken whatever action may be required. In *responsive* signaling, the sending device places a signal on the communications line and holds it there until the receiving device acknowledges receipt of the signal. Nonresponsive signaling is usually simpler but is reliable only when the sending and receiving devices are carefully synchronized, preferably on the same clock. Responsive signaling is more reliable in most cases, since it requires verification at each step in the communication process, but it requires more hardware and is usually slower than nonresponsive signaling.

Many systems employ a mixture of these two approaches to signaling, as does the printer interface of the last example. The interface holds the signal *ready* at 1 until the CPU responds with the signal *datavalid* indicating that data is on the bus. The CPU then holds the data on the bus until the interface responds with the signal *accept*. Both of these cases clearly represent responsive signaling. However, from the standpoint of the interface, the transmission of *accept* is nonresponsive, since it is held at the 1-level for just one clock period and no response is expected from the CPU. A typical timing sequence of these signals is shown in Fig. 9.17a, in which it is assumed that the CPU and the interface are on the same clock. The *ready* is shown up for an indefinite period, since it is not known whether the CPU is standing by waiting for *ready*, or is doing other things and checking *ready* periodically. When *datavalid* is detected, at step 1 of the interface sequence, *accept* is returned in the next clock period, and the CPU responds immediately by dropping *datavalid* and clearing the *IOBUS*.

This partially responsive three-line handshake is quite satisfactory for the printer interface of Example 9.3, in which the transmitter and receiver are driven by the same clock and several clock periods are required to handle the data after an *accept* is issued. Consider, however, a system in which (1) the receiver requires only one clock period to handle a data character after an *accept* is issued, and (2) the transmitter and receiver are physically separated so that a propagation delay of one or more clock periods exists on the control lines between the devices. In this case the partially responsive handshake would not be reliable, since *ready* could be returned to 1 after a character is received and processed and *the system could be looking for a new datavalid signal before the datavalid signal corresponding to the character, just received, has returned to 0.*

If the three-line control *handshake* procedure were modified to appear as shown in Fig. 9.17b, it could be considered to be completely responsive. Here the line *accept* is permitted to go to zero only after the receiving module observes that *datavalid* has returned to 0. Now, once the handshake has commenced with the appearance of a 1 on the line

351

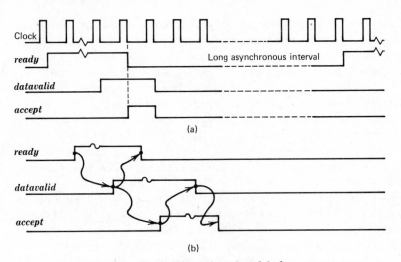

Figure 9.17. Three-line handshake.

ready, each transition occurs in response to a previous transition. In Fig. 9.17b, the ON periods of all signals are shown as being of indefinite duration, to emphasize that this can be a completely asynchronous process. No assumptions of any kind are made about the relative speeds of the devices. The process starts when *ready* goes on. From then on, every succeeding transition is triggered by some previous transition until the process ends when all signals have gone low. This *completely* responsive three-line handshake will control data communications reliably regardless of the relation between propagation delays and the storage time in receiver.

Both handshake procedures* illustrated in Fig. 9.17 will be used in the remaining chapters. The approach of Fig. 9.17a will be the most convenient and the most economical when the two communicating modules are driven synchronously by the same clock. The microprocessor to be discussed in Chapter 12 uses a two-line partially responsive handshake in which the *ready* line returns to 0 to indicate acceptance. Thus positive transitions on the line indicate *ready* while negative transitions indicate *accept*. This partially responsive approach is subject to all of the timing limitations associated with Fig. 9.17a.

In special cases one of the control signals can be eliminated completely. Following each *accept* level, the internal activities must usually take place within both the receiving and transmitting module before

---

*Although the signal names have been abbreviated, these procedures conform to the IEEE standard 488-1975 for instrument interfacing.

Figure 9.18. Control of send-limited transfers.

another character can be transferred. If, as is typically the case, one of these operations can be assumed to be consistently more time-consuming, then the start of the next transmission will depend on completion of that operation. In Example 9.3, it is the receiving device in which the speed-limiting printing operation takes place. Thus the transmitting device must be informed by a level on line *ready* that the receiver is indeed ready before a subsequent transmission can begin. Now suppose that the transmitting device were slower and could be assumed to take consistently longer to prepare for the next transmission. In this case it would not be necessary for the receiver to communicate its readiness to the transmitting device. Thus only two control lines would be required. The sequence would begin with a *datavalid* signal from the transmitter, and the receiver would respond with an *accept* as indicated in Fig. 9.18.

It might be tempting to try to reduce the number of communications control lines to two even in situations in which the data transmission rate is limited by the receiving device. One could possibly combine the *ready* and *accept* lines into a single line that might be labeled *reply*. Although this approach saves a line and can be completely responsive, it may complicate the writing of a reliable AHPL sequence.

Let us now explore communications between a master module and another arbitrary module, using three-line handshaking and the busing approach suggested by Fig. 9.15b. In addition to the 18-bit data bus, which is not shown in Fig. 9.19, there is a 12-bit *CSBUS* on which commands are transmitted from the master module to the peripheral modules, and on which status information is transmitted from the peripheral modules to the master module. A 1 will appear on a line *csrdy* from the master module whenever a command is placed on the *CSBUS*. A subset of these command bits must be used as an address, to indicate which of the peripheral modules is to receive the command. When a *csrdy* signal appears, each module will check these bits to determine if a response on its part is in order. A set of flip-flops storing various internal status information must be included in each module. A module will respond to a request-for-status command by connecting its register of status flip-flops to the *CSBUS*. Not every module will utilize all of the possible status flip-flops. Similarly, some of the command lines will be of no interest to particular modules.

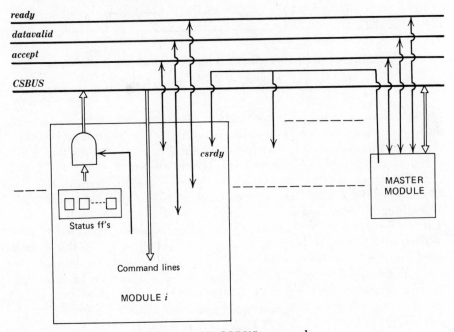

Figure 9.19. *CSBUS* approach.

    The three-line handshake control of data transfers will be the principal approach used in the remainder of the book. In general, it must be possible for any module to either transmit or receive data. Rather than provide three separate control lines to each module and three similar lines originating at each module, the lines *ready*, *datavalid*, and *accept* will each be treated as a 1-bit bus. As shown in Fig. 9.19, any module will be able to place a one-level on any of these three buses, and the bus level may be observed by any module. The only distinction between these buses and other communications buses discussed thus far rests in the fact that each is only a *1-bit* bus. For convenience the word *bus* does not appear in the names of these three control lines. *Nevertheless, ready, datavalid, and accept are communications buses in every sense and must be declared as such.* The hardware of each of these buses will be similar to the hardware for a single bit of any other communications bus.

    At any given time, only one module can be allowed to transmit data. We shall usually assume only one receiving device. If the control were not buses, it would be possible to have multiple receivers by using an ANDing of *ready* and *accept* signals from all receivers to control the handshake process. A peripheral module will be notified when it is to assume either of these roles by a command from the master module. The control of data transfers through the *IOBUS* will be as illustrated in Fig. 9.17a. This same procedure will be observed when a status vector is transferred to the master module via the *CSBUS*. Since commands are transmitted at the pleasure of the master module, only two lines are required to control a command transmission. As mentioned, the presence of a command on *CSBUS* will be signaled by a 1 on line *csrdy*. The module with the indicated device number will advise the master module of its acceptance of a command by placing a 1 on the bus *accept*.

Example 9.4

The same printing device considered in Example 9.3 is to be interfaced to the I/O system of Fig. 9.19. When a command is placed on the 12-bit *CSBUS*, the first 3 bits, $CSBUS_{0:2}$ will specify the number of the device for which the command is intended. The printer will be device #010. Although there are 9 bits, $CSBUS_{3:11}$, available for specifying commands, the printer will be subject to only two commands, which will be specified by $CSBUS_3$. If $CSBUS_3 = 0$, the printer is to accept a word for printing. If $CSBUS_3 = 1$, the printer interface is to send status information to the CPU over the *CSBUS*. Either operation is to be controlled by the three-line interactive handshake. The printer interface will have only one status bit, a flip-flop *busy*, the contents of which may be transmitted over $CSBUS_0$. The interface indicates that it cannot accept another data word by setting *busy* to 1.

Solution

The declarations are similar to those for Example 9.3 except that all the lines between the interface and the CPU, except *csrdy*, are now communications buses and must be declared after COMBUS. The following sequence is more complicated, primarily due to the need to be ready to respond to a request for status at any time.

```
MODULE: PRINTER INTERFACE
    MEMORY: DR[18]; CR[8]; busy (JK); first (JK)
    OUTPUTS: CHAR[8], print, feed
    INPUTS: wait, csrdy
    COMBUSES: IOBUS[18], CSBUS[12], ready, datavalid, accept
1.  → (csrdy ∧ $\overline{CSBUS_0}$ ∧ CSBUS₁ ∧ $\overline{CSBUS_2}$)/(1)
2.  accept = 1
    → ($\overline{CSBUS_3}$, $\overline{CSBUS_3}$, CSBUS₃)/(1, 1A, 3)
3.  → $\overline{(ready)}$/(3)
```

4. $CSBUS_0 = busy; datavalid = 1$
    $\rightarrow (\overline{accept}, accept)/(4,1)$

1A. $ready = 1$
    $\rightarrow (\overline{datavalid})/(1A)$

2A. $DR \leftarrow IOBUS; busy \leftarrow 1; accept = 1; first \leftarrow 1$

3A-6A. Same as 3-6 in Example 9.3

7A. $first \leftarrow 0; busy * \overline{first} \leftarrow 0$
    $\rightarrow (first, \overline{first})/(3A, 8A)$

8A. DEAD END

END

Step 1 waits for a *csrdy* signal occurring while device 2 is specified. Step 2 indicates that the command has been received with *accept* = 1 and determines if the command is an output data command or a request for status. If $CSBUS_3 = 0$, control branches to two parallel sequences. Steps 1A to 8A accept a data vector and print two characters as was done in Example 9.3. At the same time control returns to step 1 so that the interface is ready to respond to a request for status while the device is still busy with a printing operation. The CPU will not issue a subsequent output data command while *busy* = 1; there will be no second attempt to branch to 1A until the original control level has exited this sequence at the step 8A DEAD END.

If $CSBUS_3 = 1$ at step 2, control branches to step 3 to wait for a *ready*, which will indicate that the *CSBUS* is free. Step 4 holds *datavalid* at 1, which indicates that the requested status bit *busy* has been placed on the *CSBUS* and holds *busy* on the bus until another *accept* is received telling the device to return to step 1. The interface may be asked to respond to a request for status many times during an ongoing print operation. Clearly, the interface control unit would be much simpler if the *busy* line could be routed directly to the CPU eliminating the need for parallel sequences.

The sequence in Example 9.4 is considerably longer than that in Example 9.3, and the reader may wonder if the greater length is due to the use of the three-line interactive handshake. This is not the case. The sequence of Example 9.3 is a shorter sequence because it does not provide for control of the printer by the CPU. The sequence in that example is started by the printer indicating that it is ready to receive data. The sequence of Example 9.4 is a complete sequence, putting the CPU in control and allowing it to check the status of the printer.

Finally, it is important to note that, while the three-line interactive handshake does permit modules to operate asynchronously with respect to one another, it does not eliminate the need to synchronize control signals as they enter the control unit of a given module. Consider again the timing diagram of Fig. 9.11 but now assume that x remains at the 1-level for an indefinite period. If x goes to 1 during a clock pulse, as in

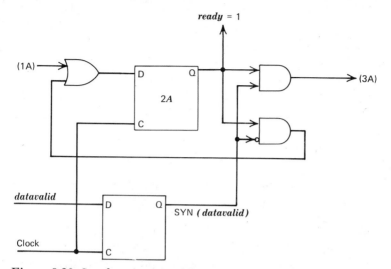

Figure 9.20. Synchronization of *datavalid* at Step 2A, Example 9.4.

Fig. 9.11, we still have the possibility that flip-flop 12 will see the change in time to react on clock-pulse 1, but flip-flop 10 will not, again resulting in double pulses moving through the system.

To eliminate such problems, the *accept, ready*, and *datavalid* must be synchronized by the circuit of Fig. 5.22 before entering a control unit. For example, the circuitry to implement step 2A of the sequence of Example 9.4 would be as shown in Fig. 9.20. To represent this accurately, step 1A should read:

1A. *ready* = 1
  → $(\overline{\text{SYN}(datavalid)})/(1\text{A})$

However, in the interest of simplicity we shall normally omit this refinement and assume that all signals are properly synchronized.

PROBLEMS

9.1 The following is an AHPL description of a counter module. Following control reset, will Z_1 ever be 1? Will Z_0? List for 12 consecutive clock periods following control reset all active control states for each clock period. Assume that $x = 0$.
   MODULE: DUAL COUNTER
   INPUTS: x
   MEMORY: A [3]; B [3]
   OUTPUTS: Z [2]

357

1. $B \leftarrow 3 \top 0$; $A \leftarrow 3 \top 0$
   $\rightarrow (x, \bar{x}, \bar{x})/(1, 2, 3)$
2. $A * B_2 \leftarrow 3 \top 0$; $Z_0 = \wedge/A$
   $\rightarrow (x, \bar{x} \wedge A_2, \bar{x})/(1, 3, 5)$
3. $B \leftarrow \text{INC}(B)$
4. DEAD END
5. $A \leftarrow \text{INC}(A)$; $Z_1 = \wedge/B$
   $\rightarrow (x, \bar{x})/(1, 2)$

END SEQUENCE
CONTROL RESET (1)
END

9.2 For the module described in Problem 9.1,
   (a) Construct a one flip-flop per control state realization of the control unit.
   (b) (For students with background in sequential circuits) Generate a state diagram for this control sequential circuit and construct a realization using a minimal number of flip-flops.

   Hint: Consider a state for each of the 16 combinations of active and inactive control steps.

9.3 The following is an AHPL description of a module designed to facilitate the transfer of data between two memories. Rewrite the module description using parallel control sequences to improve the overall transfer rate. Both the READ and WRITE operations take several clock periods to accomplish. Add a mechanism to insure that the word read from the first address will be written in the first address, etc.
   (a) Assume that the read operation will always require less time than the write operation.
   (b) Assume that the time required by both operations is variable and that it is not known which will take longer.

MODULE: TRANSFER CONTROL
   INPUTS: *XA*[12]; *XB*[12]; *DATAIN* [8]; *go; ready; done*
   OUTPUTS: *READADD; WRITEADD; read; write;*
       DATAOUT
   MEMORY: *DATA* [8]; *READADD* [12]; *WRITEADD* [12]
   1. *WRITEADD* $\leftarrow$ *XA*; *READADD* $\leftarrow$ *XB*
      $\rightarrow (\overline{go})/(1)$
   2. *WRITEADD* $\leftarrow$ INC(*WRITEADD*);
      READADD $\leftarrow$ IN(*READADD*)
      $\rightarrow (\overline{go})/(1)$

3. *read* $= 1$
   $\rightarrow (\overline{ready})/(3)$
4. **DATA** $\leftarrow$ **DATAIN**
5. *write* $= 1$
   $\rightarrow (\overline{done}, done)/(5, 2)$

END SEQUENCE
   DATAOUT = **DATA**
END

9.4   A certain special-purpose computer has only single-address memory reference instructions. Even the IOT operations are memory reference. As in SIC, the leftmost 3 bits specify the op code, and bits 3 and 4 specify indexing or indirect addressing. The only jump instruction is JPA, which causes a jump to the addressed instruction if and only if $\perp AC \leq 0$. In the programs used by this special-purpose computer, it has been shown that 1 in every 10 instructions is JPA. Write in AHPL a control sequence for the *fetch* cycle, and preparation for and termination of the *execute* cycle in this machine. The fetch of the next instruction should be accomplished in parallel with execution of the current instruction. Provide for holding up the fetch cycle while a JPA is executed. Make sure that the fetch will not interfere with use of the memory in the execution of any instruction. Assume a semiconductor memory with an access time of two clock periods. Do not include an indexing capability.

9.5   Discuss the possibility of parallel control sequences in a microprogrammed machine. Can parallel sequences exist within the microprogrammed control unit? How? Can parallel sequences be used outside the microprogrammed control unit? Can separate units be employed in a microprogrammed machine? How?

9.6   What possible source of trouble exists in the module described by the following AHPL sequence?

1. **CNT** $\leftarrow$ INC (**CNT**)
   $\rightarrow (\overline{\wedge/CNT})/(1)$
2. **Z** $= 1$

END SEQUENCE
   CNT $* x \leftarrow 8 \top 0$
END

9.7   (For students with background in sequential circuit design). Use level mode techniques to design the synchronization circuit of Fig. 9.12.

9.8 In the following partial AHPL sequence, does the input signal x require synchronization? Why or why not?

> END SEQUENCE
> $\quad a * x \leftarrow 1$
> END

9.9 Rewrite the AHPL description for the communications memory module of Example 4.3. The single-line *ready* is to be replaced by lines *ready* and *datavalid*. Lines *accept* and *word* retain their former significance. Control communications should now conform to the standard three-line handshake of Fig. 9.17a. It should no longer be necessary to assume that the communications memory is in a position to accept data whenever data are available.

9.10 Repeat Problem 9.9 for the duplicate character checker of Example 5.5. In this case the single line *data* should be replaced by lines *ready* and *datavalid*.

9.11 Add control lines and adjust the meaning of a and b in the priority store of Example 7.5 so that both input requests and output requests can be handled on a three-line handshake (Fig. 9.17a) basis. Rewrite only those AHPL steps of the priority store directly related to control communications.

9.12 Rewrite the AHPL description of the printer interface of Example 9.3 to incorporate the completely responsive three-line handshake of Fig. 9.17b.

9.13 Suppose that the duplicate character checker of Example 5.5 is connected to the busing structure suggested by Fig. 9.15a. Let the three control lines be **ready, datavalid**, and **accept**. Data is to be accepted from an 8-bit **IOBUS**. Rewrite the AHPL description of this module accordingly.

9.14 A data communications (long-distance) terminal includes its own control unit. The portion of the control unit that will cause received data to be stored in the memory of a minicomputer is to be designed. Data will pass in only one direction. Receiving data is a high-priority operation for the minicomputer. When a full buffer of data is available, the computer suspends all other activity while storing this data in memory. Connections between the terminal and the computer are shown in Fig. P9.14. The semiconductor buffer in the terminal contains (when full) 32 eight-bit characters. Pairs of consecutive characters are combined to be stored as 16-bit words in the minicomputer memory. These words can be transferred directly from **CR** in the terminal to **MD** in the minicomputer. The first portion of the terminal control sequence

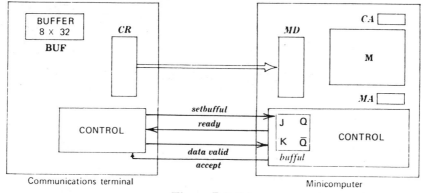

Figure P.9. 14.

is concerned with communications on a telephone line so that the 32 eight-bit characters are properly placed in the buffer. After the buffer has been filled, a level from the terminal will cause a flip-flop, *bufful*, in the computer to be set to 1. This flip-flop functions in much the same way as the interrupt flip-flops to be discussed in Chapter 10.

(a) Write the last portion of the control sequence for the terminal beginning with the step that generates the ***setbufful*** signal. This sequence will interact with the computer to cause the 32 characters to be stored in memory. Once the computer has processed the interrupt, it will respond with a signal on line *ready*. The three-line handshake then continues to completion.

(b) At step 1 in the control sequence, prior to the fetch operation, the computer pauses to examine the contents of *bufful*. If *bufful* = 0, the instruction fetch is carried out. If *bufful* = 1, control branches to step 100 to provide communications with the terminal. Write step 1. Write the sequence, beginning at step 100, which writes the data in memory. The next address at which data are to be stored in memory is available in **CA**. This address is kept current by software when a transfer sequence is not in progress.

REFERENCES

1. *IEEE Standard 488-1975*, Institute of Electrical and Electronic Engineers, New York, 1975.

2. J. C. Cluley, *Computer Interfacing and Online Operation*, Crane Russak Inc., New York, 1975.

10

INTERRUPT AND INPUT/OUTPUT

10.1 INTRODUCTION

In the last chapter we investigated the basic procedures whereby reliable communications can be provided between independent digital modules or systems. These techniques are very general and are certainly not restricted to situations involving computers. However, the most common example of digital communications is found in the communications between computers and their input/output devices. In this chapter we are concerned with the application of the techniques introduced in the last chapter to computer input/output systems. The importance of input/output in a computer system can scarcely be overstated, since this is the means by which the computer communicates with the "outside world." The computer is normally in control of the input/output process, but, as noted in the last chapter, there are situations in which a peripheral device must be able to initiate communications. Interrupt is a part of the communications problem because it is the means by which peripherals can request the "attention" of the computer when it is busy with other activities. Input/output operations are not the only reasons for interrupt, but they are probably the most common. Also, the special machine instructions dealing with interrupt are usually grouped with I/O instructions; therefore, it seems logical to consider interrupt and I/O together.

Among the more common I/O devices are card readers and punches, printers, teletypewriters, and paper tape punches and readers. These are all electromechanical devices of great complexity, but details of how they are constructed will not be considered here. We are concerned only with how the computer communicates with these devices. With regard to communications with the computer, all these devices have three special characteristics that account for the special nature of the I/O problem. First, their operation is completely asynchronous with respect to the

362

central processor. Second, their speed of operation is often orders of magnitude slower than that of the central processor. For example, the data rate of a typical card reader would be 300 words/sec, compared with a typical CPU rate of a million operations/sec. Third, their data format is usually quite different from that of the central processor.

From the standpoint of communication with the CPU, magnetic tape and disk are generally considered to be I/O devices because they share these same three special characteristics. We have previously considered these types of devices as memory, but this is simply a matter of point of view. These devices are memory in the sense that the CPU can store information in them and later retrieve it without human intervention; but they are I/O in the sense of requiring special techniques to deal with their characteristics of slow, asynchronous operation and special data formats.

There is probably more variation from computer to computer in the areas of interrupt and I/O design than in any other area of computer design. This being the case, we cannot hope to cover all possible techniques. In line with our belief that learning best proceeds from the specific to the general, we shall develop specific "typical" interrupt and I/O systems, and then comment on the variations and options open to the designer.

10.2 INTERRUPT SYSTEM FOR SIC

There are many possible situations that can call for interrupt of the main program. *Internal* interrupts are usually caused by various types of error conditions such as memory parity error or invalid memory address. *External* interrupts arise because of requests from external devices for attention. The very term *interrupt* is often misleading, as it implies an anomalous, unexpected situation that takes the CPU away from what it is "normally" doing. In situations in which the interrupt is caused by an error condition, this is the case. But errors are, hopefully, rare events; and the vast majority of interrupts come about in the course of input/output operations. In many operating environments, input/output operations occupy the bulk of the CPU's time, and interrupts are a normal occurrence. A phrase such as *request for service* would be more descriptive, but *interrupt* is the accepted term.

Interrupt systems vary widely in detail, but certain basic features are common to virtually all computers. First, there must be some means of recording the fact that an interrupt request has been made. Usually, one or more *flags* or *indicator flip-flops* will be provided for this purpose. Second, steps must be built into the control sequence whereby the CPU can check the status of these flags at regular intervals. This part of the interrupt process, the setting and checking of interrupt flags, is normally a hardware feature that proceeds automatically with little or no intervention by the programmer.

The next part of the interrupt process or system involves checking to determine where the interrupt request came from and allowing the programmer to decide whether or not the CPU should respond. This part of the process usually involves a combination of hardware and software. Finally, if the interrupt is to be responded to, the CPU must jump to a special interrupt program or subroutine. The means for jumping to the interrupt program is usually a hardware feature. The program itself, which specifies what is to be done about the interrupt, is left entirely to the discretion of the programmer.

Let us now illustrate some of these features by designing an interrupt system for SIC. The first design decision is how many interrupt flags to provide. The more flags that are provided, the more separate interrupt sources that can be identified without software interrogation. For SIC eight interrupt flags will be provided, in the form of an 8-bit register, **INTR**. The designer need not designate which interrupt sources will correspond to which positions in **INTR**. Certain internal sources of interrupt may be specified, such as arithmetic overflow, that will be permanently associated with specified positions in **INTR**. But the choice of which external (I/O) device will be associated with a given position of **INTR** will often be left as a customer option to be determined at the time of installation. For SIC the assignment of positions in **INTR** will be left open. Eight interrupt lines, **INTLINE**[8], will be added to the input declarations. These lines can be connected to any interrupt sources desired at installation. If internal interrupts are desired, appropriate output lines, e.g., **invald** for invalid memory address, may be declared, which may in turn be connected to the desired **INTLINE**. Following the END SEQUENCE statement we could then add statements of the form

$$INTR_0 * INTLINE_0 \leftarrow 1,$$

one for each position of **INTR**. As noted in Chapter 9, if **INTR** has been declared as being constructed of *J-K* flip-flops, this statement indicates that $INTLINE_0$ will be interrogated every clock period and $INTR_0$ will be set if $INTLINE_0 = 1$. There will be no synchronization problems as long as the 1 on the interrupt line lasts at least one clock period.

Although it is perfectly correct to use statements of the above form, it is inconvenient to have to write a separate statement for each bit of **INTR**. This sort of situation, in which one vector controls another vector on a bit-by-bit basis, is fairly common, so we find it convenient to define a new AHPL condition form, the element-by-element conditional, which may take either of the two following basic forms.

$$DV \circledast F \leftarrow OCLV$$
$$BUS = OCLV \circledast F$$

The vectors and the bus must be of the same dimension in statements of either form. Statements of the first form have the following meaning:

DV_i will be set to the value of $OCLV_i$ if $F_i = 1$;
DV_i will not be affected if $F_i = 0$

Statements of the second form will have the following meaning:

if $F_i = 1$, $BUS_i = OCLV_i$;
if $F_i = 0$, $OCLV_i$ will not be gated onto the bus

This form may be extended to matrices, but we shall defer discussion of this extension until Chapter 13, where a need for it first arises. In the case of the interrupt system, the control of the *INTR* register by the *INTLINES* can now be specified by the statement

$$INTR \circledast INTLINE \leftarrow \overline{8 \top 0}$$

The *OCLV* in this statement is a vector of eight 1's so that the statement specifies that a position of *INTR* will be set if the corresponding *INTLINE* = 1.

The designer's (or customer's) decision as to what interrupt sources shall be connected to the *INTR* register determines what conditions might possibly cause interrupts. It is also desirable that the programmer should be able to exercise control over which sources will actually be allowed to cause an interrupt under various conditions. In particular, the programmer may wish to establish priority among various I/O devices. For example, it may be desired to ignore a request from a slow device, such as a card reader, if a faster device, such as a disk, is already being processed.

To provide this programmer control over interrupts, we establish a *mask* register, **MR**, having the same number of positions as **INTR**. By means of a special command, to be discussed later, the programmer can set or clear any position of the mask register as desired. If a position of **MR** is set to 1, the corresponding position of **INTR** is *enabled*, i.e., when it is set by an interrupt request, it may in turn set the interrupt indicator, *intf*. If a position of **MR** is 0, the corresponding position of **INTR** is *disabled* so that its setting has no effect on *intf*. The logic by which this is accomplished is shown in Fig. 10.1.

When a condition demanding interrupt occurs, the CPU should re-

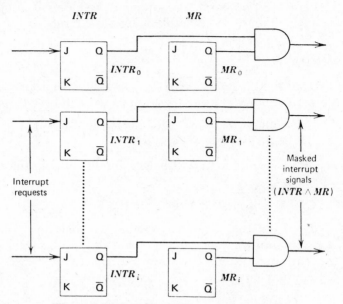

Figure 10.1. Masking of interrupt requests.

spond as quickly as possible. In most computers, the interrupt will occur as soon as the instruction currently being executed has been completed, before fetching a new instruction. Thus, before entering a new fetch cycle, the control unit should check to see if an interrupt has been requested. Referring back to Fig. 6.3, we see that a new fetch is initiated in SIC when the control unit returns to step 2 after incrementing PC (step 24) or loading a jump address into PC (step 14). Once during each instruction cycle, control must interrogate the masked interrupt signals and set the interrupt indicator, *intf*, if any are present. We then insert a new step 2, to cause a branch into an interrupt sequence if *intf* is set. The interrogation of the masked interrupt signals should come at the latest point common to all instructions, immediately before the branch at step 5. The modified control sequence will then be as follows.

1. $\rightarrow (\overline{\text{SL (SYN}(\textit{start}\text{)))}}/(1)$
2. $\rightarrow (\textit{intf})/(60)$ ←(new)
2-1. $MA \leftarrow PC$
3. $MD \leftarrow \text{BUSFN}(M; \text{DCD}(MA))$ }   no change
4. $IR \leftarrow MD;$
     $\textit{intf} * ((\bigvee/(MR \wedge INTR)) \wedge \textit{enif}) \leftarrow 1$ ←(new)

5.   As before

Step 60 is the start of the interrupt sequence; *enif* is the *enable interrupt* indicator, which provides a "master control" of the interrupt system. Its use will be more fully explained later. The modifications to the control unit logic are shown in Fig. 10.2.

The first step in the interrupt sequence is to clear *enif* and *intf* to prevent any more interrupts until the machine is in a position to deal with them. The interrupt request must be processed by a software subroutine. The hardware must place the address of the proper subroutine in the program counter so that this routine can take over. To do this, the hardware must first determine which interrupt source requires attention. The programmer has determined, by setting **MR**, which interrupt sources are to be enabled; but it is possible that more than one enabled interrupt can occur at the same time. For example, suppose that when **INTR** is interrogated (step 4), there are enabled signals present for both an overflow and an I/O request. This will result in *intf* being set, and the control unit will branch to the interrupt sequence when it returns to step 2; but which request should be dealt with first?

We shall establish priority by means of a logic circuit such that the interrupt source connected to $INTR_0$ will have highest priority, the source at $INTR_1$, next highest priority, etc. The priority circuit is described by the combinational logic subroutine PRI(A), where A is the vector of masked interrupt signals; and the output is an ρA-element vector, only 1 bit of which can take on the value 1 at any time. The combinational logic unit description is given in Fig. 10.3a, the resultant circuit for a 4-bit interrupt system is shown in Fig. 10.3b. Note that an enabled interrupt signal at any bit position is complemented and applied to AND gates at all lower-priority positions, thus blocking any lower-priority interrupts. This system establishes a fixed priority with regard to **MR** and **INTR**, but recall that the user can specify which devices are to be connected to which positions of **INTR**.

Before turning control over to a software subroutine for dealing with the interrupt request, the current contents of **PC** must be stored to provide for returning to the interrupted program. We shall permanently reserve two positions in memory for each interrupt line, one for storing the contents of **PC**, the other for a jump command. For SIC let us assign locations 00010 and 00011 to $INTR_0$, 00012 and 00013 to $INTR_1$, 0014 and 00015 to $INTR_2$, etc.

Since only one of the outputs of PRI can take on a 1 value at any one time, this output identifies the source making the interrupt request. The signal PRI(**INTR** $\wedge$ **MR**) will be fed to another logic circuit, the address coding circuit, ADDR(A), which will produce the address of the first memory location set aside for the interrupt source originating the re-

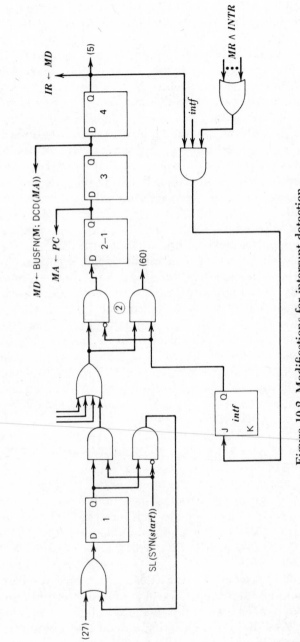

Figure 10.2. Modifications for interrupt detection.

368

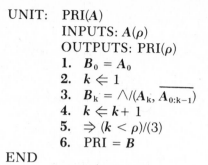

UNIT: PRI(A)

        INPUTS: $A(\rho)$

        OUTPUTS: PRI(ρ)

        1. $B_0 = A_0$

        2. $k \Leftarrow 1$

        3. $B_k = \wedge/(A_k, \overline{A_{0:k-1}})$

        4. $k \Leftarrow k + 1$

        5. $\Rightarrow (k < \rho)/(3)$

        6. PRI $= B$

END

(a)

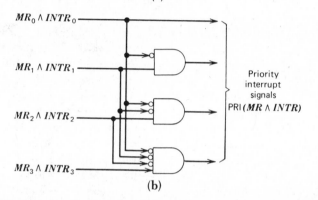

(b)

Figure 10.3. Interrupt priority network. (*a*) Combination logic unit description. (*b*) Four-bit network.

quest. For example, if the interrupt request had come from the source assigned to $INTR_0$, ADDR = 00010. This address will be loaded into *MA* and *IR*, and the current contents of *PC* will be stored at the addressed location. The address will then be transferred from *IR* to *PC* and incremented; a normal fetch cycle will then be entered. This fetch will then take the jump instruction from the second assigned location, e.g., 00011 if ADDR(PRI($INTR \wedge MR$)) = 00010. The programmer will have previously entered a jump instruction at this location, to jump to an appropriate subroutine for dealing with interrupts from the source initiating the request. This sequence, starting at step 60 is

60. *intf, enif* $\leftarrow 0, 0$

61. $IR_{5:17} \leftarrow$ ADDR(PRI(*INTR* $\wedge$ *MR*))

62. *MA* $\leftarrow IR_{5:17}$; *MD* $\leftarrow 5 \top 0, PC$

63. M $*$ DCD(*MA*) $\leftarrow$ *MD*

64. *PC* $\leftarrow IR_{5:17}$

    $\rightarrow$ (24)

The reader may note that the above sequence is similar in some respects to the JMS (jump to subroutine) sequence, and it is possible that some economy might result from sharing hardware between these two sequences. However, we are here concerned with the basic processes involved rather than minor simplifications in circuitry.

The first step in the above sequence, the clearing of *intf* and *enif*, is necessary to prevent the control unit from re-entering the interrupt sequence instead of fetching the next (jump) instruction, and to inhibit any further setting of *intf* until the programmer indicates that further interrupts are to be allowed. This is essential as the programmer must have complete control over what, if anything, is to be allowed to interrupt the interrupt program.

The reader should note carefully that the hardware sequence discussed above does not really do anything "about" the interrupt. It establishes priority among interrupts, identifies the source, and initiates a jump to a program for dealing with the interrupt. From this point on, what happens is entirely at the discretion of the programmer, and is thus largely beyond the scope of this book. However, for purposes of a fuller understanding of the interrupt process, it may be useful to discuss briefly the steps that might be involved in a typical interrupt program.

The first portion of the interrupt program may involve inquiries to find out more about the nature of the interrupt condition. For example, an I/O unit may interrupt for several reasons such as parity error, end-of-file, etc. However, each device will probably be allocated only one position in **INTR** so that it cannot directly indicate the nature of the interrupt condition. For this purpose the programmer will use STATUS TEST/device commands (to be discussed later) to interrogate the interrupting as to the exact reason for the interrupt.

Having determined the exact reason for the interrupt, the interrupt program will then take the appropriate action to deal with the interrupt condition, as specified by the programmer. If this action will require the use of the arithmetic registers, then their contents will have to be stored in order to preserve the status of the interrupted program.

One of the most difficult aspects of interrupt programming is the handling of interrupts that come in during an interrupt program. If there are no interrupt sources of such urgency that they cannot wait until the current interrupt has been processed, the program will simply leave the interrupt system disabled. Note that interrupt requests arriving while the interrupt system is disabled are not lost. They will still set the appropriate positions of **INTR** and may be responded to whenever the interrupt is enabled.

In some situations, such as real-time process control, there may be interrupt requests of such urgency that response cannot be delayed until the current interrupt program is completed. In this case the program will reenable the interrupt system, changing **MR** as required to reflect the priorities of the interrupt program. Also, the procedure for dealing with an interrupt of an interrupt may be different from that for dealing with an interrupt request from the same source but coming during the main program. The programmer may alter the interrupt program, or change the jump address associated with the interrupt source, to cause a jump to a different program.

When the appropriate action has been completed, the interrupt system will be disabled and the restoration of the main program started. It is important that the interrupt be disabled during the beginning and ending of the interrupt routine. If the computer is interrupted while in the midst of switching programs, it will be virtually impossible to keep track of the program status. The next-to-last step in the interrupt routine will reset **MR** for the main program and set *enif* to enable the interrupt system. The final command will be an indirect jump to the location where the **PC** contents were stored, to return control to the main program. For example, if the interrupt originated through $INTR_0$, the final command of the interrupt program will be

JMP I 00010

which causes a jump to the address stored in 00010, i.e., the contents of **PC** at the time the interrupt was initiated.

Note carefully that additional interrupts cannot occur until after the jump command has been executed. Prior to the next-to-last command, the interrupt has been disabled, i.e., both *enif* and *intf* have been cleared. This prevents *intf* from being set during the execution of the next-to-last command, ensuring that the jump command will be executed. The setting of *enif* will make possible the setting of *intf* during the execution of the jump command if an interrupt signal is present, but this will not cause an interrupt until the next fetch after completion of the jump command. This two-step enabling procedure, effectively delaying the enable for a full instruction cycle, is absolutely essential.

In order to clarify the above, let us consider a specific interrupt situation. In the execution of a certain program, assume that only the first three interrupt sources, $INTR_0$, $INTR_1$, and $INTR_2$ are enabled. The routines for dealing with these interrupts start at locations 00100, 00200, and 00300, respectively; the main program starts at 01000 as shown in Fig. 10.4a. Accordingly, locations 00011, 00013, and 00015 contain jumps to 00100, 00200, and 00300, while the last steps in the corresponding interrupt routines are indirect jumps through 00010, 00012, and 00014.

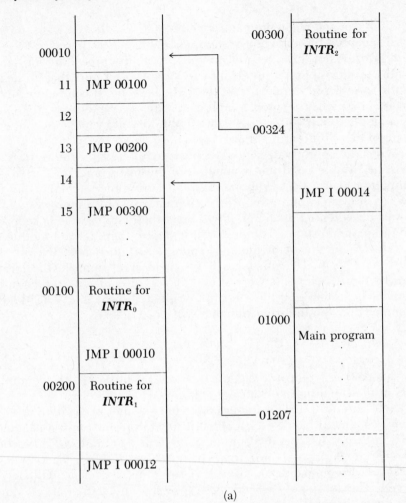

(a)

0300	DAC	370		0356	$intf \leftarrow 0;\ enif \leftarrow 0$	(APL)
0301	DFA			0357	LAC	371
0302	DAC	371		0360	DTA	
0303	DFB			0361	LAC	372
0304	DAC	372		0362	DTB	
0305	$AC \leftarrow MR$	(APL)		0363	LAC	373
0306	DAC	373		0364	$MR \leftarrow AC$	(APL)
0307	$MR \leftarrow 10000000$	(APL)		0365	LAC	370
0310	$INTR_2 \leftarrow 0;\ enif \leftarrow 1$	(APL)		0366	$enif \leftarrow 1$	(APL)
				0367	JMP I 14	

(b)

Figure 10.4. Typical interrupt routines.

372

Assume that during the execution of instruction 01205 of the main program, $INTR_2$ is set by an interrupt request. At step 4 of the next fetch cycle, $INTR$ is checked and $intf$ is set as a result of $INTR_2$ having been set. The instruction at 01206 will then be executed. At the start of the next fetch cycle (for instruction 01207), $intf$ will cause a branch to step 60, the start of the interrupt sequence. Steps 61 and 62 will load 00014, corresponding to $INTR_2$, into MA, and step 63 will load the address of the next instruction in the main program, 01207, into location 00014. Step 64 will load address 00014 into PC and this will be incremented at step 24, causing the next instruction to be fetched from 00015. This instruction, JMP 00300, causes a jump to the routine for dealing with $INTR_2$.

Figure 10.4b shows a SIC program for responding to an interrupt on $INTR_2$. Since we have yet to define a set of SIC instructions for controlling the interrupt system, some of the instructions are written in APL, simply indicating what is to be done, without regard for SIC assembly language formats. The first seven steps save the contents of AC, IA, IB, and MR, for use when returning to the interrupted program. The next instruction (307) sets the mask register so that only $INTR_0$ can interrupt the interrupt program. The instruction at 310 resets $INTR_2$ and sets $enif$ to enable a possible interrupt on $INTR_0$. We shall see shortly that it will be possible to accomplish both these operations in a single SIC instruction. The steps following 310 will take the actions necessary to respond to the particular interrupt.

Next assume that $INTR_0$ is set during the execution of instruction 00322 of the interrupt routine. During the fetch of 00323 this will cause $intf$ to be set. This will in turn cause address 00324 to be stored at 00010, followed by a jump at 00011 to 00100, to deal with $INTR_0$. On completion of the routine for $INTR_0$, the execution of JMP I 00010 will return control to 00324, to continue with the routine for $INTR_2$.

On completion of the steps that respond to $INTR_2$, $intf$ and $enif$ are first cleared (line 356) to prevent another interrupt while AC, IA, IB, and MR are restored to their original values from the main program. Step 366 sets $enif$, and the interrupt routine is completed by the indirect jump at 367, through 14 to 1207, to return to the main program. Even though a position of $INTR$ might be set during the execution of 366 and 367, $intf$ could not be set until step 4 of the fetch of 367 preventing a branch to the interrupt sequence until step 2 of the fetch following completion of the jump back to the main program.

To complete the design, we must consider the commands necessary for controlling the interrupt system. Rather than specify many different commands, we shall specify just one, $interrupt\ control$, INT, and use the same microcoding technique used for the operate instructions, in

373

which specific bits control specific operations. In this manner the programmer is given the maximum flexibility in constructing the interrupt instructions. The interrupt control INT will be one of the I/O class of instructions for which bits 0-3 are all 1's. For INT, bit-4 will also be 1, the remaining bits having the significance shown in Fig. 10.5a.

Bits $IR_{5:6}$ control MR which can be left unchanged, set to a new value equal to the 8 bits $IR_{10:17}$, or saved and restored via AC. Since this is a nonaddressed command, it is not possible to store in or retrieve directly from memory; the DAC and LAC commands must be used for that purpose. If $IR_7 = 1$, $IR_{10:17}$ corresponds on a bit-by-bit basis to $INTR_{0:7}$; if any of these bits in IR are set, the corresponding bits in $INTR$ will be cleared. Bits IR_8 and IR_9 control $intf$ and $enif$ as shown. Any combination of 1's and 0's in bits 5 to 17 is permitted. For example, the instruction shown in Fig. 10.5b would clear $intf$, set $enif$, and enable bits 0, 2, 3,

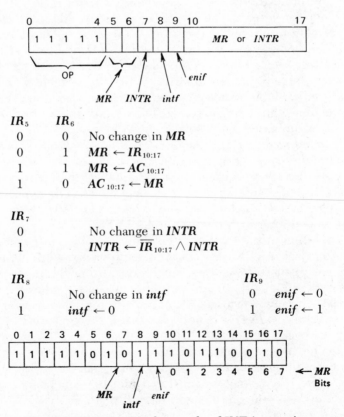

IR_5	IR_6	
0	0	No change in MR
0	1	$MR \leftarrow IR_{10:17}$
1	1	$MR \leftarrow AC_{10:17}$
1	0	$AC_{10:17} \leftarrow MR$

IR_7	
0	No change in $INTR$
1	$INTR \leftarrow \overline{IR}_{10:17} \wedge INTR$

IR_8		IR_9	
0	No change in $intf$	0	$enif \leftarrow 0$
1	$intf \leftarrow 0$	1	$enif \leftarrow 1$

Figure 10.5. Format and example of INT instruction.

and 6 of **MR**. Consideration of the hardware and control logic necessary for implementing this instruction will be deferred to a later section, in which we consider the entire I/O sequence.

The above interrupt system illustrates the essential features typical of many computer interrupt systems, but there are many variations. An address automatically generated by the hardware, as in step 61 of the above sequence, is sometimes referred to as an *interrupt vector*, presumably to convey the idea that the address "points the way" to the interrupt routine. Systems in which the hardware automatically generates these addresses are often referred to as *vectored interrupt systems*. A nonvectored system is one in which there is only one interrupt flag in the CPU, which is controlled by an ORing of all possible interrupt signals. When this flag is set, the programmer must provide a software routine to sequentially interrogate the interrupt sources to determine which one requested attention. This approach reduces the amount of hardware but at the expense of a considerable increase in the time required to service interrupts. One advantage of the nonvectored approach is that there are no hardware constraints on priority, since the programmer can interrogate the possible interrupts in any desired order. It is possible to provide programmer control of priority in a vectored system, but this requires rather elaborate hardware.

As we noted, when a program is interrupted, the contents of a number of registers may have to be preserved. The above system stores only the program counter automatically. The programmer must provide for storing the contents of other registers in the interrupt routine, a requirement that may add considerably to the length of interrupt routines. Therefore, some computers automatically store the contents of all registers whose status must be preserved and automatically restore these registers when control is returned to the main program. This approach increases the complexity of the interrupt hardware but can save a lot of time servicing interrupts, assuming that the contents of the registers need to be preserved in every case. If there are some cases in which the interrupts can be serviced without disturbing any operating registers, then the time spent storing them is wasted. The designer must decide what is best, based on the expected operating environment of the system.

An interesting and important variation on this procedure is the use of the *program status word*. Basically, replacing a main program with an interrupt program, or, for that matter, replacing any program with any other program, requires the exchange of certain information. To make this exchange as systematic as possible, we specify a *program status register*, **PSR**, which will at all times contain the information that must be preserved in order to preserve the status of any type of program. The

PSR will basically consist of the catenation of the *PC* register, the *MR*, and various indicators, the exact nature of which will depend on the computer. The contents of this register are referred to as the program status word, PSW.

Associated with interrupt source will be a reserved location in memory, in which the programmer will store the PSW for the interrupt program associated with that source. The PSW will contain the starting address of the interrupt program, the desired mask register setting, and such indicator settings as may be required. When an interrupt occurs, the CPU simply exchanges PSW's, storing the current PSW of the interrupted program in the second reserved location and loading the PSW of the interrupt program into *PSR*. The reader should note that there is nothing basically new here. This same information must be exchanged in any interrupt procedure; the PSW concept makes this exchange somewhat more systematic than it might otherwise be. This approach is very important as it is used in IBM Systems 360 and 370 and all the many imitators of those systems.

10.3   BASIC DATA TRANSFER OPERATIONS

Any data transfer operation will involve some or all of the following steps:

1. Check to see if device is available.
2. When device becomes available, activate.
3. Transfer data.
4. Deactivate.

The first step is to check to see if the desired I/O device is available. It might seem at first consideration that the CPU should "know" if it is using the device, but this is not always the case. Because I/O is slow and inefficient, software operating systems try to group I/O activities and fit them in at convenient times; as a result there may well be conflicting requests for the same device from different parts of a single program or even from different programs. It is thus desirable to have the CPU issue an inquiry as to the status of the device. This inquiry can be made in two ways; by status report or by interrupt.

In the first method, the CPU requests a status report from the I/O device and tests this report to see if the device is available, i.e., not busy with some other I/O activity. If it is busy, it executes the next command, which is a jump back to the status request, causing the CPU to remain in a loop, checking the status of the device until it becomes available.

When the status report indicates that the device is available, the jump instruction is skipped, fetching a new instruction to initiate data transfer.

The above method is undesirable unless the I/O device is likely to be immediately available, since it puts the CPU into a holding loop pending availability of the device. This can be avoided by using an interrupt inquiry. In this method, a special I/O control instruction requests the I/O device to enter an interrupt request when it becomes available. Various I/O devices may be allotted positions in the *INTR* register, which may be enabled by a suitable INT command. However, there are a number of reasons why an I/O device might issue an interrupt request, such as parity error, end-of-file, device available, etc. A special control instruction is therefore required to instruct the I/O device as to the conditions for which it should issue an interrupt request. After the above instruction has been issued, the program may go on to other tasks until it is interrupted as a result of the device's becoming available.

The exact nature of the second step, activating the device, will depend on the device, and in some cases may be skipped altogether. For example, console typewriters and CRT displays are in standby, "ready to go," any time they are available, and no activation step is necessary. On the other hand, in devices like tape units and card readers, the mechanical motion must be started, the type of code (binary, Hollerith, etc.) indicated, error indicators that are to generate interrupts enabled, etc. Similar comments apply to the deactivate step. Devices such as console typewriters and CRT displays automatically go back to standby when the transfer is complete. In a tape unit, however, the end-of-file mark must be inserted, tape motion stopped, interrupt indicators cleared, etc.

The third step, the actual transfer of the data, may be carried out by three distinct methods, which we shall designate as *programmed, buffered*, and *direct memory access* or *DMA*. In the programmed mode of transfer, the execution of one or more instructions, fetched from memory, is required for the transfer of each word. For devices requiring no activation step, the instruction to which the program skips as a result of the device's becoming available will be a READ or WRITE command to the device.

Devices requiring activation, such as tape units, generally transmit data in blocks of words, with words being transferred at a rate that is asynchronous and slow with respect to the CPU operations. In such cases the last step in the activate sequence will be to issue an instruction to interrupt when ready to transfer data. When the interrupt signal is received, the CPU goes into an interrupt procedure as described in previous sections, storing the interrupted program, fetching instructions to transfer a word or series of words, and restoring the interrupted program. This procedure can continue, with repeated interrupts of the main program until the desired number of words has been transferred, at which time the device will be deactivated.

The programmed data transfer procedure can be very inefficient if it requires a full interrupt procedure, including storage and restoration of the interrupted program, for every word transferred. For a buffered (hardware-controlled) transfer, we add sufficient control logic to eliminate the need for fetching special instructions when a word is to be transferred, plus enough additional data paths so that the main program need not be disturbed. When a word is to be transferred, execution of the main program will be suspended until the transfer is complete; but no special steps need to be taken to preserve the main program. In essence, a buffered transfer is a special interrupt procedure that requires no instructions to be fetched.

Buffered transfer is used only when a number of words are to be transferred to or from a specific area in memory, usually referred to as the *buffer area*. In some computers a certain special area of memory is permanently reserved for buffer operations, but this technique is inconvenient from a programming point of view. Usually, the programmer may specify the size and location of the buffer area. For each device to be buffered, two locations in memory are permanently reserved for storing the addresses of the buffer area. Prior to activating the buffer, the programmer will store in these locations either the first or last address of the buffer area and the number of words in the buffer area.

When the buffer is in operation, a special signal will be issued by the I/O device whenever it is ready to transfer a word. This signal will function as a special interrupt signal, transferring control to a special buffer sequence when the execution of the current instruction is complete. The buffer sequence will read the address and word count from memory, determine from them the current buffer address, transfer the word in or out of memory, update the word count and check to see if the buffer is complete (no more words to be transferred), and then return control to the main program. All of this is done by hard-wired or microprogrammed control, i.e., no instructions are fetched and sufficient extra hardware is provided so that the main program will not be affected in any way.

While buffer transfer is certainly faster than programmed transfer, we must keep in mind that the relative speeds of the CPU and the I/O devices set an upper limit on how many devices can be serviced simultaneously. When a device makes a buffer request, it must wait for the current instruction to be executed; and in the worst case, it may have to wait for the instruction with the longest execution time. For example, suppose that the longest execution time in SIC were 5 μsec and the execution time of the buffer sequence were 2 μsec. Then the fastest rate at which we could guarantee to service buffer channels would be once every 7 μsec. If there were eight buffer channels active, of equal priority and being serviced in a fixed sequence, the fastest data rate we could guarantee to handle from any single device would be one word every 56 μsec. This might not be fast enough for some devices. In that case it would be necessary to reduce the number of active buffer channels.

Even with a limited number of buffers, the buffered transfer may not be fast enough for such devices as fast parallel disks. There are two main factors limiting the speed of buffer operations. First, accesses to memory must be made to obtain the buffer addresses. This delay can be reduced by providing special registers to store the buffer addresses, either in the CPU, or in the peripheral. Second, even with the addition of special-address registers, speed is limited by the need to wait for the completion of the current instruction before starting a buffer sequence. This wait is made necessary by the fact that the buffer sequence uses the same address and data registers for accessing memory as are used by the CPU in executing other instructions. Only between instructions can we be sure that the contents of these registers need not be preserved for later use. This delay can be eliminated by providing the peripheral with *direct memory access* (DMA), an alternate path to memory that completely bypasses any registers used by the CPU for regular instructions. DMA systems vary considerably in detail, but the basic characteristic is that the CPU and the DMA channels share memory on a more-or-less equal basis, with the only delays being waits for memory to become available.

10.4 I/O SYSTEM FOR SIC

To provide specific examples of the concepts discussed above, we shall now develop an input/output system for SIC. The basic system for programmed transfer will be developed in this section, and the additions needed for buffer and DMA operation will be developed in succeeding sections. The basic block diagram of SIC, with the I/O system added, is shown in Fig. 10.6. We assume up to eight devices, all connected for programmed transfer in the manner shown in Fig. 9.15b, using an I/O bus and share control/status lines. The control/status lines will consist of a 12-bit control/status bus, **CSBUS**[12], the interrupt lines, **INTLINE**[8], and four signaling lines, *csrdy, ready, datavalid*, and *accept*. The functions of the **MR** and **INTR** have already been discussed.

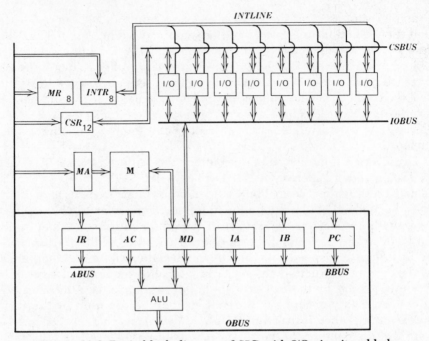

Figure 10.6. Basic block diagram of SIC with I/O circuits added.

The 12-bit control/status register, **CSR**[12], will be connected to the **CSBUS** for the purpose of transmitting instructions from the CPU to the peripherals, or status information from the peripherals to the CPU. These modifications will require the following additions to the declarations:

MEMORY: *MR*[8]; *INTR*[8]; *CSR*[12]; *intf; enif*
INPUTS: *INTLINE*[8]
OUTPUTS: *csrdy*
COMBUSES: *IOBUS*[18]; *CSBUS*[12]; *ready*;
                 datavalid; accept

There will be three basic instructions in the I/O group, i.e., instructions for which the first 4 bits are all 1. One of these, INT, has already been discussed. The TST (Test Status) command will be discussed shortly. The IOT (Input Output Transfer) command is the basic I/O command and can be considered as six different commands sharing a common 6-bit op code, 75 (octal). The formats for these instructions are shown in Fig. 10.7.

For all IOT commands, the last 12 bits comprise the command code to the peripheral device and are placed on the **CSBUS** via **CSR**. What

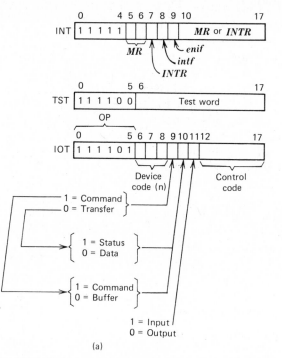

(a)

Mnemonic	$IR_{9:11}$	Meaning
ODn	000	Output data to device n
IDn	001	Input data from device n
	010	not used
ISn	011	Input status from device n and test
OBn	100	Activate output buffer, device n
IBn	101	Activate input buffer, device n
OCn	110	Command to device n
	111	not used

(b) IOT mnemonics, codes, and meanings

Figure 10.7. I/O class instructions.

happens then depends on these 12 bits. The first 6 of these bits ($IR_{6:11}$ or $CSR_{0:5}$) have a uniform meaning, regardless of which peripheral is being signaled. The last 6 bits ($IR_{12:17}$ or $CSR_{6:11}$) are device-dependent; they have no significance of any kind to the CPU and may be interpreted in different ways by different I/O devices.

The first 3 bits of the command code ($IR_{6:8}$) specify the device number, the code that indicates which of the eight possible I/O devices is to respond to the command on the *CSBUS*. The next bit, IR_9, indicates whether this command requires any further transfer of information. If $IR_9 = 0$, information is to be transferred. If $IR_9 = 1$, this is a command to take some action that requires no further interaction with the computer such as turning on a drive motor or clearing an error flag. The meaning of IR_{10} depends on IR_9. If $IR_9 = 0$, IR_{10} indicates if the information to be transferred is status (over the *CSBUS*) or data (over the *IOBUS*). If $IR_9 = 1$, IR_{10} indicates whether or not the command is to activate a buffer, a procedure that will be discussed in the next section. Finally, IR_{11} indicates the direction of transfer. The meanings of the various combination of these 3 bits is summarized in Fig. 10.7b, and corresponding assembly language mnemonics are also given.

The input data and output data instructions will each cause the transfer of one word to or from *AC* over the *IOBUS*. The command to device instruction is used primarily in the activate and deactivate steps of the I/O process. The input status instruction permits the CPU to check on the status of the peripheral devices. Each peripheral will have its own status register, made up of status flip-flops that can be set to indicate the existence of various conditions such as busy, parity error detected, out of tape, etc. A peripheral may have up to 12 status flags although few require that many. When a peripheral receives an input status command, it will connect its status register to the *CSBUS*, and the CPU will then transfer this information into the *CSR* register, where it can be tested.

The testing of the *CSR* register can be done with the input status instruction or with a separate TST instruction. For the input status instruction, the last 6 bits, $IR_{12:17}$, indicate which bits in *CSR* are to be tested. These 6 bits correspond to the last 6 bits of *CSR*. If a bit in the test word ($IR_{12:17}$) is 1, the corresponding bit in *CSR* will be tested; if that bit is 1, the next instruction will be skipped; and if none of the tested bits is 1, the next instruction will be executed. The TST instruction functions in the same way except that the test word is 12 bits ($IR_{6:17}$), permitting the entire *CSR* register to be tested. Note that the TST instruction does not cause status to be transmitted—it simply tests whatever is already in the *CSR* register. The use of an input status instruction followed by a sequence of TST instructions permits the programmer to check a number of status bits one at a time without having to call for repeated transmissions of status from the peripheral.

To clarify the use of the status check in programmed data transfer, let us consider a sequence of instructions to print out a character. The complete mnemonic for the input status instruction will be ISn xx, where xx represents the octal equivalent of the test word. Let us assume that the printer is device number 3 and that the ready indicator for the printer will be connected to $CSBUS_{11}$. Then the word to test for ready will be 000001 so that the instruction

IS3 01

will input printer status and skip if ready. Then the following sequence of instructions will print out a character initially loaded at a location CHAR in memory.

10. LAC CHAR
11. IS3 01
12. JMP 11
13. OD3

The first instruction moves the character to be printed to AC. The second instruction inputs the printer status and checks the ready flag. If the printer is not ready, the next instruction jumps back to the status check, which is thus repeated until the printer is ready, when the program skips to the output data instruction. This basic system of I/O transfer ties the program to the speed of the peripheral, but in many simple programs there is nothing that could be done in parallel with the I/O operations so that this is no disadvantage.

A partial flow chart of the I/O sequence, dealing primarily with the IOT instructions, is shown in Fig. 10.8. The branches at steps 5 and 25, part of earlier sequences, are shown to relate the I/O sequence to those already developed. The I/O sequence starts at step 50, with branches to the INT sequence, and the TST sequence, which will be left as exercises for the reader.

50. $\rightarrow (IR_4)/(\text{INT seq.})$
51. $\rightarrow (IR_5, \overline{IR}_5)/(70, \text{TST seq.})$

The IOT sequence starts at step 70 with the transfer of the command code to CSR. Step 71 places CSR on the $CSBUS$, sets $csrdy$ to 1, and waits for the return of an $accept$ signal. The $csrdy$ signal is essentially an "Attention!" signal that notifies all peripherals that a new command has been placed on the $CSBUS$ and that they should check for their device number.

70. $CSR \leftarrow IR_{6:17}$
71. $CSBUS = CSR;\ csrdy = 1$
    $\rightarrow (\overline{accept})/(71)$

The signaled device should transfer whatever part of the command it requires into its own registers for later interpretation and acknowledge receipt of the command by raising the $accept$ line. Note that even though

383

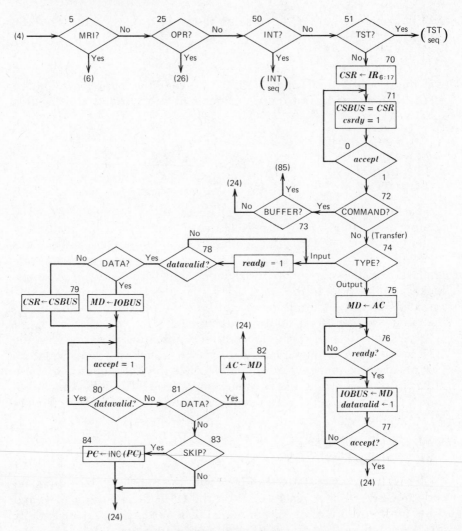

Figure 10.8. Flow chart of I/O sequence.

all devices should be constantly monitoring *csrdy*, no assumption is made about how long it will take a device to respond. The *CSR* contents are held on the *CSBUS* and *csrdy* is held at 1 until the signaled device acknowledges the command.

Step 72 checks to determine if a transfer of information is required. If not, step 73 determines if a buffer is to be activated. The activate buffer sequence will be considered in the next section. For an ordinary device command, the IOT cycle is complete and control returns to step

384

24, to prepare for fetching another instruction. If a transfer is required, step 74 determines whether it is an input or output transfer.

72. NO DELAY
$\rightarrow (\overline{IR}_9)/(74)$
73. NO DELAY
$\rightarrow (IR_{10}, \overline{IR}_{10})/(24, 85)$
74. NO DELAY
$\rightarrow (IR_{11})/(78)$

For output, step 75 moves the word to be transmitted from *AC* to *MD*, and step 76 waits for the receiving device to signal that it is ready. Note that the return of the *accept* signal at step 71 indicated only that the command was received; it did not necessarily mean that the device was ready to accept a word. On receipt of the *ready* signal, step 77 gates *MD* onto the *IOBUS*, raises *datavalid* to signal that the data is on the bus, and waits for the *accept* signal. When *accept* = 1, the bus is cleared, *datavalid* is set to 0, and control returns to the convergence point in preparation for the next instruction.

75. $MD \leftarrow AC$
76. Null
$\rightarrow (\overline{ready})/(76)$
77. $IOBUS = MD; \; datavalid = 1$
$\rightarrow (accept, \overline{accept})/(24, 77)$

For input, step 78 raises the *ready* signal and waits for the return of the *datavalid* signal, indicating that the requested word is on the bus. Step 79 checks bit IR_{10} to determine if the input word is a status word (on *CSBUS*) or a data word (on *IOBUS*), and transfers the word into *CSR* or *MD* accordingly. For ease of interpretation this is shown as a branch to separate transfers in Fig. 10.8 but is actually realized in a single step with two conditional transfers. Step 80 raises the *accept* signal, which is held at 1 until the *datavalid* signal goes down, to ensure that the bus has been cleared before proceeding. Step 81 again checks IR_{10} to determine the type of word transmitted. For a data word, step 82 moves the word to *AC* and returns to the convergence point. For a status word, step 83 compares the last 6 bits of the status word with the last 6 bits of the instruction to see if the next instruction should be skipped. Finally, step 84 provides the extra increment of *PC* to implement the skip.

78. $ready = 1$
$\rightarrow (\overline{datavalid})/(78)$
79. $CSR * IR_{10} \leftarrow CSBUS; \; MD * \overline{IR}_{10} \leftarrow IOBUS$

80. $accept = 1$
$\rightarrow (datavalid)/(80)$
81. NO DELAY
$\rightarrow (IR_{10})/(83)$
82. $AC \leftarrow MD$
$\rightarrow (24)$
83. NO DELAY
$\rightarrow (\sqrt{/(IR_{12:17} \wedge CSR_{6:11})})/(24)$
84. $PC \leftarrow INC(PC)$
$\rightarrow (24)$

The reader may note that this sequence is considerably more complex than the sequences developed in Chapter 9. The reason, of course, is that this is a general-purpose system, designed to accommodate virtually any type of peripheral device. One consequence is the use of completely interactive handshake signaling to ensure reliable operations with devices of widely varying speeds. Simpler signaling systems might be satisfactory with specific devices, but the CPU designer must try to allow for all possibilities. It should also be noted that the design of the CPU I/O system is only a part of the problem. It is usually also necessary to design interface units to match the signal requirements of the CPU and various peripheral devices. This part of the I/O design problem is the subject of the next chapter.

10.5 BUFFER SEQUENCE FOR SIC

As discussed earlier, programmed transfer is very inefficient for devices such as disks and magnetic tapes, which normally transmit data in blocks of many words, since the complete execution of a separate instruction is required for every word transferred. Also, programmed transfers are initiated by the CPU so that the rate of transfer is basically limited by the program. But devices such as disks and tape must transmit data at a certain fixed rate, and reliable transfer of data requires that the peripheral device be able to initiate each transfer. Buffering provides this capability in the form of a special interrupt procedure by means of which a peripheral can signal the CPU to carry out a transfer operation, within some maximum length of time that is independent of the program currently being executed.

Since buffered devices initiate transfers at rates determined by their own characteristics, it is clear that each buffered device must be assigned a certain amount of independent signaling hardware. That col-

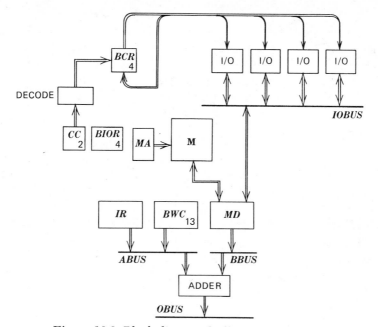

Figure 10.9. Block diagram, buffer section of SIC.

lection of hardware which is assigned to a single device and permits it to carry out buffer operations independently of any other peripheral device will be referred to as a *buffer channel*. For SIC we shall provide four buffer channels so that four peripheral devices can be buffered. These four devices are a part of the maximum of eight devices that can be accommodated by the main I/O system. These devices will utilize programmed I/O procedures for such operations as activation and status report. The buffer channel is simply that amount of extra hardware which permits these devices to transmit individual data words at rates that are essentially independent of the activities of other devices.

A partial block diagram of SIC, including only those portions used in buffer operations, is shown in Fig. 10.9. Buffer operations take place between instructions and must be performed in such a manner that the main program is not affected. Therefore, all registers whose status must be preserved from one instruction to the next have been deleted from Fig. 10.9 to emphasize that they are not available for buffer operations.

Since only three of the regular registers, *MD*, *MA*, and *IR* are available, certain special registers have to be added for buffer processing. The *buffer word counter*, *BWC*, is a 13-bit register used in processing the buffer addresses. There are two 4-bit registers, each having 1 bit for each of the four buffer channels. The positions of the *buffer* I/O register, **BIOR**, will indicate if the corresponding channel is engaged on an input or output buffer: 1 for input, 0 for output. The positions of the *buffer channel ready register*, **BCR**, will be set by signals from the corresponding channel, requesting the attention of the central processor. The *channel counter*, **CC**, is a 2-bit counting register that will contain the number of the buffer channel currently being processed.

The *buffer channel ready* lines, **BCRDY**[4], are the special interrupt lines by means of which a device requests a buffer operation. These lines set the corresponding positions of the buffer channel ready register, **BCR**[4], in exactly the same manner that **INTR** is controlled by **INTLINE**. The *buffer ready* lines, **BUFRDY**[4] are used by the CPU to acknowledge receipt of a buffer request. The *buffer end* line, *bufend*, is used by the CPU to terminate buffer operations. The buffer hardware is summarized in the following additions to the declarations.

MEMORY: **BCR**[4], **BIOR**[4], **CC**[2], **BWC**[13]
INPUTS: **BCRDY**[4]
OUTPUTS: **BUFRDY**[4], *bufend*

Although the individual transfers of data words are initiated by **BCRDY** requests from the buffered devices, a complete buffer operation, i.e., the transfer of a block of data, must be initiated by the CPU with an activate buffer instruction, OBn or IBn. An activate buffer instruction tells the peripheral to take whatever steps may be necessary to initiate the transfer of a block of words and to signal on its **BCRDY** line whenever it is ready to transfer a word. The execution of the activate buffer instruction does not involve the transfer of any data words and requires only one additional step in the CPU sequence, to set the appropriate position of **BIOR** to indicate whether an input or output buffer has been activated. If this information were not saved in **BIOR**, the CPU would have to request that information from the peripheral each time a buffer request was received. We shall assume that only devices 0, 1, 2, or 3 may be buffered so that only two bits of the device code are needed to identify the buffer channel. Step 85 sets the appropriate position of **BIOR** and returns to the convergence point for the next instruction. Thus the CPU continues with its program and no data are transferred until a **BCRDY** request is received.

85.   **BIOR** * DCD($IR_{7:8}$) ← IR_{11}
   → (24)

Whenever an active channel is ready to transfer a word, it raises its **BCRDY** line, which in turn sets the corresponding position of **BCR**.

When the sequence returns to start, the fetch of a new instruction, BCR, must be checked to see if any buffer requests have been made. For this purpose, a new step is inserted to branch to the buffer sequence if any positions of BCR have been set.

2. $\to (\vee / BCR)/(90)$
2-1. $\to (intf)/(60)$
2-2. $MA \leftarrow PC$
3.   As before

A flow chart of the buffer sequence is shown in Fig. 10.10. The first requirement is to determine which channel (or channels) made the buffer request. For this purpose we use a scanner circuit, as shown in Fig. 10.11. The output of CC is applied to a decoder circuit, which produces a signal on one of four lines that corresponds to the binary value of the contents of CC. The outputs of the decoder are ANDed with the output of BCR, and the outputs of the AND gates are OR'ed. Thus, only if the position of BCR corresponding to the contents of CC is set will there be a 1-output from the circuit. If there is not, CC is incremented, "scanning" BCR until a set position is found. This stops the scan so that CC now contains the number of the set position of BCR. It is possible that more than one position of BCR may be set, in which case the scanner circuit will stop at the first one encountered.

90. $\to (\vee / (\mathrm{DCD}(CC) \wedge BCR))/(92)$
91. $CC \leftarrow \mathrm{INC}(CC)$
      $\to (90)$

Step 90 checks to see if the scanner output is 1; if it is not, CC is incremented (step 91). A scanner output of 1, indicating that CC contains the number of a channel making a buffer request, causes a branch to step 92. For each buffer channel the programmer must have previously stored two items of information, the final address of the buffer area and minus the number of words in the buffer area. For this purpose we permanently reserve two locations in memory for each channel: locations 00040 and 00041 for channel 0, locations 00042 and 00043 for channel 1, etc. The first location of each pair will hold the negative word count, the second the final address.

To generate these addresses, we use a coding circuit, BADDR, of the same type used for the interrupt circuits. The input to BADDR is CC, which contains the number of the channel being processed. This address

389

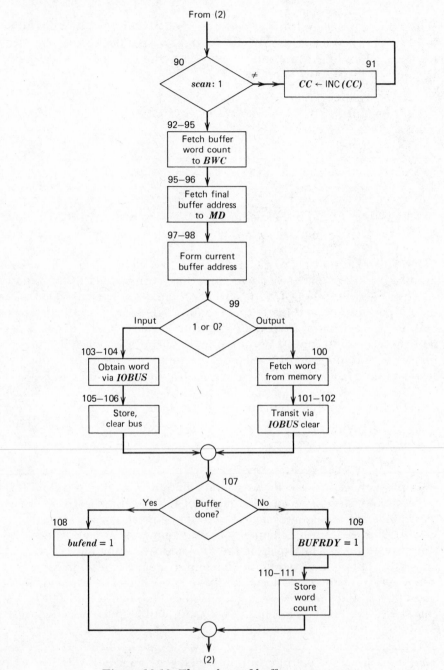

Figure 10.10. Flow chart of buffer sequence.

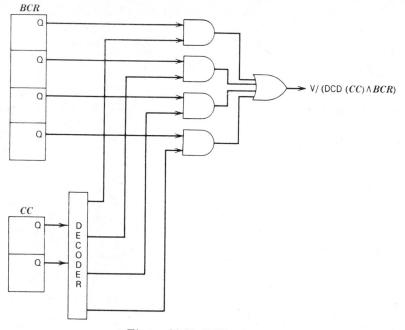

Figure 10.11. *BCR* scanner.

is sent via *IR* to *MA*; and the position of *BCR* corresponding to *CC* is cleared, since the request is now being serviced (steps 92 to 93). At step 94, the negative word count is fetched and the address in *IR* is incremented in preparation for fetching the final address. Steps 95 to 96 send the negative word count to *BWC* and fetch the final address to *MD*. Step 97 forms the current buffer address. Step 98 increments the negative word count in preparation for the next buffer cycle and sets the appropriate *BUFRDY* line to 1 to notify the peripheral that the CPU is now ready to make the data transfer.

92. $IR_{5:17} \leftarrow$ BADDR(*CC*); *BCR* $\circledast$ DCD(*CC*) $\leftarrow 0$
93. $MA \leftarrow IR_{5:17}$
94. $MD \leftarrow$ BUSFN(**M**; DCD(*MA*)); $IR_{5:17} \leftarrow$ INC($IR_{5:17}$)
95. $MA \leftarrow IR_{5:17}$; *BWC* $\leftarrow$ *MD*
96. $MD \leftarrow$ BUSFN(**M**; DCD(*MA*))
97. $MA \leftarrow$ ADD(*MD*; *BWC*)
98. *BWC* $\leftarrow$ INC(*BWC*); *BUFRDY* = DCD(*CC*)

The *BUFRDY* lines are used to acknowledge buffer requests and to indicate that the CPU is ready to proceed. Separate lines for each channel are needed because several buffer channels may have made buffer requests, in which case each of them is waiting for acknowledgment. The buffer sequence responds to whichever buffer request it detects first in the scan of **BCR** at steps 90 to 91, and the selection of the appropriate **BUFRDY** line at step 98 assures that only the selected peripheral will respond. The transfer itself, however, can be controlled by the same common signaling lines used for programmed transfers, since only the peripheral that received a **BUFRDY** signal will proceed with a transfer.

Step 99 checks **BIOR** to determine whether an input or output transfer is required. For output, step 100 fetches the desired word from memory and steps 101 to 102 complete the transfer in the same manner as for programmed transfer. For input, step 103 raises the *ready* signal and waits for *datavalid*, step 104 transfers the word to **MD**, step 105 stores the word, and step 106 completes the transfer handshake.

99.   NO DELAY

$\quad \rightarrow (\bigvee/(\text{DCD}(CC) \wedge BIOR))/(103)$

100. $MD \leftarrow \text{BUSFN}(M; \text{DCD}(MA))$

101. $\rightarrow (\overline{ready})/(101)$

102. $IOBUS = MD; datavalid = 1$

$\quad \rightarrow (accept, \overline{accept})/(107, 102)$

103. $ready = 1$

$\quad \rightarrow (\overline{datavalid})/(103)$

104. $MD \leftarrow IOBUS$

105. $M * \text{DCD}(MA) \leftarrow MD$

106. $accept = 1$

$\quad \rightarrow (datavalid)/(106)$

On completion of the input or output transfer, step 107 checks to see if the buffer is completed. Recall that **BWC** contains the negative of the number of words remaining to be stored. If the increment of **BWC** at step 98 brought this count to zero, the buffer is complete. In that event, the CPU sends *bufend* to signal the peripheral to take whatever deactivation steps may be required (step 108). If the buffer is not complete, a **BUFRDY** signal is sent (step 109), in this case signaling that the peripheral should proceed with the buffer operation. The need for this last signal may not be evident, since the presence of this signal is logically equivalent to the absence of a *bufend* signal. However, buffered devices are normally fast asynchronous devices with respect to the CPU so that the time that *bufend* should arrive cannot be accurately predicted by the peripheral. To provide fast, reliable operations, it is better to have a point in the control sequence of the peripheral at which it must receive a definite signal, either to proceed or to terminate. *This is a general principle of systems communications, that one should not rely on the absence of a signal to cause some event to take place.* If the buffer operation is to continue, steps 110 to 111 complete the sequence by storing the updated word count in the reserved location in memory.

107. NO DELAY
   $\rightarrow (\vee/\textbf{\textit{BWC}})/(109)$
108. *bufend* = 1
   $\rightarrow (2)$
109. *BUFRDY* = DCD(*CC*)
110. $MA \leftarrow \text{BADDR}(CC);\ MD \leftarrow BWC$
111. $M * \text{DCD}(MA) \leftarrow MD$
   $\rightarrow (2)$

Following completion of the buffer sequence, control returns to step 2 to check for further buffer requests. Note that step 2 gives buffer requests priority over interrupts or the fetching of new instructions. If buffer requests arrive fast enough, step 2 could result in the CPU's being completely monopolized by buffer operations. This could be prevented by having the buffer sequence return control to step 2-1, but this assignment of top priority to buffer operations is common practice. Buffered devices are generally fast sequential devices that must be serviced on request to prevent loss of data.

Also, if a peripheral is fast enough to return a new buffer request between the time it receives the signal to continue (step 109) and the time the CPU returns to step 2 following the execution of steps 110 and 111, that peripheral could monopolize the CPU. This could be prevented by reversing the order of steps 90 and 91, to increment *CC* before checking the scanner so that peripherals would be serviced in numerical order. But if only one peripheral were active, this method would waste time with four unnecessary increments of *CC* for every buffer cycle. If such monopolization by an individual channel is undesirable, the designer of the peripheral controller should limit the rate at which buffer requests can be made.

Finally, the reader should note that we have not attempted to optimize the buffer sequence with regard to speed, in the interest of maintaining the maximum possible clarity of exposition. There are many places where operations could be overlapped, particularly with memory cycles, to speed up the sequences.

10.6 DIRECT MEMORY ACCESS FOR SIC

Buffered transfer is considerably faster than programmed transfer but is limited in speed by the need to access memory to obtain addresses and the need to wait for the completion of an instruction cycle to start a buffer cycle. With *direct memory access*(DMA), separate registers are provided to keep track of the addresses, and means are provided to access memory independently of any regular CPU registers or data paths. Alternative names for DMA are *data break* and *cycle stealing*. Although usage is not entirely consistent, these two names generally imply somewhat different approaches. In a data break, the CPU simply suspends operations while the DMA transfer takes place, and then resumes its instructions cycle at the point where it stopped. This type of DMA is usually found in smaller computers, especially microprocessors.

In cycle-stealing DMA, the peripheral can execute a memory access at any time the CPU is not using memory, and the CPU continues with its normal operations. The name conveys the idea that the peripheral "steals" a memory cycle from the CPU. With this type of DMA, the CPU is not slowed down by the DMA operations unless it reaches a point where it needs memory but a DMA operation is still in progress. To provide for cycle stealing the memory usually functions as a separate subsystem to which the CPU and the DMA channels send requests for service. These requests may be granted in the order they are received, or the designer may assign some system of priority.

To illustrate these ideas, let us now develop a DMA system for SIC, assuming the memory configuration of Fig. 7.7 and the accompanying discussion. A partial block diagram of SIC, showing only that hardware involved in DMA operations, is given in Fig. 10.12. The DMA operations, like buffer operations, involve block transfers of data, and the area in memory to or from which these data are to be transferred must be specified. For this purpose two special 13-bit registers are provided, the *direct memory address* register, **DMADR**, and the *direct memory last word* register, **DMLWR**. There will be three flag flip-flops, *dmio*, *dmareq*, and *cpureq*, the purposes of which will be discussed later.

Since DMA operations take place in parallel with normal CPU operations, at any time the CPU is not accessing memory, the DMA channel must have completely independent control and data lines. Data words will be transmitted over **DMBUS**[18]. The signaling lines are DMA request, *dmar*, DMA accept, *dmacpt*, DMA valid, *dmaval*, DMA continue, *dmacon*, and DMA end, *dmaend*. The purpose of these lines will be discussed as the control sequence is developed. This DMA hardware requires the following additions to the CPU declarations. The purpose of the LABEL statement will also be discussed later.

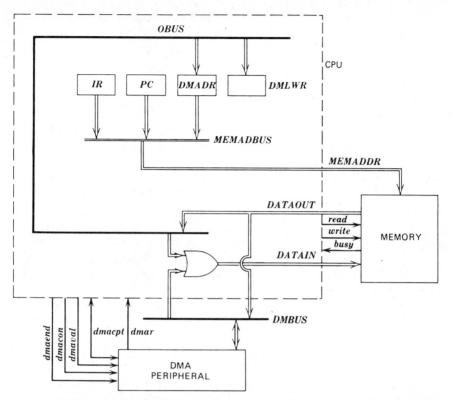

Figure 10.12. Hardware and connections for DMA in SIC.

MEMORY: *DMADR*[13]; *DMLWR*[13]; *dmio*; *dmareq*; *cpureq*
INPUTS: *dmar*
OUTPUTS: *dmaval*; *dmacon*; *dmaend*
COMBUSES: *DMBUS*[18]; *dmacpt*
LABEL: *memgnt* = CSL121

Just as is the case with buffer operations, some preliminary steps will be required to start a DMA operation: *DMLWR* must be loaded with the address of the last word in the memory area to be transferred; *DMADR* must be loaded with the address of the location immediately preceding the first location in the DMA memory area. Each DMA cycle will start by incrementing *DMADR* to provide the address of the word to be transferred. The current address is used instead of the negative word count (which was used for buffers) to eliminate the need for a special adder. For buffer operations the main CPU adder could be used, but the DMA channel cannot share any CPU hardware.

In addition to loading the addresses, the DMA activation steps must set *dmio* (0 = output, 1 = input) to indicate the direction of transfer, and the peripheral must be notified to take whatever actions may be required to prepare for DMA operations. No provision for DMA activation was made in the I/O instruction set discussed in Section 10.4. However, we note that two combinations of bits $IR_{9:11}$ were not used, and that special combinations of bits $IR_{12:17}$ could be set aside for DMA instructions. We shall leave the specification of a set of DMA activation commands as an exercise for the reader. (See Problem 10.10). In writing the DMA sequence, we shall assume that such instructions exist and that *DMADR*, *DMLWR*, and *dmio* have been properly loaded prior to the start of actual transfer operations.

A flow chart of the DMA sequence is shown in Fig. 10.13. This sequence will run in parallel with other parts of the CPU sequence. Steps 120 to 122 comprise a priority circuit that allocates memory to the CPU or to the DMA channel. Steps 123 to 131 carry out DMA transfers. Whenever the CPU or the DMA peripheral require access to memory, they will set the appropriate request flip-flop, *cpureq* or *dmareq*. The flag *cpureq* will be set by the main CPU sequence when a memory operation is required. The flag *dmareq* will constantly monitor the DMA request line, *dmar*, as indicated by the statement

$$dmareq * dmar \leftarrow 1$$

appearing after END SEQUENCE.

The first steps of the CPU sequence, as modified to accommodate DMA, and the first steps of the DMA sequence are shown below.

1.	$\rightarrow \overline{SL(SYN(start))}/(1)$
1-1.	NO DELAY
	$\rightarrow (2, 120)$
2.	NO DELAY
	$cpureq \leftarrow 1$
2-1.	$\rightarrow (\overline{memgnt})/(2\text{-}1)$
2-2.	$MEMADBUS = PC;\ read = 1$
	$\rightarrow \overline{SYN(busy)}/(2\text{-}2)$
3.	$\rightarrow (SYN(busy))/(3)$
4.	NO DELAY
	$OBUS = 0, DATAOUT;$
	$IR \leftarrow OBUS_{1:18};\ cpureq \leftarrow 0$

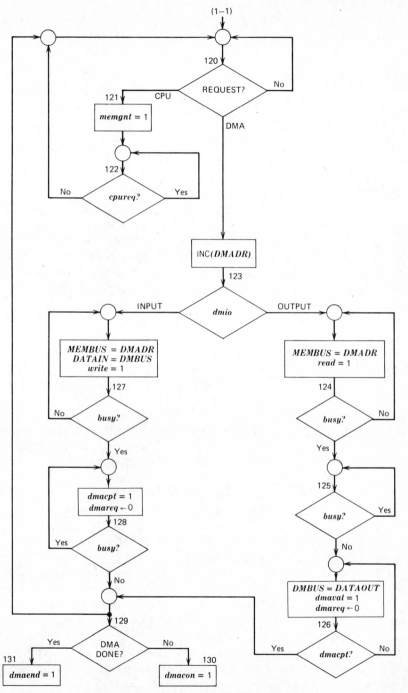

Figure 10.13. Flow chart of DMA sequence.

397

120. →$((dmareq \wedge \overline{busy})$,
$(\overline{dmareq} \wedge cpureq \wedge \overline{busy})$,
$((\overline{dmareq} \wedge \overline{cpureq}) \vee busy))/$ (123, 121, 120)

121. NO DELAY
$memgnt = 1$

122. → $(cpureq, \overline{cpureq})/$(122, 120)

123. (Start of DMA transfer)

Step 1 is the reset state, waiting for a *start* signal. Step 1-1 (which could be written as a part of step 1) provides the parallel branch to the main sequence and the DMA sequence. Step 2 is the convergence point after the completion of all instruction sequences and provides a NO DELAY set of *cpureq*, requesting memory for the fetch cycle. Control then waits at step 2-1 for the memory grant signal, *memgnt*, indicating that memory is available. In the interests of clarity, the branches to the buffer and interrupt sequences have not been shown.

In the DMA sequence, control holds at step 120 as long as the memory is busy or there are no memory requests. If the memory is not busy and a DMA request is received, control branches to step 123 to execute the transfer. If a CPU request is received and the memory is not busy and no DMA request is present, control branches to step 121 and returns the memory grant signal, which allows the CPU main sequence to proceed with the memory cycle. While this is in progress, the DMA sequence waits at step 122 until the CPU signals the end of the memory operation by clearing *cpureq*, at which time control returns to step 120 to await further memory requests. Note that step 120 gives priority to DMA requests if CPU and DMA requests arrive at the same time. This is done on the assumption that a DMA peripheral is a fast device that must be serviced quickly to prevent loss of data. By contrast, while the CPU is slowed by having to wait for memory, it does not lose data. Also note that the check of *busy* at step 120 means that the sequence need not wait for completion of the memory cycle on write operations.

In the main sequence, the return of the *memgnt* signal advances control to step 2-2, which initiates the memory operation. Steps 3 and 4 complete the operation in the same manner as discussed in Chapter 7. Step 4 also clears *cpureq* to notify the DMA sequence that memory is available. All other memory access steps in the main CPU sequence would have to be similarly modified to provide for setting *cpureq*, for waiting for the return of *memgnt*, and for clearing *cpureq* at the completion of the memory operation. (See Prob. 10.11)

To provide further clarification of the manner in which the two sequences interact, Fig. 10.14 shows the control sequence hardware for the steps discussed above. In this figure we see the reason for the LABEL statement given earlier. This is an example of a situation that can arise in parallel sequences, in which a control level in one sequence controls branching in the other sequence. If the two sequences were in separate modules, the control signal would be declared as a communication line. When the two sequences are in the same module, the LABEL statement identifies the control variable as being equal to a control signal level.

The DMA transfer sequence starts at step 123, which increments *DMADR* to obtain the address of the next word to be transferred, and checks *dmio* to see if the transfer is input or output. For output, steps 124 and 125 execute a memory read in the manner described in Section 7.3. When *busy* goes down, indicating that the word is available, step 126 clears *dmareq* so that this request will not be responded to again, gates the memory output onto *DMBUS*, raises *dmaval* to indicate that the data word is on the bus, and waits for the peripheral to acknowledge with *dmacpt*. When *dmacpt* is received, control branches in parallel to 120 to check for additional memory requests and to 129 to check for completion of the DMA operation.

123. NO DELAY
      $DMADR \leftarrow INC(DMADR)$
      $\rightarrow (dmio)/(127)$
124. $MEMADBUS = DMADR; read = 1$
      $\rightarrow (SYN(\overline{busy}))/(124)$
125. $\rightarrow (SYN(\overline{busy}))/(125)$
126. $DMBUS = DATAOUT; dmaval = 1; dmareq \leftarrow 0$
      $\rightarrow (\overline{dmacpt}, dmacpt, dmacpt)/(126, 120, 129)$

For input, step 127 initiates a memory write operation. Note that there is no wait for the peripheral to send a signal indicating that the data is on the bus. Since the *DMBUS* is not shared with other devices, the peripheral can put the word to be transferred on the bus at the same time it makes the DMA request. When *busy* goes up, indicating that the memory has accepted the word, step 128 raises *dmacpt* to notify the peripheral to clear the bus, clears *dmareq*, and branches in parallel to 120 and 129.

127. $MEMADBUS = DMADR; DATAIN = DMBUS$
      $write = 1$
      $\rightarrow (SYN(\overline{busy}))/(127)$

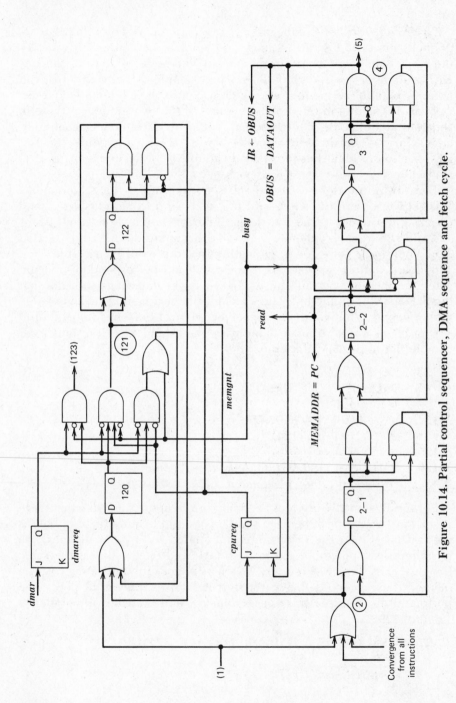

Figure 10.14. Partial control sequencer, DMA sequence and fetch cycle.

128. $dmacpt = 1; dmareq \leftarrow 0$
    $\rightarrow (120, 129)$
129. NO DELAY
    $\rightarrow ((\sqrt{/}\overline{DMADR} \oplus DMLWR), (\overline{\sqrt{/}\overline{DMADR} \oplus DMLWR}))/(130,$
    131)
130. $dmacon = 1;$ DEAD END
131. $dmaend = 1;$ DEAD END

As noted earlier, the check of *busy* at step 120 means that the sequence needs to wait only for *busy* to go up, indicating that the data to be written have been accepted. The sequence can then proceed to other steps, relying on a check of *busy* at 120 to prevent further memory operations until the memory cycle is complete. Step 129 compares the address of the word just transferred to the last-word address. If they are equal, step 131 sends the DMA end signal; if not, step 130 sends the DMA continue signal. As was the case with the buffer sequence, the peripheral receives a definite signal, to continue or to terminate.

The reader will note that the actual transfer processes are very similar for buffer transfers and for DMA transfers. From the standpoint of the peripheral device, the only difference between buffer transfer and DMA transfer is that the CPU will usually respond to a DMA request faster than to a buffer request. For the DMA transfer we have taken advantage of the fact that there is no sharing of control or data lines to simplify the handshake signaling. This simplification will make the transfer process slightly faster, but there is no logical reason why the DMA transfer sequence (steps 123 to 128) could not be made identical to the buffer transfer sequence, (steps 99 to 106) except for the names of the communications lines. If this were done, it would offer the advantage that a given peripheral could be connected either to a buffer channel or to a DMA channel with no change in the interface requirements.

In the DMA system developed above, the DMA hardware is a part of the CPU. The control hardware for the peripheral, as noted above, would be essentially the same as for a buffer channel. This approach does have advantages in simplifying synchronization between DMA operations and main CPU operations, and has no disadvantages if the DMA channel is intended to be a fixed part of the CPU design. However, manufacturers generally prefer to make expensive features like DMA optional, and doing so is simpler if DMA channels are separate modules that can be added to a system without making extensive modifications to the CPU.

As noted above, memory in a DMA system may be viewed as a separate system that provides service on request to the CPU or peripherals.

The modularity desired for easy system expansion can be achieved by extending this point of view to its logical conclusion and making the CPU, the memory, and the DMA channels separate modules. The memory will accept requests for service and addresses from the CPU or from DMA peripherals, and will execute data transfers with any of these modules. The priority hardware, performing a function similar to steps 120 to 122 of the above sequence, will be a part of the memory module. The registers and control hardware necessary to keep track of addresses and interact with memory to carry out the DMA transfers (steps 123 to 128 above) will be a part of the DMA module. When DMA operations are in progress, the CPU and the DMA channel will function completely independently, with no communications of any kind. Connections must be provided between the CPU and the peripheral for activation and deactivation of DMA operations, but the modules will otherwise be independent.

Whether DMA is a part of the CPU or provided in separate modules, the basic processes are the same. The DMA sequence developed above operates in parallel with the main sequence so that its functioning would be the same if it were in a separate module. The DMA systems in different computers vary greatly in detail, but the basic concepts of shared memory and independent communications lines are general and the system developed above is illustrative of a practical realization of these concepts.

PROBLEMS

10.1 (a) Devise a control sequence to implement the INT command in SIC, assuming hard-wired control. Start the sequence with step 140.

(b) Construct a block diagram of a control sequencer to implement the above INT sequence.

10.2 Repeat problem 10.1 for the TST command, starting the sequence with step 160.

10.3 The vectored interrupt system for SIC discussed in Section 10.2 utilizes fixed priority from the point of view of the programmer. Devise a system whereby the priority assigned to the positions of *INTR* can be controlled by the programmer. Consider both the hardware requirements and any additional instructions that might be required. Having specified the hardware and the instructions required, write the control sequence required to implement the instructions.

10.4 The programmed data transfer sequence for SIC discussed in Section 10.4 moves data through *AC*, thus creating problems with regard to the preservation of the interrupted program. Devise a system whereby programmed data transfer will not involve any general-purpose register except *MD*. Note that this may require modifications to the MRI instruction set. If so, determine the nature of any such modifications.

10.5 Assume the speed of the buffer sequence for SIC is to be increased by providing word-count registers, *BWC1* to *BWC4*, for each channel. This will eliminate two memory references per buffer cycle. Specify modifications to the instruction set to provide for loading these registers. Revise the control sequence as required to accommodate this change.

10.6 Continue Problem 10.5, assuming that the buffer speed is to be further improved by providing last word address registers, *LWA1* to *LWA4*, for each channel.

10.7 The Input Status command discussed in Section 10.4 has a disadvantage in that it requires the peripheral device to take specific action to place the status information on the *CSBUS*. If the peripheral is busy with some other operation, the CPU may be delayed waiting for the peripheral to respond to the status request. An alternative approach which eliminates such delays is to have all status information continuously available to the CPU without requiring any action by the peripheral. With such a system the status check command might be denoted Take and Test Status (TTS). Determine a possible hardware configuration to implement such a scheme, and modify the control sequence as required to implement the TTS command.

10.8 Where peripheral devices are relatively simple, such that the only status signals will be "Ready to Read" or "Ready to Write," a variant of the system of Problem 10.7 makes it possible to combine status checks and data transfers into a single command. Each device is assigned one or two positions in the processor Status Register, which it will set when it is ready for a transfer. Then a typical IOT instruction will have the meaning, "Skip and read device 3 if device 3 read flag is up." Modify SIC as required to implement such a system. Assume six peripherals, each assigned two bit positions in the 12-bit Status Register. For device #1, let SR_0 be the read flag and SR_1 the write flag; for device 2, let SR_2 be read flag and SR_3 the write flag; etc. There will be two IOT commands, SRDn—Skip and Read Device-n if device-n read flag is up, and SWTn—Skip and Write Device-n if device-n write flag is up. Determine hardware requirements, suggest appropriate instruction formats, and develop the control sequence to implement these new instructions.

10.9 The interrupt system developed for SIC in Section 10.2 saves only the contents of the program counter. If it is necessary to save the contents of other registers, this must be done by software in the interrupt routine. An alternative, which simplifies interrupt programming is to have the interrupt hardware automatically preserve all necessary registers. Modify the SIC interrupt system to provide for automatically preserving the contents of *AC, IA*, and *IB*. For this purpose set aside five locations in memory for each interrupt source, the first four for storing *PC, AC, IA*, and *IB*, in that order, the last for the address of the interrupt routine. Let these locations be 00010–00014 for *INTR$_0$*, 00020–00024 for *INTR$_1$*, etc., and assume the network ADDR has been modified to generate the addresses, 00010, 00020, etc. This approach will also require the addition of a special instruction, RFI—Return From Interrupt, to restore the registers at the completion of the interrupt routine. Indicate any hardware modifications that may be required, suggest a format for the RFI instruction, and modify the control sequence to implement this interrupt system.

10.10 Devise a set of instructions for controlling the DMA system of Section 10.6. Specify appropriate instruction formats and modify the SIC control sequence as required to implement these instructions.

10.11 In Section 10.6, the main SIC control sequence is modified to accommodate DMA only for the memory access which fetches the instructions. Modify the remainder of the SIC control sequence as required to accommodate this DMA system.

10.12 Modify the DMA sequence of Section 10.6 to utilize the same interactive signaling used in the buffer sequence, so that a given peripheral could communicate either through a buffer channel or the DMA channel, without modification of the interface circuitry.

10.13 DMA is normally an optional feature in most computer systems. It is, therefore, desirable to implement it in a modular form so that it can be added to existing systems with minimum difficulty. The DMA system of Section 10.6 does not have this characteristic, as it requires considerable modification of the CPU. A preferable approach from the standpoint of ease of modification would be to use a *Priority Memory Controller*. For non-DMA system, this controller would be omitted, and the CPU would interact with memory directly in the manner shown in Fig. 7.7. To add DMA, the controller would interconnect the CPU, the memory, and the DMA peripheral in the manner shown in Fig. P10.13. The controller would accept memory requests from the CPU or DMA peripheral, giving priority to DMA in the event of simultaneous requests. The requesting device would provide the address, and the controller would establish address and data paths between the requesting device and memory. The DMA peripheral would be responsible for keeping track of its own addresses, i.e., *DMADR* and *DMLWR* would be a part of the DMA device rather than being in the CPU. The CPU and the DMA peripheral would also be connected through the normal I/O channels to permit the CPU to issue instructions and addresses to the DMA device. Design a priority memory controller to function in the above manner. If possible this should be done in such a way as to require no modifications to the "non-DMA" version of SIC. Indicate the hardware design and write the complete AHPL description of the controller.

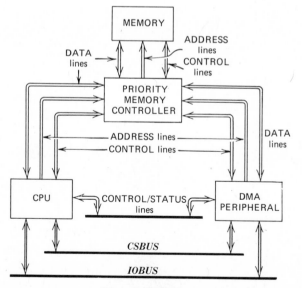

Figure. P10.13.

REFERENCES

1. Sloan, M. E., *Computer Hardware and Organization*, Science Research Associates, Chicago, 1976.
2. Korn, G. A., *Minicomputers for Engineers and Scientists*, McGraw-Hill, New York, 1973.
3. Blaauw, G. A., *Digital System Implementation*, Prentice-Hall, Englewood Cliffs, N.J., 1976.
4. Mano, M. M., *Computer System Architecture*, Prentice-Hall, Englewood Cliffs, N.J., 1976.
5. Kline, R. M., *Digital Computer Design*, Prentice-Hall, Englewood Cliffs, N.J., 1977.
6. Hellerman, H., *Digital Computer System Principles*, 2nd Edition, McGraw-Hill, New York, 1973.
7. Peatman, J. B., *The Design of Digital Systems*, McGraw-Hill, New York, 1972.
8. Davies, D. W. and D. L. A. Barber, *Communications Networks for Computers*, Wiley, New York, 1973.
9. Soucek, B., *Minicomputers in Data Processing and Simulation*, Wiley, New York, 1972.

11

PERIPHERALS AND INTERFACING

11.1 INTRODUCTION

Thus far we have looked at computer input/output only from the point of view of the CPU. Now we shall turn our attention to the problem of designing peripheral devices so that they can communicate with SIC. Often a piece of input/output equipment is designed in such a way that, by the inclusion of a small amount of additional hardware, it can be made to function with almost any computer system. The design of this additional hardware is commonly termed *interfacing*. The added hardware is itself called an *interface*. Within the framework of AHPL an interface may be a separate module or it may be part of the peripheral device module. The former will probably be most common.

In order to approach a reasonable subset of the problems encountered in designing an interface, we shall design a set of interfaces connecting SIC to a few typical peripherals. This exercise will serve a second purpose, that of familiarizing the readers with typical characteristics of each of these peripherals. Many aspects of a SIC interface will be functions of SIC itself and will be common to the various peripheral equipments. This point will be stressed in the next section as we evolve a generalized flow chart that can be followed in the design of any SIC interface. In the succeeding sections we shall consider interfaces for a paper tape reader, a printer, and a magnetic tape transport.

As an example of the design of a special-purpose peripheral equipment, in Section 11.5 we shall design a simple graphics terminal. This terminal will subsequently be interfaced to SIC. The remaining sections of the chapter will be concerned with the subject of data communications between remote digital systems. The emphasis will be on low-speed voice channel communications with only a mention of broader-

407

band systems. We shall be particularly interested in the baseband interface between a teletype and a data communications equipment and between a similar DCE and SIC.

11.2 INTERFACING TO SIC

Ordinarily, the most difficult problem associated with designing an interface is that of ascertaining the precise functions and timing of input and output lines associated with the systems to be interfaced. This problem is considerably complicated if interrupts and/or buffered I/O are to be accommodated. User manuals necessarily written in natural language format are not always equal to the task of describing the I/O characteristics of a system. For SIC input-output we have an AHPL description that precisely defines the function and timing of all input or output lines. With this AHPL description available, it is not difficult to write the AHPL description of that portion of the interface directly interacting with SIC. The designer is thus free to concentrate on properly representing the function of the peripheral equipment.

In order to provide for maximum uniformity among SIC interfaces, a standard flow chart for modules connecting to SIC has been developed. This flow chart includes in detail those aspects of the interface that must interact with the AHPL description of SIC I/O presented in Chapter 10. Aspects that are peculiar to individual peripheral devices are represented by more general blocks within the flow chart. This general SIC flow chart is shown in Figs. 11.1 and 11.2. A similar flow chart should be developed for any CPU before the task of interface design is delegated to a group of engineers who may work independently.

Figure 11.1 describes the reaction to commands received from SIC while Fig. 11.2 represents the handling of data by either input data, output data, or buffered transfers. Each peripheral will repeatedly check in a single step for a *csrdy* accompanied by the proper device number as bits 6 to 8 on the *CSBUS*. Once the command is accepted and stored and the status flip-flops are adjusted as appropriate, control diverges into two parallel sequences. One of these responds to the command while the other sequence returns to point A to await a status request that may occur while a command is in progress. The responding sequence branches into separate paths for the four types of commands. Any command requiring the status of the peripheral is responded to directly with the standard 3-line handshake sequence controlling the routing of the status vector to SIC through the *CSBUS*. The other three types of commands continue from points C, D, and E. In response to an Activate Buffer command, various initialization operations may be accomplished

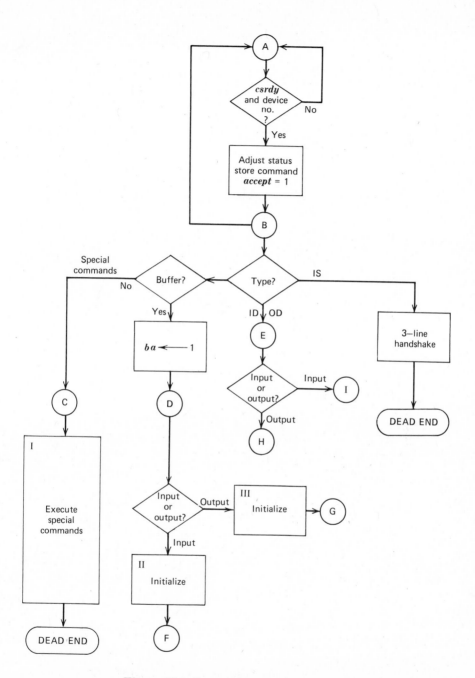

Figure 11.1. Reaction to SIC commands.

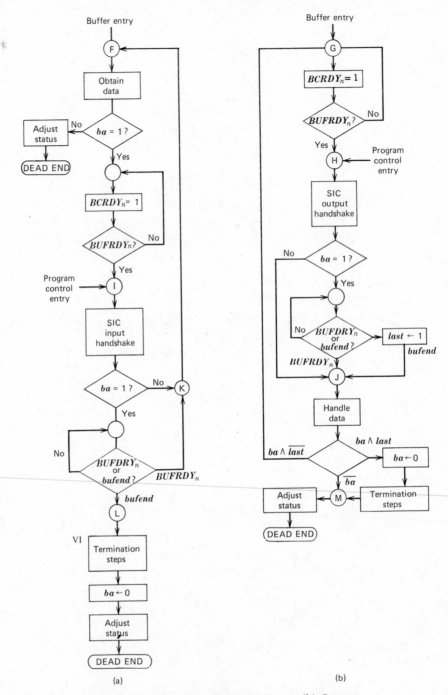

Figure 11.2. Data handling. (*a*) Input. (*b*) Output.

in both blocks II and III. Points I, H, F, and G serve as entry points into the data-handling sequence for input data, output data, and buffer commands. Block I provides for the execution of special commands that will range from none for some simple peripherals to many for more-complicated devices. Interrupts are possible from any of blocks I, II, or III. The interrupt function within SIC will not necessarily be applicable to all peripherals.

Two separate sequences are given in Figs. 11.2a and 11.2b for handling the input and output, respectively, of data to or from SIC through the IOBUS. These transfers are controlled through the standard 3-line handshakes on the control buses *ready, datavalid,* and *accept.* These same sequences are applicable to program-controlled transfers as well as buffered transfers. For buffered input to SIC, the sequence obtains a data word prior to indicating its readiness to SIC.

The response to an individual INPUT DATA command joins the data handling sequence at point I. It is assumed that a new word was obtained at the end of the previous INPUT DATA command or that the first word was obtained as a result of a special start up command. If this is not the case for a particular device, the word to be transferred must be obtained before branching to point I. Following the data transfer handshake with SIC, control must pause to get an indication from SIC as to whether a block of buffered transfers has been completed. If so, in the case of buffered input, the buffer sequence is terminated; status is adjusted; and the buffer-active flip-flip, *ba*, is cleared. After a *bufrdy* signal or if *ba* = 0, control returns to point F to obtain a new data word. For a single INPUT DATA command, control leaves the data-handling sequence and terminates once a new data word has been assembled in the output register.

In the output data handling sequence of Fig. 11.2b, *bchrdy* is held at 1 as the sequence is entered at point G. Control goes to point H immediately for a single OUTPUT DATA command or after a *bufrdy* = 1 is received in the case of buffered output. Following the data transfer handshake with SIC, it is necessary, in the case of buffered output, to wait for a possible *bufend* indicating completion of the buffer operation. Since the peripheral must handle the just-received data in all cases, a special flip-flop *last* is set to 1 if a *bufend* is received. Once the peripheral has disposed of the data, control separates for the three possible cases. If a buffer operation continues, control returns to point G. If the last buffered transfer has just been completed, *ba* is reset, any required termination steps are accomplished, status is adjusted, and the sequence terminates. For an individual OUTPUT DATA command, control goes directly to point M to adjust status and terminate. The reader should

411

note that SIC is always released at points J, K, or L in the sequences of Fig. 11.2 before the possibly time-consuming, data-handling operation by the peripheral begins.

Those activities peculiar to specific peripherals are represented by Roman-numeraled blocks I to VII in Figs. 11.1 and 11.2. The assignment of activities to these blocks will vary from device to device. It may be that even for a given device the designer may have some choice as to which block might accomplish a certain function. It might be possible, for example, to obtain the first word for a buffer input operation by way of a special command or as part of the AB command. It is also possible that interrupts may be set in SIC by the sequences in any of blocks I to VII. The reasons for the interrupts will vary from device to device. Some of the simpler peripherals will have no interrupt capability.

11.3   A SIMPLIFIED SIC INTERFACE

Even though the capacity for buffered I/O may be present in a CPU, not all peripherals will be permitted to take advantage of this flexibility. For some devices, the simplicity of the interface design might be the overriding consideration. In Fig. 11.3, we have deleted the buffered transfer capability from the flow chart of the standard SIC interface. This has made it possible to combine the sequences responding to the input status and input data commands. The distinction between these two sequences is handled by letting the statements that connect data and status information to *IOBUS* and *CSBUS* respective be conditional upon the contents of a flip-flop that stores a bit distinguishing these two commands. The simplication in Fig. 11.3 as compared to Figs. 11.1 and 11.2 is less apparent since the three-line control handshakes are illustrated in detail in Fig. 11.3.

It is possible that only part of the flow chart of Fig. 11.3 will be applicable to a given peripheral depending on the existence of special commands and on whether the peripheral is an input device, an output device, or both. As a first example, we have chosen a paper tape reader which is, of course, an input device only. The resulting interface for the reader will probably be at the compact and economical end of the spectrum of SIC interfaces.

Example 11.1
A paper tape reader is to be interfaced to SIC. Only two of the logic input lines to the reader will be used by the interface. A logical 1 for 100 μsec on line *step* will cause the reader to advance and make a new 8-bit data character available on the vector of output lines *TAPE*(8). The other input is a line called *forward*,

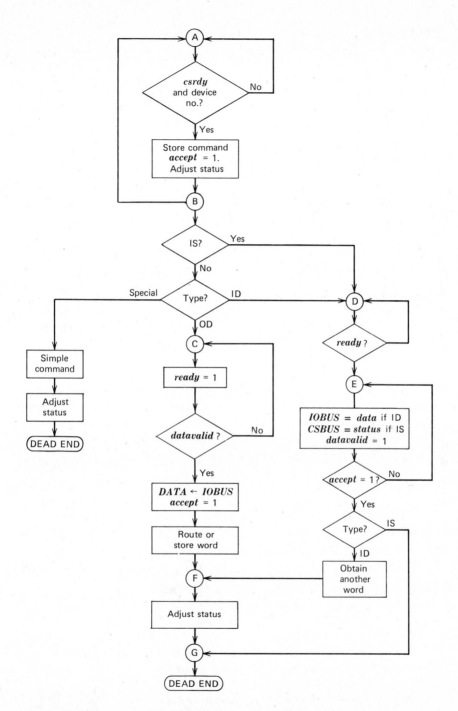

Figure 11.3. Simplified interface for SIC peripherals.

413

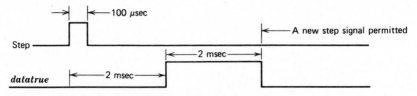

Figure 11.4. Timing of paper tape reader.

which is to be connected to the output of an interface flip-flop with the same name. If *forward* = 1, a signal on *step* will cause the tape to move forward under the read head. If *forward* = 0, the tape will move in reverse. Following a change in the value of *forward*, a 4-msec interval must precede the next signal on line *step*.

In addition to the data character, there are two output lines from the reader, *datatrue* and *prtp*. The latter will be 1 whenever the reader power is on and tape is in the reader with the latch closed. The *datatrue* line will be 1 for 2 msec after a new 8-bit character has appeared on the lines *TAPE*. The timing relationships between *step* and *datatrue* is shown in Fig. 11.4.

In addition to the INPUT STATUS command, the reader will only be required to respond to two versions of the INPUT DATA command. If the command is ID and $CSBUS_6 = 1$, the paper tape interface is to place the current character on the *IOBUS* and move the paper tape one character in the forward direction. If $CSBUS_6 = 0$, the situation is similar, but the tape is moved in the reverse direction. Status bits indicating availability and parity for the last character must be provided. The reader will be assigned device number 7.

Solution

Since the only two commands to which the paper tape interface must respond are IS and ID, the flow chart of Fig. 11.3 may be further reduced to the form given in Fig. 11.5. The status adjustment, which may be conditioned on the receipt of an ID command, has been placed ahead of the divergence of control step. The corresponding AHPL description of the interface module is as follows:

MODULE: PAPER TAPE READER INTERFACE
   MEMORY: $DR[7]$; *forward, instat, busy; pe*
   INPUTS: $TAPE[8]$; *datatrue; prtp; csrdy;*
   OUTPUTS: *step; forward*
   COMBUSES: *ready; datavalid; accept;* $IOBUS[18]$; $CSBUS[12]$
   ONE SHOTS: *change* (4 ms); *step*(100 μsec)
  1. $\rightarrow \overline{(csrdy)} \wedge (\wedge / CSBUS_{0:2}) / (1)$
  2. *forward* * $\overline{CSBUS_4} \leftarrow CSBUS_6$; *accept* = 1; *change* * $(\overline{CSBUS_4}$
     $\wedge$ (*forward* $\oplus CSBUS_6$)) $\leftarrow$ 1; *instat* $\leftarrow CSBUS_4$; *busy* * $\overline{CSBUS_4} \leftarrow$ 1;
     $\rightarrow$ (3, 1)

414

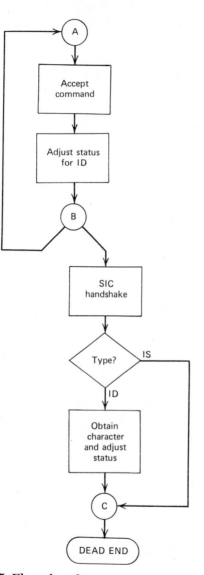

Figure 11.5. Flow chart for paper tape reader interface.

3. Null
   $\rightarrow \overline{ready}/(3)$
4. $CSBUS_{0:2} * instat = (prtp, busy, pe)$
   $IOBUS_{11:17} = DR * \overline{instat}; datavalid = 1$
   $\rightarrow (\overline{accept}, accept \wedge instat, accept \wedge \overline{instat})/(4, 8, 5)$
5. $step * \overline{change} \leftarrow 1$
   $\rightarrow change/(5)$
6. $(DR, pe) * datatrue \leftarrow (TAPE_{0:6}, ODDPAR (TAPE))$
   $\rightarrow \overline{datatrue}/(6)$
7. $busy * \overline{datatrue} \leftarrow 0$
   $\rightarrow (datatrue, \overline{datatrue})/(7, 8)$
8. DEAD END
END SEQUENCE

The only bit of the command that is merely stored at step 2 is $CSBUS_4$, which is a 1 for input status and a 0 for input data. This bit is stored in the flip-flop *instat*. If the command is INPUT DATA, the status flip-flop *busy* is set to 1. It may appear that *instat* and *busy* are storing the same information. This is not the case. For INPUT DATA *busy* will remain 1 until a new character has been obtained from the tape. The flip-flop *instat*, which is initially 0, will be set to 1 as soon as a request for status occurs while the reader is busy.

We assume that bit 6 of the *CSBUS* will indicate whether the tape should move forward or in reverse. This bit is stored in flip-flop *forward* if the command is input data. If the value of *forward* is changed, the one shot *change* is triggered to prevent an input on line *step* for at least 4 msec. Following step 2, control diverges into two parallel sequences, returning to step 1 to wait for another status request and continuing to step 3 to execute a data or status transfer to SIC. Another status request will not occur until this interchange is complete so that the divergence of control could equally well have taken place at step 4.

The interface waits for a *ready* at step 3. At step 4, the appropriate bus connection is established depending on *instat*, and a *datavalid* signal is issued. Notice that *DR* is only large enough to accommodate a 7-bit character; therefore, only 7 bits of the 18-bit *IOBUS* are used. Following an *accept* level, control branches to step 5 if it is necessary to read another data character from tape, or to step 8 if an INPUT STATUS has just been executed.

Control is held at step 5 until *change* has returned to 0, if the read direction has changed, before the 100 μsec one-shot *step* is triggered. At step 6, a new character is placed in the data register *DR* upon the appearance of a signal on the line *datatrue*. The output of the parity check network ODDPAR is placed in the flip-flop *pe* at the same time. If parity was odd, SIC will be able to observe the parity error at the time of its next status check. Control is held at step 7 until *datatrue* has returned to 0, thus preventing a premature *step* signal.

416

11.4 A MAGNETIC TAPE TRANSPORT CONTROLLER

Perhaps the most complicated of all peripheral equipments is the magnetic tape transport. The transport is subject to a relatively large number of commands, and the variety of activities involved gives rise to numerous status bits. Information is stored on tape in records, many characters in length, which are written on the tape and read from the tape as units. The reading or writing of a record almost demands handling as a buffer operation. Several circumstances can occur in the course of a magnetic tape operation that cannot be anticipated by the CPU. If interrupt is available in a computer system, one would expect an interrupt line to be assigned to a magnetic tape transport.

Interfacing a tape transport to a CPU is sufficiently complicated that the task is usually referred to as designing a controller. Sometimes a single controller will control more than one tape transport. In this section we shall design a controller for controlling the interaction of a single 7-track tape transport with the SIC I/O system. The controller will be able to generate interrupts and will read and write records as buffered block transfers. In other respects, the controller will be kept as uncomplicated as possible. The number of commands to which it will respond and the amount of status information reported will be less than in most commercially available transports.

One of the special characteristics of I/O devices is that the data format is generally different from that used in the central processor or main memory. On magnetic tape, information is arranged in characters of 6 to 8 bits (see Fig. 3.27); the same sort of arrangement is used on paper tape. Punched cards generally consist of 80 columns of 12 positions each, normally read one column at a time. For teletypewriters, information arrives one character at a time. High-speed printers may require that all the characters for one line (100 to 150 characters) be supplied at one time, or they may accept data one character at a time.

The word length of main memory, i.e., the number of bits accessed in a single read-write cycle generally matches none of these I/O data formats. It is therefore necessary to provide means of assembling smaller data groups into larger, and disassembling larger data groups into smaller, as data flows between memory and the I/O devices. This assembly and disassembly may be done by the central processor, but it is more common to provide separate assembly and disassembly logic within the individual I/O devices, for two reasons. First, a single computer may have to communicate with many different types of I/O devices, each with its own special requirements so that supplying sufficient flexibility in a single CPU would be difficult. Second, providing

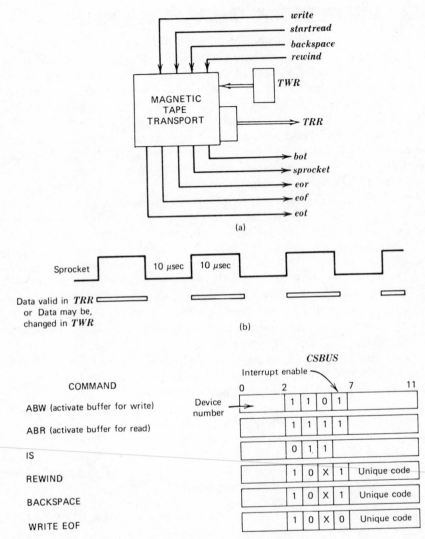

(a)

(b)

(c) Commands to tape controller

Figure 11.6. Tape transport specifications.

all these data conversion services would leave the CPU with little time to do anything else. A small computer like SIC might use the CPU for these activities in conjunction with devices, such as the paper tape reader discussed in the previous section, with which it communicates only a small portion of the time. The SIC computer has been provided with an 18-bit *IOBUS*. The more heavily-used tape transport will be assigned the task of disassembling each 18-bit word from the *IOBUS* into three 6-bit characters to be written on tape. As part of the read operation, the controller will assemble sets of three consecutive characters into the 18-bit register *TDR* for transmission to SIC on the *IOBUS*.

The tape transport will be assumed to conform to the model of Fig. 3.28 (repeated as Fig. 11.6a) with input control lines *write, startread, backspace*, and *rewind* and output control lines *eot, sprocket, eor, bot*, and *eof*. All changes in output levels will be assumed to be synchronized with the controller clock. When the controller wishes to write a block on tape, it holds a 1-level on line *write* until the operation is complete. The tape transport will respond with periodic 1-levels on line *sprocket* of 10-μsec duration and separated by intervals of at least 10 μsec. The next data character to be written on tape may be placed in the 7-bit tape write register, *TWR*, at any time when *sprocket* = 1 (Figure 11.6b). After a longitudinal parity check character (*LPC*) is written on tape, the controller *write* level will go to zero. As a result, no further sprocket signals will appear at the tape transport output. The tape will stop in about ¾ in., thus generating an end of record (*eor*) gap.

A read operation may be initiated by a one-period level on the line *startread*. Each time a new 10-μsec level appears on line *sprocket*, a new character will be available on lines *TRR*. A valid character can be expected on these lines during the entire 10-μsec interval. (Figure 11.6b). During a read operation, each *sprocket* level is triggered by the OR combination of the 7 bits in the odd parity data character, so the interval between sprocket levels will be similar to the interval generated during the write operation. A read operation may be terminated by the appearance of a 1 on any of the lines *eor, eof*, or *eot*.

A level on line *backspace* will cause the tape to move backward past one record. A level on line *rewind* will cause the tape to be rewound until the beginning of tape mark is under the read head.

The commands to which the tape transport controller will be expected to respond are given in Fig. 11.6c. The values for bits appearing on the *CSBUS* corresponding to each command are also shown. A bit with a special meaning applicable for activate buffer commands and the REWIND and BACKSPACE commands has been assigned to bit $CSBUS_6$. If this bit is 1, the controller is instructed to interrupt SIC after comple-

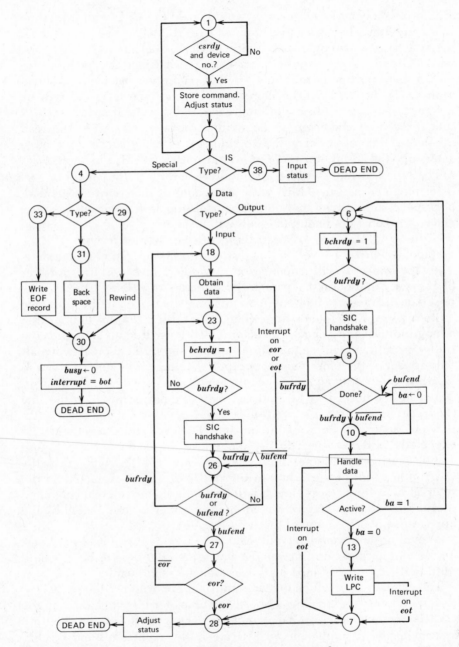

Figure 11.7. Tape transport control.

tion of the command or if an error is encountered prior to completion. The codes corresponding to the last three special tape transport commands are not specified, and recognition of these commands will be expressed in function notation and the corresponding combinational logic unit descriptions will not be provided.

The only means provided for reading and writing data on tape is by way of buffered transfers. It is, therefore, convenient to provide the special WRITE EOF command to write the two-character *end-of-file* record. The execution of this command will automatically provide the three blank character spaces on tape.

Since SIC can conveniently test only 6 status bits, status information describing the controller will be reduced to the following:

CSBUS	0	1	2	3	4	5
	Power and tape	*busy*	*pe*	*eor*	*endfile*	*eot*

The first 3 bits are consistent with their use in the previous paper tape reader example. The beginning of tape signal will be be passed on to SICPAC. It will be assumed that the SICPAC operating system will recall if the last command issued to the tape transport was REWIND. Since the *eof* signal is transient, a flip-flop *endfile* will be set whenever an end-of-file record is encountered. The *eor* and *eot* signals will be assumed to be constant levels generated by sensors of a gap or end-of-tape mark.

Since the tape controller will not be required to respond to input data and output data commands, the general data-handling sequence for SIC peripherals, as depicted in Fig. 11.2, may be simplified. A complete flow chart for the transport controller is given in Fig. 11.7. Entry points from the input data and output data commands have been omitted from the data-handling sequences as have several checks of *ba* which were required to separate control for the completed program controlled transfers. The flip-flop *last* is not needed, since *ba* can now be reset to zero immediately when *bufend* is encountered during a buffered output operation.

The three special commands are indicated separately in Fig. 11.7. An interrupt must be generated following completion of the REWIND and BACKSPACE commands. An interrupt is also appropriate if an *eor* or *eof* is encountered during a buffered input operation. If the SIC operating system is properly aware of the number of words in each record, it should be able to avoid receiving an *eor* interrupt, but one is included as a precaution. A buffered output operation will be interrupted by an *end-of-tape* (*eot*) signal. The operating system will rely on this signal to make a program aware that no more files can be written on a given tape. Both types of interrupts are shown in Fig. 11.7. Except as discussed above, this figure conforms to the general SIC peripheral control sequence of Figs. 11.1 and 11.2.

The input-output connections to the tape transport controller are shown in Fig. 11.8. The lines to and from the tape transport are as shown in Fig. 11.6a. The usual connections to the SIC communications buses are shown. Since more than one identical tape transport will be connected into the SIC system, the device number will be left unspecified until the physical connection is actually established. At that time, three

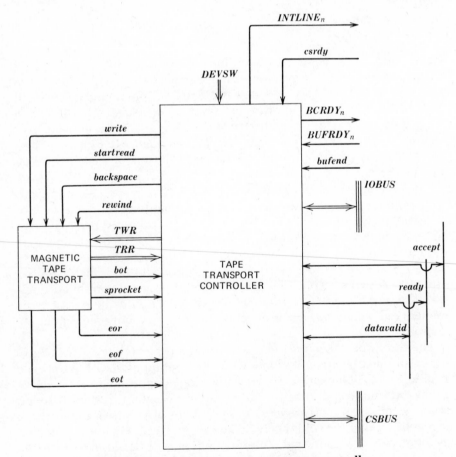

Figure 11.8 Connections to tape transport controller.

switches labeled as the vector **DEVSW** will be semipermanently set. The number $\perp$**DEVSW** will be the tape controller device number. The variable subscript n indicating individual lines in the vectors **INTLINE**, **BCRDY** and **BUFRDY**, thus, becomes equal to $\perp$**DEVSW**.

The AHPL description of the tape transport controller begins with a declaration of the input and output lines given in Fig. 11.8. As required, those I/O lines that are buses are declared as such. The register **DR** is provided to store an 18-bit data word that will be broken into, or assembled from, three 6-bit data characters. The register **LPC** stores longitudinal odd parity over the characters so far read from, or written, on tape; **CNT** is a two-bit counter used primarily to select one of the three 6-bit character spaces in **DR**. The flip-flop **ba** is set at the beginning of an activate buffer command while **enint** is used to store the interrupt enable bit from a command. The flip-flops **busy**, **pe**, and **endfile** all store status information. Since **INTLINE**$_n$, **BCRDY**$_n$, and **BUFRDY**$_n$ are all scalars, they are relabeled with lower-case strings for convenience in describing the controller itself.

MODULE: TAPE CONTROLLER
   INPUTS: **TRR**[7]; *csrdy; bot; eot; sprocket; eor; eof;*
           DEVSW[3]; **BUFRDY**$_n$; *bufend*
   OUTPUTS: **BCRDY**$_n$; **TWR**[7]; *write; startread;*
           backspace; rewind; **INTLINE**$_n$
   COMBUSES: **IOBUS**[18]; **CSBUS**[12]; *ready; datavalid; accept*
   MEMORY: **TWR**[7]; *ba;* **LPC**[7]; **DR**[18]; **CNT**[2];
           enint; busy; pe; endfile; write
   LABELS: **INTLINE**$_n$ = *interrupt;* **BCRDY**$_n$ = *bcrdy;*
          BUFRDY$_n$ = *bufrdy*

1. $\rightarrow ((\vee/(\textbf{DEVSW} \oplus \textbf{CSBUS}_{0:2})) \wedge csrdy)/(1)$
2. *accept* $= 1$; *enint* $\leftarrow$ **CSBUS**$_6$
   $\rightarrow$ (**CSBUS**$_3$, **CSBUS**$_3$, 1)/(38, 3, 1)
3. *ba* $\leftarrow$ **CSBUS**$_4$; *busy* $\leftarrow$ 1; *pe* $\leftarrow$ 0; *endfile* $\leftarrow$ 0 NO DELAY
   $\rightarrow$ (**CSBUS**$_4$)/(5)
4. NO DELAY
   $\rightarrow$ (RWND(**CSBUS**$_{7:11}$), BKSP(**CSBUS**$_{7:11}$),
   WREOF(**CSBUS**$_{7:11}$))/(29, 31, 33)

Some of the principal step numbers are shown in Fig. 11.7 to facilitate understanding of the sequence. The first five steps accept and store a command and effect branching to the six commands that can be executed by the tape transport controller. Using NO DELAY steps, all branching to commands is accomplished during the clock period in which *accept* $= 1$. Thus the only command bit stored is the interrupt enable bit from

$CSBUS_6$. Step 3 initializes three status flip-flops and sets ba for an AB_n command. Three minterm function expressions separate the three special commands at step 4. The buffered I/O operations are initiated at step 5, which separates these two data-handling sequences.

5. $LPC \leftarrow 7 \top 0;$ *write* $\leftarrow \overline{CSBUS_5}$;
   startread $= CSBUS_5$ NO DELAY
   $\rightarrow (\overline{CSBUS_5}, CSBUS_5)/(6, 18)$
6. $bcrdy = sprocket$
   $\rightarrow (\overline{bufrdy})/(6)$
7. *ready* $= 1$
   $\rightarrow (\overline{datavalid})/(7)$
8. $DR \leftarrow IOBUS;$ *accept* $= 1; CNT \leftarrow 0, 0$
9. $ba * bufend \leftarrow 0$
   $\rightarrow (bufend \wedge \overline{bufrdy})/(9)$
10. $TWR_{1:6} \leftarrow BUSFN((DR_{0:5} ! DR_{6:11} ! DR_{12:17}) * DCD_{0:2} (CNT));$
    $CNT \leftarrow INC(CNT);$
    $LPC_{1:6} \leftarrow LPC_{1:6} \oplus BUSFN(DR_{0:5} ! DR_{6:11} ! DR_{12:17}) *$
    $DCD_{0:2} (CNT));$
    $TWR_0 \leftarrow ODDPAR(BUSFN(DR_{0:5} ! DR_{6:11} ! DR_{12:17}) *$
    $DCD_{0:2} (CNT)))$
    $LPC_0 \leftarrow LPC_0 \oplus EVENPAR(BUSFN(DR_{0:5} ! DR_{6:11} ! DR_{12:17}) *$
    $DCD_{0:2} (CNT)))$

The write operation continues at step 6 with the activation of $bcrdy$ as soon as the first *sprocket* level appears. A data word is accepted at step 8, and control waits at step 9 for an indication from SIC as to whether more words will follow. At step 10, one of the three 6-bit characters from DR is loaded into the tape write register depending on the value of CNT. Bit 0 of this register is used to establish odd lateral parity, and the 7-bit character is exclusive ORed with the contents of LPC. Thus at all times this register contains 1's corresponding to longitudinal odd parity. Step 11 waits for *sprocket* to return to 0 or for an *eot* indication. If an *eot* is observed, the buffer sequence terminates at step 17 after an interrupt is established. After a new *sprocket* level appears at step 12, control either returns to step 10 to write the next character, or to step 6 to receive a new data word or to step 13 if ba has been reset by a *bufend* level. Steps 13 to 16 provide for writing the LPC character on tape following three blank character spaces.

11. *interrupt* $= eot \wedge enint$
    $\rightarrow (sprocket \wedge \overline{eot}, sprocket \wedge \overline{eot}, eot)/(11, 12, 17)$
12. $\rightarrow (\overline{sprocket}, sprocket \wedge (\overline{\wedge/CNT}), sprocket \wedge (\wedge/CNT) \wedge ba,$
    $sprocket \wedge (\wedge/CNT) \wedge \overline{ba})/(12, 10, 6, 13)$

13. $CNT \leftarrow 0, 0; TWR \leftarrow 7 \top 0$
14. $TWR \leftarrow LPC * (\wedge/CNT);$
    $CNT \leftarrow INC(CNT)$
15 $interrupt = eot \wedge enint$
    $\rightarrow (sprocket \wedge \overline{eot}, \overline{sprocket} \wedge \overline{eot}, eot)/(15, 16, 17)$
16. $\rightarrow (\overline{sprocket}, sprocket \wedge (\vee/CNT), sprocket \wedge (\overline{\vee/CNT}))/(16, 14, 17)$
17. $write \leftarrow 0; busy \leftarrow 0$
    DEAD END

The input buffer sequence continues at step 18, where control waits until the tape has accelerated to speed and the end of record gap is no longer under the read head. Step 20 waits for a *sprocket* signal indicating data available in *TRR*. If an *eof* or *eor* is encountered, an interrupt is generated and the sequence terminates at step 28. Step 21 places three consecutive characters in *DR*, checks for a lateral parity error, and keeps track of longitudinal parity. After the *sprocket* level returns to zero at step 22, control either returns to step 20 to await another character or goes to step 23 to alert SIC that a data word is ready. The SIC handshake is completed at step 25 and step 26 waits to see if the buffer operation has been completed. If not, control returns to step 19 to read another sequence of three characters. If so, control waits at step 27 until an end of record gap is encountered. Thus the controller continues reading through a record even though SIC may want only the first part of the record.

18. $\rightarrow (eor)/(18)$
19. $CNT \leftarrow 0, 0$ NO DELAY
20. $endfile \leftarrow eof; interrupt = enint \wedge (eof \vee eor)$
    $\rightarrow (\overline{eor} \wedge sprocket \wedge \overline{eof}, eor \vee eof, \overline{eor} \wedge sprocket \wedge \overline{eof})/(20, 28, 21)$
21. $(DR_{0:5} ! DR_{6:11} ! DR_{12:17}) * DCD_{0:2}(CNT) \leftarrow TRR_{0:5};$
    $CNT \leftarrow INC(CNT);$
    $pe * EVENPAR(TRR) \leftarrow 1;$
    $LPC \leftarrow LPC \oplus TRR$
22. $\rightarrow (sprocket, \overline{sprocket} \wedge (\overline{\wedge/CNT}), sprocket \wedge (\wedge/CNT))/(22, 20, 23)$
23. $bcrdy = 1$
    $\rightarrow (\overline{bufrdy})/(23)$
24. $\rightarrow (\overline{ready})/(24)$
25. $IOBUS = DR; datavalid = 1$
    $\rightarrow (\overline{accept})/(25)$
26. $pe * ((\vee/LPC) \wedge bufend) \leftarrow 1$
    $\rightarrow (bufrdy \wedge \overline{bufend}, bufrdy, bufend)/(26, 19, 27)$
27. $\rightarrow \overline{eor}/(27)$
28. $busy \leftarrow 0; ba \leftarrow 0$ NO DELAY
    DEAD END

Steps 29 and 30 execute the REWIND command that generates an interrupt upon completion. Similarly, the backspace sequence is only two steps, with step 32 waiting for either an end-of-record or beginning of tape level. Steps 33 to 37 write an end-of-file record that consists of the character 1, 0, 0, 1, 1, 1, 1 followed by three blank character spaces followed by another 1, 0, 0, 1, 1, 1, 1.

The input status command is accomplished by steps 38 and 39. The 6 status bits connected to the $CSBUS$ at step 39 are as previously listed.

29. $rewind = 1$
$\rightarrow (\overline{bot})/(29)$

30. $busy \leftarrow 0;\ interrupt = bot$
DEAD END

31. $backspace = 1$
$\rightarrow(\overline{eor})/(31)$

32. $\rightarrow((\overline{eor \vee bot}),\ (eor \vee bot))/(32, 30)$

33. $write \leftarrow 1;\ CNT \leftarrow 0, 0$
$\rightarrow (\overline{sprocket})/(33)$

34. $TWR \leftarrow (1, 0, 0, 0, 1, 1, 1) * (\overline{CNT}_0 \wedge \overline{CNT}_1)$ NO DELAY

35. $\rightarrow (\overline{sprocket})/(35)$

36. $\rightarrow (\overline{sprocket},\ sprocket \wedge endfile,\ sprocket \wedge \overline{endfile})/(36, 30, 37)$

37. $CNT \leftarrow INC(CNT);\ endfile * (CNT_0 \wedge CNT_1) \leftarrow 1$
NO DELAY
$\rightarrow (34)$

38. $\rightarrow (\overline{ready})/(38)$

39. $CSBUS_{0:5} = prtp,\ busy,\ pe,\ eor,\ endfile,\ eot;$
$datavalid = 1$
$\rightarrow (\overline{accept},\ accept)/(39,\ DEAD\ END)$

END

11.5   DISPLAY PROCESSOR

In the last several years the use of computers to control the display on cathode ray tubes has become common. Such systems are often called *graphics terminals*. In this section a simple special-purpose processor will be designed for this function. Whether or not it is a computer is arguable. To permit a single-section discussion, the system has been kept as simple as possible. Still, many of the pertinent considerations are introduced, and some interesting design approaches are illustrated. In this section, we shall carry out the design of this typical special-purpose peripheral. In the next section, we shall interface it to SIC. The reader should notice the convenience resulting from the separation of these two tasks.

Our system will provide the display of a picture consisting of alpha-numeric characters and interconnected line segments. This picture may be modified by the user sitting in front of the tube. To be of value, the system must have the capability of permanently storing or outputting a data description of the picture to other systems. Although not discussed, we presume this capability to be present. One application example would be the construction of a diffusion mask for an LSI circuit on a graphics terminal. When completed, the data description would be fed to a controller for an automatic drafting machine to initiate the mask-making process.

User control of the system will be effected by typing commands on a keyboard or by operating what has become known as a *joy stick*. The joy stick is simply a lever, movable in two dimensions, which positions a small cross (+) on the tube. This cross indicates the starting point for the next line segment to be placed on the display. If a character is entered, the lower left corner of the character will rest on the center of the cross. For simplicity, the keyboard will include a separate key for each command in addition to the alphanumeric keys. In more complex systems, commands are typed in. This, of course, implies software for compiling the commands.

A skeleton hardware configuration is depicted in Fig. 11.9. The memory **M** is not random access. Only the word in $\mathbf{M}^0$ can be read out at any given time. The same pulse that will cause $\mathbf{M}^0$ to be placed in the register **R** will rotate the remaining rows up one position and place the contents of **R** in the last location of **M**. Very likely, **M** will be constructed using inexpensive MOS shift registers.

Three units, which we shall not design in detail, actually control the movement of the beam on the CRT (cathode ray tube). A control pulse to the *beam position* unit will cause the beam to be blanked while it is moved to the (x,y) position specified by the two 8-bit segments of the 16-bit register, **BP**. This unit must convert the two numbers in **BP** to analog form and take control of the beam from the other two units. A control pulse to the *line segment* generator will cause the beam to trace a line on the scope from its current position on the CRT to the position specified by the coordinates stored in **LS**. A pulse to the *character* generator will cause two characters to be written on the CRT.

In the absence of inputs from the user, information specifying commands to the three activity units are continuously circulated in **M**. Each time a display command emerges from **M**, the corresponding line or character is refreshed on the CRT. The formats of the display commands are given in Fig. 11.10. All commands contain 17 bits so that the word length of **M** is 17 bits. A 1 in the leftmost bit position indicates a com-

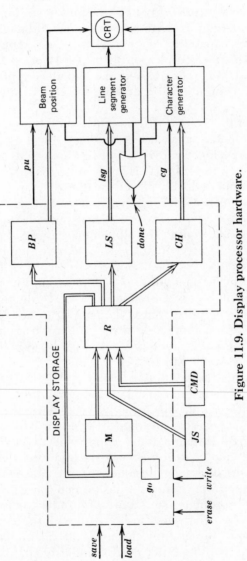

Figure 11.9. Display processor hardware.

mand to reposition the beam. Eight bits indicate the new x coordinate and 8 bits the new y coordinate. If the leftmost 2 bits are both 0, the word is blank and available for storing a new user command. The format of Fig. 11.10c specifies tracing a line segment of length and direction given by (Δx, Δy). Sign bits are included. The last command specifies the tracing of two alphanumeric characters.

How often must a character or line be retraced on the scope in order that the user will not notice a flicker? This will depend on many factors, an excellent discussion of which may be found in Reference [10]. For the more commonly used CRT phosphors, a repetition rate of between 35 and 50 Hz is recommended. The times required for positioning and line and character drawing vary widely in existing systems. Let us assume the relatively fast positioning time of 20 μsec, a two-character writing time of 20 μsec, and a line-tracing time of 20 μsec. Input command processing and other operations will require negligible time by comparison. We assume that each command must be retraced 40 times in a second. Therefore, each command in **M** will occupy the processor 800 μsec out of each second; and **M** should be constructed to store less than $10^6/800 = 1250$ words.

User inputs to the system are accomplished through registers **JS** and **CMD**, as illustrated in Fig. 11.9. The 16-bit register, **JS**, which is formatted according to the rightmost 16 bits of Fig. 11.10a, instantaneously reflects the position of the joy stick. The format of **CMD** will normally reflect the 17 bits in Figs. 11.10c,d. Data and commands are entered into this register from the keyboard.

Only the module labeled "Display Storage," which provides overall control of the display process, will be designed in this section. Like the beam position and character and line segment display units, the registers **JS** and **CMD** will not be part of the display storage module. Thus we shall not be concerned with the logic between the keyboard and the register **CMD**.

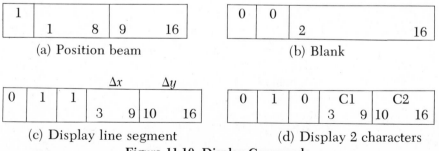

(a) Position beam (b) Blank

(c) Display line segment (d) Display 2 characters

Figure 11.10. Display Commands.

429

The registers *JS* and *CMD* will affect the display only when the user causes the flip-flop **go** to set to 1 or establishes a 1 on line **erase**. If **go** = 1, a new command is to be displayed and stored in **M**. If **erase** = 1, control searches for any positioning command with coordinates equal to the present contents of *JS*. All such commands and the corresponding display commands are eliminated by changing the leftmost 2 bits to 0, indicating blanks. The search continues as long as **erase** = 1, even though all commands corresponding to the beam position stored in *JS* may have been erased. It is assumed that the user will release the *erase* button before repositioning the joy stick.

The first step of the control sequence for the display storage model is included as a reset state, which will assure that at least one beam position command is always stored in memory. This provides a synchronizing mechanism, since a new pair of commands can be added to a display only at the end of the series of already stored pairs (see step 17).

Step 2 of the control sequence for the display processor rotates a new command out of memory into *R* and moves the just-executed command from the principal register *R* to the last row of memory. Step 3 causes a branch back to step 2 and another rotation of **M** if the command in *R* was not a positioning command. Rotations continue until a positioning command is found. Since the commands are treated in pairs, the above feature will serve to keep the system synchronized. If either of the inputs **load** or **save** is 1, control branches out of the normal sequence to provide for reading or replacing the entire contents of **M**. The sequence for accomplishing this, which begin at steps 21 and 23, will be discussed in the next section in conjunction with the interface of the display storage module to SIC.

The sequence separates at step 3 depending on the presence of an *erase*. In the absence of this user input, the positioning command in *R* is executed by steps 4 and 5. Line *pu* is the control line to the positioning unit. After a memory rotation at step 6, step 7 causes a branch to step 11 to prevent the writing of garbage on the screen by a blank command. Steps 8 and 9 cause the appropriate display commands to be executed.

MODULE DISPLAY STORAGE
    MEMORY: M[1024, 17]; *R*[17]; go(JK); *BP*[16];
                LS[16]; *CH*[16]
    INPUTS: *JS*[16]; *CMD*[17]; *start; write; done;*
              erase; load; save
    OUTPUTS: *R*[17]; *go; pu; cg; lsg; BP*[16],
              LS[16]; *CH*[16]

1. $R \leftarrow (1, 16 \top 0)$
2. $R \leftarrow M^0; M \leftarrow M^{1:1023}! R$
   $\rightarrow (\overline{load \vee save}, load, save)/(3, 21, 24)$
3. $\rightarrow (\overline{R_0}, R_0 \wedge erase, R_0 \wedge \overline{erase})/(2, 12, 4)$
4. $BP \leftarrow R_{1:16}; pu = 1$
5. $\rightarrow \overline{done}/(5)$
6. $R \leftarrow M^0; M \leftarrow M^{1:1023} ! R$
7. $\rightarrow (\overline{R_1}, R_1 \wedge \overline{R_2}, R_1 \wedge R_2)/(11, 9, 8)$
8. $LS \leftarrow R_{3:16}; lsg = 1$
   $\rightarrow (\overline{done}, done)/(8, 11)$
9. $CH \leftarrow R_{3:16}; cg = 1$
10. $\rightarrow \overline{done}/(10)$
11. NO DELAY
    $\rightarrow (go, \overline{go})/(16, 2)$

Lines *lsg* and *cg* are the control lines to the line segment and character generation units, respectively. Following the display operation control branches to step 16 to accept a new pair of commands if *go* = 1.

Execution of an erase request begins at step 12. If the leftmost 16 bits of R match the bits of JS, zeros are placed in R_0 and R_1, and in these positions in the next command in sequence as well. If the bits of R and JS do not match, control returns to step 4 to permit a display operation.

12. NO DELAY
    $\rightarrow (\vee/(JS \oplus R_{1:16}))/(4)$
13. $R_{0:1} \leftarrow 0, 0$
14. $R \leftarrow M^0; M \leftarrow M^{1:1023} ! R$
15. $R_{0:1} \leftarrow 0, 0$
    $\rightarrow (2)$

The control sequence for inserting a new display function in the circulating sequence of commands is equally simple. After a memory rotation, step 17 checks for a blank. If one is not found, control is returned to step 3 to check for a positioning command. When a blank is found while **go** = 1, step 18 enters the contents of register *JS* as a positioning command. At step 20, the desired display command is entered in the next memory space. Control then returns to step 2 for another pass through the sequence, after a 0 is placed in **go**. The reader will note that **erase** was not similarly reset after step 15. In that case the control sequencer must continue the search for other line segments, beginning at the same position. After the desired erasure has been performed, the user must reset **erase** manually.

The *go* flip-flop may be set to cause a character or line segment to be written on the screen by a one-period level on line *write*. This write signal is accepted by the statement following END SEQUENCE.

16. $R \leftarrow M^0$; $M \leftarrow M^{1:1023} \,!\, R$
17. $\rightarrow (R_0 \vee R_1)/(3)$
18. $R \leftarrow 1, JS$
19. $R \leftarrow M^0$; $M \leftarrow M^{1:1023} \,!\, R$
20. $R \leftarrow CMD$; $go \leftarrow 0$
$\;\; \rightarrow (2)$

"load" $\begin{cases} \text{21.} & \rightarrow (\overline{go})/(21) \\ \text{22.} & R \leftarrow CMD; go \leftarrow 0 \\ \text{23.} & \rightarrow (2) \\ \text{24.} & \rightarrow (go \wedge save, \overline{save})/(24,2) \end{cases}$

"save" $\begin{cases} \text{25.} & R \leftarrow M^0; M \leftarrow M^{1:1023} \,!\, R \\ \text{26.} & go \leftarrow 0 \\ & \rightarrow (4) \end{cases}$

END SEQUENCE
$go \ast write \leftarrow 1$
CONTROL RESET (1)
END

11.6   SIC INTERFACE FOR DISPLAY PROCESSOR

The display processor designed in the previous section could have been intended for use as a stand-alone device. Most likely, it would have been designed to be controlled through a minicomputer. In this section we shall interface this unit to SIC. Since SIC will have a separate keyboard input device, it will no longer be necessary to provide a separate keyboard for the graphics display. The register *CMD* will thus become part of the interface module, and the lines *write, erase, load*, and *save* will be outputs of this module. The interface is to be designed so that a SIC program can be written to permit the user to issue requests through the SIC keyboard. The reader will first position the joy stick and then, via this program, cause a line segment or character generation command to be outputted to the display interface. The manual capability of erasing characters of line segments at the position specified by the joy stick remains, but the button will now be designated *localerase*.

The SIC computer can also provide the capability for storage of a completed display for future reference. The entire contents of the display memory could be routed through SIC to and from magnetic tape.

The same SIC display program discussed above could act on user requests to transfer files between tape and the display memory.

In order to accommodate the above activities, the display interface module must be capable of responding to the following four commands.

IS	Input status
OD	Output data and display
AB input	Buffered input
AB output	Buffered output

The output data command will only be used by the display program in response to a user request for display of a character or line segment. The retrieving and replacing of the contents of the display memory will be accomplished as 1024-word buffered transfers.

A block diagram of the interface module as it relates to SIC and the display processor is provided in Fig. 11.11. The function of each line into or out of the display interface and of the memory elements declared below should become clear as we consider the control sequence. The first steps will separate the sequences for the four possible commands much the same as shown in Fig. 11.1. There are no special commands and no ID (input data) commands. The output buffer initializa-

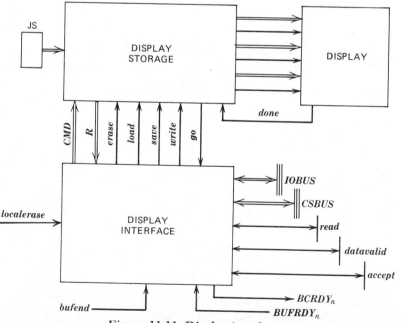

Figure 11.11. Display interface.

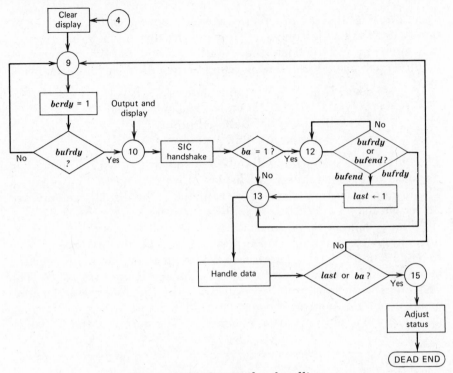

Figure 11.12. Output data handling.

tion block of Fig. 11.1 consists of clearing all commands from the display memory. The resulting two-step approach is time-consuming but eliminates the need for counting the number of entries in the new display prior to clearing the remaining memory. The flow chart of Fig. 11.12, which depicts both buffered and program-controlled output from SIC, conforms closely to the standard format of Fig. 11.2b. The input data sequence similarly conforms to the standard. The buffer output sequence begins at step 9 and is joined by the output data command at step 10. The buffer input sequence begins at 16 and the input status sequence at step 24.

The AHPL description of the SIC interface module begins as follows. Steps 2 and 3 separate the four commands while steps 4 through 8 clear the display by interacting with load sequences (steps 21 to 23) of the display memory. The one-shot *clear* is set to 1 at step 7 and remains 1 for 30 msec, ample time for the entire memory to circulate through **R**.

MODULE: DISPLAY INTERFACE
   MEMORY: **CMD**[17]; **ba**(JK); **busy**(JK);
            load (JK); *save*(JK); *last*

ONE SHOT: $clear(30$ msec$)$
COMBUS: $CSBUS[12]$; $IOBUS[18]$; $ready$; $datavalid$; $accept$
INPUTS: $accept$; $R[17]$; go; $csrdy$; $BUFRDY_{13}$; $localerase$
OUTPUTS: $CMD[17]$; $write$; $BCRDY_n$; $erase$; $load$; $save$
LABELS: $BCRDY_n = bcrdy$; $BUFRDY_n = bufrdy$

1. $\rightarrow \overline{(CSBUS_0 \wedge CSBUS_1 \wedge CSBUS_2 \wedge csrdy)}/(1)$
2. $accept = 1$; $busy * \overline{(CSBUS_3 \wedge CSBUS_4)} \leftarrow 1$
   $\rightarrow (CSBUS_3 \wedge CUBUS_4, \overline{CUBUS}_3 \wedge CUBUS_4, 1)/(10, 24, 1)$
3. $ba \leftarrow 1$;
   $\rightarrow CSBUS_5/(16)$
4. $clear \leftarrow 1$; $load \leftarrow 1$
5. $CMD \leftarrow 17 \top 0$
6. $write = 1$
7. $\rightarrow (go)/(7)$
8. $\rightarrow clear/(5)$

A 17-bit vector from the $IOBUS$ is accepted at step 11. In the program control mode this vector will be a line segment or character generation command to be loaded into the display memory following a position command from JS. In the buffer output mode, beam position commands as well as line segment and character generation commands are accepted from the $IOBUS$. After loading CMD, control proceeds directly to step 13 for a program-controlled transfer or to this step after $bufrdy$ or $bufend$ for a buffered transfer. Step 13 sets flip-flop go in the display storage module. A single command through the SIC keyboard will be transferred from CMD to R following a position from JS by step 20 of the display storage module. Because $load = 1$ during a buffered output, each command from the $IOBUS$ is inserted in memory by steps 21 to 23 of the display module. As soon as the display interface observes $go = 1$, control branches to step 15 to reset all status and control flip-flops or to step 9 to issue a new $bcrdy$.

9. $bcrdy = 1$
   $\rightarrow bufrdy/(9)$
10. $ready = 1$
    $\rightarrow \overline{datavalid}/(10)$
11. $CMD \leftarrow IOBUS_{1:17}$; $accept = 1$
    $\rightarrow \overline{ba}/(13)$
12. $last * bufend \leftarrow 1$
    $\rightarrow (\overline{bufend \vee bufrdy})/(12)$
13. $write = 1$
14. $\rightarrow (\overline{go}, go \wedge (last \vee \overline{ba}), go \wedge (\overline{last \vee \overline{ba}}))/(14, 9, 15)$
15. $ba \leftarrow 0$; $busy \leftarrow 0$; $load \leftarrow 0$; $save \leftarrow 0$
    DEAD END

435

If the contents of the display memory are to be saved through a buff-ered transfer to SIC, control in the display interface branches to step 16 to set flip-flop *save*. Steps 17 through 19 of the interface interact with steps 24 through 26 of the display storage module to load data from the display memory into **CMD**. This data moves on to SIC via the buffer handshake and data handshake of steps 20 through 22. We assume that SIC will count the number of words received and issue a *bufend* after the receipt of 1024 words. When *bufend* appears, control branches from step 23 back to step 15 to clear the status and control flip-flops.

16. $save \leftarrow 1$
17. $write = 1; \rightarrow \overline{go}/(17)$
18. $\rightarrow go/(18)$
19. $CMD \leftarrow R$
20. $bcrdy = 1$
    $\rightarrow \overline{bufrdy}/(20)$
21. $\rightarrow \overline{ready}/(21)$
22. $IOBUS_{1:17} = CMD; datavalid = 1$
    $\rightarrow \overline{accept}/(22)$
23. $\rightarrow (\overline{bufrdy \vee bufend}, bufrdy, bufend)/(23, 17, 15)$
END SEQUENCE
    $erase = localerase$
    CONTROL RESET (1)
END

The design of the modules discussed in the last two sections is typical of a design task that might be encountered by a group within a special-purpose, minicomputer-based facility. The design language approach made possible division of the task into two modules that might be de-signed simultaneously by two engineers. The AHPL syntax is suffi-ciently powerful to permit the expression of interconnections between the two modules and to SIC. At the same time it will provide the means of communication between the two engineers necessary for the coor-dination of their designs.

11.7 NON-RESPONSIVE SERIAL COMMUNICATIONS

Up to this point in this chapter we have limited our discussion to com-munication between digital devices in close physical proximity and linked together by a common busing configuration. Let us now increase the distance between two devices until they are certainly not housed in the same building and are quite possibly separated by a considerable

1. *ready* $= 1$
   $\rightarrow \overline{datavalid}/(1)$
2. *accept* $= 1$
   $\rightarrow datavalid/(2)$

3. "Begin storage"

   .
   .
   .
   .

n - 1. "End storage"
   $\rightarrow (1)$

(a)

1. *ready* $= 1$
   $\rightarrow \overline{datavalid}/(1)$
2. *accept* $= 1$
   $\rightarrow (datavalid, \overline{datavalid}, 1)/(2, n, 3)$

3. "Begin storage"

   .
   .
   .

n-1. "End storage"
n. CONVERGE $(n - 1, 2)$
   $\rightarrow (1)$

(b)

Figure 11.13. Receiver sequences.

distance. Now the problem of communications between the devices is governed by a new set of constraints. As the distance increases, the use of eight or more data lines in parallel often becomes economically unattractive. The three-line handshake approach may also appear less attractive simply because it requires three separate control lines.

The handshake or responsive approach to data transmission will also impose an increasingly significant time delay on the communications process as distance increases. As pointed out in Chapter 9, a completely responsive handshake should be used if the propagation delay between receiver and transmitter exceeds one or two clock periods. This avoids the possibility of the receiver's issuing a new *ready* before the previous *accept* has been observed by the transmitter. The completely responsive control sequence for the receiver shown in Fig. 11.13a. does not begin to store a received data character until *accept* has been returned to 0.

Figure 11.14 depicts the timing of a moderate distance data transmission controlled by the completely responsive three-line handshake of Fig. 11.13a. The delay associated with the propagation of a control signal between devices is T. For open-wire transmission the delay is 3.2 μsec/km., but for a coaxial cable it may typically by 6 μsec/km. Beginning at a point where the transmitter has a character ready and has just been made aware that the receiver is also ready, the transmitter establishes **datavalid** $= 1$ which is observed by receiver after a delay T. The receiver then issues an **accept** $= 1$, which is observed by the transmitter again after delay T. The transmitter drops **datavalid** upon receiving **accept**. After another delay of T, the receiver sees that **datavalid** $= 0$. It then drops **accept** and begins to store the data just received. After this

437

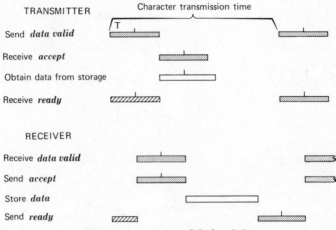

Figure 11.14. Handshake delay.

data is stored, receiver control returns to step 1 to issue a new *ready* = 1, puts a new data character on line, and sets *datavalid* to 1. This completes the cycle associated with the transmission of one character. It can be seen from Fig. 11.14 that the total transmission time for a character is $S + 4T$. For N bit characters the data transmission rate in bits/sec is thus given by Eq. 11.1. where S is the time required for storage of a character.

$$R = \frac{N}{S + 4T} \tag{11.1}$$

It is possible for the receiver to begin storage of a character while still holding *accept* at 1. This is implemented by the partially-parallel control sequence of Fig. 11.13b. In this case the data transmission rate is given by Eq. 11.2 if $S > 2T$.

$$R = \frac{N}{S + 2T} \tag{11.2}$$

The corresponding data rate for $S \leqslant 2T$ is given by Eq. 11.3.

$$R = \frac{N}{4T} \tag{11.3}$$

Example 11.2

Assuming completely responsive signaling, compute the maximum data transmission rate, R, for eight data lines (one character) in parallel and for only one data line. Assume that the slower of the receiving and transmitting devices has a storage time, S, of 20 μsec. The distance between the devices is 30 miles; the propagation delay is 10 μsec/mile. Could either of the communicating devices be a tape transport that reads at a rate of 50,000 characters/sec?

Solution

The propagation time delay is given by

$T = 30 \text{ miles} \times 10 \ \mu\text{sec/mile} = 300 \ \mu\text{sec}$

For serial transmission the data rate may be computed using Eq. 11.3.

$$R_{\text{serial}} = \frac{1}{4 \times 300 \ (10^6)} = 833 \text{ bits/sec}$$

If 8 bits are transmitted in parallel on eight wires, the data rate is then

$$R_{\text{parallel}} = \frac{8}{4 \times 300(10^6)} = 6667 \text{ bits/sec}$$

Even the data rate for 8-bit parallel transmission is insufficient to permit the continuous flow of data from the magnetic tape transport into the communications channel. The alternatives would be to consider a random access data buffer with intermittent reading from the tape transport or, as we shall see, broadband nonresponsive transmission.

Often the requirement to extend data communications networks over greater distances coincides with the need to include a larger variety of devices within the network. Typical networks will include equipment from more than one manufacturer. Sometimes CPU's from different manufacturers will be interconnected. These machines will have a variety of word lengths, and communications on an I/O bus equal in length to the word length of one of the machines in the network is usually not practical. Instead a standard specifying communications in the form of series of 8-bit characters has been agreed upon. Sequences of characters are arranged in messages with specific characters used to identify the beginning and end of messages. It then becomes a job of the receiving device to identify messages and to translate the information contained in these messages to a form locally usable. This task will usually be accomplished by a combination of hardware and software. This approach is *nonresponsive* transmission. Data rates for nonresponsive transmission will not depend directly on the distance between communicating terminals.

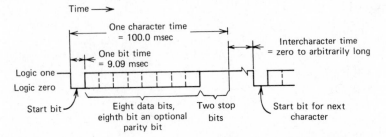

Figure 11.15. Asynchronous 10-character/sec serial transmission.

The message format is usually severely constrained when communications are confined to a computer and a set of remote time-sharing terminals. In this case message identification may be handled entirely by hardware. The only message translation at the terminal involves recoding of individual characters to a form representable on a CRT. This is also a hardware function. Time sharing will be discussed in more detail in Chapter 16.

By far the most common approach to the transmission of 8 bit bytes is in a serial-by-bit fashion. This mode in which only one communications line or channel is required serves as a standard for communications between equipments supplied by various manufacturers [4]. Serial-by-bit communications may be either synchronous or asynchronous at the byte level, and individual bits may be either clocked or unclocked. These two distinct concepts will now be discussed.

The most common asynchronous serial communications mode is the 11-bit/character, 10-character/sec teletype format. In this mode the line is normally at the logical 1 level between characters as shown in Fig. 11.15. The transmission of a character is signaled by a logical-0 start bit at the beginning of a character. The start bit is of 9.09-msec duration, as are each of the remaining 10 bits in the character. The start bit is followed by 8 information bits and then two logical-1 stop bits. The line must be at logical-1 for at least 2 × 9.09 msec following the last information bit before another start bit can appear. The actual time at which the line remains logical-1 before another start bit occurs may, of course, be much longer.

The 11-bit/character mode provides for communication without additional clocking or synchronization regardless of the characteristics of the communications channel. Asynchronous unclocked serial transmission may be extended to 30 characters/sec (300 bit/sec). For this mode the second stop bit is eliminated, resulting in 10-bit characters.

For transmission rates greater than 300 bits/sec the data are usually clocked. If the data transmission is accomplished by a direct wire link

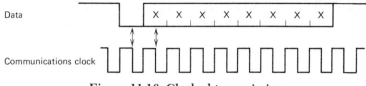

Data

Communications clock

Figure 11.16. Clocked transmission.

between the transmitter and receiver, a second connecting wire can be used by the transmitter to provide timing information. The Electronics Industry Association Standard RS-232 specifies clocking as illustrated in Fig. 11.16. Notice that there is one clock cycle/data bit, with the 1- to-0 transition on the clock line occurring at the midpoint of each bit. The receiver can depend on this transition to indicate times when the data line can be reliably sampled. The reader should not confuse the low-frequency communications clock with the much faster logic clock, which synchronizes all register transfers and control state transitions.

Clocked data transmission may be either asynchronous or synchronous by character. Synchronous transmission requires that successive 8-bit characters be packed together so that the first bit of each succeeding character will follow immediately after the last bit of the preceding character. Some method of synchronization must be employed at the beginning of a message so that the receiving system will be able to identify the first bit of each character. Synchronization procedures are discussed in References [1, 2].

Various combinations of clocked and unclocked, synchronous and asynchronous communications modes are employed over voice-grade telephone channels, which will be discussed in the next section. Typical applications of each mode are listed in Fig. 11.17.

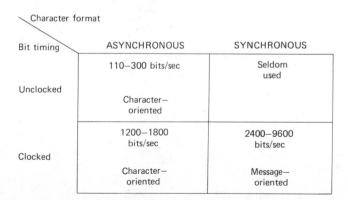

Character format Bit timing	ASYNCHRONOUS	SYNCHRONOUS
Unclocked	110–300 bits/sec Character— oriented	Seldom used
Clocked	1200–1800 bits/sec Character— oriented	2400–9600 bits/sec Message— oriented

Figure 11.17. Serial nonresponsive data transmission modes.

11.8 VOICE-GRADE COMMUNICATIONS CHANNELS

One natural advantage of nonresponsive serial-by-bit data transmission is that it can readily be carried out utilizing the voice-grade telephone network. A standard voice channel has a bandwidth of 3200 Hz. Thus, some means of modulating the baseband (sequence of logic levels) data signal is required, so that it may be represented by frequencies within this range. This fact makes necessary another piece of equipment between a data terminal, or serial interface to a computer or other digital device, and the communications channel. This piece of equipment may be referred to as a MODEM (modulator-demodulator) or as a data communications equipment (DCE). The place of the MODEM in a data communications link is illustrated in Fig. 11.18.

A few remarks on the communications channel and typical MODEM's are in order. The reader's appreciation of the discussion of this channel will depend to some extent on his previous background. Our primary goal, however, in these last three sections of Chapter 11 is a mastery of the design of an interface between a MODEM and a data terminal. This topic is independent of the reader's background in communications.

A typical MODEM designed to transmit and receive data at the lowest data rates of 110 and 300 bits/sec will utilize the simplest possible means of modulation, FSK, or frequency-shift keying. This simply means that the channel will be driven by a sinusoidal signal of one frequency, perhaps 980 Hz, during each interval when the MODEM input is logical 1 and by a different frequency, perhaps 1180 Hz, when the MODEM input is logical 0. The logic levels can then be recovered in the receiving MODEM by a simple filtering scheme.

MODEM's designed for use at higher data rates will use other types of modulation schemes. A theoretical upper limit for the data rate for any channel with bandwidth W was derived by Shannon [5]. In Eq. 11.4, C is the upper limit of the data rate and S/N is the ratio of the magnitude of the transmitted signal to the magnitude of spurious noise signals caused by imperfections in the network.

$$C = W \log_2 (1 + S/N) \tag{11.4}$$

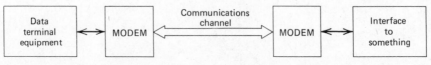

Figure 11.18. Data communications link.

	MODEM Type			
	103	202	201	203
Data rate on switched telephone network	≤ 300 bits/sec	≤ 1200	2000	3600, 4800
Private line data rate	≤ 300 bits/sec	≤ 1800	2400	4800, 7200, 9600; 10,800
Type of modulation	FSK	FSK	Phase modulation	Amplitude modulation
Synchronous/ asynchronous	Asyn-chronous	Asyn-chronous	Synchronous	Synchronous
Clocking	Clocked or unclocked	Clocked	Clocked	Clocked
Directional capability	Full duplex or half duplex	Half duplex	Half duplex	Half duplex

Fig. 11.19 Western Electric Voice Channel Specifications

A value of $S/N = 1000$ is considered very satisfactory. For this signal-to-noise ratio the upper limit of the data rate that can be transmitted on a voice-grade telephone channel would be given by Eq. 11.5.

$$C = 3200 \log_2 (1000) = 32,000 \text{ bits/sec} \qquad (11.5)$$

Due to limitations in all existing modulation schemes and to imperfections within the switched telephone network, data rates that can be handled by available MODEM's all fall considerably short of the limit obtained above. A list of MODEM's available from the telephone company with their respective characteristics is given in Fig. 11.19.

The term *full-duplex* listed under the MODEM 103 indicates that this device is capable of transmitting data and receiving data simultaneously from the communications channel. The term *half-duplex* listed for the other MODEM's indicates that transmission may be accomplished in either direction but in only one direction at a time. A period of time is required to reverse the direction of transmission in a half-duplex system. Depending on the nature of the telephone circuit established, this time

443

can vary from several milliseconds to as much as 10 sec. It is interesting to note that simultaneous bidirectional transmission is available on a two-wire pair only at the slowest data rate.

The reader may be aware that most long distance telephone transmission is accomplished via microwave links. Using three levels of frequency multiplexing, as many as 1800 voice channels are superimposed on a single microwave radio beam. The bandwidth of this carrier channel must be 4kHz × 1800 = 7.2 MHz. It is possible to transmit data at higher rates by entering the multiplexing process above the voice channel level. For example, the bandwidth of 60 voice channels or 240 kHz could be used as a single data transmission channel. This approach requires special equipment for local transmission from the user's site to a telephone central office. Few readers will be involved in larger bandwidth/higher data rate transmission at the hardware level; for this reason it will not be treated further. The interested reader is referred to Reference [1].

We are now ready to turn our attention to the design of a data terminal to function in conjunction with an asynchronous MODEM such as the Western Electric 103 and to the interfacing of other digital devices to a MODEM. The EIA Standard RS 232 specifies all lines interconnecting a data terminal equipment (DTE) and a MODEM or DCE for serial data transmission. This specification also describes in detail the function of each line. There are a total of 21 standard lines that can interconnect the two devices. Not every line will be used in every interface. The subset of these lines with which we shall concern ourselves is shown in Fig. 11.20. Each line is named and is assigned a two-letter symbol for use in AHPL. The letters bear no relation to the names but are consistent with the RS-232 identifiers. The first letter of the identifiers for the two data lines is b; the first letter of each control line identifier is c; and each clock line identifier begins with d.

The same lines in Fig. 11.20 are used whether the DTE and DCE are to be used full-duplex or half-duplex. The function of a line may differ slightly for the two cases, however.

Lines ba and bb must be held at logical 1 (mark) when inactive. If the operation is full-duplex, both lines may be active simultaneously. Otherwise only one may be active. When the DTE wishes to transmit data, a 1 level is placed on line ca. The DCE will respond with a 1 on "clear to send" if the channel is available. Line ca should never be raised if line cb is already high, indicating that a previous transmission is not yet complete. Lines cc and cd continually indicate whether the DTE and DCE are turned on and functioning. Whenever the DCE is receiving a character from the channel, a 1 level is placed on line cf to alert the DTE to monitor the "received data" line.

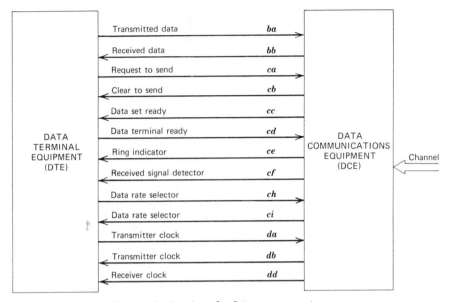

Figure 11.20. Standard interconnections.

If two MODEM's are to be connected through the switched telephone network, a channel must be established using a dialing procedure. Dialing may be a feature of the MODEM or may be accomplished by an auxiliary telephone. During the dialing process the MODEM appears not ready to the initiating terminal. Whenever a ring frequency is detected by the receiving MODEM, this fact is passed on to its DTE by a 1 on line ce. If the receiving DTE is not ready ($cd = 0$), its MODEM will appear as busy. If the DTE is ready to respond, it will issue a "request to send" and transmit a mark for a period of time followed by a message of greeting.

A logical 1 on line cf indicates that the MODEM is currently receiving information from the communications channel. Some MODEM's are designed to function at more than one data rate. Lines ch and ci are provided so that a single switch can be designed into either the DTE or DCE to select one of two data rates. If information transmission is to be carried out in the clocked mode, the clock signal is always generated at the transmitting end. As indicated by the presence of two lines da and db, the transmitter clock may be located in either the DTE or DCE. The synchronizing signal is transmitted on the communications channel and detected at the receiving end by various methods that will not be discussed here [1, 7]. The received clock signal is passed on to the DTE on line dd.

445

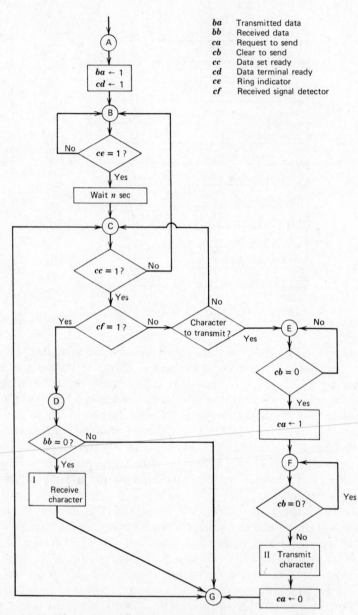

Figure 11.21. Flow chart of noninitiating, serial, asynchronous data terminal.

The flow chart of Fig. 11.21 describes the function of a noninitiating, serial, asynchronous data terminal as it relates to a compatible MODEM in a half-duplex communications system. This flow chart has been carefully worked out to conform to the RS 232 functional description of the seven lines listed in the figure. Details of these functional descriptions are most easily understood by references to this flow chart. From the reset state the terminal sets flip-flops to indicate "data terminal ready" and to establish a mark on line ba. It then waits for a ring indicator. When a ring is received, the terminal waits a period of time for the circuit to be established and then goes to point C in readiness to transmit or receive data. Usually, the first activity will be to transmit an acknowledgment. A terminal that can initiate communications will differ from Fig. 11.21 only in that point C can be reached without receiving a ring indication. The dialing function is incorporated in the MODEM and would not be reflected in the flow chart.

Point C is the point of convergence following either transmission or reception of a data character. For this reason a check at this point is made to ascertain that the data set ready signal remains 1. Next, line cf is checked to determine if data are being received by the MODEM. If so, the control moves to point D to check for a start bit and then circulates in a loop until a start bit is found or the received signal indicator goes off.

If $cf = 0$, a local check is made to determine if the terminal or device interfaced to the terminal desires to transmit a character. If a character is ready for transmission and $cb = 0$, flip-flop ca is set to 1 to signal a "request to send," to the MODEM. After a delay to switch to transmit mode, the modem will raise cb to 1 and start transmitting whatever appears on line ba. After transmitting the character, the DTE drops ca and returns to point C. If the data terminal at the other end of the communications link operates in the same manner, it is possible for both terminals to start transmitting at the same time, resulting in loss of data. To prevent this, half-duplex systems should employ some system of message protocol by means of which terminals exchange permission to transmit. The nature of the transmit and receive blocks will depend on the particular situation. One possibility will be illustrated by the following example.

Example 11.3

Design an interface for the simple printer of Example 9.3 so that it will serve as a receiving terminal for a 10-character/sec, asynchronous unclocked communications channel. It will be recalled that the printer has a vector of 8 input data lines **CHAR** [8]. It has only two control inputs *print* and *feed*. The only control output is labeled *wait*. Following a *print* level, *wait* will be 1 for 0.09 sec; following a *feed* level, *wait* will be 1 for 0.18 sec.

It may be assumed that each line of received characters will be followed by a carriage-return character and then a line-feed character. This is standard practice where the output terminals are teletypewriters.

Solution

The printer will be a receiving terminal only and will have no opportunity to communicate the signal on line *wait* back along the communications channel. The interface must, therefore, provide for receiving a continuous stream of characters at a rate of 10 characters/sec while ignoring line *wait*. Since the printing of a character requires 0.09 sec., some provision must be made for a one-character buffer register, i.e., for receiving the next character while the preceding character is printed. For this purpose we use the registers *DATA* [8] and *CHAR* [8]. The bits from *bb* are initially shifted into *DATA* and then transferred to *CHAR*, after which *DATA* is reloaded.

Notice that the carriage-return/line-feed operation initiated by a one-period level on the line, *feed*, requires almost 0.2 sec. This operation, which will be initiated by a carriage-return character in *CHAR*, will not be completed in time to allow the following character to be printed. Fortunately, this following character will always be a line feed that may be safely ignored, since a line feed has already been initiated. A special flip-flop *pass* will be included which can be set to 1 to cause the next character following a carriage return to be ignored.

The "receive character" block of Fig. 11.21 has been expanded, and the portion of this flow chart associated with transmitting has been deleted in forming the printer terminal flow chart of Fig. 11.22. The delay following the detected ring has been eliminated so that the printer begins to look for received characters immediately. Two one-shots, one of 9.09 msec or 1-bit duration and one of 4.55 msec or ½–bit duration, are included to cause line *bb* to be sampled at the midpoint of each bit. Notice that the total delay is 9.09 msec + 4.55 msec between the onset of the start bit and the midpoint of the first data bit. A 3-bit counter to count inputs bits is also required. In light of Fig. 11.22 the following AHPL sequence is self-explanatory.

> MODULE: PRINTER TERMINAL
>   INPUTS: *bb, cc, ce, cf*
>   MEMORY: *CHAR* [8]; *DATA* [8]; *CNT* [3]; *pass; cd*
>   OUTPUTS: *CHAR* [8]; *feed; print; cd.*
>   ONE-SHOTS: *period* (9.09 msec); *half* (4.55 msec)
> **1.** $cd \leftarrow 1$; *pass* $\leftarrow 0$
> **2.** $\rightarrow (\overline{ce}) / (2)$

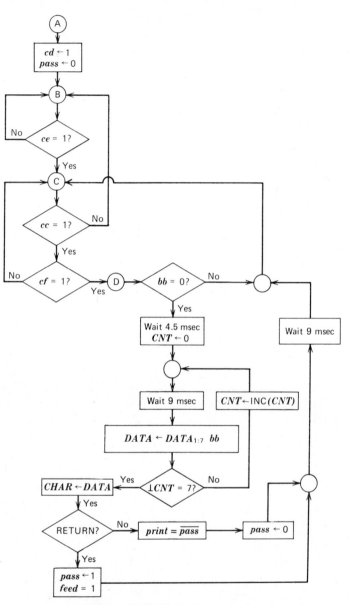

Figure 11.22. Printer terminal.

3. $half * (cc \land cf \land \overline{bb}) \leftarrow 1$
   $\rightarrow (\overline{cc}, (cc \land (\overline{cf} \lor bb)), (cc \land (\overline{\overline{cf} \lor bb})))/(2, 3, 4)$
4. $CNT \leftarrow 0, 0, 0$
   $\rightarrow (half)/(4)$
5. $period \leftarrow 1$
6. $\rightarrow (period)/(6)$
7. $DATA \leftarrow DATA_{1:7}, bb$
   $\rightarrow (\land CNT)/(9)$
8. $CNT \leftarrow \text{INC}(CNT); \rightarrow (5)$
9. $CHAR \leftarrow DATA$
   $\rightarrow (\text{RETURN } (DATA))/(11)$
10. $print = \overline{pass}; pass \leftarrow 0$
    $\rightarrow (12)$
11. $feed = 1; pass \leftarrow 1$
12. $period \leftarrow 1$
13. $\rightarrow (\overline{period}, period)/(3, 13)$
    END SEQUENCE
    CONTROL RESET (1)
    END

11.9   SIC AS A DATA TERMINAL

We are now ready to consider the design of a more complicated data terminal with the capability of both sending and receiving information. The reader should now be ready to approach the design of a teletype replacement CRT terminal such as might be used in a computer time-sharing application. Such a design, although straightforward, would be somewhat lengthy for our purposes here. An equally-interesting situation lies at the other end of the communications channel from the user terminal. If a computer is to be connected to a communications terminal, a DTE must be designed to interface with its input/output buses as illustrated in Fig. 11.23. We shall now consider the design of such a DTE for SIC.

The SIC communications interface is to be designed to operate exclusively in the serial asynchronous, clocked, 30 characters/sec mode. Therefore, each character will consist of 10 bits, only the last of which is a stop bit. The transmit clock is to be generated by the data terminal on line *da*. The system is to operate half duplex. Each DTE will be connected to only one MODEM so that a separate DTE would be required for each phone line connected to the computer. A special DTE/DCE capable of simultaneous connection to a large number of lines would be used in a typical time-sharing system. Such a system would certainly be designed around a CPU with much more capability

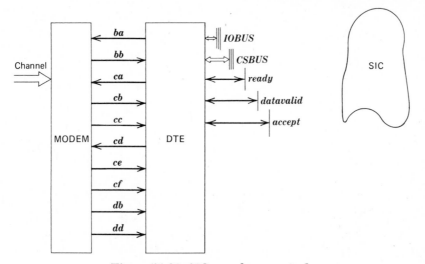

Figure 11.23. SIC as a data terminal.

than SIC. As with time-sharing, we shall assume that the channel will not be established by SIC and that SIC will always respond to a ring with an initial transmission.

Only one 8-bit character will be accepted from SIC during each OD command. These 8 bits will be $\textbf{IOBUS}_{10:17}$. The terminal will be designed under the assumption that SIC is in control of communications. That is, the device at the other end of the communications channel will transmit only when told by SIC that it may do so. Therefore, the terminal need not check for a received signal once an output data command has been received.

The SIC data terminal must be designed consistent with both Fig. 11.3, the flow chart for simplified SIC peripherals, and Fig. 11.21, the flow chart for asynchronous data terminals. A combined flow chart is given in Fig. 11.24. Once out of the reset state, the DTE module will consist of two independent parallel sequences. The DTE could be expressed as two separate modules, although this would result in an unnatural division of hardware and would require extra declarations, and extra lines of AHPL to specify intermodule communications. The parallelism is necessary, since the terminal must simultaneously watch for a possible IS or OD command as well as a received data signal. The terminal itself will be unaware whether or not the remote station has been granted permission to transmit. Therefore, it cannot know whether to expect an OUTPUT DATA command or a received data signal. The hypothetical

451

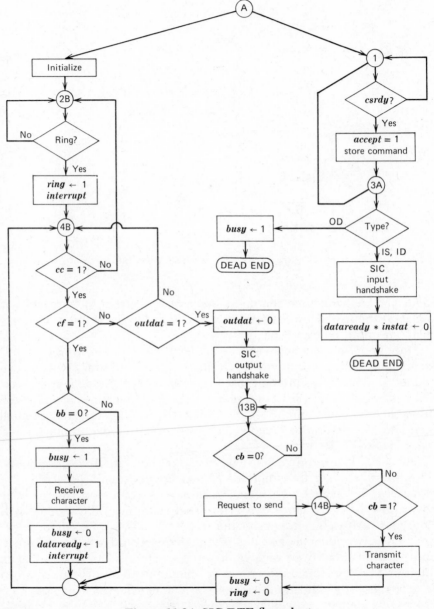

Figure 11.24. SIC DTE flow chart.

case in which SIC and the remote station attempt to transmit simultaneously will not happen and is a "don't care" condition.

The right portion of the flow chart beginning at step 1 responds to SIC commands. Two flip-flops are provided to store the command received. The flip-flop *outdat* will be set to 1 whenever the command is OD. The flip-flop *instat* will distinguish between IS and ID as in previous sections. The storage of the command is especially important in this case because the entire output data operation will be accomplished by the leftmost sequence.

On the left there are two points that specify sending an interrupt to SIC. First, SIC is interrupted following a ring signal. The detection of a ring will also cause the flip-flop *ring* to be set to 1. This will be a status bit observable by the SIC interrupt routine. Thus SIC will be able to distinguish a ring from an interrupt generated following the receipt of a character from the MODEM. In the latter case the status flip-flop *dataready* is set at the time of the interrupt.

The SIC computer must complete its response to the interrupt requesting an ID command within a period of 3.3 msec (1 stop bit). Should SIC fail to do so, the terminal may begin to replace the character waiting in its only data register, *CHAR*, with the next character from the channel. For a computer 3.3 msec is ample time so that no buffer register is included.

If an OD command has been stored and no receive signal is present, control branches to the SIC output handshake. Once a "clear to send" is observed, the data character is passed on to the MODEM. The status flip-flop *busy* remains one during this operation to prevent a subsequent OD command. Thus the terminal forces SIC to transmit at the prescribed data rate.

The following is an AHPL description of the SIC terminal. The elements declared are familiar SIC input-output variables or DTE variables except for *time*. We assume that *time* is a periodic square wave of 30 Hz. We assume also that this line is the output of another module consisting of a basic clock of some multiple of 30 Hz and a counter.* The SIC DTE will be synchronized to the SIC clock. The line *time* will not be synchronized to this clock and a synchronizer will be required. Since the SIC clock is much higher frequency than *time*, the variation of the duration of the on and off intervals of SYN(*time*) will be negligible.

---

*The counting function cannot be included in the DTE module, since this would require defining more than one clock and specifying which applies at each step. This feature has not been included in the version of AHPL presented herein.

MODULE: SIC TERMINAL
  INPUTS: *bb; cb; cc; ce; cf; dd; db*
  MEMORY: *CHAR* [8]; *ring, busy; dataready; outdat;*
                instat; ba; ca; cd; CNT [3]
  OUTPUTS: *ba; ca; cd; INTLINE$_6$*
  COMBUSES: *IOBUS* [18]; *CSBUS* [12]; *ready; datavalid; accept*

1. $ba \leftarrow 1; cd \leftarrow 1$
      $\rightarrow \overline{(2A, 2B)}$

2A. $\rightarrow \overline{(csrdy \wedge CSBUS_0 \wedge CSBUS_1 \wedge CSBUS_2)}/(2A)$

3A. *accept* $= 1$; *instat* $\leftarrow \overline{CSBUS}_4$; *outdat* $\leftarrow \overline{CSBUS}_4 \wedge \overline{CSBUS}_5$
      $\rightarrow (1, \overline{CSBUS}_5, CSBUS_5)/(2A, 4A, 6A)$

4A. *busy* $\leftarrow 1$

5A. DEAD END

6A. $\rightarrow \overline{ready}/(6A)$

7A. $IOBUS_{10:17} = CHAR$; *datavalid* $= 1$
      $CSBUS_{0:4} = cc$; *busy*, 0, *ring, dataready*
      $\rightarrow \overline{accept}/(7A.)$

8A. *dataready* $* \overline{instat} \leftarrow 0$

9A. DEAD END

Steps 2A through 9A specify the control sequence that interacts with SIC. The DTE is device 6. Steps 6A through 8A place information on the *CSBUS* and *IOBUS* in response to an ID or IS command. The 5 status bits are consistent with other SIC peripherals. The line *cc* indicates the "channel on" condition. Parity is not checked by the terminal, so a 0 is connected in place of a parity error flip-flop. The last 2 status bits have special meanings, as indicated.

Step 1 initializes the system and 2B checks for a ring. When one is encountered, a two-period interrupt level is sent to SIC. Step 4B checks for a received signal or an indication in *outdat* that an OD command has been received. Step 5B checks for a stop bit. Steps 7B, 8B, and 9B effect a sampling of each data level on line *bb* at the point of a zero going transition on line *dd*. Each successive information bit is shifted into **CHAR** at step 9B. Once a character has been received, an interrupt is generated; and **busy** is cleared.

Steps 11B through 20B receive a character from SIC and shift it out serially on line *ba*. Most of the steps are included to ascertain that the midpoint of a data bit coincides with a 1 to 0 transition of SYN (*time*). This timing signal is connected as an output on line *da*. In particular a start bit is generated at the time that control exits step 14. This bit (ba = 0) continues for one full period of (*time*) until the first time control exits step 16. The 8 data bits are placed on the line by steps 15 and 16 while a stop bit is generated by steps 17 and 18. Once a "request to send" is removed, control waits at step 19B until "clear to send" is also 0. Only then is the flip-flop busy cleared.

2B. $INTLINE_6 = ce$
    $\rightarrow (\overline{ce})/(2B)$

3B. $ring \leftarrow 1; INTLINE_6 = 1$

4B. $\rightarrow (\overline{cc}, cc \wedge cf, cc \wedge \overline{cf} \wedge outdat, cc \wedge \overline{cf} \wedge \overline{outdat})/(2B, 5B, 11B, 4B)$

5B. $busy * \overline{bb} \leftarrow 1$
    $\dashrightarrow (\overline{dd \wedge \overline{bb}})/(4B)$

6B. $CNT \leftarrow 0, 0, 0$
    $\rightarrow (\overline{dd})/(6B)$

7B. $\rightarrow (\overline{\overline{dd}})/(7B)$

8B. $\rightarrow (dd)/(8B)$

9B. $CHAR \leftarrow CHAR_{1:7}, bb; INTLINE_6 = \wedge /CNT$
    $CNT \leftarrow INC\ (CNT)$
    $\rightarrow (\overline{\wedge/CNT})/(7B)$

10B. $busy \leftarrow 0; dataready \leftarrow 1; INTLINE_6 = 1; \rightarrow (4B)$

11B. $outdat \leftarrow 0; ready = 1$
    $\rightarrow (\overline{datavalid})/(11B)$

12B. $CHAR = IOBUS_{10:17}; accept = 1$

13B. $\rightarrow (cb)/(13B)$

14B. $ca \leftarrow 1; \rightarrow (\overline{cb \wedge \overline{db}})/(14B)$

15B. $ba * db \leftarrow 0; CNT \leftarrow 0, 0$
    $\rightarrow (\overline{\overline{db}})/(15B)$

16B. $\rightarrow (db)/(16B)$

17B. $CNT * db \leftarrow INC(CNT)$
    $ba, CHAR_{0:6} * db \leftarrow CHAR$
    $\rightarrow (\overline{db}, db \wedge (\overline{\wedge/CNT}))/(17B, 16B)$

18B. $\rightarrow (db)/(18B)$

19B. $ba * db \leftarrow 1$
    $\rightarrow (\overline{db})/(19B)$

20B. $\rightarrow (db)/(20B)$

21B. $busy \leftarrow 0; ring \leftarrow 0$
    $\rightarrow (4B)$

END

Much of the hardware associated with the above control sequence is associated with converting parallel 8-bit vectors to and from serial 10-bit characters; LSI components are available for accomplishing this task. Although most such devices require a clock input that is some multiple of the desired bit frequency, they can be utilized to reduce the overall parts count in an interface.

455

PROBLEMS

11.1 Revise the interface for the printer in Example 9.4 so that it can receive buffered as well as program-controlled output. The interface is to be consistent with the flow charts of Fig. 11.1 and 11.2 and the *CSBUS* bit designations as given in Chapter 10.

11.2 Suppose that SIC did not inform its peripherals that it had completed a buffer operation until a *bchrdy* = 1 signal is received indicating that the peripheral device is ready to receive another character. Modify the flow charts of Figs. 11.2a and 11.2b to conform to this situation. Could the input and output flow charts be combined? If so, would this result in more economical realizations? What problems would be caused for particular peripherals?

11.3 A digital magnetic tape cassette unit is to be interfaced to SIC. A digital cassette unit is simpler and slower than an ordinary tape transport. As with a paper tape reader or punch the characters are treated individually rather than in blocks. Each time the cassette receives a one-period level on an input line labeled *read*, it reads one 7-bit character from tape and makes it available on seven-level output lines designated by the vector Z. Similarly, a one-period level on line *write* will cause the cassette unit to enter the values present on seven input lines designated by the vector X as a 7-bit character on tape. The maximum frequency of reading or writing is 500 characters/sec. Therefore, a period of 2 msec must be allowed between successive *read* or *write* levels. An output line labeled *cassetteready* from the cassette unit is provided to prevent too-frequent requests. If the unit is presently engaged in a read, write or rewind operation, *cassetteready* = 0. Once such an operation has been completed, *cassetteready* will be 1 until another *read* or *write* pulse is received.

    If the characters on tape are visualized as a numbered string, the unit, when *cassetteready* = 1, may be considered as resting between character $i - 1$ and character i. Either of these characters can be read or overwritten by the next *read* or *write* pulse. An input line to the cassette unit labeled *reverse* is provided to distinguish between these two cases. If *reverse* = 1 when a pulse arrives, character $i - 1$ is read or overwritten and the unit ends up between characters $i - 2$ and $i - 1$. If *reverse* = 0, character i is read or overwritten and the unit advances one character. The remaining input line to the cassette is labeled *rewind.* A pulse on this line will cause the tape to be rewound. After *cassetteready* returns to 1, the unit will be resting before the first character on tape. When in this state the unit will not respond to a reverse read or write.

A digital system is to be designed that will interface the cassette unit to SIC to operate in the *program-controlled* mode only (Fig. 11.3). It will not be connected to a buffer channel. The cassette unit will be considered as device 4 in SIC and will be required to respond to only those four SIC instructions tabulated.

Type	Octal	Function
OC4	754601	Rewind
OD4	754000	Output one 18-bit word
ID4	754100	Input one 18-bit word
IS4	754300	Input status

An 18-bit SIC word is to be stored as three successive characters on a cassette tape. Both the input and output commands assume that the tape will be advanced three characters in the forward direction. Only 4 bits will be included in the cassette device status register, SR, which will be connected to $CSBUS_{0:3}$. Bit $SR_0 = 1$, when power is on. Bit SR_1 will be 1, when the cassette is busy. Bit SR_2 will be 1 if a parity error has been detected in the currently available word. Bit SR_3 will be 1 if the tape has just been rewound.

The interface unit must include an 18-bit register DR in which 18-bit words are assembled and disassembled. The next 18-bit word must be ready in DR before SR_1 is set to 0 to avoid holding up SIC. Similarly, SIC must not be held up while a word is being written on tape.

The seventh bit of each character is used as a parity bit. The interface must generate this bit to form even parity over each character written on tape. The interface must check parity as each character is read from tape.

List and identify the purpose of all registers and individual memory elements needed in the interface unit. Write a complete module description in AHPL for the interface unit. The cassette interface will be assumed to operate using the SIC clock.

11.4 Suppose the line *cassetteready* will remain 0 when the cassette described in Problem 11.3 has reached the end-of-tape condition. Add a fifth status bit SR_4 to convey this information to SIC. Revise the module description of Problem 11.3, so that SR_4 can be set to 1 whenever an end-of-tape is reached. Provide for sending an interrupt signal to SIC whenever this happens.

11.5   Modify the module description of Problem 11.3 so that the cassette interface can respond to an activate buffer command and data can be delivered to, and received from, SIC on a buffer channel.

11.6   Design an interface for a card reader, to interact with the buffer sequence of SIC, as characterized by Figs. 11.1 and 11.2. The reader has two inputs, *feed*, which causes a card to move from the supply hopper to the read position, and *advance*, which moves the card under the read head, from one column to the next. After 80 *advance* pulses, the card will automatically move to the output hopper. You may assume that a one-clock-period logical 1 on either line will activate *feed* or *advance*. The output, in 12-bit Hollerith code, will appear on lines *CHAR* [12]. A line *read* will go to logical 1 when a column is in position under the read head and the data on *CHAR* is valid; *read* also indicates that the *advance* signal can be sent at any time. A logical 1 on line *empty* indicates that there are no cards in the supply hopper.
   You may assume the availability of a logic circuit CODE, which converts the 12-bit Hollerith code to 8-bit ASCII code. As a card is read, the entire card image is to be stored in an 18-bit, 40-word buffer memory, two characters to a word, the first character in positions 10 to 17, the second in positions 1 to 8. The buffer memory satisfies the model of the clocked RAM described in Chapter 7 and reads or writes in one clock period. Input or output is over lines *BUFMEM* [18], and the address lines are *BUFADD* [6]. Note that these are logic lines; there is no address register or data register intrinsic to the memory. When an entire card image of 80 characters has been stored, the interface should then interact with the buffer sequence to transmit the 40 words to memory. This process should be repeated until the CPU signals the end of the buffer or until there are no more cards to read.
   The card reader will be device 3. The operation will be initiated by an activate buffer command, which will cause the reader to read the first character. The only other command this device will respond to is an input status request. There are two error conditions that will cause the reader to stop and send an interrupt over *INTLINE*$_3$. If it runs out of cards it should set *CSR*$_1$ and interrupt. If the CPU ends the buffer with only part of a card image transmitted or while a card is being read, the reader should set *CSR*$_2$, and interrupt. Write in AHPL a complete module description of the card-reader interface.

11.7   Rewrite the module description of the paper tape reader interface of Example 11.1 so that it can transfer information to SIC in response to an activate buffer command.

11.8 Rewrite the module description for the card reader of problem 11.6 so that it will respond to program controlled ID and OD commands so that the buffer channel can be omitted. Data handling should remain the same in all other respects. Your design should be consistent with the simplified SIC interface flow chart of Fig. 11.3.

11.9 The control and data connections to a simplified 360 RPM magnetic disk recording system are shown in Fig. P.11.9a. The data is formated internally so that 8-bit bytes may be received at the data input and will appear at the data output. The system consists of 4 disks with 64 tracks/disk. When a pulse of at least 0.1 μsec (one-period level) appears on line *seek*, the disk system will select a disk and orient the corresponding read/write head on a track as specified by an 8-bit address. This address will be assumed to be present on the eight data input lines at the time of the *seek* pulse. Each track is formatted so that each actual data record is preceded by several bytes of record identifying information. Thus the search for a particular record within a track may be accomplished by software. Data bytes and identifier bytes are all accepted and supplied indiscriminantly by the disk

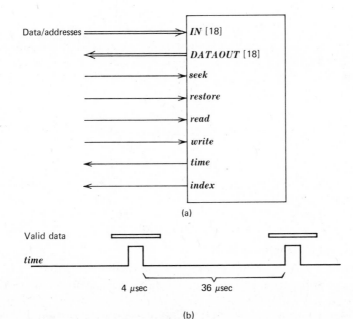

(a)

(b)

Figure P.11.9.

system. A pulse on line *restore* will reorient each read/write head
to a position at the center of the corresponding disk. The seek
and restore operations will require between 10 and 320 msec
depending on the track in question.

When *read* = 1, 4 μsec timing pulses will appear on line *time* at 36
μsec intervals as shown in Fig 11.9b. A valid data byte is available as
DATOUT for a 10 μsec period around each 4 μsec *time* pulse. If write
= 1, a byte from vector *IN* will be accepted for recording on disk while
time = 1. Once during each revolution of the disks, the line *index* will
be logical 1 for 40 μsec. This marks the beginning of a track, and no
pulse will appear on *time* during (and in the case of read for 40 μsec
after) this interval.

Design a SIC I/O interface (device 3) for the above disk system. Assume that 8-bit data bytes are transferred on $IOBUS_{10:17}$. The interface
must respond to IS, OD, and ID commands. It must also respond
to the following special command, OUTPUT ADDRESS (753402) by
seeking a track specified by $IOBUS_{10:17}$. The restore function should be
automatic when the interface is inactive. Write a complete module description in AHPL for the disk interface.

11.10 Redesign the disk interface of Problem 11.9 so that input and
output may take place using the buffer channel.

11.11 Approximately how many *bits,* including identifier bytes, may
be recorded on each track of the disk system of Problem 11.9?
If the system were left unchanged except that the speed were
increased to 3600 RPM, would program-controlled data transfer
be adequate? Under what conditions?

11.12 Rewrite the AHPL module description of the tape transport controller of Section 11.5 so that both the input and the output of
data can be accomplished using program controlled transfers.
Assume that the transport will never be connected to a buffer
channel.

11.13 Suppose that the SIC interface to the graphics terminal of Section 11.6 is driven by the SIC clock but that the graphics terminal
is driven by a separate clock. Indicate the necessary modifications in the appropriate steps of the interface control sequence.

11.14 Suppose that a special communications channel of 32-kHz bandwidth is available through the telephone company. Assume that
the modulation scheme used will permit data transmission at rate
equal to 25 percent of the maximum predicted by Shannon's
equation for S/N = 1000. Suppose that an 8-bit parallel respon-

sive (three-line handshake) approach is also under consideration. Which approach will permit transmission at the highest data rate over short distances? Which approach will permit transmission at the highest data rate over very long distances? Assuming a delay of 6 μsec/km. on the responsive control lines, for what distance would the maximum data rate for the two transmission schemes be exactly the same?

11.15 Write in AHPL a complete module description for an interface between the display storage module of Section 11.5 and an RS 232 asynchronous, serial MODEM operating at 10 characters/sec. The communications channel will be connected to a computer for the purpose of storage and recall of a complete display. Each 17-bit vector to be transmitted to and from R will be formatted in three 8-bit characters as given in Fig. P.11.15. The register CMD will be connected locally to a keyboard and will not be part of the interface. If the character 00010011 is received, the interface terminal will immediately proceed to transmit the entire contents of the display store (one pair of words per refresh cycle). Otherwise each set of six characters received following the format of Fig. P.11.15 will be assumed to specify a beam position and a display command. These two 17-bit words will be entered in the store overwriting any entry currently stored at the corresponding beam position.

$$\boxed{0, 1, 0, R_{0:4}} \quad \boxed{1, 0, R_{5:10}} \quad \boxed{1, 1, R_{11:16}}$$

11.16 Revise the AHPL module description of the printer terminal in Example 11.3 so that it will function at 30 characters/sec with a received clock signal available on line dd. Eliminate as many one-shots as possible from the original design.

11.17 Repeat Problem 11.16 with the data-rate selector line, ci, implemented. If $ci = 0$, 11-bit characters will be received asynchronously up to 10 characters/sec. If $ci = 1$, 10-bit characters will be received at up to 30 characters/sec. The clock line dd is applicable in both cases.

11.18 Suppose the printer terminal of Example 11.3 is modified so that print takes 0.03 sec and feed 0.06 sec to permit operation at 30 characters/sec. Replace the one-shots *period* and *half* by a counter with an appropriate number of bits. Assume that the printer terminal is driven by a clock of frequency 307.2 kHz. Rewrite the AHPL module description accordingly. Now let the module just designed be driven by a 300 kHz clock. (Assume that the printer will work this fast.) How far from the midpoint of the last data bit will sampling take place? Will the module still work? What prevents the errors from becoming cumulative from character to character?

11.19 Revise the AHPL module description of the SIC terminal in Section 11.9 by replacing the one-shot *half* and the external timing module with an internal counter. Assume that the SIC clock frequency is exactly 1.23 MHz.

11.20 Consider the signal SYN(*time*) used in the SIC terminal module of Section 11.9. Suppose that the SIC clock is 1 MHz. What portion of the logical 1 half periods of SYN(*time*) will be exactly 1/60 sec in duration? What portion will be longer than 1/60 sec? How long? What portion will be shorter than 1/60 sec? How long?

11.21 Write control sequences for execution of the following two additional commands that could be included in the display processor of Section 11.5. Assume separate flip-flops for these commands similar to *go* and *erase*.
(a) Erase one line of characters.
(b) Erase the entire screen.

11.22 (For electrical engineers.) Design the line segment generator used in the display processor. Use gates, flip-flops, operational amplifiers, and FET analog switches. Your outputs should be the inputs of the vertical and horizontal deflection amplifiers and the beam emission control. Assume typical signal levels.)

REFERENCES

1. Abramson, N., and F. F. Kuo. *Computer Communications Networks*, Prentice Hall, Englewood Cliffs, N.J., 1973.

2. Eisenbies, J. L., "Conventions for Digital Data Communications Link Design," *IBM Syst. J.*, 6(4) (1967), 267–302.

3. Lohse, E. L., ed., Proposed USA Standard, Data Communications Control Procedures for the USA Standard Code for Information Interchange," *Commun. ACM*, 12(3) (1969), 166–178.

4. Publications of the ANSI Standards Committee on Data Processing, Technical Committee X353 on Data Communications, Business Manufacturers Association, New York.

5. Shannon, C. E., "The Mathematical Theory of Communication," *Bell System Technical Journal*, July and October 1948.

6. Holzman, L. N. and W. J. Lawless, "Data Set 203 A New High Speed Voiceband MODEM," *Computer*, Sept./Oct. 1970, pp. 24–30.

7. Davies, D. W. and D. L. A. Barber, *Communications Networks for Computers*, John Wiley & Sons, London, 1973.

8. Flores, I., *Peripheral Devices*, Prentice Hall, Englewood Cliffs, N.J., 1973.

9. *M6800 Applications Manual*, Motorola Semiconductor Products Inc., Phoenix, Ariz., 1975.

10. *Disk File Applications*, American Data Processing Inc., Detroit, Mich., 1964.

11. Sebestyen, L. L., *Digital Magnetic Tape Recording for Computer Applications*, Chapman and Hall, London, 1973.

12. Cluley, J. C., *Computer Interfacing and Online Operation*, Crane, Russak Inc., New York, 1975.

13. Watson, R. W., et al., "A Design of a Display Processor," *Proceedings AFIPS Fall Joint Computer Conference*, 1969, p. 209.

12

MICROPROCESSORS

12.1 INTRODUCTION

Probably, no recent development in electronics has created as much interest and enthusiasm as the microprocessor. Many persons believe that the microprocessor is the most significant development in electronics since the integrated circuit. Very impressive if true, but just what is a microprocessor? And why are so many people so excited about the prospects of microprocessors?

A *microprocessor* is basically a computer CPU on a single integrated circuit chip. Combine a microprocessor chip with a few other chips to provide memory and some I/O control and you have a *microcomputer*. Note that a microprocessor is no more a complete computer system than is any other "bare" CPU. It must be combined with memory and I/O before it can do anything useful.

The importance of microprocessors (or microcomputers) is not that they do anything basically different from what any full-sized computer does. They are important because their small size and low cost make the power of computers available for a vast new range of applications. In this connection it is important to recognize that there are two basic markets for computers. Medium and large computers are normally found in independent, "stand-alone" installations, such as in computer centers, in data processing for banks and insurance companies, etc. When most people think of computers, it is this sort of application they have in mind.

Minicomputers are often used in such "stand-alone" applications, but the majority of minicomputer sales are to the OEM (Original Equipment Manufacturers) market. That is, they are not sold directly to the ultimate user but are sold to a manufacturer who incorporates the computer as a

464

component of some larger system, which is in turn sold to the actual user. An example is a numerically controlled machine tool. The components of the system are the machine tool itself, the motors and actuators that drive it, the switches and relays that control the electric power, sensors to measure position and speed, and a minicomputer to control the whole system.

The range of OEM applications of minicomputers is surprisingly large but is limited by cost and size factors. A typical minicomputer costs from $1,000 to $10,000 and occupies 1 to 2 ft^3 of space. By contrast, a typical microcomputer costs less than $100 and requires only a few inches of space. This order-of-magnitude reduction in cost and size opens up an almost unlimited range of new OEM applications. Every cash register can incorporate a microcomputer that will not only replace the electromechanical innards of the conventional cash register but can also provide communications to a central computer for credit checks, accounting, and inventory control. A microcomputer can be installed in every car to control timing and carburetion to achieve optimum power and economy and emission control. Every TV set can include a microcomputer to provide electronic games.

The above examples are some of the more obvious ones, things that we always knew computers could do if we could just afford them. Perhaps even more important is the vast range of applications that are entirely new. As the cost of microprocessors continues to decrease, designers find ways to use them in applications in which nobody ever even considered using computers before.

The microprocessor also has a special kind of impact on the designer of electronics systems, in that it requires an approach to design from a very different point of view. Design is now not only a process of specifying components and designing logic but is also a process of programming a microprocessor to do as much as possible. As we shall see, microprocessors can be programmed to do all manner of things that no one ever thought of doing by computer. At this point in the book the reader is in a good position to make this transition in design philosophy. First, as noted earlier, microprocessors function in very much the same way as the conventional computers we have been studying. Second, and even more important, we have already adopted a programming point of view of design. When we set up flow charts and write an AHPL control sequence, we are writing a program for the internal functioning of the computer. With a microprocessor we shall write programs for what we want the microprocessor to do as an internal component of a larger system.

12.2 EVOLUTION OF THE MICROPROCESSOR

The microprocessor is a result of continued development of the techniques of Large Scale Integration (LSI). When the first LSI circuits were developed, it was obvious that LSI would have an important impact on reducing the component count in computers, but it is doubtful that even the most optimistic LSI proponents seriously believed that an entire CPU could be put on a single chip. However, when the single-chip pocket calculator emerged as a practical reality, it became evident that a single-chip CPU of some sort was just a matter of time, and the calculator chip was the logical starting point for the development of a CPU chip.

The conventional calculator is not a computer, but it does possess three of the five basic characteristics of a computer stated in Chapter 1. Obviously, it has a calculating section; it has input (keyboard); and it has output (a display). It lacks memory to store data and instructions, and the decision capability necessary to sequence through a stored program. The problem faced by the designers of the first microprocessors was how to modify the calculator chips to provide these additional features.

The decision and sequencing capability required that additional control logic be put on the chip. This was not too difficult a problem, particularly as advances in LSI technology made it possible to fit more and more logic on a chip. The memory posed a more difficult problem. It was possible to put a few memory registers on a calculator chip, but there was no way to fit enough memory on the calculator chip to provide any significant computing capability. Thus it was obvious that the memory would have to be on separate chips. Suitable LSI memory chips were readily available, but these chips had to be connected to the processor chip, raising the problem of pin-out limitations.

There are two basic limitations to the complexity of LSI devices. One is, of course, the amount of logic that can be crammed onto a chip. The second is the number of connections that can be made to the chip. Continuing advances in LSI technology have steadily increased the density of the circuits on the chips, but increasing the number of pins has been more difficult. Since connections are basically made by fastening wires to the chip, it is the chip size that limits the number of connections. For a variety of technical reasons, it has proved easier to increase circuit density than chip size, and the number of connections has generally been a more serious limitation than circuit density.

The designers were thus faced with the problem of providing connections between the processor chip and the memory chips without significantly increasing the number of pins on the processor chip. They did this by using the same lines for both I/O and memory. This is a logical approach since, from the standpoint of the processor, there is no basic difference between data and instructions transmitted to or from input/output devices, and data and instructions obtained from or stored in a memory. Thus "input/output" was generalized to include communications with any device not on the processor chips. This approach is not peculiar to microprocessors. The PDP/11 and similar minicomputers treat memory and I/O devices in the same way, as addressed locations. It is a subject of some debate as to whether this approach is desirable from the user's point of view, but it is almost a necessity in microprocessors because of pin-out limitations. A few microprocessors have separate lines for memory and I/O devices, but they are very much the exception to the rule.

Another problem associated with adding memory to a calculator was how to address it. In the full-size computers we have studied, there are separate lines for addresses and data, but the pin-out limitations in the early microprocessors made this approach impractical. As a result, most early microprocessors time-shared the same lines for addresses and data, sending out the addresses at one time, and transmitting the data at a later time. A final characteristic of the first microprocessors that reflects their calculator heritage is the 4-bit word size. Calculators are decimally oriented. Decimal characters are entered serially from the keyboard and they are processed serially, as decimal digits. The digits are represented internally by 4-bit binary codes so that internal registers and data paths are primarily 4 bits in length. Even though microprocessors generally do not work in decimal, the 4-bit word length was retained.

In summary then, the first microprocessors, while similar in many respects to full-size computers, had the following rather distinctive characteristics:

1. They were 4-bit machines.
2. They had a single communications bus for memory and I/O.
3. The single bus was time-shared for both addresses and data.

These microprocessors worked well for some applications, but it was quickly found that they had some serious limitations. The 4-bit word length meant that many more steps were required for any given task than with larger machines, and that they were very difficult to program. The instruction sets were very limited and many data words were required to accommodate data of any reasonable precision. To address any significant amount of memory, addresses had to be sent serially in groups of several 4-bit words. This in turn required external hardware to assemble the addresses and store them for the time required to read or write memory.

The first improvement introduced to correct these deficiencies was to increase the word size to 8 bits. Next, as soon as improvements in the technology made it possible to increase the number of pins, separate output lines were provided for addresses. Because even 8 bits is not enough to address a large memory, most microprocessors have larger address buses (12 to 16 bits) than data buses (8 bits). As we shall see in the next section, the problem of generating addresses longer than the basic word length has led to rather elaborate addressing techniques in microprocessors. As the technology has continued to develop, 12-bit and 16-bit microprocessors have appeared. But the 8-bit units remain the most popular.

12.3 ORGANIZATION OF A TYPICAL MICROPROCESSOR

In this section we shall consider the organization of a specific micro-processor in some detail. At the time of this writing, the most popular microprocessors (all 8-bit units) are the Intel 8080, the Fairchild F-8, and the Motorola M6800. To the extent that one believes in the selection process of the open market, one could then argue that these three units are in some sense the "best" microprocessors. These three units differ significantly in organization, and each has its own advantages and weak-nesses with respect to specific applications. We have chosen to study the M6800, not because it is better than the others in any particular way, but because its architecture is more like that of conventional minicom-puters than is the case with the other two units. It will thus be easier to explain its operation in terms of the background developed in preceding chapters.

The basic block diagram of the 6800 is shown in Fig. 12.1. Commu-nications between the processor chip and other units are provided by an 8-bit data bus, *DBUS*, and a 16-bit address bus, *ADBUS*, and 11 control/status lines. The data bus *DBUS* provides for transmission of data and instructions between the processor and memory or I/O devices, *ADBUS* is a one-way bus used to transmit 16-bit addresses from the processor to other devices, chiefly memory. Associated with the buses are two buffer registers, the data buffer register, *DBR*, and the address buffer register, *ADBR*.

Communications within the chip are via two buses, the 8-bit internal data bus, *IDBUS*, and the 16-bit internal address bus, *IABUS*. Accessible to the programmer are two 8-bit accumulators, *ACCA* and *ACCB*; the 8-

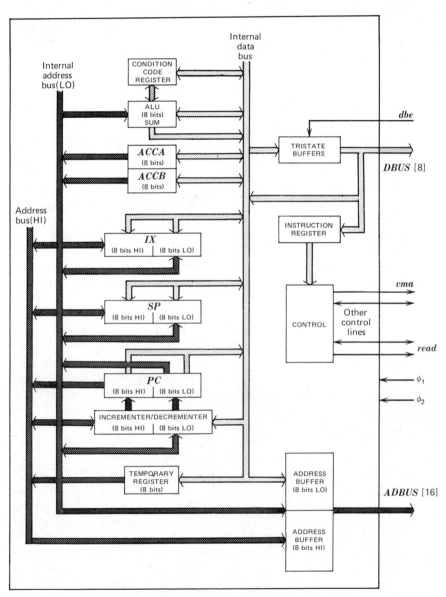

Figure 12.1. M6800 microprocessor block diagram.

bit condition code register, *CCR*; and three 16-bit registers, the stack pointer, *SP*, an index register, *IX*, and the program counter, *PC*. The temporary register, which stores an address byte during extended addressing, and the incrementer/decrementer, which functions in conjunction with the program counter, are not accessible to the programmer. Also inaccessible to the programmer are the 8-bit instruction register and two 8-bit address buffers.

Since there are both 16-bit registers and 8-bit registers, the reader may wonder why this is considered an 8-bit microprocessor. The reason is that all data are transmitted to and from other devices via the 8-bit *DBUS*, and all processing of data is done by the 8-bit accumulators and the 8-bit ALU. The 16-bit buses and registers are used for the generation, storage, and transmission of addresses. When addresses must be processed, they can be transmitted in 8-bit segments over the *IDBUS* to the ALU, and data can be transmitted from the accumulators to the ALU via the low-order 8 bits of *IABUS*. There is, thus, some mixing of data and address functions, as there is in all computers, but this is clearly an 8-bit CPU with 16-bit addresses.

This configuration has many points in common with SIC. The instruction register, the program counter, and the index register serve precisely the same functions they did in SIC. There are two accumulators instead of one, but this is just a particular case of a multiregister configuration. There are two registers rather different in function than any we have seen before, *SP* and *CCR*. The stack pointer, *SP*, will be discussed later, in conjunction with a discussion of its operation. The condition code register, *CCR*, is affected by many instructions and will be considered now to facilitate discussion of the instruction set.

All branching in the 6800 is based on the condition code register. Recall that SIC features branching on the accumulator and link. Clearly, branching on the index registers would be useful in some applications, but the microcoding scheme used in SIC could not accommodate additional branches. In general, the more registers a machine has, the more difficult it is to provide separate branch commands for each register. An approach used in many full-sized machines, as well as most microprocessors is the use of *flags* that are set by each operation and can then be tested. For example, a *carry flag* will be set any time an arithmetic operation, in any register, results in an output carry. A *zero flag* is set any time an operation produces a zero result, in any register. In the 6800 there are six flags, which for notational convenience are considered to be the six low-order bits of the command code register, *CCR*. The two high-order bits are not used. It should be noted that the *CCR* register is not a register in the usual sense that the contents have some homog-

TABLE 12.1   Command Code Register Bits in M6800

CCR Bit[a]	Symbol[b]	Significance
CCR_2	h	Half-carry bit. Set if there is a carry out of bit 4 in arithmetic operations, cleared if no carry
CCR_3	i	Interrupt mask bit
CCR_4	n	Negative bit. Equal to the most significant bit (sign bit) of the result
CCR_5	z	Zero bit. Set if an operation produces a zero result, cleared otherwise.
CCR_6	v	Overflow bit. Set if an arithmetic operation results in an overflow, cleared if no overflow
CCR_7	c	Carry bit. Set if there is a carry out of bit-0 in arithmetic operations, cleared if no carry

[a]In the 6800 manual, bits are numbered in the opposite order to that used in this book, i.e., the least significant bit is denoted as bit-0. Thus what we call bit-0 in this table would be bit-7 in a 6800 manual.
[b]The listed symbols are lower case equivalents of the symbols used in the 6800 manual. This notation will sometimes be used in place of subscripted bits of CCR for clarity.

enous significance as a single unit of information. The six flag bits are set, cleared, and tested completely independently of one another. The treatment of these six flags as a part of a register has a parallel in the concept of a program status word, discussed in Chapter 10.

Although the 6 flag bits are considered as parts of the CCR register, they are also each denoted by a separate symbol as shown in Table 12.1. The interrupt mask bit (i) is not actually a flag bit and is used in a manner quite different from the other 5 bits, as will be discussed in the section on interrupt in the 6800. The n and z bits are set or cleared in accordance with the above table on the basis of the result of any operation that changes the contents of *ACCA, ACCB, IX,* or *SP*.

The c bit is set or cleared by add or subtract commands and is included in shift operations, as will be discussed later. The c bit is also used as an input in ADC and SBC instructions. This feature is included to facilitate multiple-word arithmetic. If a data vector cannot be accommodated by a single byte, it may be spread across any required number of bytes. When addition (or subtraction) is carried out, the least-signif-

471

icant bytes of the operands are added to form the least-significant byte of the sum and the carry into the next byte is saved in c. The next two bytes are then added together with the carry, and this process can be repeated with any number of bytes. The c bit thus performs essentially the same function as the link in SIC.

The h bit is affected only by addition operations. This bit is used to facilitate decimal operations, in which each byte contains two 4-bit BCD digits. The v bit is primarily affected by add and subtract commands. It also has special meaning for some other commands, for details of which the reader should consult the 6800 manual.

In addition to being set or cleared as the result of various register operations as discussed above, the *CCR* can be set by commands that test, but do not change, the contents of various registers. These commands, TST, CMP, and BIT, will be discussed later. Finally, the c, v, and i bits can be individually set or cleared by separate instructions.

Instructions in the 6800 may consist of 1, 2, or 3 bytes.* The first byte is always the op code, including address mode control bits. The second and third bytes, if present, may be data (immediate addressing) or may be an address. Since the op codes are 8 bits, it is customary to represent them as two hex digits, e.g., 0100 1101 = 4D. In the 6800 the first digit of the op code, i.e., the first 4 bits, indicates the basic type of instruction. For purposes of discussion it is convenient to classify the instruction into eight categories, as indicated by the first digit of the op code (Table 12.2). As was the case with the ISZ command in SIC, there are some instructions that do not fit neatly into any category. For example, in terms of the above classification, the jump instructions are grouped with the memory and register-and-memory operations, because they use the same forms of addressing, even though they do not access memory.

Let us further consider these instruction classes with reference to the discussion of instruction and address types of Chapter 6. Referring to the types of Table 12.2 by the first digit of their op codes, we see that types 0, 1, 4, and 5 are *implied address* instructions. The location of the operand to be processed is implied by the op code, e.g., COMA, complement *ACCA*. No reference is made to memory to fetch or store an operand. Instructions of this type correspond to the operate instructions in SIC and may also be referred to as register instructions. These are all 1-byte instructions.

The branch instructions (Type 2) are comparable to the jump instruction in SIC, in that they are addressed instructions but make no refer-

---

*In discussing the 6800, we shall use the terms *byte* and *word* interchangeably, since an 8-bit word is a byte.

TABLE 12.2   Op Code Classification of M6800 Instructions

First Digit of Op Code	Type of Instruction	Number of Bytes
0	*CCR* operations	1
1	Accumulator-to-accumulator	1
2	Branch	2
3	Stack and Interrupt	1
4	*ACCA* operations	1
5	*ACCB* operations	1
6, 7	Memory operations	2 or 3
8-F	Register-and-memory operations	2 or 3

ence to memory. These are 2-byte instructions, employing a special form of relative addressing. The second byte is interpreted as a two's complement number and is added to the program counter plus 2. This allows branching over a range of -125 to $+129$ bytes from the current instruction.

Types 6 to F are the memory reference instructions, which access memory to obtain or store an operand. Types 8 to F are similar to the memory reference instructions in SIC, involving a memory location and one of the addressable registers, i.e., *ACCA*, *ACCB*, *IX*, or *SP*. Types 6 and 7 are memory-to-memory instructions, in which an operand is obtained from memory, processed in some manner—shifted, complemented, etc.—and then returned to the same memory location, without changing the contents of any of the addressable registers.

For the register-and-memory instructions (Types 8 to F) there are four types of addressing, specified by the last 2 bits of the first digit of the op code, as shown in Table 12.3. Immediate addressing provides the operand itself in locations immediately following the op code. For instructions involving the accumulators, immediate addressing requires a 2-byte instruction, the first byte being the op code, the second byte being the 8-bit operand. For instructions involving *IX* or *SP*, immediate addressing requires a 3-byte instruction, the first byte being the op code, the next 2 bytes providing a 16-bit operand.

Direct and extended addressing are similar to direct addressing in SIC, in that the address is provided as a part of the instruction. The only difference is that the short word length makes it necessary to use multiword instructions. Direct addressing requires a 2-byte instruction, the

TABLE 12.3   Types of Addressing for Register-
                       and-Memory Instructions

First Digit of Op Code	$IR_2 \, IR_3$	Type of Addressing
8 or C	0 0	Immediate
9 or D	0 1	Direct
B or F	1 1	Extended
A or E	1 0	Indexed

first byte, as always, containing the op code, the second byte containing
an 8-bit address, which permits access to locations 0 to 255 in memory.
*Extended addressing, which requires a three-byte instruction, is the
normal mode. The second and third bytes provide a 16-bit address, thus
allowing access to a full 65K of memory.* Indexed addressing requires
a 2-byte instruction, with the 8-bit unsigned address in the second byte
being added to the index register to obtain a full 16-bit address. The
effective address is stored in a temporary register and the contents of
the index register are not changed. For the memory-to-memory instructions, only indexed (Type 6) and extended (Type 7) addressing are used.

The stack and interrupt instructions (Type 3) are one-byte instructions. Some use implied addressing and some access memory at an address obtained from the *SP* (stack pointer) register. In SIC the interrupt
instructions were considered a part of the I/O class of instructions. In
the 6800 there are no special I/O instructions. As discussed earlier, in
most microprocessors (including the 6800) memory and I/O devices are
addressed and communicated with in the same general manner so that
there is no need for a special class of I/O instructions.

It will likely seem to the reader that addressing in the 6800 is quite
complicated. Such addressing complexity is characteristic of microprocessors, and the 6800 is in fact simpler than most in this respect. Such
complexity comes about primarily as an attempt to compensate for short
word lengths. With 8-bit words it is obviously impossible to provide an
op code and any useful address in one word. The most obvious solution,
employed in direct and extended addressing in the 6800, is to use multiword instructions. But this approach exacts a speed penalty, since two
or three words must be fetched from memory for each such instruction.

Immediate addressing saves time, since the operands are fetched directly from memory without the intermediate step of obtaining addresses from memory. However, this technique is really only useful for

constants. Loading data into the body of a program is next to impossible, particularly in microcomputers, in which the programs are generally stored in ROM.

Indexed addressing conserves storage relative to extended addressing, since a full 16-bit address can be obtained with a 2-byte instruction. Depending on the type of program, some of this advantage will be lost by the need to include instructions to process the index register. It might be noted in passing that indexed addressing as found in the 6800 is more like base addressing in terms of the discussion in Chapter 6.

Perhaps the most common technique used to reduce addressing delays in microprocessors is *pointer addressing*. Basically, a pointer register is any CPU register that can be referred to to obtain an address. In that sense, the program counter could just as well be referred to as the program pointer. The 6800 has one pointer, the stack pointer, but most microprocessors provide more pointers. Indeed, some users feel that this is a weakness of the 6800, that it does not provide more pointers. Pointer addressing, particularly with regard to stacks, will be more fully discussed later.

As we have seen, the first digit of the op code specifies the basic type of instruction and the addressing mode. Within these groups, the second digit specifies the operation. We shall now consider the operations available in the various groups. For the two groups of accumulator instructions the second digit codes are the same, the only difference being that type 4 instructions process *ACCA* and type 5 instructions process *ACCB*. These instructions are summarized in Table 12.4. The codes not listed are not used. The "Cycles" column indicates the execution time and is included for future reference.

These operations are mostly self-explanatory. In the shift and rotate commands (ROR, LSR, ASR, ASL, ROL), c is the carry bit in the **CCR**. The c bit performs much the same function as the link in SIC. The command ASR is a special arithmetic shift that preserves the sign bit (bit-0) but shifts the rest of the word right. The test instructions (TSTA, TSTB) compare the contents of the specified accumulator to zero and set the n and z bits as shown. Although not shown in the table, n and z are similarly updated by any operation that alter the contents of the accumulators.

For instruction types 6 and 7, the operations and 2nd-digit codes are exactly the same as for types 4 and 5. The difference is that the operations are performed on operands obtained from memory, by extended or indexed addressing, and the results are returned to the same locations. The mnemonics are also the same, except that the A or B designating

475

TABLE 12.4   M6800 Accumulator Commands

2nd Digit of Op Code	Mnemonic Type		Cycles	Operation[a]
	4	5		
0	NEGA	NEGB	2	2's complement $ACCx$
3	COMA	COMB	2	Logical (1's) complement $ACCx$
4	LSRA	LSRB	2	$ACCx, c \leftarrow 0, ACCx$
6	RORA	RORB	2	$ACCx, c \leftarrow c, ACCx$
7	ASRA	ASRB	2	$ACCx, c \leftarrow ACCX_0, ACCX$
8	ASLA	ASLB	2	$c, ACCx \leftarrow ACCx, 0$
9	ROLA	ROLB	2	$c, ACCx \leftarrow ACCx, c$
A	DECA	DECB	2	Decrement $ACCx$
C	INCA	INCB	2	Increment $ACCX$
D	TSTA	TSTB	2	$n \leftarrow ACCx_0; z \leftarrow \overline{\vee/ACCx}$
F	CLRA	CLRB	2	Clear $ACCx$

[a] $ACCx = ACCA$ for Type 4, $ACCB$ for Type 5.

the accumulator is omitted, e.g., NEG, COM, INC, DEC. The execution times are six cycles for type 7 (extended) and seven cycles for type six (indexed).

For type 8-to-F, as with types 4 and 5, the second digit of the op code has a uniform meaning in specifying the operation to be performed. The first digit (type number) specifies the type of addressing and which register is to be used. Eleven of the 16 codes in this group specify accumulator-and-memory operations, as specified in Table 12.5. For types 8, 9, A, and B, the operations involve $ACCA$; for types C, D, E, and F, the operations involve $ACCB$. The mnemonics are as shown, except that A or B is added to the mnemonic according to which accumulator is being used. The type number also indicates the type of addressing, as shown in Table 12.3. The above codes are uniform for all four addressing types, except that the Store Accumulator (STAx) command is undefined for immediate addressing. The cycle times are dependent on the type of addressing. They are 2, 3, 4, and 5 cycles for immediate, direct, extended, and indexed, respectively, except for STAx, for which they are 4, 5, and 6 cycles for direct, extended, and indexed, respectively.

The command SUBx is a binary subtraction of the contents of the memory location from the accumulator contents; SBCx is the same except that the c bit of CCR is also subtracted. The commands CMPx and BITx, respectively, make arithmetic and logical comparisons of the con-

TABLE 12.5   M6800 Accumulator-and-Memory Commands.

Second Digit of Op Code	Mnemonic[a]	Operation[a,b]
0	SUBx	$ACCx \leftarrow SUB_{1:8}(ACCx; M^i)$
1	CMPx	$c, n \leftarrow SUB_{0:1}(ACCx; M^i); v \leftarrow Overflow$ $z \leftarrow \overline{\sqrt{/}SUB_{1:8}(ACCx; M^i)}$
2	SBCx	$ACCx \leftarrow SUBC(ACCx; M^i; c)$
4	ANDx	$ACCx \leftarrow ACCx \wedge M^i$
5	BITx	$n \leftarrow ACCx_0 \wedge M_0{}^i; z \leftarrow \overline{\sqrt{/}(ACCx \wedge M^i)}$
6	LDAx	$ACCx \leftarrow M^i$
7	STAx	$M^i \leftarrow ACCx$
8	EORx	$ACCx \leftarrow ACCx \oplus M^i$
9	ADCx	$ACCx \leftarrow ADD(ACCx; M^i; c)$
A	ORAx	$ACCX \leftarrow ACCx \vee M^i$
B	ADDx	$ACCx \leftarrow ADD(ACCx; M^i)$

[a] x stands for A for types 8, 9, A, and B;
x stands for B for types C, D, E, and F.
[b] M^i represents the addressed location in memory. SUB and SBC are binary subtract functions with 9 output bits.

tents of the memory location and the accumulator contents without affecting the register; CMPx executes a subtraction and updates c, n, v, and z as shown, while BITx executes a logical AND and updates only n and z, as shown in Table 12.5.

Second-digit op codes E and F are, respectively, load and store commands, for **SP** for types 8, 9, A, B, and for **IX** for types C, D, E, F, with the type of address determined as for others in these types. Code C designates Compare Index (CPX) for types 8, 9, A, and B. This compares the upper half of **IX** ($IX_{0:7}$) with the addressed location, and the lower half of **IX** with the location following the addressed location, and sets **CCR** accordingly. These and other special operations will be depicted later in Fig. 12.2.

There are five accumulator-to-accumulator (Type 1) commands, as listed in Table 12.6. All are 1-byte instructions requiring two cycles.

Type 0 commands are used for initialization and resetting of the condition code flip-flops. The operations CLC (0C), SEC (0D), CLV (0A), SEV (0B), CLI (0E), and SEI (0F) clear or set flip-flops c, v, and i, respectively. Op code 02 is NOP (no operation).

The type-2 commands are the branch commands. There are 15 branch

TABLE 12.6   Accumulator-to-Accumulator Instructions, M6800

Op Code	Mnemonic	Cycles	Operation
10	SBA	2	$ACCA \leftarrow \text{SUB}(ACCA; ACCB)$
11	CBA	2	Compare $ACCA$ to $ACCB$, and update c, n, and z
16	TAB	2	$ACCB \leftarrow ACCA$
17	TBA	2	$ACCA \leftarrow ACCB$
1B	ABA	2	$ACCA \leftarrow \text{ADD}(ACCA; ACCB)$

commands, as listed in Table 12.7. All are two-byte commands using relative addressing, as discussed earlier. If the branch condition is satisfied, the second byte, considered as signed two's complement number, is added to the program counter to obtain the address of the next instruction. All branch commands require four cycles. Note that only the c, v, n, and z bits are used in branching. The h bit is used only to facilitate decimal arithmetic, as discussed above. The unconditional branch and

TABLE 12.7   M6800 Branch Commands

Op Code	Mnemonic	Branch Condition
20	BRA	Branch always (unconditional)
24	BCC	$c = 0$
25	BCS	$c = 1$
28	BVC	$v = 0$
29	BVS	$v = 1$
26	BNE	$z = 0$
27	BEQ	$z = 1$
2A	BPL	$n = 0$
2B	BMI	$n = 1$
2C	BGE	$n \oplus V = 0$
2D	BLT	$n \oplus V = 1$
2E	BGT	$z \vee (n \oplus v) = 0$
2F	BLE	$z \vee (n \oplus v) = 1$
22	BHI	$c \vee z = 0$
23	BLS	$c \vee z = 1$

the eight branches on the four individual flag bits are self-explanatory. The other six branches are more complex and require some explanation. For example, what is the difference between BPL (Branch on Plus), which tests only the sign bit, and BGE (Branch if Greater than or Equal to 0), which tests both the sign bit and the overflow bit? To answer this, the meaning of the v bit must be more carefully considered.

The v bit is set when an addition or subtraction operation produces an arithmetic overflow. For purposes of determining overflow, the numbers being added or subtracted are considered to be 2's complement numbers, consisting of a sign bit and 7 numeric bits, giving a range -128 to $+127$. If an operation produces a positive result without overflow, clearly both the sign bit and the overflow bit will be 0 $(n \oplus v) = 0$. Consider, however, the situation if two positive numbers are added and produce an overflow, as follows.

$$
\begin{array}{cccccccccc}
v & 0 & 1 & 2 & 3 & 4 & 5 & 6 & 7 & \\
 & 0 & 1 & 1 & 0 & 0 & 1 & 1 & 1 & (+103) \\
 & 0 & 0 & 1 & 1 & 0 & 0 & 0 & 1 & (+49) \\
\hline
1 & 1 & 0 & 0 & 1 & 1 & 0 & 0 & 0 & (152)
\end{array}
$$

Now $v = 1$ due to the overflow, and the sign bit has changed to 1 $(n \oplus v = 0)$ because the 8-bit adder treats the sign bits of the operand as numeric bits. Although there is an overflow, the sum is still a positive number; indeed, the 8-bit sum does represent the correct sum without the sign bit. Thus the BGE command allows us to test for positive results even though there is overflow. Similar arguments apply for BLT (Branch on Less Than 0), BGT (Branch on Greater Than 0), and BLE (Branch on Less than or Equal to 0).

The BHI (Branch on Higher) and BLS (Branch on Less than or the Same) are used with the subtract or compare commands to compare the magnitude of numbers. Note first that for subtract operations, c is set if there is a borrow out. Thus, if you subtract the number in B from the number in A and there is no borrow out and the result is not 0, then the number in A was the larger number.

A limitation of all the branch commands is that the branch is restricted to a limited range around the current instruction location. The jump command (JMP) has the same effect as BRA, except that it uses extended (7E) or indexed (6E) addressing to form a full 16-bit address. Thus a combination of a conditional branch and jump provides a conditional jump to any location in memory. The jump command is not a memory reference command in the usual sense but is clearly an addressed command, as are the Type 6 and 7 commands. It is therefore assigned the

		Address Type				
Mnemonic	**Meaning**	**Rel.**	**Immed.**	**Direct**	**Index**	**Exten.**
JMP	Uncond. jump				6E	7E
BSR	Branch to subroutine	8D				
JSR	Jump to subroutine				AD	BD
LDS	Load stack pntr		8E	9E	AE	BE
STS	Store stack pntr			9F	AF	BF
LDI	Load index reg		CE	DE	EE	FE
STI	Store index reg			DF	EF	FF
CPX	Compare IX to mem		8C	9C	AC	BC

Op Codes

Figure 12.2. Special Instructions.

codes 6E (JMP indexed) and 7E (JMP extended). Figure 12.2 summarizes the op codes for jump and a number of other instructions that do not quite fit the eight categories of Table 12.2. The BSR and JSR commands will be discussed in a later section.

12.4 STACK HANDLING AND SUBROUTINES

The only class of instructions we have not discussed is Type-3, the stack instructions. A stack can be any list of data stored in sequential locations in memory that can be accessed from one end by use of the stack pointer register, *SP* and the "push" and "pull" instructions. The operation of the PSHA instruction (push *ACCA* on stack) is illustrated in Fig. 12.3. Assume that immediately prior to the execution of the PSHA instruction, *SP* contains the address 0500. Then *SP* is said to *point* to location 0500. Also assume that *ACCA* contains the data byte 37 (Fig. 12.3a). When PSHA is executed, the word from *ACCA* is stored in location 0500 and *SP* is then *decremented* to 04FF so that *SP* now points to that location in the stack. As successive PSHA instructions are executed, each successive word from *ACCA* is added "on top" of the stack.

Words may be "pulled" or "popped" from the stack by the PULA command (pull from stack to *ACCA*) as shown in Fig. 12.4. Assume that immediately prior to execution of the PULA instruction, *SP* points to location 04FF (Fig. 12.4a). When the PULA instruction is executed, *SP* is *incremented* to 0500 and the contents of that location are read out to *ACCA* (Fig. 12.4b). As successive PULA instructions are executed, the words in the stack will be read out in succession, in the opposite order

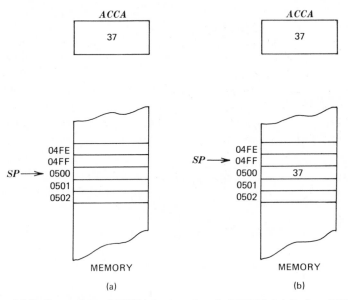

Figure 12.3. Operation of PSHA instruction in M6800 (*a*) Before PSHA.
(*b*) After PSHA.

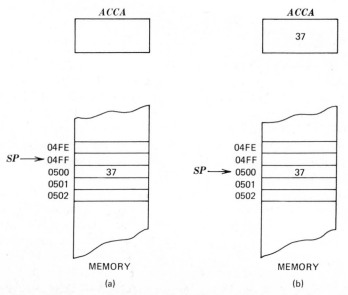

Figure 12.4. Operation of PULA instruction in M6800. (*a*) Before PULA.
(*b*) After PULA.

to that in which they were stored. Because of this ordering, stacks are often referred to as "last-in, first-out" (LIFO) lists. Stacks are also referred to as "push-down stacks," but this name may be misleading as it may suggest that words already in the stack are moved down as each new word is added.

The type 3 commands affecting the stack or the stack pointer are summarized in Table 12.8. All are 1-byte, four-cycle commands. Also affecting the stack pointer are the load stack pointer (LDS) and store stack pointer (STS) commands in groups 8, 9, A, B, as discussed earlier.

TABLE 12.8   Stack Commands in M6800

Op Code	Mnemonic	Operation
32	PULA	1. $SP \leftarrow \text{INC}(SP)$
		2. $ACCA \leftarrow \text{BUSFN}(M; SP)$
33	PULB	1. $SP \leftarrow \text{INC}(SP)$
		2. $ACCA \leftarrow \text{BUSFN}(M; SP)$
36	PSHA	$M * \text{DCD}(SP) \leftarrow ACCA; SP \leftarrow \text{DEC}(SP)$
37	PSHB	$M * \text{DCD}(SP) \leftarrow ACCB; SP \leftarrow \text{DEC}(SP)$
30	TSX	$IX \leftarrow \text{INC}(SP)$
35	TXS	$SP \leftarrow \text{DEC}(IX)$
31	INS	$SP \leftarrow \text{INC}(SP)$
34	DES	$SP \leftarrow \text{DEC}(SP)$

Stack addressing offers considerable speed advantage in processing data. Once the stack pointer has been initialized, by an LDS command, for example, a whole list of data can be stored and recovered without further reference to memory for addresses. Since the stack pointer can be initialized to any value, stacks can be located anywhere in memory and their size is limited only by available memory space. The LIFO ordering may be an advantage or disadvantage, depending on the type of problem.

Although the stack can be used for handling data arrays, one of the most important applications of the stack in the 6800 is for subroutine linkage. The reader will recall that the JSR command in SIC loaded the return address, i.e., the address of the next instruction in the main routine, in the first location in the subroutine. Control was subsequently returned to the main routine by an indirect jump through the first location in the subroutine. In the 6800 the return address is saved on the stack, by two commands, Branch to Subroutine (BSR) and Jump to Subroutine (JSR). The only difference between the two is the type of addressing: BSR (8D) uses relative addressing while JSR uses indexed (AD) or extended (BD) addressing.

Let us now consider the control sequence for the JSR extended (BD) command and the results of execution in a particular case. Assume that the JSR command is at location 0500 in the main program and that the subroutine is located at 0860. Because JSR extended is a 3-byte command, locations 0500, 0501, and 0502 contain the op code and the 2 bytes of the address. Also assume that the stack pointer currently points to 01A7. The status of memory immediately prior to fetching the JSR instruction is shown in Fig. 12.5a.

The control sequence starts with the fetch of the op code (BD) into **IR**.* This is followed by a number of branch instructions as required to decode the op code. For purposes of discussion assume that the JSR sequence starts at step 50. Step 50 increments the **PC** to obtain the next byte of instruction. Step 51 fetches this byte, the upper half of the sub-routine address, into the upper half of **IDR**. Steps 52 and 53 repeat this process to obtain the lower half of the subroutine address. Step 54 then increments **PC** again, to obtain the address of the next instruction in the main program. Steps 55 and 56 store the lower half of this address on the stack and increment **SP**. Steps 57 and 58 repeat this process to store the upper half of the return address on the stack. Finally, step 59 moves

*Control sequences given for the 6800 in this chapter do not show the data paths and may not conform to actual timing. They are intended to show only the sequences of operations that must take place.

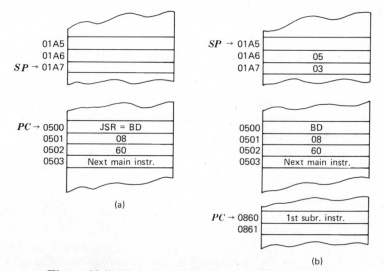

Figure 12.5. Execution of JSR (extended) command.

the subroutine address into *PC* and returns to step 1 to fetch the first subroutine instruction. The status of memory at this point is shown in Fig. 12.5b.

1. *IR* ← BUSFN(M; DCD(*PC*))
   branches

50. *PC* ← INC(*PC*)
51. $IDR_{0:7}$ ← BUSFN(M; DCD(*PC*))
52. *PC* ← INC(*PC*)
53. $IDR_{8:15}$ ← BUSFN(M; DCD(*PC*))
54. *PC* ← INC(*PC*)
55. M * DCD(*SP*) ← $PC_{8:15}$
56. *SP* ← DEC(*SP*)
57. M * DCD(*SP*) ← $PC_{0:7}$
58. *SP* ← *DEC(SP)*
59. *PC* ← *IDR*
    → (1)

The return from subroutine is accomplished by the RTS (39) instruction. This simply pulls the return address off the stack and places it in the *PC*. The program counter must be stored on the stack and retrieved by a special instruction rather than by an indirect jump, as in SIC, because a microprocessor subroutine may very well be stored in read-only memory.

12.5 CLOCKING AND CONTROL

The M6800 requires a two-phase non-overlapping clock (see Fig. 12.6) with a frequency in the range of 200 kHz to 1 MHz. This is generated by an external oscillator and applied to the ϕ_1 and ϕ_2 input pins. One complete clock cycle, i.e., one pulse of each phase, is referred to as a *machine cycle*. The execution time of each instruction is measured in machine cycles. The range of execution times is from two to nine cycles, depending on the number of memory references required.

Internally, the 6800 is implemented in terms of dynamic MOS. Both clock phases are used and are necessary for the storage of data. If either clock phase is witheld for a period greater than 5 μsec, all internally stored data will be lost.

For our purposes it is not necessary to examine the timing of information transfers within the 6800. We need only understand that *the 6800 is a clocked system* and how its clock is to be interpreted by interconnecting modules. As illustrated in Fig. 12.6, *the leading edge of ϕ_1 is to be regarded as the clocking transition* of all transfers that may involve

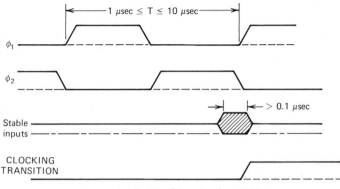

Figure 12.6. Clocking in the 6800.

externally supplied information. As also shown in Fig. 12.6, inputs to the 6800 must be stable at least 100 nsec in advance of this transition, which also approximately coincides with the trailing edge of ϕ_2.

The above stability constraint on inputs to the 6800 will be quite easy to satisfy given the long clock period of the system. Most devices which will be interfaced to the 6800 will be clocked by ϕ_2. In this chapter we shall specify the trailing edge of ϕ_2 as the clocking transition in these devices. Since the trailing edge of ϕ_2 immediately precedes the leading edge of ϕ_1, a data transition clocked by ϕ_2 will not be recognized by the 6800 until a full clock period later, at the next leading edge of ϕ_1. Two systems thus clocked by ϕ_1 and ϕ_2 may be assumed to be operating synchronously. The consistency of this notion with our earlier definition of a clocked system is shown by the timing diagram of Fig. 12.7b, which corresponds to the hypothetical AHPL sequence in Fig. 12.7a.

The sequence of Fig. 12.7a may represent outputs of the 6800 triggered by ϕ_1 or terminals within a peripheral clocked by the trailing edge of ϕ_2. Notice that, as in earlier chapters, the step 2 bus connection statement causes data to be placed on the **QBUS** during the corresponding clock period while the transfer specified by step 2 takes place at the end of that period. Sometimes data appear on lines interconnecting the 6800 and supporting modules only during the duration of ϕ_2. This will be represented in AHPL by bus connections conditional on ϕ_2, as illustrated by the third statement in step 2 of Fig. 12.7a.

The reader may have noticed **dbe**, the only input control line to the 6800 specifically identified in Fig. 12.1. Data may be routed from the internal data bus to the **DBUS** only if **dbe** = 1. This line is provided to permit locking out the CPU during communications between peripherals in more complex microprocessor systems. Normally, **dbe** = ϕ_2.

485

1.
2. $z \leftarrow 1$
    QBUS = REG
    OUTBUS = REG $* \phi_2$

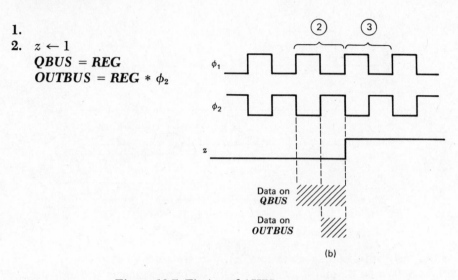

Figure 12.7. Timing of AHPL statements.

Thus the placing of data on the **DBUS** is conditional on ϕ_2, e.g., **DBUS = IDBUS** $* \phi_2$.

Both READ and WRITE operations between the 6800 and attached memory units must be accomplished during one clock period. Throughout this period the 6800 will hold a 1 on the output control line **vma** (valid memory address). The following AHPL sequence describes the control generated within the 6800 by a read operation.

  9. **read** $\leftarrow 1$
10. **ADBUS** = "address"
     vma = 1; **IDBUS = DBUS**
     "destination register" $\leftarrow$ **IDBUS**

A flip-flop, **read**, connected to an output line, is set to 1 to permit the addressed peripheral to distinguish between a READ or WRITE request. Step 10 holds the "address" (which may have originated in one of several registers) on the **ADBUS**, holds **vma** at 1 and establishes a path to the "destination register" in anticipation of the data word to be received. This data word is clocked into the destination register by the ϕ_1 transition at the end of step 10. As illustrated in Fig. 12.8, the data word must be available at the 6800 input port 100 nsec ahead of this transition.

The 6800 implements the following AHPL sequence to accomplish a WRITE operation. This sequence can be easily translated into a timing diagram for WRITE.

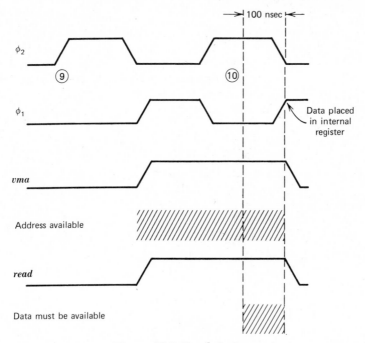

Figure 12.8. Read timing.

19. *read* ← 0
20. *ADBUS* = "address"
    IDBUS = "data"
    DBUS = *IDBUS* * ϕ_2 "*dbe* = ϕ_2"
    vma = 1

By overlapping steps internally, the 6800 can read or write data at the rate of one word/clock period. A peripheral must be able to respond to consecutive requests if *vma* remains 1.

It will be noted that the above procedure is totally nonresponsive. The MPU sends out the *vma* signal to indicate the start of a transfer operation and then proceeds on to the next cycle, assuming that the data have been picked up or delivered at the right time. There is no input corresponding to *dataready* in Chapter 10 allowing the peripheral to signal that it is ready to proceed. If the peripheral device is fast enough to meet the timing requirements set forth above, this causes no problems. But many commonly used memory devices are not fast enough to keep up with the 6800 MPU running at its maximum clock rate of 1 MHz. One means of solving this problem is to slow the clock. This can be done easily, since the clock is externally generated, but such an approach has the obvious disadvantage of slowing the entire system to a rate dictated by the slowest memory device.

Another approach is to allow the slow peripheral to control the duration of ϕ_2. Note that it is the duration of ϕ_2 that controls the speed with which the peripheral must respond. For read, the MPU reads whatever is on the bus for the last 100 nsec of ϕ_2, whatever the duration of ϕ_2. For write, the data are available on the bus from 200 nsec after the start of ϕ_2 until the end of ϕ_2, whatever the duration of ϕ_2. Slow devices may thus be accommodated by delaying the end of ϕ_2 until the device is ready to continue. The only limitation on this is that ϕ_2 must not exceed 5 μsec, since if ϕ_1 is down more than 5 μsec, a loss of data stored in internal registers will result.

The two-phase clock and the special control of ϕ_2 can be provided by the control module described by the following sequence.

MODULE: 6800 CONTROL
CLOCK PERIOD: 500 nsec
INPUTS: *slow*, *vma*.
OUTPUTS: ϕ_1, ϕ_2, *enable*, $\overline{enable}$
1. $z_1 = 1$
2. $z_2 = 1$
  $\rightarrow (\overline{slow}, slow)/(1, 2)$
END SEQUENCE
$\phi_1 = z_1 \wedge \overline{z_2}$
$\phi_2 = \overline{z_1} \wedge z_2$
enable $= \phi_2 \wedge vma$
END

The input *slow* is a line that can be set to 1 by a slow peripheral to delay the end of ϕ_2. The reader will note a new feature in this sequence, the declaration of the clock rate. This information is not essential to the design of the module but is useful information to emphasize the function of the circuit in setting the basic operating speed of the system. This is a generally useful feature of AHPL, that declaration statements may be added whenever useful to clarify the system design, as individual circumstances may suggest.

The input *slow* is a signal from a device that requires extra time to respond. As long as *slow* is at the 0 level, control cycles pass through steps 1 and 2 at the maximum rate, producing a symmetrical 1-Mhz, two-phase clock signal. If *slow* is high, the circuit holds at step 2, lengthening the ϕ_2 pulse in increments of 500 nsec. A peripheral generating a *slow* signal must be timed by the clock module to assure that changes in *slow*

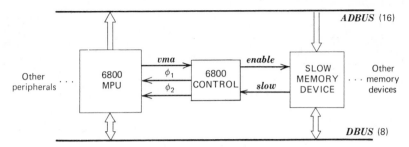

Figure 12.9. Typical system interconnections.

are properly synchronized. The ANDing of z_1 and z_2 to produce ϕ_1 and ϕ_2 assures that the clock phases will be nonoverlapping. The *enable* output provides a signal that goes high coincident with ϕ_2 during transfer operations. Recall that *vma* goes high at the same time that the address is placed on *ADBUS*. Some memory devices require an activate (enable) signal that goes high only after the address has stabilized. The *enable* output satisfies this requirement. Its complement, *enable*, is also provided, since some devices require a signal that goes low to enable. Figure 12.9 shows the manner in which the 6800 MPU, the control module, and a slow memory might be interconnected in a typical system.

12.6 TYPICAL MEMORY SYSTEMS

As is the case with any computer system, the size and speed of the memory in a minicomputer is a critical factor in determining the overall system capabilities. The 16-bit *ADBUS* provides an addressing capability of 65K bytes. Since the 6800 addresses all peripherals in the same manner, some of these addresses must be reserved for I/O devices so that the actual memory capability is slightly less than 65K.

The 6800 is theoretically capable of working with any type of memory devices, but practical and economic considerations effectively limit main memory to electronic memory devices that are directly compatible with the 6800 MPU. For most microcomputer systems the main memory will consist of both RAM and ROM. Since ROM's are commonly used for microprogramming, the use of ROM's with microcomputers sometimes misleads people to think that microcomputer systems are user microprogrammed. This is not generally the case. The M6800 is internally microprogrammed, with a ROM on the MPU chip controlling internal operations in the general manner discussed in Chapter 8. However, the 6800 is not user-microprogrammable. The external ROM is simply a part of the main memory, being used to store programs written

489

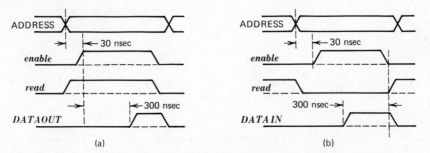

Figure 12.10. Read and write timing in 6810 RAM. (*a*) Read. (*b*) Write.

in machine language in the same manner as any other memory device. Microcomputers, like any size computers, must have nonvolatile storage for programs that must be preserved even if the computer is turned off. Indeed, such programs are the primary programs for microcomputers, since they are used mostly in dedicated applications, with fixed programs. Electronic ROM's are the most practical form of nonvolatile storage for use with microprocessors. In most microcomputer systems the bulk of memory is in ROM, with only enough RAM being provided to allow for temporary storage of data.

The 6800 can work with any memory chips that are TTL compatible and meet the MPU timing constraints, either directly or through slowing of the clock, as discussed in the last section. Two memory devices commonly used with the 6800 are the 6810 static RAM and 6830 ROM. The communication lines to the 6810 are the address lines and the data lines, and two control inputs. The input *read** specifies whether a read or write operation is required and the Chip Enable (Chip Select) line causes the specified operation to take place. The timing constraints on read and write operations in the 6810 are shown in Fig. 12.10. For both read and write the *enable* signal must be at the 1-level for a minimum of 400 nsec; *read* must be stable at the appropriate level for the same period; and the address lines must be stable from 30 nsec before *enable* goes up until *enable* goes down. For read the output data will be stable from 300 nsec after *enable* goes up until 10 nsec after *enable* goes down. For write the datain must be stable for at least 300 nsec prior to the time the *enable* goes down. For the 6830 ROM the timing is the same as for the read operation in the 6810, the only difference being that no *read* input is required. A comparison of these timing requirements with the

---

*In the 6800 and the 6810 the read/write control line is named R/W. We use the name *read*, since R/W is not permitted as a variable name in the AHPL syntax.

timing of the read and write cycles of the 6810 will show that they are compatible at any clock rate up to the maximum 1 MHz, provided that

$$enable = \phi_2 \wedge vma$$

is used for the chip enable on the 6810 or 6830.

The complete memory will normally be made up of several chips of both RAM and ROM. The low-order bits of the address will be used to address a specific word on a chip; the higher-order bits will be used to select a particular chip. Figure 12.11a shows the functional block diagram of the 6810 RAM. This chip provides storage for 128 eight-bit words, requiring seven address bits to select a word. There are six enable inputs E_0, E_3, $\bar{E}_1$, $\bar{E}_2$, $\bar{E}_4$, and $\bar{E}_5$ to which address leads can be connected. All lead to a single AND gate, the latter four through inverters so that the chip is enabled (selected) only if

$$\wedge/E = 1$$

Typically, the $(vma \wedge \phi_2)$ signal will be applied to one enable input to provide memory timing and some combination of higher-order address bits will be applied to the remaining enable inputs to select the chip. Figure 12.11b shows the functional block diagram of a 6830 ROM. It resembles the 6810 except that it has 10 address lines to select one out of 1024 8-bit words, and has only four *enable* lines, for which the purchaser specifies the active levels, i.e., whether 0 or 1 enables.

The designer has considerable freedom in assigning addresses to the

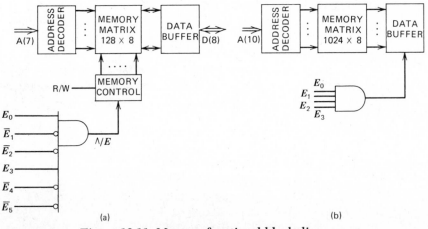

Figure 12.11. Memory functional block diagrams.
(*a*) **6810 RAM** (*b*) **6830 ROM.**

memory devices. The address field has a range of 65K locations, but systems rarely use this full capacity. The designer determines the addresses corresponding to a specific memory chip by specifying which bits of *ADBUS* will be connected to the various enable inputs. One constraint is that fixed locations have been set aside for dealing with interrupts, just as was done in SIC. These addresses are the highest eight addresses, FFF8 to FFFF so that it is usual to assign ROM to the high-order addresses. We also recall that direct addressing refers to the first 256 locations in the address field so that it is usual to assign RAM to the low-order addresses. Addresses between RAM and ROM are available for I/O devices.

Example 12.1

Let us now consider a specific example of the manner in which memory addresses are assigned. Assume that a system is to be designed with 2048 words of ROM and 512 words of RAM, using two 6830's and four 6810's. The first step is to set up a *memory map*, showing the range of addresses assigned to each chip (Fig. 12.12). In all cases the word address on the chip will be obtained from the low-order address bits on *ADBUS*.

To select the chips we could, of course, fully decode the high-order bits. This would clearly be a waste of effort, since we only need to select one chip out of six. By using less bits for the selection, we can take advantage of the on-chip decoding provided by the enable AND gates on the memory chips.

First, we note that we could use any of the high-order five bits to select between RAM and ROM, so we will use $ADBUS_0$ for this purpose. To select between the two ROM chips, we use $ADBUS_5$, which is 0 for the second hex digit in the range 8 to B, and 1 for the second digit in the range C to F. To select among the four RAM chips, an inspection of the address ranges shows that bit $ADBUS_{7:8}$ provides the desired differentiation. Figure 12.13 shows the manner in which the chips would be connected to achieve the above assignments. Note that the ROM chips have been specified with two of the enable inputs, $\bar{E}_2$ and $\bar{E}_3$, as active low. As the 6810 chips have more active low enable inputs, we

Chip	Address range (HEX)
6830 No. 1	FC00 to FFFF
6830 No. 2	F800 to FBFF
6810 No. 1	0000 to 007F
6810 No. 2	0080 to 00FF
6810 No. 3	0100 to 017F
6810 No. 4	0180 to 01FF

Figure 12.12. Memory map, Ex. 12.1.

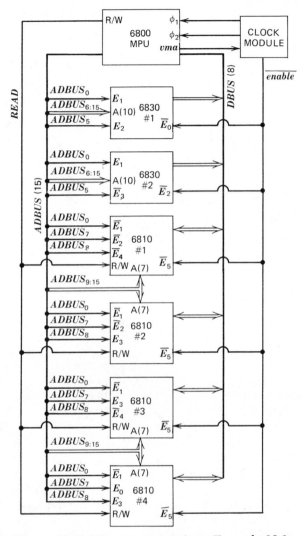

Figure 12.13. Memory connections, Example 12.1.

have used the $\overline{enable}$ signal from the clock module. Since we have not fully decoded the high-order address bits, there are many addresses other than those listed in the memory map that would access memory. For example, any address in the range XC00 to XFFF, where X stands for any hex digit from 8 to F, will access 6830 No. 1, so that bits $ADBUS_{1:4}$ are "don't-cares" for ROM addresses. However, from the standpoint of program consistency and clarity, only addresses

493

in the ranges shown in the memory map should be used. Finally, it is assumed in Fig. 12.13 that any enable inputs now shown are wired high or low in such manner as to have no effect on enable operation.

The *slow* input to the clock module must be wired low, since these memory chips are capable of operating at full MPU speed.

It is possible to write AHPL descriptions of the memory modules, specifying both their operation and their connections to the remainder of the system. For 6810 chip No. 1 in Example 12.1, the AHPL description would be as follows:

MODULE: RAM 6810-1
    INPUTS: *ADBUS* [16]; *read; $\overline{enable}$*
    COMBUS: *DBUS* [8]
    MEMORY: **M** [128; 8]
END SEQUENCE
    $\overline{E}_1 = ADBUS_0$
    $\overline{E}_2 = ADBUS_7$
    $\overline{E}_4 = ADBUS_8$
    $E_0 = E_3 = 1$
    $\overline{E}_5 = enable$
    DBUS = BUSFN (**M**; DCD(*ADBUS*$_{9:15}$)) * (($\wedge$/E) $\wedge$ *read*)
    M * (DCD(*ADBUS*$_{9:15}$) $\wedge$ (($\wedge$/E) $\wedge$ $\overline{read}$)) ←o *DBUS*
END

The symbol ←o is used to indicate an unclocked transfer, unclocked in the sense that the contents of the memory elements are not synchronously changed by a clock transition. The memory elements are effectively unclocked flip-flops, or *latches*, with the data being routed to their inputs during the entire interval in which

$$enable = vma \wedge \phi_2 = 1$$

There are no synchronization problems, since the data are stable on the *DBUS* throughout this interval.

The above basic technique of memory assignment can be used for any size of memory within the addressing capacity of the MPU. As more chips are used, more high-order bits must be decoded, in which event it may be necessary to use external decoding logic to supplement the on-chip decoding provided by the enable AND gates. Other types of memory chips may have only one enable input, in which case all decoding must be done in external logic, and the resultant decoded select signal must be externally ANDed with the *enable* (or $\overline{enable}$, as required) signal from the clock module. If slow modules are used, the clock must be slowed, or provision must be included in the memory module to generate the *slow* signal. If devices are to be used that are too slow to respond in the maximum ϕ_2 duration of 5 sec, the I/O techniques to be described in a later section must be used.

12.7 INTERRUPT HANDLING

The handling of interrupts is an important aspect of any computer system, but it is especially critical in microcomputers. The most common applications of microcomputers are in control and communications systems, where they primarily interact with devices that are much slower, often on an irregular, unscheduled basis. Consider, for example, a microcomputer controlling a point-of-sale terminal. Between transactions the computer will be in a standby condition, or possibly carrying out background computations or communications with a central computer. The start of a transaction, which may come at any time, will call for service by interrupting the computer. When the transaction has started, the interval between key entries by the clerk will be very long in terms of electronic speeds. The normal procedure will be to have each key stroke interrupt the computer. This is an example of what is often referred to as an "interrupt-driven environment," in which the primary task the computer is to respond to requests for service in the form of interrupt signals.

In the M6800 interrupts are also important because of the nonresponsive signaling techniques used for communications with peripherals. As noted earlier, when the MPU sends out an address and *vma* signal, it then proceeds to read or write on the *DBUS* at a fixed time, without waiting for any acknowledgment from the peripheral. When dealing with peripherals that are too slow to respond in the allotted time, the usual procedure is for the MPU to notify the peripheral that it is ready for a transfer, and then wait for the peripheral to interrupt, as an indication that it is ready to proceed. There are many variations on this procedure, depending on which device is initiating operations, but the main point is that interrupts are necessary to communications with slow peripherals, as they are the only means by which such devices can exchange signals with the MPU.

The 6800 provides for three types of hardware interrupts and one software interrupt. The hardware interrupts are initiated by signals on three input lines, $\overline{irq}$, $\overline{nmi}$, and $\overline{res}$. The primary interrupt line is $\overline{irq}$, Interrupt Request. Any peripheral may request an interrupt by driving $\overline{irq}$ low. Each time the MPU completes an instruction, it checks the state of $\overline{irq}$. If $\overline{irq}$ = 0, the processor then checks i, the interrupt mask bit

(CCR_3). If $CCR_3 = 1$, the interrupt request is ignored and the MPU proceeds to execute the next instruction. If $CCR_3 = 0$, the MPU enters the hardware interrupt routine, which consists of three parts. First, the contents of *PC*, *IX*, *ACCA*, *ACCB*, and *CCR* are loaded onto the stack, to preserve them for restoration of the main program after the interrupt has been dealt with. Second, the *i* bit (CCR_3) is set to 1, to prevent additional responses to the same interrupt. Third, the contents of memory locations FFF8 and FFF9 are loaded into the program counter, and a new instruction is then fetched. Locations FFF8 and FFF9, normally in ROM, must contain the starting address of the software interrupt routine; the net result of the hardware interrupt routine is thus to preserve the status of the main program and jump to the interrupt program.

The interrupt program will be of the same general sort as discussed in Chapter 10. Since the 6800 has no register corresponding to *INTR* in SIC, an important part of the interrupt routine is a polling of the possible interrupt sources to determine which is to be serviced. If more than one device may have made a request, the routine must include priority procedures to determine which will be serviced first. The absence of an interrupt register also means that *irq* must be held low until the MPU responds. The peripheral will normally have an interrupt flag which drives the *irq* line; the interrupt routine must include provision for clearing this flag to prevent a second response to the same request. The last instruction in any interrupt routine will be RTI, Return from Interrupt (Op Code = 3B), which restores the contents of the main registers from the stack and fetches a new instruction, thus jumping back to the main program.

The second type of interrupt is initiated by a low on *nmi*, Nonmaskable Interrupt, which, as the name implies, cannot be disabled by the *i* bit. If *nmi* is low when the MPU completes an instruction, the interrupt routine will be entered regardless of the state of *i*. The interrupt routine for *nmi* is the same as for *irq* except that the interrupt address loaded into *PC* is taken from locations FFFC and FFFD. Unlike *irq*, holding *nmi* low will not cause additional interrupts; *nmi* must go high for at least one cycle and then low again to cause another interrupt. The third type of hardware interrupt is initiated by the *res* line (Reset). This is a special interrupt procedure used to initialize the system after start-up, or to restart it after a power failure. The *res* line must go low for at least eight machine cycles; when it goes high after this period, the *i* bit will be set to 1 and the address of a start-up program will be loaded into *PC* from memory locations FFFE and FFFF. There is no saving of registers on the stack, since the purpose of this type of interrupt is to start over, rather than to preserve an existing program. The routine to which $\overline{res}$ causes a jump will not be an interrupt routine in the usual sense but rather a start-up routine for initializing the MPU and peripherals to appropriate starting conditions.

The fourth type of interrupt is initiated by execution of the instruction SWI, Software Interrupt (Op Code = 3F). This is not an interrupt in the sense of being initiated by an external device but produces the same results as a hardware interrupt. The contents of the registers are preserved on the stack, the i bit is set, and the address of the interrupt program is loaded into PC from locations FFFA and FFFB. This command is useful for debugging and troubleshooting, as it stops the program in place and loads the operating registers into memory, where they can be easily examined or displayed.

A special interrupt instruction is WAI, Wait for Interrupt (Op Code - 3E). This instruction saves the register contents in the stack and then waits for a hardware interrupt initiated by $\overline{irq}$ or $\overline{nmi}$. When either of these interrupts occurs, the process proceeds in the manner described above, except that the registers have already been saved so that the interrupt response time is correspondingly shortened. The final two commands related to the interrupt system are SEI, Set i (0F), and CLI, Clear i (0E), which set and clear the interrupt mask bit, respectively. The flow chart of Figure 12.14 will clarify the operation of the various interrupt procedures.

12.8 INPUT/OUTPUT AND THE PERIPHERAL INTERFACE ADAPTER

Input/output procedures in the 6800 are similar to the programmed transfer procedures used in SIC but are somewhat complicated by the lack of signaling lines and the consequent use of nonresponsive signaling. First, since there is no separate bus corresponding to the *CSBUS*, the *DBUS* must be time-shared for the transfer of both data and control/status information. This means that procedures that require only a single program step in SIC may require several steps in the 6800. Second, the lack of signaling lines corresponding to *ready, accept*, and *datavalid*, as discussed in Chapter 9, means that interrupts must normally be relied on to provide responsive signaling for devices too slow to meet the timing requirements discussed in Section 12.6. The time-consuming sequences required for interrupt response can be avoided by the use of status-checking, but this approach may waste processor time by holding the MPU in waiting loops for long periods of time.

Assume that it is desired to transfer data between the 6800 and a tape unit that transfers data in blocks of 8-bit words. A straightforward ap-

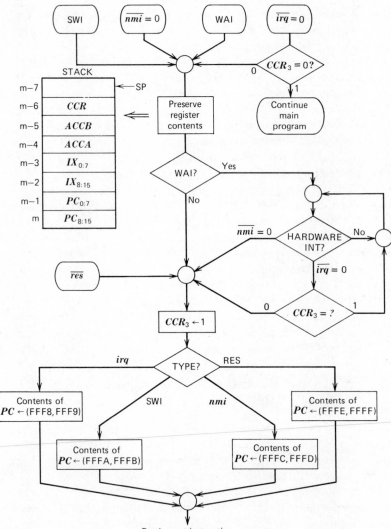

Figure 12.14. Flow chart of interrupt sequences.

proach would be to have the 6800 first send a command word to the tape unit to start tape motion and to interrupt whenever it is ready to transfer a word. Whenever an interrupt is received, the MPU will jump to an interrupt routine that will transfer the word and also keep a count of the number of words transferred. When the desired number of words has been transferred, a deactivate command will be sent to the tape unit.

Let us now consider some of the interface requirements implied by this scheme. First, the tape unit must have a command register capable of accepting a command word at any time, in a nonresponsive manner. This differs from the system discussed in Chapter 10 in that there is no *csrdy* signal to identify the word as a command word. Assuming that the tape unit is also capable of receiving data from the MPU, some other means of differentiating between data words and command words must be found. The usual procedure is to have separate data and command registers, each with a different address. Recall that all peripheral devices in a 6800 system are addressed as memory locations. We are not limited to a small range of device numbers, as in SIC, so each I/O device can have a number of registers. The function of a word can thus be identified by the address associated with it, rather than by a special signaling line.

Recall that the interrupt line, $\overline{irq}$, must be held low until the MPU responds. The tape interface must therefore include an interrupt flag that will drive $\overline{irq}$ low when set. If the tape unit is one of several devices that can generate interrupts, interrupt flag must be accessible to the MPU for purposes of polling to determine which device interrupted. It must also be possible to clear this interrupt flag on command by the MPU. For data transfer, the tape unit must have a register capable of receiving data nonresponsively on MPU write cycles, and it must be capable of gating data onto the DBUS in a manner consistent with the timing of the MPU read cycle.

Interface circuitry to satisfy the above requirements can, of course, be designed for any specific device, but such custom design can be largely eliminated by the use of the 6820 Peripheral Interface Adapter (PIA). This device meets all the requirements above and is sufficiently flexible so that a great variety of peripherals can be interfaced to the 6800 MPU with little or no additional electronics. A simplified block diagram of the PIA, which emphasizes logical organization rather than electronic details is shown in Fig. 12.15.

The PIA is divided into two nearly identical sections, denoted A and B. Communication to the MPU takes place via the *DBUS*, and data are relayed to or from the peripherals via the *PABUS* or *PBBUS*. The PIA

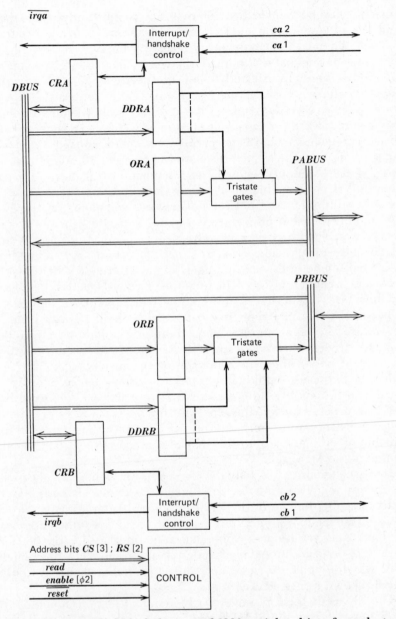

Figure 12.15. Simplified block diagram of 6820 peripheral interface adapter.

is addressed by three lines, CS_0, CS_1, and $\overline{CS_2}$, the chip being selected when

$$\wedge CS = 1$$

The line *read* controls the direction of data transfer, from MPU to PIA for *read* = 0, from PIA to MPU for *read* = 1. Driving the $\overline{reset}$ input low will clear all PIA registers. The PIA has no internal clock, and a single step occurs whenever a pulse appears on the *enable* line. Although there is no requirement that the *enable* pulses be periodic, this line is always tied to the ϕ_2 clock so that it is effectively a clock input, and the PIA will be considered a clocked device in the ensuing discussion.

As seen by the MPU, the PIA consists of four locations, consisting of two control registers, *CRA* and *CRB*, and two peripheral ports, *PPA* and *PPB*. These locations are selected by the *RS* inputs as shown in Table 12.9, with RS_1 selecting the A or B side, and RS_0 selecting the control register or the peripheral port on the side selected. Each peripheral port consists of an output register, *ORA* or *ORB*, a data direction register, *DDRA* or *DDRB*, and the two 8-bit bidirectional peripheral data buses, *PABUS* and *PBBUS*. When a peripheral port is addressed for a WRITE operation, data may be written in either the data direction register (*DDRA* or *DDRB*) or the output register (*ORA* or *ORB*), depending on the setting of CRA_5. The results of a READ operation on a peripheral port will be discussed later.

If either of the control registers are addressed ($RS_0 = 1$) a read or write cycle by the MPU will read or write in the selected register in the same manner as any memory location, except that a write operation affects only the low-order 6 bits. The 2 high-order bits of the control registers

TABLE 12.9 PIA On-Chip Addressing

RS_0	RS_1	Location Addressed	WRITE Destination	
			$CRA_5=0$	$CRA_5=1$
0	0	Port A	*DDRA*	*ORA*
1	0	*CRA*	*CRA*	*CRA*
			$CRB_5=0$	$CRB_5=1$
0	1	Port B	*DDRB*	*ORB*
1	1	*CRB*	*CRB*	*CRB*

501

serve as interrupt flags and cannot be directly set or reset by the MPU. However, a READ of the corresponding peripheral port will automatically reset these bits.

Associated with each port are two control lines to the peripheral devices ($ca1$ and $ca2$ for Port A) and an interrupt line to the MPU. These interrupt lines ($\overline{irqa}$ and $\overline{irqb}$) go low when an interrupt flag is set and may be tied together with other active/low interrupt lines to drive the $\overline{irq}$ line of the MPU.

Wiring to the PIA and the control of connections to the buses and transfers from the buses may be specified unambiguously in AHPL. This requires only declarations and unlabeled statements following END SEQUENCE. The control sequence, describing interactions with the peripherals, will be filled in during later discussion.

MODULE: PIA
INPUTS: "appropriate $ADBUS$ bits";
              $read$; $reset$; $ca1$; $cb1$;
OUTPUTS: $\overline{irqa}$; $\overline{irqb}$;
MEMORY: $CRA[8]$; $ORA[8]$; $DDRA[8]$;
              $CRB[8]$; $ORB[8]$; $DDRB[8]$; caf; cbf;
COMBUSES: $DBUS[8]$; $PABUS[8]$; $PBBUS[8]$;
              $ca2$; $cb2$
LABELS: $CS_{0:2}$, $RS_{0:1}$ = "appropriate $ADBUS$ bits"
CLOCK: ϕ_2 (trailing edge)

END SEQUENCE

$(ORA\ !\ DDRA\ !\ ORB\ !\ DDRB) * (((DCD_0(RS) \wedge (CRA_5, \overline{CRA_5})),$
$(DCD_1(RS) \wedge (CRB_5, \overline{CRB_5}))) \wedge ((CS_0 \wedge CS_1 \wedge CS_2) \wedge \overline{read})) \leftarrow$
$\quad DBUS$
$(CRA_{2:7}\ !\ CRB_{2:7}) * ((DCD_2(RS), DCD_3(RS))$
$\quad \wedge ((CS_0 \wedge CS_1 \wedge CS_2) \wedge \overline{read})) \leftarrow DBUS_{2:7}$
$PBBUS = ORB \circledast DDRB$
$PABUS = ORA \circledast DDRA$
$DBUS = (DDRA\ !\ PABUS\ !\ CRA\ !\ DDRB\ !\ PBBUS\ !\ CRB) *$
$\quad ((DCD_0(RS) \wedge (\overline{CRA_5}, CRA_5), DCD_2(RS),$
$\quad DCD_1(RS) \wedge (\overline{CRB_5}, CRB_5), DCD_3(RS))$
$\quad \wedge (\wedge/CS) \wedge read \wedge \phi_2)$
$(CRA_{0:1}\ !\ CRB_{0:1}) * (((\overline{RS_1} \wedge CRA_5), (RS_1 \wedge CRB_5)) \wedge RS_0 \wedge$
$\quad (\wedge/CS) \wedge read) \leftarrow 0, 0$

END

For WRITE operations, data from the $DBUS$ can be stored in the control registers, the direction registers, or the output registers, as specified by the RS bits and CRA_5. The first two statements following END SEQUENCE describe the WRITE transfers. The output registers (ORA and ORB) serve as buffer registers, providing temporary storage for data from the MPU until a peripheral is ready to accept it. Any time a WRITE operation is executed with an output register addressed as indicated above, the data from the MPU will be stored in the output register. However, the outputting of this data over the peripheral buses ($PABUS$ or $PBBUS$) is not automatic but is controlled by the data direction registers.

The data direction registers are used to program the peripheral data lines for input or output. A 1 in a given bit position of the data direction register will connect the corresponding bit of the output register to the corresponding peripheral data line, thus programming that line as an output, driven by the output register. A 0 in a given bit of the data direction register will place the tristate gate connecting the corresponding data line to the output register in the high-impedance state. That line is thus programmed to act as an input, driven by an input line from a peripheral device. These bus connections are specified by the third and fourth statements following END SEQUENCE. Recall, from Chapter 10, that $\circledast$ is the element-by-element conditional. Thus $PABUS_i = ORA_i$ if $DDRB_i = 1$. If $DDRB_i = 0$, $PABUS_i$ is disconnected from ORA_i by the tristate gate, and that bus line is controlled by other sources connected to the line. Statements 3 and 4 following END SEQUENCE specify the control of the peripheral buses in this manner. The fifth statement specifies the READ of the control registers of buses, as determined by RS. In summary, a WRITE to an output register will always transfer 8 bits to the register, but only those bits programmed as outputs will appear on the peripheral bus. A READ of the peripheral bus will similarly always read 8 bits. For those bit positions programmed as inputs, the data read will be that placed on the bus by a peripheral device; for those positions programmed as outputs, the data read will be the contents of the output register. The final statement following END SEQUENCE specifies the clearing of the interrupt flags by a READ operation.

In addition to providing for data input and output, the PIA also provides control and status communications, via the ca and $irqa$ lines on the A side, and the cb and $irqb$ lines on the B side. The functioning of these lines is controlled by various bits in the respective control registers. The $ca1$ and $ca2$ lines are used for interrupts. Since both function in exactly the same way, we shall discuss only the A side, in the interests of clarity. The CRA_0 bit serves as an interrupt flag, which is set by transitions on the $ca1$ line. The direction of transition, which sets CRA_0,

TABLE 12.10 Control of *ca1* Interrupts
(Similar for *cb1* and *CRB*$_0$)

CRA_6	CRA_0	$\overline{irqa}$	CRA_7
0	Set on ↓ transition of *ca1*	Not affected by setting of CRA_0	0
		Low if $CRA_0 = 1$	1
1	Set on ↑ transition of *ca1*	Not affected by setting of CRA_0	0
		Low if $CRA_0 = 1$	1

is controlled by CRA_6. If $CRA_6 = 0$, negative-going transitions of *ca1* will set CRA_0; if $CRA_6 = 1$, positive-going transitions of *ca1* will set CRA_0. The interrupt *line ca1* cannot be masked off; CRA_6 only determines the direction of transition that will set the interrupt flag. However, the interrupt *flag* may be masked by CRA_7 in the same way that *MR* masks *INTR* in SIC. If $CRA_7 = 0$, the interrupt flag will have no effect on the interrupt line, $\overline{irqa}$; if $CRA_7 = 1$, $\overline{irqa}$ will go low when CRA_0 is set. The above behavior is exactly duplicated on the B side. Table 12.10 summarizes the control of the *ca1* interrupts.

The *ca2* and *cb2* lines can be used either as interrupt inputs or as control outputs. If $CRA(B)_2 = 0$, CRA_1 and CRB_1 function as interrupt flags, with $CRA(B)_3$ and $CRA(B)_4$ controlling the transitions and masking in the same manner as $CRA(B)_6$ and $CRA(B)_7$. When both interrupt flags are enabled on either side, either flag being set will drive $\overline{irqa(b)}$ low.

If $CRA(B)_2 = 1$, *ca(b)2* functions as a control output, and the CRA $(B)_1$ interrupt flag is inactive, being held low. When programmed as outputs, these lines function to provide control communications between the MPU and peripherals, but the two sides function in different manners. The *ca2* line is set up to provide handshaking for read operations, while *cb2* is set up to provide handshaking for write operations. On each side there are three modes of operation, controlled by $CRA(B)_3$ and $CRA(B)_4$. If $CRA(B)_3 = 1$, *ca(b)2* follows $CRA(B)_4$. This provides a programmed mode of control, whereby the MPU can send control signals to the peripherals by setting or clearing bit 4 in the control register. This mode of control functions in the same way on both the A and B sides.

If $CRA_3 = 0$, *ca2* provides handshake control for read operations in

TABLE 12.11   Control of $ca2$ Line (Similar for $cb2$, except that handshake follows WRITE in ORB)

CRA_2	CRA_3	$ca2$		CRA_4
0		$ca2$ functions as an interrupt line, setting CRA_1 under control of CRA_3 and CRA_4, in the same manner $ca1$ is controlled by CRA_6 and CRA_7		
1	0	Handshake, goes low following READ of $PABUS$.	Remains low until active transition on $ca1$.	0
			Remains low for one clock time	1
	1	Follows CRA_4	$ca2 = 0$	0
			$ca2 = 1$	1

two different modes, controlled by CRA_4. If $CRA_4 = 1$, $ca2$ provides a pulse handshake for read operations, going low for one clock period following a read of the PA data lines. If $CRA_4 = 0$, $ca2$ goes low following a read of the $PABUS$ and remains low until an active transition of $ca1$. (An *active* transition is a transition programmed to set the interrupt flag by CRA_6). On the B side the operation is the same except that $cb2$ goes low following a write into ORB. The control of $ca2$ is summarized in Table 12.11.

This variety of operating modes provides great flexibility to the designer in setting up signaling sequences to match the requirements of a wide variety of peripheral devices. Figure 12.16 shows the sequence of signals in a typical read operation. In this example $CRA_{2:4} = 100$ so that $ca2$ is programmed as an output, to go low following a read of the data lines and high on an active transition of $ca1$. Since $CRA_{6:7} = 11$, positive transitions on $ca1$ are active and CRA_0 is enabled. At the start of the sequence we assume that $ca2$ is low as a result of a previous read operation. At 1 the peripheral places new data on the $PABUS$, which we assume has been programmed 'for input. At 2 the peripheral sends a positive interrupt transition on $ca1$ as a signal that new data are ready. This signal sets the interrupt flag CRA_0, which in turn drives $\overline{irqa}$ low and also drives $ca2$ high. On sensing the interrupt, the MPU begins the

505

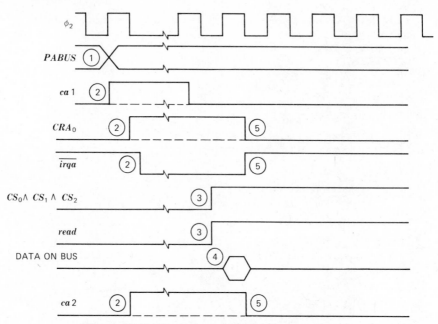

Figure 12.16. Typical read handshake sequence.

interrupt routine, which at 3 sends the appropriate address and sets *read* to 1. The PIA gates the requested data onto the *DBUS* at 4. When the read operation is complete at 5, *ca2* goes low as a signal to the peripheral that the data has been accepted. Also at 5, the interrupt flag is cleared and *irqa* goes back to 1. A read of the data lines always clears the interrupt flags on that side.

To implement the control communication just discussed, we add the following control sequence to the AHPL description of the PIA module.

1. $\rightarrow ((\overline{(\wedge/CS)} \wedge \overline{RS}_0 \wedge (RS_1 \oplus read) \wedge \overline{CRB_5})/(1)$
2. NO DELAY
   $\rightarrow(\overline{read})/(5)$
3. $caf * (CRA_2 \wedge \overline{CRA}_3) \leftarrow 0$ NO DELAY
   $\rightarrow \overline{(CRA_2 \wedge \overline{CRA}_3 \wedge CRA_4)}/(1)$
4. $caf \leftarrow 1$
   $\rightarrow (1)$
5. $cbf * (CRB_2 \wedge \overline{CRB}_3) \leftarrow 0$
   $\rightarrow \overline{(CRB_2 \wedge \overline{CRB}_3 \wedge CRB_4)}/(1)$
6. $cbf \leftarrow 1$
   $\rightarrow (1)$

END SEQUENCE

Step 1 waits for the PIA to be addressed for either a read of *PABUS* or a write to *ORB*. Since *ca2* and *cb2* must be held low for one or more clock periods for handshake operations, it is necessary to specify flip-flops *caf* and *cbf* to drive these lines. For read operations, control branches to step 3 to set *caf* to 0 if handshaking is specified. For pulse handshake ($CRA_4 = 1$), step four sets *caf* back to 1 and returns control to step 1. Otherwise, control returns to step 1 from step 3, and *caf*, if low, remains low until set high by a transition on *ca1*. Steps 5 and 6 similarly clear and set *cbf*, which controls *cb2* for write handshaking.

It is also necessary to add some statements followimg END SE-QUENCE. The first two statements tie *ca2* to CRA_4 or *caf* when that line is programmed as a control output. The third statement connects *irqa* to the interrupt flags when they are enabled. Flip-flops *y1a* and *y2a* are updated to the values on lines *ca1* and *ca2* each clock period. If *y1a* and *c1a* differ, indicating a transition, the fifth statement sets *caf* if the transition is in the direction specified by CRA_6. This same transition establishes an interrupt in CRA_0. The next statement similarly establishes an interrupt in CRA_1 upon a transition an *ca2* if this line has been programmed as an interrupt input. The last statement initializes *caf* to 1 when *ca2* is established as an output.

> END SEQUENCE "additional statements"
> $ca2 = CRA_1 * (CRA_2 \wedge CRA_3)$
> $ca2 = caf * (CRA_2 \wedge \overline{CRA_3})$
> $irqa = \overline{(CRA_7 \wedge CRA_0)} \wedge \overline{(CRA_4 \wedge CRA_1)}$
> $y1a \leftarrow ca1; y2a \leftarrow ca2$
> $(caf, CRA_0) * ((\overline{y1a} \wedge CRA_6 \wedge ca1) \vee (y1a \wedge \overline{CRA_6} \wedge \overline{ca1})) \leftarrow 1, 1$
> $CRA_1 * (\overline{CRA_2} \wedge ((\overline{y2a} \wedge CRA_3 \wedge ca2) \vee (y2a \wedge \overline{CRA_3} \wedge \overline{ca2}))) \leftarrow 1$
> $caf * (RS_0 \wedge \overline{RS_1} \wedge DBUS_2 \wedge \overline{DBUS_3}) \leftarrow 1$
> "similar statements for Port B"
> END

To conclude this section, a few comments about some of the special features of the PIA may be useful. First, the reader may wonder why the data direction registers are provided for programming the data lines for input or output. Since the A side is set up for read handshaking and the B side for write handshaking, it might seem reasonable to use the A side only for input and the B side only for output. When the PIA is used to interface devices that both read and write in 8-bit words, this is exactly what is done, the A side is programmed for input, the B side for output. However, such situations are the exception to the rule in micro-computer applications. Microcomputers are very likely to be commu-nicating with a variety of individual single-bit devices, such as switches, relays, indicator lamps, actuators, etc. In such cases it is very useful to be able to program each data line on an individual basis.

Another consideration is that programming considerations often make some bit positions more convenient for input or output than others. In this connection it is important to keep in mind that the 6800 has many instructions that operate on memory locations in the same manner as internal registers and that peripherals are addressed in that same manner as memory locations. As a result, peripherals can often be tested or controlled directly, in the same manner as internal registers, without the need to explicitly transfer control or status information. As an example, assume that an indicator light has to be turned on and off frequently as a signal to an operator. If this light is connected to $PBBUS_7$ programmed as an output, the light can be turned on and off by alternately incrementing and decrementing ORB, without affecting any other positions of ORB. As another example, inputs that need to be tested frequently should be tied to $PABUS_0$ or $PBBUS_0$, since this bit corresponds to the sign-bit and can be easily tested. It is for this reason that the high-order bits of control registers are used as the primary interrupt flags.

12.9   DESIGNING MICROCOMPUTER-BASED SYSTEMS

In this section we shall consider some of the techniques of designing systems using microcomputers, with an emphasis on the problems of interfacing to the "noncomputer" parts of the system. The hardware design of the microcomputer itself is usually a trivial problem, consisting primarily of deciding how much memory and how many interface adapters are needed. The main design task can be conveniently broken into three parts. The first is deciding how the various system components should be interconnected, including a decision as to what tasks should be done in hardware and in software. The second is the design of such special-purpose hardware as may be required. The third is the actual programming of the microcomputer. Clearly, the three parts of the design process interact strongly, and the design process is usually iterative, as is the case with most design. The topic of designing microcomputer systems is far too large to treat comprehensively in this section. Indeed, a complete system of sufficient complexity to justify the use of a microprocessor would likely require the better part of a chapter just to describe what it was supposed to do. Rather than try to design any complex systems, we shall consider some typical problems encountered in the design of microcomputer systems and some of the design choices open to the designer in solving such problems.

Before proceeding to actual examples, some preliminaries must be established in the interests of brevity in later discussions. A number of these examples will require the writing of 6800 programs, for which we shall use a simplified assembly language based on the cross-assembler provided for by Motorola for the 6800 system [1]. Typical statements in this language follow.

```
0000    * TYPICAL ASSEMBLY LANGUAGE STATEMENTS
0010    BEGIN   LDAA    #$24      LOAD  ACCA  WITH  HEX
                                  24
0020            ADDA    #CONST   ADD CONSTANT
0030            STAA    SUM      STORE AT SUM
0040            BRA     BEGIN    BRANCH TO BEGIN
0050    CONST   EQU     $F8
0060    SUM     EQU     $0100
```

Each statement begins with a line number. These numbers may be consecutive at intervals, as shown, to allow for later insertion of new steps. If the first character following the line number is an asterisk, the entire line is a comment. A regular statement consists of four fields in addition to the line number: the label, the opcode, the operand, and the comment. The label is optional and is generally used only if the statement is the destination of a branch or jump. The op code is a three- or-four-letter mnemonic, as defined in earlier sections. The operand is required for instructions other than those using implied addressing and may consist of a hex number or a variable name. The comment field is optional.

In the operand field, # indicates immediate addressing, and $ indicates a hex number. Thus line 10 will cause hex 24 to be loaded into the byte following the code for LDAA, and execution of the instruction will cause this number to be loaded into *ACCA*. Variable names are defined by the assembly directive EQU. Thus CONST is defined as hex F8 and SUM as hex 0100. Line 20 will cause hex F8 to be loaded into the byte following the op code for ADDA, and execution will add this number to *ACCA*. Line 30 will load hex 0100 into the two bytes following the op code for STAA and execution will store the contents of *ACCA* at location 0100, since the absence of # means the operand is to be treated as an address. An operand followed by ",X", i.e., 465,X, indicates indexed addressing.

For purposes of design examples, it will be convenient to assume a standard microcomputer configuration. We shall assume a system as shown in Fig. 12.13, with the memory map of Fig. 12.12, with the addition of one PIA, which will be assigned addresses 4000 to 4003. (Since the addresses are not fully decoded in Fig. 12.13, the addition of the PIA will require changes in the address connections to the RAM. See Problem 12.5.) The register selection bits in the PIA, RS_0, RS_1, will be

TABLE 12.12   PIA Addresses in
Example System

Address	Register
4000	*PPA*
4001	*PPB*
4002	*CRA*
4003	*CRB*

connected to $ADBUS_{14}$, $ADBUS_{15}$, so that the addresses of the PIA will be as shown in Table 12.12. Further, we shall assume that any program written for this system will include the statements,

PPA	EQU	4000
PPB	EQU	4001
CRA	EQU	4002
CRB	EQU	4003

so that we can use the symbolic names in programs.

There are certain problems that arise frequently in the design of many different systems, and it is important that the designer have a repertoire of standard techniques for solving these problems. Since microcomputer systems involve both hardware and software, the standard solutions may involve hardware, in the form of standard circuits; or software, in the form of standard subroutines; or a mixture of both.

A typical microcomputer system will have a number of devices capable of interrupting. As we have seen, however, the 6800 has only one interrupt line so that the first part of any interrupt routine will be a check to determine which devices have interrupted. If interrupt handling is done by means of PIA's, determination of the interrupt source will be done by testing the interrupt flags of the PIA's. The simplest method is a sequential poll of the PIA control registers, as provided by the following subroutine.

Line 110 loads *ACCA* with the mask word 11000000. Line 120 AND's the contents of *CRA* with this word, setting *Z* if neither interrupt flag is set and setting *N* if CRA_0 is set. If neither is set, line 130 branches to check the other side of the PIA. If CRA_0 is set, line 140 branches to a routine to service this interrupt. Only if $CRA_0 = 0$ and $CRA_1 = 1$ will the routine reach line 150, which branches to the service routine for that interrupt. The remainder of the routine checks *CRB* for interrupts. The routine can be easily extended to poll any number of PIA's.

```
0100    *  SUBROUTINE TO POLL PIA INTERRUPT FLAGS
0110    POLL  LDAA  #$CO  LOAD MASK
0120          BITA  CRA   CHECK FOR FLAGS SET
0130          BEQ   NEXT  NOT SET, GO TO NEXT CHECK
0140          BMI   SER1  BIT-0 SET, GO TO SERVICE ROUTINE
0150          BRA   SER2  BIT-1 SET, GO TO SERVICE ROUTINE
0160    NEXT  BITA  CRB   CHECK FOR FLAGS SET
0170          BEQ   RTRN  NOT SET, RETURN
0200          BMI   SER3  BIT-0 SET, GO TO SERVICE ROUTINE
0210          BRA   SER4  BIT-1 SET, GO TO SERVICE ROUTINE
0220    RTRN  RTS         RETURN FROM SUBROUTINE
```

This routine illustrates the power of the BIT test command. The ability of the 6800 to address a peripheral location with this command enables a test of peripheral status without separate steps to input the status. In addition, the BIT command does not change the accumulator contents so that the mask needs to be loaded only once to check any number of control registers. It should also be noted that this routine is suitable even if CRA_1 or CRB_1 are not programmed as interrupts, since they are held low in that case.

In the event of simultaneous interrupts, the interrupts will be serviced in the order they are polled, which is fixed in the above program. In some cases a fixed priority for servicing may be satisfactory, but in other cases the order in which interrupts should be serviced may depend on the current program status. For example, the priority assigned to an interrupt source may depend on how long an interval has passed since it was last serviced. Such situations can be handled by more elaborate polling routines, in which the order of polling may be varied. Such routines will require more steps and will thus take longer to execute. It should be noted that the hardware interrupt routine, i.e., stacking the registers and jumping to the software interrupt routine, requires 10 cycles (10 μsec) to execute, and the RTI instruction requires another 10 cycles. If the time for complex polling and priority routines must be added to this minimum of 20 cycles associated with any interrupt, the time to service interrupts may be too long for fast peripherals. In that event it may be necessary to add external priority circuitry.

The interrupt system in the 6800 is a nonvectored system. The speed of interrupt response may be significantly increased by adding external hardware to convert it to a vectored system, i.e., one in which the hardware generates an address associated with the specific interrupt. All interrupt sources are OR-tied to the $\overline{irq}$ line in the usual manner. When

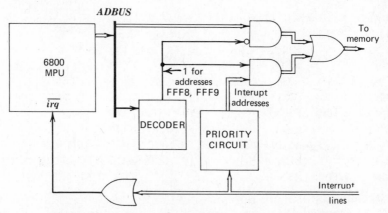

Figure 12.17. External generation of interrupt vector.

this line goes low, the MPU stacks the registers and generates the addresses FFF8 and FFF9. The address lines from the MPU are not routed directly to the memory chips; instead, they go to address generation network, which also receives an individual interrupt line from each source. A decoder must be included to check for the addresses FFF8 and FFF9. Any other addresses are routed to the memory without change. If either of these two addresses is detected, the network generates the addresses corresponding to highest priority interrupt present. The block diagram of Fig. 12.17 illustrates the basic approach.

Example 12.2
Design an external priority interrupt circuit to generate the interrupt vectors for the highest priority active interrupt from four interrupt lines.*

Solution
In response to the interrupt signal on $\overline{irq}$, the MPU will generate two addresses, FFF8 and FFF9. The priority circuit must convert these to the addresses of the pairs of locations, where the pointers to the interrupt routines for the four sources have been stored. The pairs of addresses that must be generated from each source are shown in Table 12.13. It would be possible to locate the interrupt pointers anywhere in memory and have the priority circuit generate the full addresses. However, if the pointers are grouped near FFF8 and FFF9 as shown, only three bits ($ADBUS_{12:14}$) of the addresses generated by the MPU

---

*We have limited the number of sources to four in the interest of simplicity. In practice, this approach would be justified only for a much larger number of sources.

TABLE 12.13   Interrupt Vectors for Example 12.2

	Address from 6800	
Source	FFF9	FFF8
1	FFF9	FFF8
2	FFF7	FFF6
3	FFF5	FFF4
4	FFF3	FFF2

need to be altered. Figure 12.18 shows the block diagram of the system, assuming the memory map of Fig. 12.12, which places the interrupt locations in ROM module 6830 No. 1. The AHPL description of the module follows.

MODULE: VECTOR
    MEMORY: *INTREG* [4]
    INPUTS: $ADBUS_{6:14}$; *INTLINES* [4]
    OUTPUTS: *ADOUT* [3]
    CLOCK: $\phi 2$
END SEQUENCE
    INTREG $* \overline{intsig} \leftarrow$ *INTLINES*
    $intsig = (\wedge /ADBUS_{6:12}) \wedge \overline{ADBUS}_{13} \wedge \overline{ADBUS}_{14}$
    ADOUT $= ((ADBUS_{12:14})$! $(ADDRF(PRI(INTREG)))) * (\overline{intsig}, intsig)$
END

Although no control sequence is required, the module VECTOR is a sequential circuit. The 4-bit register **INTREG** is updated each clock period from the interrupt lines unless the addresses FFF8 or FFF9 appear on the **ADBUS**. In that event a 1 appears on line **intsig**. This signal inhibits the updating of **INTREG**, to ensure that both addresses will be generated even if a higher-priority interrupt should arrive while a pointer is being fetched. If **intsig** is low, the last statement passes bits 12 to 14 of the address through without change; if **intsig** is high, the appropriate bits to generate the desired vectors are gated out. In this example PRI is left undefined—it could be a simple combinational priority circuit such as used in SIC or a complex module permitting variable priority. The ADDRF network generates the appropriate address bits based on the output of PRI.

Another very common problem in systems using microcomputers is the generation of time delay. Many applications require the computer to take some action and then wait a fixed length for time before taking

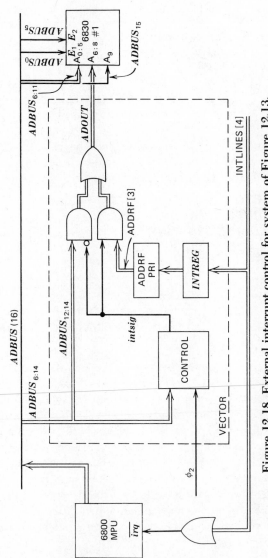

Figure 12.18. External interrupt control for system of Figure 12.13.

some other action. One approach is to load a register in the MPU and then decrement the register until it reaches zero, by means of a program segment such as

```
0400                 LDAA    #COUNT
0410     TIME        DECA
0420                 BNE     TIME
0430                 continue
```

Each pass through the loop requires six cycles so that this segment will introduce a delay (in microseconds) of $2 + (6 \times COUNT)$. Since the maximum value for COUNT is 253 (decimal), the maximum interval with this segment is 380 μsec. Longer intervals can be generated by incrementing the 16-bit index register, or incrementing memory locations, which take longer to access. In general, this programming approach should be used only for relatively short delays, since it makes the MPU unavailable for other tasks. When long intervals are required, it is generally preferable to have the MPU trigger external time-delay circuitry that will then interrupt when the specified interval is complete.

Keyboards of various types are often used as inputs in microcomputer systems. Typically, whenever a key is pressed, a corresponding code should be entered into register or memory location. Switches in a keyboard are typically arranged in a matrix as shown in Fig. 12.19. When a switch is closed, a connection is made between a horizontal and a vertical line. In a fully decoded keyboard, electronics will be provided to determine which lines have been connected, and to generate a corresponding code, along with a strobe signal to indicate that the coded output is ready. The keyboard electronics will also "debounce" the switches. Most switches involve some sort of mechanical spring action, and the contacts will usually bounce when operated, resulting in several rapid openings and closings of the circuit. In conventional applications, such as turning on lights, this bouncing action is too fast to be noticed, but digital devices are fast enough to follow the bounce action, possibly resulting in erroneous operation. As a result, switches that drive digital systems are usually equipped with "debounce" circuits that provide a single level change for each operation of a switch.

Keyboards equipped with all necessary electronics for debouncing and coding are readily available. However, if a keyboard is to be used with a microprocessor, the extra electronics can be eliminated by letting the processor perform the debouncing and coding functions. The bouncing action of a switch normally continues for no more than a millisecond, although the manufacturer's specifications should be checked in any particular instance. Debouncing can thus be accomplished by delaying

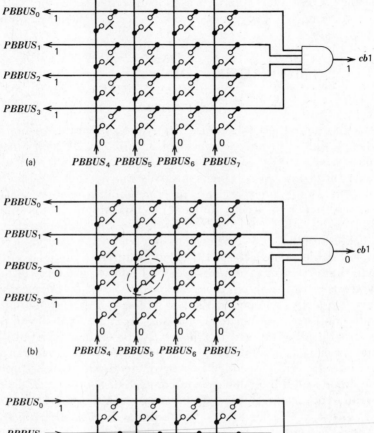

(a)

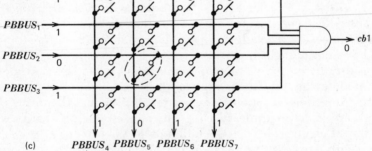

(b)

(c)

Figure 12.19. Read of data from a keyboard.

interrogation of the switch until it has stopped bouncing. Determining which switch is closed is accomplished in most micoprocessors by some kind of scanning routine, which sequentially checks each line of the matrix. The capability to set each peripheral line for input or output in the PIA can be utilized for an interrogation routine that eliminates the need for a line-by-line scan.

Example 12.3

Write a keyboard scan routine for a keyboard of 16 keys arranged in a 4×4 matrix. This routine should load *ACCA* with a code corresponding to the key pressed. In the event of two or more keys being pressed at the same time, it should generate a signal to sound a buzzer, to indicate that the clerk should reenter the data.

Solution

The complete program is shown in Fig. 12.20. The initializing subroutine sets up control register *CRB* to enable interrupts on negative-going transitions on *cb1* and to enable access to *DDRB*. It enables *PBBUS*$_{0:3}$ as inputs and *PBBUS*$_{4:7}$ as outputs and then loads *ORB* with 11110000. The horizontal lines of the matrix are connected to *PBBUS*$_{0:3}$, the vertical lines to *PBBUS*$_{4:7}$, and the horizontal lines are also ANDed to *cb1*. The initial situation is thus as shown in Fig. 12.19a. The four open-circuit lines leading to *PBBUS*$_{0:3}$ are interpreted by the input circuitry as logical 1's.

Now assume that the circled switch in Fig. 12.19b is closed. This will result in a negative transition on *cb1*, causing an interrupt, and will place a 0 on line *PBBUS*$_2$. After stacking the registers in response to the interrupts and polling to determine that the keyboard is the source of the interrupt, the MPU then branches to a delay loop, such as discussed earlier, to wait for the switch bounce to end, after which it reads the peripheral data into *ACCA*. Recall that a read of lines programmed as outputs reads the output register, so the word read into *ACCA* will be 11010000.

The MPU now has enough information to determine the horizontal line on which the switch is located but also needs to determine the vertical line. For this purpose, we now complement *DDRB*, to program *PBBUS*$_{0:3}$ as outputs and *PBBUS*$_{4:7}$ as inputs. We then OR *ACCA* with $0F and load the result, 11011111, into *ORB*. The resultant situation at the switch matrix is shown in Fig. 12.19c. The peripheral output is now read back into *ACCA*, producing the word 11011011 in that register. We see that this procedure will always result in a word in *ACCA* with six 1's and two 0's, the locations of the two 0's corresponding to the two lines connected by the key closure.

At this point, line 400, all data required to identify the switch is in ACCA. The remainder of the routine is concerned with generating a code corresponding to

```
0100    INIT    LDAA    #$01    *LOAD CRB TO ENABLE CB1 AND
0110            STAA    CRB     *ACCESS DDRB
0120    BUZZ    LDAA    #$0F    *SET UP PB0-PB3 AS INPUTS,
0130            STAA    PPB     *PB4-PB7 AS OUTPUTS
0140            LDAA    #$05    *SET CRB TO ACCESS ORB
0150            STAA    CRB
0160            LDAA    #$F0    *LOAD 11110000 IN ORB
0170            STAA    PPB
0200            RTS
0300    KBRD    JSR     DELAY   *DELAY UNTIL BOUNCE ENDS
0310            LDAA    PPB     *LOAD SWITCH DATA
0320            CLR     CRB     *ACCESS DDRB, SET PB0-PB3 AS
0330            COM     PPB     *OUTPUTS, PB4-PB7 AS INPUTS
0340            LDAB    #$05    *ACCESS ORB
0350            STAB    CRB
0360            ORAA    #$0F    *OR READ DATA WITH 00001111,
0370            STAA    PPB     *STORE IN ORB
0400            LDAA    PPB     *READ SWITCH DATA
0410            LDX     KLIST   *LOAD INDEX WITH ADDRESS OF
                                 KLIST
0420            CLRB
0430    CHECK   CMPA    0,X     *COMPARE SWITCH DATA TO
                                 KLIST
0440            BEQ     CODE    *IF MATCH, GO TO LOOK UP
                                 CODE
0450            INCB            *NO MATCH, INCREMENT ACCB
0460            CMPB    #$10    *ALL CHECKED WITHOUT
                                 MATCH?
0470            BEQ     ERROR   *YES, GO TO ERROR
0500            INX             *NO, INCR. KLIST ADDRESS,
0510            BRA     CHECK   *GO BACK TO CHECK NEXT
0520    CODE    STAB    TEMP    *TRANSFER COUNT TO
0530            LDX     TEMP    *INDEX REGISTER, TRANSFER
0540            LDAA    CADD,X  *CODE WORD TO ACCA
0550            BRS     INIT    *INITIATE FOR NEXT KEY CLO-
                                 SURE
0560            RTI             *RETURN TO MAIN PROGRAM
0570    ERROR   LDAA    #$21    *SET UP CRB FOR WRITE
0600            STAA    CRB     *TO SIGNAL ERROR
0610            BRS     BUZZ    *BRANCH TO SIGNAL ERRO-
                                 NEOUS ENTRY
0620            RTI             *RETURN TO MAIN PROGRAM
```

Figure 12.20. Keyboard read program.

the key. Some form of table look-up will normally be involved, and a variety of techniques are available. This routine assumes that the 16 possible words corresponding to a single switch closure have been stored at location KLIST. Lines 410 to 510 search this list for a match, counting the number of words checked in *ACCB*. If a match is found, lines 520 to 560 obtain the corresponding code from a list for which the starting address is CADD. If no match is found, the read data corresponds to a multiple-switch closure, which is considered to be an error. In that event the steps starting in line 570 set up *cb2* as an output for write handshake and then go back to 120 to set up for the next character. The write to *ORB* at line 170 will then drop *cb2*, as a signal to activate a buzzer indicating an erroneous entry, and the interrupt corresponding to the next entry will then restore *cb2* to the high level.

This example illustrates several interesting points about the use of microcomputers. First, it is a good illustration of the tremendous speed of microprocessors in terms of a human time frame. Here we have a program of over 30 instructions, including a loop that may be executed 16 times, that must be executed every time a key is pressed. An experienced operator might be able to press four keys per second, allowing one quarter of a second for the program. But one quarter of a second is 250,000 μsec, and the average execution time of the 6800 is about 5 μsec. The microprocessor could thus execute 50,000 instructions in the interval between closures. Indeed, it is so fast that we have to deliberately introduce delay to allow for switch bounce. If this were all the processor were doing, it would be idling more than 99 percent of the time.

The use of the microprocessor to "debounce" the switches is an example of something mentioned earlier, the use of microcomputers to do things that one would not usually think of doing by computer. An electronic "debounce" circuit is quite simple and one could not justify using a microcomputer for that task alone, but if a microcomputer is being used anyway and "can spare the time," then using it for that purpose is entirely reasonable. Another aspect of the replacement of logic circuitry by programming is that one should consider the *function* of the logic circuitry to be replaced rather than its *structure*. Some manufacturers of microcomputer systems offer program packages that simulate standard logic devices, enabling the designer to simulate complete systems by linking these packages together in a manner analogous to the interconnections of the logic devices. This is seldom the best design approach. Instead, one should consider the basic function of the entire logic system and design to achieve that function with the simplest possible program structure.

All of the examples in this section also bring in the familiar problem of cost-speed tradeoff. Performing a task by external electronics will almost always be faster than doing it by programming but will probably be more expensive. The cost factor is usually strongly affected by volume considerations. Programming is primarily a one-time cost, for the initial programming and generation of the ROM patterns, with a very small incremental cost for each additional unit produced. The initial design cost for custom electronics may be less than programming costs, but there is a much higher unit cost for manufacturing the electronics for each unit produced. As a result the choice between the two methods will often depend on the number of units to be produced.

Example 12.4

Let us now interface the paper tape reader of Example 11.1 to the 6800, using a 6820 PIA. The reader will recall that this reader has two input lines, *step* and *forward*, 8-bit data output lines, *TAPE*[8], and two output control lines, *datatrue* and *prtp*. A pulse with a minimum duration of 100 μsec on *step* will cause the tape to move to the next character, in the direction indicated by the level signal on *forward* (1 = forward, 0 = reverse). The minimum interval between pulses on *step* is 4 msec, and a change in the level on *forward* must be followed by a 4-msec delay before another *step* pulse can be sent. The line *prtp* will be at the 1-level whenever the reader power is on. Line *datatrue* will go to the 1-level 2 msec after the start of the *step* pulse to indicate that the new character is available on the *TAPE* lines, and will go back to the 0-level 2 msec later to indicate that a new *step* pulse can be accepted. Note that the return of *datatrue* to the 0-level is provided only to indicate that the 4-msec interval is complete; the data are valid on *TAPE* from the time *datatrue* goes high until the tape starts moving as a result of the next *step* pulse. In designing an interface for this reader

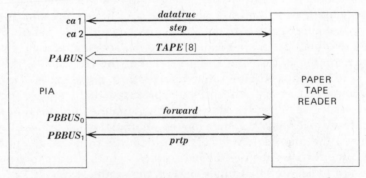

Figure 12.21. Connections between paper tape reader and PIA in Example 12.4.

it is important to note that the standard procedure is to read the character currently under the read head and *then* advance the tape. Since our objective is to minimize the amount of external electronics, parity checking will be done within the 6800, after the word has been transmitted to *ACCA*.

The connections between the tape reader and the PIA are shown in Fig. 12.21. Primary communications will be through the A side; *forward* and *prtp* occupy 2 bits on the B side, the remainder of the B side being available for other purposes. The *ca2* command will be used to issue the *step* pulses and will be programmed to follow *CRA*$_4$. Negative transitions of *datatrue* will be used as interrupts on *ca1* to signal that the reader is ready for a new *step* pulse. The data input will be through the *PABUS*.

0210	PTINIT	CLR	CRA	* SET CONTROL REGISTERS
0220		LDAA	CRB	* FOR ACCESS TO
0230		ANDA	#$FB	* DATA DIRECTION
0240		STAA	CRB	* REGISTERS.
0250		CLR	PPA	* SET DDRA FOR INPUT
0260		LDAA	PPB	* SET PB1
0270		ANDA	#$BF	* FOR INPUT,
0300		ORAA	#$80	* PB0 FOR
0310		STAA	PPB	* OUTPUT.
0320		LDAA	CRB	* SET CRB5
0330		ORAA	#$04	* FOR ACCESS
0340		STAA	CRB	* TO ORB,
0350		LDAA	#$40	* CHECK PRTP,
0360		BITA	PPB	* POWER ON?
0370		BNE	NXT1	* YES, GO TO NXT1
0400		JSR	ALRM	* NO, NOTIFY OPERATOR.
0410	NXT1	LDAA	#$FC	* SET PA LINES FOR INPUT,
0420		STAA	CRA	* CA1 FOR INTERRUPT ON
0430	* NEG TRANSITION, CA2 TO FOLLOW CRA4, TURN ON CA2.			
0440		JSR	D100	* DELAY 100 MICROSEC
0450		LDAA	CRA	* TURN OFF
0460		ANDA	#$F7	* CA2,
0470		ORAA	#$01	* ENABLE
0500		STAA	CRA	* INTERRUPT
0510		RTS		* RETURN TO MAIN PROGRAM

The subroutine PTINIT is used to set up the PIA for interfacing with the paper tape reader. Lines 210 to 240 set the control registers for access to the data direction registers. Since all of the A side is used for the reader, we simply clear *CRA*. The B side, however, is used for other purposes so that we wish to clear only bit CRB_5, providing access to $DDRB$. Steps 220 to 240 illustrate a procedure used repeatedly in the program when it is desired to alter only certain bits in a word and leave other bits undisturbed. To set bits to 0, a mask word, with 0's in the bit positions to be cleared and 1's in all other positions, is ANDed with the word to be altered. To set bits to 1, a mask word, with 1's in the bit positions to be set and 0's in all other positions, is ORed with the word to be altered.

Lines 250 to 310 set $PABUS$ and $PBBUS_1$ for input and $PBBUS_0$ for output. Lines 320 to 340 set CRB_5 to provide access to ORB and the $PBBUS$ lines. Lines 350 to 370 check $prtp$ to verify that the paper tape reader is turned on. This illustrates another standard procedure for testing individual bits in words. We load the accumulator with a mask word of all 0's except for a 1 in the bit position to be tested. The execution of the BIT command then ANDs the word to be tested with the mask word, without changing the test word, and sets the CCR bits accordingly. If the tested bit is 0, the ANDing produces all zeros and the z bit in CCR is set; if the tested bit is 1, the z bit is not set. In this case, if the power is on, the program skips to NXT1 to continue the setup process. If power is not on, it jumps to subroutine ALRM, which notifies the operator and waits for $prtp$ to go up. We shall not consider ALRM here, since it would depend on the peripherals available for notifying the operator.

With the power on, the routine continues at NXT1 to load the CRA register with the control word 11111100, which provides for setting of interrupt flag CRA_0 by negative transitions on $ca1$, provides access to the $PABUS$ for input, sets up $ca2$ to follow CRA_4 as an output, and sets CRA_4 to drive $ca2$ to 1, initiating the 100-μsec pulse on $step$. Line 440 then jumps to a subroutine to generate a 100-μsec delay. On completion of this delay, lines 450 to 500 turn off CRA_4, thus ending the $step$ pulse, and enable the interrupt on $irqa$. Control then returns to the main program to await the interrupt generated by the negative transition on $datatrue$ after 4 msec.

Note that this routine does not actually read a character. Paper tape is always loaded initially on a blank section so that no characters will be lost by stepping the tape one position before reading. This initial step is provided solely to generate the first interrupt by $datatrue$ that will start the actual reading of the tape.

When the interrupt occurs on the negative transition of $datatrue$, the interrupt routine, after identifying the tape reader as the source, will jump to one of two routines, TAPEF or TAPER, depending on whether it is desired to step forward or backward following the read of a character. The TAPEF routine starts by reading the data word into $ACCA$. Line 610 checks the status of $forward$. Recall that when a line is programmed for output, a READ of that line will read the corresponding bit of the output register, which in turn drives that line. Since $forward$ will have to be checked each time a character is read, it has been connected to $PBBUS_0$, which is the simplest line to test. This bit corresponds to the sign bit for numeric data. The TEST command compares the tested word to 0 and sets bit n in CCR if the word is negative. If *forward* is set, line 620 branches to NXT2 to step the tape. If *forward* = 0, lines 630 to 660 set it to 1 and wait 4 msec before proceeding to NXT2. The remainder of the program generates the 100-μsec *step* pulse and enables the interrupt in the same manner as the PTINIT routine discussed above. The TAPER routine will be the same except for clearing *forward* instead of setting it.

0600	TAPEF	LDAA	PPA	* READ DATA WORD
0610		TEST	PPB	* FORWARD SET?
0620		BMI	NXT2	* YES, GO TO NXT2
0630		LDAB	PPB	* NO, SET FORWARD
0640		ORAB	#$80	
0650		STAB	PPB	
0660		JSR	D4M	* DELAY 4 MILLISEC
0670	NXT2	LDAB	CRA	* PROCEED TO STEP TAPE
0700		ORAB	#$08	* TURN ON CA2
0710		ANDB	#$FE	* DISABLE INTERRUPT
0720		STAB	CRA	
0730		JSR	D100	* DELAY 100 MICROSEC
0740		LDAB	CRA	
0750		ANDB	#$F7	* TURN OFF CA2
0760		ORAB	#$01	* ENABLE INTERRUPT
0770		STAB	CRA	
1000		RTI		* RETURN TO MAIN PROGRAM

The interface routine designed above assumes that once tape reading is commenced, it is desirable to interrupt the MPU whenever a new character is available. In some cases it might be preferable to let the MPU control the timing. This could be done by disabling the *irqa* line (by setting CRA_7 to 0). The flag CRA_0 would still be set by negative transitions of *datatrue*, thus serving as a status flag indicating when the reader has data available. When a character was desired, the program would test this bit (with the command TEST CRA) and proceed with other activities and check again at intervals, or go into a loop waiting for the data to become available. The above routine also permits changing from forward read to reverse read at any time. In many situations, the direction of read would be changed infrequently, if at all. In that event, the PTINIT routine could set the desired direction and the checking and setting of *forward* in the tape read routines could be eliminated.

As the final design example in this chapter, let us consider the use of a 6800 system as a controller for a floppy disk unit. This poses a very different sort of problem, since a floppy disk is very fast, so fast that we shall find it necessary to use external electronics to perform some tasks the MPU is too slow to handle. A floppy disk stores data on a flexible plastic disk coated with magnetic recording material. Data are recorded serially on concentric tracks, at a nominal rate of 250 kHZ, i.e., 1 bit every 4 μsec. If the controller is to interface directly to this serial data train, it must be capable of reading or writing at this rate. It is obvious that the 6800 cannot meet this speed requirement. For example, the minimum possible write sequence would consist of pulling successive words off the stack, shifting them to form a serial bit string, and transmitting them to the PIA output register, 1 bit at a time. But the pull instruction alone requires 4 μsec to execute.

As an alternative, let us consider external electronics to convert from serial to parallel on read and from parallel to serial on write. On read this circuitry would shift the serial data from the disk into an 8-bit shift register. When a byte had been assembled, it would be transferred to an 8-bit output register. The PIA would be signaled that a word was ready, and the next word would be assembled in the shift register. The procedure would be similar for write, except in the opposite direction. With this method the controller must be capable of sending or receiving a word every 8-bit times, i.e., every 32 μsec. Let us now see if the 6800 is fast enough to meet this requirement.

The most ovious approach is to interrupt via the $\overline{irq}$ line whenever the disk is ready for a transfer. However, because of the stacking and unstacking of the registers, 20 cycles are required to jump to an interrupt routine and return. Further, an interrupt request via irq cannot be serviced until the current instruction is completed. Thus there is a minimum "overhead" of about 30 cycles associated with responding to interrupts on irq so that we could not reliably respond to requests for data transfer every 32 μsec. An alternate approach is to disable irq and continuously monitor the interrupt flag in the PIA via a program loop. If the interrupt from the disk is connected to $ca1$, the following instructions will hold the MPU in a loop until CRA_0 is set by a transition on $ca1$.

INTEST BITB CRA

BPL   INTEST

We use the BIT command instead of TST because it is 2 cycles faster. It requires that $ACCB_0 = 1$, but this can be set during initialization, after which the loop can be used any number of times, since BIT does not change the accumulator contents. This loop requires 8 cycles to execute, but a transition in $ca1$ may come just after execution of the BITB command has started so it may take nearly 16 cycles (16 μsec) to detect an interrupt.

Most floppy disks store data in the IBM 3740 format, in which data are stored in fixed-length record, or *fields*, of 128 bytes. There is no special signal to indicate the end of a field, as there is with magnetic tape; therefore, the controller must count the number of bytes read and terminate read operations when 128 bytes have been received. On that basis the simplest possible read loop would be the following, in which we assume that the A side of the PIA is used for input.

1200	RDLOOP	BITB	CRA	*TEST FOR
1210		BPL	RDLOOP	*BYTE READY
1220		LDAA	PPA	*GET BYTE
1230		PSHA		*STORE BYTE
1240		INCB		*INCR BYTE COUNTER
1250		BNE	RDLOOP	*LOOP UNTIL LAST BYTE

The *ACCB* register is used as a byte counter, being initially set to -128, which also sets bit 0 to 1 as required for the BITB test at line 1200. Allowing for the maximum 16 cycles to recognize a byte-ready signal, this loop requires 30 μsec per byte transferred, just barely fast enough. Some margin for variations in MPU clock rate or disk speed can be provided by noting that the loop at lines 1200 and 1210 requires a minimum of 8 cycles to respond so that the byte-ready signal could be issued up to 8 μsec before the byte was actually ready for transfer. This look-ahead does not alter the average transfer rate of 1 byte every 32 μsec, but the worst case of 16 cycles to detect a byte-ready signal will occur only occasionally. Also note that the read of the peripheral data lines at line 1220 automatically clears the interrupt flag CRA_0. This characteristic of the PIA is very useful here, since there is no time to spare for separate clearing of the flag.

In order to design the external read circuitry necessary to convert data from serial to parallel, we must consider the signal formats from the disk. In the 3740 format, information is recorded in the form of alternate clock and data pulses. Special electronics are provided as a part of the disk unit to separate the clock and data trains. The read electronics provide three output lines, a data line, *data*, a clock line, *datatime*, which indicate when data are valid, and a line *mark*, which will be discussed below. The relative timing of *data* and *datatime* is illustrated in Fig. 12.22a.

The *datatime* pulses will be used to time the reading of the *data* line, but we also need a means to determine the start time for each byte. In

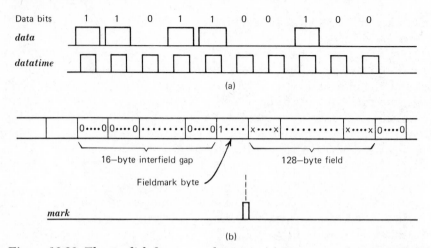

Figure 12.22. Floppy disk formats and timing. (*a*) Timing on data and clock lines. (*b*) Portion of typical data track and relative timing of *mark*.

the 3740 format, each data field (record) is preceded by an interrecord gap of at least 16 bytes of all zeros. Preceding each field is a *field mark* byte, in which the first bit is always 1. There are several special marks used in the 3740 format, which consist not only of a particular byte pattern in the data but also of a particular clock pattern. The clock separation circuitry places a 1 on the *mark* line at bit 7 time if this special clock pattern is received.

When the controller wishes to read a field, it sends a read-enable signal to the read module. This module then starts monitoring the *data* line. As soon as a 1 is detected on the *data* line, the module starts counting bits as they are shifted into a register. When 8 bits have been received, the module signals the controller that a byte is available, and the controller checks the *mark* line and this byte to see if it is the field mark. If the read-enable signal was sent while an interrecord gap was being read, the first 1 on the data line will be the start of the field mark and reading of the bytes in the field can now proceed. If the read module was enabled while a data field was under the read head, the first 1 detected will not be the start of the field mark, and the first 8 bits sent will not correspond to that mark. In that event the controller will turn off the read module and then turn it on again. This process will be repeated until a field mark is detected. The process requires less than 3 byte times per byte checked so that the first interrecord gap to come under the head will be detected.

With this background we are now in a position to design a read module to interface between the floppy disk unit and the 6800 controller mod-

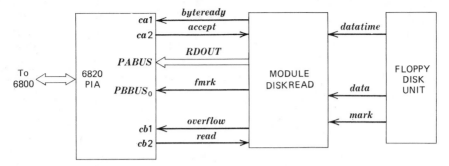

Figure 12.23. System connections to module DISKREAD.

ule. The system interconnections are shown in Fig. 12.23. The **byte-ready** line, indicating that a byte is ready for transmission, is connected to **ca1**, which is programmed to set CRA_0 on positive transitions. An **accept** signal is provided by **ca2** programmed to function in the read handshake mode. This line will go high on the active transition of **ca1** and will go low on the read of the peripheral data lines. If this line has not gone low when the next byte is ready, the module will issue an **overflow** signal, connected to interrupt on $\overline{irqb}$ via **cb1**. The **read** signal (read-enable) will be provided by **cb2**, programmed to follow CRB_4. The **mark** signal will be stored by the read module and made available to the PIA on line **fmrk**, connected to $PBBUS_0$. The data are transmitted over line **RDOUT** [8] to the PABUS inputs of the PIA.

The block diagram of the DISKREAD module is shown in Fig. 12.24.

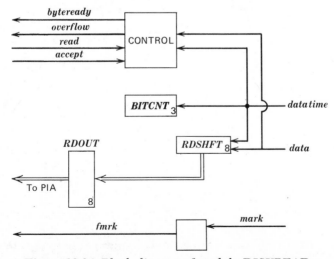

Figure 12.24. Block diagram of module DISKREAD.

The 8-bit shift register **RDSHFT** is used to assemble the serial bits into bytes and **RDOUT** stores the assembled byte for transmission. The modulo-8 counter **BITCNT** counts the bits as they are shifted in, and *fmrk* stores the *mark* bit. The module is clocked by *datatime*.

The control sequence for the module follows.

MODULE: DISKREAD
  MEMORY: **BITCNT** [3]; **RDOUT** [8]; **RDSHFT** [8]; *fmrk*
  INPUTS: *datatime; data; read; accept; mark*
  OUTPUTS: **RDOUT** [8]; *byteready; overflow; fmrk*
  CLOCK: *datatime*
  1. $\rightarrow (\overline{\text{SYN}(read)})/(1)$
  2. **RDSHFT** $\leftarrow$ **RDSHFT**$_{1:7}$, *data*; **BITCNT** * *data* $\leftarrow$ 0, 0, 0
     $\rightarrow (\overline{data})/(2)$
  3. **RDSHFT** $\leftarrow$ **RDSHFT**$_{1:7}$, *data*; **BITCNT** $\leftarrow$ INC(**BITCNT**);
     fmrk * $(\overline{BITCNT_0 \wedge BITCNT_1 \wedge \overline{BITCNT_2}}) \leftarrow$ *mark*
     $\rightarrow (BITCNT_0 \wedge BITCNT_1 \wedge \overline{BITCNT_2})/(3)$
  4. **RDSHFT** $\leftarrow$ **RDSHFT**$_{1:7}$, *data*; **BITCNT** $\leftarrow$ INC(**BITCNT**):
     byteready = $\overline{\text{SYN}(accept)}$; **RDOUT** $\leftarrow$ **RDSHFT**
     $\rightarrow (\text{SYN}(accept))/(6)$
  5. NO DELAY
     $\rightarrow (\text{SYN}(read), \overline{\text{SYN}(read)})/(3, 1)$
  6. *overflow* = 1
     $\rightarrow (\text{SYN}(read), \overline{\text{SYN}(read)})/(6, 1)$
END

Step 1 holds in a waiting loop until the PIA raises the *read* line. Step 2 starts shifting bits in to **RDSHFT** but does not start counting bits until a 1 is received, at which time **BITCNT** is reset, indicating that bit-0 of a byte has been received. Control then proceeds to step 3, where the rest of the bits in the byte are shifted in and counted. The data arrives most significant bit first, so data is shifted left into **RDSHFT**. Note that **BITCNT** always indicates the number of the bit that was shifted in at the last clock time. Thus $\perp$**BITCNT** = 6 indicates bit-7 time, when *mark* is available to be loaded into *fmrk*.

When $\perp$**BITCNT** = 6, indicating that the last bit in the byte is being shifted in, control branches to step 4 to transfer the asembled byte to **RDOUT**. There is no gap between bytes in the data train so that the first bit of the next byte must also be shifted in at the same time. Step 4 also issues the *byteready* signal, provided that *accept* is low, indicating that the previous byte has been picked up. If *accept* is still high, control branches to step 6 to issue the *overflow* signal, which will interrupt the

MPU. The control holds at step 6 until *read* goes low, indicating that the processor has responded to the interrupt by terminating the read operation, after which the control returns to step 1 to await a new read operation.

Note the timing of the **byteready** signal. Since this is a connection statement, **byteready** will go high at the beginning of step 4, while the data being transferred to **RDOUT** will not be available until the end of step 4. The PIA thus has 4 μsec of "advance notice" that a word will be available, as discussed earlier. The handshake operation provided by the *accept* signal is needed since, as noted earlier, the MPU is just barely fast enough to keep up with the disk and may fall behind due to disk speed or clock variations. If there is no overflow, control continues from step 4 to step 5 to determine if the read operation has been terminated. If it has not, control returns to step 3 to continue the read process.

Note that syncronization is specified for the signals *accept* and *read*, which enter the DISKREAD module from the ϕ2-clocked PIA. If these signals are not synchronized to *datatime*, DISKREAD could be driven to two simultaneous control states, as discussed in Chapter 9. In the reverse the *byteready* and *overflow* signals enter the PIA as interrupts. Interrupt signals are clocked into flip-flops before being sampled by a control sequence, and no further synchronization is required. This is a general feature of interrupt inputs in microprocessors, that synchronization is automatically provided, so that the designer need not be concerned with synchronization of interrupt signals.

Let us now consider a program to interract with this read module, to read a 128-byte record. We assume that the PIA has been initialized to program the lines to function as discussed above. The address of the buffer area where the 128 bytes are to be stored is located at **BUFADR** and the test pattern corresponding to the field identification mark is stored at **TSTMKR**. The complete program is shown in Fig. 12.25.

The program begins by loading the buffer address into the stack pointer, the test mark into the index register, and -128 into **ACCB**, which will serve as the byte counter. The next three steps, starting at RDSTRT, set **CRB**$_4$, which raises *cb2*, issuing the **read** signal to the module. The portion of the program starting at TSTLP waits for the **byteready** signal indicating that the first byte is ready and compares this byte to the test mark stored in the index register. The index register is used because the field mark is 9 bits, consisting of the field mark byte and *fmrk*, which is connected to **PBBUS**$_0$. The data ports, **PPA** and **PPB**, are assigned consecutive addresses, so that the single command CMX compares both to the 16-bit index register.

1500	FDSKRD	LDS	BUFADR	* LOAD SP WITH BUFFER ADDR.
1510		LDX	TSTMRK	* LOAD IX WITH TEST MARK.
1520		LDAB	#$80	* LOAD-128 IN ACCB.
1530	RDSTRT	LDAA	#$08	* SET CRB-4 TO
1540		ORAA	CRB	* RAISE CB-2 AND
1550		STAA	CRB	* ENABLE READ.
1560	TSTLP	BITB	CRA	* WAIT FOR
1570		BPL	TSTLP	* BYTEREADY.
1600		CMX	PPA	* MATCH TO TEST MARK?
1610		BEQ	RDLOOP	* YES, GO TO RDLOOP.
1620		LDAA	#$F7	* NO, CLEAR CRB-4 TO
1630		ANDA	CRB	* END READ AND
1640		STAA	CRB	* GO BACK TO
1650		BRA	RDSTRT	* RDSTRT AND LOOK AGAIN.
1660	RDLOOP	BITB	CRA	* TEST FOR
1670		BPL	RDLOOP	* BYTE READY.
1700		LDAA	PPA	* GET BYTE.
1710		PSHA		* STORE BYTE
1720		INCB		* INCR BYTE COUNTER.
1730		BNE	RDLOOP	* LOOP UNTIL LAST BYTE
1740		LDAA	#$F7	* CLEAR CRB-4 TO
1750		ANDA	CRB	* END READ AND
1760		STAA	CRB	* CONTINUE AS REQUIRED

Figure 12.25. Program to read record from disk.

If a match is found, the program branches to RDLOOP to begin reading the field. The byte counter is not incremented at this point, as the identification mark is not included in the 128 bytes of the data field. If a match is not found, the final steps in the TSTLP section turn off the *read* signal and return to RDSTRT to try again. The section starting at RDLOOP, as discussed earlier, pushes the successive words onto the stack and increments the byte counter until the entire field has been stored. The last three steps then clear the *read* signal, and the program then continues on to whatever next steps may be appropriate.

In this discussion we have simplified the problems of controlling a disk in the interests of clarity. The above program will read whatever field first comes under the head. A more sophisticated program would include provision for searching for a particular record. The write interface has not been considered at all. This would require another module, similar to the above, to serialize the data from the processor. A complete controller system must also include provision for moving the head to a desired track. The controller will keep a record of the current location of the head. When a new track is to be accessed, the new track address will be compared to the current track address to determine the direction of motion and the number of tracks over which the head must move. For most disks, the head will move one track each time a *step* line is pulsed. The controller must thus issue the appropriate number of *step* pulses at the appropriate rate, typically about 10 msec/track. This is slow by electronic standards so that the microprocessor can easily handle head motion control without external electronics. There are many other factors we could consider in the design of a floppy disk controller, but our objective here is only to illustrate the basic design approach and some typical problems that the designer may encounter. For the interested reader, Reference [1] details a complete design for a floppy disk controller.

12.10 SUMMARY

In this chapter we have hardly scratched the surface of the vast topic of microprocessors. We have discussed only one specific model of the dozens now available. We have considered only a few typical applications, most of them simple; but we hope that the reader will realize that the application of microprocessors involves only minor extensions of concepts already studied. The architecture of microprocessors is not basically different from that of full-size computers. With the background developed in this book, the reader should have little difficulty understanding the structure of any microprocessor. Programming a microprocessor is not very different from programming a minicomputer. Anyone capable of programming a minicomputer to perform a given task should be able to program a microcomputer to do the same thing.

As we noted at the beginning of the chapter, the only really different characteristic of microprocessors is that they are smaller and cheaper than full-size computers. This fact makes them practical for all kinds of new applications. They can be used to do tasks that have never been done by computers before, in areas where computers have never been considered. Thus the chief new demand on the designer is a demand for a new perspective about where, when, and how computers can be used.

In considering applications of microprocessors, we have focused primary attention on the problem of interfacing with peripherals and specially-designed modules. In some cases the peripherals and microprocessor taken together may form a complete system. In other cases the microprocessor may be simply controlling the peripherals in support of a larger system. The former situation is probably the more common. However, the designer should be alert for situations in which large systems can be partitioned into subunits in which the microprocessor can play a central role.

PROBLEMS

12.1 Devise a circuit to realize the control sequence given in Section 12.5 for the MODULE: 6800 CONTROL.

12.2 Assume an M6800 system with the memory configuration shown in Example 12.1. A programmer who does not understand memory maps writes a program including a number of addresses not in the ranges shown in the map. A list of addresses is given below. For each address, determine the chip accessed and the location accessed on that chip. Example: Address FFFF accesses location 3FF on ROM No. 1. For 6830, on-chip addresses are in the range 000 to 3FF; for 6810, in the range 00 to 7F. (All addresses in hexadecimal.)
(a) 9D41 (b) C541 (c) F95B (d) D964
(e) 01C4 (f) 7BC4 (g) 0144 (h) 007D (i) 00FD

12.3 For the memory system of Example 12.1, write AHPL descriptions for memory modules 6810-2, 6810-3, 6810-4, 6830-1, 6830-2, in the same manner as the description given in the text for 6810-1.

12.4 Assume that the system of Example 12.1 is to be expanded to accommodate 1024 words of RAM, in the form of eight 6810's. Show the revised memory map, and revise the connection diagram of Fig. 12.13 as required. (*Hint*: this may require external logic to partially decode the addresses.)

12.5 Again modify the system of Fig. 12.13, this time to accommodate a PIA, assigned addresses 4000 to 4003, as discussed in Section 12.9. Location 4000 is assigned to *PPA*, 4001 to *PPB*, 4002 to *CRA* and 4003 to *CRB*.

12.6 Modify the interrupt polling routine of Section 12.9 to poll the interrupts from three PIA's.

12.7 For the vectored interrupt system of Example 12.2, assume a fixed priority system, with source 1 having the highest priority, source 2 the second-highest priority, etc. Write AHPL unit descriptions of the networks PRI and ADDRF.

12.8   We now wish to design a vectored interrupt system similar to
that of Example 12.2, except that the priorities will be variable,
subject to control of the 6800 MPU. Let us assume the four interrupt sources are two PIA's. The memory map will be that of
Example 12.1, modified to assign locations 4000 to 4007 to the
PIA's. The interrupt system will include an 8-bit priority control
register, **PRIREG**, which is connected to the **DBUS** and is assigned address 4010. Whenever the priorities are to be changed,
the 6800 will send a new control word to **PRIREG**. The four
interrupt sources will be renumbered 0, 1, 2, 3. The desired
priorities may be indicated in either of two ways. One way is to
let the first two bits of **PRIREG** indicate the number of the device
which is to have the highest priority, the second two bits the
number of the device which is to have the second-highest priority, etc. The second approach is to let the first two bits indicate
the priority (0 for highest priority to 3 for lowest priority) of
device 0, the second two bits the priority for device 1, etc. You
may use whichever approach leads to the simplest design for the
associated circuitry. Modify the control sequence as required,
and redesign the networks PRI and ADDRF as required.

12.9   Write a delay loop program similar to that given in Section 12.9,
except that the program should increment two memory locations
catenated as a single 16-bit counter. What is the range of delays
that can be obtained with such a program, assuming the usual
clock rate of 1.0 MHz?

12.10 For long delays, programs such as written in Problem 12.9 are
often unsatisfactory, as they tie up the MPU for the entire period
of the delay. A preferable approach may be to use an external
counter which can be preset to count for some specified period
and then interrupt the MPU, which can thus be working at other
tasks in the interval. One convenient approach is to use a set of
cascaded decimal counters to divide the 1 MHz clock frequency
by multiples of 10, to provide frequencies of 100 KHz, 10 KHz,
1 KHz, etc. These lower frequencies are then used to drive a
presettable counter which produces an output pulse to interrupt
the MPU when the count reaches 10. For example, if we wished
to provide a delay of 4 msec., we would preset the counter to six
and trigger it with the 1 KHz signal. After four pulses, the counter
would reach 10 and produce a pulse to interrupt the MPU. For
this problem we wish to design such an interval timer to interact
with the MPU through the B side of a PIA.

All counters will be SN74192 counters, the pin diagram of

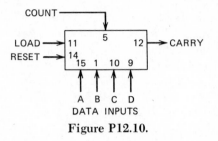

Figure P12.10.

which is shown in Figure P12.10. Negative-going pulses are required at the COUNT input. With LOAD held high, the counter functions as a decade counter, producing a negative pulse on the CARRY output for every ten COUNT pulses. The counters can thus be cascaded simply by connecting the CARRY output of one stage to the COUNT input of the next stage. When the LOAD input is driven low, the counter will be preset to the value appearing at data inputs A, B, C, D (D most significant). When LOAD goes high, the counter will then count to 10 in response to COUNT pulses, starting from the preset value. Driving the RESET line low will reset the count to zero. Five counters will be cascaded to divide the 1 MHZ clock down. Four output lines from the PIA, $PBBUS_{0:3}$, will be used to select one of four frequencies, 10 KHZ, 1 KHz, 100 Hz, or 10 Hz, to drive the presettable counter. The data inputs to the presettable counter will be driven by $PBBUS_{4:7}$, and the CARRY output of the presettable counter will interrupt via $cb1$. Line $cb2$ will drive the LOAD line of the presettable counter and the RESET lines of the decade counters. Draw the block diagram of the interval timer, showing the connections to the PIA, and write the AHPL description of the timer module. Write a segment of 6800 code to provide a delay of 40 msec. using this timer, including the steps necessary to initialize the PIA. What is the range of delays available with this timer? Would it be possible to obtain a delay of 25 msec? How?

12.11 The keyboard scan routine of Example 12.3 is based on the capability of the 6820 PIA of programming lines to function as either inputs or outputs. In other microprocessor systems this may not be the case, that is, certain lines are permanently dedicated for output, others for input. In such a situation a sequential scan will generally be the best approach. In this approach the output lines are connected to the horizontal lines of the matrix, the input lines to the vertical (or vice-versa, as may be convenient). The matrix is scanned by sequentially applying voltage to one output line at a time and checking the input lines. A voltage will appear on a vertical line only when voltage is applied to the horizontal line to which the closed switch is connected. To illustrate this method, assume that an 8 × 8 (64-switch) matrix is to be scanned using a PIA, with the *PABUS* available only for input, the *PBBUS* only for output. Write a program to carry out a sequential scan of this matrix, including provision for detecting multiple closures. Compare the complexity of this approach with that used in Example 12.3.

12.12 In Example 12.5 reference is made to a subroutine ALRM which notifies the operator that the power to the paper tape reader is not turned on. Assume that the alarm is in the form of light controlled by $PBBUS_7$ programmed as an output, 0 for OFF, 1 for ON. Modify the routine PTINIT to initialize $PBBUS_7$ with the light off. Write the subroutine ALRM, which should turn on the light, then monitor *prtp* until the power is turned on, then turn off the light and return to the main program.

12.13 Write a program to control the paper tape reader via status testing, as described immediately following Example 12.4.

12.14 A slower version of the tape transport described in Section 11.4 is to be interfaced to the 6800 MPU. The functioning of all input and output lines will remain the same except that the period on the line *sprocket* will be 50 μsec. Two PIA's will be required. Connect the 7 low-order bits of the two data buses of one PIA to the input and output data lines from the transport. Connect the *sprocket* line to a data input line on the other PIA. The remaining input and output lines may be connected to available PIA lines as appropriate. Write subroutines which will respond to *sprocket* signals by reading or writing characters. Include lateral parity checking and generation. Six-bit characters are to stored as the low-order 6 bits on data stacks. You need not consider routines for creating or initializing stacks or keeping track of record length. Write subroutines for generating commands on lines *write, startread, backspace*, and *rewind*. Also write a subroutine to react to signals on lines *bot, eor, eof*, and *eot*. Include a block diagram showing all connections between the PIA's and the transport. Define all addresses of PIA registers used in your program.

535

12.15 The recording scheme used in the floppy disc unit described in Section 12.9 requires rather elaborate and expensive electronics. In less expensive disc units and in tape cassette units, simpler schemes are used in which there are no byte synchronization marks or special field marks. Let us assume a tape cassette unit in which there are only two output lines, a *data* line and a *datatime* line, serving exactly the same purpose as in the floppy disc. We shall also assume that the bit rate is sufficiently low that the MPU can do the converting from serial to parallel, i.e., there will be no external electronics between the cassette unit and the microcomputer system. Records will have the format shown in Fig. P12.15. (This format has been used in low-cost systems using the 6800 and other microcomputers.) Each record starts with 100 "SYN" bytes (ASCII 16), followed by a (∗) character (ASCII 2A). The next two bytes are the low and high bytes (SAL and SAH) of the starting address of the area in memory where the record is to be stored as it is read from tape. This address is followed by the bytes making up the record, which may be of any length. The end of the record is indicated by a (/) character (ASCII 2F). The input program will begin by reading in 8 bits and checking to see if these bits make up a SYN character. If they do not, it may indicate that the character is not from the SYN section of the record, or it may indicate that the first bit read was not the first bit of a byte. So the program skips one bit, effectively shifting ahead one bit in the data train, and then repeats the check for a SYN byte. This process is repeated until a SYN byte is found. However, an apparent SYN byte might occur in the data section due to reading across a byte boundary. Therefore, when an apparent SYN byte is found the program then checks the next 10 bytes to see if they are also SYN bytes. If not, the program returns to the search for a SYN byte; if so, the program waits for the (∗) byte. The next two bytes are taken as the address, and the record is then read and stored, terminating when the (/) byte is detected. Write a 6800 program for the above input process. Assume that the cassette interfaces to the MPU via an PIA. Indicate which PIA lines will be used and

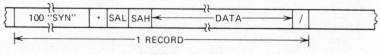

Figure P.12.25

describe how the PIA will be set up, but you need not write the PIA initialization routine. From the timing of the program determine the fastest bit rate that can be handled.

12.16 For the recording format mentioned in the last problem, the tape routines are designed to work with very simple decks which provide no *datatime* signals. The only output is a *data* line, which alternately switches between the 0 and 1 levels. The beginning of a character is marked by a transition from 0 to 1. If the bit is a logical-1, *data* stays at the 1-level for 2/3 of the bit time and then goes back to the 0-level. For a logical-0, *data* stays at the 1-level for 1/3 of the bit time and then goes back to the 0-level. The end of a bit (and the beginning of the next bit) is indicated by another 0-to-1 transition. Write a subroutine to decode data recorded in this form and load the resultant bit (0 or 1) into the sign bit of *ACCA*. Again, indicate which PIA lines will be used and how they will be set up, but do not write the initialization program. You may assume delay subroutines as required. Assume the bit period is 6.0 msec.

12.17 When data is transmitted in serial form by an MPU it is usual to use the asynchronous data format of Fig. 11.15, with each byte being transmitted as an 11-bit serial character. The conversion between parallel and serial can be accomplished with a special purpose integrated circuit, the Universal Asynchronous Receiver-Transmitter (UART). Also, Motorola provides a special form of UART, the 6850 Asynchronous Communications Interface Adapter (ACIA) for use in 6800 systems. However, extra devices increase system cost and, just as debounce circuits can be replaced by programming, so UARTs can be replaced by programming if MPU time is available. Write a 6800 program to convert data bytes taken from memory to the serial format of Fig. 11.15, to be transmitted via an output line from a PIA.

REFERENCES

1. ———, *M6800 Microprocessor Applications Manual*, Motorola, Inc., Phoenix, Ariz., 1975.

2. Soucek, B., *Microprocessors and Microcomputers*, Wiley, New York, 1976.

3. Peatman, J. B., *Microcomputer-Based Design*, McGraw-Hill, New York, 1977.

13

13.1 OVERVIEW

Up to this point in the book we have restricted our treatment to small computers. In this chapter and in Chapter 14 we shall turn our attention to large machines that are designed to accomplish many computations per unit time and as much computation as possible per unit cost.

Many large computer systems are operated in either the batch-processing or the time-sharing mode. In both situations a queue of programs awaiting execution is always present at the input terminals to the system. Thus the computer system takes on many of the characteristics of a production process. The goal becomes to maximize the number of jobs (weighted of course by their complexity) that are inputed to the system and executed per unit of time. A measure of accomplishment of this goal is called the machine's *throughput*.

The raw material of the production process is programs rather than parts of an automobile to be assembled together. Programs as contrasted to sets of automobile parts are conceived and constructed independently by many different individuals, with little thought given to the convenience of the production process. Some of the largest installations can afford the luxury of assigning different types of jobs to different machines. Other batch-oriented installations attempt to improve throughput by spacing jobs in time, according to memory requirements or other apparent features that provide information as to job type. It is, of course, impossible to completely anticipate the requirements of a program until it is executed. In general, it is the same flexibility that makes the computer program so very useful that renders it so hard to treat as a production item. Perhaps more than any other one feature, it is the conditional branch instruction that limits the applicability of mass production techniques on program execution.

There are two obvious approaches to improving a machine's throughput. The speed with which the central processor can perform arithmetic can be increased. It is also possible to increase the speed at which data can be moved about in the machine. This includes input/output rates, memory access times, etc. In general, an efficient machine represents a balance between the two capabilities. For example, it would be wasteful of computation capability to utilize an extremely fast central processor with a slow random access memory and a minimum input/output capability. When a central processor is forced to stand idle for significant periods of time because the system I/O is unable to deliver programs or carry off results fast enough, we say the system is *I/O bound*. Because batch processing facilities must handle many small programs and many I/O-oriented data processing assignments, such systems usually operate I/O bound.

Memory organization is often the determining factor with respect to the speed at which data can be moved about within a computer system. This chapter is thus devoted to memory organization while Chapter 17 is concerned with other approaches to increasing machine throughput.

In Fig. 13.1 we see a block diagram of a computer system that will allow us to outline the data flow problem in more detail. Here we classify the major subunits of a computer system into three sections according to response time. A memory unit is included in each section. As mentioned in Chapter 3, the capacity and speeds of the three memory units vary inversely. The high-speed memory in block 3 has the smallest capacity while the mass memories of block 1 are slowest. The random access memory is intermediate in both categories. The set of memories of differing characteristics may be termed a *memory hierarchy*. In some systems it is possible to divide the hierarchy into more than three blocks. For example, the mass memory is assumed to include both magnetic disk and magnetic tape memories, which have different speeds and capacities. Three blocks are convenient for this discussion, however.

The high-speed memory may consist of a few data registers, as will be discussed in Section 13.2, or a larger number of registers capable of accommodating instructions or data, such as the *scratch-pad memory* discussed in Section 13.4. In the latter case it may take on many of the characteristics of the random access memory. Reading and writing in the memory in block 3 may be accomplished in a single clock period. It is likely that considerations such as LSI chip area and power require-

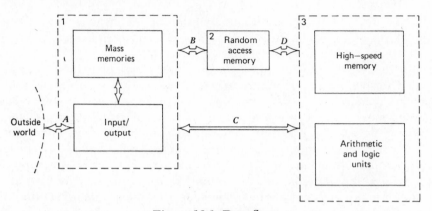

Figure 13.1. Data flow.

ments will always place a cost premium on the components of the high-speed memory. One would, therefore, expect to find in most systems a slower, cheaper, and larger capacity RAM, as shown in block 2, regardless of the organization of the high-speed memory.

Block 3 is organized so as to attempt both to minimize the cost per computation and to maximize the number of computations per unit time. Both of these parameters will be optimized for sequences of operations carried on entirely within block 3. Unfortunately, such utopian situations will be highly temporary in most real-world job environments. The overall system throughput must depend on the flow of information along paths B, C, and D in Fig. 13.1. Ideally, path C will be used only rarely, so as to avoid slowing block 3 to the data rates achievable by the devices in block 1. Thus data flow will normally be along the path ABD when the system is operating routinely in the batch mode.

Clearly, data flow along path A will occur simultaneously with other system functions without interfering in any way. This is possible primarily because the system demands the right to accept programs from users and to furnish results at its own convenience. Many organizations have been devised that will relieve the central processor in block 3 of the responsibility of data flow on path B. One of these will be discussed in Section 13.5. Thus jobs can be placed in a queue in the random access memory to be executed in order by the central processor, with the results independently removed after execution. This procedure is, of course, complicated by programs that demand large shares of the RAM or use auxiliary storage.

With independent control, data flow along path B will depend on the capacity of block 1 to provide data and the capacity of block 3 to execute programs. The cost per computation will be lowest when these capacities are matched. A quantitative model of this relation may be found in Hellerman [2]. The more common situation finds the capacity of block 1 to provide programs and data less than the capacity of block 3. We have already referred to this situation as I/O bound.

Path D is intimately involved in program execution. The high-speed memory of block 3 may contain both instructions and data so that short sequences may be executed entirely within block 3. When a branch to an instruction in the RAM of block 2 occurs, however, it often becomes necessary to replace a sequence of instructions in the high-speed memory in as little time as possible, without requiring block 3 to wait. Similarly, it may be possible to transfer arrays of data from the RAM to the high-speed memory at a data rate exceeding the maximum of the access rate for individual words in the RAM.

If the size of the user program exceeds the size of the RAM of block 2 of Fig. 13.1, it becomes necessary to periodically move portions of the program between the RAM and the semirandom access memory of block 1 in Fig. 13.1. The typical programmer does not like to bother with such details and would prefer a larger RAM, even though the average response time of this RAM might be slower. The illusion of a larger RAM can indeed be provided by modifying the hardware to permit the operating system to replace unused blocks of words in the RAM with relevant information from the SRAM as the user addresses data in a large nonexistent RAM. This concept, termed *virtual memory*, will be discussed in Section 13.5.

Implementation of both the scratch pad and the virtual memory depend on the employment of a small *associative memory*. This concept will be introduced in Section 13.3 to provide background for the scratch pad and virtual memory discussions of Sections 13.4 and 13.5. Equally fundamental and more widely used than the associative memory is the push-down stack, which will be discussed in the next section.

In Section 13.6 we shall consider a method of organizing the random access memory so that the reading and writing of individually addressed words may be overlapped. Not only will this increase the effective data rate, but this same organization will permit communication with the memory by more than one processor. As with each of the topics of this chapter, the approach of Section 13.6 may be included in a system design at the option of the designer. The designer must decide whether the performance improvement to be expected from the inclusion of one of these features is sufficient to justify the cost.

13.2 PUSH-DOWN STORAGE

A very useful, special-purpose memory feature is a *push-down storage unit* sometimes called a LIFO (last-in-first-out) list, or a *stack*. This concept was first mentioned in a problem in Chapter 10 as a facility for storing the contents of registers following an interrupt. It is similarly used in the 6800 microprocessor of Chapter 12 to store the data necessary to reenter a program following a subroutine call. Stacks are also useful in implementing compilers, since operations are usually executed in an order opposite from that in which they are encountered in the language scan process.

A stack may be implemented in any of three ways as a small, special-purpose hardware memory, within a larger RAM with special control hardware, or entirely by software within a RAM. Some microprocessors and the large-scale Burroughs 5500, 6500, and 7500 are among machines with hardware stacks. Regardless of its implementation, a stack must be capable of responding to two commands PUSH and POP (or PULL). These operations are illustrated in Fig. 13.2. The key to the implementation of the push-down store is the *stack pointer*, a register that stores the address of the next available memory location in which a new data word can be stored at the top of a list. The address contained in the stack pointer while the stack awaits a PUSH or POP command is depicted in Fig. 13.2a. Following a push command the data vector, *DATAX*, from the input register has been placed at the top of the stack and the stack pointer has been incremented to point at the next available memory location. This is illustrated in Fig. 13.2b. For a POP operation, the stack pointer is decremented to point at the first word at the top of the stack, *DATAY*, which is then transferred to an output register, as shown in Fig. 13.2c. Even though the read from the stack may be nondestructive, the location to which the stack pointer now points is considered to be empty.

The speed and timing of PUSH and POP will, of course, depend on the method of implementation of the push-down store. In any case one of the two functions will require at least two operations in sequence for completion. In Fig. 13.2, for example, POP requires that the stack pointer be decremented before the read from memory of *DATAY* can begin. If the memory were synchronous, the vector *DATAX* could be written in memory and the stack pointer incremented simultaneously in the PUSH operation. The situation would be reversed if the stack pointer normally held the address of the first data word at the top of the stack.

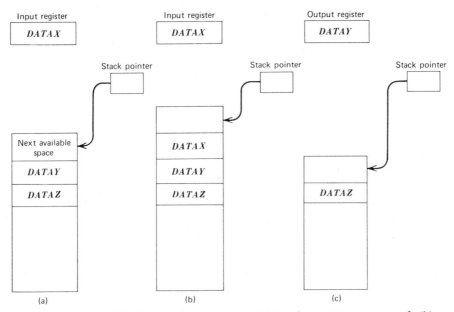

Figure 13.2. Model of push-down storage. (*a*) Stack awaiting command. (*b*) Stack following PUSH. (*c*) Stack following POP.

Both the PUSH and POP operations are slowed if the memory read and write times are greater than one clock period. The hardware implementation of a push-down store using a RAM with a response time of several clock periods is considered in the following example.

Example 13.1

Use two auxiliary data registers in conjunction with an eighteen bit 256-word, special-purpose RAM with an approximate cycle time of 10 clock periods to realize a push-down store for which the PUSH and POP operations will appear from the outside to be accomplished in 1 clock period. It may be assumed that consecutive stack operations will be separated in time by at least 20 clock periods. A third operation, LOOK, must also be possible. This operation is merely an interrogation of the word at the top of the stack without disturbing the stack. The operation may be left to the CPU control sequence by making the top word a continuous output of the stack. An input data word will be received from the **OBUS**. The PUSH and POP commands will be signaled by one-period levels on lines **push** and **pop**. When the stack is ready to receive a command, it will indicate with a continuous 1-level on line **ready**.

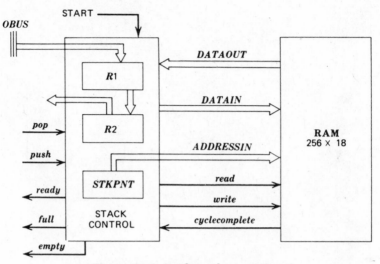

Figure 13.3. Stack implementation.

Solution

The basic block diagram of the stack modules is shown in Fig. 13.3. In addition to the RAM two 18-bit registers, $R1$ and $R2$, are included. When *ready* = 1, $R2$ will contain the word at the top of the stack; $R1$ will represent the next available space above the stack. Also, $R2$ will be connected to a vector of output lines. The 8-bit address register, *STKPNT* will point at the second word in the stack. The following is an AHPL description of the stack.

MODULE: STACK
    INPUTS: *start; OBUS*[18]; *push; pop; DATAOUT*[18]; *cyclecomplete*
    MEMORY: $R1$ [18]; $R2$ [18]; *ready; full; STKPNT* [8]
    OUTPUTS: $R2$; *ready; full; DATAIN*[18]; *ADDRESSIN*[8]; *empty readwrite*
  1. *STKPNT* $\leftarrow$ 8 $\top$ 0; *ready* $\leftarrow$ 1; *full* $\leftarrow$ 0
     $\rightarrow$ ($\overline{start}$)/(1)
  2. *ready* $*$ (*push* $\lor$ *pop*) $\leftarrow$ 0; $R1 * push \leftarrow OBUS$
     $\rightarrow$ ($\overline{push \lor pop}$, *push, pop*)/(2, 3, 5)
  3. *ADDRESSIN* = *STKPNT*; *DATAIN* = $R2$;
     write = 1
     $\rightarrow$ ($\overline{cycle\ complete}$)/(3)
  4. $R2 \leftarrow R1$; *ready* $\leftarrow$ 1; *STKPNT* $\leftarrow$ INC (*STKPNT*)
     full $*$ ($\land$ / *STKPNT*) $\leftarrow$ 1
     $\rightarrow$ (2)

Step 1 is a reset state that provides for emptying the stack by setting the address in *STKPNT* to 0. Control waits at step 2 for a PUSH or POP command.

A word to be pushed into the stack is temporarily stored in $R1$ at this step. Similarly, the output of $R2$ may be used in a LOOK or POP operation during the clock period of this step. Thus the CPU control needs to allow only one clock period for the PUSH and POP operations.

Step 3 pushes the contents of $R2$ down one place in the stack by writing it in memory at the location specified by *STKPNT*. Step 3 then completes the PUSH operation by moving the new top word to $R2$ and incrementing *STKPNT*. If the RAM has been filled, flip-flop *full* is set to 1 to inhibit further PUSH commands. If the number in *STKPNT* is 0, and *full* = 0, then the stack is empty. The *empty* signal is generated by a statement following END SEQUENCE.

The POP operation continues at step 5 with the decrementing of *STKPNT*. The top word from RAM is read at step 6 and then placed at the top of the stack in $R2$ by step 7.

    5.   *STKPNT* $\leftarrow$ DEC(*STKPNT*); *full* $\leftarrow$ 0
    6.   *ADDRESSIN* = *STKPNT*
        read = 1
        $\rightarrow$ $\overline{(cycle\ complete)}/(6)$
    7. $R2 \leftarrow$ *DATAOUT*; *ready* $\leftarrow$ 1
        $\rightarrow$ (2)
END SEQUENCE
CONTROL RESET (1)
  empty = $(\bigvee/STKPNT) \wedge \overline{full}$
END

13.3 ASSOCIATIVE MEMORY

In the next two sections we shall encounter a need to allow the scratch-pad memory and the virtual memory to function without direction from a user program. In both cases making these functions *transparent* to the programmer will require the use of an *associative* or *content-addressable* memory. In an associative memory, a data word is not obtained by supplying an address that specifies the location of that data word in memory. Instead, an identifying descriptor is provided to memory. The memory is then searched until an exact match is found between the submitted descriptor and a descriptor associated with a data word. When a match is found, the corresponding data word becomes the desired memory output. A descriptor may be part of each data word, or the descriptors may be stored separately. The human mind is often thought of as an associative memory. As an individual dwells on a particular thought, related thoughts seem to flow from memory into his consciousness.

An associative memory might be organized so that many data words will be associated with one descriptor. Here each descriptor will be unique so that only one output data word will be obtained at each memory reference. The memory search in an associative memory may be sequential or the input descriptor may attempt to match all stored descriptors simultaneously. A sequential search would be prohibitively slow in an associative memory intended for use in a high-speed processor. If the search is parallel, the large amount of combinational logic required will necessarily limit the size of an associative memory. Prior to 1970, logic costs made a combinational associative memory out of the question.

Sequential search associative memories are useful at the applications level in, e.g., information retrieval systems. As a hardware component to be designed into more complex hardware systems, we are primarily interested in the combinational search associative memory. Let us now consider the design of a combinational search associative memory with 2^n words, each with m data bits. The cost of the combinational logic involved will typically place an upper limit on n of about 10 or 12.

Consider the organization depicted in Fig. 13.4. The data are arranged in an array **AM** of 2^n m-bit words. In addition there is an array **AA** containing 2^n descriptors r bits in length. One r-bit descriptor will correspond to each word in **AM**. We shall insist that each word in **AM** have a unique descriptor so that $n < r$. In a typical application, 2^n might be the number of words in a scratch pad and 2^r might be the number of words in the main RAM. Thus n might be 8 while r might be 18.

Information can be stored in **AA** and **AM** from the vectors of input lines **AAIN** and **AMIN**. The address in both arrays of a data word and descriptor to be written is specified by the contents of the n-bit register **WRTADD**. Data are to be read from **AM** associatively. That is, the word in **AM** corresponding to the descriptor in **AA**, if any, that exactly matches the contents of the r-bit register, **DSCRPT**, will appear on the vector of output lines **AMOUT**.

Individual read and write operations can be expressed as single AHPL steps. It must be possible to replace the contents of a location in both **AA** and **AM** addressed by **WRTADD**. This write operation, effectively on a RAM with word length $r + m$, is expressed by Eq. 16.1.

$$\text{AA, AM} * \text{DCD}(\textbf{WRTADD}) \leftarrow \textbf{AAIN, AMIN} \qquad (16.1)$$
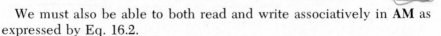

We must also be able to both read and write associatively in **AM** as expressed by Eq. 16.2.

$$\textbf{AMOUT} = \text{BUSFN (AM; ASSOC (\textbf{DSCRPT}; AA))}$$
$$\text{AM} * \text{ASSOC (\textbf{DSCRPT}; AA)} \leftarrow \textbf{AMIN} \qquad (16.2)$$

Word in **AM**

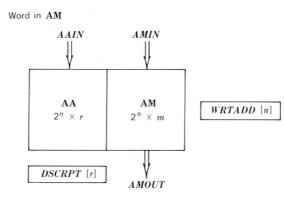

Figure 13.4. Associative memory.

The vector **AMOUT** is continuously available and may be clocked into a register to complete a read operation; BUSFN is the standard combinational logic unit developed in Chapter 7. The word lines are generated by the combinational logic unit ASSOC rather than by a decode as in a standard RAM. The ASSOC unit has 2^n outputs, one corresponding to each word of **AA** and **AM**. A bit of $ASSOC_i$ is 1 if and only if the corresponding word **AA** exactly matches the contents of the register **DSCRPT**. If there is no match, all 2^n outputs of ASSOC are 0. Each of the 2^n output functions of ASSOC are independent so that the unit may be represented in AHPL as follows, with one connection statement repeated 2^n times.

UNIT: ASSOC (**DSCRPT**; **AA**)
    INPUTS: **DSCRPT** [r]; **AA**[2 ↑ n ; r]
    OUTPUTS: ASSOC [2 ↑ n]
    1. $i \Leftarrow 0$
    2. $ASSOC_i = \overline{\vee/(\textbf{DSCRPT} \oplus \textbf{AA}^i)}$ *showing equal*
    3. $i \Leftarrow i + 1$
    4. $\Rightarrow (i < 2 \uparrow n)/(2)$
END

Clearly, $ASSOC_i = 1$ if and only if $\textbf{DSCRPT}_j = \textbf{AA}^i_j$ for all j.

13.4 SCRATCH-PAD MEMORIES

We use the term *scratch pad* to refer to a high-speed memory that is not in itself of sufficient size to satisfy the RAM requirement for the system in which it is found. There are several ways in which a scratch pad, sometimes called a buffer memory, may be organized. Some of these approaches will be discussed in this section. The portion of Fig. 13.1,

547

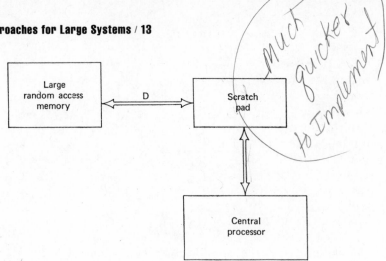

Figure 13.5. Scratch-pad memory.

which depicts path D between the large RAM and the scratch pad, is reproduced as Fig. 13.5. The simplest example of scratch-pad memory organization is the addressable register array to be discussed in Section 17.2. The use of these arrays depends on using multiaddress instructions with a small number of address bits to specify each argument. Thus the size of register arrays is limited.

If both a larger register array and the RAM are referenced by single-address instructions, the burden of when to store data in the RAM and when to use the register array is placed on the programmer. In this section we shall consider alternative organizations in which decisions between the two types of storage are made at the hardware level.

However the scratch pad is organized, the goal is to make the average access time for words requested by the central processor as near as possible to the access time of the scratch pad itself. This bound on the average access time can never be actually achieved, as the central processor will invariably request some items stored not in the scratch pad but in the large RAM. The slowing effect of references to the RAM may be lessened in the following three obvious ways. Point 3 was the topic of the previous section.

1. Keep the ratio of RAM references to scratch-pad references as small as possible.
2. Overlap references to RAM with other central processor activities. Anticipate requirements for items from RAM in advance.
3. Organize the RAM so that the average data transfer rate is greater than the reciprocal of the access time.

548

The three points are not independent. A certain anticipation of information requirements as well as the multiple use of items placed in the scratch pad are implied if sequences of items are to be profitably obtained from the RAM at an increased transfer rate.

In this section we are primarily concerned with point 1. Clearly, the number of references to the large RAM is reduced as the size of the scratch pad is increased. We may assume that the cost per bit of the scratch pad is considerably greater than that of the RAM. As the scratch pad is increased in size, the point of diminishing returns on the cost-performance curve is reached for a scratch pad with significantly less capacity than the RAM.

Critical to the organization of a small scratch pad is any advance knowledge that might exist as to the need for information from the RAM. In certain cases a program to be executed can be provided with this kind of information by the programmer. Instructions for block transfers along path D could be inserted in the program and performed in parallel with arithmetic and logical operations. For such cases a scratch pad organized merely as a fast random access memory would be satisfactory. However, the burden of providing for these block transfers cannot be passed on to the higher language programmer. The result is an extremely difficult problem for the systems programmer.

If the possibility of providing such insight within the program is discounted, what information remains as to when and if a block transfer should be performed and on what data? There is some. For example, if one word is requested from the RAM, there is a significant probability that subsequent memory locations will be accessed in the immediate future. The instruction look-ahead feature, discussed in the next section, is based on this observation. Problems remain as to how many locations to transfer, where to put the information in the scratch pad, and how to inform the central processor of its new location.

All of the above problems are solved by organizing the scratch pad in a manner so that it is completely *transparent* to the programmer. That is, the programmer may assume that he is working with the large RAM only. To the programmer every memory reference will seem to be to the RAM. The only external indication of the scratch pad will be the shorter than predicted average execution time for programs. To make the scratch pad transparent we shall organize it as an *associative memory*.

For convenience we shall detail the design of a relatively small, 256-word, associative scratch-pad memory. This memory will be operated in conjunction with a 256k-word, slow random access memory. The registers required for the implementation of this memory are shown in Fig. 13.6.

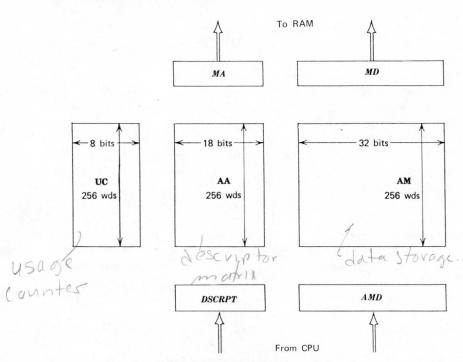

To RAM

MA

MD

8 bits

UC
256 wds

18 bits

AA
256 wds

32 bits

AM
256 wds

usage counter

descriptor matrix

data storage.

DSCRPT

AMD

From CPU

Figure 13.6. Associative scratch pad.

In addition to the matrix, **AM**, which constitutes the data storage, there are two additional 256-row matrices, **AA** and **UC**. Each word stored in **AM** is also stored in the RAM. The address of **AM**^{i} in the RAM is stored in **AA**. Thus a word retrieved from RAM that is requested by the central processor is also stored in the associative memory. The probability that this word will be requested again in the immediate future by the processor is much higher than 2^{-18}, the average request probability of a word in RAM. When the same word is subsequently requested from the associative memory, it will be obtained in only one clock period. Empirical studies on machines with associative memories have shown that up to 95 percent of the words requested by the processor have been found in the associative memory. Thus the associative memory can provide a considerable speed improvement.

Because the 256-word memory will fill up quickly, it is necessary to provide a mechanism by which words that have not recently been accessed may be replaced. Keeping track of the history of accesses is the function of counter matrix **UC**. Corresponding to each word in **AM**, there is an 8-bit counter in **UC**. Each time **AM**^{i} is accessed **UC**^{i} is set to $2^8 -$

1. With each access of **AM**, the counters corresponding to words not accessed are decremented by 1. When a counter reaches 0, it remains at that count unless set to $2^8 - 1$. Since there are 256 counters with a maximum count of 255, and only one counter is set each access, at least one of the counters will contain 0 at any given time. A word will not be deleted from the associative memory unless the corresponding count is 0. Of the remaining hardware in Fig. 13.6, **DSCRPT** and **AMD** are the address register and data registers, respectively, for the associative memory. The registers **MA** and **MD** serve this function in the RAM.

There are many possible approaches to designing control for the associative memory. Since only one clock period is required to access the associative memory itself, we shall let this be accomplished by the central processor's control unit. If an access to RAM is required, control for this function is the responsibility of the *associative memory control unit*. As we shall see, part of this function will be carried out after the cycle complete signal has been returned to the central processor. The most convenient approach to the required simultaneous but totally independent operations would seem to be two separate control units.

Within the control sequence for the CPU, the following three steps must be inserted whenever it is desired to read from memory.

1. *DSCRPT* ← "desired address"
2. *AMBUS* = ASSOC (**AA**; *DSCRPT*)
   AMD $*$ ($\vee$/ASSOC(**AA**; *DSCRPT*)) ← BUSFN (**AM**; *AMBUS*)
   UC $*$ $\overline{\text{ASSOC (\textbf{AA}; }DSCRPT)}$ ← DECZ (UC);
   UC $*$ ASSOC (**AA**; *DSCRPT*) ← $8 \top 0$
   → ($\vee$/ASSOC(**AA**; *DSCRPT*))/(4)
3. *readram* = 1
   → ($\overline{complete}$)/(3)
4. "Next CPU step"

The address of the desired word is first placed in **DSCRPT** where it is compared to each word in **AA**. If there is an address match, the corresponding data word from **AM** is placed in **AMD** at step 2. If a word is found, control passes directly from step 2 to the next CPU step. Thus a word from the associative memory is retrieved in only one clock period. If the word is found at step 2, the corresponding row of **UC** is set to all 1's. Each of the other row is decremented by the combinational logic unit DECZ. If an address match is not found, all rows of **UC** are decremented and control goes to step 3, where a read request signal is sent to the RAM control module on line *readram*.

When it is desired to write in memory, the following sequence is inserted:

1. $AMD \leftarrow$ "desired data"
   $DSCRPT \leftarrow$ "desired address"
2. $AM * \overline{\text{ASSOC (AA; }DSCRPT)} \leftarrow AMD$;
   $UC * \overline{\text{ASSOC (AA; }DSCRPT)} \leftarrow \overline{\text{DECZ (UC)}}$;
   $UC * \text{ASSOC (AA; }DSCRPT) \leftarrow \overline{8 \top 0}$
   $\rightarrow (\vee/\text{ASSOC (AA; }DSCRPT))/4$
3. $writeram = 1$
   $\rightarrow (\overline{complete})/(3)$
4. "Next CPU step"

If the address in which a word has been written has been moved into **AA**, the data are merely written in the corresponding row of **AM**, to be moved to the RAM by the memory control at a later time. The rows of **UC** are modified as in the read sequence. If the address is not in **AA**, a *writeram* signal is sent to the memory control module.

In the above two sequences the combinational logic unit ASSOC functions as discussed in the previous section. Note that in the read sequence the output of this unit is routed to the BUSFN unit for **AM** through a bus, *AMBUS*. This permits sharing of the BUSFN network with another control vector generated by the sequence for the RAM controller.

If a desired address is not found in the associative memory, control passes to the memory control module, which facilitates communication between the associative memory and the slower asynchronous RAM. A reference to RAM will cause the CPU to wait a much longer period of time than if the address had been found in **AA**. The interface between the associative memory and the RAM is illustrated in Fig. 13.7. The

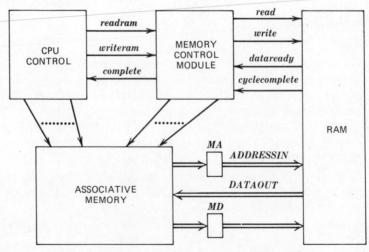

Figure 13.7. Associative memory/RAM interface.

memory control module is separate from the CPU control but both are capable of controlling data transfers within the associative memory. This departure from the convention of Chapter 9 will cause no problems, since the CPU control is always waiting for a **complete** signal whenever the memory control is active. The AHPL description of the memory control module begins as follows.

MODULE: MEMORY CONTROL

INPUTS: *readram; writeram; DATAOUT* [32]; *DSCRPT* [18]; *busy*

OUTPUTS: *complete; DATAIN*[32], *ADDRESSIN* [18]; *read; write*

MEMORY: *AMD* [32]; *MA* [18]

UC [256:8]; AA [256:18]; AM [256:32]; *MD* [32]

1. $\rightarrow$ ($\overline{readram \wedge writeram}$)/(1)
2. *AMBUS* = FIRSTFREE (UC)
   MA $\leftarrow$ BUSFN (AA; FIRSTFREE (UC))
   MD $\leftarrow$ BUSFN (AM; *AMBUS*)
3. *write* = 1
   $\rightarrow$ ($\overline{busy}$)/(3)

Finds the first place that is free.

The receipt of either a *readram* or a *writeram* signal indicates that a space must be found in the associative memory for a new data word. In the case of *writeram* this word is already in *AMD*. For *readram* the word will eventually come from the RAM. Step 2 selects some row i in the associative memory for which $UC^i = 8 \top 0$. This is accomplished by the combinational logic unit FIRSTFREE which has 256 output lines, only one of which is 1 corresponding to a row for which $UC^i = 8 \top 0$. The address stored in row i of *AA* is transfered to *MA* and the data word from AM^i to *MD*. The output of FIRSTFREE is connected to *AMBUS* so that the BUSFN network is shared with the associative read from **AM**.

Control separates at step 4 so that a word can be obtained from the RAM to satisfy a read request. In the case of a write, the data is already waiting in *AMD* to be placed in the associative memory. The address is placed in *MA* at step 5, and the word is obtained from memory and placed in *AMD* by step 7.

4. $\rightarrow$ (*busy*, $\overline{busy} \wedge readram$, $\overline{busy} \wedge writeram$)/(4, 5, 8)
5. *MA* $\leftarrow$ *DSCRPT*
6. *read* = 1
   $\rightarrow$ ($\overline{busy}$)/(6)
7. *AMD* $*$ $\overline{busy}$ $\leftarrow$ *DATAOUT*
   $\rightarrow$ ($\overline{busy}$)/(7)

553

8. (**AA, AM**) $*$ FIRSTFREE (**UC**) $\leftarrow$ *DSCRPT, AMD;*
    UC $*$ FIRSTFREE (**UC**) $\leftarrow \overline{8 \top 0}$
    complete = 1
9. $\rightarrow$ (*readram* $\lor$ *writeram*)/(9)
10. NO DELAY $\rightarrow$ (1)
END SEQUENCE
   ADDRESSIN = MA
   DATAIN = MD
END

Control converges at step 8 for the read and write operations. The word to be placed in the associative memory and its address are now available in *AMD* and *DSCRPT*, respectively. The output of FIRST-FREE is used to cause these vectors to be placed in the appropriate registers of **AM** and **AA**. At the same time a vector of eight 1's is placed in the same **ROW** of **UC**. The other rows of **UC** were decremented before the RAM request was made. A complete signal is now returned to the CPU. For a read, the desired word remains in *AMD* for use by the CPU control. For a write, the word will not be placed in the RAM until it is later removed from the associative memory.

Not included in the above control module is a sequence to sweep the entire associative memory into the RAM. Such a command, which would also clear each row of **UC**, might be helpful to the operating system at the completion of a program.

13.5 VIRTUAL MEMORY

Somewhat analogous to the associative scratch pad is *virtual memory*. Although the scratch pad is included to shorten the effective access time of memory references, virtual memory is an organizational technique for increasing the apparent size of the random access memory. That is, the number of random access addresses available to the programmer is substantially greater than the number of locations in the physical RAM. These additional data are actually stored in a semirandom access memory (SRAM). The actual location of a particular data word is transparent to the programmer. Hence the term, *virtual memory*. To be of any value, the virtual memory control must operate so as to make the probability large that a piece of data will be residing in RAM when it is requested.

In Chapter 3 we observed that identifying and retrieving data files from an SRAM, particularly a magnetic disk, was usually a software function. If a word in the virtual memory, but not currently in the RAM, is addressed by an individual instruction, this fact must be noted by the hardware control sequence; also, provision must be made to transfer

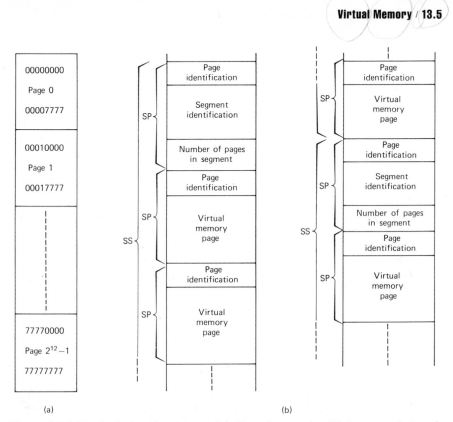

Figure 13.8. Typical virtual memory. (*a*) **Virtual memory.** (*b*) **Storage of virtual memory in SRAM.**

control to a software routine that will obtain this word and the entire *page* of data in which it resides from the SRAM. This implies a very close coordination of hardware control sequences and software routines, as was the case in interrupt processing in Chapter 10. In fact, in our example of a virtual memory implementation we shall rely on an interrupt to initiate a software search for a page of data.

A typical virtual memory will be organized into pages of data words with between 2^{10} and 2^{12} words in each page. Since the object of the virtual memory is to provide a very large memory of apprently individually addressable words, one would expect to find at least 2^{10} pages in a virtual memory. A virtual memory consisting of 2^{12} pages of 2^{12} words each is depicted in Fig. 13.8a. Each word in the virtual memory is assigned a 24-bit address, called a *virtual address*. This address will consist of 12 bits specifying the *virtual page number* and 12 bits specifying the address within the page, i.e., the *page address*. Each memory address instruction must contain 24 address bits so as to precisely specify the location of each operand in the virtual memory.

No practical random access memory large enough to store the entire contents of the virtual memory of Fig. 13.8a exists. Typically, only a small subset of the virtual memory pages, perhaps 64, pages are actually stored in RAM. The remaining pages must be stored in an SRAM. The reader will recall that individual records were usually obtained from a track on a magnetic disk by a software search process. If the SRAM is organized to support a virtual memory, the *SRAM page* labeled, SP, in Fig. 13.8b will replace the record as the smallest addressable unit of data in the SRAM. Thus each SRAM page will consist of a virtual memory page and a page identifier to permit it to be located by search.

Storage in an SRAM must also be organized into files that constitute individual user programs or user-specified data structures. A file will usually include several records. The storage of each file must include identifying data as well as some form password to prevent unauthorized use or alteration of the files. In an SRAM organized to support a virtual memory, the term *segment*, labeled SS in Fig. 13.8, is typically used in place of file. A segment will consist of a variable number of SRAM pages, up to a system-specified maximum, headed by a segment identification page containing the identifying data mentioned above and the number of pages to be expected in the segment. Segments are manipulated by the operating system. The special hardware control sequences necessary to identify missing pages in the RAM will not be cognizant of any partitioning of the virtual memory into segments. Since we shall not attempt to design an operating system in this section, it will not be necessary to structure the segment identification page in more detail.

The operating system together with pertinent tables must be stored continuously in RAM. Since this information must not be removed from the RAM to make room for missing pages, the RAM will be typically organized as illustrated in Fig. 13.9. It is assumed that each page contains 2^{12} words as in the virtual memory pages of Fig. 13.8 so that a page from virtual memory can be stored in each page of RAM. The RAM of Fig. 13.9 consists of 64 pages or a total of 2^{18} words. We have arbitrarily set aside 8 RAM pages or ⅛ of the total memory for storage of the operating system and related tables. Therefore, only 56 pages of memory are available for storage of user pages from the virtual memory. Of the 2^{12} virtual memory pages only those currently in use will be stored in the RAM. Others must be obtained from the SRAM as needed, replacing pages in RAM with the longest histories of disuse. The first two locations in RAM will be used by the hardware to inform the operating system of the number of a needed page that is missing from the RAM and the

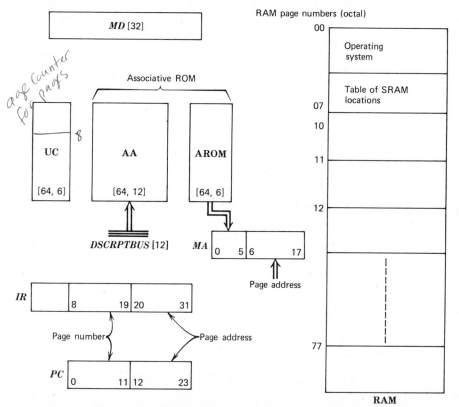

Figure 13.9. RAM organization for virtual memory.

number of the page that has had the least recent use and can be deleted from the RAM.

Also shown in Fig. 13.9 are a 32-bit instruction register and a 24-bit program counter. The least-significant 12 bits of each specify the *page address*, i.e., the address of a word within a 2^{12}-word page. The next 12 bits in each case specify a *page number* in virtual memory. Together these 24 bits are the virtual address. If a particular page of the virtual memory is stored in RAM, it may be located by reference to the small *associative read only memory* **AROM**. When a virtual memory page number is connected to the bus **DSCRPTBUS**, the output of the associative memory is the corresponding 6-bit RAM page number. The catenation of these 6 bits with the page address specifies the location of a desired word in RAM. The first 8 pages of RAM must always contain the operating system that cannot be removed to the SRAM. For the purpose of memory reference commands within the operating system, these RAM pages will be assumed to correspond to the first 8 pages of virtual memory. Therefore, the first 8 rows of **AA** will contain the binary equivalent of the fixed values 0000 to 0007 while the first 8 rows of **AROM** will be 00 to 07. The use counter array **UC** will function in the same manner as in the previous section except that each row of $\mathbf{UC}_{0:7}$ will be fixed at 111111.

A flow chart illustrating the functions involved in executing a program in a virtual memory system is shown in Fig. 13.10. The process is shown as beginning with an operating system fetch from SRAM of a segment containing a user program or perhaps only a subset of the pages in a segment. Only a portion of the segment will be retrieved if the segment exceeds the 56 pages available in RAM or if the program must share the RAM with other programs. The treatment of a segment by the operating system will depend in part on control information supplied by the user.

The implementation of block 2 of Fig. 13.10 with virtual memory will require some special features in the hardware control sequence. Block 3 is entirely a hardware function while blocks 1 and 4 can be accomplished by software using ordinarily available assembly language instructions.

The following sequence must be included at each read from virtual memory in the CPU control sequence.

R1. **DSCRPTBUS** = "virtual page number"
$\quad$ **MA** ← BUSFN (**AROM;** ASSOC (**AA; DSCRPTBUS**)), "page address";
$\quad$ **MD** * $\overline{(\vee/\text{ASSOC} (\mathbf{AA; DSCRPTBUS}))}$ ← 20 $\top$ 0, "virtual page number"
$\quad$ → $(\vee/\text{ASSOC} (\mathbf{AA; DSCRPTBUS}))/(100)$

R2. **DSCRPTBUS** = "virtual page number";
$\quad$ **UC** * (ASSOC (**AA; DSCRPTBUS**)) ← 6 $\top$ 55;
$\quad$ **UC** * $\overline{(\text{ASSOC} (\mathbf{AA, DSCRPTBUS}))}$ ← DECZ (**UC**);
$\quad$ **MD** ← BUSFN (**M;** DCD (**MA**))

R3. Next step

The first step connects the page number from **PC** or **IR** as appropriate to **DSCRPTBUS**. If any output of ASSOC (**AA, DSCRPTBUS**) is 1, 6 bits from **AROM** catenated with the page address from the appropriate source are placed in **MA**. Control then passes to step 2 where the desired word is read from the RAM. If $\vee/\text{ASSOC} = 0$ indicating a missing page, then the page number is placed in the last 12 bits of **MD** and control branches to step 100 where the implementation of block 3 of Fig. 13.10 begins.

If the page is found in RAM, the corresponding row of **UC** is set to the binary equivalent of 55 at step 2. The remaining rows of **UC** are decremented, and the read from RAM is accomplished.

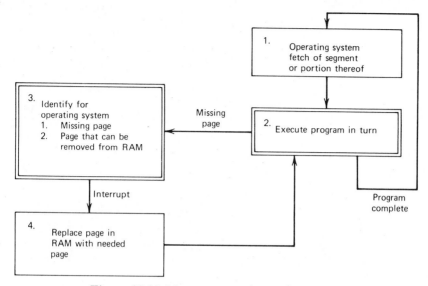

Figure 13.10. Management of virtual memory.

The following, very similar pair of steps will be inserted in the main control sequence wherever it is necessary to effect a write in RAM.

W1. $\textbf{\textit{DSCRPTBUS}}$ = "virtual page number";
$\textbf{\textit{MA}} \leftarrow \textbf{BUSFN}~(\textbf{AROM};~\textbf{ASSOC}~(\textbf{AA};~\textbf{\textit{DSCRPTBUS}}))$, "page address";
$\textbf{\textit{MD}} * (\overline{\bigvee(/\textbf{ASSOC}~(\textbf{AA};~\textbf{\textit{DSCRPTBUS}}))} \leftarrow 20 \top 0$, "virtual page number"
$\rightarrow (\overline{\bigvee/\textbf{ASSOC}~(\textbf{AA};~\textbf{\textit{DSCRPTBUS}})})/(100)$

W2. $\textbf{\textit{DSCRPTBUS}}$ = "virtual page number"
$\textbf{UC} * (\textbf{ASSOC}~(\textbf{AA},~\textbf{\textit{DSCRPTBUS}})) \leftarrow 6 \top 55;$
$\textbf{UC} * \overline{(\textbf{ASSOC}~(\textbf{AA},~\textbf{\textit{DSCRPTBUS}}))} \leftarrow \textbf{DECZ}~(\textbf{UC});$
$\textbf{M} * \textbf{DCD}~(\textbf{\textit{MA}}) \leftarrow \textbf{\textit{MD}}$

Only the last line of step W2 differs from the previous sequence to permit the actual write in memory. It is assumed that the data has already been placed in $\textbf{\textit{MD}}$. We note that $\textbf{\textit{MD}}$ is affected by steps R2 and W2 only in the event of a missing page. In this case execution of the instruction has been interrupted and will be restarted once the missing page is obtained. Thus there is no conflict in the use of $\textbf{\textit{MD}}$.

Table 13.1 lists the information that must be provided to the operating system to retrieve a missing page and indicates where this information is to be found. It is the function of the sequence beginning at step 100 to obtain or store the appropriate page numbers in these first two locations of RAM. The number of the missing page is already in $\textbf{\textit{MD}}$ so that

TABLE 13.1

Eventual RAM location	Virtual page numbers
000000	Number of missing virtual page
000001	Virtual page to be moved from RAM
	Where Page Numbers Can Be Found
000000	$MD_{20:31}$
000001	BUSFN (**AA**; FIRSTFREE (**UC**))

step 100 merely places address 0 in **MA** and step 101 writes the missing page number in RAM. Step 102 increments **MA** and places the number of the virtual page to be moved from RAM in **MD** so that it can be written in location 000001 by step 103. The page to be replaced is determined by the combinational logic unit FIRSTFREE, which finds a row of **UC** that contains all 0's. The virtual page number is then obtained from the corresponding row of **AA**.

100. $MA \leftarrow 18 \top 0$
101. $M * DCD(MA) \leftarrow MD$
102. $MA \leftarrow INC(MA)$
      $MD_{20:31} \leftarrow BUSFN\ (\mathbf{AA};\ FIRSTFREE(\mathbf{UC}))$
      $AA * FIRSTFREE(\mathbf{UC}) \leftarrow MD_{20:31}$
103. $M * DCD(MA) \leftarrow MD$

At the same time that step 102 places the number of the page to be replaced in **MD**, it writes the number of the missing virtual page in **AA** at the row identified by FIRSTFREE. Thus the corresponding page in RAM will from now on be referenced using the new page number. The simultaneous shift of information between two registers is, of course, allowed in a clocked system. Step 104 now places 110111 in the row of **UC** corresponding to the page to be replaced, decrements the remaining rows of **UC** and generates an interrupt.

104. $UC * FIRSTFREE(\mathbf{UC}) \leftarrow 6 \top 55$
      $UC * \overline{FIRSTFREE(\mathbf{UC})} \leftarrow DECZ(UC)$
      interrupt $= 1$

With the generation of the interrupt, further responsibility for exchanging pages in RAM is passed to the operating system software. This function can be accomplished using ordinarily available assembly language instructions. The new virtual page number (missing page) is now stored in **AA**. Therefore, this number must be used in addressing the

RAM page to be rewritten both in removing old information and replacing it with new. The virtual page number of the page to be removed is used only to identify the SRAM page to be updated. The data in the virtual page to be placed in SRAM will probably be quite different from the old data that it will replace. These data have not changed since they were copied into RAM in an earlier exchange. The discussion of virtual memory is complete except for the design of the operating system, which will not be considered here.

13.6 MULTIPLE-MEMORY BANKS

The speed at which a magnetic core RAM may be operated is limited by physical considerations. The situation is only slightly more complex for a large semiconductor RAM. Once the cost per bit to be allowed for such a memory is fixed by design decision, the available technologies are constrained and a limit on the operating speed is the result.

There will always be applications of a random access memory in which its overall performance cannot be improved beyond a point dictated by the basic read and write times. There are circumstances, however, when the need for information from two consecutive memory locations becomes known at one time. It is possible to organize a slow random access memory so that several such memory references can be handled almost simultaneously. We shall first accomplish this by dividing the memory into several independent banks. The method of assigning addresses to these banks is called *interleaving*.

A memory consisting of 16 interleaved banks is partially depicted in Fig. 13.11. The complete memory contains 2^{18} words, 2^{14} in each bank. The assignment of memory addresses is shown in octal in the figure. Notice that the first overall address, 000000, is found in **M0**, while the next address, 000001, is found in **M1**, with 000002 in **M2**, etc. Thus the first 16 addresses are distributed over the 16 banks, the second 16 are similarly distributed, etc. This is interleaving.

A sophisticated central processor will often find it advantageous to obtain the contents of several consecutive addresses from memory simultaneously. Typically, this information will be transferred to a scratch-pad memory. The reader will see more clearly how these blocks of data may be used in the next section.

It should be apparent that the memory in Fig. 13.11 can be in the process of retrieving up to 16 consecutive data words simultaneously. The feasibility of this set up depends on a disparity between the access time of the individual memory banks and the basic clock period of the central processor. Suppose, for example, that core or MOS memories

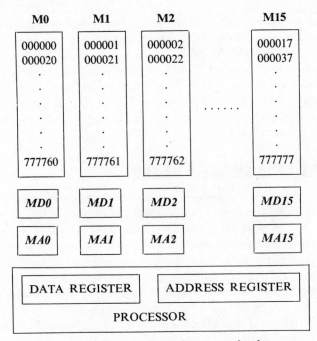

Figure 13.11. Interleaved memory banks.

with access times of 500 nsec are used while the clock period is 20 nsec. Thus as many as 25 high-speed register transfers could be accomplished while a word was obtained from a memory bank.

Suppose that the processor in Fig. 13.11 becomes aware of a need to read data from several consecutive memory addresses. It begins by placing the first address in the processor address register shown. It can place a second address in this register while the master memory controller routes the first address to the memory address register of the appropriate memory bank. This process can continue until an address in the processor address register is found to be located in a memory bank that is busy servicing a prior request. In the case of the transfer of a very long block of data, the memory controller will begin transferring data into the processor data register at the same time new addresses are routed to other memory banks.

The writing of the control sequence for the memory in Fig. 13.11 will be left as a problem for the reader. In the next section a control sequence will be written for a somewhat more complicated situation.

An alternative approach to 16 interleaved banks would be organizing the memory with words equal in length to 16 processor words. When a block of processor words are requested, a long word is read from memory and broken into segments as it is transferred to the processor. For several reasons (left to the insight of the reader) this approach is less flexible than interleaving.

13.7 INTERLEAVED BANKS WITH MULTIPLE ENTRY POINTS

Once the decision has been made to include multiple-memory banks in a system, an additional advantage accrues: the memory can be accessed simultaneously from more than one entry point. These entry points may be connected to separate processors in a multiprocessing situation. Alternatively, they can be regarded as DMA points to speed up I/O operations and accomplish this in parallel with the execution of other programs. In this section we shall construct a control sequence for a four-bank memory with four entry points. This sequence should serve to illustrate problems that will occur in other complex multipath data routing situations.

Our basic configuration will consist of four separate memory banks as illustrated in Fig. 13.12. Each bank has a separate memory data register and memory address register as shown. Any of the four memory banks may communicate with any of four entry points through the respective communications address register, CA, and communications data register, CD. The memory unit and the processors are operated from the same clock source. Thus a processor can place a word in its CA register in one clock period, and this word may be taken from the register in the next clock period by memory control. The data communications process may take place in either direction through a CD register.

Two flip-flops, r ($r0$ to $r3$) and w, are associated with each CA register for control purposes. If the corresponding r flip-flop is set to 1, a read is being requested. If $w = 1$, a word to be written in memory is waiting in the communications data register with the address in the corresponding address register. If $r = w = 0$, the address and data communications registers are available to the entry point control unit. This indicates to the processor that it must take the next action.

The transfer of addresses between the CA and MA registers is accomplished by way of the bus, $ADBUS$. Data are routed between the memory data registers and the CD registers by way of the $DBUS$. Data may pass through the $DBUS$ in both directions.

Some provision must be made for keeping track of which entry point is currently served by a given memory bank so that word read out can be routed to the proper CD register. As the time required to access memory or to write in memory is many clock periods, it is possible for

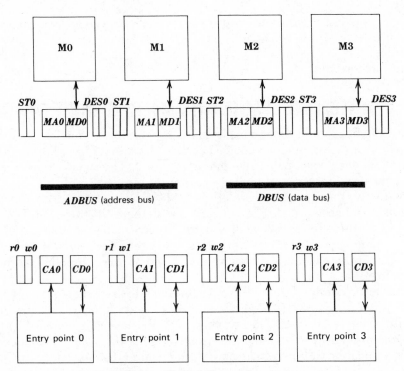

Figure 13.12. Memory layout.

all four memory banks to be simultaneously in the process of retrieving four separate data words for the same entry point. Therefore, we include a 2-bit register **DES** with each memory bank element to identify the entry point that will receive the word, if any, currently being read from the memory bank. Also associated with each bank is a 2-bit status register, **ST**. If $ST = 00$, the bank is inactive. The status register will be 01 whenever a write or read operation is in progress. If $ST = 10$, the bank has just completed a read operation; and the data is waiting in the memory data register.

The hardware associated with a typical memory bank **M0** is detailed in Fig.13.13a. The hardware associated with a typical entry point is given in Fig.13.13b. Notice in particular that the communications address register, **CA2**, contains 18 bits while the memory address register has space for only 16 bits. The two least-significant-bits in **CA2** indicate the number of the bank containing the requested data while the most-significant 16 bits specify the address within the bank. Thus each bank contains the data for every fourth address, as illustrated in Fig. 13.14, where the addresses are listed in octal.

564

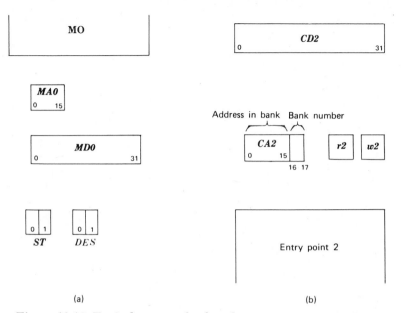

Figure 13.13. Typical memory bank and communications hardare.

If the other three entry points are not requesting data at a given time, one processor can supply four consecutive addresses to the four memory banks in only two clock periods per address. We make the assumption that if an entry point requests four words to be read from memory, this point will be ready to receive the words as they become available. Otherwise, the data words may not be transferred to *CD* in the same order as requested. In general, the control sequencers must in some way keep track of the requests for data that they have made. In particular, a pro-

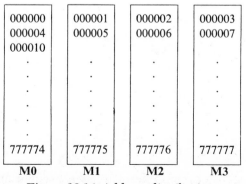

Figure 13.14. Address distribution.

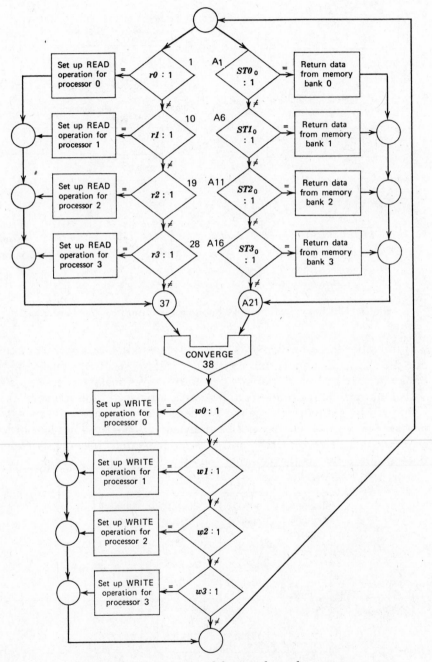

Figure 13.15. Bus control for interleaved memory.

cessor must not attempt to write in a bank if a read request is outstanding.

We are now ready to begin consideration of the control sequence for our multibank memory. Control of this unit may be thought of as managing traffic through the address and data buses. In order to avoid slowing the process unnecessarily, we must permit simultaneous transfers on the two buses. As depicted in Fig. 13.15, the control sequence is divided into two sections. The first part of the sequence will accept a new READ request and simultaneously deliver the data from a completed READ. The upper left path in Fig. 13.15 specifies the interrogation of each entry point for a possible READ request. The first request encountered is set up by passing the address to the appropriate memory bank through the *ADBUS*. At the same time, a word may be returned to an entry point through the *DBUS*. Control for the latter activity is depicted in the upper right path of Fig. 13.15.

Following the processing of no more than one read request and one data return, control converges to permit a search for a possible WRITE request. We represent control convergence in the flow chart by the hardware symbol for this operation. Only the first WRITE request encountered is set up by the lower sequence in Fig. 13.15. Write requests are considered separately, since both data and an address must be passed to a memory bank. This ties up both buses, precluding any parallel transfer.

The reader may notice a priority system built into the flow chart in which the lower-numbered entry points and memory banks enjoy highest priority. It may even appear that repeated requests from the high-priority units will be honored, effectively causing the low-priority units to be ignored. This will not be the case. The actual read and write times for the memory banks are much longer than the time required for several passes through the bus control sequence. Each transfer of address or data between processor and memory bank takes only one clock period.

The details of the control sequence implementing a typical READ request (entry point 0) follow.

1. $\rightarrow (r0 \wedge DCD(CA0_{16:17}), \overline{r0})/(2, 4, 6, 8, 10)$
2. NO DELAY
   $\rightarrow (ST0_0 \vee ST0_1)/(10)$
3. $DES0, ST0, r0 \leftarrow 0, 0, 0, 1, 0; ADBUS = CA0$
   $MA0 \leftarrow ADBUS; read0 = 1;$ NO DELAY
   $\rightarrow (37)$

Sequences for the other entry points are similar. If a read request by entry point 0 is encountered at step 1, a four-way branch depending on the bank addressed by **CA0** is executed. If that bank is inactive, step 3 causes the appropriate status changes and connects the **ADBUS** for the transfer of the address from **CA0** to the proper memory address register (**MA0** for the case shown). Step 3 also carries out the address transfer and sends a read request to bank 0. Three separate two-step sequences, 4 to 5, 6 to 7, and 8 to 9, are required to handle cases in which banks 1, 2, and 3, respectively, are addressed. Steps 10 to 37 process requests made by the other three entry points.

The concurrent sequence for returning data is given by steps A1 to A5, which handle returns from bank 0. Similar sequences in steps A6 to A20 will service the remaining three memory banks. Step A1 causes a branch, depending on the destination of the data as specified by **DES0**.

A1. $\rightarrow (STO_0 \wedge DCD(DES0), \overline{STO}_0)/(A2, A3, A4, A5, A6)$

A2. $STO \leftarrow 0, 0; DBUS = MD0;$
$CD0 \leftarrow DBUS;$
$dataready0 = 1$ NO DELAY
$\rightarrow (A21)$

Step A2 establishes bus connections, returns the status of the memory bank to idle, transmits the desired data word to **CD0**, and announces this fact with a **dataready0** signal. Steps A3, A4, and A5 will similarly effect transfers back to the remaining three entry points from bank 0.

From steps 37 and A21 control is routed to the convergence step 38. From this point the sequence to service write requests begin.

A21. NO DELAY $\rightarrow$ (38)

37. NO DELAY $\rightarrow$ (38)

38. CONVERGE (A18, 37)

39. $\rightarrow (w0 \wedge DCD(CA0_{16:17}), \overline{w0})/(40, 42, 44, 46, 48)$

40. NO DELAY
$\rightarrow (STO_0 \vee STO_1)/(48)$

41. $STO, w0 \leftarrow 0, 1, 0; ADBUS = CA0;$
$DBUS = CD0; MA0 \leftarrow ADBUS; MD0 \leftarrow DBUS;$
$write0 = 1$
$\rightarrow$ (66)

66. DIVERGE (1, A1)

Steps 42-47 handle the cases in which banks 1, 2, and 3 are addressed. Steps 48 to 65 handle WRITE requests made by entry points 1, 2, and 3. The above sequence is not necessarily the fastest or most efficient. A pass through the sequence will require at most four clock periods. If the memory read-write cycle is 50 to 100 times the clock period (a possibility), the four clock period service time is not significant. If the read-write cycle is 10 or fewer clock periods, this delay may become significant. Clearly, a speed improvement could be realized by replacing the buses with direct transfers. Further improvement might be realized by eliminating the transfers altogether in favor of combinational logic routing of addresses. The result, of course, would be a formidable combinational logic network.

The hardware configuration discussed above was made as general as possible to illustrate the techniques involved. If certain of the entry points can be satisfied with lower grade service, various less costly approaches can be used. When a larger number of memory banks are interleaved, a saving could be realized by advancing addresses from address register to address register in shift register fashion until a match of bank identification bits is obtained. Data could be shifted out in the same fashion. The number of variations of such schemes is almost endless.

PROBLEMS

13.1 As mentioned in Section 13.2, a push-down stack can be implemented in three ways. Special control hardware in conjunction with a large RAM is the approach in the 6800 microprocessor while completely independent hardware is used in Example 13.1. Write a software realization of a stack in SIC assembly language with subroutines implementing PUSH, POP, and LOOK.

13.2 Assume that the stack module in Example 13.1 is implemented using a RAM for which both READ and WRITE operations take just slightly less than two clock periods. Rewrite the module description such that a PUSH or POP operation is completed and *ready* restored to 1 in the fewest possible clock periods after the one period level appears on line *push* or line *pop*.

13.3 The module description STACK in Example 13.1 fails to make use of location 0 in the RAM. When the first data word is placed in $R2$, the original "don't care" contents of $R2$ are placed in location 0. Thus the capacity of the stack is 255 words in RAM plus 1 word in $R2$. Rewrite the module description so that location 0 is utilized efficiently to provide a 257-word stack.

13.4 Combine the control sequences of Section 13.4 so that all memory references are handled by a Memory Control Sequencer. All memory references in the main control sequence will require a transfer of control to this unit. Write this sequence in AHPL. Discuss the advantages and disadvantages of the approach.

13.5 Write in AHPL a combinational logic unit description for FIRST-FREE as used in Section 13.4.

13.6 The first eight pages of the RAM in Fig. 13.9 will never be replaced by pages from virtual memory. The first eight vectors in the arrays **UC, AA**, and **AROM** serve only to identify the locations of these pages, which are never moved. Modify the main control unit sequences labeled R1, R2, and R3 and W1, W2, and W3 so that reference to these pages is identified and the least-significant 6 bits of the page number shifted directly into $MA_{0:5}$ without reference to **AROM**. This would permit the number of rows in **UC, AA**, and **AROM** to be reduced to 56 and would eliminate ⅛ of the logic in ASSOC (**DSCRPTBUS, AA**).

13.7 In step 102 of the sequence that identifies the missing virtual page (see Table 13.1) for the operating system, the missing page number is placed in $MD_{20:31}$ by step 102 and loaded into the least-significant 12 bits of the RAM location 0 by step 103. What benefit would result from placing this number instead in $MD_{8:19}$ and storing it in the corresponding bit positions in location 0?

13.8 Rewrite the control sequence for managing the interleaved memory banks of Problem 13.7 making maximum possible use of conditional transfers to reduce the time for reading and writing in the multibank memory.

13.9 Write a control sequence that will manage access to the 16-bank memory of Fig. 13.11 from a single entry point.

13.10 Consider a machine whose slow, large-capacity RAM is arranged in blocks of 16 words. Each time a request is made for one of the words in a block, the entire block is read into a memory data register in one operation. Suppose that a single central processor will request words from this memory at a rate exceeding the reciprocal of the read time of this memory. Often the requests will be for data from consecutive memory locations and hence can be serviced at an increased rate. Write a control sequence for this memory so that it will satisfy as nearly as possible the needs of the mentioned central processor. Define control and data registers as needed.

13.11 Compare the efficiencies of the memory of Problem 13.10 and the multiple-bank arrangement of Fig. 13.11. Form a conjecture as to their respective abilities to satisfy the requests of a processor that may request data at a rate four times the reciprocal of the memory cycle time. How might hard data be obtained to substantiate this conjecture? Supply some details.

13.12 The associative memory controller of Section 13.4 requests only one word at a time from the RAM. Modify the control sequence so that each request for a word in RAM will cause the three succeeding words to be placed in the associative memory as well. Assume that the associative memory is dealing with an interleaved multibank RAM so that these transfers can take place approximately in parallel.

13.13 In Fig. 13.9 the **AROM** serves only to encode a 1 of 64 code (only one of the 64 terminals represented by ASSOC (**AM;** **DSCRPTBUS**) will be 1) to form $MA_{0:5}$. This vector must be decoded later by the RAM decoder. Write a combinational logic unit description for the elimination of **AROM**. The decoder will have as inputs ASSOC (**AM; DSCRPTBUS**) and $MA_{6:17}$.

13.14 Write an AHPL control sequence that will sweep the entire contents of the associative scratch pad of Section 13.4 into RAM and will clear each row of **UC** to 0.

REFERENCES

1. Hellerman, H., *Digital System Principles*, 2nd ed., McGraw-Hill, New York, 1973.

2. *M6800 Microprocessor Applications Manual*, Motorola Incorporated, Phoenix, Ariz., 1975.

3. Meade, R. M., "How a Cache Memory Enhances a Computer's Performance," *Electronics*, Jan. 1972, pp. 58–62.

4. Meade, R.M., "Design Approaches for Cache Memory Control," Computer Design, Jan. 1971, p. 87.

5 Jones, R. M., "Factors Affecting the Efficiency of a Virtual Memory." *IEEE Trans. Computers*, Nov. 1969, p. 1004.

6. "The Multics Virtual Memory," *Honeywell Information Systems REPORT 1L02, 1L12*, Phoenix, Ariz., 1972.

7. "Control Data ,7600 Computer System," *Reference Manual*, Publication No. 60258200.

8. Chu, Y., *Computer Organization and Programming*, Prentice Hall, Englewood Cliffs, N.J., 1972.

9. Laliotis, T. A., "Main Memory Technology," *Computer*, Sept. 1973, pp. 21–27.

14

HIGH-SPEED ADDITION

14.1 INTRODUCTION

One of the main concerns of the computer designer is obtaining the highest possible operating speed, subject to various technical and economic constraints. As we have seen, the adder plays a central role in the operation of the computer, and is thus a major factor in determining the overall speed of most machines. As a result, the design of high-speed adders has been the subject of exhaustive study from the very beginning of the computer era.

Over the years a number of fast-adders have been developed, but today the majority of fast-adder designs utilize some version of the *carry look-ahead* principle. The carry look-ahead adder was first described by Weinberger and Smith [1] in 1956. The design was further refined in the design of the *Stretch* computer; this version was described by MacSorley [2] in a 1961 article that is the basic reference on the subject. Flores (1963) [3] presented the first description in a textbook, and his description is probably the most complete to date.

A particular problem of notation arises in describing adders. It is standard practice in articles on adders to number the bit positions starting with the least-significant-digit (l.s.d.) position as bit 0, the next most significant as bit 1, etc. However, as we have seen, the practice in numbering registers is exactly the opposite, the most-significant-digit (m.s.d.) position being bit 0. The former convention is convenient from the point of view of keeping the equations simple, since we start writing equations with the l.s.d. position. If we adopt the latter convention, in a p-bit adder the l.s.d. is bit $(p\text{-}1)$, the next digit is bit $(p\text{-}2)$, etc., which makes for very cumbersome notation. To keep things as simple as possible while remaining consistent with the register notation, throughout this

572

chapter we shall discuss a fixed-length adder of 64 bits, from bit 0 (m.s.d.) to bit 63 (l.s.d.). The reader should have no trouble adapting the equations to adders of any other length, and we believe that the slight loss of generality will be more than compensated for by the advantages of a consistent system of notation.

14.2 RIPPLE-CARRY ADDER

The simplest form of parallel adder is the ripple-carry adder, which consists of full-adders connected as shown in Fig. 14.1. The combinational logic subroutine generating this adder was presented in Section 7.7, but we wish to analyze it in detail at this time to set the stage for the discussion to follow. The adder combines an addend and an augend, **A** and **B**, to develop a sum, **S**. A given full adder, in the *j*th bit position, receives the *j*th bits of the addend and augend, A_j and B_j, together with a carry-in from the next-least-significant digit, C_j+1, and produces the sum bit, S_j, and the carry-out C_j. The truth table for a full adder is shown in Fig. 14.2, and the equations for the sum and carry bits are given in Eqs. 14.1 and 14.2.

$$S_j = (A_j \wedge \bar{B}_j \wedge \bar{C}_{j+1}) \vee (\bar{A}_j \wedge \bar{B}_j \wedge C_{j+1}) \vee (\bar{A}_j \wedge B_j \wedge \bar{C}_{j+1}) \vee (A_j \wedge B_j \wedge C_{j+1}) \ (14.1)$$

$$C_j = (A_j \wedge B_j) \vee (A_j \wedge C_{j+1}) \vee (B_j \wedge C_{j+1}) \tag{14.2}$$

Note that these equations are written in the second-order, sum-of-products form; so that there are two levels of gating (AND-OR) between the input and output. If we let the delay through a single level of gating be Δt, then the delay in a single stage is $2\Delta t$, which is the minimum possible. We assume that all bits of the addend and augend arrive at the same time, but each individual adder cannot develop its sum until $2\Delta t$ after it receives the carry from the previous stage. Further, if the addend

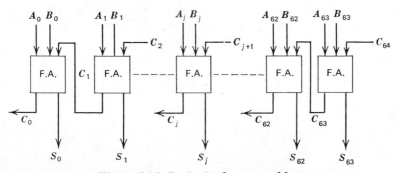

Figure 14.1. Basic ripple-carry adder.

A_j	B_j	C_{j+1}	S_j	C_j
0	0	0	0	0
0	0	1	1	0
0	1	0	1	0
0	1	1	0	1
1	0	0	1	0
1	0	1	0	1
1	1	0	0	1
1	1	1	1	1

Figure 14.2. Truth table for a full adder.

bit is 1 and the augend bit 0 (or vice versa), the carry-out will not be developed until $2\Delta t$ after the arrival of the carry-in. In the worst possible case the carry may have to propagate ("ripple-through") the adder from one end to the other, with a delay of $2\Delta t$ in each stage and a total delay of $\rho 2\Delta t$ for the whole adder. The worst case will rarely occur; if the addend and augend bits are both 0 or both 1, then the output carry is independent of the input carry. But we must allow for the worst case. Thus, for a 64-bit adder, we must allow $128\Delta t$ for addition; and even with very fast electronics, this can be an intolerable delay. As a result, the ripple-carry adder will generally be found only in small, inexpensive computers.

14.3 THE MINIMUM-DELAY ADDER

A basic theorem of Boolean algebra states that any Boolean function, no matter how complex, can be realized in a second-order (sum-of-products or product-of-sums) form. All the bits of the addend and augend are assumed to be available simultaneously so that there would seem to be no theoretical reason why we cannot develop a second-order equation for each sum bit and eliminate the delays of carry propagation. Let us investigate this possibility for the 64-bit adder.

For the l.s.d. position we have

$$S_{63} = (A_{63} \wedge \bar{B}_{63} \wedge \bar{C}_{64}) \vee (\bar{A}_{63} \wedge B_{63} \wedge \bar{C}_{64}) \vee (\bar{A}_{63} \wedge \bar{B}_{63} \wedge C_{64}) \vee (A_{63} \wedge B_{63} \wedge C_{64}) \quad (14.3)$$

and

$$C_{63} = (A_{63} \wedge B_{63}) \vee (A_{63} \wedge C_{64}) \vee (B_{63} \wedge C_{64}) \quad (14.4)$$

For the next stage we have

$$S_{62} = (A_{62} \wedge \bar{B}_{62} \wedge \bar{C}_{63}) \vee (\bar{A}_{62} \wedge B_{62} \wedge \bar{C}_{63}) \vee (\bar{A}_{62} \wedge \bar{B}_{62} \wedge C_{63}) \vee (A_{62} \wedge B_{62} \wedge C_{63}) \quad (14.5)$$

Substituting Eq. 14.4 into Eq. 14.5 to eliminate the propagated carry,* we have

$$
\begin{aligned}
S_{62} = {} & (A_{62} \wedge B_{62} \wedge A_{63} \wedge B_{63}) \vee (A_{62} \wedge B_{62} \wedge A_{63} \wedge C_{64}) \vee (A_{62} \wedge B_{62} \wedge B_{63} \wedge C_{64}) \\
& \vee (A_{62} \wedge \overline{B}_{62} \wedge \overline{A}_{63} \wedge \overline{B}_{63}) \vee (A_{62} \wedge \overline{B}_{62} \wedge \overline{A}_{63} \wedge \overline{C}_{64}) \vee (A_{62} \wedge \overline{B}_{62} \wedge \overline{B}_{63} \wedge \overline{C}_{64}) \\
& \vee (\overline{A}_{62} \wedge \overline{B}_{62} \wedge A_{63} \wedge B_{63}) \vee (\overline{A}_{62} \wedge \overline{B}_{62} \wedge A_{63} \wedge C_{64}) \vee (\overline{A}_{62} \wedge \overline{B}_{62} \wedge B_{63} \wedge C_{64}) \\
& \vee (\overline{A}_{62} \wedge B_{62} \wedge \overline{A}_{63} \wedge \overline{B}_{63}) \vee (\overline{A}_{62} \wedge B_{62} \wedge \overline{A}_{63} \wedge \overline{C}_{64}) \vee (\overline{A}_{62} \wedge B_{62} \wedge \overline{B}_{63} \wedge \overline{C}_{64}) \quad (14.6)
\end{aligned}
$$

Here we have a second-order equation exclusively in terms of the original inputs to the adder; so S_{62} will be developed with the same delay as S_{63}. However, Eq. 14.3 requires only 4 three-input AND gates while Eq. 14.6 requires 12 four-input AND gates. If we carry the same process on further, we find that S_{61} requires 4 four-input and 24 five-input gates, and S_{60} requires 4 four-input, 8 five-input, and 48 six-input AND gates. It is obvious that the number and size of gates very rapidly becomes totally impractical: S_0 would require approximately 10^{20} gates!

14.4 THE CARRY LOOK-AHEAD PRINCIPLE

We have seen that the ripple-carry adder is too slow and the minimum-delay adder impractical; therefore, we look for something in between. In one sense, we need to find a way to factor the equations of the minimum-delay adder into groupings of practical size. There are an infinite number of ways of factoring the equations, and many have been tried; but the most successful designs all utilize the *carry look-ahead* principle.

We begin by taking a slightly different approach to the implementation of the individual full adder. Notice from Fig. 14.2 that if $A_j = B_j = 0$, then $C_j = 0$ regardless of the value of C_{j+1}. Similarly, if $A_j = B_j = 1$, then $C_j = 1$ regardless of C_{j+1}. If $A_j \neq B_j$, then the carry-out C_j is the same as the carry-in C_{j+1}. In the latter case we say that the carry propagates through stage j. When the carry-out stage j is a 1 regardless of the carry-in, we say that stage j is a *generate* stage. This interpretation of an adder stage is given in Fig. 14.3.

Stage j is a generate stage if and only if G_j as defined by Eq. 14.7 is 1:

$$
G_j = A_j \wedge B_j \quad (14.7)
$$

---

*The input carry to the first stage, C_{64}, is used in complement arithmetic and is assumed to be available at the same time as the addend and augend.

A_j	B_j	C_j	
0	0	0	
0	1	C_{j+1}	Propagate stage
1	0	C_{j+1}	Propagate stage
1	1	1	Generate stage

Figure 14.3. Carry propagation.

Stage j is a propagate stage if and only if P_j is defined by Eq. 14.8 is 1:

$$P_j = A_j \oplus B_j = (A_j \wedge \overline{B}_j) \vee (\overline{A}_j \wedge B_j) \tag{14.8}$$

From Fig. 14.3 we observe that we have a carry-out stage whenever $G_j = 1$ or when $P_j = 1$ and there is a carry into stage j. This yields Eq. 14.10 as an expression for C_j.

$$C_j = (A_j \wedge B_j) \vee (((A_j \wedge \overline{B}_j) \vee (\overline{A}_j \wedge B_j)) \wedge C_{j+1}) \tag{14.9}$$

$$C_j = G_j \vee (P_j \wedge C_{j+1}) \tag{14.10}$$

It is also possible to express the sum S_j as a function of G_j, P_j, and C_{j+1}. This is most easily accomplished by algebraic manipulation of the basic expression for S_j.

$$S_j = (A_j \wedge \overline{B}_j \wedge \overline{C}_{j+1}) \vee (\overline{A}_j \wedge B_j \wedge \overline{C}_{j+1}) \vee (\overline{A}_j \wedge \overline{B}_j \wedge C_{j+1})$$
$$\vee (A_j \wedge B_j \wedge C_{j+1}) \tag{14.11}$$

$$= (((A_j \wedge B_j) \vee (\overline{A}_j \wedge \overline{B}_j)) \wedge C_{j+1}) \vee (((A_j \wedge \overline{B}_j) \vee (\overline{A}_j \wedge B_j)) \wedge \overline{C}_{j+1})$$

$$S_j = (\overline{P}_j \wedge C_{j+1}) \vee (P_j \wedge \overline{C}_{j+1}) \tag{14.12}$$

Equations 14.12 and 14.10 are certainly simpler in form than the original sum and carry equations, but it is not yet evident what effect they will have on the speed or complexity of the circuit. For this purpose let us now apply these equations to the design of the 64-bit adder starting as usual with the l.s.d. position:

$$\begin{aligned}
S_{63} &= (\overline{P}_{63} \wedge C_{64}) \vee (P_{63} \wedge \overline{C}_{64}) \\
S_{62} &= (\overline{P}_{62} \wedge C_{63}) \vee (P_{62} \wedge \overline{C}_{63}) \\
S_{61} &= (\overline{P}_{61} \wedge C_{62}) \vee (P_{61} \wedge \overline{C}_{62}) \\
S_{60} &= (\overline{P}_{60} \wedge C_{61}) \vee (P_{60} \wedge \overline{C}_{61})
\end{aligned} \tag{14.13}$$

The sum equations obviously all have the same form so that we shall implement them with a special form of full-adder circuit, as shown in Fig. 14.4. For later convenience, we shall divide this circuit into two sections, the *PG section* and the *SUM section*, as shown.

HIGH–SPEED ADDITION/14

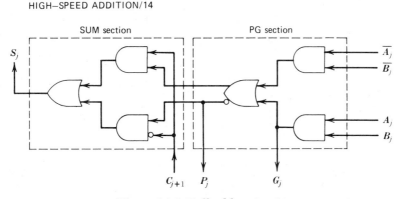

Figure 14.4. Full-adder circuit.

The carry-in terms to the sum circuits will be developed as shown in the following equations:

$$C_{63} = G_{63} \vee (P_{63} \wedge C_{64}) \tag{14.14}$$

$$\begin{aligned} C_{62} &= G_{62} \vee (P_{62} \wedge C_{63}) \\ &= G_{62} \vee (P_{62} \wedge G_{63}) \vee (P_{62} \wedge P_{63} \wedge C_{64}) \end{aligned} \tag{14.15}$$

$$\begin{aligned} C_{61} &= G_{61} \vee (P_{61} \wedge C_{62}) \\ &= G_{61} \vee (P_{61} \wedge G_{62}) \vee (P_{61} \wedge P_{62} \wedge G_{63}) \vee (P_{61} \wedge P_{62} \wedge P_{63} \wedge C_{64}) \end{aligned}$$
$$\tag{14.16}$$

These three equations are implemented in the carry look-ahead (CLA) unit, shown in Fig. 14.5. (This unit also implements some additional equations, which will be discussed shortly.) Since the CLA unit may be used with any set of four bit-positions, we have used generalized subscripts in Fig. 14.5. For implementation of the above equations, $j = 63$.

The interconnection of the CLA unit with the adder units for bits 60 to 63 is shown in Fig. 14.6. Noting that each unit (SUM, PG, CLA) is a second-order circuit, we can analyze the propagation delays. Let us consider the worst case, a carry generated in bit 63 and propagated through to bit 60. The carry is generated in PG_{63} with a delay of $2\Delta t$, propagated through the CLA to C_{61} in $2\Delta t$, and propagated through SUM_{60} to develop S_{60} in $2\Delta t$, for a total delay of $6\Delta t$. This compares with a delay of $8\Delta t$ for ripple-carry through 4 bits. This is only a minor improvement; but this is just the beginning of the design, as we shall see.

If we examine Eqs. 14.14, 14.15, 14.16, we see that they are iterative in form; there is no reason why we could not continue the same process to write equations for C_{60}, C_{59}, etc. These equations would also be sec-

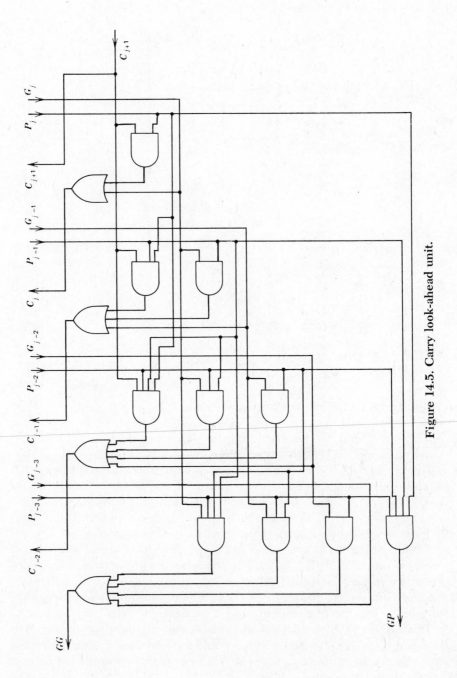

Figure 14.5. Carry look-ahead unit.

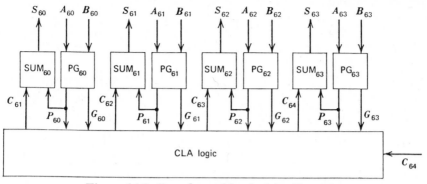

Figure 14.6. Complete adder for bits 60 to 63.

ond-order, so the CLA unit could be extended to cover more bits, with no increase in delay. However, as we increase the number of bits, the size and number of gates also increases: C_{61} requires four-input gates, C_{60} would require five-input gates, C_{59} would require six-input gates; etc. So the number of bits the CLA unit can cover is limited by the fan-in capability of our gates. Circuit technology makes it generally impractical to go beyond about 8 bits in the basic CLA unit.

14.5 GROUP CARRY LOOK-AHEAD

As the next step in our design, we shall divide the 64-bit adder into 4-bit groups, bits 0 to 3 comprising group 0, bits 4 to 7, group 1, etc. We then define *group generate*, **GG**, and group propagate, **GP**, terms, as shown for group 15 (bits 60 to 63). The group generate term corresponds to the situation

$$GG_{15} = G_{60} \vee (P_{60} \wedge G_{61}) \vee (P_{60} \wedge P_{61} \wedge G_{62}) \vee (P_{60} \wedge P_{61} \wedge P_{62} \wedge G_{63}) \quad (14.17)$$

$$GP_{15} = P_{60} \wedge P_{61} \wedge P_{62} \wedge P_{63} \quad (14.18)$$

where a carry has been generated somewhere in the group and all more-significant positions are in the propagate condition so that the carry propagates on out of the group. The group propagate corresponds to the condition in which all bits in the group are in the propagate condition so that a carry into the group should pass right through the group. Note that these terms are implemented by the leftmost five gates in the CLA unit (Fig. 14.5).

Next, we note that there is a carry-out of the group if a carry is generated in the group and propagated out or if there is a carry into the group that is propagated through the group. Thus we can define the *group carry*, GC_{15}, which is equal to C_{60}, by the following equation:

$$C_{60} = GC_{15} = GG_{15} \lor (GP_{15} \land GC_{16}) \qquad (14.19)$$

where $GC_{16} = C_{64}$, the carry into the group. In a similar fashion we can develop equations for the group carries from succeeding 4-bit groups.

$$C_{56} = GC_{14} = GG_{14} \lor (GP_{14} \land GC_{15})$$
$$= GG_{14} \lor (GP_{14} \land GC_{15}) \lor (GP_{14} \land GP_{15} \land GC_{16}) \quad 14.20)$$

and

$$C_{52} = GC_{13} = GG_{13} \lor (GP_{13} \land GC_{14})$$
$$= GG_{13} \lor (GP_{13} \land GC_{14}) \lor (GP_{13} \land GP_{14} \land GC_{14})$$
$$\lor (GP_{13} \land GP_{14} \land GP_{15} \land GC_{16}) \qquad (14.21)$$

Except for the names of the variables, Eqs. 14.19, 14.20, and 14.21 are seen to be identical to Eqs. 14.14, 14.15, and 14.16. Thus the group carry terms can be developed by the same type of CLA circuit as used for the ordinary carries (14.5). The interconnection of adders and CLA units for bits 48 to 63 is shown in Fig. 14.7. (The group carry unit is labeled GCLA for purposes of identification but is the same circuit as the CLA units.)

Now let us consider the delay for these 16 bits, again considering the worst case. The carry is generated in PG_{63} in $2\Delta t$, propagates through CLA_{15} to develop GG_{15} in $2\Delta t$, through $GCLA_3$ to develop GC_{13} in $2\Delta t$ and through CLA_{12} to develop C_{48} in $2\Delta t$. Thus the carry propagation delay in Fig. 14.7 is $8\Delta t$ compared to $32\Delta t$ for 16 bits of a ripple-carry adder. We are now beginning to see some significant improvements in delay times, but we are not done yet.

14.6 SECTION CARRY LOOK-AHEAD

We now divide the 64-bit adder into four 16-bit sections and define *section generate*, *SG*, and *section propagate*, *SP*, terms, in a manner exactly analogous to the group terms. These equations will be seen to have the same form as Eqs. 14.17 and 14.18 for the group generate and propagate terms. Thus the

$$SG_3 = GG_{12} \lor (GP_{12} \land GG_{13}) \lor (GP_{12} \land GP_{13} \land GG_{14})$$
$$\lor (GP_{12} \land GP_{13} \land GP_{14} \land GG_{15}) \qquad (14.22)$$

and

$$SP_3 = GP_{12} \land GP_{13} \land GP_{14} \land GP_{15} \qquad (14.23)$$

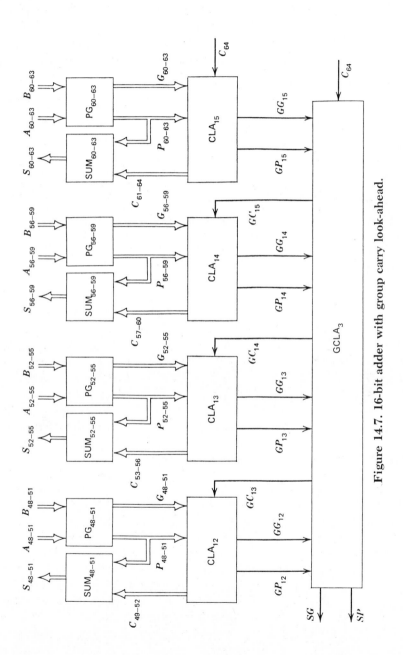

Figure 14.7. 16-bit adder with group carry look-ahead.

five leftmost gates of Fig. 14.5 will form SG and SP terms when the inputs are GG and GP terms. The SG and SP outputs from GCLA are shown in Fig. 14.7.

We now develop equations for *section carry-out* in the same manner as for the group carry-outs. These equations are seen to have the same form as

$$C_{48} = GC_{12} = SC_3 = SG_3 \vee (SP_3 \wedge SC_4) \tag{14.24}$$

$$\begin{aligned} C_{32} = GC_8 = SC_2 &= SG_2 \vee (SP_2 \wedge SC_3) \\ &= SG_2 \vee (SP_2 \wedge SG_3) \vee (SP_2 \wedge SP_3 \wedge SC_4) \end{aligned} \tag{14.25}$$

$$\begin{aligned} C_{16} = GC_4 = SC_1 &= SG_1 \vee (SP_1 \wedge SC_2) \\ &= SG_1 \vee (SP_1 \wedge SG_2) \vee (SP_1 \wedge SP_2 \wedge SG_3) \\ &\quad \vee (SP_1 \wedge SP_2 \wedge SP_3 \wedge SC_4) \end{aligned} \tag{14.26}$$

those for the original CLA unit so that the same form of circuit can be used again, with one small change. Since there will be no further levels of look-ahead, the final output carry, C_0, must be developed. To develop this term,

$$\begin{aligned} C_0 &= SG_0 \vee (SP_0 \wedge SG_1) \vee (SP_0 \wedge SP_1 \wedge SG_2) \vee (SP_0 \wedge SP_1 \\ &\quad \wedge SP_2 \wedge SG_3) \vee (SP_0 \wedge SP_1 \wedge SP_2 \wedge SP_3 \wedge SC_4) \end{aligned} \tag{14.27}$$

connect a SC_4 input to the gate in Fig. 14.5 that develops GP, and connect the output of this gate to the OR gate that develops GG in Fig. 14.5; this gate will now develop C_0. The complete block diagram of the 64-bit adder with three levels of carry look-ahead is shown in Fig. 14.8.

Applying the same sort of analysis as before, the reader should be able to convince himself that the worst case delay through this adder would be $14\Delta t$, compared to $128\Delta t$ for the 64-bit, ripple-carry adder. Thus we have achieved about 9:1 improvement in speed, certainly a worthwhile accomplishment. However, we must also consider the cost of this speed improvement. An exact cost analysis would depend on the hardware chosen, but a good measure of the cost of a logic circuit is the total number of gate terminals (inputs and outputs), since this number will generally be proportional to the total number of active devices.

The full-adder of Fig. 14.4 has 22 terminals, giving a total of 1408 for 64-bits. The CLA unit of Fig. 14.5 has 56 terminals, and there are 21 CLA units in the complete adder of Fig. 14.8. If we include the two extra inputs in the SCLA required for C_0, this gives a grand total of 2586 terminals for the complete adder. The cost of a ripple-carry adder will depend on the full-adder configuration chosen. The simplest circuit known to the authors [4] has 27 terminals, giving a total of 1728 terminals

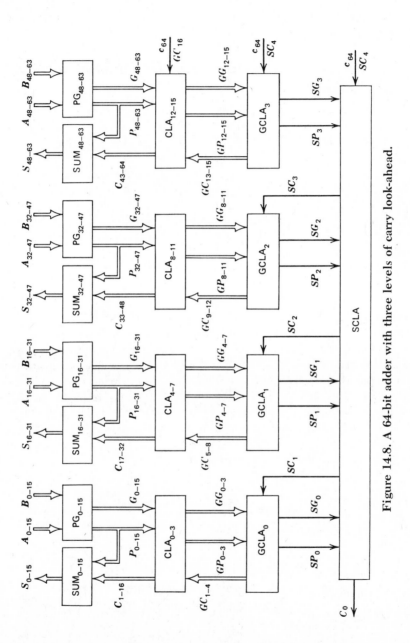

Figure 14.8. A 64-bit adder with three levels of carry look-ahead.

for 64 bits. Thus, for less than a 50 percent increase in cost, we have achieved about a 9:1 increase in speed, a remarkable speed/cost trade-off.

14.7 GENERATION OF ADDER LOGIC BY COMBINATIONAL LOGIC UNIT

We have now completed our discussion of the principles of the carry look-ahead adder, but we have actually generated only a sample of the equations describing it. The structure of the adder is highly repetitive in form, with the same form of equations occurring many times, so that it is ideally suited to description by combinational logic unit description.

The complete adder is made up of two types of units, the full adders, and the CLA units so that we start by writing AHPL descriptions of these units.

Example 14.1
Write an AHPL combinational logic unit description for the full adder of Fig. 14.4.

Solution
Because of the way in which the various units are interconnected in the complete adder, it is preferable to consider the full adder as two separate units, corresponding to the SUM and PG sections in Fig. 14.4. The descriptions are given below. For the PG units, inputs w and x correspond to A_j and B_j, and outputs PG_0, PG_1, and PG_2 correspond to $\overline{P}_j$, P_j, and G_j, respectively, in Fig. 14.4. For the SUM unit, inputs y and z correspond to $\overline{P}_j$ and P_j from the PG unit, cin corresponds to C_{j+1}, and output SUM corresponds to S_j.

> UNIT: PG(w; x)
>   INPUTS: (w; x; $\overline{w}$; $\overline{x}$)
>   OUTPUTS: PG[3]
>   1. $a = w \wedge x$
>   2. $b = \overline{w} \wedge \overline{x}$
>   3. $c = a \vee b$
>   4. $d = \overline{c}$
>   6. $PG_0 = c$
>   7. $PG_1 = d$
>   8. $PG_2 = a$
> END
> UNIT: SUM(y; z; cin)
>   INPUTS: (y; z; cin)

OUTPUT: SUM
1. $a = \overline{cin}$
2. $b = a \wedge z$
3. $c = cin \wedge y$
4. SUM $= b \vee c$
END

Example 14.2
Write an AHPL combinational logic unit description of the carry look-ahead unit of Fig. 14.5.

Solution
We note that the structure of this unit is repetitive in character so that an iterative form of description is appropriate. For this purpose it is convenient to assign subscripted names to the signal lines as shown in Fig. 14.9. The main portion of the subroutine consists of statements 4, 5, and 7, which iteratively generate the various A_i, B_i, and C_i terms. The subroutine starts by setting $i = 3$ and jumping to step 7 to generate A_3. Note that we enter the loop at this point because there is no C_3 or B_3 term. Next, i is decremented to 2 and control jumps back to step 5 to generate B_2, after which step 6 checks for $i = 0$. Since $i \neq 0$ at this point, control passes to step 7 to generate A_2. This general process is repeated until $i = 0$, when step 7 branches to step 10 to generate A_0, which is of

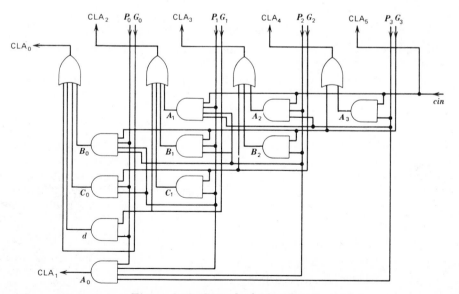

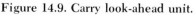

Figure 14.9. Carry look-ahead unit.

a slightly different form than the other A terms. Steps 11 to 16 then generate the six output terms, corresponding to the four carry terms, and the group generate and group propagate terms.

UNIT: CLA(P; G; cin)
         INPUTS: $P[4]$; $G[4]$; cin
         OUTPUTS: CLA[6]
         1. $i \Leftarrow 3$
         2. $\Rightarrow (7)$
         3. $d = G_1 \wedge P_0$
         4. $C_i = G_2 \wedge (\wedge/P_{i:1})$
         5. $B_i = G_3 \wedge (\wedge/P_{i:2})$
         6. $\Rightarrow (i = 0)/(10)$
         7. $A_i = cin \wedge (\wedge/P_{i:3})$
         8. $i \Leftarrow i - 1$
         9. $\Rightarrow (i + 3)$
         10. $A_0 = \wedge/P_{0:3})$
         11. $CLA_0 = G_0 \vee B_0 \vee C_0 \vee d$
         12. $CLA_1 = A_0$
         13. $CLA_2 = G_1 \vee A_1 \vee B_1 \vee C_1$
         14. $CLA_3 = G_2 \vee A_2 \vee B_2$
         15. $CLA_4 = G_3 \vee A_3$
         16. $CLA_5 = cin$
END

The CLA unit contains 14 gates so that a noniterative subroutine consisting of 14 gate-defining statements would be quite practical. We chose to use an iterative approach in the interests of further illustrating the use of iteration in generating complex circuits. For the full 64-bit adder, the iterative approach is clearly preferable.

Example 14.3
Write an AHPL combinational logic description of the 64-bit adder of Fig. 14.8.

Solution
The complete routine follows. All variable names correspond to the notation of Fig. 14.8. The index variable i is the bit index, j is the group index, and k is the section index.

UNIT: CLADD(A; B; cin)
         INPUTS: $A[64]$; $B[64]$; cin
         OUTPUTS: CLADD[65]
         1. $i \Leftarrow 64$

2. $C_i = cin$
3. $i \Leftarrow i - 1$
4. $NOTP_i, P_i, G_i = \text{PG}(A_i; B_i)$
5. $S_i = \text{SUM}(NOTP_i; P_i; C_{i+1})$
6. $\Rightarrow (i \neq 0)/(3)$
7. $i \Leftarrow 60$
8. $j \Leftarrow 16$
9. $GC_j = cin$
10. $j \Leftarrow j - 1$
11. $GG_j, GP_j, C_{i+1:i+4} = \text{CLA}(P_{i:i+3}; G_{i:i+3}; GC_{j+1})$
12. $i \Leftarrow i - 4$
13. $\Rightarrow (j \neq 0)/(10)$
14. $j \Leftarrow 12$
15. $k \Leftarrow 4$
16. $SC_k = cin$
17. $k \Leftarrow k - 1$
18. $SG_k, SP_k, GC_{j+1:j+3} = \text{CLA}_{0:4} (GP_{j:j+3}; GG_{j:j+3}; SC_{k+1})$
19. $j \Leftarrow j - 4$
20. $\Rightarrow (k \neq 0)/(17)$
21. $AG, AP, SC_{1:3} = \text{CLA}_{0:4} (SP_{0:3}; SG_{0:3}; SC)$
22. $C_0 = AG \vee (AP \wedge SC_4)$
23. $\text{CLADD} = C_0, S_{0:63}$

END

The first loop, statements 3 to 6, connects all PG and SUM units. For the PG units, the inputs are the 64 A_i and 64 B_i lines, and the outputs are defined as the corresponding $NOTP_i$, P_i, and G_i lines. For the sum units, the outputs are defined as the 64 sum bits. The inputs are $NOTP_i$, P_i, and input carry bits. There is one special problem here, in that the c bits (other than c_{64}) have not been defined at this point. The compiler generating the network would therefore have to make a note that these are undefined inputs, to be connected when they are defined by later statements.

The next loop, steps 10 to 13 generates the first level of carry look-ahead, units CLA_0 to CLA_{15} in Fig. 14.8. On the first pass through this loop, $i = 60$ and $j = 15$. Statement 11 will define GG_{15}, GP_{15}, and $C_{61:64}$ as the outputs of CLA units connected with $P_{60:63}$, $G_{60:63}$, and GC_{16} (C_{64}) as inputs. Reference to Fig. 14.7 will verify that these are the required inputs and outputs for CLA_{15}. On the next pass, $i = 56$ and $j = 14$; the reader can also easily verify that step 11 will then connect the proper inputs and outputs for CLA_{14} as shown in Fig. 14.7. The process continues in this manner until all 16 first-level CLA units have been connected. Note that this stage defines the c lines, which can now be connected as the appropriate inputs to SUM units. Also, the GC inputs have not been defined at this point so that the compiler would again have to make a note that these must be defined by later operations.

The next loop, steps 17 to 20, connects the second level of CLA units, $GCLA_0$ to $GCLA_3$ in Fig. 14.8. The functioning of this loop is basically the same as that connecting the first level of CLA units. The only difference is that only three of the carry outputs from the CLA, corresponding to $CLA_{2:4}$ in Fig. 14.9 are used. The output CLA_5 is needed only in the first level of carry look-ahead. We shall leave it to the reader to verify from a review of the discussion of group look-ahead in Section 14.5 that this is correct.

Finally, steps 21 to 22 define the SCLA unit of Fig. 14.8. Note that there are no propagate and generate outputs specified for the SCLA unit. As discussed in Section 14.6, the carry-out term is generated from these terms and the carry-in. Therefore, step 21 defines generate and propagate outputs of this CLA unit as internal variables AG and AP (for Adder Generate and Adder Propagate), which are then combined with the input carry to generate the output carry.

The situation encountered in the above example, of connection statements requiring inputs that were not defined until later in the routine, warrants further comment. In the routine generating the ripple-carry adder in Chapter 7, this situation did not occur. All the logic involved in processing each bit was fully specified before going on to the next bit. At no time was an input required that had not yet been specified. Clearly, the need to keep track of which inputs have not been specified and to check for them later will complicate the hardware compiler. Therefore, it is reasonable to ask why this situation occurs and if it could not in some way be avoided.

The situation occurs because we have grouped the carry look-ahead process in terms of 4-bit modules. Consider Fig. 14.7, with special attention to the relationship between CLA_{14} and $GCLA_3$. CLA_{14} requires GC_{15} as an input, but GC_{15} is an output of $GCLA_3$ which in turn requires the outputs of CLA_{14} as inputs. There is apparently a circular signal path that makes it impossible to completely define either unit independently of the other. If we consider the equations, we find that there is not in fact any circular relationship; GC_{15} is a function only of GG_{15}, GP_{15}, and C_{64}, all of which will have been defined earlier in the compilation process. But the grouping of the processing of $GG_{12:15}$ and $GP_{12:15}$ into a single CLA module makes it impossible to separate these terms in the writing of the CL subroutine. The problem could be avoided by not treating the CLA units as modules but rather writing appropriate equations for each bit of the look-ahead process, and there would be no objection to this if the CLA units were actually being generated from discrete gates. However, 4-bit CLA units are available as standard integrated circuits, and realization of an adder would almost certainly be in terms of such modules.

14.8 THE CARRY COMPLETION ADDER

There is another type of adder that applies a completely different approach, and therefore deserves some comment. We have noted that the worst case, the carry propagating from one end of the adder to the other, will occur only with certain combinations of operands. In most cases there will be stages in either the *generate* or *no propagate* condition every few bits so that any given carry is likely to propagate through only a few stages. It has been shown [5] that the average maximum carry length for a 64-bit adder is about 7 bits. Thus the *average* time for addition in a ripple-carry adder would be about $14\Delta t$, the same as for the full CLA adder designed in previous sections.

In the carry completion adder, circuitry is added to detect when all carries have fully propagated and issue a completion signal. Upon receipt of the completion signal, the computer can then go on to the next step without waiting to allow time for the rare worst case. A carry completion adder of typical design [3] has a cost about halfway between that of the ripple-carry and the CLA adders. This type of adder has been used in a few machines but has not met with much acceptance. The main problem is that it is difficult to make effective use of the time "saved" by the carry completion adder. If the add time is fixed, we can schedule other activities to be going on at the same time. But if the add times may vary over a range of 64:1, it becomes very difficult to synchronize other operations with the adder.

14.9 SUMMARY

The carry look-ahead adder has been considered in detail for two reasons: first, it is probably the most popular form of fast adder; second, it is a classic example of the ingenious application of logic design to the problem of obtaining increased speed at minimum cost.

The validity of the first reason may change with time due to developments in device technology. However, it is interesting to note that the carry look-ahead principle, which was first applied to vacuum-tube circuits, has also been applied to integrated circuits, resulting in CLA adders nearly a thousand times faster than the original vacuum-tube versions. A design principle that has remained viable while component speeds have increased by several orders of magnitude has certainly demonstrated some intrinsic validity.

589

On the other hand, as basic logic speeds continue to increase, the ordinary ripple-carry adder may become so fast compared to other system components, such as memory, that the CLA adder will be less attractive economically. But whatever the future may bring for the CLA adder, the logic design principles it illustrates will remain important. The careful analysis of the arithmetic process and the resultant factoring of the equations into iterative forms are basic ideas that will remain applicable to any technology.

REFERENCES

1. Weinberger, A., and J. L. Smith, "The Logical Design of a One-Micro-second Adder Using One-Megacycle Circuitry," *IRE Trans. Elec. Computers*, Vol. EC-5, No. 2 (June 1956), pp. 65–73.

2. MacSorley, O. L., "High-Speed Arithmetic in Binary Computers," *Proc. IRE*, Vol. 49, No. 1 (Jan. 1961), pp. 67–91.

3. Flores, I., *The Logic of Computer Arithmetic*, Prentice-Hall, Englewood Cliffs, N.J., 1963, Chaps. 4, 5, and 6.

4. Maley, G. A., and J. Earle, *The Logic Design of Transistor Digital Computers*, Prentice-Hall, Englewood Cliffs, N.J., 1963, p. 163.

5. Hendrickson, H. C., "Fast High-Accuracy Binary Parallel Addition," *IRE Trans. Elec. Computers*, Vol. EC-9, No. 4 (Dec. 1960), pp. 469–479.

15

MULTIPLICATION AND DIVISION

15.1 SIGNED MULTIPLICATION

In Chapter 6 the multiplication of negative numbers in complement form was accomplished by first determining the sign of the product, converting the operands to magnitude form, and then carrying out the multiplication. For numbers stored in one's-complement form, this conversion can be accomplished by merely reading the operand bits from the complement side of each flip-flop in the respective register. Thus, for one's-complement machines, sign and magnitude provide a satisfactory approach to multiplication.

In the two's-complement system, the process of complementing requires extra addition cycles, which may be considered to consume time unnecessarily. Recall that in Chapter 6 multiplication was initiated with the multiplicand in the *MD* register and the multiplier in the *AC* register. As the multiplication progressed, the multiplier was first transferred to *MQ* and the product was gradually formed in *AC* and shifted, least-significant bit first, into the *MQ* register. At the conclusion of this operation, the product is found spanning *AC* and *MQ*.

We now propose to carry out multiplication in the same manner without first converting the operands to magnitude form. Thus *MD* and *MQ* may contain two's-complement numbers. As we shall see, it will be necessary to modify the hardware program slightly. Our goal in doing so will be to accomplish any corrections in the same time intervals as the basic shift and add operations.

We see in Fig. 15.1 a tabulation of the possible contents of *MD* and *MQ*. We let a and b represent the respective numerical values, which may be either positive or negative. If both a and b are positive, then

a	b	$\perp MQ$	$\perp MD$	Desired Result $\perp(AC, MQ)$
$+$	$+$	a	b	ab
$+$	$-$	a	$2^n - |b|$	$2^{2n} - a \cdot |b|$
$-$	$+$	$2^n - |a|$	b	$2^{2n} - |a| \cdot b$
$-$	$-$	$2^n - |a|$	$2^n - |b|$	$|a| \cdot |b|$

Figure 15.1.

two's complement and signed-magnitude multiplication are identical. As we shall see, the program to be specified for two's-complement multiplication will reduce to the program of Chapter 6 for this case.

Now consider the second case; the multiplier is still positive but the multiplicand is negative so that the product should be negative. Recall that the basic multiplication process consists of repeated cycles of adding the multiplicand to partial products in AC, followed by right shifts of the new partial product. If we add a negative multiplicand in the proper complement form to negative partial products in the proper complement form, the result will be a negative product in the proper complement form.

We aleady know that complement addition works so that the only special precaution we must observe is to see that the shifting process produces a proper complement. Assume that the number y is loaded into an n-bit AC register, i.e.,

$$\perp AC = y$$

If we shift this number one place right, the effect is to reduce the value by 2^{-1}, i.e.,

$$\perp (0, AC_{0:n-2}) = 2^{-1} \times y$$

The correct complement form for the negative value of the shifted quantity would be a binary vector such that

$$\perp AC = 2^n - 2^{-1}y$$

Now suppose that the complement of y, $2^n - y$, has been stored in AC and is shifted one place right. The result is

$$\perp(0, AC_{0:n-2}) = 2^{-1}(2^n - y) = 2^{n-1} - 2^{-1}y$$

which is not the correct complement of the shifted number. To correct it, we must add 2^{n-1}, which gives

$$2^{n-1} - 2^{-1}y + 2^{n-1} = 2^n - 2^{-1}y$$

i.e., a 1 is inserted in the vacated most-significant-digit position.

In summary, for both cases in which the multiplier is positive, we add the multiplicand and shift, the only difference being that a 0 is inserted in the vacated position for positive multiplicand and a 1 for negative multiplicand. This is equivalent to saying that the inserted bit is equal to the multiplicand sign; therefore, the desired shifting can be accomplished by the statement

$$AC, MQ \leftarrow MD_0, AC, MQ_{0:n-2}$$

Next we consider the situation in which the multiplier is negative. When this occurs, both the multiplier and multiplicand are complemented, thus giving the proper sign for the product. The complementation can be accomplished without lengthening the multiplication process. Recall that in the routine of Chapter 6 the multiplier is inspected 1 bit at a time to determine whether the multiplicand is to be added to the current partial product. We also recall that a bit-by-bit algorithm for taking the two's-complement of a number was discussed in Chapter 2. The bits of the number are examined and corrected sequentially from right to left. Until a 1 is encountered, 0's are left unchanged. The first 1 from the right is also left unchanged, but all remaining bits are complemented. We shall use this complementing process for each bit of the multiplier as that bit is used to control addition of the multiplicand to the partial product.

With a negative multiplier, the sign of the product will be the opposite of the sign of the multiplicand. Thus, if the multiplicand is positive, it must be complemented to the negative form before adding in order to produce a negative product, and vice versa for a negative multiplicand. Noting that an alternate procedure for taking the two's-complement is to take the logical complement (one's-complement) and add 1 in the least-significant-digit position, we see that the multiplicand can be complemented as it is added to the partial product. We need only gate the complement of **MD** to the adder and insert a 1 on the input carry line. Finally, the proper shifting algorithm must be followed, inserting 0 when a positive product is to be developed and 1 when the product is to be negative.

On the basis of the above discussion we can now set up a flow chart for the complete signed multiplication procedure, as shown in Fig. 15.2. As in Chapter 6 we shall assume 18-bit registers and shall assume that we start with the multiplier in **AC** and the multiplicand in **MD**.

Steps 1 and 2 check for zero operands, in which case steps 18 and 19 set the product to zero and exit:

1. $\rightarrow (\overline{\vee/AC})/(19)$
2. $\rightarrow (\overline{\vee/MD})/(18)$

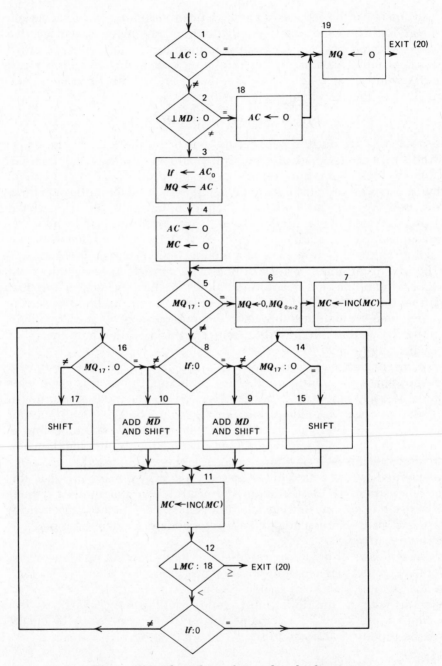

Figure 15.2. Flow chart of signed multiplication.

Step 3 stores the multiplier sign in the link and transfers the multiplier to MQ. The storage of the multiplier sign is required because the shifting will move the sign into a different position of MQ after every cycle. Step 4 clears AC and the multiplication counter, MC:

  3. $lf \leftarrow AC_0;\ MQ \leftarrow AC$
  4. $AC \leftarrow 18 \top 0;\ MC \leftarrow 5 \top 0$

Step 5 commences the actual multiplication by checking the least-significant digit of the multiplier. As long as the multiplier bits remain zero, the product is to remain zero, regardless of the ultimate sign of the product. Thus we remain in the steps 5, 6, 7 loop, shifting only the multiplier, until the first 1 of the multiplier is encountered:

  5. $\rightarrow (MQ_{17})/(8)$
  6. $MQ \leftarrow 0, MQ_{0:16}$
  7. $MC \leftarrow \mathrm{INC}(MC)$
      $\rightarrow (5)$

Step 8 checks the sign of the multiplier to determine whether the true or complemented contents of MD should be added. For a positive multiplier, step 9 adds the true contents of MD to AC and shifts right, inserting MD_0 in the vacated position. For a negative multiplier, step 10 adds the complement of the contents of MD and shifts right, inserting $\overline{MD}_0$ in the vacated position:

  8. $\rightarrow (lf)/(10)$
  9. $AC, MQ \leftarrow MD_0, \mathrm{ADD}(AC;\ MD;\ 0), MQ_{0:16}$
      $\rightarrow (11)$
 10. $AC, MQ \leftarrow \overline{MD}_0, \mathrm{ADD}(AC;\ \overline{MD};\ 1), MQ_{0:16}$

Whichever addition was made, step 11 increments the multiplication counter and step 12 checks to see if the multiplication is complete. If not, step 13 checks the multiplier sign, branching to step 14 for positive multiplier, to step 16 for negative multiplier. Step 8, which also checks the multiplier sign, is encountered only on the first 1 in the multiplier, which must be treated differently from succeeding 1's for negative multipliers.

 11. $MC \leftarrow \mathrm{INC}(MC)$
 12. $\rightarrow (MC_0 \wedge MC_3)/(20)$
 13. $\rightarrow (lf)/(16)$

For positive multipliers, step 14 checks the current least-significant bit of the multiplier, branching to step 15 for a shift if it is 0 and to step 9 for add-and-shift if it is 1. Step 16 makes a similar check for negative multipliers, branching to step 17 for a shift for a 1-bit or to step 10 for add-and-shift for a 0-bit.

14. $\rightarrow (MQ_{17})/(9)$
15. $AC, MQ \leftarrow MD_0, AC, MQ_{0:16}$
    $\rightarrow (11)$
16. $\rightarrow (\overline{MQ_{17}})/(10)$
17. $AC, MQ \leftarrow \overline{MD}_0, AC, MQ_{0:16}$
    $\rightarrow (11)$
18. $AC \leftarrow 18 \top 0$
19. $MQ \leftarrow 18 \top 0$

After each shift or add-and-shift, control returns to step 11 to increment MC and check for completion. Steps 18 and 19 set the product to zero for zero operands as determined in steps 1 and 2.

15.2 MULTIPLICATION SPEED-UP—CARRY-SAVE

The time-saving offered by the technique discussed in the last section is relatively small. At best, it eliminates two additions required for complementing; since there may be n additions required for an n-bit multiplier, this is a minor saving. It is often included, since it requires little extra hardware. In order to make any significant reductions in multiplication time, we must reduce either the number of additions or the addition time. If multiplication is to be provided, we shall almost certainly use a fast adder, such as the CLA adder discussed in the last chapter; but the necessity for n complete additions will still make multiplication relatively slow. Many techniques for multiplication speed-up have been proposed, most of which are discussed in Flores [1]. We shall consider only a few of the more significant and representative techniques.

Certainly, the best method of speed-up, in terms of cost/performance ratio, is the *carry-save* technique. This technique provides very significant increases in speed with relatively little extra hardware, and there are few multipliers of any size that do not include this feature in some form. The basic notion of carry-save is simple. The addition process may be visualized as developing a set of sum and carry bits, shifting of the carry bits right, and updating the sum and carry bits. The process continues until the carry has been formed and shifted $n - 1$ times. This is actually a synchronous interpretation of the usual carry propagation process. Now, suppose a series of numbers is to be added together, one at a time. Since addition is associative, the process is not changed if the next argument is added at the same time as the shifted carry. The process continues, with a new carry word formed and shifted with each addition, until the list of numbers to be added is exhausted. From that point the carry is allowed to propagate normally through $n - 1$ stages to complete the arithmetic.

Multiplication is an example of the process described above with the ith argument consisting of the multiplicand shifted $i - 1$ bits to the left if the ith bit of the multiplier is 1. Otherwise, the ith entry is zero. The process is illustrated for a simple example in Fig. 15.3. The process consists of four steps of additions to the partial product, followed by a fifth step, representing completion of the carry propagation. In this figure we have shown the computer form of the process, with the relative left shift of the carry-save word, **CS**, and the multiplicand actually provided by a right shift of the partial product. The **CS** word is shown boxed for emphasis, and the space in the **AC, MQ** word indicates the boundary between partial product and the shifted remainder of the multiplier.

	0000 1011	*AC, MQ*	
	0000	*CS*	
	1111	$MD \cdot 1$	Step 1
1st Partial sum	1111 1011	*AC, MQ*	
	0000	*CS*	
Shift	01111 101	*AC, MQ*	
	1111	$MD \cdot 1$	Step 2
2nd Partial sum	10001 101	*AC, MQ*	
	0111	*CS*	
Shift	010001 10	*AC, MQ*	
	0000	$MD \cdot 0$	Step 3
3rd Partial sum	001101 10	*AC, MQ*	
	0100	*CS*	
Shift	0001101 1	*AC, MQ*	
	1111	$MD \cdot 1$	Step 4
4th Partial sum	1010101 1	*AC, MQ*	
	0101	*CS*	
Shift	01010101	*AC, MQ*	Step 5
Propagate add	10100101	*AC, MQ*	

$$1011 \times 1111 = 10100101$$

Figure 15.3. Example of carry-save multiplication.

In analyzing the example, note that the contents of the **AC, MQ** registers, in each step prior to the last, do not represent the binary sum of the three inputs but rather represent the bit-by-bit exclusive-OR'ing of the three input vectors. For example, at step 2,

$$(1, 0, 0, 0, 1) = (1, 1, 1, 1, 0) \oplus (0, 0, 0, 0, 0) \oplus (0, 1, 1, 1, 1)$$

and the carry bits, 0111, are shifted and added in step 3. The reader should follow the process step by step; and if necessary, check by carrying out the multiplication in the usual manner.

In most computers the same adder is used for multiplication as for all other operations involving addition so that provision must be made to modify this adder when carry-save is to be implemented. If we assume an 18-bit ripple-carry adder, the configuration for carry-save would be as shown in Fig. 15.4. The output-carry from each stage, instead of going directly to the input-carry line of the next stage, is stored in a position of the **CS** register. On the next cycle, this stored carry will become the input-carry to the same stage. It might seem that each stage of the **CS** register should provide the input-carry to the next stage to the left, until we recall that the partial sum is shifted to the right before the next cycle, providing the logical equivalent of a left shift of the carries. A two-level switching network on each carry-input can be added so that the same adder can function as given in Fig. 14.1 or Fig. 15.4, depending on the value of a single control signal.

The basic control program for the carry-save multiplication can now be written. Note that steps 2 and 3, representing formation of the carries and partial sums, occur simultaneously and are written on separate lines

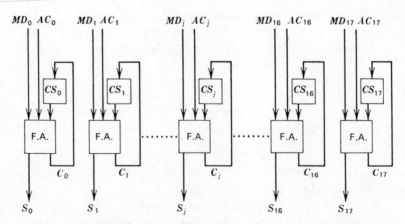

Figure 15.4. Ripple-carry adder converted to carry-save adder.

solely for clarity. Also note that circuitry of the adder would require gating to

1. $MC \leftarrow 5 \top 0$; $CS \leftarrow 18 \top 0$
2. $AC \leftarrow AC \oplus CS \oplus (MD \wedge MQ_{17})$
3. $CS \leftarrow (CS \wedge AC) \vee (CS \wedge (MD \wedge MQ_{17})) \vee (AC \wedge (MD \wedge MQ_{17}))$
4. $AC, MQ \leftarrow 0, AC, MQ_{0:16}$
5. $MC \leftarrow \mathrm{INC}(MC)$
6. $\rightarrow (\overline{MC_0 \wedge MC_3})/(2)$
7. $AC \leftarrow \mathrm{ADD}(AC; CS)$

convert from a conventional adder to a carry-save adder, and the complete program would probably include the setting and clearing of some sort of indicator to control this gating.

The above program considers the multiplication of magnitudes only. We leave it as an exercise for the reader to modify the signed multiplication routine to incorporate carry-save. Carry-save can be used with virtually any type of adder or other type of speed-up method.

15.3 MULTIPLE-BIT SPEED-UP TECHNIQUES

So far we have assumed that only one multiplier bit is to be handled each cycle. By carrying out multiplication for several bits at a time, the number of cycles can be reduced. This will reduce the overall multiply time if extra hardware is provided to process multiple bits in the same time as single bits. First, we must provide for multiple shifts in the same time as single shifts; second, we must provide means of adding multiples of the multiplicand in a single addition cycle.

The simplest multiple-bit techniques is *shifting over zeros*. We inspect two or more of the multiplier bits. If they are all zero, we make a multiple shift over the corresponding number of bits. The speed advantage of this technique depends on the statistical likelihood that strings of zeros of various lengths may occur. The technique is fairly simple and frequently used.

A closely related technique is *shifting over ones*. Assume that we have three ones in a row in the multiplier. Essentially, this requires adding seven times the multiplicand, which can be accomplished by *subtracting* the multiplicand, shifting three places—which multiplies by eight—and then adding the multiplicand. Since this method requires two addition cycles, there must be at least three consecutive ones before it is worth doing; it is therefore less popular than shifting over zeros.

Next let us consider the handling of arbitrary pairs of multiplier bits. If at a given step the least-significant-multiplier bits are 00, a 2-bit shift is carried out. If the bits are 01, the multiplicand is added and then a 2-bit shift is made. If the bits are 10, there are two possible techniques. The first is to revert to the single-bit method, i.e., make a single shift to take care of the 0 and then pair the 1 with the next bit in the multiplier for the next cycle. Alternatively, we can shift the multiplicand one position to the left as it enters the adder—thus multiplying it by two—and then make a 2-bit shift of the sum. If the bits are 11, there are also two possibilities. We can add, shift once, and pair the second 1 with the next multiplier bit. Or we can provide a special register, **TR**, in which we store three times the multiplicand at the start of the multiplication cycle. Then when 11 occurs, we add **TR** to the partial product and shift twice. Note that the use of **TR** and the use of multiplicand shifting will require the addition of an extra bit position to **AC** and the adder.

A control sequence for bit-pair multiplication, using **TR** and multiplicand shifting, follows. Note in step 4 that there are two separate shifts indicated. There is a two-bit shift of the catenation of the adder output and the **MQ** register, and a shift of the multiplicand as it is gated to the adder, indicated by the use of $(0, MD)$ or $(MD, 0)$ as an adder argument.

1. $AC \leftarrow MD, 0$
2. $TR \leftarrow \text{ADD}(AC; (0, MD))$
3. $MC \leftarrow 5 \top 0;$ *lf*, $AC \leftarrow 20 \top 0$
4. *lf*, $AC, MQ \leftarrow ((0, 0, \textit{lf}, AC, MQ_{0:15})$
   $! (0, 0, \text{ADD}(AC; (0, MD)), MQ_{0:15})$
   $! (0, 0, \text{ADD}(AC; (MD, 0)), MQ_{0:15})$
   $! (0, 0, \text{ADD}(AC; TR), MQ_{0:15})$
   $* ((\overline{MQ}_{16} \wedge \overline{MQ}_{17}), (\overline{MQ}_{16} \wedge MQ_{17}),$
   $(MQ_{16} \wedge \overline{MQ}_{17}), (MQ_{16} \wedge MQ_{17}))$
5. $MC \leftarrow \text{INC}(MC)$
6. $\rightarrow (\overline{MC_1 \wedge MC_4})/(4)$

An alternate scheme for handling bit-pairs, known as *ternary* multiplication, is discussed by Flores [1].

Groups of 3 multiplier bits can be handled by techniques quite similar to those already discussed. In the table of Fig. 15.5 are listed the actions taken for various bit combinations. We see that this method requires the capability for both single and double shifts of **MD**, and single shifts of **TR**. For bit triplets 101 and 111, we revert to bit-pair methods, letting the third bit form part of the next triplet. Alternatively, we could provide special registers for storing $5 \times (\perp MD)$ and $7 \times (\perp MD)$.

One might expect to achieve further improvement by handling more than 3 bits at a time. However, extending the above approach directly

Multiplier Bits	Action
0 0 0	Triple shift
0 0 1	Add *MD*, triple shift
0 1 0	Add 2 × *MD*, triple shift
0 1 1	Add *TR*, triple shift
1 0 0	Add 4 × *MD*, triple shift
1 0 1	Add *MD*, double shift
1 1 0	Add 2 × *TR*, triple shift
1 1 1	Add *TR*, double shift

Figure 15.5. Bit-triplet multiplication.

would imply the use of a large number of registers to store the products of the multiplicand and various prime numbers. To compute the contents of these registers serially prior to the multiplication would tend to negate any speed advantage that might be obtained. At some point one would expect a decrease in speed with the consideration of additional bits.

Alternatively, the multibit partial products could be expressed as a combinational logic subroutine. These products could then be added to the contents of *AC, MQ*, employing carry-save. Each addition of an r-bit partial product would be followed by a shift of r-bits. This approach will be considered in Section 15.5. Until recently, such lavish use of combinational logic would have been prohibitively expensive. With the continuing decrease in cost of large-scale integrated circuits, such approaches are becoming practical. The limiting case is a completely combinational-logic multiplier.

15.4 SPEED ANALYSIS

Before proceeding further it will be instructive to derive some expressions that will allow us to compare the speed of various multiplier configurations. In order to carry out this analysis, it is necessary to make some assumptions regarding the speed of various operations relative to the basic clock rate of the computer. Let σ represent the propagation delay through two levels of logic. The time required to change the contents of a register will then be on the order to 2σ to 4σ, depending on the logic family used. To allow time for logical operations during transfer and some tolerance for stray delays, the clock period might typically be set to $\tau_c = 8\sigma$. As we saw in the last chapter, the carry propagation time for a very fast adder might be $\tau_p = 7\sigma$. On this basis we shall assume that a shift operation requires one clock period, an add-and-shift operation, two clock periods.

First, let us consider bit-by-bit multiplication without carry-save. If the multiplier bit is 0, we shift in one clock period; if it is 1, we add and shift in two clock periods. The probabilities of a multiplier bit being 1 or 0 are both 0.5. Therefore, the average time for accomplishing multiplication is given by Eq. 15.1:

$$T_1 = 0.5N\tau_c + 0.5N(2\tau_c) = 1.5N\tau_c = 12N\sigma \tag{15.1}$$

where N is the word length. Becoming slightly more general, suppose that a slower adder were employed, requiring k clock periods to complete an addition. In this case, Eq. 15.1 takes the form of Eq. 15.2:

$$T_1 = 0.5N\tau_c + 0.5N(k\tau_c) = \frac{N\tau_c}{2} \times (1 + k) \tag{15.2}$$

If carry-save is employed, the partial-add requires a delay of only σ so that each cycle except the last requires only one clock period for a partial-add and shift. Thus the time for an N-bit multiplication is given by Eq. 15.3:

$$T_2 = (N - 1)\tau_c + k\tau_c = (N - 1 + k)\tau_c \tag{15.3}$$

For $k = 2$, we have $T_2 = (N + 1)\tau_c$, which approaches $\frac{2}{3}T_1$ for large N. For a slower adder ($k > 2$), the improvement achieved by carry-save is more noticeable.

Consider next the bit-pair process described in the previous section. Let us assume that $k = 2$ and carry-save is not employed. Thus $N/2$ cycles will be required. Since an addition is required in all but the case in which both multiplier bits are zero, three quarters of the cycles will require two clock periods while one quarter will require one period. Therefore, the average bit-pair multiplication time is given by Eq. 15.4.

$$T_3 = \frac{N}{2}[0.75(2\tau_c) + 0.25\tau_c] + 2\tau_c = (0.875N + 2)\tau_c \tag{15.4}$$

The $2\tau_c$ on the right accounts for the addition time necessary to compute the contents of the **TR** register. If bit-pairs and carry-save are used, only one clock period is required for all but the last of the $N/2$ shift cycles. For this case we express the multiplication time in Eq. 15.5.

$$T_4 = \left(\frac{N}{2} - 1\right)\tau_c + 2\tau_c + 2\tau_c$$
$$= \left(\frac{N}{2} + 3\right)\tau_c \tag{15.5}$$

For bit-triplets with carry-save, the average multiplication time is given by Eq. 15.6,

$$T_5 = \left(\frac{N}{2.75} + 3 \right) \tau_c \qquad (15.6)$$

The derivation of this expression will be left as an exercise. The various expressions for multiplication times are summarized in the table in Fig. 15.6.

15.5 LARGE, FAST PARALLEL MULTIPLIERS

For a large, fast machine with a heavy investment in memory and peripheral equipment, an additional investment in logic circuitry to speed up arithmetic and increase the machine's throughput is usually considered money well spent. The time for multiplication can be decreased from the level discussed in the previous sections by decreasing the number of intermediate storage times required. This must be accomplished while holding the propagation time preceding each storage time to a minimum.

Consider the "paper-and-pencil" multiplication of two 4-bit binary numbers, shown here as a specific example and in general terms. The P terms represent the bit-by-bit partial products, i.e., $P_{33} = X_3 \wedge Y_3$, $P_{23} = X_2 \wedge Y_3$, $P_{32} = X_3 \wedge Y_2$, etc. The multiplication process can be divided into two parts, the development of the array of partial products and the summation of these partial products.

Multiplication Scheme	Multiplication Time	Time for $N = 64$
Bit-by-bit	$1.5N\tau_c$	$96\tau_c$
Bit-by-bit with carry-save	$(N + 1)\tau_c$	$65\tau_c$
Bit-pairs	$(0.875N \times 2)\tau_c$	$58\tau_c$
Bit-pairs with carry-save	$\left(\dfrac{N}{2} + 3 \right) \tau_c$	$35\tau_c$
Bit-triplets with carry-save	$\left(\dfrac{N}{2.75} + 3 \right) \tau_c$	$26\tau_c$

Figure 15.6. Multiplication times for two clock periods per addition ($2\tau_0$)

1011	$X_0\ X_1\ X_2\ X_3$
1101	$Y_0\ Y_1\ Y_2\ Y_3$

1011	$P_{03}\,P_{13}\,P_{23}\,P_{33}$
0000	$P_{02}\,P_{12}\,P_{22}\,P_{32}$
1011	$P_{01}\,P_{11}\,P_{21}\,P_{31}$
1011	$P_{00}\,P_{10}\,P_{20}\,P_{30}$

10001111	$Z_0\ Z_1\ Z_2\ Z_3\ Z_4\ Z_5\ Z_6\ Z_7$

The array of partial products can be developed in the time of a single gate delay, $\sigma/2$, by an array of N^2 AND gates for the multiplication of two N-bit numbers. With all N^2 partial product terms available simultaneously, the addition of these terms can then be carried out in a single combinational logic adder, with no intermediate storage. The speed of the addition is limited primarily by adder complexity considered to be economically feasible.

The most straightforward, multiple-operand adder is the combinational carry-save adder, shown in Fig. 15.7. This circuit consists of an array of full-adders. In the top row of adders, the first two rows of partial products are partially added. The sums and carries from this addition are combined with the third row of partial products in the second row of adders. These sums and carries are in turn combined with the last row of partial products in the third row of adders. The last row of adders ripple the carries through to complete the addition. Note that the worst case for carry propagation would be through a path of six adders, for a delay of 6σ. The complete multiplication, including formation of the partial product in an array of 16 AND gates, summation of the partial products, and shifting or storage of the product, can thus be completed in $2\tau_c$. This compares with a time of $5\tau_c$ for the sequential carry-save multiplier, for 4 bits.

This basic technique can be extended to any number of bits, with an additional delay of 2σ for each additional bit. The general relationship is

$$\tau_p = 2(N - 1)\sigma$$

Thus, assuming $\tau_c = 8\sigma$, as before, the time for a 64-bit multiplication would be $16\tau_c$, compared with a low of $26\tau_c$ for the methods previously discussed. Also note that this assumes ripple-carry for completion of the addition. The use of carry look-ahead in the last stage would reduce the time to $9\tau_c$.

Although this approach can theoretically be extended to any number

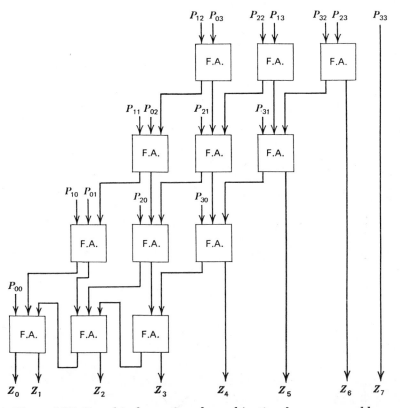

Figure 15.7. Four-bit, four-operand, combinational carry-save adder.

of bits, the cost may become prohibitive for large numbers of bits, even with large-scale integrated circuits. For 64 bits this technique requires an array of 4096 AND gates and an array of 4032 full-adders for the ripple-carry version. As an alternative we could use a combination of combinational and sequential techniques. In one large machine, using 48-bit words, the multiplier is divided in half. The multiplicand is first multiplied by the lower half of the multiplier, using a 24 × 48 array of AND gates to form the partial products and an array of adders to form 72-bit, partial-sum and partial-carry terms, which are saved in registers. The same arrays are then used to multiply the multiplicand by the upper half of the multiplier, forming two more 72-bit, partial-sum and partial-carry terms. The four partial terms are then added in a 4 × 96 carry-save adder to form two 96-bit, partial-sum and partial-carry terms, which are then added in a 96-bit, carry look-ahead adder to form the complete product. Depending on the exact form of the adder arrays, the time for this technique would be about $12\tau_c$.

There are many other possible ways of reducing multiplication time. If we consider the complexity of the operation, it is hardly surprising that a tremendous variety of techniques has been used, and many more will doubtless be developed in the future. We have tried here to indicate the basic ideas behind some of the more popular techniques, not to provide an exhaustive survey. Further, no general evaluation of the various techniques is practical, since so much depends on the characteristics of the system in which the multiplier is being used.

15.6 DIVISION

In most computers, division is a considerably slower operation than multiplication. Its logical nature is such that it does not lend itself to speed-up as well as multiplication; and it occurs less frequently than multiplication in the general mix of problems so that slow speed can be better tolerated. In the machine using the complex 48-bit multiplication scheme described earlier, division takes four times as long as multiplication.

The basic technique of division is the comparison, or trial-and-error, method. In decimal division we compare the divisor to the dividend or current partial remainder, estimate how many times it "fits," and then check the estimate by multiplying the divisor by the quotient digit and subtracting the resultant product from the partial remainder. If it does not "fit," we make a new estimate; hence the name "trial-and-error."

Binary division is considerably simpler, since the quotient bit is either 0 or 1. If the divisor is smaller than the partial remainder, the quotient bit is 1 and we subtract; if it is larger, the quotient bit is 0 and we do not subtract. An example of "paper-and-pencil" binary division of two 7-bit (including sign) numbers is shown in Fig. 15.8.

Consideration of this example indicates several special problems of division. First, placement of the binary point in the quotient requires not only knowledge of the position of the binary point in the divisor and dividend, but also some information as to the relative magnitudes of the two operands. For example, both divisor and dividend can be fractional (binary point to the left, as in Fig. 15.8); but if the divisor is smaller than the dividend, the quotient will not be fractional. It is usual to assume both operands fractional and to require that the divisor be larger than the dividend, thus ensuring a fractional quotient. Provisions to ensure this condition may be included in either the hardware or software of the

```
           0.101110
0.011010)0.010011
         −011010          Divisor larger than dividend, shift
         ───────
          001100          Subtract, enter 1
          011010          Shift divisor, enter 0
         −011010          Shift divisor
         ───────
          010110          Subtract, enter 1
         −011010          Shift divisor
         ───────
          010010          Subtract, enter 1
         −011010          Shift divisor
         ───────
          001010          Subtract, enter 1
          011010          Shift divisor, enter 0
```

Figure 15.8. Binary division, trial-and-error method.

machine. We shall assume that this condition is met in the remainder of this chapter.

In the manual technique, we determine whether or not to subtract by a visual comparison of the shifted divisor and partial remainder. Unfortunately, the usual method of comparing the magnitudes of two numbers in a computer is to subtract one from the other and note the sign of the result. Thus we must subtract on every cycle. Further, since a negative difference will be indicated by a carry-out of the most-significant-digit position, we must allow time for the carry to propagate all the way through; so carry-save is ruled out.

In the manual technique we shift the divisor right to make it smaller than the partial remainder. In a computer, since the adder is fixed in position relative to the registers, we accomplish the same result by shifting the partial remainder left. As we do so, we shift the quotient into the MQ register. Figure 15.9 illustrates the computer implementation of division for the same example as Fig. 15.8.

The process starts with the divisor in MD, the dividend in AC, and the MQ register cleared. In the following we shall assume positive operands and shall write the AHPL statements for 18-bit division as we describe the process. Since the divisor is known to be larger than the dividend, step 1 shifts AC, MQ and enters the sign bit of the quotient (0 for this example) in the vacated position.

1. $AC, MQ \leftarrow AC_{1:17}, MQ, 0; \; MC \leftarrow 5 \top 0$

Step 2 examines the result of a trial subtraction. Note that we have to make a subtraction in any case; but the subtraction is "completed," in the sense of entering the result into AC, only if the difference is positive,

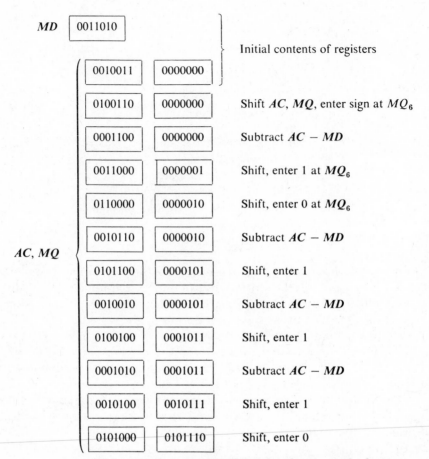

Figure 15.9. Computer division by trial-and-error method.

i.e., the divisor "fits" into the partial remainder. Note that the subtraction is accomplished by using the logical (one's) complement of MD and injecting a 1 on the input-carry line.

2. $\rightarrow (\text{ADD}_0(AC; \overline{MD}; 1))/(5)$

Step 3 enters the difference into AC, and step 4 shifts AC, MQ, entering a 1 into MQ. These two steps can be combined, but we have shown them separate for clarity. At step 5, if the subtraction did not work, AC, MQ is shifted, with a 0 entered in MQ.

3. $AC \leftarrow \text{ADD}_{1:18}(AC; \overline{MD}; 1)$
4. $AC, MQ \leftarrow AC_{1:17}, MQ, 1$
      $\rightarrow (6)$

5. $AC, MQ \leftarrow AC_{1:17}, MQ, 0$

Step 6 increments the multiplication counter, MC, which we assume was set to zero at the start; step 7 checks to see if the division is complete. At the finish the quotient is in MQ and the remainder in AC. The designer may add a step to switch their positions if it is desired that all arithmetic operations terminate with the answer in AC. In this discussion we have considered only positive operands. We shall leave it as an exercise for the reader to devise procedures for handling negative operands.

6. $MC \leftarrow INC(MC)$
7. $\rightarrow (\overline{MC_0 \wedge MC_4})/(2)$
8. EXIT

As we mentioned earlier, it is relatively difficult to increase the speed of division significantly, but we might indicate the general nature of a few techniques that have been used. One technique is known as *nonperforming* division. The basic idea is to find some faster method of comparing the magnitudes of two numbers than subtracting them. One possibility is to use some type of carry-completion adder, in which a change in the sign of the difference can be detected in less time than it takes to complete the subtraction; or one might provide a combinational circuit for comparing the magnitudes of two numbers. With the increasing availability of large-scale integrated circuits, this last approach may be the most attractive.

The concept of shifting over 0's can be applied to division, but practical application requires that the divisor be normalized. For example, if the divisor is 0.1xxxxxxxx and the dividend is 0.00001xxx, we can see that four shifts will be required before a subtraction can possibly be successful. Thus we can shift four places and enter four 0's in the quotient before trying a subtraction. On the other hand, if there were leading 0's in the divisor, it would be more difficult to determine how many shifts should be made.

Shifting over 1's and other multibit techniques, analogous to those used in multiplication, are possible; but they are so complex that their practicality is questionable. The interested reader is referred to Flores [1] for a full discussion.

15.7 SUMMARY

Our goal in this chapter has been to suggest some of the problems and options available in the implementation of multiplication and division. We have not attempted to provide all of the information that may be required to make a design decision. The reader will, hopefully, have gained sufficient insight to consider in more detail the various aspects of multiplication and division as the need arises. As before, we have utilized AHPL as much as possible so that the reader will retain the confidence that he can fill in the details of a hardware realization in a straightforward way.

We have restricted ourselves to fixed-point arithmetic. Floating point is the topic of the next chapter. As we shall see, however, most of the material of this chapter is applicable to floating point. It is only necessary to add a few registers for handling the exponents and some additional control logic.

PROBLEMS

15.1 Suppose that a special-purpose computer is to be designed that will be called upon frequently to compute x^3 in fixed point. The number x may be positive or two's-complement. Write an AHPL routine for accomplishing this operation. The sign should be developed directly as part of the multiplication operation, as discussed in Section 15.1. Assume an 18-bit word length.

15.2 Rewrite the carry-save routine of Section 15.2 to allow for two's-complement multipliers and multiplicands.

15.3 Improve the AHPL routine of Section 15.2 by adding a hardware capability to detect strings of 0's in the multiplier and providing for a multiple shift of that number of bits in **AC**.

15.4 Refer to the time for bit-by-bit multiplication with carry-save given in Fig. 15.6. Develop a similar expression valid where the capability for shifting over unlimited strings of 0's is provided. Assume that only one clock period is required to shift over a string. Suppose that the hardware could not detect strings longer than 5 bits. How would this affect your expression?

15.5 Compile a table similar to Fig. 15.5 for bit-quadruplet multiplication. How many multiple multiplier registers would you recommend? What would be the average number of bits handled in a cycle by this scheme?

15.6 Develop an expression for the multiplication time of a multiplier using bit-triplets without carry-save.

15.7 Modify the AHPL routine for elementary division in Section 15.6 to allow for negative arguments.

15.8 Write an AHPL routine for division that allows for shifting over strings of 0's. Assume that both divisor and dividend are positive.

REFERENCES

1. Flores, Ivan, *The Logic of Computer Arithmetic*, Prentice-Hall, Englewood Cliffs, N.J., 1963.

2. Chu, Yaohan, *Digital Computer Design Fundamentals*, McGraw-Hill, New York, 1962.

3. Habibi, A., and P. A. Wintz, "Fast Multipliers," *IEEETEC*, Vol. C-19, Feb. 1970, pp. 153–157.

4. Pezaris, S. D., "A 40-ns 17-Bit by 17-Bit Array Multiplier," *IEEE-TEC*, Vol. C-20, April 1971, pp. 442–448.

5. Braun, E. L., *Digital Computer Design*, Academic Press, New York, 1963.

6. Ling, H., "High-Speed Computer Multiplication Using a Multiple-Bit Decoding Algorithm," *IEEETEC*, Vol. C-19, Aug. 1970, pp. 706–710.

16

FLOATING-POINT ARITHMETIC

16.1 INTRODUCTION

Floating-point notation is the computer equivalent of the familiar scientific notation. For example, rather than write the speed of light as

$$300,000,000 \text{ m/sec}$$

we generally write

$$3 \times 10^8 \text{ m/sec}$$

or the FORTRAN equivalent

$$3.0E08$$

Virtually all high-level programming languages provide for this type of notation, and provision for handling numbers in this form can be included either in the software (the compiler) or in the hardware. We are concerned in this chapter with the hardware procedures for handling numbers in this form.

All our discussions of computer arithmetic up to now have assumed *fixed-point* operation.* The radix (decimal or binary) point is not physically present in a computer register, but its assumed position clearly must be known. When we add two numbers together, such as

$$
\begin{array}{r}
36.81 \\
+1.041 \\
\hline
37.851
\end{array}
$$

the decimal points must be aligned, whatever the length of the numbers. When we add the contents of two registers, the corresponding bit po-

---

*This should not be confused with the *fixed format* (F format) of FORTRAN, which concerns only the form of the numbers for input-output.

612

sitions are combined; therefore, we must assume the same position for the radix point in both registers for the results to have any meaning.

It is general practice in computers to assume the radix point immediately to the left of the most-significant digit, as was done for the division process in Chapter 15. The chief reason for this practice is to preserve alignment of the radix point in multiplication and division. For example, consider multiplication in a computer with three-digit decimal registers. Multiplication inherently produces a double-length product;

$$\begin{array}{r} 0.361 \\ \times 0.483 \\ \hline 0.174363 \end{array}$$

but because our registers are only 3-digits, we can retain only the three most-significant digits. We note that the decimal point in the product is in the correct position, to the left of the m.s.d. With any other position of the decimal point in the multiplier and mulltiplicand, the decimal point of the product would be in the wrong position.

Not all numbers are fractions, so how can we use a fixed-point computer? The answer is that, at input, each number must have a scale factor assigned to it to convert it to a fraction. Thus 531 will have a scale factor of 1000 assigned and will enter the machine as 0.531. This assignment is done by the loading program and must be done even for floating-point machines. The difference between fixed- and floating-point machines is in what is done with the scale factor after it is assigned. In a fixed-point machine, the programmer must keep track of the scale factor and take it properly into account in all operations This can be done, but it is very complicated. When compilers are written for fixed-point machines, the scaling is provided in the compiler; so users of the machine writing in the high-level language are not aware of the problem.

Although it is possible to handle scaling problems by programming, the resultant programs or compilers tend to be inefficient because of the many extra steps required to keep track of the scale factors. In floating-point machines we substitute hardware for software, or in some cases we microprogram the computer to handle the scale factors. The scale factors become part of the data words and are handled automatically by the hardware. The resultant hardware is relatively complex and obviously adds to the cost of the computer. However, the operation of the machine is so much more efficient that floating-point hardware is usually considered a good investment and is omitted only on small computers.

Another important reason for floating point is the increased range of the computer. Consider a fixed-point computer with 48-bit word length.

With one bit reserved for the sign, the range of numbers that can be represented is $\pm 2^{47}$, which is approximately $\pm 10^{14}$. Although this seems very large, there are many classes of problems for which it is inadequate. For example, in electronic circuit problems we frequently deal with resistance in megohms (10^6) and capacitance in picofarads (10^{-12}), a range of values of 10^{18}, too large for a 48-bit fixed-point machine.

In floating point, each data word A is divided into two parts, the mantissa and the exponent. If A stores a positive floating-point variable a, then a is given by

$$a = \perp AM \times 2^{\perp AE}$$

where AM and AE are the mantissa and exponent, respectively. In a typical 48-bit machine, the mantissa might be 37 bits including sign, and the exponent 11 bits. Now the range of numbers that can be represented is

$$\pm 2^{36} \times 2^{2^{11}} = \pm 2^{36} \times 2^{2048} \approx \pm 10^{630}$$

The increase in range has a cost in accuracy, since we have lost 11 bits of precision, or about three decimal digits. However, 36 bits still provide about 10 decimal digits of accuracy, adequate for most problems. In addition, most machines with floating-point arithmetic also provide fixed-point arithmetic for greater accuracy and may also provide double-precision arithmetic for even greater accuracy.

16.2 NOTATION AND FORMAT

The first decision we have to make in designing a floating-point system is the number of bits to be used in the exponent. This depends to an extent on the total word length but is generally between 7 and 14 bits. The choice obviously involves a compromise between range and accuracy. For our examples in this chapter, we shall specify a 48-bit machine with 11-bit exponents.

The next question is the arrangement of the various parts of the data word. The most common arrangement places the sign of the mantissa in the bit-0 position, followed by the exponent and then the mantissa, as shown in Fig. 16.1. The separation of the mantissa and its sign may seem awkward, but this arrangement offers some advantages. First, the bit-0 position will be the sign for fixed-point format; this position may be specially set up for sign manipulation. Since the mantissa is handled as a fixed-point number, it seems reasonable to preserve its sign position. Similarly, the rightmost bit position is set up for receiving the input carry required in certain complement arithmetic so that it is desirable

Mantissa   Exponent   Mantissa   Typical Order
Sign

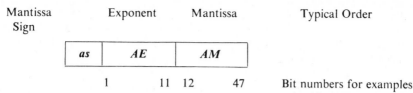

1   11 12   47   Bit numbers for examples
in this chapter

Figure 16.1. Floating-point data format.

to keep the l.s.d. of the mantissa in this position. Third, the exponent is more significant than the mantissa so that placing the exponent to the left of the mantissa means that relative magnitude comparisons can be made by the same algorithms as for fixed-point numbers. We shall therefore adopt the format shown in Fig. 16.1. Notice in the figure that the sign of the mantissa (i.e., the sign of the floating-point number) is denoted separately as as; as, AM will be considered to be in two's-complement form.

Next, consider the matter of exponent representation. Obviously, we must provide for both positive and negative exponents. The most straightforward approach is to use the same representation used for the mantissa and fixed-point numbers, i.e., signed magnitude, two's complement, or one's complement, as the case may be, with the exponent sign in the m.s.d. position of the exponent section (bit 1 in the format of Fig. 13.1). This system has been used in many machines.

Another system of representation, known as *biased exponents*, adds a positive constant to each exponent as the floating-point number is formed so that internally all exponents are positive. For example, with an 11-bit exponent section, 2^{10} is added to each exponent so that (in octal notation) exponents range from 0000 to 3777 with 2000 corresponding to a true exponent value of zero. There are at least two major reasons for the use of biased exponents. One is that the absence of negative exponents may provide some simplification of the exponent arithmetic.

The second factor relates to the manner in which zero is represented in floating-point form. Formally, zero times anything is zero, so that the exponent associated with a zero mantissa is apparently arbitrary. In some machines, when a computation results in a zero mantissa, the exponent is left at whatever value it happens to have, resulting in a "dirty" zero. However, as we shall see later, dirty zeros may result in a loss of significance in some computations. As a result, most machines assign the smallest possible exponent to a zero mantissa, producing a "clean" zero. With unbiased exponents, the smallest possible exponent is the most negative possible exponent; but with biased exponents it is zero. The

615

floating-point representation of zero is then the same as the fixed-point, i.e., all zeros. This means that the same circuitry and the same commands can be used to test for zero, regardless of the type of arithmetic. The biased exponents corresponding to various floating-point values are shown in Fig. 16.2. Note that -2^{10} and $2^{10} - 1$ are the smallest and largest possible exponents, respectively.

Finally, note that there is no particular problem converting to and from the biased form. Numbers have to be converted between decimal and floating-point binary on input and output in any case, and the biasing of the exponent does not make the conversion any more difficult.

Another question about representation arises from the fact that in floating-point notation there is no unique representation for a given number. For example, 0.5×10^2 and 0.05×10^3 represent the same number. Since the number of bits (or digits) in a register is fixed, we obviously reduce the number of possible significant digits if we carry along nonsignificant leading zeros. Therefore, it is standard practice on the input of floating-point numbers to adjust the exponent so that the leading bit or digit of the mantissa is nonzero. Numbers in this form are said to be *normalized*.

Now consider the subtraction of one normalized number from another.

$$
\begin{array}{r}
0.10011 \times 2^9 \\
-0.10010 \times 2^9 \\
\hline
0.00001 \times 2^9
\end{array}
$$

The result is unnormalized. In most machines postnormalization is performed after every operation, to ensure that all operands are always in the normalized form. In the above example, the result would be normalized to 0.1×2^5. There are some who feel that postnormalization is undesirable because it may hide a progressive loss of significance in a sequence of calculations. Most computers either use normalized arithmetic at all times or else offer the programmer the choice of using it or not. We shall use it in all our examples.

Floating-Point Number	AE	$\perp AE$
$\perp AM \cdot 2^{-2^{10}}$	0,0,0,0,0,0,0,0,0,0,0	0
$\perp AM \cdot 2^0$	1,0,0,0,0,0,0,0,0,0,0	2^{10}
$\perp AM \cdot 2^{2^{10}-1}$	1,1,1,1,1,1,1,1,1,1,1	$2^{11} - 1$
$\perp AM \cdot 2^b$	1,(10)$\top$ b	$2^{10} + b$
$\perp AM = 0$	0,0,0,0,0,0,0,0,0,0,0	0

Figure 16.2. Biased exponent representation.

16.3 FLOATING-POINT ADDITION AND SUBTRACTION

In this section we shall develop an AHPL routine for handling floating-point addition and subtraction. The emphasis will be on presenting an understandable treatment of the arithmetic operations without worrying about details of the hardware configuration. The existence of necessary registers, data paths, and combinational logic circuits will be assumed. In the last section of the chapter a specific hardware configuration will be developed.

In these analyses, two input operands will be A and B; the result will be C; and the sign, exponent, and mantissa sections will be denoted by adding the letters s, E, or M, respectively. Thus the operand A is made up of the catenation of its three components.

$$A \leftarrow as, AE, AM$$

For addition and subtraction, the exponents must be equal before the mantissa can be added or subtracted. For example, if $A = 0.111010 \times 2^7$ and $B = 0.101010 \times 2^5$, then B must be converted to 0.001010×2^7 before the mantissas can be combined. Thus the first steps are to compare the exponents, subtract the smaller from the larger, and then shift the mantissa having the smaller exponent right a number of places equal to the difference between the exponents.

Note that significant digits will be lost from the number shifted; and if the difference between exponents is larger than the number of digits in the mantissa, the smaller number will be shifted right out. In the above example, if $B = 0.101010 \times 2^1$, then after shifting to equalize exponents, $B = 0.000000 \times 2^7$. Thus, if the difference between the exponents is larger than the number of digits in the mantissa, the answer is taken as equal to the large operand.

This preshifting also accounts for the loss of significance with dirty zeros. Assume that one operand is a dirty zero with a large exponent and the other is a nonzero number with a small exponent. Then the nonzero operand may be shifted right out, giving an incorrect zero answer.

After exponent equalization, the mantissas are added or subtracted in the usual fashion. If the result overflows, the control sequence then checks for *exponent overflow*. If the exponent of the inputs was the largest possible for the machine, then increasing it by one as a result of mantissa overflow will result in exponent overflow, indicating a result too large to be represented by the computer. If there is no exponent overflow, the mantissa is shifted one place right and the exponent is increased by one.

If there is no mantissa overflow, a check is made to see if the result is normalized. If not, the result is shifted left until a nonzero digit appears in the m.s.d. position, decreasing the result exponent by one for each shift. In the event of an all-zero result, the postnormalization step should be skipped. After normalization, a check for *exponent underflow* is required. If the input exponent was close to the most negative possible, decreasing it further for normalization may result in underflow, indicating that the result is too small to be represented by the computer.

The complete flow chart for the process is shown in Fig. 16.3. At step 1 we subtract BE from AE. Recall that subtraction is accomplished by adding the two's complement of the subtrahend to the minuend, and that the two's complement of a number is equal to the logical complement (one's complement) plus 1 on the carry-in line. This requires no extra time because the 1 is added as part of the regular add cycle. Step 2 then

1. $CE \leftarrow \text{ADD}(AE; \overline{BE};1)$
2. $\rightarrow ((\overline{CE}_0 \wedge (\vee /CE)), CE_0, (\wedge /CE))/(3, 9, 8)$

checks to determine if the difference is positive, negative, or zero. If it is positive (AE larger than BE), step 3 checks to see if the difference is larger than 36, the number of bits in the mantissa, in which case step 4 sets the result equal to A. The CGTM function is a combinational logic function such that

$$\text{CGTM}(CE) = 1 \qquad \text{if } (\perp CE) > 36.$$

If the exponent difference is not greater than 36, the mantissa BM, corresponding to the smaller exponent, is shifted right at step 5. Step 6 decrements the exponent difference and step 7 checks to determine if the exponent difference has been reduced to zero, looping back to step 5 to shift again if it has not. When the shifting is complete, step 8 sets the sum exponent equal to the larger operand exponent. Step 2 also branches to step 8 for the case of zero exponent difference, since the result exponent is equal to either AE or BE for that case.

3. $\rightarrow (\overline{\text{CGTM}(CE)})/(5)$
4. $C \leftarrow A$
    $\rightarrow (30)$
5. $BM \leftarrow 0, BM_{0:34}$
6. $CE \leftarrow \text{DEC}(CE)$
7. $\rightarrow (\vee /CE)/(5)$
8. $CE \leftarrow AE$
    $\rightarrow (16)$

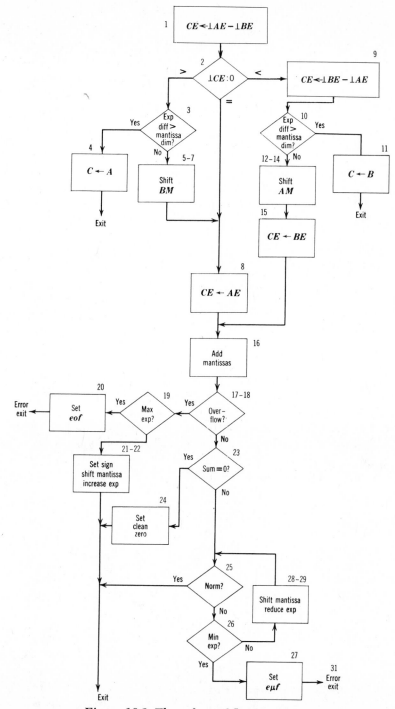

Figure 16.3. Flow chart of floating ADD.

For the case in which the exponent difference is negative (**BE** greater than **AE**), step 2 branches to step 9, where **BE** is subtracted from **AE**, to obtain the positive exponent difference. Steps 10 to 15 repeat the functions of steps 3 to 8, for the case in which **BE** is the larger exponent.

9. $CE \leftarrow \text{ADD}(\overline{AE}; BE; 1)$
10. $\rightarrow (\overline{\text{CGTM}(CE)})/(12)$
11. $C \leftarrow B$
    $\rightarrow (30)$
12. $AM \leftarrow 0, AM_{0:34}$
13. $CE \leftarrow \text{DEC}(CE)$
14. $\rightarrow (\vee /CE)/(12)$
15. $CE \leftarrow BE$

At step 16 the mantissas are added, after which we check for overflow. This could be done in a single step, but we have broken it up into two steps for ease of analysis. At step 17 we check for like signs, since there can be no overflow if the operands are of opposite sign. At step 18 we check to see if the addition of like-signed operands has produced an overflow. We shall leave it as an exercise for the reader to show that overflow will result in an apparent change in the sign of the result. (See Problem 16.1). If there is an overflow, step 19 checks to see if the exponent already has the maximum value. If it does, incrementing it would produce exponent overflow so that the exponent overflow indicator, *eof*, is set and control exits the routine. If there is no exponent overflow, steps 21 and 22 shift the mantissa, set the sign bit, and increment the exponent. The setting of the sign bit is necessary because the bit placed in *cs* by the addition is not the sign bit, but the carry-out from the addition, i.e., the most significant bit of the sum.

16. $cs, CM \leftarrow \text{ADD}((as, AM); (bs, BM); 0)$
17. $\rightarrow (as \oplus bs)/(23)$
18. $\rightarrow (\overline{as \oplus cs})/(23)$
19. $\rightarrow (\wedge /CE)/(21)$
20. $eof \leftarrow 1$
    $\rightarrow (31)$
21. $cs, CM \leftarrow as, cs, CM_{0:46}$
22. $CE \leftarrow \text{INC}(CE)$
    $\rightarrow (30)$

If there was no overflow, a check is made at step 23 for a zero mantissa. If $\perp CM = 0$, **CE** is set equal to zero to provide a clean zero (step 24).

23. $\rightarrow (\overline{\vee /CM})/(25)$

24. $\boldsymbol{CE} \leftarrow 11 \top 0$
$\rightarrow (30)$

Step 25 checks for an unnormalized result. For positive numbers we wish to bring a 1 into the m.s.d. position; for negative numbers in complement form, it is just the opposite: a normalized number has a 0 in the m.s.d. position. Thus, in normalized numbers, the most significant bit and the sign bit will be opposite.

25. $\rightarrow (\boldsymbol{CM}_0 \oplus \boldsymbol{cs})/(30)$

If the result is not normalized, a check is made to see if the exponent is already zero (step 26), in which case decrementing it would produce exponent underflow, indicated by setting the exponent underflow indicator, *euf* (step 27).

26. $\rightarrow (\vee/\boldsymbol{CE})/(28)$
27. $euf \leftarrow 1$
$\rightarrow (31)$

If there is no underflow, the mantissa is shifted (step 28), the exponent is decremented (step 29), and control is returned to step 25 to see if the result is now normalized. The normalization process continues in this manner until the result is normalized.

28. $\boldsymbol{CM} \leftarrow \boldsymbol{CM}_{1:47}, 0$
29. $\boldsymbol{CE} \leftarrow \mathrm{DEC}(\boldsymbol{CE})$
$\rightarrow (25)$
30. NORMAL EXIT
31. ERROR EXIT

Small computers, such as SIC, generally do not have a SUBTRACT instruction, and subtraction is accomplished by taking the complement of the subtrahend by program steps. If a computer is large enough to have a floating-point unit, however, it will certainly have a SUBTRACT instruction. This feature requires sufficient extra hardware to take the two's complement of subtrahend, which we shall assume to be the $\boldsymbol{B}$ operand in terms of the previous discussion.

Recalling our previous discussion of subtraction by addition of the two's complement of the subtrahend, we can change the floating-add routine to a subtract routine by changing just three steps. Step 11 is modified to generate the complement of $\boldsymbol{BM}$ as the mantissa of the result for the case in which the $\boldsymbol{B}$ exponent is so much larger than the $\boldsymbol{A}$ exponent that the answer is simply $-\perp\boldsymbol{B}$.

11. $\boldsymbol{C} \leftarrow \boldsymbol{bs}, \boldsymbol{BE}, \mathrm{ADD}(0; \overline{\boldsymbol{BM}}; 1); \rightarrow (30)$

621

Step 16 is modified so that the adder will perform subtraction, as discussed

16. $cs, CM \leftarrow \text{ADD}(as, AM; bs, \overline{BM}; 1)$

above; and step 17 must be changed, since the addition of like-signed numbers is equivalent to the subtraction of oppositely signed numbers, and vice versa. With these changes, the program will produce the difference, $\perp C = \perp A - \perp B$.

17. $\rightarrow \overline{(as \oplus bs)}/(23)$

16.4   FLOATING-POINT MULTIPLICATION AND DIVISION

For floating-point multiplication we add the exponents and multiply the mantissas. The mantissa multiplication may be done by any of the various methods discussed in the previous chapter, and thus may be fairly simple or quite complex. In other respects floating multiplication is somewhat simpler than floating addition or subtraction, as there are fewer special conditions to worry about. There is no preshifting required and no possibility of mantissa overflow.

A flow chart for floating multiplication is shown in Fig. 16.4. Step 1 checks for either operand equal to zero and sets the product to zero at step 2 if this condition occurs.

1. $\rightarrow (\overline{(\vee/AM)} \vee \overline{(\vee/BM)})/(3)$
2. $C \leftarrow 48 \top 0$
       $\rightarrow (21)$

Step 3 adds the exponents. Note that the link must be connected to receive any additive overflow. Since both exponents are biased by the addition of 2^{10}, the exponent sum will have to be corrected by subtracting 2^{10}. Before doing this, however, a check is made for exponent overflow and underflow. Overflow will occur if the exponent sum is larger than $2^{11} - 1 + 2^{10}$ so that the subtraction of 2^{10} will leave an exponent larger than the largest legal biased value, $2^{11} - 1$. We leave it to the reader to satisfy himself that this condition will be indicated by both the link and the most-significant digit of CE being 1. Step 4 checks for this condition, and step 5 sets the *eof* indicator if the condition occurs.

3. $lf, CE \leftarrow \text{ADD}(AE; BE; 0)$
4. $\rightarrow (lf \wedge CE_0)/(6)$
5. $eof \leftarrow 1$
       $\rightarrow (22)$

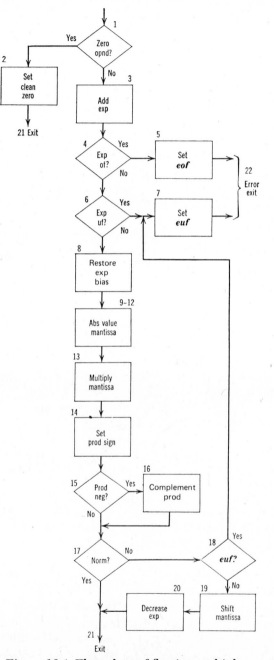

Figure 16.4. Flow chart of floating multiply.

If both of these bits are 0, the subtraction of 2^{10} will produce exponent underflow, i.e., a biased exponent less than zero. Step 6 checks for this condition, and step 7 sets the *euf* indicator if appropriate.

6. $\rightarrow (lf \vee CE_0)/(8)$
7. $euf \leftarrow 1$
     $\rightarrow (22)$

If neither overflow nor underflow occurs, the exponent is corrected. Since the two's complement (2^{11}'s complement) of 2^{10} is 2^{10}, this is accomplished at step 8 by adding 2^{10}, with the carry-out ignored.

8. $CE \leftarrow \text{ADD}(11 \top 1024; CE; 0)$

As discussed in the last chapter, there are ways of handling complemented operands directly in multiplication; but we shall use the technique of recomplementing negative operands and multiplying magnitudes. Steps 9 to 12 complement negative operands.

  9. $\rightarrow (\overline{as})/(11)$
10. $AM \leftarrow \text{ADD}(\overline{AM}; 36 \top 0; 1)$
11. $\rightarrow (\overline{bs})/(13)$
12. $BM \leftarrow \text{ADD}(36 \top 0; \overline{BM}; 1)$
13. $CM \leftarrow \text{MULTIPLY}(AM; BM)$ (SEQUENCE)

At step 13 we multiply the mantissa magnitudes by any of the magnitude multiplication methods discussed in the last chapter. At this point we should normally insert a complete sequence for multiplication. Alternately, we could use the declaration statements to establish connections to a multiplication module. In this case, since we are not dealing with details of hardware, we shall use the informal "shorthand" notation above to indicate that the multiplication of mantissas has taken place.

Steps 14 to 16 set the sign of the product and complement the product if it is negative.

14. $cs \leftarrow as \oplus bs$
15. $\rightarrow (\overline{cs})/(17)$
16. $CM \leftarrow \text{ADD}(\overline{CM}; 36 \top 0; 1)$

Step 17 checks to see if the product mantissa is normalized. If not, step 18 checks for zero exponent, indicating exponent underflow. If there is no underflow, steps 19 and 20 shift the mantissa and reduce the exponent. Note that only one normalization shift is necessary; the smallest normalized operand is 0.1000. . . . . so that the smallest possible product is 0.01000. . . . .

17. $\rightarrow (CM_0 \oplus cs)/(21)$
18. $\rightarrow (\sqrt{/CE})/(7)$
19. $CM \leftarrow CM_{1:35}, 0$
20. $CE \leftarrow \text{DEC}(CE)$
21. NORMAL EXIT
22. ERROR EXIT

Division is very similar. The exponents are subtracted and the mantissas divided. A zero divisor leads to an overflow, a zero dividend to a zero quotient. We shall leave the writing of a program for floating-point divide as an exercise for the reader.

16.5 HARDWARE ORGANIZATION FOR FLOATING-POINT ARITHMETIC

In the previous sections the exact hardware configurations were not specified. Separate registers were assumed for all operands and results, and no separate MQ register was specified for multiplication. In practice, the register layout for floating-point multiplication and division is quite similar to the layout for the corresponding fixed-point operations.

In view of the complexity of the floating-point processes, it is hardly surprising that there are many different hardware arrangements used for implementation. As a general rule, the same registers and adder used for fixed-point or integer arithmetic are used for processing the mantissas. The variety lies chiefly in the way the exponents are handled. One possibility is to "split" the registers electronically, so that the same registers are used for all parts of the floating-point data words. An alternate approach, which is probably more commonly used, is to *unpack* the exponents and place them in separate registers.

Even if separate mantissa and exponent registers are used, the arithmetic and logic circuits may be split, or shared by the mantissa and exponent registers. Alternately, completely separate arithmetic and logic facilities may be provided for the exponent processing. Just which approach is used may depend on the manner in which address modification, particularly indexing, is handled. If index addition is done in the main adder, then the main adder will probably also be used for both exponent and mantissa processing. If a separate adder is used for index addition, this adder will probably also be used for exponent processing. This latter alternative is particularly attractive if the exponents and the index quantities are comparable in size, which they often are.

One possible organization for floating-point operation is shown in Fig. 16.5. This arrangement provides much greater clarity in analyzing the

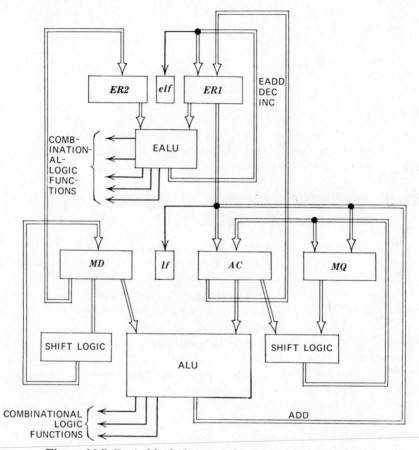

Figure 16.5. Basic block diagram, floating-point hardware.

various aspects of floating point than does any shared-hardware approach. The mantissas will be handled in the same three 48-bit registers that would be used for fixed-point, or integer, arithmetic: **MD**, the memory data register; **AC**, the accumulator register; and **MQ**, the multiplier-quotient register. All three registers will be provided with logic for 1-bit right or left shifts; and **AC** and **MQ** may be connected for shifting if desired.

Rather than indicate just an adder, we indicate an arithmetic logic unit, ALU. As we have seen in our analysis of the floating-point operations, it is necessary to be able to detect certain special conditions such as a mantissa equal to zero. These conditions will be detected by combinational logic circuits with the appropriate register positions as inputs.

Often these logic circuits may be wholly or partially realized by sharing the logic of the adder. For example, in a carry look-ahead adder, the condition of equal signs would be indicated by $\overline{P}_0 = 1$. For this reason we simply specify the ALU, a package of combinational logic to realize the desired functions.

The *ER1* and *ER2* registers are 11-bit exponent registers connected to bits 1 to 11 of the *AC* and *MD* registers. Exponent processing is handled by the exponent arithmetic logic unit, EALU, which, in addition to exponent arithmetic, provides a variety of combinational logic functions. For instance, INC and DEC provide for counting up and counting down in the *ER1* register; EADD is any conventional adder, with the output carry connected to a special link, *elf*, for detection of exponent overflow, as discussed earlier.

We have shown in Fig. 16.5 only those registers and interconnections actually involved in the execution of the floating-point operations. As we have indicated, the exponent logic might well be used for index addition and other aspects of address processing; but we are not concerned with such matters here. We have also omitted any paths required for fetching the operands. A floating-point command normally includes the fetching of one operand from memory, with the other operand having been placed in the appropriate register by previous commands. For example, addition would start with one operand already in the *AC* register, with the other to be fetched from memory and loaded into the *MD* register as a part of the Floating-Add sequence. The first steps in execution would *unpack* the arguments in *AC* and *MD*, placing the exponents in *ER1* and *ER2*. The control sequence of Section 13.3 would then follow, modified as necessary to fit the specific hardware configuration (see Problem 13.4). The sequence would conclude by *packing* (assembling) the complete floating-point sum in *AC*.

PROBLEMS

16.1 As noted in Section 16.3, the handling of overflow in floating-point addition is different from that in fixed-point addition. The addition of two 36-bit mantissas can produce a 37-bit sum, but this need not mean an overflow. Unless the exponent already has its largest possible value, the mantissa sum can be shifted one place right and the exponent increased. To do this, however, it is necessary that all 37 bits of the sum be preserved, i.e., that the carry-out from the most significant numeric bit not be dropped. For this reason, step 16 of the floating-add sequence calls for the addition of two 37-bit mantissas, sign plus magnitude, resulting in a 37-bit sum.

    (a) For all combinations of mantissa signs and relative magnitudes, show the most-significant bit of the sum is the proper sign bit for nonoverflow conditions, and is the most-significant numeric bit for overflow conditions.

    (b) For all possible combinations of signs and relative magnitudes, show that step 18 is a correct test for overflow.

    (c) Show that the shift of step 21 produces the proper shifted mantissa sum for positive or negative sums.

16.2 At step 9 of the floating add sequence we perform a second exponent subtraction to obtain a positive exponent difference for the case in which **BE** is larger than **AE**. Obviously, the required number of shifts could be determined from the negative exponent difference resulting from the first subtraction, thus eliminating the need for the second subtraction. Alter the sequence as necessary to incorporate this alternate approach, and indicate any additional hardware that may be needed. If additional hardware is needed, comment on whether the potential savings in time are likely to justify the additional cost.

16.3 The exponent subtractions could be entirely eliminated by using a combinational logic unit to compare the exponents. Write a combinational logic unit description of a circuit to develop three outputs, AEG, AEB, and AEL, defined as follows:

    AEG $= 1$ if and only if $(\perp AE) > (\perp BE)$

    AEB $= 1$ if and only if $(\perp AE) = (\perp BE)$

    AEL $= 1$ if and only if $(\perp AE) < (\perp BE)$.

Comment on whether the time saved by eliminating the exponent subtractions is likely to justify the added cost of the combinational logic unit.

16.4 Adapt the control sequence for Floating-Add to the hardware configuration of Fig. 16.5. Start with the operands in the **AC** and **MD** registers. Include steps to unpack the operands and pack the sum. Convert all operand designations to the appropriate register designations. Define any combinational logic functions required. Note that **AC** and **MQ** are equipped for shifting only 1 bit at a time.

16.5 Repeat Problem 16.4 for the Floating-Multiply sequence of Section 13.4. Start with the multiplier in **AC** and the multiplicand in **MD**. Use the basic add-and-shift multiply routine described in Chapter 6 for the mantissa multiplication.

16.6 Write a control sequence for division, in the same general form as the multiplication sequence of Section 16.4, i.e., in terms of general operands rather than a specific hardware configuration.

16.7 Repeat Problem 16.5 for the Floating-Divide sequence developed in Problem 16.6. Start with the dividend in *AC* and the divisor in *MD*. Use the basic division technique of Chapter 15 for division of the mantissa magnitudes.

17

INCREASING CPU CAPABILITY

17.1 INTRODUCTION

Chapter 13 we introduced the concept of throughput. We saw in that chapter that throughput could be improved by organizing the main memory and supplementary memories so as to minimize the time used up in retrieving data and instructions from memory. Throughput is also a function of the speed in which operations can be accomplished within the CPU. The speed of all computer functions can be increased by increasing component speed. In Chapters 14, 15, and 16 we saw that the speed of arithmetic operations could be increased up to a point by using more complex logic. Component speeds are limited by the state of the art, and a point of diminishing returns is always reached in speeding-up individual arithmetic operations. In this chapter we shall be concerned with further increasing computer throughput by organizational innovation.

In Chapter 12 a multiregister organization was considered in connection with a microprocessor. These registers were used to reduce the number of references to an *off*-chip memory. In Section 17.2 we shall consider a more general multiregister organization as it might be used in a large machine, where the speed of data flow and throughput are reflected in the cost effectiveness of the machine. In Sections 17.3, 17.4, and 17.5 we shall investigate organizational innovations aimed at increasing the number of computations per unit time that can be performed by a central processor. In general, we shall try to organize machines so that more than one computation can be accomplished simultaneously or in parallel. We shall find that it is impossible to completely separate computation and data movement. Thus there will be considerable interrelation between this chapter and Chapter 13.

Time-sharing is the topic of Section 17.6. The purpose of time-sharing is user convenience. We shall be concerned with maintaining as high a throughput as possible while operating in the time-sharing mode. Sections 17.7 and 17.8 consider byte-oriented machines, which are of interest in a wide variety of business data-processing applications. The chapter concludes with a descriptive section on large, special-purpose computer organizations. These machines operate very efficiently on a particular class of complex computational problems.

17.2 REGISTER SYMMETRY AND MULTIADDRESS INSTRUCTIONS

Among the most time-consuming aspects of instruction execution are the continual references to the main random access memory for instructions and data. As solid-state random access memories become common, an improvement in access time will be inevitable. However, the speed-cost trade-off will remain. Economics will continue to force the use of slower, cheaper technologies for the main memory than are used for the high-speed registers within the central processor. In the next several sections we shall discuss a number of organization techniques intended to minimize the time consumed by access to the main memory.

One approach to reducing the number of memory references was incorporated into most third-generation machines. By adding a small number of registers to form a very small high-speed memory, it is possible to reduce both the number of instruction fetches and the number of data requests from the RAM. The number of instruction fetches is reduced through the use of multiaddress instructions. A single ADD instruction, for example, might cause an argument at address A to be added to an argument obtained from address B and the result placed in address C. Because all three of these addresses are part of one instruction word, two instruction fetches are avoided. Multiaddress instructions were mentioned earlier and were first considered in the early days of computing. Their efficient application, however, depends on the use of the small set of high-speed data registers. It will usually be impractical to employ instruction words long enough to specify three addresses in the RAM. The number, or address, of a high-speed register can be specified by just a few bits. When data in the high-speed registers can be used repeatedly, the number of data requests to the RAM is also reduced. Clearly, the relative improvement that may be achieved by this approach is program-dependent.

The diagram in Fig. 17.1 is suggestive of a multiregister configuration for a large, general-purpose computer. We have resorted to many notational simplifications in order to leave the diagram tractable. Single ar-

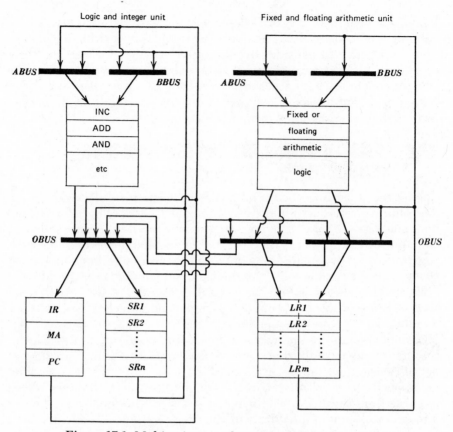

Figure 17.1. Multiregister configuration for large machine.

rows are used to indicate vector data paths, and registers as well as logic units are grouped together in banks. An arrow from a register bank to a bus, for example, should be interpreted as representative of the network of connections of individual registers to the bus.

The configuration at the left handles logical and integer operations while that at the right handles the more complex arithmetic operations. Notice that the special registers **IR**, **MA**, and **PC** can serve as logic and integer arguments.

Two separate busing configurations are provided, one for simple fixed-point and logical operations and one for multiplication, division, and floating-point instructions. The general-purpose registers at the right, labeled **LR1**, etc., would generally be longer than the **SR** registers, to accommodate the longer floating-point operands. Notice that the OBUS at the input to the long registers is split into two sections. This makes it possible to provide communication with the short register **OBUS**. The number of **LR** and **SR** registers is variable. Under certain circumstances, the numbers *n* and *m* may be quite large.

Clearly, many of the complexities involved in the execution of instructions on the configuration of Fig. 17.1 remain unmentioned. No purpose would be served by attempting to treat such a mass of details here. We have presented this configuration first only because it is typical of what may be found in certain existing large-scale computers.

Let us remove completely the right-hand busing configuration from Fig. 17.1 and further specify 13 short registers, plus registers **IR, MA**, and **PC** as registers 13, 14, and 15, so that these registers may be addressed in the same manner as the **SR** registers. The modified configuration as depicted in Fig. 17.2 is something of a superminicomputer, which we can describe in more detail. Notice that the data lines from memory are connected to the **ABUS** with a direct connection between the **ABUS** and **OBUS** to provide for loading any of the 16 registers from memory.

For convenience we shall assume 24-bit words throughout. We shall allow two types of instruction words. The first type, shown in Fig. 17.3a, provides for obtaining an argument from or depositing a result in the random access memory. The second type of instruction, illustrated in Fig. 17.3b, calls for obtaining both arguments from the 16 data registers and placing the result in one of these registers.

Indexing, as indicated by bit 3, is possible when a reference to the random access memory is specified. If $IR_3 = 0$, bits 4 to 7 may be used to specify some form of indirect addressing. Any of the 16 data registers may be used as an index register, as specified by bits 4 to 7, if $IR_3 = 1$. Consider the instruction

$$2 \quad 4 \quad 4 \quad 3 \quad 0 \quad 0 \quad 4 \quad 0 \quad \text{(octal)} \tag{17.1}$$

Using the SIC op code, we may interpret this instruction as calling for ANDing the contents of the word in **RAM** with the contents of **SR3**. The address of the word in **RAM** is given by 40 plus the contents of **SR2**. The result must replace the argument in **SR3**.

We can express the above sequence of transfers in AHPL if we represent the 16 data registers as the rows of a matrix **SR**. This implies, for example, that

$$SR^3 = SR3$$

and

$$SR^{15} = PC$$

The following sequence begins with the execution phase of the instruc-

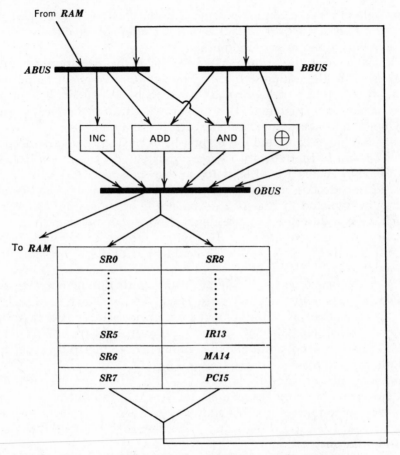

Figure 17.2. Simplified multiregister configuration.

tion given by expression 17.1. The execution sequences of other Type I instructions will be similar.

1. $ABUS, BBUS = \overline{12 \top 0}, IR_{12:23}, \overline{12 \top 0}, BUSFN_{12:23}$ $(SR; DCD(IR_{4:7}))$;
   $MA \leftarrow ADD(ABUS; BBUS)$
2. $read = 1$
   $\rightarrow (\overline{dataready})/(2)$
3. $ABUS = DATAOUT; BBUS = BUSFN(SR; DCD(IR_{8:11}))$
   $SR * DCD(IR_{8:11}) \leftarrow ABUS \wedge BBUS$

Type II instructions are indicated by an op code consisting of three 1's. The particular Type II instructions are specified by bits 3 to 11. A large number of Type II instructions are possible, including most func-

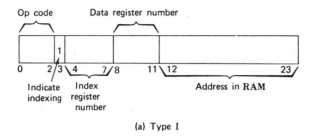

(a) Type I

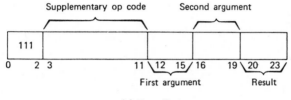

(b) Type II

Figure 17.3. Instructions for configuration of Fig. 17.3.

tions accomplished by SIC operate instructions. The three sets of 4 bits at the right of the Type II instruction indicate the data registers containing the arguments of each operation, together with the register into which the result is to be deposited.

The following sequence accomplishes a Type II AND operation. It is quite similar to the Type I AND sequence presented above except that no memory reference is required and the result need not replace either argument. No indexing is carried out.

1. $ABUS = $ BUSFN(SR; DCD($IR_{12:15}$))
   $BBUS = $ BUSFN(SR; DCD($IR_{16:19}$))
   $SR * $ DCD($IR_{20:23}$) $\leftarrow ABUS \wedge BBUS$

Although the $ABUS$ and $BBUS$ inputs have been completely specified in the above, the $OBUS$ inputs have not been directly stated. Since the $OBUS$ input connections are not affected by the multiple register configuration, we assume that the final register transfer statement is sufficient to implicitly difine the necessary connections from the ALU to the $OBUS$.

The savings to be achieved by reducing the number of memory references required by execution cycles seems less significant when we remind ourselves that a memory reference is still required for fetching each instruction. One would clearly like to reduce the average fetch time also. This is a more difficult problem, which will be approached by techniques presented in some of the next few sections.

17.3 INSTRUCTION LOOK-AHEAD

The savings achieved by minimizing the number of storage references during instruction execution can never seem quite satisfying as long as a reference to memory is required by the fetch phase of each instruction. If a scratch-pad memory is not used, one might attempt to reduce the number of fetch cycles that require reference to the main RAM by allowing short sequences of instructions to be stored in high-speed electronic registers, as were data in Section 17.2. If the number of *look-ahead* registers is sufficiently large, short loops in the program can be traversed entirely within the look-ahead unit. If a cache memory with an access time equivalent to the look-ahead registers is used, the same saving may be achieved by looping within the cache memory. This assumes block transfers into the cache, as discussed in Problem 13.12. As the buffer memory may in some cases be quite large, the likelihood of storing a complete loop within the cache is great.

Thus, if a cache is used, a very large number of registers within the look-ahead unit would be redundant. There is further advantage in a look-ahead unit with a few registers, however. The time consumed by the memory references may be approximately cut in half by overlapping the fetch and execution phases. That is, while one instruction is being executed, the next instruction can be fetched, placed in the instruction register, and readied for execution. This approach would be particularly advantageous in places where more than one word from memory are required to form an instruction. As other aspects of this machine are well understood, we can most simply illustrate the design of this simple form of look-ahead unit in terms of SIC. In practice, it is unlikely that this feature would be included in such an otherwise elementary computer.

Given the simple 8k memory originally provided for SIC, very little could be accomplished by adding a look-ahead unit. We must have the possibility of obtaining an instruction word and data word from memory simultaneously, or serially in a very short time period. This would imply an interleaved RAM, a buffer memory, or both. For purposes of illustration we replace the original SIC memory with a four-way interleaved memory of the form described in Section 13.7. The memory will be identical to the one in Section 13.7. except that the four banks will contain 2^{11} or approximately 2k eighteen-bit words each. The memory address registers will, therefore, be 13 bits. Only two of the entry points to the memory will be used in the discussion. The other two ports might be used for DMA input/output transfers. A scratch-pad memory will not be included in the design.

Given the above configuration, the principal payoff of the look-ahead unit to be discussed will be simultaneous fetch and execution memory references approximately 75 percent of the time. On the average, 25 percent of the data addresses will be found in the same bank as the instruction addresses. The resulting design will be the most elementary form of a look-ahead unit, but it should serve as an introduction to some of the awkward problems that are created when look-ahead is included in a design.

Other than the memory, the only registers added to facilitate look-ahead are shown in Fig. 17.4. The instruction register *IR1* contains the instruction under execution while *IR2* and *IR3* are provided for the next two instructions in sequence. If at the beginning of the control sequence the special flip-flop *sh* (short) contains a 0, the registers *IR1* and *IR2* contain the next two instructions in order. If *sh* = 1, only *IR1* contains the proper instruction. These two situations are illustrated in Fig. 17.4a and 17.4b. We shall see that *sh* will be 1 following a jump or skip instruction.

The control sequence will cause the instruction in *IR1* to be executed while at the same time causing the next two instructions to be placed in *IR2* and *IR3*. The program counter will contain the address of the next instruction to be obtained from memory, whether this instruction is to be placed in *IR2* or *IR3*. The first step separates control for the JMP instruction. In effect, the execution of JMP and determination of the next instruction are the same operation.

1. $\rightarrow (IR1_0 \wedge IR1_1 \wedge \overline{IR1}_2)/(17)$
2. NO DELAY
   $\rightarrow (A3, 3)$
   A3.—AX Execution
   AX + 1. $\rightarrow (11)$

Step 2 causes control to diverge to accomplish execution and fetch simultaneously. The A sequence executes all but the conditional skips at the end of the ISZ instruction and in the last event time of operate instructions. The execution sequence uses memory communications registers *CA1* and *CD1*.

3. $CA0, ro \leftarrow PC, 1$
   $\rightarrow (\overline{sh})/(9)$
4. $PC \leftarrow INC(PC)$
5. $\rightarrow (ro)/(5)$
6. $CA0, ro \leftarrow PC, 1$
7. $\rightarrow (\overline{dataready})/(7)$

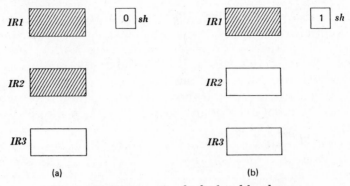

Figure 17.4. Instruction look-ahead hardware.

8. $IR2, wo \leftarrow CD0, 0$
9. $\rightarrow (dataready)/(9)$
10. $IR3 \leftarrow CD0$
11. CONVERGE

Step 3 provides the memory communications register with the address of the next instruction. If $sh = 0$, control branches to step 9 to wait for the remaining instruction to be retrieved. This instruction is subsequently placed in **IR3**. If $sh = 1$, the program counter is incremented and control circulates in a loop until **CA0** is free to accept another address. The second address is supplied at step 6. Control then waits for both instructions, placing the first in **IR2** and the second in **IR3**. Notice that at step 8 only **wo** is reset to 0, since the processor does not know whether the second address has as yet been accepted by memory from **CA0**. There is no danger of saddling memory with a dummy read operation, however, as only one memory bank is addressed.

Control converges at step 11 to permit completion of any possible skip operation. We leave the combinational logic determining the skip operation to the reader. We merely define the function, f, which is to be 1 if and only if any sort of skip instruction is called for *and* the skip condition is satisfied.

12. $\rightarrow (\bar{f})/(14)$
13. $IR1, IR2, sh \leftarrow IR2, IR3, 1$
     $\rightarrow (15)$
14. $sh \leftarrow 0$
15. $IR1, IR2 \leftarrow IR2, IR3$

If $f = 1$, the instructions are advanced in the look-ahead unit at step 13 and **sh** is set to 1. If $f = 0$, **sh** is cleared to 0. At step 18 the instructions are advanced for all cases. Thus the instructions were advanced twice in the case of a skip.

16. $PC \leftarrow INC(PC)$
    $\rightarrow (1)$

Prior to step 16 the *PC* is always set at the last instruction already entered in the look-ahead unit. After *PC* is incremented at step 16, it contains the address of the next instruction to be obtained from memory.

Control branched at step 1 to step 17 for separate execution of the JMP instruction. Indirect addressing is possible, and is provided for by steps 19, 20, and 21. Step 22 completes the jump operation by placing the new instruction in *IR1* and setting *sh* to 1. As the address of this instruction has already been inserted in *PC*, the situation is the same as at step 15 following a skip instruction. This completes the discussion of the elementary look-ahead unit.

17. $CA0, PC, ro \leftarrow IR_{5:17}, IR_{5:17}, 1$
18. $\rightarrow (\overline{dataready})/(18)$
19. $\rightarrow (\overline{IRI_4})/(22)$
20. $CA0 \leftarrow CD0_{5:17}; PC \leftarrow CD0_{15:17}; ro \leftarrow 1$
21. $\rightarrow (\overline{dataready})/(21)$
22. $IR1 \leftarrow CD0; sh \leftarrow 1; PC \leftarrow INC$
    $\rightarrow (1)$

If a scratch-pad memory is included in a computer, the actual execution of certain longer instructions will be more time-consuming than the instruction fetch or the data fetch operation. In this case, further advantage would be realized by overlapping the execution phases of several instructions. This approach would considerably complicate the design of the look-ahead unit. Some instructions use as arguments the result computed by the immediately previous instructions. Other sequences of instructions are independent. It would be the responsibility of the look-ahead unit to distinguish these two situations and to allow the execution of instructions only after the required arguments become available. Further complication is introduced by conditional branch instructions. These will either terminate a sequence of overlapping instructions or possibly cause partially computed results to be discarded.

The above example should have made clear the fact that the design of a control sequence for even an elementary look-ahead unit is quite involved. The difficulties involved in handling jump and skip instructions were apparent. As we shall note in the next section, the handling of these instructions in a more sophisticated look-ahead unit requires a very powerful memory organization.

17.4 EXECUTION OVERLAP

So far we have limited our discussion of throughput improvement to speeding up the movement of data. If many of these innovations are included in the design of a machine, the execution of instructions by the central processor can become the bottleneck. A preferable situation would have the data movement and computation capabilities approximately matched. In this section we begin our discussion of organizational techniques for speeding up instruction execution.

The notion of operating a computer like an assembly line with an unending series of instructions in various stages of completion has intrigued designers for many years. The instruction look-ahead problem, as discussed in the last section, and the hardware costs involved acted to keep the idea on the shelf during the early history of computing. With the advent of LSI this concept has been reexamined and in some cases put into practice. Our goal in this section will be to define the reservation control and routing system for a computer featuring simultaneous execution of instructions. Once again our system is only intended to suggest one possible approach. We begin by considering an example of overlap within a single *functional unit*.

Example 17.1

Design a multiplication unit capable of an average execution rate of one 18-bit multiplication per clock period, which will complete a given multiplication operation in three clock periods.

Solution.

The reader will recall from Chapter 14 that many approaches to multiplication are possible, some requiring considerable combinational logic. We propose here a simple approach that satisfies the problem statement. No claim is made that this is a particularly efficient approach in terms of the cost of the combinational logic required. The method is illustrated in Fig. 17.5.

The multiplier is shown as composed of six strings of 3 bits each. The first step of the multiplication process computes, in parallel, six partial products by performing multiplication of each 3-bit segment times the multiplicand, *MTND*. Each product consists of 36-bits with the significant bits of each partial product vector shifted left 3 bits (multiplied by 8) from those of the product immediately above. Those memory elements in the 36-bit products that always contain zeros would not be included in the actual physical implementation.

MTND   Multiplicand
A, B, C, D, E, F   Multiplier in 3-bit segments

$$P1 = (36)\top(\perp MTND \times \perp F)$$
$$P2 = (36)\top(\perp MTND \times 8 \times \perp E)$$
$$P3 = (36)\top(\perp MTND \times 64 \times \perp D) \qquad \text{36-bit partial products}$$
$$P4 \qquad\qquad\qquad \text{etc.}$$
$$P5$$
$$P6$$

PROD

Figure 17.5. Multiplication in six segments.

The second step of the operation will consist of adding $P1$, $P2$, and $P3$ to form $SUM1$ and adding $P4$, $P5$, and $P6$ to form $SUM2$. The last step consists of merely adding $SUM1$ and $SUM2$. Two very fast adders are assumed, which can perform the additions in a single clock period. Note that a complete carry propagation must be provided for each step. Once again we point out that quite likely breaking the process up in some other manner might permit a shorter carry propagation. The approach here was chosen for reasons of simplicity.

The registers required are illustrated in Fig. 17.6. The multiplier is stored in the register, **MLTR**. Five control flip-flops, $c1$, $c2$, $c3$, $c4$, and $c5$, are included to control the flow of information through the multiplier. The values of $c1$ and $c5$ are supplied externally while $c2$, $c3$, and $c4$ are under control of the multiplier control unit. Also, $c1 = 1$ indicates the presence of arguments in **MTND** and **MLTR**; $c2 = 1$ indicates that a set of six partial products are stored; $c3 = 1$ indicates the existence of numbers in **SUM1** and **SUM2**; $c4 = 1$ indicates the existence of a product in **PROD**; and $c5 = 1$ indicates that the present stored product will remain in **PROD** after the next clock period.

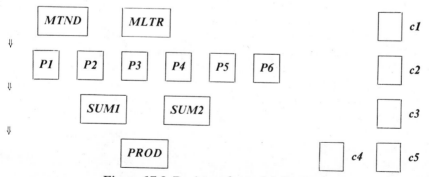

Figure 17.6. Registers for multiplication.

1. $PROD * (\overline{c4 \wedge c5}) \leftarrow ADD(SUM1; SUM2)$

   $(SUM1, SUM2) * (\overline{c3 \wedge c4 \wedge c5}) \leftarrow (ADD3(P1; P2; P3), ADD3(P4; P5; P6)$

   $(P1, P2, P3, P4, P5, P6) * (c2 \wedge c3 \wedge c4 \wedge c5) \leftarrow TIMES(MTND; MLTR)$

   $c4, c3, c2 \leftarrow c3 \vee (c4 \wedge c5), c2 \vee (c3 \wedge c4 \wedge c5), c1 \vee (c2 \wedge c3 \wedge c4 \wedge c5)$

   $\rightarrow (1)$

The multiplication control routine consists of a single step as shown. As discussed in Chapter 7, the control unit might consist of only combinational logic connected directly to the clock. At every clock period in which arguments are entered in **MTND** and **MLTR**, a 1 is entered in **c1**. With each clock pulse, the contents of the registers at each level in Fig. 17.6 are replaced by more nearly completed results in the next lower level of registers. An exception occurs if the external reservation control indicates, by inserting a 1 in **c5**, that the result currently in **PROD** will not be removed during a given step. In this case, information will be advanced within the multiplication unit only insofar as empty registers exist within the unit.

Execution overlap is facilitated by programming so that many consecutive instructions specify the same operation on different arguments. This is the assumption in the CDC STAR (see Section 17.9). Under these circumstances, execution overlap is referred to as *pipelining*. We shall find it convenient to refer to the array of registers containing arguments on which computation is in various stages of completion as *pipelines*.

Let us assume that a particular computer has only two arithmetic functional units, multiplication and division, which require more than 1 clock period for execution. Execution overlap for multiplication is as discussed in the above example. The division unit will accept arguments every 4 clock periods while requiring 12 clock periods to complete a given computation. Several additional logic units that require only 1 clock period for execution also exist within the machine.

Consider the look-ahead and reservation control unit required to manage this setup. Space will not permit complete development of this design, but we shall attempt to illustrate some of the complications involved. Let us assume that the machine under discussion has at least 10 general-purpose data registers, along the lines discussed in Section 17.2. These are labeled a through j, as shown in Fig. 17.7a. In Fig. 17.7b we see 10 arbitrary operations strung together to form an assembly language program. Although written in a distortion of APL, each step corresponds to a plausible assembly language operation. The lettered arguments refer to numerical values stored in the general-purpose data registers while three arguments are identified by their location in RAM. These

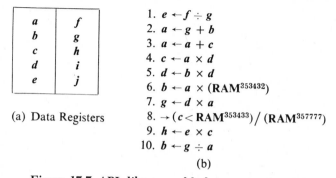

(a) Data Registers

1. $e \leftarrow f \div g$
2. $a \leftarrow g + b$
3. $a \leftarrow a + c$
4. $c \leftarrow a \times d$
5. $d \leftarrow b \times d$
6. $b \leftarrow a \times (\mathrm{RAM}^{353432})$
7. $g \leftarrow d \times a$
8. $\rightarrow (c < \mathrm{RAM}^{353433}) / (\mathrm{RAM}^{357777})$
9. $h \leftarrow e \times c$
10. $b \leftarrow g \div a$

(b)

Figure 17.7. APL-like assembly language program.

three arguments may or may not be in the associative memory.

We assume that following a branch operation, the 10 instructions of Fig. 17.7 were placed in the look-ahead unit. From the point of view of the look-ahead unit, we have the unusual good fortune of only 1 branch instruction out of 10 instructions. Let us proceed to identify the tasks that must be accomplished by the look-ahead unit during each time period. We assume that nothing has previously been done for any of these instructions. The pipelines are empty, etc.

During step 1, arguments f and g must be entered into the division pipeline. They must somehow be tagged so that the result will be recognized later. An identifier must in some way be associated with register e so that this register will not be used as an argument for the next 12 clock periods. Memory references must be initiated for the three arguments stored in RAM. The instructions must be shifted ahead in the look-ahead unit with a memory reference initiated to replace instruction 10. These last operations, which must be repeated each step, will not be mentioned again.

Instructions 2 and 3 are conveniently executed in one step each. At steps 4 and 5, two sets of arguments are entered into the multiplication pipeline. If the data word in memory location 353432 was in the associative memory, all but the register **PROD** of the multiplication pipeline would be filled at step 6.

At first glance it would appear that a multiplication pipeline will be completely filled at step 7. However, the look-ahead unit must observe that the argument, d, is tagged and that the new value has not yet emerged from the multiplication pipeline. The control unit must wait two clock periods before instruction 7 can be initiated.

In the meantime, look-ahead control advances to step 8. Conveniently, the new value of c emerges from the multiplication pipeline at this step so that it may be compared with the contents of memory location 353433 if available. If c is smaller, a new string of instructions must be placed in the look-ahead unit while the instructions prior to 8 are completed.

If c is larger, instruction 9 may be initiated. Depending on holdups in prior instructions, the new value of e may or may not have emerged from the division pipeline. Also at step 9, instruction 7 may be initiated as the argument, d, is now available.

Clearly, the design of a control unit able to keep track of all of the details discussed above would be a formidable task; also, many of the details, particularly those involving new instructions being entered in the look-ahead unit, were not even mentioned.

The above discussion reflected an attempt to handle one instruction per time step. If we consider all that must be done, it would be difficult indeed to realize this goal in the actual design of a look-ahead unit. Nonetheless it is necessary if one processor is to have any chance of keeping up with the multiplication pipeline. Given the achievement of the goal of one instruction per time step, it is doubtful that one processor could have more than one computation in the pipeline often enough to be worth the cost of the multiplication unit. Filling the pipelines would require an extremely cooperative programmer or compiler.

Given the possibility of multiprocessing, execution overlap may be viewed in a different light. This is the topic of the next section.

17.5 MULTIPROCESSING

In the previous section it was implied that in order to justify the cost of highly combinational, arithmetic functional units, they must be kept reasonably busy. Whether this is so or not is an economic question. Factors such as the cost of LSI, on which an answer to such a question might be based, change continuously.

If the answer is "yes, they must be kept busy," then two approaches are possible. One approach is to use the computer system primarily in an environment of special problems in which the proportion of arithmetic operations to other instructions is greater than average. The highly parallel ILLIAC IV, which will be discussed in Section 17.9, is based on the premise that this is possible. Unfortunately, there may be only a few such special problem environments that can afford a large-scale machine.

The other approach is to increase the rate of execution of instructions to a point at which the utilization of a particular functional unit is sufficient to justify its inclusion. In the case of the multiplication unit of the previous section, satisfactory utilization may mean only intermittent occurrences of more than one computation in the pipeline. The notion of continuously full pipelines within a general-purpose computing system may be wishful thinking.

The look-ahead unit, touched on in the previous section, represents an effort to increase the utilization rate of functional units. There it was assumed that only one program was in the process of execution at a given time. Relaxing this assumption leads to the concept of *multiprocessing*. That is, let us postulate a set of n separate control units, each executing a separate program in central memory. Such a system is illustrated in Fig. 17.8. The processors share the items requiring the heaviest investment: the very large random access memory, peripheral equipments, and certain highly combinational functional units. The several processors should have less trouble keeping the pipelines filled than a single look-ahead unit.

The advantage of the system in Fig. 17.8 is efficiency. The obvious disadvantage is that it is so large, and therefore so expensive, as to be

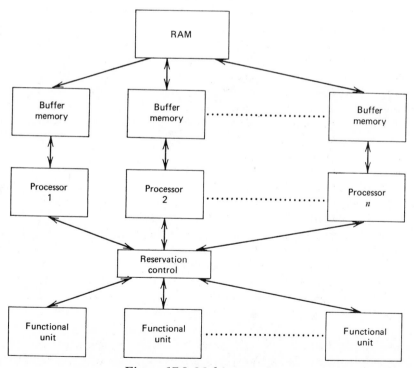

Figure 17.8. Multiprocessing.

of interest to relatively few installations. Perhaps it could be sold in modular, or building block, fashion. Unfortunately, the purchaser of a single processor would find at least some hardware in the system for which the only justification is that it will make an n processor system operate more efficiently.

With the intention of returning to the system of Fig. 17.8 later, let us consider multiprocessing as a general term. This term has been given different meanings in different contexts. For example, multiprocessing has been used in a purely software sense to refer to an operating system switching back and forth from the execution of one program to another. Some advantage may be derived from this technique if one program under execution arrives at a point where extensive I/O is required. Where DMA is employed, there can be simultaneous operations contributing to the execution of two programs. As no more then one instruction can be fetched and considered for execution at a given time, the above technique is properly referred to as *multiprogramming*. The term *multiprocessing* is reserved to refer to separate hardware control units executing separate programs simultaneously.

Various forms of actual hardware multiprocessing may be found in existing machines. One of the earliest examples may be found in the CDC 6400, which is organized along the lines depicted in Fig. 17.9. Here the central processor executes programs simultaneously with 10 *peripheral processors*. The peripheral processors handle the chores of managing input/output, preparing programs for execution, and loading the main memory. No functional units are shared by the central processor and the peripherals. The main random access memory is not shared, in the sense that only the central processor executes programs in this memory. The peripheral processors merely load and unload central memory. There is extensive hardware sharing among the peripheral processors. It might even be argued that the specialized design employed actually binds the ten peripheral processors together as one processor under a single control unit. For further details the reader is referred to the CDC reference manuals. In any case there are at least two independent control units in Fig. 17.9.

We now return to consider the configuration of Fig. 17.8 in more detail. The question might arise as to why the RAM is shared, rather than providing a separate smaller RAM for each processor. The reason is greater flexibility. If certain processors use less than their share of memory, this memory is available to a larger program that may be in the process of execution by another processor. Certain programs may even require the entire large memory. Although this situation would idle all

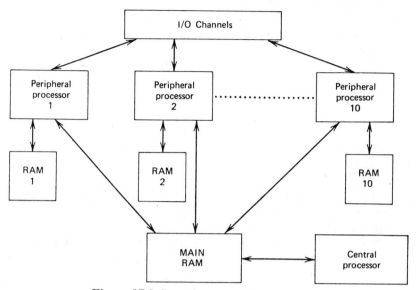

Figure 17.9. Input/output multiprocessing.

but one processor, it still might be more economical than a frequent shuffling of overlays in a smaller memory.

Dedicating the entire configuration of Fig. 17.8 to a single program raises the question "Why can't all of the processors work in parallel on the same program?" Clearly, if a program is serial in nature, i.e., if most program steps depend on results of immediately preceding steps, it is not possible for more than one processor to work on the problem at a given time. But perhaps many problems are not all that serial. Perhaps they just look that way after being reduced to program form. Which problems can be formulated for parallel processing given the latitude to change even the numerical techniques or models used? Which, if any, programs written in the usual manner in a high-level language could be compiled for parallel processing? How difficult would be the writing of such a compiler? These are questions that the authors cannot answer but which must be faced by a designer contemplating a system relying on parallel processing for efficiency. Some work in this direction has been accomplished in research in support of ILLIAC IV. Section 17.9 will be devoted to ILLIAC IV.

One more feature of Fig. 17.8, the reservation control block, merits further consideration. The interaction of more than one separate control unit has been encountered in the text. In most cases this was a limited cooperative interaction between a processor and a supporting peripheral equipment. In Fig. 17.8 the processors are completely independent and competitive. That, at some point in time, two processors will attempt to supply arguments to one functional unit simultaneously, is unavoidable. At the minimum, some priority network must be included. More likely, the reservation control will be a separate control unit similar to the memory bank control of Section 13.7.

The reservation control cannot afford the luxury of sequential searching for requests, as was the case in the memory control. It must complete service of each request for a functional unit in only one or two clock periods. In the process it must determine the priority of conflicting requests, check availability of the functional unit, and tag arguments so that results may be returned to the correct processor. Simultaneous with servicing requests, it must return computed results. Again, no more than one or two clock periods can be allowed for this operation. Space limitations preclude presentation of the design of the reservation control. The design of a stripped-down version will be left as a problem for the reader.

17.6   TIME-SHARING

Time-sharing as a medium for executing programs is not special purpose. Most any program that can be executed by a batch processing facility can also be executed by a time-sharing system. The need for special-purpose hardware, except for the input/output terminals, is not apparent either. Many functioning time-sharing systems consist of a general-purpose computer connected through its normal I/O channels to remote time-sharing terminals. Only the software operating system is special purpose.

It is the authors' contention that time-sharing using general-purpose hardware uses this hardware less efficiently than a time-sharing system with hardware particularly adapted to this task. In this section we shall discuss the general functioning of a time-sharing system, pointing out where special-purpose hardware might effectively be used; AHPL sequences describing the system will not be presented. The overall system is far too complex to permit detailing the design in a single section.

A block diagram of one approach to time-sharing is shown in Fig. 17.10. Two processors are used. One processor, the *master*, controls the overall function of the system and assembles information from the user terminals. The larger *slave* computer does nothing but compile and execute user programs. The slave computer may be a large general-purpose computer. The only saving to be made by tailoring the design of

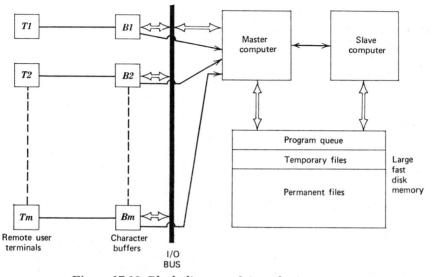

Figure 17.10. Block diagram of time-sharing system.

the slave would lie in simplifying its I/O handling capability, since it only needs to communicate with the master computer, the disk memory, and a control console (not shown). The hardware included in the master computer will be most efficiently utilized if this machine is designed as a special-purpose computer.

The master computer is the less-expensive machine and must never be the limiting factor in system performance. The goal is to match the computing capability of the slave computer to a planned customer load. That is, the computer must be able to compile and execute programs submitted by the customers with satisfactory promptness, at a time when an expected maximum portion of the terminals is in operation. In order that a long program not tie up the slave and exclude other users, execution of a program is carried on for a maximum of t_r sec. At the end of this time, another program from a queue of programs stored in the disk memory is loaded into the slave computer for execution. If execution of the first program was not completed, this program is restored in the disk memory at the bottom of the queue. Execution is continued with each "turn" in the central processor, until completed. It is the responsibility of the master computer to enter programs in the queue as requested by the user terminals, and to transmit output information from the disk file to the terminals. The slave relates only to the program queue, except that program *swaps* are made on command from the master and data may be obtained from other files in the disk memory.

The time required to swap programs in the slave computer will be denoted t_s. The number of terminals connected to the system is m. The expected maximum number of programs in the queue (on a typical day) is n. The maximum time a program must wait for a turn in the slave is given by Eq. 17.2.

$$\text{wait time} = n(t_r + t_s) \tag{17.2}$$

The worst case ratio of expected computation time for one terminal to real time is given by Eq. 17.3. This expression assumes that a program requested by the terminal is reentered in the queue each time it is swapped out of the slave.

$$\text{terminal computation time ratio} = \frac{t_r}{n(t_r + t_s)} \tag{17.3}$$

The above expressions are plotted in Fig. 17.11 for various values of n. An optimistic swap time of $t_s = 20$ msec was assumed. This is slightly more than the time required for one rotation of a disk rotating at 3600 rpm. To achieve this swap time, a separate read-write head would be required for each track on the disk. A longer swap time would significantly degrade the potential performance plotted in Fig. 17.11. The following example illustrates how data of the form given in Fig. 17.11 might be used in planning a time-sharing system.

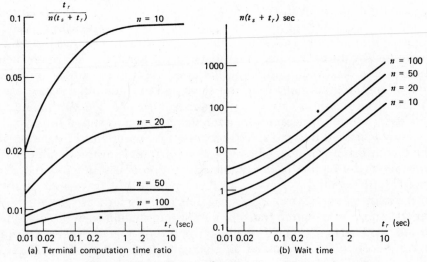

Figure 17.11. Time utilization ($t_s = 20$ msec.).

Example 17.2

A time-sharing system is to be planned for a particular set of customers. It has been determined that the average program likely to be submitted to the system could be compiled in less than 0.5 sec. Similarly, the execution time of an average program for the system is envisioned as 3 sec. These figures, of course, assume a particular slave processor selected for use in the system. It has also been estimated that 50 percent of all terminals will have a program in the queue at a time of maximum activity. The maximum number of terminals, m, that can be connected to the system is to be determined.

Solution.

Assuming all of the rather uncertain assumptions made in the above paragraph, the determination of m remains in part subjective. A critical question is, "How poor a level of service will the customers tolerate during hours of peak activity?" It may be advantageous to overload the system to insure efficient use of the slave at other than peak periods.* Let us assume that a competitive time-sharing service is available; therefore, the customer must be kept happy.

Typical time-sharing users debug their programs on-line by alternately compiling and editing their programs. We assume that users' irritation increases rapidly if required to wait longer than 60 sec for compilation of a simple program. We, therefore, let $t_r = 0.5$ and specify a run wait time less than 60 sec. For these figures Eq. 17.2 yields $n = 120$. This point is denoted by an asterisk in Fig. 17.11b.

The user will usually tolerate a longer wait during execution of a program. Let us assume that a 15-min execution time (which could coincide with a coffee break) will be tolerated for a 3-sec program. This implies a terminal computation time ratio of $3/900 = 0.0033$. A point corresponding to this value and $t_r = 0.5$ is denoted by an asterisk in Fig. 17.11a. For $t_r = 0.5$, $1/n$ 0.033, so that $n = 300$.

From Fig. 17.11 we see that a tolerable wait time is more difficult to achieve. We therefore conclude that $n = 120$ will satisfy both the wait and the execution time requirements. Then, $m = 240$ becomes a design parameter for the system. As we shall see, this number is important in the design of the master processor.

The value of t_r chosen in the above example will result in fairly efficient utilization of the slave. The ratio of computation time to real time $t_r/(t_s + t_r)$ is a measure of efficiency. For $t_r = 0.5$ this ratio is 0.96 (for the assumed very short swap time of 20 msec). This measure of efficiency drops to 0.5 for $t_r = 20$ msec. This relatively inefficient mode of operation could result if the system were connected to a very large number of terminals for the execution of very short programs. A similarly

---

*In many systems efficiency is maintained by running large batch processing jobs during slack periods.

low efficiency would result from use of a slower-disk memory, employing movable read-write heads. The impact of swap time on system efficiency can be lessened significantly by providing for the storage of two programs in the random access memory of the slave processor. In this way one program can be executed while a new program is simultaneously read from the disk to replace the program just executed. Most existing time-sharing systems possess this capability, which is a form of multiprogramming, as mentioned in Section 17.5. We leave the analysis of this technique as a problem for the reader.

The number of terminals, m, is the key parameter in the design of the master processor. This unit must be able to accept a steady stream of characters from all m terminals and to respond to all system commands. From the previous discussion we conclude that service would be very poor if all terminals were in use. Such a situation will be self-limiting in that users would give up if told to wait or if programs took an excessively long time to execute. In any case, the user would be aware of the overload condition. Failure of the system to accept an input character is a much graver sin, a hardware failure. Under certain conditions, chaos could be the result.

Standard telecommunications allows 11 bits (8 information bits, a parity bit, and 2 bits marking the beginning and ending of a character) per character. These bits are transmitted serially. They are received and stored in an 11-bit buffer, as illustrated in Fig. 17.10. When a complete character is present in the buffer, an interrupt is transmitted to the master. In the absolute worst case, interrupts could issue from all m buffers simultaneously. The master must respond to all of these interrupts by accepting all m characters before another bit arrives. For a character rate, r (typically between 10 and 20 characters/sec), the interval between bits will be $1/11r$. Since the processor must respond to m interrupts $1/11rm$ sec are available for the processing of a single interrupt. For $r = 20$ and $m = 240$, 19 μsec are available to service each buffer. This is ample time for servicing an interrupt by a hardware control sequence. It would very likely not be sufficient time to service an interrupt via software.

Let us assume that $t_c \leq 1/11rm$ sec are used to input or output each character. If all m processors are in constant communication at the rate of r characters/sec, the portion of master processing time devoted to input/output is $t_c rm \leq 1/11$. The remainder of the master time is devoted to other tasks. A very general list of the functions that must be accomplished by the master and the attached buffers are listed in Fig. 17.12.

Characters taken from the character buffers are stored in a line buffer. A line buffer, consisting of between 70 and 200 characters, must be

Activity	Special Hardware
Storage of incoming bits in character buffers	Yes
Filling of line buffers	Possibly
Maintain temporary files	Possibly
Respond to user commands	
Control program queue and slave operation	
Handle output	

Figure 17.12. Master activities.

provided for each terminal connected to the system. The line buffers may consist of sections of the master processor RAM. Where speed is crucial, special hardware line buffers may be provided. Just as the master must respond to interrupts from full character buffers, it must check for end-of-line characters in the line buffer. A completed line in the line buffer may be a systems command or it may be a line to be stored in a file. In many systems these two types of lines are easily distinguished by the presence or absence of a line number. If a line number is present, the line must be removed from the line buffer and placed in what we shall define as a *temporary file*. If $r = 10$ characters/sec, this operation must be accomplished within 0.1 sec.

A temporary file must be provided corresponding to each terminal that is connected. As many as 256 lines are allowed for a temporary file. For illustration, consider a system with 128 characters per line, 128 lines per temporary file, and four characters per word in the master RAM. This implies 4k words per temporary file. For large m it may not be practical to store complete temporary files in the master RAM. If not, a special parallel control sequence must be provided to transfer groups of temporary file lines from RAM to disk while other activities are in progress. This implies cycle stealing or multiple-memory banks.

The order of lines in the temporary files is immaterial. This format is convenient for implementing the various EDIT commands by which the user can alter or replace lines in the temporary file. Editing is accomplished by the master. The command SAVE causes lines from the temporary file to be inserted in the permanent file. Lines in the permanent file are in numerical order. A line from the temporary file is inserted in the permanent file between permanent lines with the next higher and next lower line numbers. When line numbers are identical, the line from the temporary file replaces the line in the permanent file.

Other commands that must be processed by the master are tabulated in Fig. 17.13. Some response must be made to each command in not

653

NEW	Calls for a new file to be established
OLD	Requests retrieval of an old file
LIST	Calls for teletype listing of file
SAVE	Temporary file inserted in permanent file
UNSAVE	Eliminate permanent file
COMPILE (FILE NAME)	Compile permanent file and store as named file
RUN	Execute file (compile if needed)
EDIT	Miscellaneous text editing commands available
BYE	Disconnects terminal

Figure 17.13. Minimal set of time-sharing commands.

much more than one second. In some cases the immediate response will consist of printing the word WAIT, indicating that a period of time is required before execution of the command is complete. In other cases the master may respond to a command with a question. In response to the command OLD, for example, the master will ask for the name of the permanent file with which the user wishes to work.

The master must output various sorts of information, including responses to commands, results of programs, and listings. The procedures for each case are somewhat different. All output procedures are approximately the reverse of the input procedure already discussed in detail. We shall omit further discussion of output.

As the reader has observed, the master computer is required to perform a great variety of tasks. The timing of these tasks is not completely under control of this computer. To make possible timely response to all outside demands, the master operating system must be very carefully written to interlace the various activities. Large systems will tend to impose difficult-to-meet performance specifications on the master. Such circumstances suggest the design of a special-purpose processor, with a control sequencer providing a maximum of concurrent activity.

The commands in Fig. 17.13 suggest a very simple, time-sharing system. More commands could be added to permit more flexible utilization of the slave computer. Commands requesting access to magnetic tape files, operation in the remote batch mode, or paper tape input are possibilities.

17.7 VARIABLE WORD-LENGTH COMPUTERS

All of the machine organizations we have studied so far have assumed that all operations involve operands of a fixed length. No matter how complex the organization, we have assumed that each memory access involves one complete operand. The choice of the word length for such a machine necessarily involves a number of compromises. In Chapter 1 we discussed the compromises involved in choice of word length, memory size, and instruction complexity. With regard to operand size, the word length should be large enough to handle the largest operands anticipated but not so large as to waste excessive memory space on operands of average size.

For typical engineering and scientific computations, in which data are primarily numeric and the precision of data does not vary widely, reasonable compromises on a fixed word length are possible. However, in many business data-processing applications, the size of basic data items varies over too wide a range to make any single word length satisfactory.

First, the size of numeric data items may vary widely. For example, an inventory program may involve thousands of individual item prices, requiring only a few digits each, and a small number of inventory totals, each requiring many digits. Even more of a problem is the fact that most data in business problems consist of alphanumeric characters. A single data item, such as a name or address, may require 20 or 30 characters; but such operations as sorting and editing require the ability to access and process individual characters.

Alphanumeric characters are coded in combinations of 6 to 8 bits, the most common length being 8 bits, with an 8-bit data unit generally referred to as a *byte*, as mentioned earlier. We could thus provide for processing individual characters in a fixed word-length machine by making the basic word length equal to 1 byte, i.e., 8 bits. However, this arrangement would require separate instructions for each byte processed, a requirement that would lead to intolerably long programs for even simple data processing problems. (Although the problems are not exactly the same, the reader who has tried to write character-handling programs in ordinary FORTRAN will have some conception of the difficulties involved.)

One answer to the problem of achieving efficient processing character-oriented programs is provided by a *variable word-length* organization, in which single instructions may specify operands of any number of bytes to be processed 1 byte at a time. Thus the word length will always be some multiple of 8, and a word will be referenced by addressing the first byte in the word. Because machines with this organization are most useful for business data processing, they have been traditionally referred to as "business" computers, in contrast to "scientific," or fixed word-length, computers.

Since a complete operand may be very long, up to 256 bytes in typical variable word-length computers, it is not practical to provide an accumulator capable of storing a complete operand. Without an accumulator to serve as the implied source of one operand and implied destination of the results, the one-address instruction is impractical. For this reason, most variable word-length computers use two-address replacement instructions. For example, an ADD instruction would have the basic format.

| ADD | LOCA | LOCB |

and the meaning, "Add the operand found in LOCA to the operand found in LOCB and store the sum in LOCA, replacing the first operand." The replacement aspect of this format causes difficulties when it is necessary to preserve both operands so that it might seem that the three-address format would be preferable. However, since variable word-length machines require addressing down to the byte level, they require such long addresses that three-address instructions would generally be impractically long.

Although addressing is at the byte level, this does not mean that the memory should be byte-oriented. If the basic memory word length is 1 byte, then n accesses will be required for an n-character operand; since memory is relatively slow, this is very undesirable. Most variable word-length machines access several bytes at a time, with 4 bytes (32 bits) probably being the most common memory word length. This is the length we shall assume for the remainder of this chapter. It might seem that we are defeating our original objective of conserving memory space by using a 4-byte word, but operands of less than four characters will occur relatively infrequently. Our primary concern in the variable word-length organization is to provide for handling very long operands with reasonable efficiency.

Next let us consider the implications of our choice of memory word length on the addressing problems. First, we note that addressing to the byte level will require 2 more bits than addressing to the word level, with 4 bytes/word. For example, with a memory of 128k words, there will be 512k bytes, requiring 19-bit addresses. Two addresses will, therefore, require 38 bits so that an instruction cannot be fitted into a single memory word. We can make two accesses to memory for each instruction fetch, but we would like to avoid that if possible.

One way to reduce the number of address bits required in the instruction is *base-addressing*. We divide the 128k words of memory into 64 segments of 2k words each and specify a 6-bit, *base address register*, into which we place the 6 most-significant bits of the address of the first word in the 2k segment we wish to address. The address in the instruction then need specify only which byte out of 8k (2k words of 4 bytes each) is desired, which requires only 13 bits; so our two addresses will fit into a single memory word.

Although this scheme saves address bits, it is inconvenient from the programmer's point of view. Any time he wants an operand or instruction not in the current 2k segment, he must reset the base address register. This problem may be alleviated by having several base address registers, and adding bits to the instruction to indicate which one is to be used. For example, we could have four base address registers and add 2 bits to the instruction to designate which one is to be used. An instruction could then access any of 8k words in memory, in any four 2k groups in memory.

With the 2 bits added for base address designation, we need 28 bits for addressing, leaving 4 bits for the op code for memory reference instructions. This might be sufficient but we have not yet indicated the length of the operands. The addresses will specify the first bytes in each operand, but the number of bytes must also be specified. There are two methods used to specify operand length. The most obvious is to add bits to the instruction, but this gets us right back into problems with the instruction length. A widely used alternative is to use a special symbol, the *word mark*, in the operand itself, to identify the last byte. There are a variety of ways of coding the word mark, but the simplest is to set aside 1 bit position in each byte, which will be 1 only for the last byte of an operand.

Let us now consider a partial organization and instruction sequence for a computer embodying the features discussed above. The memory word length will consist of 128k words of 32 bits (4 bytes) each. The instruction format will be as shown; *BA* is the number of the base address register.

OP	*BA*	ADDRESS *A*	ADDRESS *B*

0   3 4   5 6   18 19   31

The two low-order bits of each address will be the byte number, i.e., 00 will signify the first byte in the word (bit 0 to bit 7), 01 will signify the second byte (bit 8 to bit 15), etc. The catenation of the upper 11 bits in the address, with the 6 bits of the specified base address register, will form the address of the word in memory. Operands will start with the byte addressed and will be processed from left to right in each word, through consecutive memory locations, until the word mark is encountered. The word mark will be a 1 in the high-order bit of a byte.

A partial block diagram of the computer is shown in Fig. 17.14. There are two 32-bit operand registers, **MDA** and **MDB**, and two 1-byte op-

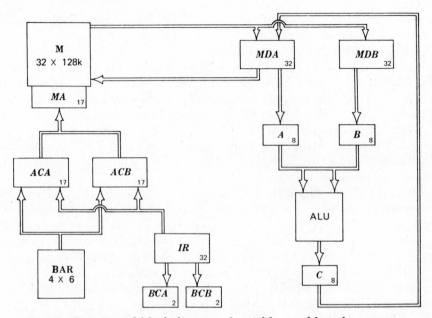

Figure 17.14. Partial block diagram of variable word-length computer.

erand registers, *A* and *B*, which provide the operands for the ALU. The ALU provides the logic to carry out various operations such as AND, OR, ADD, etc. The results go to a third 1-byte register, *C*, from which they are returned to *MDA*. The byte counters, *BCA* and *BCB*, are 2-bit counters to keep track of which bytes in *MDA* and *MDB* are currently being processed. The instruction register, *IR*, holds the 32-bit instruction currently being executed; *BAR* is the matrix of four 6-bit, base address registers. The two 17-bit address counters, *ACA* and *ACB*, keep track of the addresses of the operand words.

Now let us consider the control sequence for the implementation of typical memory reference instruction. These instructions will obtain variable length arguments specified by addresses *A* and *B*, perform a logical or arithmetic computation, and place the result in the memory space specified by address *A*. We shall assume that the instruction has been fetched and loaded into *IR* and that the base address registers have been loaded by previous instructions. The basic flow chart of the sequence is shown in Fig. 17.15.

We start with step 5, assuming that the first four steps fetched the instruction and branched to the appropriate sequence. Steps 5 and 6 form the initial word addresses from the upper 11 bits of the addresses

658

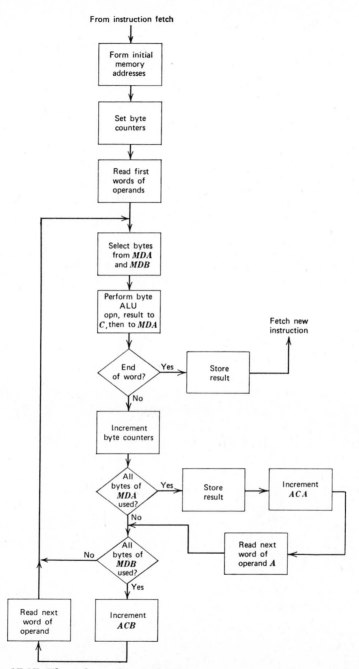

Figure 17.15. Flow chart of typical *MRI* sequence in variable word-length computer.

in the instruction and the 6 bits of the selected base address register. Step 7 loads the low-

   5. $ACA \leftarrow BUSFN(BAR; DCD(IR_{4:5})), IR_{6:16}$
   6. $ACB \leftarrow BUSFN(BAR; DCD(IR_{4:5})), IR_{19:29}$
   7. $BCA \leftarrow IR_{17:18}; BCB \leftarrow IR_{30:31}$
   8. $MA \leftarrow ACA$
   9. $MDA \leftarrow BUSFN(M; DCD(MA))$
   10. $MA \leftarrow ACB$
   11. $MDB \leftarrow BUSFN(M; DCD(MA))$

order 2 bits of each address into the byte counters. Steps 8 to 11 fetch the first words of the two operands from memory. In order to select bytes from a 32-bit vector, we must arrange the bytes in a four-row matrix. This may be accomplished by the following LABEL statements which we shall assume to be part of the module declaration.

   LABEL: **ARRAYMDA** $= MDA_{0:7} \mathbin{!} MDA_{8:15} \mathbin{!} MDA_{16:23} \mathbin{!} MDA_{24:31}$
   LABEL: **ARRAYMDB** $= MDB_{0:7} \mathbin{!} MDB_{8:15} \mathbin{!} MDB_{16:23} \mathbin{!} MDB_{24:31}$

Step 12 loads the appropriate bytes into A and B.

   12. $A \leftarrow BUSFN(\textbf{ARRAYMDA}; DCD(BCA))$
        $B \leftarrow BUSFN(\textbf{ARRAYMDB}; DCD(BCB))$
   13. $C \leftarrow ALOP(A; B; IR_{0:3})$
   14. **ARRAYMDA** $* DCD(BCA) \leftarrow C$
        $\rightarrow (A_0)/(17)$

At step 13, ALOP represents the appropriate operation by the ALU, as specified by the op code. We are assuming any "byte-by-byte" operation, i.e., one in which there is no carry-over from 1 byte to the next. At step 14 the result from C is returned to the appropriate byte destination in MDA.

This completes the operations on 1 byte. The remainder of the sequence consists of "bookkeeping" operations to sequence through the remaining bytes of the operands. Step 14 checks to see if the end of the operand has been reached. For this example we assume that both operands are the same

   15. $MA \leftarrow ACA$
   16. $M * DCD(MA) \leftarrow MDA$
        $\rightarrow$ (fetch new instruction)

length, so the byte of operand A just processed is checked for an end-of-word mark. If an end-of-word mark is sensed, steps 15 and 16 store the result, and branch to fetch a new instruction. If the end of the operands has not been

17. $BCA \leftarrow \text{INC}(BCA); BCB \leftarrow \text{INC}(BCB)$
18. $\rightarrow (\vee/BCA)/(24)$
19. $MA \leftarrow ACA$
20. $M * \text{DCD}(MA) \leftarrow MDA$
21. $ACA \leftarrow \text{INC}(ACA)$
22. $MA \leftarrow ACA$
23. $MDA \leftarrow \text{BUSFN}(M; \text{DCD}(MA))$
24. $\rightarrow (\vee/BCB)/(12)$ NO DELAY
25. $BCB \leftarrow \text{INC}(ACB)$
26. $MA \leftarrow ACB$
27. $MDB \leftarrow \text{BUSFN}(M; \text{DCD}(MA))$
    $\rightarrow (12)$

reached, step 17 increments the byte counters and step 18 checks to see if all the bytes in **MDA** have been processed. The byte counters are modulo-2 counters, with the sequence 00, 01, 10, 11, then returning to 00. If the counter reads 00 after incrementing, all bytes in the word have been processed. In that event, the result in **MDA** is stored, **ACA** is incremented, and the next word of operand A is read out. Steps 24–27 check to see if the operand in **MDB** has been fully processed and read out a new word if required. After any new word has been accessed, control returns to step 12 to continue the byte processing. Note that independent byte counters are provided, on the assumption that the two operands need not start in the same byte-position of a word.

Another distinct feature of the variable word-length computer is the manner of performing arithmetic. In the fixed word-length computer, numeric operators are fully converted from decimal to binary on input, e.g., 169 is converted to 10101001 so that there is no correlation between any specific binary bits and any specific decimal digits. Performing this conversion to a variable word-length format is considerably more complicated. Therefore, numeric operators, like alphanumeric, are converted into binary code on a digit-by-digit basis. There are a variety of codes used, but the most common is the direct 4-bit binary equivalent, generally referred to as binary-coded-decimal, or BCD. Thus the BCD equivalent for 169 would be 0001 0110 1001. (The spaces between digits are shown only for clarity, and would not be present in the computer.) Since a decimal digit requires only 4 bits for code, there is a question of how best to arrange them in 8-bit bytes. They may be stored one digit to a byte in the low-order 4 bits, with the upper 4 bits 0 except in the case of end-of-word mark, or they may be packed two digits to a byte.

The use of BCD representation obviously requires that arithmetic be done on a digit-by-digit basis. To illustrate the difference, the addition

Decimal	Binary	BCD
73	1001001	0111 0011
62	0111110	0110 0010
135	10000111	0001 0011 0101

Figure 17.16. Addition in decimal, binary, and BCD.

of two numbers is shown in Fig. 17.16 in both binary and BCD. In the BCD mode, addition in each digit position forms a BCD sum digit, with a carry into the next digit if the sum exceed 9. The addition of two BCD digits is generally done in two steps. First, the digits are added as conventional 4-bit binary numbers, producing a 4- or 5-bit binary sum. If the sum exceeds 9, a carry is stored for addition to the next digit position; the sum digit is corrected to the correct BCD value. The correction is done by adding binary 6 to the sum. We shall leave it to the reader to satisfy himself that adding binary 6 to a binary number between 10 and 18 will produce the correct BCD value of the lower-order digit in the 4 lower-order bits of the sum.

To further illustrate the process of addition, as well as some other features of variable word-length computers, let us consider the process of addition in a computer of the IBM System/360-370 family, as in Example 17.3. The various models of System/360-370, although "program-compatible," differ considerably in details of organization and functioning; thus the following should be considered as representative rather than exactly descriptive of any particular computer.

Example 17.3

System/360-370 computers can operate in either a fixed or variable word-length mode. For operations in the variable word-length mode, instructions are in the SS (Storage-to-Storage) format, and have the same replacement meaning as covered above. There are two important distinctions between the SS instructions and those discussed earlier. First, 4 bits are used to designate 1 of up to 16 possible base address registers, and a separate base address may be specified for each address. Second, the length of the operand, up to 256 bytes, is specified in the instruction so that no word marks are needed.

The SS format is shown in Fig. 17.17. The total length of the instruction is 6 bytes (48 bits) and the lengths of the various segments are shown in bytes in Fig. 17.17. The memory word length in various System/360-370 models may be 16, 32, or 64 bits; so the fetch of an SS instruction may require one, two, or three memory accesses. We shall again assume a 32-bit memory word length, requiring two accesses for an SS instruction, with the right half of the second word being discarded; BAA and BAB are the designators for the base address registers. As before, the lower-order 2 bits in the addresses will designate the byte address,

OP	Length	BAA	Address A	BAB	Address B

$|\leftarrow 1 \rightarrow|\leftarrow 1 \longrightarrow| \quad \frac{1}{2} \quad |\longleftarrow 1\frac{1}{2}\longrightarrow| \quad \frac{1}{2} \quad |\longleftarrow 1\frac{1}{2}\longrightarrow|$

Figure 17.17. SS instruction format.

with the upper 10 forming the lower-order portion of the word address. The base address registers are 24 bits in length, and are *added* to the 10-bit addresses from the instruction, to generate 24-bit addresses.

The register configuration will be only slightly different from that shown in Fig. 17.14. The *ACA, ACB*, and *MA* registers will be 24 bits in length, and the dimensions of *BAR* will be 16 × 24. There will be one new register, *LR*, an 8-bit counter used to keep track of the number of bytes processed; the *C* register will be 9 bits, to provide for storage of the carry. Also, we shall assume a direct path from memory to *IR* for instruction fetches.

Since the fetch process is somewhat more complex, we shall include it in our program. The first two steps read the first word, containing the op code, length, and first address, into *IR*.

1. $MA \leftarrow PC$
2. $IR \leftarrow \text{BUSFN}(M; \text{DCD}(MA))$
3. $\rightarrow (\overline{IR_0 \wedge IR_1})/\text{``other instruction types''}$
4. $ACA \leftarrow \text{BUSFN}(BAR; \text{DCD}(IR_{16:19})), IR_{20:29}$
5. $BCA \leftarrow IR_{30:31}$

An *SS* instruction is indicated by the first 2 bits of the op code being 1. Step 3 checks for this condition, and branches to other sequences if the instruction is not of the *SS* type. Step 4 forms the word address of the first operand in *ACA* and step 5 loads the byte address into *BCA*. Steps 6 to 10 fetch the second word of the instruction and load *ACB* and *BCB*.

6. $PC \leftarrow \text{INC}(PC)$
7. $MA \leftarrow PC$
8. $IR_{16:31} \leftarrow \text{BUSFN}_{0:15} (M; \text{DCD}(MA))$
9. $ACB \leftarrow \text{BUSFN}(BAR; \text{DCD}(IR_{16:19})), IR_{20:29}$
10. $BCB \leftarrow IR_{30:31}$

Step 11 loads the operand length (in bytes) into *LR*, and steps 12 to 15 load the first words of the operands into *MDA* and *MDB*.

11. $LR \leftarrow IR_{8:15}$
12. $MA \leftarrow ACA$
13. $MDA \leftarrow \text{BUSFN}(M; \text{DCD}(MA)$
14. $MA \leftarrow ACB$
15. $MDB \leftarrow \text{BUSFN}(M; \text{DCD}(MA))$

Step 16 checks the op code and branches accordingly. The remainder of our program will consider the sequence for ADD only. In System/360-370 computers, decimal digits may be stored one or two to a byte; but for arithmetic operations they are packed two to a byte, in standard BCD code. The decimal adder, which we shall call by the combinational logic subroutine DECADD, combines two digits of each operand and an input carry from the previous two digits, to form two digits of the sum and an output carry. To accommodate these, the C register is enlarged to 9 bits, with the output carry going to C_0.

17. $C_0 \leftarrow 0$
18. $A \leftarrow$ BUSFN(**ARRAYMDA**; DCD(**BCA**));
     $B \leftarrow$ BUSFN(**ARRAYMDB**; DCD(**BCB**))
19. $C \leftarrow$ DECADD(A; B; C_0)
20. ARRAYMDA $*$ DCD(**BCA**) $\leftarrow C_{1:8}$

Step 17 sets the input carry to zero, step 18 moves the proper bytes into A and B, step 19 carries out the addition, and step 20 stores the two digits of sum, leaving the input carry for the next two digits in C_0. This completes the addition of two digits, and the remainder of the program consists of the "bookkeeping" operations required to sequence the digits through the added in the proper sequence.

Step 21 decrements the byte count in LR by one, and step 22 checks to see if the end of the operands has been reached. If so, steps 23 and 24 store the final word of the result and exit to the next instruction fetch.

21. $LR \leftarrow$ DEC(LR)
22. $\rightarrow (\vee /LR)/(25)$
23. $MA \leftarrow ACA$
24. $M * $ DCD(MA) $\leftarrow MDA$
     $\rightarrow$ (fetch new instruction)

The remaining steps in the program are the same as presented previously, except for the direction of sequencing through the successive bytes and words. When processing alphanumeric characters, it is convenient to proceed from left to right, as one does in reading or writing normal text. But arithmetic operation must proceed from right to left, starting with the least-significant digit. When data are read in, they are normally read from left to right, as they would appear, for example, on punched cards; they are stored in sequentially increasing locations in memory. One could store decimal numbers in the opposite order, but this would be very inconvenient because it would mean specifying in advance whether those data may be considered only as alphanumeric or decimal. It is more usual to specify that arithmetic operations will sequence through the operands in the opposite direction. To accomplish this, the byte counters and address counters are decremented instead of incremented. Except for this, steps

25 to 35 of this example correspond exactly to steps 18 to 28 of the previous presentation.

25. $BCA \leftarrow \text{DEC}(BCA); \ BCB \leftarrow \text{DEC}(BCB)$
26. $\rightarrow (\overline{BCA_0 \wedge BCA_1})/(32)$
27. $MA \leftarrow ACA$
28. $M * \text{DCD}(MA) \leftarrow MDA$
29. $ACA \leftarrow \text{DEC}(ACA)$
30. $MA \leftarrow ACA$
31. $MDA \leftarrow \text{BUSFN}(M; \text{DCD}(MA)$
32. $\rightarrow (\overline{BCB_0 \wedge BCB_1})/(18)$
33. $ACB \leftarrow \text{DEC}(ACB)$
34. $MA \leftarrow ACB$
35. $MDB \leftarrow \text{BUSFN}(M; \text{DCD}(MA)$
    $\rightarrow (1)$

As the previous examples illustrate, the internal organization and functioning of the variable word-length computer will be considerably more complex than that of the fixed word-length machine. Nevertheless, the increased efficiency of these machines for business-oriented problems generally justifies the increased complexity. For example, decimal arithmetic is definitely slower than binary. However, business processing generally involves a great many I/O operations and character-oriented operations and relatively few arithmetic operations. Thus the relative inefficiency of arithmetic operations is more than compensated for by the greater efficiency of I/O conversions using the BCD format.

One of the biggest problems in this type of computer is the time penalty involved in the multiple-memory accesses, and a great variety of techniques have been applied to minimize this penalty. One common technique is the use of a split cycle in memory, to take advantage of the fact that since the A operand is to be replaced, there is no reason to rewrite it after reading. Rewriting typically requires about 60 percent of the time of a full memory cycle in a core memory, and a split cycle allows one the option of reading without rewriting. Thus the A operand is read first in a read-only operation, leaving the location cleared. The B operand is then read, and the rewrite takes place while processing continues. When ready, the result is stored in the already-cleared location with a write-only operation. The net result is a saving of one memory cycle out of three. The reader can probably identify other points in the program where memory accesses can overlap processing steps.

Interrupts also present a special problem in this type of computer. We have seen that certain interrupts must be serviced in a relatively short time. With the variable word-length organization, the duration of any given operation is unpredictable so that it may be necessary to interrupt in the middle of the execution of an instruction. Preserving the status of an incompletely executed instruction will obviously be more difficult than for one that has been completed.

The relative merits of the two types of organizations, fixed and variable word length, is still a subject of considerable debate. In a sense, IBM has avoided the debate by providing both types of operations in the System/360-370 machines. Naturally, providing both types of operations requires even more complex organization than providing either separately. However, as advances in integrated circuits make ever-more-complex functions available at ever-decreasing cost, it is quite possible that the general trend in computer design will be toward more-and-more complex machines.

17.8   SORT PROCESSOR

One of the most time-consuming activities in business data processing is the sorting, ordering, or alphabetizing of lists of data. This process can be made much more efficient through the use of special-purpose hardware. In this section the implementation of specific instructions intended to perform operations related to the sorting problem will be considered. A complete design of the computer will not be presented.

The computer under consideration has a memory of 2^{16}, or 64k, words of 24 bits each. As this computer is to be dedicated to a particular inventory control application, the memory is permanently allocated as shown in Fig. 17.18. The last half of the memory consists of a set of data files that require frequent updating and resorting. All of the remaining storage, except for the first 1024 words, are allocated to program and working storage. The first 1024 words are a working key file. This section of memory may be accessed through a separate address pointer and data register as well as through the usual **MA** and **MD**. This is possible, since the entire memory may be assumed to be implemented using semiconductors.

Each file in the 32k file area is divided into a set of file blocks, as illustrated in Fig. 17.18. The first word in each block is an identifying number called a *key*. No two blocks in the same file will have the same key. The first word in each file contains the address of the last key in the file; the second word in the file contains the number of words per block, which is the same for all blocks in a file; and the third word contains the number of blocks.

Several instruction formats are permitted. Only two formats will con-

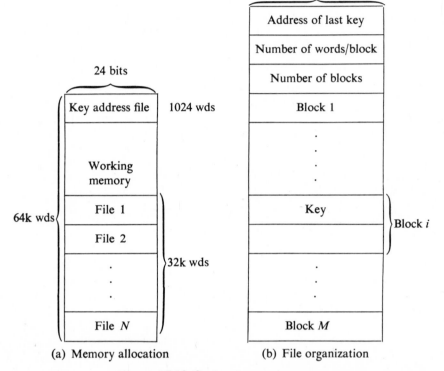

Figure 17.18. Sort processor memory.

cern us. One of these is the single-word format of Fig. 17.19. As with all instructions for this machine, the op code consists of 6 bits. Bits 6 and 7 allow for specifications of indexing or indirect addressing, or both, depending on the op code. The last 16 bits are the address. The first word of the two-word instruction in Fig. 17.19 is interpreted just like a one-word instruction. The second word contains a second address in the leftmost 16 bits. The rightmost 8 bits contain a constant, n, which may be used in various ways. Indirect addressing is not permitted by either of these two instruction formats. It may be employed by other formats, however.

Let us suppose that op codes 64 and 65 (octal) specify two special sort instructions, as described in Fig. 17.20.

The registers directly involved in the sort instructions are listed in Fig. 17.21. The use of these registers will become clear with the presentation of the control sequence. The listed sequence begins followng

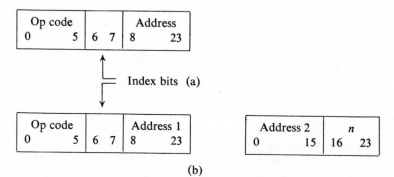

Index bits (a)

(b)

Figure 17.19. Two instruction formats.

| 6 | 4 | | | A | |

specifies sorting the file whose first word is located at address A (indexed if specified). Sorting consists of placing the addresses of the keys (for the various blocks) in descending order of key magnitude in the first several locations in memory. That is, the address of the largest key is placed in location 0.

| 6 | 5 | | | A | |

is the same except that the addresses are arranged according to the ascending order of key magnitude.

Figure 17.20. Sorting instructions.

Register	Number of bits	Description
AC	24	Accumulator
NBLKS	8	Number of blocks in file
LKA	16	Address of key to last block in file
IR1	24	Instruction register
KEYAD	16	Address of key under consideration
NWDS	8	Number of words per block
MA	16	Memory address register
MD	24	Memory data register
MAC1	10	Counting address register for first 1024 addresses
MAC2	10	Counting address register for first 1024 addresses
POINT	8	Address of selected key

Figure 17.21. Register used in sort instruction.

668

the fetch cycle and separation of control from other instructions. We assume that indexing has been completed with the indexed address remaining in *IR1*.

1. $MA \leftarrow IR1_{8:23}$
2. $MD \leftarrow \text{BUSFN}(M; \text{DCD}(MA))$
3. $LKA \leftarrow MD_{14:23}; \ MA \leftarrow \text{INC}(MA)$
4. $MD \leftarrow \text{BUSFN}(M; \text{DCD}(MA))$
5. $NWDS \leftarrow MD_{16:23}; \ MA \leftarrow \text{INC}(MA)$
6. $MD \leftarrow \text{BUSFN}(M; \text{DCD}(MA))$
7. $MAC1 \leftarrow 10 \top 128; \ NBLKS \leftarrow MD_{16:23}$
8. $MA \leftarrow \text{INC}(MA)$

The first seven steps obtain the address of the last key in the file, the number of words per block, and the number of blocks, and place this information in the registers provided for this purpose, *LKA*, *NWDS*, and *NBLKS*. Step 7 initializes two counters. The special counters, *MAC1* and *MAC2* serve as separate memory address registers for the first 1024 locations in memory. The *addressing networks* associated with these registers are completely separate from the *MA* network. The memory address register, *MD*, is used in conjunction with any of the three address registers. To be completely correct BUSFN(M; DCD(*MA*)) should be interpreted as

$$\text{BUSFN}(M^{1024:65535}; \ \text{DCD}_{1024:65535}(MA))$$

The range of addresses should be similarly interpreted for write operations. Steps 8 to 12 obtain the key numbers and place them in a separate list beginning at memory location 128. The process of comparing key magnitudes begins at step 16, following the reinitializing of the address registers. The memory address register, *MA*, is used to keep track of the key under consideration.

9. $MD \leftarrow \text{BUSFN}(M; \text{DCD}(MA))$
10. $ADDRBUS = MAC1;$
    $M^{0:1023} * \text{DCD}(ADDRBUS) \leftarrow MD$
    $\rightarrow (\vee/(MA \oplus LKA)/(13)$
11. $MA \leftarrow \text{ADD}_{9:24}(MA; NWDS)$
12. $MAC1 \leftarrow \text{INC}(MAC1)$
    $\rightarrow (9)$
13. $MAC2 \leftarrow 10 \top 0; \ IR1 \leftarrow \text{INC}(IR1)$
14. $IR1 \leftarrow \text{INC}(IR1)$
15. $IR1 \leftarrow \text{INC}(IR1)$
16. $MA \leftarrow IR1_{8:23}; \ MAC1 \leftarrow 10 \top 128$

17. $MD \leftarrow MA$
18. $ADDRBUS = MAC2;\ M^{0:1023} * \mathrm{DCD}(ADDRBUS) \leftarrow MD$
19. $ADDRBUS = MAC1;\ MD \leftarrow \mathrm{BUSFN}(M^{0:1023};\ \mathrm{DCD}(ADDRBUS))$
20. $AC \leftarrow MD$
21. $MA \leftarrow \mathrm{ADD}(MA;\ NWDS)$
22. $MAC1 \leftarrow \mathrm{INC}(MAC1)$
23. $ADDRBUS = MAC1;\ MD \leftarrow \mathrm{BUSFN}(M^{0:1023};\ \mathrm{DCD}(ADDRBUS))$
24. $\rightarrow (\overline{\mathrm{LARGER}\ (MD;\ AC)})/(27)$
25. $AC \leftarrow MD;\ MD \leftarrow MA;\ POINT \leftarrow MAC1$
26. $ADDRBUS = MAC2;\ M^{0:1023} * \mathrm{DCD}(ADDRBUS) \leftarrow MD$
    $\rightarrow (\sqrt{/(MA \oplus LKA)})/(22)$
27. $MAC2 \leftarrow \mathrm{INC}(MAC2)$
28. $\rightarrow (\overline{\sqrt{/(MAC2 \oplus NBLKS)}})/(31)$
29. $MAC1 \leftarrow POINT;\ MD \leftarrow 24 \top 0$
30. $ADDRBUS = MAC1;\ M^{0:1023} * \mathrm{DCD}(ADDRBUS) \leftarrow MD$
    $\rightarrow (16)$
31. EXIT

Each pass through the inner loop, beginning at step 22, represents a pass through the list of keys to find the largest key remaining in the list. The address (in the original file) of the largest key is placed in M^0 on the first pass. The address of the second largest key is placed in M^1 on the second pass, and so on. Once an address corresponding to a key is entered in the list, that key is replaced by zero so that it will not be entered in the list twice. We assume that all keys are greater than zero. At the beginning of each pass, the first key is placed in AC. This key is compared to subsequent keys. When a larger one is found, it replaces the original key in AC; $MAC1$ is used to count through the list of keys in the inner loop. With each step, the number of words per block is added to MA; thus MA stores the file address of each key, which is compared to AC.

The $MAC2$ register contains the address of the location in the list where the next key address is to be placed. The contents of $MAC2$ are updated each pass through the outer loop. Also, the address in $POINT$ is used to replace the selected key by zero each pass through the outer loop.

The major operation is the combinational logic subroutine LARGER $(MD;\ AC)$, which is used to control a branch at step 24. The output of the logic unit will be 1 if the first argument, MD, is larger than the magnitude of the second argument, AC. The output is 0 otherwise. The writing of this subroutine will be left to the reader. The subroutine LARGER causes the keys to be arranged in descending order to execute the single-address instruction 64. The execution of instruction 65 requires only a slight modification of the routine LARGER.

No software sorting routine will be written to verify the saving that can be provided by the above special-purpose processor. However, the savings should be considerable. In a software version, each AHPL step in the routine listed above would be replaced by at least one fetch and execution memory cycle. Merely avoiding the fetch cycle will result in nearly a 50 percent saving. Many of the bookkeeping steps that are accomplished above in single register transfers will require a sequence of two or three instructions to accomplish by software. Overall, one can be confident of achieving at least a 3:1 speed improvement by using a hardware sorter. This is achieved at the expense of adding several hardware registers and a number of special data paths. Some of the registers can be used by other instructions. In any case, the sorting instruction could be justified only in situations where it is used frequently.

In addition to sorting files, it is likely that the same processor will be called upon to rearrange the blocks in the file. The storage of key addresses in the first few words of memory can only be temporary. The MOVE instruction described in Fig. 17.22 may be used in the rearrangement of data. If the first 3 bits of the op code are octal 5, then the instruction is recognized as a two-address instruction and the next word in the instruction sequence is placed in the supplementary instruction register, *IR2*. Op code 57 indicates an instruction that will move a block of words from one section of memory to another. Address 1 specifies the address of the first word in the block to be moved; address 2 specifies the new location of the first word in the block. The number of words in the block to be moved is given by the 8-bit binary number, n. The MOVE instruction described above may be used in a variety of ways.

17.9 LARGE, SPECIAL-PURPOSE MACHINES

Although not installed or constructed on campus, ILLIAC IV, is the fourth of a series of computers developed at the University of Illinois.

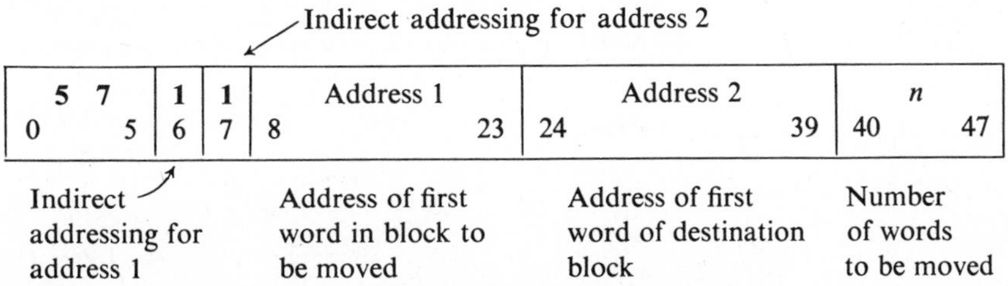

Indirect addressing for address 2

5 7	1	1	Address 1	Address 2	n
0 5	6	7	8 23	24 39	40 47

Indirect addressing for address 1   Address of first word in block to be moved   Address of first word of destination block   Number of words to be moved

Figure 17.22. A MOVE instruction.

Most of the special-purpose machines discussed so far in this chapter have been small machines dedicated to one specific task. ILLIAC IV is a very large multispecial-purpose machine. That is, it is intended for use for a variety of problems that consume extremely large amounts of time on ordinary computers. Not all programs can be run efficiently on ILLIAC IV, however.

A simplified hardware layout of one of four identical quadrants of ILLIAC IV is shown in Fig. 17.23. The disk memory and the Burroughs 6500 computer used for I/O communications are actually shared by all four quadrants. The quadrants can work independently or they can be joined together in a single array for large problems.

The 64 processing elements are actually independent arithmetic units. The basic clock period is 80 nsec. The use of emitter-coupled logic permits addition to be accomplished in three clock periods. The carry-save multiplication requires five clock periods. These figures are for 64-bit operations within each individual processing element (P.E.). The processing element memories are constructed using thin film technology

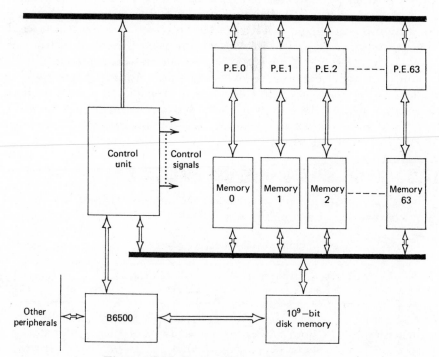

Figure 17.23. One quadrant of ILLIAC IV.

to permit an access time of 120 nsec. The reader will note the close match achieved between the addition time and the memory access time.

The distinguishing feature of the ILLIAC IV organization is that the 64 processing elements do not possess individual control units. All P.E.'s are under control of the single control unit shown. This feature constrains their operations such that all P.E.'s must simultaneously execute the same operation on different data. The only local control available to the individual P.E.'s is an 8-bit register, *RGM*, which stores the results of tests and specifies whether the P.E. will actually execute or will ignore an instruction issued by the control unit. The control unit depicted in Fig. 17.23 includes arithmetic and indexing capability, two 64-word buffer memories for accepting blocks of instructions from the P.E. memories, and broadcast registers to supply identical data items to all processing elements.

A principal advantage of the ILLIAC IV organization is necessarily the economy achieved in the sharing of a single control unit by 64 processing elements. An additional advantage in some applications is the fast transfer of information between operating registers in individual P.E.'s. Interconnections between the P.E.'s are provided so that they may be arranged in a two-dimensional (8 × 8) array or a 64-element linear array. Actual realization of these advantages depends on keeping the processing elements busy. If control signals are disabled by all but a few processors, most of the time, then ILLIAC IV is operating very inefficiently indeed. Achieving a high-P.E. utilization rate requires careful choice of problems and careful programming. Among the problems that seem suited to ILLIAC IV are matrix algebra, partial differential equations including hydrodynamic flow and weather modeling, linear programming, multiple target tracking, and logic simulation for test sequence generation in LSI circuits.

The above discussion has necessarily been brief. For details the reader is referred to References 6 and 7. The notion of an array of processing elements under control of a single control unit is interesting and worth including. It is the view of the authors that the usefulness of this concept is not limited to huge machines like ILLIAC IV. A smaller array of processors might be efficiently dedicated to any of a variety of special-purpose applications. There is currently considerable interest in the possibility of using arrays of microprocessors under control of a larger computer for special-purpose applications.

Another form of large special-purpose computer seems to be suited to the very same set of applications as is ILLIAC IV. These are super-pipeline machines. The CDC STAR is the first of these machines to become operational. The pipeline processor, illustrated figuratively in

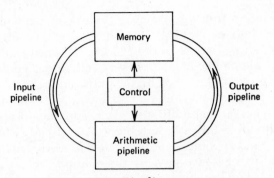

Figure 17.24. Pipeline processor.

Fig. 17.24, gains its advantage by starting the retrieval of subsequent sets of operands, each located in memory adjacent to the first, before the first result has been returned to memory. To take maximum advantage of the pipeline concept, data on which similar operations are to be performed must be arranged in adjacent locations in memory. Thus such sets of identical operations must actually exist in the application algorithm as they will, to a sufficient extent, in those applications pointed out in the above discussion of ILLIAC IV.

The arithmetic unit of Fig. 17.24 is arranged to perform arithmetic in pipeline form (see Section 17.5). In the special-purpose pipeline processor, the memory read and write operations are also overlapped in pipeline form. Thus retrieval, arithmetic, and storage operations are performed in step as data move around the loop in Fig. 17.24. In most cases, all data in the pipeline must be subject to the same arithmetic operation. As an exception, the CDC STAR can perform the inner or dot product of two vectors as their elements pass through the pipeline in pairs.

Reference 8 attempts to compare ILLIAC IV and the CDC STAR with each other and with a more conventional large machine. The issue is left somewhat in doubt. Final verdict must await extended operation of the two machines in a production environment. Must will depend on software development and the skill at efficient use of the machines eventually achieved by programmers.

17.10 SUMMARY

In this chapter, as has been the case throughout most of the book, the emphasis has been on how to design rather than on what to design. Various factors that influence design decisions in large machines have been pointed out, but no systematic procedure for evaluating these factors has been presented. The reader can no doubt see the advantage of an analytical model that will indicate whether such features as look-ahead, pipelining, or multiprocessing should be employed in a given design. Models of this type have in fact been developed but have generally been very complex and applicable only to specific situations.

Rather than attempt to present a representative sampling of decision models, we merely call the reader's attention to their general use. As the costs implied by a design decision in the computer area are often very great, the designer must endeavor to take advantage of any analytical aids available.

PROBLEMS

17.1 Write in AHPL the control sequences for Type I and Type II increment instructions in terms of the hardware configuration of Fig. 17.2.

17.2 Write in AHPL the control sequence for the complete fetch cycle of the machine in Fig. 17.2. Continue the sequence for Type I and Type II instructions to the point where control must separate for the execution of individual instructions.

17.3 Step 12 of Section 17.3 uses a Boolean function, f, to control whether or not a skip is to be executed. Write a Boolean algebraic expression for f.

17.4 Consider a look-ahead unit similar to the unit discussed in Section 17.3, but containing a block of 16 instruction registers, so that small loops can be contained within the unit. Assume that the instructions are replaced as a block after the last one is executed, or upon a jump out of the block. Write an AHPL control sequence for this look-ahead unit. Assume a 16-bank RAM but no scratch pad. Execution of the first instruction in a new book should begin as soon as it is received from memory.

17.5 Design the control sequence to a single computer that will appear as eight separate copies of SIC. Consider memory reference instructions only. The machine will have a 64k core memory. Devise an economic technique for achieving an access time for each processor equal to the overall access time of the machine.

Hint: Consider CDC 6400 peripheral processors.

17.6 Write the control sequence for the reservation control in Fig. 17.8. Assume that each request for a functional unit must be accomplished in no more than two clock periods.

17.7 Suppose the slave processor in the time-sharing system of Fig. 17.10 is organized so that two user programs can be stored in memory at one time. While one of the programs is being executed, the other may be replaced by a new program from the queue in the disk memory. Assume that a special DMA control sequencer is included in the slave for this purpose. Suppose that a more economical disk memory system, requiring some head movement, is used so that the average swap time, t_s, is 100 msec. Replot Fig. 17.11a and 17.11b taking these changes into consideration.

   Would it be advantageous to include a larger RAM in the slave so that up to five user programs could be stored at once? Why? Under what circumstances? How would this affect Fig. 17.11?

17.8 Assume an average compilation time of 0.5 sec and an execution time of 3 sec. How many terminals may be handled by the modified version of Fig. 17.12 discussed in Problem 17.7, if a 15-min wait for a run would be tolerated and 50 percent of the terminals are active in peak periods.

17.9 Write the portion of the control sequencer for the master computer in Fig. 17.10 that assembles lines of characters in a temporary file in disk storage. A special character is supplied by the teletype to indicate the end of a line. Define registers, buses, and buffer storage as needed. The configuration should be economically reasonable.

Hint: The only character whose contents is of any interest to this sequencer is the end-of-line character (carriage return). The sequencer must keep track of the number of lines in each file so that users can be warned when approaching file limits.

   Software in the master will accomplish editing and issue warnings. Suggest an approach for integrating the above control sequencer with the primary sequencer for executing instructions.

17.10 For a shift command in a variable word-length computer, only one address is needed. System/360 computers use several formats for shift instructions; one is the same as the SS format (Fig. 17.17) except that the *B* address is omitted. For such a command, the shift is one digit left or right, the direction of shift being indicated by the last bit of the op code: 0 indicating right and 1, left. Write a control sequence for shifting in a machine having the configuration described in Example 17.3.

17.11 Multiplication in a variable word-length computer may be done as follows: the first digit of the multiplicand is multiplied by the first digit of the multiplier; the low-order digit of the resultant product is stored in the low-order position of the product location, the second digit being saved for the next cycle; the second digit of the multiplicand is then multiplied by the first multiplier digit; and the low-order digit of this product is added to the carry from the first multiplication, the sum being stored in the second digit position of the product location. This procedure is repeated until the multiplicand is completely multiplied by the first multiplier digit. The same process is then carried out for the second multiplier digit, with the resultant partial product, shifted one place left, being added to the first partial product. This is repeated for each multiplier digit in turn until the multiplication is completed. Assume a machine having the configuration of Example 17.3 and the SS instruction format of Fig. 17.17. Since both the multiplier and multiplicand must be preserved for the entire sequence, the product cannot replace either operand. Assume that operand A is the multiplier, operand B is the multiplicand, and the product is to be stored in the appropriate number of sequential locations immediately following the multiplicand. Write a control sequence for multiplication in this machine.

17.12 One of the character-handling commands in System/360 is TRANSLATE, which functions as follows. The instruction, in the SS format, specifies two addresses. The first address specifies an operand ranging from 1 to 256 bytes in length. The second address specifies the origin of a function table of bytes defining the desired translation. In execution, each byte of the argument, scanning from left to right, is in turn replaced by a function byte from the table. The location of the function byte is obtained by adding the argument byte to the table origin. Write a control sequence for executing the TRANSLATE instruction in the configuration of Example 17.3.

17.13. Assume that the key for the first block of a file as described in Fig. 17.18 sometimes serves as an overall key for the file. Write the control sequence for an instruction that will arrange the addresses of these file keys in the first several memory locations in descending order of key magnitude. Is an address required for this instruction? If not, suggest ways in which the address bits might be used to specify variations of the basic instruction.

17.14. Write a subroutine in SIC assembly language that will accomplish the sort function, described in Section 17.8. Merely lengthen the SIC word length to 21 bits so that 16 bits can be used to address a 64k memory. Assume that the basic clock rates and memory access times are the same for SIC and the sort processor. Compare the actual times required to accomplish the sort operation by the two methods.

17.15 Write the combinational logic subroutine LARGER used in Section 17.8. Arrange the logic network so that most of it is also applicable to instruction 65 (octal).

17.16 Lay out a minicomputer version of ILLIAC IV. Assume that a single control unit will control eight processors, each processing the approximate capability of SIC. Status flip-flops and a routing network must be included. Assume the processors to be arranged in a line.

Specify all registers required in the processors and the controller. Define a complete list of commands for the system. Include commands for routing data between the control memory and the individual processor memories. Also include commands providing for the testing and setting of status bits.

REFERENCES

1. Flores, Ivan, *Computer Organization*, Prentice-Hall, Englewood Cliffs, N.J., 1969.

2. Hellerman, H., *Digital System Principles*, 2nd ed., McGraw-Hill, New York, 1973.

3. Murphy, J. O., and R. M. Wade, "The IBM 360/195 in a World of Mixed Jobstreams," *Datamation*, Apr. 1970, p. 72.

4. Thorton, J. E., *Design of a Computer, The CDC 6600*, Scott-Foresman and Company, 1970.

5. Chen, T. C., "Parallelism, Pipelining and Computer Efficiency," *Computer Design*, Jan. 1971, p. 69.

6. Barnes, G. H., et al., "The ILLIAC IV Computer," *IEEE Trans. Computers*, Aug. 1968, p. 746.

7. McIntyre, D. E., "An Introduction to the ILLIAC IV Computer," *Datamation*, Apr. 1970.

8. Graham, W. R., "The Parallel and the Pipeline Computers," *Datamation*, Apr. 1970, p. 68.

9. "Control Data 7600 Computer System," *Reference Manual*, Publication No. 60258200.

10. *A Guide to the IBM System/370 Model 165*, GC20-1730-0.

11. "Control Data 6400/6500/6600 Computer System," *Reference Manual*, Publication No. 60100000.

12. Barsamian, H., "Firmware Sort Processor with LSI Components," *Proceedings AFIPS Spring Joint Computer Conference*, 1970, p. 183.

Most of the syntax of AHPL was presented in Chapter 5, but a few conventions were added in subsequent chapters. For easy reference we include the following complete catalog of AHPL syntax, written in the same informal style as Chapter 5. References to semantics are given.

I BASIC STRUCTURE

The AHPL descriptions of systems are organized as shown in Fig. A.1. The components of the systems are classified as *modules* or *units*. *Modules* are subsystems containing memory. *Units* describe purely combinational logic networks.

II VARIABLES

Variables include scalars (lower-case boldface italic), vectors (upper-case boldface italic), and arrays (upper-case boldface Roman). Elements of vectors and columns of arrays are selected by subscripts, e.g., A_j and M_j. Rows of arrays are selected by superscripts, e.g., M^j. The dimensions of vectors and arrays are indicated in declaration statements. Array M [n, m] indicates n rows and m columns and A [n] indicates n elements. Vectors are assumed to be arranged as rows.

III MODULE DESCRIPTIONS

A. Name

The name of a module will be stated in the form,

MODULE: NAME.

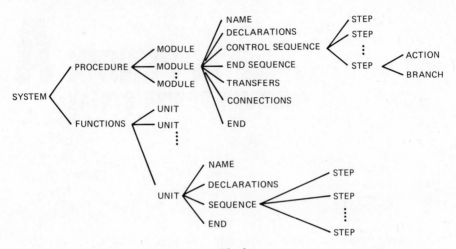

Figure A.1. Block structure.

B. Declarations

All elements making up the module must be declared and dimensioned. A variable cannot be referred to elsewhere in the description unless it has been declared. The declarations include

MEMORY   (Flip-flops, registers, memory arrays)
INPUTS
OUTPUTS
BUSES
COMBUSES
LABELS   (Section 5.6)
ONE SHOTS   (Section 5.9)

Buses are internal communications lines with more than one source and/or destination. A COMBUS is a bus between modules. Inputs and outputs are lines between modules with only one source and one destination. Refer to Section 5.6 for an example of declarations and to Sections 5.6 and 5.9 for discussions of LABEL and ONE-SHOT.

C. Control Sequence

A control sequence is made up of sequentially numbered steps. Each step may include transfer statements, connection statements, and a branch statement, as shown in Fig. A.2.

682

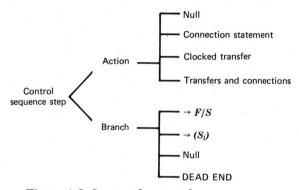

Figure A.2. Syntax of a control sequence step.

The action part of a step may consist of any number of transfers and connections. The allowed forms of connections and transfers are given in Fig. A.3. References are given for the semantics of each form.

The destinations on the right in Fig. A.3 may be selected by the selection operators listed in Fig. A.4a. In **OCLV**'s and **OCLM**'s arguments selected by the selection operators may be operated on by the logic operators of Fig. A.4b. The arguments may consist of memory elements, inputs, functions, buses, and constants. An n-bit constant vector whose elements consist of the bits of the binary equivalent of the decimal number, p, may be expressed $n \top p$. If the $\leftarrow$ is replaced by $\leftarrow$o, the corresponding expression becomes an unclocked transfer. See Section 12.6 for the semantics of the operator $\leftarrow$o.

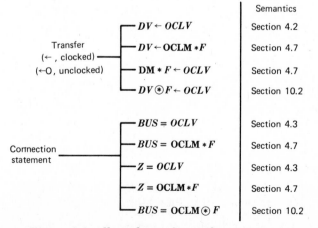

Figure A.3. Allowed transfers and connections.

A_j	The jth column of A
$A_{m:n}$	Columns m through n of A
,	Catenation (Section 5.3)
$A!B$	Row catenation (Section 5.3)
M^j	The jth row of M
$M^{m:n}$	Row m through row n of M

(a)   Selection operators

$\wedge$	And
$\vee$	Or
Overbar	Not
$\wedge/$	And over elements of a vector
$\vee/$	Or over elements of a vector
$\oplus$	Exclusive Or
SL	Single level (Section 7.2)
SYN	Synchronization (Sections 5.9 and 9.4)

(b) AHPL logic operators

Figure A.4.

The precedence structure established for AHPL operators is (1) Not and SYN and SL, (2) all selection operators except catenate, (3) $\wedge$, (4) $\vee$ or $\oplus$, and (5) catenate.

The basic form of branch statement is

$$\rightarrow (F)/(N)$$

where F is a vector of Boolean elements, formed by the same rules as the elements of $OCLV$'s and N is a vector of statement numbers. The meaning of this form is

"Go to N_i if $F_i = 1$.

If there are only two branch conditions, and one points to the next step in sequence, this condition and next statement number may be omitted from the expression. If more than one N_i is 1, then the sequence branches to more than one step in parallel. For a treatment of parallel sequences and the semantics of DEAD END and CONVERGE, the reader is referred to Section 9.2.

The phrase NO DELAY appended to a control sequence step indicates that this step is accomplished simultaneously with the prior step in the sequence.

D. Following END SEQUENCE

All statements following END SEQUENCE are executed every clock period. The syntax of this section is the same as that of the ACTION part of a control sequence step except that a single CONTROL RESET statement can be included. (See Section 7.2).

IV COMBINATIONAL LOGIC UNIT DESCRIPTION

The UNIT name as indicated in Fig. A.1 is the same as the calling identifier of the network. Only INPUTS and OUTPUTS are declared, but these declarations take the same form as for MODULES. The output vector will ordinarily be identified by the module name. The three types of steps in the combinational logic unit description are depicted in Fig. A.5.

The logic operators in the *OCLV* of Fig. A.5 are the same as in a module. Row compression U/X, U/M, and column compression $U//M$ are added to the list of selection operators. See Fig. 5.6 for semantics. The subscripts and superscripts in the selection operators may be index variables to be defined by index transfers. The index branch and the index transfer are executed at compile time. These statements may use any of the APL operators listed in Figs. 5.5 and 5.6 and the exponentiation operator $\uparrow$ (Section 7.7). Index branch statements take the general form

$$\Rightarrow (E)$$

where E is any APL expression that reduces to a statement number. Compile time transfer statements will use a double arrow

$$\Leftarrow$$

to distinguish these transfers from control sequence transfers.

For a more complete discussion of the semantics of the combinational logic unit description, see Section 7.7.

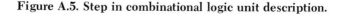

STEP—

— Connection $A = OCLV$

— Index transfer (Any APL transfer)

— Index branch (Any APL branch)

Figure A.5. Step in combinational logic unit description.

A hardware compiler and a function level simulator* have been implemented from AHPL. In order to make these programs as widely usable as possible, we have adopted an equivalent set of symbols for AHPL using only the 128 symbol ASCII character set. Only characters from this set were used in the compiler and simulator. This same set of symbols might be a good choice for any implementation of AHPL that might be contemplated by the reader.

Only upper-case characters are available so that arrays, vectors, and scalers can be distinguished only by noting the declarations. Subscripts and superscripts are, of course, not implementable; therefore, these selection operations must be accomplished in some other manner. The ASCII representation of these and other selection operators are given in Part I of Table B.1. The same symbols must be used for row and column declaration as for superscripting and subscripting, respectively. For example M<9> [4] could be element 4 of row 9 of array M, or could be a declaration of array M with 9 rows and 4 columns.

The ASCII equivalents of the APHL logic operators are given in Part II of Table B.1. Equivalents of the remaining AHPL symbols are given in Part III of the table.

*See Reference 5 of Chapter 7.

TABLE B.1

Meaning	AHPL Symbols	Machine-Readable AHPL Symbols
I. Selection Operators		
The jth column of A	A_j	$A\ [j]$
Columns m through n of A	$A_{m:n}$	$A\ [m{:}n]$
Column catenation	,	,
Row catenation	$A\ !\ B$	$A\ !\ B$
The jth row of $\mathbf{M}$	$\mathbf{M}^j$	$M <j>$
Rows j through k of $\mathbf{M}$	$\mathbf{M}^{j:k}$	$M <j;\,k>$
II Logic Operators		
AND	$\wedge$	&
OR	$\vee$	+
Exclusive OR	$\oplus$	@
AND elements of vector	$\wedge/$	&/
OR elements of vector	$\vee/$	+/
NOT*	Overbar	$\rceil$
III. Other Symbols		
Memory element transfer	$\leftarrow$	$< =$ (two characters)
Compile time transfer	$\Leftarrow$	$<=$ $''$
Control branch	$\rightarrow$	$=>$ $''$
Compile time branch	$\Rightarrow$	$=>$ $''$
Conditional	$*$	$*$
Encode	$\top$	$\$$
Conditional	$\circledast$	$**$ $''$

*The computer character for the NOT operation will depend on the printer used. In some cases it will be ↑ or ∧. In any case it is the character corresponding to ASCII code 5E.

APPENDIX C

SIC CONTROL SEQUENCE

For ease of reference, the complete control sequence for SIC is listed here, as developed in Chapters 6, 7, and 10. This includes the interrupt, I/O, and buffer sequences but does not include DMA. The sequences for the INT and TST commands are not given, as they were left as exercises for the reader. A fully synchronous memory, requiring only one clock period for read or write has been assumed throughout the sequence.

MODULE: SIC

MEMORY: $M[8192; 18]$; $AC[18]$; $MD[18]$; $IR[18]$; $PC[13]$; $MA[13]$; $IA[13]$; $IB[13]$; $MR[8]$; $INTR[8]$; $CSR[12]$: $BWC[13]$; $BCR[4]$; $BIOR[4]$; $CC[2]$; lf; $intf$; $enif$

INPUTS: $INTLINE[8]$; $BCRDY[4]$; $start$; $ready$; $datavalid$; $accept$

OUTPUTS: $BUFRDY[4]$; $csrdy$; $ready$; $datavalid$; $accept$; $bufend$

BUSES: $ABUS[18]$; $BBUS[18]$; $OBUS[19]$

COMBUSES: $IOBUS[18]$; $CSBUS[12]$

1. $\rightarrow (\overline{SL(SYN(start))})/(1)$
2. $\rightarrow (\vee/BCR)/(90)$
2-1. $\rightarrow (intf)/(60)$
2-2. $MA \leftarrow PC$
3. $MD \leftarrow \text{BUSFN}(M; \text{DCD}(MA))$
4. $IR \leftarrow MD$;
   $intf * ((\vee/(MR \wedge INTR)) \wedge enif) \leftarrow 1$
5. $\rightarrow (IR_0 \wedge IR_1 \wedge IR_2)/(25)$
6. NO DELAY
   $\rightarrow ((\overline{IR_3} \wedge \overline{IR_4}), (\overline{IR_3} \wedge IR_4), IR_3)/(13, 7, 10)$
7. $MA \leftarrow IR_{5:17}$
8. $MD \leftarrow \text{BUSFN}(M; \text{DCD}(MA))$
9. $IR_{5:17} \leftarrow MD_{5:17}$
   $\rightarrow (13)$

Fetch cycle

10. NO DELAY $\quad\quad\quad\quad\quad$ } Fetch
$\quad\rightarrow (IR_4)/(12)$ $\quad\quad\quad\quad$ cycle

11. $IR_{5:17} \leftarrow \text{ADD}(IR_{5:17} ; IA)$
$\quad\rightarrow (13)$

12. $IR_{5:17} \leftarrow \text{ADD}(IR_{5:17} ; IB)$

13. NO DELAY
$\quad\rightarrow (\overline{IR_0 \wedge IR_1})/(15)$

14. $PC \leftarrow IR_{5:17}$
$\quad\rightarrow (2)$

15. $MA \leftarrow IR_{5:17}$
$\quad\rightarrow (IR_0)/(21)$

16. $MD \leftarrow \text{BUSFN}(M; \text{DCD}(MA))$
$\quad\rightarrow (\overline{IR_1} \wedge \overline{IR_2})/(18)$

17. $AC \leftarrow (MD \: ! \: (MD \wedge AC \: ! \: \text{ADD}(MD; AC)))$
$\quad\quad * ((\overline{IR_1} \wedge IR_2), (IR_1 \wedge \overline{IR_2}), (IR_1 \wedge IR_2));$
$\quad lf * (IR_1 \wedge IR_2) \leftarrow \text{ADD}_0(MD; AC)$ $\quad$ Memory
$\quad\rightarrow (24)$ $\quad\quad\quad\quad\quad\quad\quad\quad\quad\quad$ reference
$\quad\quad\quad\quad\quad\quad\quad\quad\quad\quad\quad\quad\quad\quad\quad$ insts

18. $MD \leftarrow \text{INC}(MD)$

19. $M * \text{DCD}(MA) \leftarrow MD$
$\quad\rightarrow (\vee/MD)/(24)$

20. $PC \leftarrow \text{INC}(PC)$
$\quad\rightarrow (24)$

21. $MD \leftarrow (AC \: ! \: (5 \top 0, \text{INC}(PC))) * (IR_2, \overline{IR_2})$

22. $M * \text{DCD}(MA) \leftarrow MD$
$\quad\rightarrow (IR_2)/(24)$

23. $PC \leftarrow IR_{5:17}$

24. $PC \leftarrow \text{INC}(PC)$
$\quad\rightarrow (2)$

25. NO DELAY
$\quad\rightarrow (IR_3)/(50)$

26. NO DELAY
$\quad\rightarrow (IR_5)/(30)$

27. NO DELAY
$\quad\rightarrow ((IR_6 \wedge IR_7), (\overline{IR_6 \wedge IR_7}))/(1, 29)$

(No Step 28)

29. $AC * (IR_8 \vee IR_9) \leftarrow ((\overline{18 \top 0}) \: ! \: (18 \top 0) \: ! \: \overline{AC})$
$\quad\quad * ((\overline{IR_8} \wedge IR_9), (IR_8 \wedge \overline{IR_9}), (IR_8 \wedge IR_9));$
$\quad lf * IR_6 \leftarrow 0; \: lf * IR_7 \leftarrow 1$
$\quad\rightarrow (33)$ $\quad\quad\quad\quad\quad\quad\quad\quad\quad\quad\quad$ Operate
$\quad\quad\quad\quad\quad\quad\quad\quad\quad\quad\quad\quad\quad\quad\quad$ insts

30. $\rightarrow (IR_4)/(32) \quad$ NO DELAY

31. $lf, AC \leftarrow AC, lf$
$\quad\rightarrow (33)$

689

32. $lf, AC \leftarrow AC_{17}, lf, AC_{0:16}$
33. NO DELAY
    $\rightarrow (IR_{10})/(40)$
34. NO DELAY
    $\rightarrow ((\overline{IR}_{11} \wedge \overline{IR}_{12}), (\overline{IR}_{11} \wedge IR_{12}), (IR_{11} \wedge \overline{IR}_{12}),$
    $(IR_{11} \wedge IR_{12}))/(35, 37, 38, 39)$
35. NO DELAY
    $\rightarrow (\overline{IR_{13} \wedge lf})/(43)$
36. $PC \leftarrow INC(PC)$
    $\rightarrow (24)$
37. $AC \leftarrow (5 \top 0, IA \mathbin{!} 5 \top 0, IB) * (\overline{IR}_{13}, IR_{13})$
    $\rightarrow (43)$
38. $IA \leftarrow ((AC_{5:17}) \mathbin{!} (INC(IA))) * (\overline{IR}_{13}, IR_{13})$
    $\rightarrow (43)$
39. $IB \leftarrow ((AC_{5:17}) \mathbin{!} (INC(IB))) * (\overline{IR}_{13}, IR_{13})$
    $\rightarrow (43)$
40. NO DELAY
    $\rightarrow (IR_4)/(42)$
41. $lf, AC \leftarrow AC, lf$
    $\rightarrow (43)$
42. $lf, AC \leftarrow AC_{17}, lf, AC_{0:16}$
43. NO DELAY
44. $\rightarrow (IR_{14})/(45)$
44. $\rightarrow (f, \bar{f})/(36, 24)$
    $(f = (AC_0 \wedge IR_{15}) \vee ((\overline{\vee/AC}) \wedge IR_{16})$
    $\vee (\overline{AC}_0 \wedge (\vee/AC) \wedge IR_{17}))$
45. NO DELAY
    $\rightarrow (IR_4)/(47)$
46. $lf, AC \leftarrow AC, lf$
    $\rightarrow (24)$
47. $lf, AC \leftarrow AC_{17}, lf, AC_{0:16}$
    $\rightarrow (24)$

} Operate insts

50. $\rightarrow (IR_4)/(\text{INT seq})$
51. $\rightarrow (IR_5, \overline{IR}_5)/(70, \text{TST seq})$
60. $intf, enif \leftarrow 0, 0$
61. $IR_{5:17} \leftarrow ADDR(PRI(INTR \wedge MR))$
62. $MA \leftarrow IR_{5:17}; MD \leftarrow 5 \top 0, PC$
63. $M * DCD(MA) \leftarrow MD$
64. $PC \leftarrow IR_{5:17}$
    $\rightarrow (24)$

} Interrupt sequence

70. $CSR \leftarrow IR_{6:17}$
71. $CSBUS = CSR;\ csrdy = 1$
    $\rightarrow (\overline{accept})/(71)$
72. NO DELAY
    $\rightarrow (\overline{IR_9})/(74)$
73. NO DELAY
    $\rightarrow (IR_{10},\ \overline{IR_{10}})/(24,\ 85)$
74. NO DELAY
    $\rightarrow (IR_{11})/(78)$
75. $MD \leftarrow AC$
76. Null
    $\rightarrow (\overline{ready})/(76)$
77. $IOBUS = MD;\ datavalid = 1$
    $\rightarrow (accept,\ \overline{accept})/(24,\ 77)$
78. $ready = 1$
    $\rightarrow (\overline{datavalid})/(78)$
79. $CSR * IR_{10} \leftarrow CSBUS;\ MD * \overline{IR}_{10} \leftarrow IOBUS$
80. $accept = 1$
    $\rightarrow (datavalid)/(80)$
81. NO DELAY
    $\rightarrow (IR_{10})/(83)$
82. $AC \leftarrow MD$
    $\rightarrow (24)$
83. NO DELAY
    $\rightarrow (\bigvee/IR_{12:17} \wedge \overline{CSR_{6:11}}))/(24)$
84. $PC \leftarrow INC(PC)$
    $\rightarrow (24)$
85. $BIOR * DCD(IR_{7:8}) \leftarrow (IR_{11} \wedge \overline{4 \top 0})$
    $\rightarrow (24)$

Input/Output Sequence

90. $\rightarrow (\bigvee/(DCD(CC) \wedge BCR))/(92)$
91. $CC \leftarrow INC(CC)$
    $\rightarrow (90)$
92. $IR_{5:17} \leftarrow BADDR(CC);$
    $\qquad BCR * DCD(CC) \leftarrow 4 \top 0$
93. $MA \leftarrow IR_{5:17}$
94. $MD \leftarrow BUSFN(M;\ DCD(MA));$
    $\qquad IR_{5:17} \leftarrow INC(IR_{5:17})$
95. $MA \leftarrow IR_{5:17};\ BWC \leftarrow MD$
96. $MD \leftarrow BUSFN(M;\ DCD(MA))$
97. $MA \leftarrow ADD(MD;\ BWC)$

Buffer sequence

98. $BWC \leftarrow \text{INC}(BWC); BUFRDY = \text{DCD}(CC)$
99. NO DELAY
  $\rightarrow (\bigvee/(\text{DCD}(CC) \wedge BIOR))/(103)$
100. $MD \leftarrow \text{BUSFN}(M; \text{DCD}(MA))$
101. Null
  $\rightarrow (\overline{ready})/(101)$
102. $IOBUS = MD; datavalid = 1$
  $\rightarrow (accept, \overline{accept})/(107, 102)$
103. $ready = 1$
  $\rightarrow (\overline{datavalid})/(103)$
104. $MD \leftarrow IOBUS$
105. $M * \text{DCD}(MA) \leftarrow MD$
106. $accept = 1$
  $\rightarrow (datavalid)/(106)$
107. NO DELAY
  $\rightarrow (\bigvee/(BWC)/(109)$
108. $bufend = 1$
  $\rightarrow (2)$
109. $BUFRDY = \text{DCD}(CC)$
110. $MA \leftarrow \text{BADDR}(CC); MD \leftarrow BWC$
111. $M * \text{DCD}(MA) \leftarrow MD$
  $\rightarrow (2)$

APPENDIX D

INSTRUCTION SET— M6800 MICROPROCESSOR

| Type 0 CCR Instructions | | | | Type 2 Branch Instructions | | |
| Address Mode—Implied | | | | Address Mode—Relative | | |
Instruction	Mnemonic	Op Code		Instruction	Mnemonic	Op Code
No operation	NOP	02		Branch	BRA	20
Trans. ACCA to CCR	TAP	06		Br. if higher	BHI	22
Trans. CCR to ACCA	TPA	07		Br. if lower or same	BLS	23
Incr. IX	INX	08		Br. if carry clear	BCC	24
Decr. IX	DEX	09		Br. if carry set	BCS	25
Clear V	CLV	0A		Br. if ≠ 0	BNE	26
Set V	SEV	0B		Br. if = 0	BEQ	27
Clear C	CLC	0C		Br. if overflow clear	BVC	28
Set C	SEC	0D		Br. if overflow set	BVS	29
Clear I	CLI	0E		Br. if plus	BPL	2A
Set I	SEI	0F		Br. if minus	BMI	2B
				Br. if ≥ 0	BGE	2C
Type 1 Accum. to Accum.				Br. if < 0	BLT	2D
Address Mode—Implied				Br. if > 0	BGT	2E
Subtract Accum	SBA	10		Br. if ≤ 0	BLE	2F
Compare Accum	CBA	11				
Tran. ACCA to ACCB	TAB	16				
Tran. ACCB to ACCA	TBA	17				
Dec. Adj. ACCA	DAA	19				
Add ACCB to ACCA	ADBA	1B				

Type 3   Stack Instructions
Address Mode—Implied

Tran. SP to IX	TSX	30
Increment SP	INS	31
Pull stack to ACCA	PULA	32
Pull stack to ACCB	PULB	33
Decrement SP	DES	34
Tran. IX to SP	TXS	35
Push ACCA to stack	PSHA	36
Push ACCB to stack	PSHB	37
Return fr. subroutine	RTS	39
Return fr. interrupt	RTI	3B
Wait for interrupt	WAI	3E
Software interrupt	SWI	3F

Types 4, 5   Accumulator Instructions

Address Mode—Implied

Type 6, 7   Memory Instructions
Address Mode—Extended or indexed

Instruction	ACCA Mnemonic	Op Code	ACCB Mnemonic	Op Code	Mnemonic	Op Code Extended	Indexed
Negate (2's Compl.)	NEGA	40	NEGB	50	NEG	70	60
Complement (logical)	COMA	43	COMB	53	COM	73	63
Log. Shift Right	LSRA	44	LSRB	54	LSR	74	64
Rotate Right	RORA	46	RORB	56	ROR	76	66
Arith. Shift Right	ASRA	47	ASRB	57	ASR	77	67
Arith Shift Left	ASLA	48	ASLB	58	ASL	78	68
Rotate left	ROLA	49	ROLB	59	ROL	79	69
Decrement	DECA	4A	DECB	5A	DEC	7A	6A
Increment	INCA	4C	INCB	5C	INC	7C	6C
Test	TSTA	4D	TSTB	5D	TST	7D	6D
Clear	CLRA	4F	CLRB	5F	CLR	7F	6F
Jump					JMP	7E	6E

Types 8,9,A,B,C,D,E,F   Register—Memory Instructions

Instruction	Mnemonic	Op Code			
		Immediate	Direct	Extended	Indexed Relative
Subt. from ACCA	SUBA	80	90	B0	A0
Subt. from ACCB	SUBB	C0	D0	F0	E0
Compare to ACCA	CMPA	81	91	B1	A1
Compare to ACCB	CMPB	C1	D1	F1	E1
Subt. from ACCA w/carry	SBCA	82	92	B2	A2
Subt. from ACCB w/carry	SBCB	C2	D2	F2	E2
AND with ACCA	ANDA	84	94	B4	A4
AND with ACCB	ANDB	C4	D4	F4	E4
Bit test w/ACCA	BITA	85	95	B5	A5
Bit test w/ACCB	BITB	C5	D5	F5	E5
Load ACCA	LDAA	86	96	B6	A6
Load ACCB	LDAB	C6	D6	F6	E6
Store ACCA	STAA		97	B7	A7
Store ACCB	STAB		D7	F7	E7
Ex-OR with ACCA	EORA	88	98	B8	A8
Ex-OR with ACCB	EORB	C8	D8	F8	E8
Add to ACCA w/carry	ADCA	89	99	B9	A9
Add to ACCB w/carry	ADCB	C9	D9	F9	E9
OR with ACCA	ORAA	8A	9A	BA	AA
OR with ACCB	ORAB	CA	DA	FA	EA
Add to ACCA	ADDA	8B	9B	BB	AB
Add to ACCB	ADDB	CB	DB	FB	EB
Compare to IX	CPX	8C	9C	BC	AC
Branch to subroutine	BSR				8D
Jump to Subroutine	JSR			BD	AD
Load SP	LDS	8E	9E	BE	AE
Load IX	LDX	CE	DE	FE	EE
Store SP	STS		9F	BF	AF
Store IX	STX		DF	FF	EF